Linux Kernel Progra

A comprehensive guide to kernel internals, writing kernel modules, and kernel synchronization

Kaiwan N Billimoria

BIRMINGHAM - MUMBAI

Linux Kernel Programming

Copyright © 2021 Packt Publishing

All rights reserved. No part of this book may be reproduced, stored in a retrieval system, or transmitted in any form or by any means, without the prior written permission of the publisher, except in the case of brief quotations embedded in critical articles or reviews.

Every effort has been made in the preparation of this book to ensure the accuracy of the information presented. However, the information contained in this book is sold without warranty, either express or implied. Neither the author, nor Packt Publishing or its dealers and distributors, will be held liable for any damages caused or alleged to have been caused directly or indirectly by this book.

Packt Publishing has endeavored to provide trademark information about all of the companies and products mentioned in this book by the appropriate use of capitals. However, Packt Publishing cannot guarantee the accuracy of this information.

Group Product Manager: Wilson D'souza
Publishing Product Manager: Vijin Boricha
Content Development Editor: Romy Dias
Senior Editor: Rahul D'souza
Technical Editor: Nithik Cheruvakodan
Copy Editor: Safis Editing
Project Coordinator: Neil Dmello
Proofreader: Safis Editing
Indexer: Manju Arasan
Production Designer: Joshua Misquitta

First published: March 2021

Production reference: 2170321

Published by Packt Publishing Ltd.
Livery Place
35 Livery Street
Birmingham
B3 2PB, UK.

ISBN 978-1-78995-343-5

www.packt.com

First, to my dear parents, Diana and Nadir "Nads", for showing me how to live a happy and productive life. To my dear wife, Dilshad (an accomplished financial advisor herself), and our amazing kids, Sheroy and Danesh – thanks for all your love and patience.

– Kaiwan N Billimoria

Contributors

About the author

Kaiwan N Billimoria taught himself BASIC programming on his dad's IBM PC back in 1983. He was programming in C and Assembly on DOS until he discovered the joys of Unix, and by around 1997, Linux!

Kaiwan has worked on many aspects of the Linux system programming stack, including Bash scripting, system programming in C, kernel internals, device drivers, and embedded Linux work. He has actively worked on several commercial/FOSS projects. His contributions include drivers to the mainline Linux OS and many smaller projects hosted on GitHub. His Linux passion feeds well into his passion for teaching these topics to engineers, which he has done for well over two decades now. He's also the author of *Hands-On System Programming with Linux*. It doesn't hurt that he is a recreational ultrarunner too.

> *Writing this book took a long while; I'd like to thank the team from Packt for their patience and skill! Carlton Borges, Romy Dias, Vijin Boricha, Rohit Rajkumar, Vivek Anantharaman, Nithin Varghese, and all the others. It was indeed a pleasure working with you.*
>
> *I owe a debt of gratitude to the very able technical reviewers – Donald "Donnie" Tevault and Anil Kumar. They caught a lot of my mistakes and omissions and greatly helped make this book better.*

About the reviewers

Donald A. Tevault, but you can call him Donnie, got involved with Linux way back in 2006 and has been working with it ever since. He holds the Linux Professional Institute Level 3 Security certification, and the GIAC Incident Handler certification. Donnie is a professional Linux trainer, and thanks to the magic of the internet, teaches Linux classes literally the world over from the comfort of his living room. He's also a Linux security researcher for an IoT security company.

Anil Kumar is a Linux BSP and firmware developer at Intel. He has over 12 years of software development experience across many verticals, including IoT, mobile chipsets, laptops/Chromebooks, media encoders, and transcoders. He has a master's degree in electronics design from the Indian Institute of Science and a bachelor's degree in electronics and communication from BMS College of Engineering, India. He is an electronics enthusiast and blogger and loves tinkering to create fun DIY projects.

Table of Contents

Preface — 1

Section 1: The Basics

Chapter 1: Kernel Workspace Setup — 13
  Technical requirements — 14
  Running Linux as a guest VM — 15
    Installing a 64-bit Linux guest — 15
      Turn on your x86 system's virtualization extension support — 16
      Allocate sufficient space to the disk — 18
      Install the Oracle VirtualBox Guest Additions — 18
    Experimenting with the Raspberry Pi — 21
  Setting up the software – distribution and packages — 24
    Installing software packages — 26
      Installing the Oracle VirtualBox guest additions — 27
      Installing required software packages — 27
      Installing a cross toolchain and QEMU — 28
      Installing a cross compiler — 29
    Important installation notes — 30
  Additional useful projects — 31
    Using the Linux man pages — 31
      The tldr variant — 32
    Locating and using the Linux kernel documentation — 33
      Generating the kernel documentation from source — 35
    Static analysis tools for the Linux kernel — 35
    Linux Trace Toolkit next generation — 36
    The procmap utility — 37
    Simple Embedded ARM Linux System FOSS project — 39
    Modern tracing and performance analysis with [e]BPF — 39
    The LDV - Linux Driver Verification - project — 40
  Summary — 42
  Questions — 42
  Further reading — 42

Chapter 2: Building the 5.x Linux Kernel from Source - Part 1 — 43
  Technical requirements — 44
  Preliminaries for the kernel build — 44
    Kernel release nomenclature — 45
    Kernel development workflow – the basics — 46
    Types of kernel source trees — 49
  Steps to build the kernel from source — 52

Table of Contents

Step 1 – obtaining a Linux kernel source tree — 53
- Downloading a specific kernel tree — 54
- Cloning a Git tree — 55

Step 2 – extracting the kernel source tree — 57
- A brief tour of the kernel source tree — 58

Step 3 – configuring the Linux kernel — 63
- Understanding the kbuild build system — 64
- Arriving at a default configuration — 65
- Obtaining a good starting point for kernel configuration — 66
  - Kernel config for typical embedded Linux systems — 67
  - Kernel config using distribution config as a starting point — 68
  - Tuned kernel config via the localmodconfig approach — 69
- Getting started with the localmodconfig approach — 71
- Tuning our kernel configuration via the make menuconfig UI — 74
  - Sample usage of the make menuconfig UI — 77
- More on kbuild — 85
  - Looking up the differences in configuration — 86

Customizing the kernel menu – adding our own menu item — 88
- The Kconfig* files — 89
- Creating a new menu item in the Kconfig file — 90
- A few details on the Kconfig language — 93

Summary — 96
Questions — 96
Further reading — 96

Chapter 3: Building the 5.x Linux Kernel from Source - Part 2 — 97
Technical requirements — 98
Step 4 – building the kernel image and modules — 98
Step 5 – installing the kernel modules — 104
- Locating the kernel modules within the kernel source — 104
- Getting the kernel modules installed — 106

Step 6 – generating the initramfs image and bootloader setup — 108
- Generating the initramfs image on Fedora 30 and above — 109
- Generating the initramfs image – under the hood — 110

Understanding the initramfs framework — 112
- Why the initramfs framework? — 112
- Understanding the basics of the boot process on the x86 — 115
- More on the initramfs framework — 116

Step 7 – customizing the GRUB bootloader — 119
- Customizing GRUB – the basics — 120
- Selecting the default kernel to boot into — 121
- Booting our VM via the GNU GRUB bootloader — 123
- Experimenting with the GRUB prompt — 125

Verifying our new kernel's configuration — 127
Kernel build for the Raspberry Pi — 129

[ii]

Step 1 – cloning the kernel source tree	130
Step 2 – installing a cross-toolchain	131
First method – package install via apt	132
Second method – installation via the source repo	132
Step 3 – configuring and building the kernel	133
Miscellaneous tips on the kernel build	**136**
Minimum version requirements	137
Building a kernel for another site	137
Watching the kernel build run	138
A shortcut shell syntax to the build procedure	139
Dealing with compiler switch issues	140
Dealing with missing OpenSSL development headers	140
Summary	**142**
Questions	**142**
Further reading	**142**
Chapter 4: Writing Your First Kernel Module - LKMs Part 1	**145**
Technical requirements	**146**
Understanding kernel architecture – part 1	**147**
User space and kernel space	147
Library and system call APIs	148
Kernel space components	149
Exploring LKMs	**152**
The LKM framework	152
Kernel modules within the kernel source tree	154
Writing our very first kernel module	**157**
Introducing our Hello, world LKM C code	157
Breaking it down	158
Kernel headers	159
Module macros	160
Entry and exit points	160
Return values	161
The 0/-E return convention	161
The ERR_PTR and PTR_ERR macros	163
The __init and __exit keywords	164
Common operations on kernel modules	**165**
Building the kernel module	165
Running the kernel module	167
A quick first look at the kernel printk()	168
Listing the live kernel modules	171
Unloading the module from kernel memory	172
Our lkm convenience script	173
Understanding kernel logging and printk	**175**
Using the kernel memory ring buffer	176
Kernel logging and systemd's journalctl	178
Using printk log levels	180

Table of Contents

        The pr_<foo> convenience macros   182
        Wiring to the console   183
        Writing output to the Raspberry Pi console   185
        Enabling the pr_debug() kernel messages   188
    Rate limiting the printk instances   190
    Generating kernel messages from the user space   193
    Standardizing printk output via the pr_fmt macro   194
    Portability and the printk format specifiers   196

Understanding the basics of a kernel module Makefile   197
Summary   200
Questions   200
Further reading   200

Chapter 5: Writing Your First Kernel Module - LKMs Part 2   201
Technical requirements   202
A "better" Makefile template for your kernel modules   202
    Configuring a "debug" kernel   204
Cross-compiling a kernel module   206
    Setting up the system for cross-compilation   207
    Attempt 1 – setting the "special" environment variables   208
    Attempt 2 – pointing the Makefile to the correct kernel source tree for the target   211
    Attempt 3 – cross-compiling our kernel module   213
    Attempt 4 – cross-compiling our kernel module   217
Gathering minimal system information   219
    Being a bit more security-aware   222
Licensing kernel modules   224
Emulating "library-like" features for kernel modules   226
    Performing library emulation via multiple source files   226
    Understanding function and variable scope in a kernel module   227
    Understanding module stacking   231
        Trying out module stacking   234
Passing parameters to a kernel module   241
    Declaring and using module parameters   241
    Getting/setting module parameters after insertion   244
    Module parameter data types and validation   247
        Validating kernel module parameters   247
        Overriding the module parameter's name   248
        Hardware-related kernel parameters   249
Floating point not allowed in the kernel   250
Auto-loading modules on system boot   252
    Module auto-loading – additional details   256
Kernel modules and security – an overview   258
    Proc filesystem tunables affecting the system log   259
    The cryptographic signing of kernel modules   261
    Disabling kernel modules altogether   263

Coding style guidelines for kernel developers	264
Contributing to the mainline kernel	265
Getting started with contributing to the kernel	265
Summary	266
Questions	267
Further reading	267

Section 2: Understanding and Working with the Kernel

Chapter 6: Kernel Internals Essentials - Processes and Threads	271
Technical requirements	272
Understanding process and interrupt contexts	272
Understanding the basics of the process VAS	274
Organizing processes, threads, and their stacks – user and kernel space	277
User space organization	280
Kernel space organization	282
Summarizing the current situation	284
Viewing the user and kernel stacks	285
Traditional approach to viewing the stacks	286
Viewing the kernel space stack of a given thread or process	286
Viewing the user space stack of a given thread or process	287
[e]BPF – the modern approach to viewing both stacks	288
The 10,000-foot view of the process VAS	292
Understanding and accessing the kernel task structure	294
Looking into the task structure	296
Accessing the task structure with current	298
Determining the context	299
Working with the task structure via current	301
Built-in kernel helper methods and optimizations	302
Trying out the kernel module to print process context info	304
Seeing that the Linux OS is monolithic	305
Coding for security with printk	305
Iterating over the kernel's task lists	307
Iterating over the task list I – displaying all processes	307
Iterating over the task list II – displaying all threads	308
Differentiating between the process and thread – the TGID and the PID	310
Iterating over the task list III – the code	312
Summary	315
Questions	316
Further reading	316
Chapter 7: Memory Management Internals - Essentials	317
Technical requirements	318
Understanding the VM split	318

Looking under the hood – the Hello, world C program	319
Going beyond the printf() API	321
VM split on 64-bit Linux systems	324
Virtual addressing and address translation	324
The process VAS – the full view	330
Examining the process VAS	**331**
Examining the user VAS in detail	332
Directly viewing the process memory map using procfs	333
Interpreting the /proc/PID/maps output	333
The vsyscall page	336
Frontends to view the process memory map	336
The procmap process VAS visualization utility	337
Understanding VMA basics	342
Examining the kernel segment	**344**
High memory on 32-bit systems	347
Writing a kernel module to show information about the kernel segment	348
Viewing the kernel segment on a Raspberry Pi via dmesg	348
Macros and variables describing the kernel segment layout	350
Trying it out – viewing kernel segment details	353
The kernel VAS via procmap	357
Trying it out – the user segment	362
The null trap page	364
Viewing kernel documentation on the memory layout	365
Randomizing the memory layout – KASLR	**366**
User-mode ASLR	367
KASLR	368
Querying/setting KASLR status with a script	368
Physical memory	**372**
Physical RAM organization	372
Nodes	372
Zones	375
Direct-mapped RAM and address translation	377
Summary	**382**
Questions	**382**
Further reading	**382**
Chapter 8: Kernel Memory Allocation for Module Authors - Part 1	**383**
Technical requirements	**384**
Introducing kernel memory allocators	**384**
Understanding and using the kernel page allocator (or BSA)	**386**
The fundamental workings of the page allocator	387
Freelist organization	387
The workings of the page allocator	390
Working through a few scenarios	392
The simplest case	392
A more complex case	392
The downfall case	392
Page allocator internals – a few more details	393

Learning how to use the page allocator APIs	395
Dealing with the GFP flags	397
Freeing pages with the page allocator	399
Writing a kernel module to demo using the page allocator APIs	401
Deploying our lowlevel_mem_lkm kernel module	407
The page allocator and internal fragmentation	411
The exact page allocator APIs	411
The GFP flags – digging deeper	413
Never sleep in interrupt or atomic contexts	413
Understanding and using the kernel slab allocator	**415**
The object caching idea	416
Learning how to use the slab allocator APIs	419
Allocating slab memory	419
Freeing slab memory	421
Data structures – a few design tips	423
The actual slab caches in use for kmalloc	424
Writing a kernel module to use the basic slab APIs	426
Size limitations of the kmalloc API	**429**
Testing the limits – memory allocation with a single call	430
Checking via the /proc/buddyinfo pseudo-file	433
Slab allocator – a few additional details	**435**
Using the kernel's resource-managed memory allocation APIs	435
Additional slab helper APIs	436
Control groups and memory	437
Caveats when using the slab allocator	**438**
Background details and conclusions	438
Testing slab allocation with ksize() – case 1	439
Testing slab allocation with ksize() – case 2	440
Interpreting the output from case 2	442
Graphing it	443
Slab layer implementations within the kernel	444
Summary	**445**
Questions	**445**
Further reading	**445**
Chapter 9: Kernel Memory Allocation for Module Authors - Part 2	**447**
Technical requirements	**447**
Creating a custom slab cache	**448**
Creating and using a custom slab cache within a kernel module	448
Creating a custom slab cache	449
Using the new slab cache's memory	452
Destroying the custom cache	453
Custom slab – a demo kernel module	453
Understanding slab shrinkers	458
The slab allocator – pros and cons – a summation	459
Debugging at the slab layer	**460**
Debugging through slab poisoning	460

Table of Contents

Trying it out – triggering a UAF bug	462
SLUB debug options at boot and runtime	465
Understanding and using the kernel vmalloc() API	**466**
Learning to use the vmalloc family of APIs	467
A brief note on memory allocations and demand paging	471
Friends of vmalloc()	473
Specifying the memory protections	477
Testing it – a quick Proof of Concept	478
Why make memory read-only?	480
The kmalloc() and vmalloc() APIs – a quick comparison	480
Memory allocation in the kernel – which APIs to use when	**481**
Visualizing the kernel memory allocation API set	482
Selecting an appropriate API for kernel memory allocation	483
A word on DMA and CMA	486
Stayin' alive – the OOM killer	**487**
Reclaiming memory – a kernel housekeeping task and OOM	487
Deliberately invoking the OOM killer	488
Invoking the OOM killer via Magic SysRq	489
Invoking the OOM killer with a crazy allocator program	489
Understanding the rationale behind the OOM killer	491
Case 1 – vm.overcommit set to 2, overcommit turned off	492
Case 2 – vm.overcommit set to 0, overcommit on, the default	493
Demand paging and OOM	494
Understanding the OOM score	498
Summary	**499**
Questions	**500**
Further reading	**500**
Chapter 10: The CPU Scheduler - Part 1	**501**
Technical requirements	**502**
Learning about the CPU scheduling internals – part 1 – essential background	**502**
What is the KSE on Linux?	502
The POSIX scheduling policies	503
Visualizing the flow	**506**
Using perf to visualize the flow	506
Visualizing the flow via alternate (CLI) approaches	510
Learning about the CPU scheduling internals – part 2	**511**
Understanding modular scheduling classes	511
Asking the scheduling class	517
A word on CFS and the vruntime value	519
Threads – which scheduling policy and priority	**521**
Learning about the CPU scheduling internals – part 3	**525**
Who runs the scheduler code?	525
When does the scheduler run?	525
The timer interrupt part	526

The process context part	527
Preemptible kernel	528
CPU scheduler entry points	530
The context switch	532
Summary	533
Questions	533
Further reading	533

Chapter 11: The CPU Scheduler - Part 2 — 535

Technical requirements	535
Visualizing the flow with LTTng and trace-cmd	536
Visualization with LTTng and Trace Compass	536
Recording a kernel tracing session with LTTng	537
Reporting with a GUI – Trace Compass	538
Visualizing with trace-cmd	539
Recording a sample session with trace-cmd record	540
Reporting and interpretation with trace-cmd report (CLI)	542
Reporting and interpretation with a GUI frontend	547
Understanding, querying, and setting the CPU affinity mask	548
Querying and setting a thread's CPU affinity mask	550
Using taskset(1) to perform CPU affinity	554
Setting the CPU affinity mask on a kernel thread	554
Querying and setting a thread's scheduling policy and priority	555
Within the kernel – on a kernel thread	556
CPU bandwidth control with cgroups	557
Looking up cgroups v2 on a Linux system	559
Trying it out – a cgroups v2 CPU controller	561
Converting mainline Linux into an RTOS	566
Building RTL for the mainline 5.x kernel (on x86_64)	568
Obtaining the RTL patches	568
Applying the RTL patch	571
Configuring and building the RTL kernel	571
Mainline and RTL – technical differences summarized	575
Latency and its measurement	576
Measuring scheduling latency with cyclictest	578
Getting and applying the RTL patchset	579
Installing cyclictest (and other required packages) on the device	582
Running the test cases	583
Viewing the results	585
Measuring scheduler latency via modern BPF tools	588
Summary	589
Questions	590
Further reading	590

Section 3: Delving Deeper

Chapter 12: Kernel Synchronization - Part 1 — 593

Table of Contents

Critical sections, exclusive execution, and atomicity — 594
- What is a critical section? — 594
- A classic case – the global i ++ — 597
- Concepts – the lock — 600
  - A summary of key points — 603

Concurrency concerns within the Linux kernel — 604
- Multicore SMP systems and data races — 605
- Preemptible kernels, blocking I/O, and data races — 606
- Hardware interrupts and data races — 607
- Locking guidelines and deadlocks — 608

Mutex or spinlock? Which to use when — 611
- Determining which lock to use – in theory — 613
- Determining which lock to use – in practice — 614

Using the mutex lock — 615
- Initializing the mutex lock — 616
- Correctly using the mutex lock — 617
- Mutex lock and unlock APIs and their usage — 618
  - Mutex lock – via [un]interruptible sleep? — 620
- Mutex locking – an example driver — 621
- The mutex lock – a few remaining points — 626
  - Mutex lock API variants — 626
    - The mutex trylock variant — 626
    - The mutex interruptible and killable variants — 628
    - The mutex io variant — 629
  - The semaphore and the mutex — 629
  - Priority inversion and the RT-mutex — 630
  - Internal design — 631

Using the spinlock — 632
- Spinlock – simple usage — 632
- Spinlock – an example driver — 634
- Test – sleep in an atomic context — 636
  - Testing on a 5.4 debug kernel — 637
  - Testing on a 5.4 non-debug distro kernel — 642

Locking and interrupts — 645
- Using spinlocks – a quick summary — 652

Summary — 653
Questions — 653
Further reading — 653

Chapter 13: Kernel Synchronization - Part 2 — 655
Using the atomic_t and refcount_t interfaces — 656
- The newer refcount_t versus older atomic_t interfaces — 657
- The simpler atomic_t and refcount_t interfaces — 659
  - Examples of using refcount_t within the kernel code base — 661
- 64-bit atomic integer operators — 663

Using the RMW atomic operators — 665

RMW atomic operations – operating on device registers	665
Using the RMW bitwise operators	668
Using bitwise atomic operators – an example	670
Efficiently searching a bitmask	673
Using the reader-writer spinlock	**673**
Reader-writer spinlock interfaces	674
A word of caution	676
The reader-writer semaphore	677
Cache effects and false sharing	**678**
Lock-free programming with per-CPU variables	**680**
Per-CPU variables	681
Working with per-CPU	682
Allocating, initialization, and freeing per-CPU variables	682
Performing I/O (reads and writes) on per-CPU variables	683
Per-CPU – an example kernel module	685
Per-CPU usage within the kernel	689
Lock debugging within the kernel	**691**
Configuring a debug kernel for lock debugging	692
The lock validator lockdep – catching locking issues early	694
Examples – catching deadlock bugs with lockdep	697
Example 1 – catching a self deadlock bug with lockdep	697
Fixing it	701
Example 2 – catching an AB-BA deadlock with lockdep	702
lockdep – annotations and issues	707
lockdep annotations	707
lockdep issues	708
Lock statistics	709
Viewing lock stats	709
Memory barriers – an introduction	**711**
An example of using memory barriers in a device driver	712
Summary	**714**
Questions	**715**
Further reading	**715**
	717
Other Books You May Enjoy	**719**
Index	**723**

Preface

This book has been explicitly written with a view to helping you learn Linux kernel development in a practical, hands-on fashion, along with the necessary theoretical background to give you a well-rounded view of this vast and interesting topic area. It deliberately focuses on kernel development via the powerful **Loadable Kernel Module (LKM)** framework; the vast majority of kernel projects and products, which includes device driver development, are done in this manner.

The focus is kept on both working hands-on with, and understanding at a sufficiently deep level, the internals of the Linux OS. In these regards, we cover everything from building the Linux kernel from source through understanding and working with complex topics such as synchronization within the kernel.

To guide you on this exciting journey, we divide this book into three sections. The first section covers the basics – setting up a workspace required for kernel development, building the kernel from source, and writing your first kernel module.

The next section, a key one, will help you understand important and essential kernel internals – the Linux kernel architecture, the task structure, and user and kernel-mode stacks. Memory management is a key and interesting topic – we devote three whole chapters to it (covering the internals to a sufficient extent, and importantly, how exactly to allocate any free kernel memory). The working and deeper details of CPU scheduling on Linux round off this section.

The last section of the book deals with the more advanced topic of kernel synchronization – a necessity for professional design and code on the Linux kernel. We devote two whole chapters to covering key topics within this.

The book uses the, at the time of writing, latest 5.4 **Long Term Support (LTS)** Linux kernel. It's a kernel that will be maintained (both bug and security fixes) from November 2019 right through December 2025! This is a key point, ensuring that this book's content remains current and valid for years to come!

We very much believe in a hands-on approach: over 20 kernel modules (besides several user apps and shell scripts) on this book's GitHub repository make the learning come alive, making it fun, interesting, and useful.

We highly recommend you also make use of this book's companion guide, *Linux Kernel Programming (Part 2)*.

It's an excellent industry-aligned beginner's guide to writing `misc` character drivers, performing I/O on peripheral chip memory and handling hardware interrupts. You can get this book for free along with your copy, alternately you can also find this eBook in the GitHub repository at: `https://github.com/PacktPublishing/Linux-Kernel-Programming/tree/master/Linux-Kernel-Programming-(Part-2)`.

We really hope you learn from and enjoy this book. Happy reading!

Who this book is for

This book is primarily for those of you beginning your journey in the vast arena of Linux kernel module development and, to some extent, Linux device driver development. It's also very much targeted at those of you who have already been working on Linux modules and/or drivers, who wish to gain a much deeper, well-structured understanding of Linux kernel architecture, memory management, and synchronization. This level of knowledge about the underlying OS, covered in a properly structured manner, will help you no end when you face difficult-to-debug real-world situations.

What this book covers

`Chapter 1`, *Kernel Workspace Setup*, guides you on setting up a full-fledged Linux kernel development workspace (typically, as a fully virtualized guest system). You will learn how to install all required software packages on it, including a cross toolchain. You will also learn about several other open source projects that will be useful on your journey to becoming a professional kernel/driver developer. Once this chapter is done, you will be ready to build a Linux kernel as well as to start writing and testing kernel code (via the loadable kernel module framework). In our view, it's very important for you to actually use this book in a hands-on fashion, trying out and experimenting with code. The best way to learn something is to do so empirically – not taking anyone's word on anything at all, but by trying it out and experiencing it for yourself.

Chapter 2, *Building the 5.x Linux Kernel from Source – Part 1*, is the first part of explaining how to build the modern Linux kernel from scratch with source code. In this part, you will be given necessary background information – the version nomenclature, the different source trees, the layout of the kernel source – on the kernel source tree. Next, you will be shown in detail how exactly to download a stable vanilla Linux kernel source tree onto the VM. We shall then learn a little regarding the layout of the kernel source code, getting, in effect, a "10,000-foot view" of the kernel code base. The actual work of extracting and configuring the Linux kernel then follows. Creating and using a custom menu entry for kernel configuration is also shown.

Chapter 3, *Building the 5.x Linux Kernel from Source – Part 2*, is the second part on performing kernel builds from source code. In this part, you will continue from the previous chapter, now actually building the kernel, installing kernel modules, understanding what exactly `initramfs (initrd)` is and how to generate it, as well as setting up the bootloader (for x86). Also, as a valuable add-on, this chapter then explains how to cross-compile the kernel for a typical embedded ARM target (using the popular Raspberry Pi as a target device). Several tips and tricks on kernel builds, and even kernel security (hardening), are mentioned as well.

Chapter 4, *Writing Your First Kernel Module – LKMs Part 1*, is the first of two parts that cover a fundamental aspect of Linux kernel development – the LKM framework, and how it is to be understood and used by the "module user," by you – the kernel module or device driver programmer. It covers the basics of the Linux kernel architecture and then, in great detail, every step involved in writing a simple "Hello, world" kernel module, compiling, inserting, checking, and removing it from the kernel space. We also cover kernel logging via the ubiquitous printk API in detail.

Chapter 5, *Writing Your First Kernel Module – LKMs Part 2*, is the second part that covers the LKM framework. Here, we begin with something critical – learning how to use a "better" Makefile, which will help you generate more robust code (having several code-checking, correction, static analysis targets, and so on). We then show in detail the steps to successfully cross-compile a kernel module for an alternate architecture, how to emulate "library-like" code in the kernel (via both the "linking" and the module-stacking approaches), defining and using passing parameters to your kernel module. Additional topics include the auto-loading of modules at boot, important security guidelines, and some information on the kernel documentation and how to access it. Several example kernel modules make the learning more interesting.

Preface

Chapter 6, *Kernel Internals Essentials – Processes and Threads*, delves into some essential kernel internals topics. We begin with what is meant by execution in process and interrupt contexts, and minimal but required coverage of the process user **virtual address space** (**VAS**) layout. This sets the stage for you; you'll then learn about Linux kernel architecture in more depth, focusing on the organization of process/thread task structures and their corresponding stacks – user- and kernel-mode. We then show you more on the kernel task structure (a "root" data structure), how to practically glean information from it, and even iterate over various (task) lists. Several kernel modules make the topic come alive.

Chapter 7, *Memory Management Internals – Essentials*, a key chapter, delves into essential internals of the Linux memory management subsystem, to the level of detail required for the typical module author or driver developer. This coverage is thus necessarily more theoretical in nature; nevertheless, the knowledge gained here is crucial to you, the kernel developer, both for deep understanding and usage of appropriate kernel memory APIs as well as for performing meaningful debugging at the level of the kernel. We cover the VM split (and how it is on various actual architectures), gaining deep insight into the user VAS (our procmap utility will be an eye-opener), as well as the kernel segment (or kernel VAS). We then briefly delve into the security technique of memory layout randomization ([K]ASLR), and end this chapter with a discussion on physical memory organization within Linux.

Chapter 8, *Kernel Memory Allocation for Module Authors Part 1*, gets our hands dirty with the kernel memory allocation (and obviously, deallocation) APIs. You will first learn about the two allocation "layers" within Linux – the slab allocator that's layered above the kernel memory allocation "engine," and the page allocator (or BSA). We shall briefly learn about the underpinnings of the page allocator algorithm and its "freelist" data structure; this information is valuable when deciding which layer to use. Next, we dive straight into the hands-on work of learning about the usage of these key APIs. The ideas behind the slab allocator (or cache) and the primary kernel allocator APIs – the `kzalloc/kfree` – are covered. Importantly, the size limitations, downsides, and caveats when using these common APIs are covered in detail as well. Also, especially useful for driver authors, we cover the kernel's modern resource-managed memory allocation APIs (the `devm_*()` routines).

Chapter 9, *Kernel Memory Allocation for Module Authors Part 2*, goes further, in a logical fashion, from the previous chapter. Here, you will learn how to create custom slab caches (useful for high-frequency (de)allocations for, say, a custom driver), along with some help regarding debugging memory allocations at the slab layer. Next, you'll understand and use the `vmalloc()` API (and friends). Very importantly, having covered many APIs for kernel memory (de)allocation, you will now learn how to pick and choose an appropriate API given the real-world situation you find yourself in. This chapter is rounded off with important coverage of the kernel's **Out Of Memory (OOM)** "killer" framework. Understanding it will also lead to a much deeper understanding of how user space memory allocation really works, via the demand paging technique.

Chapter 10, *The CPU Scheduler - Part 1*, the first part of two chapters, covers a useful mix of theory and practice regarding CPU scheduling on the Linux OS. The minimal necessary theoretical background on the thread as the KSE and available kernel scheduling policies are topics initially covered. Next, sufficient kernel internal details on CPU scheduling are covered to have you understand how scheduling on the modern Linux OS works. Along the way, you will learn how to "visualize" PU scheduling with powerful tools such as perf; thread scheduling attributes (policy and real-time priority) are delved into as well.

Chapter 11, *The CPU Scheduler – Part 2*, the second part on CPU scheduling, continues to cover the topic in more depth. Here, we cover further visualization tools for CPU scheduling (leveraging powerful software such as LTTng and the trace-cmd utility). Next, the CPU affinity mask and how to query/set it, controlling scheduling policy and priority on a per-thread basis – such a powerful feature! – are delved into. An overview of the meaning and importance of control groups (cgroups), along with an interesting example on CPU bandwidth allocation via cgroups v2 is seen. Can you run Linux as an RTOS? Indeed you can! The details on actually doing so are then shown. We round off this chapter with a discussion on (scheduling) latencies and how to measure them.

Chapter 12, *Kernel Synchronization – Part 1*, first covers the key concepts regarding critical sections, atomicity, what a lock conceptually achieves and, very importantly, the why of all this. We then cover concurrency concerns when working within the Linux kernel; this moves us naturally on to important locking guidelines, what deadlock means, and key approaches to preventing deadlock. Two of the most popular kernel locking technologies – the mutex lock and the spinlock – are then discussed in depth along with several (driver) code examples.

Preface

Chapter 13, *Kernel Synchronization – Part 2*, continues the journey on kernel synchronization. Here, you'll learn about key locking optimizations – using lightweight atomic and (the more recent) refcount operators to safely operate on integers, RMW bit operators to safely perform bit ops, and the usage of the reader-writer spinlock over the regular one. Inherent risks, such as cache "false sharing" are discussed as well. An overview of lock-free programming techniques (with an emphasis on per-CPU variables and their usage, along with examples) is then covered. A critical topic – lock debugging techniques, including the usage of the kernel's powerful "lockdep" lock validator, is then covered. The chapter is rounded off with a brief look at memory barriers (along with an example).

To get the most out of this book

To get the most out of this book, we expect you to have knowledge and experience in the following:

- Know your way around a Linux system, on the command line (the shell).
- The C programming language.
- It's not mandatory but experience with Linux system programming concepts and technologies will greatly help.

The details on hardware and software requirements, as well as their installation, are covered completely and in depth in Chapter 1, *Kernel Workspace Setup*. It's critical that you read it in detail and follow the instructions therein.

Also, we have tested all the code in this book (it has its own GitHub repository as well) on these platforms:

- x86_64 Ubuntu 18.04 LTS guest OS (running on Oracle VirtualBox 6.1)
- x86_64 Ubuntu 20.04.1 LTS guest OS (running on Oracle VirtualBox 6.1)
- x86_64 Ubuntu 20.04.1 LTS native OS
- ARM Raspberry Pi 3B+ (running both its "distro" kernel as well as our custom 5.4 kernel); lightly tested
- x86_64 CentOS 8 guest OS (running on Oracle VirtualBox 6.1); lightly tested

We assume that, when running Linux as a guest (VM), the host system is either Windows 10 or later (of course, even Windows 7 will work), or a recent Linux distribution (for example, Ubuntu or Fedora), or even macOS.

If you are using the digital version of this book, we advise you to type the code yourself or, better, access the code via the GitHub repository (link available in the next section). Doing so will help you avoid any potential errors related to the copying and pasting of code.

I strongly recommend that you follow the *empirical approach: not taking anyone's word on anything at all, but trying it out and experiencing it for yourself*. Hence, this book gives you many hands-on experiments and kernel code examples that you can and must try out yourself; this will greatly aid you in making real progress and deeply learning and understanding various aspects of Linux kernel development.

Download the example code files

You can download the example code files for this book from GitHub at `https://github.com/PacktPublishing/Linux-Kernel-Programming`. In case there's an update to the code, it will be updated on the existing GitHub repository.

We also have other code bundles from our rich catalog of books and videos available at `https://github.com/PacktPublishing/`. Check them out!

Download the color images

We also provide a PDF file that has color images of the screenshots/diagrams used in this book. You can download it here: `http://www.packtpub.com/sites/default/files/downloads/9781789953435_ColorImages.pdf`.

Conventions used

There are a number of text conventions used throughout this book.

`CodeInText`: Indicates code words in text, database table names, folder names, filenames, file extensions, pathnames, dummy URLs, user input, and Twitter handles. Here is an example: "The `ioremap()` API returns a KVA of the `void *` type (since it's an address location)"

A block of code is set as follows:

```
static int __init miscdrv_init(void)
{
    int ret;
    struct device *dev;
```

Preface

When we wish to draw your attention to a particular part of a code block, the relevant lines or items are set in bold:

```
#define pr_fmt(fmt) "%s:%s(): " fmt, KBUILD_MODNAME, __func__
[...]
#include <linux/miscdevice.h>
#include <linux/fs.h>
[...]
```

Any command-line input or output is written as follows:

```
pi@raspberrypi:~ $ sudo cat /proc/iomem
```

Bold: Indicates a new term, an important word, or words that you see onscreen. For example, words in menus or dialog boxes appear in the text like this. Here is an example: "Select **System info** from the **Administration** panel."

Warnings or important notes appear like this.

Tips and tricks appear like this.

Get in touch

Feedback from our readers is always welcome.

General feedback: If you have questions about any aspect of this book, mention the book title in the subject of your message and email us at `customercare@packtpub.com`.

Errata: Although we have taken every care to ensure the accuracy of our content, mistakes do happen. If you have found a mistake in this book, we would be grateful if you would report this to us. Please visit `www.packtpub.com/support/errata`, selecting your book, clicking on the Errata Submission Form link, and entering the details.

Piracy: If you come across any illegal copies of our works in any form on the Internet, we would be grateful if you would provide us with the location address or website name. Please contact us at copyright@packt.com with a link to the material.

If you are interested in becoming an author: If there is a topic that you have expertise in and you are interested in either writing or contributing to a book, please visit authors.packtpub.com.

Reviews

Please leave a review. Once you have read and used this book, why not leave a review on the site that you purchased it from? Potential readers can then see and use your unbiased opinion to make purchase decisions, we at Packt can understand what you think about our products, and our authors can see your feedback on their book. Thank you!

For more information about Packt, please visit packt.com.

Section 1: The Basics

Here, you will learn how to perform basic kernel development tasks. You will set up a kernel development workspace, build a Linux kernel from source, learn about the LKM framework, and write a "Hello, world" kernel module.

This section comprises the following chapters:

- Chapter 1, *Kernel Workspace Setup*
- Chapter 2, *Building the 5.x Linux Kernel from Source, Part 1*
- Chapter 3, *Building the 5.x Linux Kernel from Source, Part 2*
- Chapter 4, *Writing Your First Kernel Module – LKMs Part 1*
- Chapter 5, *Writing Your First Kernel Module – LKMs Part 2*

Section 1: The Basics

We highly recommend you also make use of this book's companion guide, *Linux Kernel Programming (Part 2)*.

It's an excellent industry-aligned beginner's guide to writing `misc` character drivers, performing I/O on peripheral chip memory and handling hardware interrupts. This book is primarily for Linux programmers beginning to find their way with device driver development. Linux device driver developers looking to overcome frequent and common kernel/driver development issues, as well as understand and learn to perform common driver tasks - the modern **Linux Device Model (LDM)** framework, user-kernel interfaces, performing peripheral I/O, handling hardware interrupts, dealing with concurrency and more - will benefit from this book. A basic understanding of Linux kernel internals (and common APIs), kernel module development and C programming is required.

You can get this book for free along with your copy, alternately you can also find this eBook in the GitHub repository: `https://github.com/PacktPublishing/Linux-Kernel-Programming/tree/master/Linux-Kernel-Programming-(Part-2)`.

Kernel Workspace Setup

Hello, and welcome to this book on learning Linux kernel development. To get the most out of this book, it is very important that you first set up the workspace environment that we will be using throughout the book. This chapter will teach you exactly how to do this and get started.

We will install a recent Linux distribution, preferably as a **Virtual Machine** (**VM**), and set it up to include all the required software packages. We will also clone this book's code repository on GitHub, and learn about a few useful projects that will help along this journey.

The best way to learn something is to do so *empirically* – not taking anyone's word on anything at all, but trying it out and experiencing it for yourself. Hence, this book gives you many hands-on experiments and kernel code examples that you can and indeed must try out yourself; this will greatly aid in your making real progress and deeply learning and understanding various aspects of Linux kernel and driver development. So, let's begin!

This chapter will take us through the following topics, which will help us set up our environment:

- Running Linux as a guest VM
- Setting up the software – distribution and packages
- A few additional useful projects

Technical requirements

You will need a modern desktop PC or laptop. Ubuntu Desktop specifies the following as "recommended system requirements" for the installation and usage of the distribution:

- A 2 GHz dual core processor or better.
- RAM:
    - Running on physical host: 2 GB or more system memory (more will certainly help).
    - Running as a guest VM: The host system should have at least 4 GB RAM (the more the better and the smoother the experience).
- 25 GB of free hard drive space (I suggest more, at least double this).
- Either a DVD drive or a USB port for the installer media (not required when setting up Ubuntu as a guest VM).
- Internet access is definitely helpful and required at times.

As performing tasks such as building a Linux kernel from source is a very memory- and CPU-intensive process, I highly recommend that you try it out on a powerful Linux system with plenty of RAM and disk space to spare as well. It should be pretty obvious – the more RAM and CPU power the host system has, the better!

Like any seasoned kernel contributor, I would say that working on a native Linux system is best. However, for the purposes of this book, we cannot assume that you will always have a dedicated native Linux box available to you. So, we will assume that you are working on a Linux guest. Working within a guest VM also adds an additional layer of isolation and thus safety.

Cloning our code repository: The complete source code for this book is freely available on GitHub at `https://github.com/PacktPublishing/Linux-Kernel-Programming`. You can clone and work on it by cloning the `git` tree, like so:

```
git clone
https://github.com/PacktPublishing/Linux-Kernel-Programming.git
```

The source code is organized chapter-wise. Each chapter is represented as a directory – for example, `ch1/` has the source code for this chapter. The root of the source tree has some code that is common to all chapters, such as the source files `convenient.h`, `klib_llkd.c`, as well as others.

Chapter 1

For efficient code browsing, I would strongly recommend that you always index the code base with `ctags(1)` and/or `cscope(1)`. For example, to set up the `ctags` index, just `cd` to the root of the source tree and type `ctags -R`.

Unless noted otherwise, the code output we show in the book is the output as seen on an x86-64 *Ubuntu 18.04.3 LTS* guest VM (running under Oracle VirtualBox 6.1). You should realize that due to (usually minor) distribution – and even within the same distributions but differing versions – differences, the output shown here may not perfectly match what you see on your Linux system.

Running Linux as a guest VM

As discussed previously, a practical and convenient alternative to using a native Linux system is to install and use the Linux distribution as a guest OS on a VM. It's key that you install a recent Linux distribution, preferably as a VM to be safe and avoid unpleasant data loss or other surprises. The fact is when working at the level of the kernel, abruptly crashing the system (and the data loss risks that arise thereof) is actually a commonplace occurrence. I recommend using **Oracle VirtualBox 6.x** (or the latest stable version) or other virtualization software, such as **VMware Workstation**.

Both of these are freely available. It's just that the code for this book has been tested on *VirtualBox 6.1*. Oracle VirtualBox is considered **Open Source Software (OSS)** and is licensed under the GPL v2 (the same as the Linux kernel). You can download it from `https://www.virtualbox.org/wiki/Downloads`. Its documentation can be found here: `https://www.virtualbox.org/wiki/End-user_documentation`.

The host system should be either MS Windows 10 or later (of course, even Windows 7 will work), a recent Linux distribution (for example, Ubuntu or Fedora), or macOS. So, let's get started by installing our Linux guest.

Installing a 64-bit Linux guest

Here, I won't delve into the minutiae of installing Linux as a guest on Oracle VirtualBox, the reason being that this installation is *not* directly related to Linux kernel development. There are many ways to set up a Linux VM; we really don't want to get into the details and the pros and cons of each of them here.

[15]

Kernel Workspace Setup

But if you are not familiar with this, don't worry. For your convenience, here are some excellent resources that will help you out:

- A very clearly written tutorial entitled *Install Linux Inside Windows Using VirtualBox* by Abhishek Prakash (*It's FOSS!, August 2019*): `https://itsfoss.com/install-linux-in-virtualbox/`.

- An alternate, similarly excellent resource is *Install Ubuntu on Oracle VirtualBox:* `https://brb.nci.nih.gov/seqtools/installUbuntu.html`.

Also, you can look up useful resources for installing a Linux guest on VirtualBox in the *Further reading* section at the end of this chapter.

While you install the Linux VM, keep the following things in mind.

Turn on your x86 system's virtualization extension support

Installing a 64-bit Linux guest requires that CPU virtualization extension support (Intel VT-x or AMD-SV) be turned on within the host system's **basic input/output system** (**BIOS**) settings. Let's see how to do this:

1. Our first step is to ensure that our CPU supports virtualization:
    1. **There are two broad ways to check this while on a Windows host**:
        - One, run the Task Manager app and switch to the **Performance** tab. Below the CPU graph, you will see, among several other things, **Virtualization**, with **Enabled** or **Disabled** following it.
        - A second way to check on Windows systems is to open a Command window (**cmd**). In Command Prompt, type `systeminfo` and press *Enter*. Among the output seen will be the `Virtualization Enabled in firmware` line. It will be followed by either `Yes` or `No`.

2. **To check this while on a Linux host,** from Terminal, issue the following commands (processor virtualization extension support: vmx is the check for Intel processors, smv is the check for AMD processors):

   ```
   egrep --color "vmx|svm" /proc/cpuinfo
   ```

   For Intel CPUs, the vmx flag will show up (in color) if virtualization is supported. In the case of AMD CPUs, svm will show up (in color). With this, we know that our CPU supports virtualization. But in order to use it, we need to enable it in the computer BIOS.

2. Enter the BIOS by pressing *Del* or *F12* while booting (the precise key to press varies with the BIOS). Please refer to your system's manual to see which key to use. Search for terms such as Virtualization or Virtualization Technology (VT-x). Here is an example for Award BIOS:

Figure 1.1 – Setting the BIOS Virtualization option to the Enabled state

 If you are using an Asus EFI-BIOS, you will have to set the entry to [Enabled] if it is not set by default. Visit https://superuser.com/questions/367290/how-to-enable-hardware-virtualization-on-asus-motherboard/375351#375351.

Kernel Workspace Setup

3. Now, choose to use hardware virtualization in VirtualBox's **Settings** menu for your VM. To do this, click on **System** and then **Acceleration**. After that, check the boxes, as shown in the following screenshot:

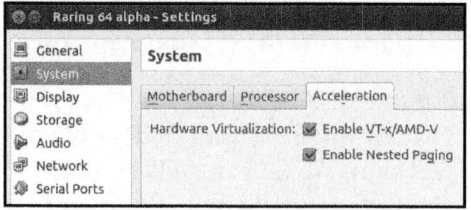

Figure 1.2 – Enabling hardware virtualization options within the VirtualBox VM settings

This is how we enable our host processor's hardware virtualization features for optimal performance.

Allocate sufficient space to the disk

For most desktop/laptop systems, allocating a gigabyte of RAM and two CPUs to the guest VM should be sufficient.

However, when allocating space for the guest's disk, please be generous. Instead of the usual/default 8 GB suggested, I strongly recommend you make it 50 GB or even more. Of course, this implies that the host system has more disk space than this available! Also, you can specify this amount to be *dynamically allocated* or *allocated on-demand*. The hypervisor will "grow" the virtual disk optimally, not giving it the entire space to begin with.

Install the Oracle VirtualBox Guest Additions

For best performance, it's important to install the Oracle VirtualBox Guest Additions as well within the guest VM. These are essentially para-virtualization accelerator software, which greatly helps with optimal performance. Let's see how to do this on an Ubuntu guest session:

1. First, update your Ubuntu guest OS's software packages. You can do so using the following command:

    ```
    sudo apt update

    sudo apt upgrade
    ```

[18]

2. On completion, reboot your Ubuntu guest OS and then install the required packages using the following command:

   ```
   sudo apt install build-essential dkms linux-headers-$(uname -r)
   ```

3. Now, from the VM menu bar, go to **Devices | Insert Guest Additions CD image...**. This will mount the `Guest Additions ISO` file inside your VM. The following screenshot shows what it looks like doing this:

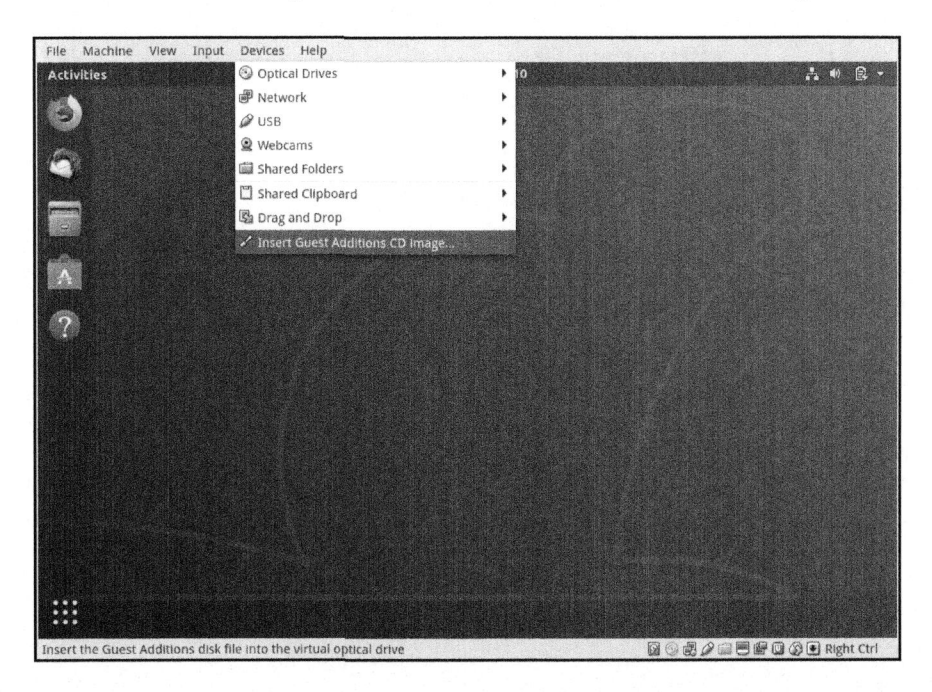

Figure 1.3 – VirtualBox | Devices | Insert Guest Additions CD image

4. Now, a dialog window will pop up that will prompt you to run the installer in order to launch it. Select **Run**.
5. The Guest Additions installation will now take place in a Terminal window that shows up. Once complete, hit the *Enter* key to close the window. Then, power off your Ubuntu guest OS in order to change some settings from the VirtualBox manager, as explained next.

Kernel Workspace Setup

6. Now, to enable **Shared Clipboard** and **Drag'n'Drop** functionalities between the guest and host machines, go to **General | Advanced** and enable the two options (**Shared Clipboard** and **Drag'n'Drop**) as you wish with the dropdowns:

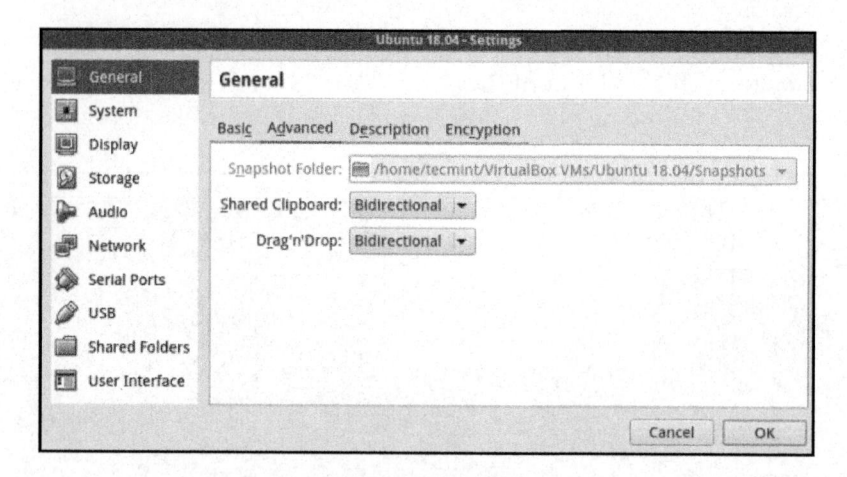

Figure 1.4 – VirtualBox: enabling functionality between the host and guest

7. Then, click **OK** to save the settings. Now boot into your guest system, log in, and test that everything is working fine.

> As of the time of writing, Fedora 29 has an issue with the installation of the `vboxsf` kernel module required for the **Shared Folders** feature. I refer you to the following resource to attempt to rectify the situation: *Bug 1576832 - virtualbox-guest-additions does not mount shared folder* (`https://bugzilla.redhat.com/show_bug.cgi?id=1576832`).
>
> If this refuses to work, you can simply transfer files between your host and guest VM over SSH (using `scp(1)`); to do so, install and start up the SSH daemon with the following commands:
> ```
> sudo yum install openssh-server
> sudo systemctl start sshd
> ```

Remember to update the guest VM regularly and when prompted. This is an essential security requirement. You can do so manually by using the following:

```
sudo /usr/bin/update-manager
```

Finally, to be safe, please do not keep any important data on the guest VM. We will be working on kernel development. Crashing the guest kernel is actually a commonplace occurrence. While this usually does not cause data loss, you can never tell! To be safe, always back up any important data. This applies to Fedora as well. To learn how to install Fedora as a VirtualBox guest, visit `https://fedoramagazine.org/install-fedora-virtualbox-guest/`.

> **TIP**
> Sometimes, especially when the overhead of the X Window System (or Wayland) GUI is too high, it's preferable to simply work in console mode. You can do so by appending 3 (the run level) to the kernel command line via the bootloader. However, working in console mode within VirtualBox may not be that pleasant an experience (for one, the clipboard is unavailable, and the screen size and fonts are less than desirable). Thus, simply doing a remote login (via `ssh`, `putty`, or equivalent) into the VM from the host system can be a great way to work.

Experimenting with the Raspberry Pi

The Raspberry Pi is a popular credit card-sized **Single-Board Computer** (**SBC**), much like a small-factor PC that has USB ports, a microSD card, HDMI, audio, Ethernet, GPIO, and more. The **System on Chip** (**SoC**) that powers it is from Broadcom, and in it is an ARM core or cluster of cores. Though not mandatory, of course, in this book, we strive to also test and run our code on a Raspberry Pi 3 Model B+ target. Running your code on different target architectures is always a good eye-opener to possible defects and helps with testing. I encourage you to do the same:

Figure 1.5 – The Raspberry Pi with a USB-to-serial adapter cable attached to its GPIO pins

Kernel Workspace Setup

You can work on the Raspberry Pi target either using a digital monitor/TV via HDMI as the output device and a traditional keyboard/mouse over its USB ports or, more commonly for developers, over a remote shell via `ssh(1)`. However, the SSH approach does not cut it in all circumstances. Having a *serial console* on the Raspberry Pi helps, especially when doing kernel debugging.

> I would recommend that you check out the following article, which will help you set up a USB-to-serial connection, thus getting a console login to the Raspberry Pi from a PC/laptop: *WORKING ON THE CONSOLE WITH THE RASPBERRY PI*, kaiwanTECH: `https://kaiwantech.wordpress.com/2018/12/16/working-on-the-console-with-the-raspberry-pi/`.

To set up your Raspberry Pi, please refer to the official documentation: `https://www.raspberrypi.org/documentation/`. Our Raspberry Pi system runs the "official" Raspbian (Debian for Raspberry Pi) Linux OS with a recent (as of the time of writing) 4.14 Linux kernel. On the console of the Raspberry Pi, we run the following commands:

```
rpi $ lsb_release -a
No LSB modules are available.
Distributor ID: Raspbian
Description:    Raspbian GNU/Linux 9.6 (stretch)
Release:        9.6
Codename:       stretch
rpi $ uname -a
Linux raspberrypi 4.14.79-v7+ #1159 SMP Sun Nov 4 17:50:20 GMT 2018 armv7l GNU/Linux
rpi $
```

What if you don't have a Raspberry Pi, or it's not handy? Well, there's always a way – emulation! Though not as good as having the real thing, emulating the Raspberry Pi with the powerful **Free and Open Source Software** (**FOSS**) emulator called **QEMU** or **Quick Emulator** is a nice way to get started, at least.

> As the details of setting up the emulated Raspberry Pi via QEMU go beyond the scope of this book, we will not be covering it. However, you can check out the following links to find out more: *Emulating Raspberry Pi on Linux*: http://embedonix.com/articles/linux/emulating-raspberry-pi-on-linux/ and *qemu-rpi-kernel*, *GitHub*: https://github.com/dhruvvyas90/qemu-rpi-kernel/wiki.

Also, of course, you do not have to confine yourself to the Raspberry Pi family; there are several other excellent prototyping boards available. One that springs to mind is the popular **BeagleBone Black (BBB)** board.

> In fact, for professional development and product work, the Raspberry Pi is really not the best choice, for several reasons... a bit of googling will help you understand this. Having said that, as a learning and basic prototyping environment it's hard to beat, with the strong community (and tech hobbyist) support it enjoys.
>
> Several modern choices of microprocessors for embedded Linux (and much more) are discussed and contrasted in this excellent in-depth article: *SO YOU WANT TO BUILD AN EMBEDDED LINUX SYSTEM?*, Jay Carlson, Oct 2020 : https://jaycarlson.net/embedded-linux/; do check it out.

By now, I expect that you have set up Linux as a guest machine (or are using a native "test" Linux box) and have cloned the book's GitHub code repository. So far, we have covered some information regarding setting up Linux as a guest VM (as well as optionally using boards such as the Raspberry Pi or the BeagleBone). Let's now move on to a key step: actually installing software components on our Linux guest system so that we can learn and write Linux kernel code on the system!

Setting up the software – distribution and packages

It is recommended to use one of the following or later stable version Linux distributions. As mentioned in the previous section, they can always be installed as a guest OS on a Windows or Linux host system, with the clear first choice being Ubuntu Linux 18.04 LTS Desktop. The following screenshot shows you the recommended version and the user interface:

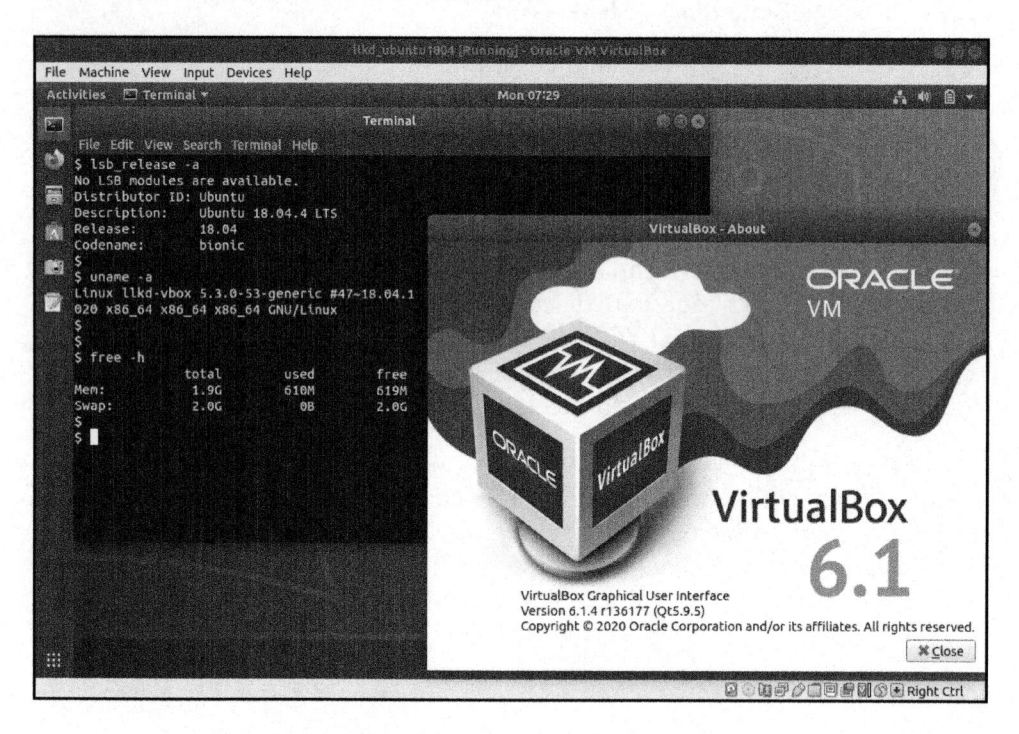

Figure 1.6 – Oracle VirtualBox 6.1 running Ubuntu 18.04.4 LTS as a guest VM

The preceding version – Ubuntu 18.04 LTS Desktop – is the version of choice for this book, at least. The two primary reasons for this are straightforward:

- Ubuntu Linux is one of the, if not *the*, most popular Linux (kernel) development workstation environments in industry use today.
- We cannot always, for lack of space and clarity, show the code/build output of multiple environments in this book. Hence, we have chosen to show the output as seen on Ubuntu 18.04 LTS Desktop.

> Ubuntu 16.04 LTS Desktop is a good choice too (it has **Long-Term Support (LTS)** as well), and everything should work. To download it, visit https://www.ubuntu.com/download/desktop.

Some other Linux distributions that can also be considered include the following:

- **CentOS 8 Linux (not CentOS Stream)**: CentOS Linux is a distribution that's essentially a clone of the popular enterprise server distribution from RedHat (RHEL 8, in our case). You can download it from here: https://www.centos.org/download/.
- **Fedora Workstation**: Fedora is a very well-known FOSS Linux distribution as well. You can think of it as being a kind of test-bed for projects and code that will eventually land up within RedHat's enterprise products. Download it from https://getfedora.org/ (download the **Fedora Workstation** image).
- **Raspberry Pi as a target**: It's really best to refer to the official documentation to set up your Raspberry Pi (*Raspberry Pi documentation*: https://www.raspberrypi.org/documentation/). It's perhaps worth noting that Raspberry Pi "kits" are widely available that come completely pre-installed and with some hardware accessories as well.

> If you want to learn how to install a Raspberry Pi OS image on an SD card, visit https://www.raspberrypi.org/documentation/installation/installing-images/.

- **BeagleBone Black as a target**: The BBB is, like the Raspberry Pi, an extremely popular embedded ARM SBC for hobbyists and pros. You can get started here: https://beagleboard.org/black. The System Reference Manual for the BBB can be found here: https://cdn.sparkfun.com/datasheets/Dev/Beagle/BBB_SRM_C.pdf. Though we don't present examples running on the BBB, nevertheless, it's a valid embedded Linux system that, once properly set up, you can run this book's code on.

Kernel Workspace Setup

Before we conclude our discussion on selecting our software distribution for the book, here are a few more points to note:

- These distributions are, in their default form, FOSS and non-proprietary, and free to use as an end user.
- Though our aim is to be Linux distribution-neutral, the code has only been tested on Ubuntu 18.04 LTS and "lightly" tested on CentOS 8, and a Raspberry Pi 3 Model B+ running the Raspbian GNU/Linux 9.9 (stretch) Debian-based Linux OS.
- We will, as far as is possible, use the very latest (as of the time of writing) **stable LTS Linux kernel version 5.4** for our kernel build and code runs. Being an LTS kernel, the 5.4 kernel is an excellent choice to run on and learn with.

> It is interesting to know that the 5.4 LTS kernel will indeed have a long lifespan; from November 2019 right up to December 2025! This is good news: this book's content remains current and valid for years to come!

- For this book, we'll log in as the user account named `llkd`.

> It's important to realize, for maximized security (with the latest defenses and fixes), that you must run the most recent **Long Term Support** (**LTS**) kernel possible for your project or product.

Now that we have chosen our Linux distribution and/or hardware boards and VMs, it's time we install essential software packages.

Installing software packages

The packages that are installed by default when you use a typical Linux desktop distribution, such as any recent Ubuntu, CentOS, or Fedora Linux system, will include the minimal set required by a systems programmer: the native toolchain, which includes the `gcc` compiler along with headers, and the `make` utility/packages.

In this book, though, we are going to learn how to write kernel-space code using a VM and/or a target system running on a foreign processor (ARM or AArch64 being the typical cases). To effectively develop kernel code on these systems, we will need to install some software packages. Read on.

Installing the Oracle VirtualBox guest additions

Make sure you have installed the guest VM (as explained previously). Then, follow along:

1. Log in to your Linux guest VM and first run the following commands within a Terminal window (on a shell):

    ```
    sudo apt update
    sudo apt install gcc make perl
    ```

2. Install the Oracle VirtualBox Guest Additions now. Refer to *How to Install VirtualBox Guest Additions in Ubuntu*: https://www.tecmint.com/install-virtualbox-guest-additions-in-ubuntu/.

> This only applies if you are running Ubuntu as a VM using Oracle VirtualBox as the hypervisor app.

Installing required software packages

To install the packages, take the following steps:

1. Within the Ubuntu VM, first do the following:

    ```
    sudo apt update
    ```

2. Now, run the following command in a single line:

    ```
    sudo apt install git fakeroot build-essential tar ncurses-dev
    tar xz-utils libssl-dev bc stress python3-distutils libelf-dev
    linux-headers-$(uname -r) bison flex libncurses5-dev util-
    linux net-tools linux-tools-$(uname -r) exuberant-ctags cscope
    sysfsutils gnome-system-monitor curl perf-tools-unstable
    gnuplot rt-tests indent tree pstree smem libnuma-dev numactl
    hwloc bpfcc-tools sparse flawfinder cppcheck tuna hexdump
    openjdk-14-jre trace-cmd virt-what
    ```

The command installing `gcc`, `make`, and `perl` is done first so that the Oracle VirtualBox Guest Additions can be properly installed straight after. These (Guest Additions) are essentially para-virtualization accelerator software. It's important to install them for optimal performance.

This book, at times, mentions that running a program on another CPU architecture – typically ARM – might be a useful exercise. If you want to try (interesting!) stuff like this, please read on; otherwise, feel free to skip ahead to the *Important installation notes* section.

Installing a cross toolchain and QEMU

One way to try things on an ARM machine is to actually do so on a physical ARM-based SBC; for example, the Raspberry Pi is a very popular choice. In this case, the typical development workflow is to first build the ARM code on your x86-64 host system. But to do so, we need to install a **cross toolchain** – a set of tools allowing you to build software on one host CPU designed to execute on a different *target* CPU. An x86-64 *host* building programs for an ARM *target* is a very common case, and indeed is our use case here. Details on installing the cross compiler follow shortly.

Often, an alternate way to just trying things out is to have an ARM/Linux system emulated – this alleviates the need for hardware! To do so, we recommend using the superb **QEMU** project (https://www.qemu.org/).

To install the required QEMU packages, do the following:

- For installation on Ubuntu, use the following:

    `sudo apt install qemu-system-arm`

- For installation on Fedora, use the following:

    `sudo dnf install qemu-system-arm-<version#>`

To get the version number on Fedora, just type the preceding command and after typing the required package name (here, `qemu-system-arm-`), press the *Tab* key twice. It will auto-complete, providing a list of choices. Choose the latest version and press *Enter*.

CentOS 8 does not seem to have a simple means to install the QEMU package we require. (You could always install a cross toolchain via the source, but that's challenging; or, obtain an appropriate binary package.) Due to these difficulties, we will skip showing cross-compilation on CentOS.

Installing a cross compiler

If you intend to write a C program that is compiled on a certain host system but must execute on another target system, then you need to compile it with what's known as a cross compiler or cross toolchain. For example, in our use case, we want to work on an x86-64 host machine. It could even be an x86-64 guest VM, no issues, but run our code on an ARM-32 target:

- On Ubuntu, you can install the cross toolchain with the following:

    ```
    sudo apt install crossbuild-essential-armhf
    ```

    The preceding command installs an x86_64-to-ARM-32 toolchain appropriate for ARM-32 "hard float" (armhf) systems (such as the Raspberry Pi); this is usually just fine. It results in the `arm-linux-gnueabihf-<foo>` set of tools being installed; where `<foo>` represents cross tools such as `addr2line`, `as`, `g++`, `gcc`, `gcov`, `gprof`, `ld`, `nm`, `objcopy`, `objdump`, `readelf`, `size`, `strip`, and so on. (The cross compiler prefix in this case is `arm-linux-gnueabihf-`). In addition, though not mandatory, you can install the `arm-linux-gnueabi-<foo>` cross toolset like this:

    ```
    sudo apt install gcc-arm-linux-gnueabi binutils-arm-linux-gnueabi
    ```

- On Fedora, you can install the cross toolchain with the following:

    ```
    sudo dnf install arm-none-eabi-binutils-cs-<ver#> arm-none-eabi-gcc-cs-<ver#>
    ```

> For Fedora Linux, the same tip as earlier applies – use the *Tab* key to help auto-complete the command.

Installing and using a cross toolchain might require some reading up for newbie users. You can visit the *Further reading* section where I have placed a few useful links that will surely be of great help.

Important installation notes

We will now mention a few remaining points, most of them pertaining to software installation or other issues when working on particular distributions:

- On CentOS 8, you can install Python with the following command:

  ```
  sudo dnf install python3
  ```

  However, this does not actually create the (required) **symbolic link (symlink)**, `/usr/bin/python`; why not? Check out this link for details: https://developers.redhat.com/blog/2019/05/07/what-no-python-in-red-hat-enterprise-linux-8/.

  To manually create the symlink to, for example, `python3`, do the following:

  ```
  sudo alternatives --set python /usr/bin/python3
  ```

- The kernel build might fail if the OpenSSL header files aren't installed. Fix this on CentOS 8 with the following:

  ```
  sudo dnf install openssl-devel
  ```

- On CentOS 8, the `lsb_release` utility can be installed with the following:

  ```
  sudo dnf install redhat-lsb-core
  ```

- On Fedora, do the following:
    - Install these two packages, ensuring the dependencies are met when building a kernel on Fedora systems:
      `sudo dnf install openssl-devel-1:1.1.1d-2.fc31 elfutils-libelf-devel`
      (the preceding `openssl-devel` package is suffixed with the relevant Fedora version number (`.fc31` here; adjust it as required for your system).
    - In order to use the `lsb_release` command, you must install the `redhat-lsb-core` package.

Congratulations! This completes the software setup, and your kernel journey begins! Now, let's check out a few additional and useful projects to complete this chapter. It's certainly recommended that you read through these as well.

Chapter 1

Additional useful projects

This section brings you details of some additional miscellaneous projects that you might find very useful indeed. In a few appropriate places in this book, we refer to or directly make use of some of them, thus making them important to understand.

Let's get started with the well-known and important Linux *man pages* project.

Using the Linux man pages

You must have noticed the convention followed in most Linux/Unix literature:

- The suffixing of *user commands* with (1) – for example, `gcc(1)` or `gcc.1`
- *System calls* with (2) – for example, `fork(2)` or `fork().2`
- *Library APIs* with (3) – for example, `pthread_create(3)` or `pthread_create().3`

As you are no doubt aware, the number in parentheses (or after the period) denotes the section of the **manual** (the **man** pages) that the command/API in question belongs to. A quick check with `man(1)`, via the `man man` command (that's why we love Unix/Linux!) reveals the sections of the Unix/Linux manual:

```
$ man man
[...]
A section, if provided, will direct man to look only in that section
of
the manual. [...]

       The table below shows the section numbers of the manual
followed by the types of pages they contain.

            1   Executable programs or shell commands
            2   System calls (functions provided by the kernel)
            3   Library calls (functions within program libraries)
            4   Special files (usually found in /dev)
            5   File formats and conventions eg /etc/passwd
            6   Games
            7   Miscellaneous (including macro packages and conventions),
    e.g.
                man(7), groff(7)
            8   System administration commands (usually only for root)
            9   Kernel routines [Non standard]
    [...]
```

[31]

So, for example, to look up the man page on the `stat(2)` system call, you would use the following:

```
man 2 stat  # (or: man stat.2)
```

At times (quite often, in fact), the `man` pages are simply too detailed to warrant reading through when a quick answer is all that's required. Enter the `tldr` project – read on!

The tldr variant

While we're discussing `man` pages, a common annoyance is that the `man` page on a command is, at times, too large. Take the `ps(1)` utility as an example. It has a large `man` page as, of course, it has a huge number of option switches. Wouldn't it be nice, though, to have a simplified and summarized "common usage" page? This is precisely what the `tldr` pages project aims to do.

> **TL;DR** literally means **Too Long; Didn't Read**.

In their own words, they provide "simplified and community-driven man pages." So, once installed, `tldr ps` provides a neat brief summary on the most commonly used `ps` command option switches to do something useful:

```
~ $ tldr ps

ps

Information about running processes.

- List all running processes:
  ps aux

- List all running processes including the full command string:
  ps auxww

- Search for a process that matches a string:
  ps aux | grep string

- List all processes of the current user in extra full format:
  ps --user $(id -u) -F

- List all processes of the current user as a tree:
  ps --user $(id -u) f

- Get the parent pid of a process:
  ps -o ppid= -p pid

~ $
```

Figure 1.7 – A screenshot of the tldr utility in action: tldr ps

> **TIP**: All Ubuntu repos have the `tldr` package. Install it with `sudo apt install tldr`.

It's indeed worth checking out. If you're interested in knowing more, visit https://tldr.sh/.

Earlier, recall that we said that userspace system calls fall under section 2 of the man pages, library subroutines under section 3, and kernel APIs under section 9. Given this, then, in this book, why don't we specify the, say, `printk` kernel function (or API) as `printk(9)` – as `man man` shows us that section 9 of the manual is *Kernel routines*? Well, it's fiction, really (at least on today's Linux): *no man pages actually exist for kernel APIs!* So, how do you get documentation on the kernel APIs and so on? That's just what we will briefly delve into in the following section.

Locating and using the Linux kernel documentation

The community has developed and evolved the Linux kernel documentation into a good state over many years of effort. The *latest version* of the kernel documentation, presented in a nice and modern "web" style, can always be accessed online here: https://www.kernel.org/doc/html/latest/.

> Of course, as we will mention in the next chapter, the kernel documentation is always available for that kernel version within the kernel source tree itself, in the directory called `Documentation/`.

Kernel Workspace Setup

As just one example of the online kernel documentation, see the following partial screenshot of the page on *Core Kernel Documentation/Basic C Library Functions* (`https://www.kernel.org/doc/html/latest/core-api/kernel-api.html#basic-c-library-functions`):

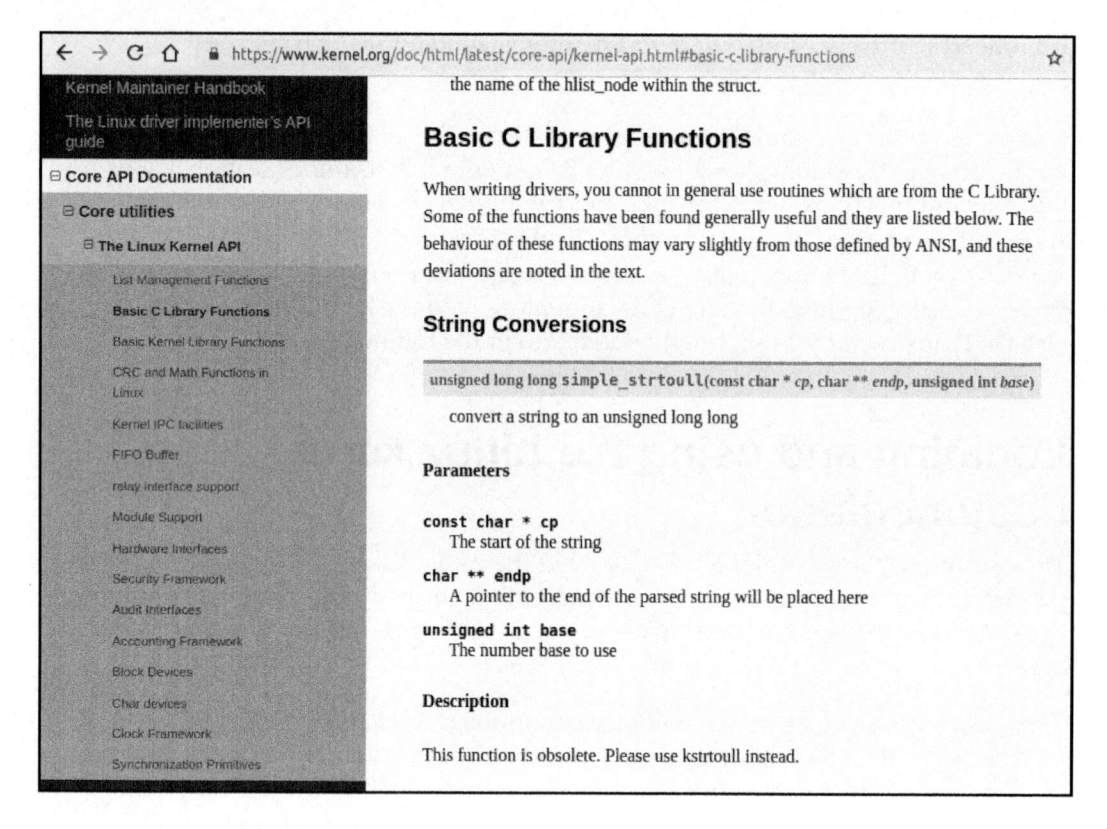

Figure 1.8 – Partial screenshot showing a small part of the modern online Linux kernel documentation

As can be gleaned from the screenshot, the modern documentation is pretty comprehensive.

Generating the kernel documentation from source

You can literally generate the full Linux kernel documentation from within the kernel source tree in various popular formats (including PDF, HTML, LaTeX, EPUB, or XML), in a *Javadoc* or *Doxygen-like* style. The modern documentation system used internally by the kernel is called **Sphinx**. Using `make help` within the kernel source tree will reveal several *documentation targets*, among them `htmldocs`, `pdfdocs`, and more. So, you can, for example, `cd` to the kernel source tree and run `make pdfdocs` to build the complete Linux kernel documentation as PDF documents (the PDFs, as well as some other meta-docs, will be placed in `Documentation/output/latex`). The first time, at least, you will likely be prompted to install several packages and utilities (we don't show this explicitly).

> **TIP**
> Don't worry if the preceding details are not crystal clear yet. I suggest you first read `Chapter 2`, *Building the 5.x Linux Kernel from Source – Part 1*, and `Chapter 3`, *Building the 5.x Linux Kernel from Source – Part 2*, and then revisit these details.

Static analysis tools for the Linux kernel

Static analyzers are tools that, by examining the source code, attempt to identify potential errors within it. They can be tremendously useful to you as the developer, though you must learn how to "tame" them – in the sense that they can result in false positives.

Several useful static analysis tools exist. Among them, the ones that are more relevant for Linux kernel code analysis include the following:

- Sparse: `https://sparse.wiki.kernel.org/index.php/Main_Page`
- Coccinelle: `http://coccinelle.lip6.fr/` (requires the `ocaml` package installed)
- Smatch: `http://smatch.sourceforge.net/`, `http://repo.or.cz/w/smatch.git`
- Flawfinder: `https://dwheeler.com/flawfinder/`
- Cppcheck: `https://github.com/danmar/cppcheck`

For example, to install and try Sparse, do the following:

```
sudo apt install sparse
cd <kernel-src-tree>
make C=1 CHECK="/usr/bin/sparse"
```

Kernel Workspace Setup

There are also several high-quality commercial static analysis tools available. Among them are the following:

- SonarQube: `https://www.sonarqube.org/` (a free and open source community edition is available)
- Coverity Scan: `https://scan.coverity.com/`
- Klocwork: `https://www.meteonic.com/klocwork`

> **TIP:** `clang` is a frontend to GCC that is becoming more popular even for kernel builds. You can install it on Ubuntu with `sudo apt install clang clang-tools`.

Static analysis tools can save the day. Time spent learning to use them effectively is time well spent!

Linux Trace Toolkit next generation

A superb tool for *tracing* and *profiling* is the powerful **Linux Tracing Toolkit next generation** (**LTTng**) toolset, a Linux Foundation project. LTTng allows you to trace both userspace (applications) and/or the kernel code paths in minute detail. This can tremendously aid you in understanding where performance bottlenecks occur, as well as aiding you in understanding the overall code flow and thus in learning about how the code actually performs its tasks.

In order to learn how to install and use it, I refer you to its very good documentation here: `https://lttng.org/docs` (try `https://lttng.org/download/` for installation for common Linux distributions). It is also highly recommended that you install the Trace Compass GUI: `https://www.eclipse.org/tracecompass/`. It provides an excellent GUI for examining and interpreting LTTng's output.

> **TIP:** Trace Compass minimally requires a **Java Runtime Environment** (**JRE**) to be installed as well. I installed one on my Ubuntu 20.04 LTS system with `sudo apt install openjdk-14-jre`.

As an example (I can't resist!), here's a screenshot of a capture by LTTng being "visualized" by the superb Trace Compass GUI. Here, I show a couple of hardware interrupts (IRQ lines 1 and 130, the interrupt lines for the i8042 and Wi-Fi chipset, respectively, on my native x86_64 system.):

[36]

Chapter 1

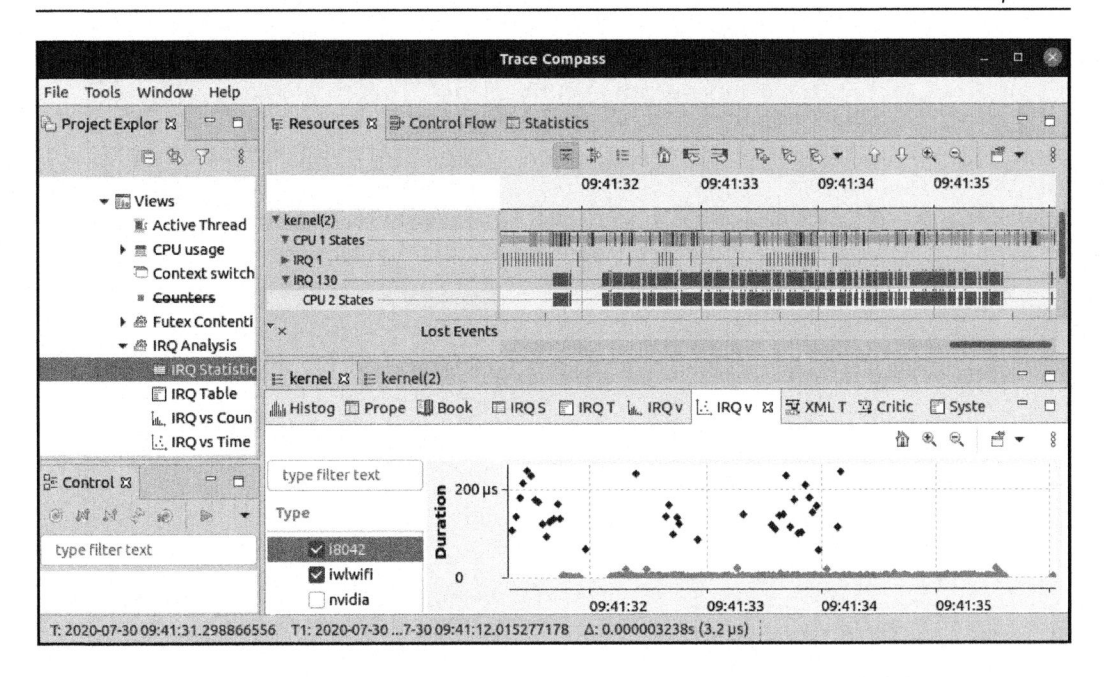

Figure 1.9 – Sample screenshot of the Trace Compass GUI; samples recorded by LTTng showing IRQ lines 1 and 130

The pink color in the upper part of the preceding screenshot represents the occurrence of a hardware interrupt. Underneath that, in the **IRQ vs Time** tab (it's only partially visible), the interrupt distribution is seen. (In the distribution graph, the y axis is the time taken; interestingly, the network interrupt handler – in red – seems to take very little time, the i8042 keyboard/mouse controller chip's handler – in blue – takes more time, even exceeding 200 microseconds!)

The procmap utility

Visualizing the complete memory map of the kernel **Virtual Address Space (VAS)** as well as any given process's user VAS is what the `procmap` utility is designed to do.

The description on its GitHub page sums it up:

It outputs a simple visualization of the complete memory map of a given process in a vertically-tiled format ordered by descending virtual address. The script has the intelligence to show kernel and userspace mappings as well as calculate and show the sparse memory regions that will be present. Also, each segment or mapping is scaled by relative size (and color-coded for readability). On 64-bit systems, it also shows the so-called non-canonical sparse region or 'hole' (typically close to 16,384 PB on the x86_64).

[37]

Kernel Workspace Setup

The utility includes options to see only kernel space or userspace, verbose and debug modes, the ability to export its output in convenient CSV format to a specified file, as well as other options. It has a kernel component as well and currently works (and auto-detects) on x86_64, AArch32, and Aarch64 CPUs.

> Do note, though, that I am still working on this utility; it's currently under development... there are several caveats. Feedback and contributions are most appreciated!

Download/clone it from https://github.com/kaiwan/procmap:

```
[==================---   P R O C M A P    ---==================]
Process Virtual Address Space (VAS) Visualization utility
https://github.com/kaiwan/procmap

Sun Dec 27 09:47:44 IST 2020
[=====---  Start memory map for 1:systemd  ---=====]
[Pathname: /usr/lib/systemd/systemd ]
VAS mappings:   name    [ size,perms,u:maptype,u:0xfile-offset]
+----------------  K E R N E L  V A S     end kva -----------------+ ffffffffffffffff
|<... K sparse region ...> [   8.00 MB,--- ]                       |
|                                                                  |
|                                                                  |
+------------------------------------------------------------------+ fffffffffff7ff000
|         fixmap region [   2.52 MB,r-- ]                          |
|                                                                  |
+------------------------------------------------------------------+ fffffffffff579000  <-- FIXADDR_START
|<... K sparse region ...> [   5.47 MB,--- ]                       |
|                                                                  |
+------------------------------------------------------------------+ fffffffffff000000  <-- MODULES_END
|         module region [1008.00 MB,rwx ]                          |
|                                                                  |
|                                                                  |
|                                                                  |
+------------------------------------------------------------------+ ffffffffc0000000  <-- MODULES_VADDR
|<... K sparse region ...> [  40.60 TB,--- ]                       |
|                                                                  |
|                                                                  |
|                                                                  |
|                                                                  |
|                                                                  |
|                                                                  |
|                                                                  |
|                                                                  |
|                                                                  |
|                                                                  |
+------------------------------------------------------------------+ ffffd764bfffffff  <-- VMALLOC_END
|         vmalloc region [  31.99 TB,rw- ]                         |
|                                                                  |
```

Figure 1.10 – A partial screenshot of the procmap utility's output, showing only the top portion of kernel VAS on x86_64

We make good use of this utility in Chapter 7, *Memory Management Internals - Essentials*.

Simple Embedded ARM Linux System FOSS project

SEALS or **Simple Embedded ARM Linux System** is a very simple "skeleton" Linux base system running on an emulated ARM machine. It provides a primary Bash script that asks the end user what functionality they want via a menu, then accordingly proceeds to cross-compile a Linux kernel for ARM, then creates and initializes a simple root filesystem. It can then call upon QEMU (`qemu-system-arm`) to emulate and run an ARM platform (the Versatile Express CA-9 is the default board emulated). The useful thing is, the script builds the target kernel, the root filesystem, and the root filesystem image file, and sets things up for boot. It even has a simple GUI (or console) frontend, to make usage a bit simpler for the end user. The project's GitHub page is here: `https://github.com/kaiwan/seals/`. Clone it and give it a try... we definitely recommend you have a look at its wiki section pages at `https://github.com/kaiwan/seals/wiki` for help.

Modern tracing and performance analysis with [e]BPF

An extension of the well-known **Berkeley Packet Filter** or **BPF**, **eBPF** is the **extended BPF**. (FYI, modern usage of the term is simply to refer to it as **BPF**, dropping the 'e' prefix). Very briefly, BPF used to provide the supporting infrastructure within the kernel to effectively trace network packets. BPF is a very recent kernel innovation – available only from the Linux 4.0 kernel onward. It extends the BPF notion, allowing you to trace much more than just the network stack. Also, it works for tracing both kernel space as well as userspace apps. *In effect, BPF and its frontends are the modern approach to tracing and performance analysis on a Linux system.*

To use BPF, you will need a system with the following:

- Linux kernel 4.0 or later
- Kernel support for BPF (`https://github.com/iovisor/bcc/blob/master/INSTALL.md#kernel-configuration`)
- The **BCC** or `bpftrace` frontends installed (link to install them on popular Linux distributions: `https://github.com/iovisor/bcc/blob/master/INSTALL.md#installing-bcc`)
- Root access on the target system

Using the BPF kernel feature directly is very hard, so there are several easier front ends to use. Among them, BCC and `bpftrace` are regarded as useful. Check out the following link to a picture that opens your eyes to just how many powerful BCC tools are available to help trace different Linux subsystems and hardware: https://github.com/iovisor/bcc/blob/master/images/bcc_tracing_tools_2019.png.

> **Important**: You can install the BCC tools for your regular host Linux distro by reading the installation instructions here: https://github.com/iovisor/bcc/blob/master/INSTALL.md. Why not on our guest Linux VM? You can, when running a distro kernel (such as an Ubuntu- or Fedora-supplied kernel). The reason: the installation of the BCC toolset includes (and depends upon) the installation of the `linux-headers-$(uname -r)` package; this `linux-headers` package exists *only for* distro kernels (and not for our custom 5.4 kernel that we shall often be running on the guest).

The main site for BCC can be found at https://github.com/iovisor/bcc.

The LDV - Linux Driver Verification - project

The Russian Linux Verification Center, founded in 2005, is an opensource project; it has specialists in, and thus specializes in, automated testing of complex software projects. This includes comprehensive test suites, frameworks, and detailed analyses (both static and dynamic) being performed on the core Linux kernel as well as on the primarily device drivers within the kernel. This project puts a great deal of focus on the testing and verification of *kernel modules* as well, which many similar projects tend to skim.

Of particular interest to us here is the Online Linux Driver Verification Service page (http://linuxtesting.org/ldv/online?action=rules); it contains a list of a few verified **Rules** (Figure 1.11):

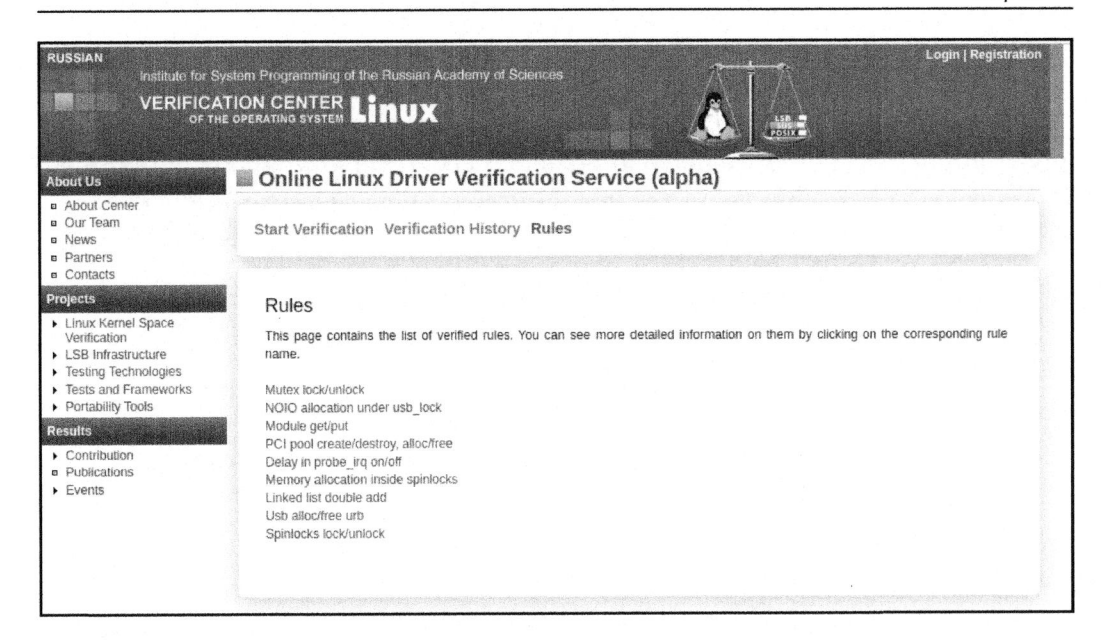

Figure 1.11 – Screenshot of the 'Rules' page of the Linux Driver Verification (LDV) project site

By glancing through these rules, we'll be able to not only see the rule but also instances of actual cases where these rules were violated by driver/kernel code within the mainline kernel, thus introducing bugs. The LDV project has successfully discovered and fixed (by sending in patches in the usual manner) several driver/kernel bugs. In a few of the upcoming chapters, we shall mention instances of these LDV rule violations (for example, memory leakage, **Use After Free** (**UAF**) bugs, and locking violations) having been uncovered, and (probably) even fixed.

Here are some useful links on the LDV website:

- The Linux Verification Center home page; http://linuxtesting.org/
- Linux Kernel Space Verification; http://linuxtesting.org/kernel
- Online Linux Driver Verification Service page **with verified Rules** : http://linuxtesting.org/ldv/online?action=rules
- *Problems in Linux Kernel* page; lists over 400 issues found in existing drivers (mostly fixed as well); http://linuxtesting.org/results/ldv

Summary

In this chapter, we covered in detail the hardware and software requirements to set up an appropriate development environment for beginning to work on Linux kernel development. In addition, we mentioned the basics and provided links, wherever appropriate, for setting up a Raspberry Pi device, installing powerful tools such as QEMU and a cross toolchain, and so on. We also threw some light on other "miscellaneous" tools and projects that you, as a budding kernel and/or device driver developer, might find useful, as well as information on how to begin looking up kernel documentation.

In this book, we definitely recommend and expect you to try out and work on kernel code in a hands-on fashion. To do so, you must have a proper kernel workspace environment set up, which we have successfully done in this chapter.

Now that our environment is ready, let's move on and explore the brave world of Linux kernel development! The next two chapters will teach you how to download, extract, configure, and build a Linux kernel from source.

Questions

As we conclude, here is a list of questions for you to test your knowledge regarding this chapter's material: `https://github.com/PacktPublishing/Linux-Kernel-Programming/tree/master/questions`. You will find some of the questions answered in the book's GitHub repo: `https://github.com/PacktPublishing/Linux-Kernel-Programming/tree/master/solutions_to_assgn`.

Further reading

To help you delve deeper into the subject with useful materials, we provide a rather detailed list of online references and links (and at times, even books) in a Further reading document in this book's GitHub repository. The *Further reading* document is available here: `https://github.com/PacktPublishing/Linux-Kernel-Programming/blob/master/Further_Reading.md`.

2
Building the 5.x Linux Kernel from Source - Part 1

Building the Linux kernel from source code is an interesting way to begin your kernel development journey! Rest assured, it's a long and arduous journey, but that's the fun of it, right? The kernel build topic itself is large enough to merit being divided into two chapters, this one and the next.

The primary purpose of this chapter and the next is to describe in detail how exactly you can build a Linux kernel from scratch, from source code. In this chapter, you will initially learn how to download a stable vanilla Linux kernel source tree onto a guest Linux **Virtual Machine** (**VM**) (by vanilla kernel, we mean the plain and regular default kernel source code released by the Linux kernel community on its repository, `https://www.kernel.org`). Next, we will learn a little bit about the layout of the kernel source code – getting, in effect, a 10,000-foot view of the kernel code base. The actual kernel build recipe then follows.

Before proceeding, a key piece of information: any Linux system, be it a supercomputer or a tiny embedded device, has three required components: a bootloader, an **Operating System** (**OS**) kernel, and a root filesystem. In this chapter, we concern ourselves only with the building of the Linux kernel from source. We do not delve into the root filesystem details, and (in the next chapter) learn to minimally configure the (very x86-specific) GNU GRUB bootloader.

In this chapter, we will cover the following topics:

- Preliminaries for the kernel build
- Steps to build the kernel from source
- Step 1 – obtaining a Linux kernel source tree

- Step 2 – extracting the kernel source tree
- Step 3 – configuring the Linux kernel
- Customizing the kernel menu – adding our own menu item

Technical requirements

I assume that you have gone through `Chapter 1`, *Kernel Workspace Setup*, and have appropriately prepared a guest VM running Ubuntu 18.04 LTS (or CentOS 8, or later stable releases of these distributions) and installed all the required packages. If not, I highly recommend you do this first.

To get the most out of this book, I strongly recommend you first set up the workspace environment, including cloning this book's GitHub repository (`https://github.com/PacktPublishing/Linux-Kernel-Programming`) for the code, and work on it in a hands-on fashion.

Preliminaries for the kernel build

It's important to understand a few things right from the outset that will help you as we proceed on our journey of building and working with a Linux kernel. Firstly, the Linux kernel and its sister projects are completely decentralized - it's a virtual, online open-source community! The closest we come to an office is this: stewardship of the Linux kernel (as well as several dozen related projects) is in the capable hands of the Linux Foundation (`https://linuxfoundation.org/`); further, it manages the Linux Kernel Organization, a private foundation that distributes the Linux kernel to the public for no charge (`https://www.kernel.org/nonprofit.html`).

Some of the key points we discuss in this section includes the following:

- The kernel release, or version number nomenclature
- The typical kernel development workflow
- The existence of different types of kernel source trees within the repository

With this information in place, you will be better armed to move through the kernel build procedure. All right, let's go over each of the preceding points.

Kernel release nomenclature

To see the kernel version number, simply run `uname -r` on your shell. How do you precisely interpret the output of `uname -r`? On our Ubuntu distribution version 18.04 LTS guest VM, we run `uname(1)`, passing the `-r` option switch to display just the current kernel release or version:

```
$ uname -r
5.0.0-36-generic
```

> Of course, by the time you read this, the Ubuntu 18.04 LTS kernel has certainly been upgraded to a later release; that's perfectly normal. The 5.0.0-36-generic kernel was the one I encountered with the Ubuntu 18.04.3 LTS at the time of writing this chapter.

The modern Linux kernel release number nomenclature is as follows:

```
major#.minor#[.patchlevel][-EXTRAVERSION]
```

This is also often written or described as `w.x[.y][-z]`.

The square brackets around the `patchlevel` and `EXTRAVERSION` components indicate that they are optional. The following table summarizes the meaning of the components of the release number:

Release # component	Meaning	Example numbers
Major # (or w)	Main or major number; currently, we are on the 5.x kernel series, thus the major number is 5.	2, 3, 4, and 5
Minor # (or x)	The minor number, hierarchically under the major number.	0 onward
[patchlevel] (or y)	Hierarchically under the minor number – also called the ABI or revision – applied on occasion to the stable kernel when significant bug/security fixes are required.	0 onward
[-EXTRAVERSION] (or -z)	Also called `localversion`; typically used by distribution kernels to track their internal changes.	Varies; Ubuntu uses `w.x.y-'n'-generic`

Table 2.1 – Linux kernel release nomenclature

So, we can now interpret our Ubuntu 18.04 LTS distribution's kernel release number, `5.0.0-36-generic`:

- **Major # (or w)**: 5
- **Minor # (or x)**: 0
- **[patchlevel] (or y)**: 0
- **[-EXTRAVERSION] (or -z)**: `-36-generic`

Note that distribution kernels may or may not precisely follow these conventions, it's really up to them. The regular or vanilla kernels released on `https://www.kernel.org/` do follow these conventions (at least until Linus decides to change them).

> (a) As part of an interesting exercise configuring the kernel, we will later change the `localversion` (aka `-EXTRAVERSION`) component of the kernel we build.
> (b) Historically, in kernels before 2.6 (IOW, ancient stuff now), the *minor number* held a special meaning; if an even number, it indicated a stable kernel release, if odd, an unstable or beta release. This is no longer the case.

Kernel development workflow – the basics

Here, we provide a brief overview of the typical kernel development workflow. Anyone like you who is interested in kernel development should at least minimally understand the process.

> A detailed description can be found within the kernel documentation here: `https://www.kernel.org/doc/html/latest/process/2.Process.html#how-the-development-process-works`.

A common misconception, especially in its baby years, was that the Linux kernel is developed in a very ad hoc fashion. This is not true at all! The kernel development process has evolved to become a (mostly) well-oiled system with a thoroughly documented process and expectation of what a kernel contributor should know in order to use it well. I refer you to the preceding link for the complete details.

In order for us to take a peek into a typical development cycle, let's assume we have the latest mainline Linux Git kernel tree cloned on to our system.

> The details regarding the use of the powerful `git(1)` **Source Code Management (SCM)** tool is beyond the scope of this book. Please see the *Further reading* section for useful links on learning how to use Git. Obviously, I highly recommend gaining at least basic familiarity with using `git(1)`.

As mentioned earlier, as of the time of writing, **the 5.4 kernel** is the latest **Long-Term Stable (LTS)** version, so we shall use it in the materials that follow. So, how did it come to be? Obviously, it has evolved from the **release candidate (rc)** kernels and the previous stable kernel release that precedes it, which in this case would be the *v5.4-rc'n'* kernels and the stable *v5.3* one before it. We use the `git log` command as follows to get a human-readable log of the tags in the kernel Git tree ordered by date. Here, we are only interested in the work that has lead to the release of the 5.4 LTS kernel, hence we have deliberately truncated the following output to reveal only that portion:

> The `git log` command (that we use in the following code block, and in fact any other `git` sub-commands) will only work on a `git` tree. We use the following one purely for demonstrating the evolution of the kernel. A bit later, we will show how you can clone a Git tree.

```
$ git log --date-order --graph --tags --simplify-by-decoration --pretty=format:'%ai %h %d'
* 2019-11-24 16:32:01 -0800 219d54332a09  (tag: v5.4)
* 2019-11-17 14:47:30 -0800 af42d3466bdc  (tag: v5.4-rc8)
* 2019-11-10 16:17:15 -0800 31f4f5b495a6  (tag: v5.4-rc7)
* 2019-11-03 14:07:26 -0800 a99d8080aaf3  (tag: v5.4-rc6)
* 2019-10-27 13:19:19 -0400 d6d5df1db6e9  (tag: v5.4-rc5)
* 2019-10-20 15:56:22 -0400 7d194c2100ad  (tag: v5.4-rc4)
* 2019-10-13 16:37:36 -0700 4f5cafb5cb84  (tag: v5.4-rc3)
* 2019-10-06 14:27:30 -0700 da0c9ea146cb  (tag: v5.4-rc2)
* 2019-09-30 10:35:40 -0700 54ecb8f7028c  (tag: v5.4-rc1)
* 2019-09-15 14:19:32 -0700 4d856f72c10e  (tag: v5.3)
* 2019-09-08 13:33:15 -0700 f74c2bb98776  (tag: v5.3-rc8)
* 2019-09-02 09:57:40 -0700 089cf7f6ecb2  (tag: v5.3-rc7)
* 2019-08-25 12:01:23 -0700 a55aa89aab90  (tag: v5.3-rc6)
[...]
```

Aha! In the preceding code block, you can clearly see that the stable 5.4 kernel was released on 24 November 2019 and the 5.3 tree on 15 September 2019 (you can also verify this by looking up other useful kernel resources, such as https://kernelnewbies.org/LinuxVersions).

Building the 5.x Linux Kernel from Source - Part 1

For the development series that ultimately led to the 5.4 kernel, this latter date (15 September 2019) marks the start of what is called the **merge window** for the next stable kernel for a period of (approximately) two weeks. In this period, developers are allowed to submit new code to the kernel tree (in reality, the actual work would have been going on from a lot earlier; the fruit of this work is now merged into mainline at this time).

Two weeks later (on 30 September 2019), the merge window was closed and the `rc` kernel work started, with `5.4-rc1` being the first of the `rc` versions, of course. The `-rc` (also known as prepatch) trees work primarily on merging patches and fixing (regression) bugs, ultimately leading to what is determined by the chief maintainers (Linus Torvalds and Andrew Morton) to be a "stable" kernel tree. The number of prepatches (`-rc` releases) varies. Typically, though, this "bugfix" window takes anywhere between 6 to 10 weeks, after which the new stable kernel is released. In the preceding code block, we can see that eight release candidate kernels finally resulted in the stable release of the v5.4 tree on 24 November 2019 (taking a total of 70 days).

The same can be seen more visually via the releases page at `https://github.com/torvalds/linux/releases`:

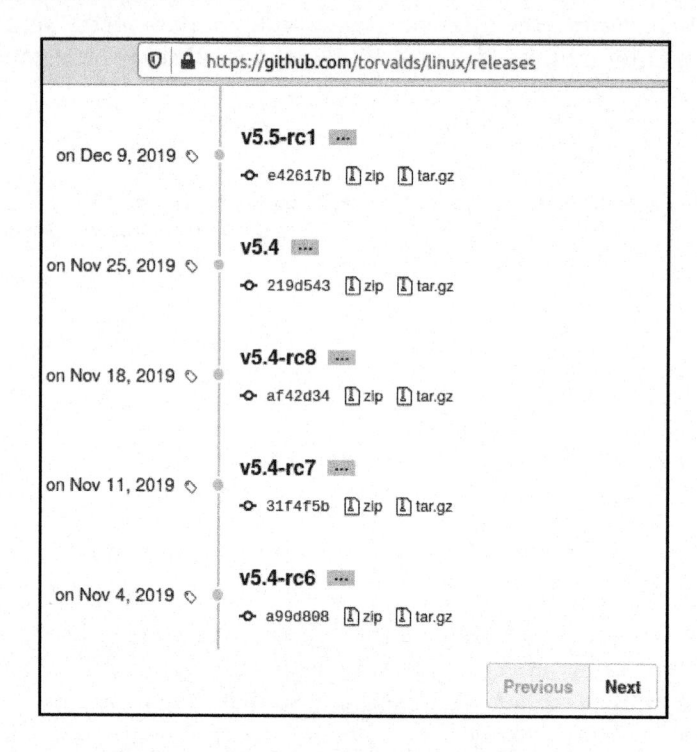

Figure 2.1 – The releases leading up to the 5.4 LTS kernel (read it bottom-up)

[48]

Chapter 2

The preceding screenshot is a partial screenshot showing how various *v5.4-rc'n'* release candidate kernels ultimately resulted in the release of the LTS 5.4 tree (on 25 November 2019, with *v5.4-rc8* being the last `rc` release). The work never really stops: by early December 2019, the *v5.5-rc1* release candidate went out.

Generically, taking the 5.x kernel series as an example (the same holds true for any other recent `major` kernel series), the kernel development workflow is as follows:

1. The 5.x stable release is made. Thus, the merge window for the 5.x+1 (mainline) kernel has begun.
2. The merge window remains open for about 2 weeks and new patches are merged into the mainline.
3. Once (typically) 2 weeks have elapsed, the merge window is closed.
4. `rc` (aka mainline, prepatch) kernels start. *5.x+1-rc1, 5.x+1-rc2, ..., 5.x+1-rcn* are released. This process takes anywhere between 6 to 8 weeks.
5. The stable release has arrived: the new *5.x+1* stable kernel is released.
6. The release is handed off to the "stable team":
   - Significant bug or security fixes result in the release of *5.x+1.y* : *5.x+1.1, 5.x+1.2, ... , 5.x+1.n*.
   - Maintained until the next stable release or **End Of Life** (**EOL**) date reached

...and the whole process repeats.

So, when you now see Linux kernel releases, the names and the process involved will make sense. Let's now move on to looking at the different types of kernel source trees out there.

Types of kernel source trees

There are several types of Linux kernel source trees. The key one is the **Long Term Support** (**LTS**) kernel. Okay, so what exactly is an LTS release kernel? It's simply a "special" release in the sense that the kernel maintainers will continue to backport important bug and security fixes upon it (well, security issues are typically nothing but bugs), until a given EOL date.

The "life" of an LTS kernel will usually be a minimum of 2 years, and it can go for several more (it's extended at times). The **5.4 LTS kernel** that we will use throughout this book is the 20th LTS kernel and has **a lifespan of just over 6 years – from November 2019 to December 2025**.

There are several types of release kernels in the repository. However, here, we mention an incomplete list, ordered from least to most stable (thus, their life, from shortest to longest time span):

- **-next trees**: This is indeed the bleeding edge, subsystem trees with new patches collected here for testing and review. This is what an upstream kernel contributor will work on.
- **Prepatches, also known as -rc or mainline**: These are release candidate kernels that get generated prior to a release.
- **Stable kernels**: As the name implies, this is the business end. These kernels are typically picked up by distributions and other projects (at least to begin with). They are also known as vanilla kernels.
- **Distribution and LTS kernels**: Distribution kernels are (obviously) the kernels provided by the distributions. They typically begin with a base vanilla/stable kernel. LTS kernels are the specially maintained-for-a-longer-while kernels, making them especially useful for industry/production projects and products.

> In this book, we will work throughout on the latest LTS kernel as of the time of writing, which is the 5.4 LTS kernel. As I mentioned in `Chapter 1`, *Kernel Workspace Setup*, the 5.4 LTS kernel was initially slated to have an EOL of "at least December 2021." Recently (June 2020), it's now been pushed **to December 2025**, keeping this book's content current and valid for years to come!

- **Super LTS (SLTS) kernels**: Even longer maintained LTS kernels (by the *Civil Infrastructure Platform* (`https://www.cip-project.org/`), a Linux Foundation project).

It's quite intuitive. Nevertheless, I refer you to kernel.org's **Releases** page to obtain details on the type of release kernels: `https://www.kernel.org/releases.html`. Again, for even more detail, visit *How the development process works* (`https://www.kernel.org/doc/html/latest/process/2.Process.html#how-the-development-process-works`).

As an interesting aside, certain LTS kernels are very long-term releases, the aptly named **SLTS** or **Super LTS** kernels. As an example, the 4.4 Linux kernel (the 16th LTS release) is considered to be an SLTS kernel. As the first kernel selected for SLTS, the Civil Infrastructure Platform will provide support until at least 2026, possibly until 2036.

Querying the repository, `www.kernel.org`, in a non-interactive scriptable fashion can be done using `curl(1)` (the following output is the state of Linux as of 05 January 2021):

```
$ curl -L https://www.kernel.org/finger_banner
The latest stable version of the Linux kernel is: 5.10.4
The latest mainline version of the Linux kernel is: 5.11-rc2
The latest stable 5.10 version of the Linux kernel is: 5.10.4
The latest stable 5.9 version of the Linux kernel is: 5.9.16 (EOL)
The latest longterm 5.4 version of the Linux kernel is: 5.4.86
The latest longterm 4.19 version of the Linux kernel is: 4.19.164
The latest longterm 4.14 version of the Linux kernel is: 4.14.213
The latest longterm 4.9 version of the Linux kernel is: 4.9.249
The latest longterm 4.4 version of the Linux kernel is: 4.4.249
The latest linux-next version of the Linux kernel is: next-20210105
$
```

Of course, by the time you read this, it's extremely likely (certain, in fact) that the kernel has evolved further and later versions show up. For a book such as this one, the best I could do is pick the latest LTS kernel at the time of writing.

> Of course, it's happened already! The 5.10 kernel was released on 13 December 2020 and, as of the time of writing (just before going to print), the work on the 5.11 kernel is in progress...

Finally, yet another safe way to download a given kernel is provided by the kernel maintainers who offer a script to safely download a given Linux kernel source tree, verifying its PGP signature. The script is available here: `https://git.kernel.org/pub/scm/linux/kernel/git/mricon/korg-helpers.git/tree/get-verified-tarball`.

Right, now that we're armed with the knowledge on kernel version nomenclature and types of kernel source trees, it's time to begin our journey of building our kernel.

Steps to build the kernel from source

As a convenient and quick reference, the following are the key steps required to build a Linux kernel from source. As the explanation for each of them is pretty detailed, you can refer back to this summary to see the bigger picture. The steps are as follows:

1. Obtain a Linux kernel source tree through either of the following options:
   - Downloading a specific kernel source as a compressed file
   - Cloning a (kernel) Git tree
2. Extract the kernel source tree into some location in your home directory (skip this step if you obtained a kernel by cloning a Git tree).
3. Configuration: Select the kernel support options as required for the new kernel,
   `make [x|g|menu]config`, with `make menuconfig` being the preferred way.
4. Build the kernel's loadable modules and any **Device Tree Blobs** (**DTBs**) with `make [-j'n'] all`. This builds the compressed kernel image (`arch/<arch>/boot/[b|z|u]image`), the uncompressed kernel image (`vmlinux`), `System.map`, the kernel module objects, and any configured DTB(s) files.
5. Install the just-built kernel modules with `sudo make modules_install`. This step installs kernel modules by default under `/lib/modules/$(uname -r)/`.
6. Set up the GRUB bootloader and the `initramfs` (earlier called `initrd`) image (x86-specific):
   `sudo make install`:
   - This creates and installs the `initramfs` (or `initrd`) image under `/boot`.
   - It updates the bootloader configuration file to boot the new kernel (first entry).
7. Customize the GRUB bootloader menu (optional).

This chapter, being the first of two on this topic, will essentially cover *steps 1 to 3*, with a lot of required background material thrown in as well. The next chapter will cover the remaining steps, *4 to 7*. So, let's begin with *step 1*.

Step 1 – obtaining a Linux kernel source tree

In this section, we will see two broad ways in which you can obtain a Linux kernel source tree:

- By downloading and extracting a specific kernel source tree from the Linux kernel public repository (https://www.kernel.org)
- By cloning Linus Torvalds' source tree (or others') – for example, the `linux-next` Git tree

But how do you decide which approach to use? For the majority of developers like you working on a project or product, the decision has already been made – the project uses a very specific Linux kernel version. You will thus download that particular kernel source tree, quite possibly apply project-specific patches to it if required, and use it.

For folks whose intention is to contribute or "upstream" code to the mainline kernel, the second approach – cloning the Git tree – is the way to go for you. (Of course, there's more to it; we described some details in the *Types of kernel source trees* section).

In the following section, we demonstrate both approaches. First, we describe the approach where a particular kernel source tree (not a Git tree) is downloaded from the kernel repository. We choose, as of the time of writing, the **latest LTS 5.4 Linux kernel** for this purpose. In the second approach, we clone a Git tree.

Building the 5.x Linux Kernel from Source - Part 1

Downloading a specific kernel tree

Firstly, where is the kernel source code? The short answer is that it's on the public kernel repository server visible at `https://www.kernel.org`. The home page of this site displays the latest stable Linux kernel version, as well as the latest `longterm` and `linux-next` releases (the following screenshot shows the site as of 29 November 2019. It shows dates in the well-known `yyyy-mm-dd` format):

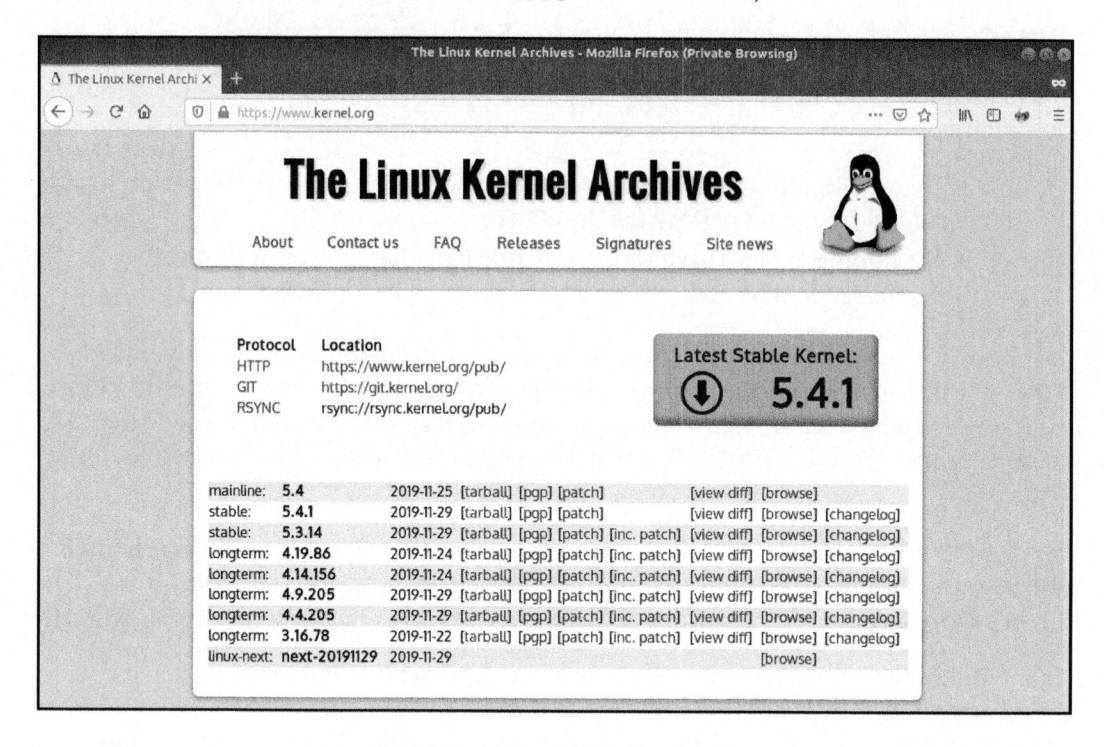

Figure 2.2 – The kernel.org site (as of 29 November 2019)

> **TIP**: A quick reminder: we also provide a PDF file that has the full-color images of the screenshots/diagrams used in this book. You can download it here: `https://static.packt-cdn.com/downloads/9781789953435_ColorImages.pdf`.

[54]

Chapter 2

There are many ways to download a (compressed) kernel source file. Let's look at two of them:

- An interactive, and perhaps simplest way, is to visit the preceding website and simply click on the appropriate `tarball` link. The browser will download the image file (in `.tar.xz` format) to your system.
- Alternatively, you can download it from the command line (a shell or the CLI) using the `wget(1)` utility (we can also use the powerful `curl(1)` utility to do so). For example, to download the stable 5.4.0 kernel source compressed file, we can do the following:

   ```
   wget --https-only -O ~/Downloads/linux-5.4.0.tar.xz
   https://mirrors.edge.kernel.org/pub/linux/kernel/v5.x/linux-5.4.0.tar.xz
   ```

> **TIP**
> If the preceding `wget(1)` utility doesn't work, it's likely because the kernel (compressed) `tarball` link changed. For example, if it didn't work for `5.4.0.tar.xz`, try the same `wget` utility but change the version to `5.4.1.tar.xz`.

This will securely download the 5.4.0 compressed kernel source tree to your computer's `~/Downloads` folder. Of course, you may not want the versions of the kernel that are displayed on the repository's home page. For example, what if, for my particular project, I require the latest 4.19 stable (LTS) kernel, the 19th LTS release? Simple: via the browser, just click on the `https://www.kernel.org/pub/` (or the mirror `https://mirrors.edge.kernel.org/pub/`) link (immediately to the right of the "HTTP" link shown in the first few lines) and navigate to the `linux/kernel/v4.x/` directory on the server (you might be directed to a mirror site). Or, simply point `wget(1)` at the URL (here, as of the time of writing, it happens to be `https://mirrors.edge.kernel.org/pub/linux/kernel/v4.x/linux-4.19.164.tar.xz`).

Cloning a Git tree

For a developer like you working on and looking to contribute code upstream, you *must* work on the very latest version of the Linux kernel code base. Well, there are fine gradations of the latest version within the kernel community. As mentioned earlier, the `linux-next` tree, and some specific branch or tag within it, is the one to work on for this purpose.

Building the 5.x Linux Kernel from Source - Part 1

In this book, though, we do not intend to delve into the gory details of setting up a `linux-next` tree. This process is already very well documented and we would prefer not to merely repeat instructions (see the *Further reading* section for detailed links). The detailed page on how exactly you should clone a `linux-next` tree is here: *Working with linux-next*, https://www.kernel.org/doc/man-pages/linux-next.html, and, as mentioned there, the *linux-next tree*, http://git.kernel.org/cgit/linux/kernel/git/next/linux-next.git, is the holding area for patches aimed at the next kernel merge window. If you're doing bleeding-edge kernel development, you may want to work from that tree rather than Linus Torvalds' mainline tree.

For our purposes, cloning the *mainline* Linux Git repository (Torvalds' Git tree) is more than sufficient. Do so like this (type this on one line):

```
git clone
https://git.kernel.org/pub/scm/linux/kernel/git/torvalds/linux.git
```

> **TIP**
>
> Note that cloning a complete Linux kernel tree is a time-, network-, and disk-consuming operation! Ensure you have sufficient disk space free (at least a few gigabytes worth).
>
> Performing `git clone --depth n <...>`, where n is an integer value, is very useful to limit the depth of history (commits) and thus keep the download/disk usage low(er). As the man page on `git-clone(1)` mentions for the `--depth` option: "Create a shallow clone with a history truncated to a specified number of commits."

As per the preceding tip, why not do the following (again, type this on one line)?

```
git clone --depth=3
https://git.kernel.org/pub/scm/linux/kernel/git/torvalds/linux.git
```

If you intend to work on this mainline Git tree, please skip the *Step 2 – extracting the kernel source tree* section (as the `git clone` operation will, in any case, extract the source tree) and continue with the section that follows it (*Step 3 – configuring the Linux kernel*).

Step 2 – extracting the kernel source tree

As mentioned earlier, this section is meant for those of you who have downloaded a particular Linux kernel from the repository, https://www.kernel.org, and aim to build it. In this book, we use the 5.4 LTS kernel release. On the other hand, if you have performed `git clone` on the mainline Linux Git tree, as shown in the immediately preceding section, you can safely skip this section and move on to the next one on kernel configuration.

Now that the download is done, let's proceed further. The next step is to extract the kernel source tree – remember, it's a tar-ed and compressed (typically `.tar.xz`) file.

We assume that, as shown in detail earlier in this chapter, you have by now downloaded the Linux kernel version 5.4 code base as a compressed file (into the `~/Downloads` directory):

```
$ cd ~/Downloads ; ls -lh linux-5.4.tar.xz
-rw-rw-r-- 1 llkd llkd 105M Nov 26 08:04 linux-5.4.tar.xz
```

The simple way to extract this file is by using the ubiquitous `tar(1)` utility to do so:

```
tar xf ~/Downloads/linux-5.4.tar.xz
```

This will extract the kernel source tree into a directory named `linux-5.4` within the `~/Downloads` directory. But what if we would like to extract it into another folder, say `~/kernels`? Then, do it like so:

```
mkdir -p ~/kernels
tar xf ~/Downloads/linux-5.4.tar.xz --directory=${HOME}/kernels/
```

This will extract the kernel source into the `~/kernels/linux-5.4/` folder. As a convenience, and good practice, let's set up an *environment variable* to point to the location of the root of our kernel source tree:

```
export LLKD_KSRC=${HOME}/kernels/linux-5.4
```

> Note that, going forward, we will assume that this variable holds the location of the kernel source tree.

While you could always use a GUI file manager application (such as `Nautilus(1)`) to extract the compressed file, I strongly urge you to get familiar with using the Linux CLI to perform these operations.

> **TIP:** Don't forget `tldr(1)` when you need to quickly lookup the most frequently used options to common commands! For example, for `tar(1)`, simply use `tldr tar` to look it up.

Did you notice? We extract the kernel source tree into *any* directory under our home directory (or even elsewhere), unlike in the old days when the tree was always extracted under a root-writeable location (often, `/usr/src/`). Nowadays, just say no (to that).

If all you wish to do now is proceed with the kernel build recipe, skip the following section and move along. If interested (we certainly hope so!), the next section is a brief but important deviation into looking at the structure and layout of the kernel source tree.

A brief tour of the kernel source tree

The kernel source code is now available on your system! Cool, let's take a quick look at it:

```
$ ls
arch/      crypto/          include/    kernel/       mm/        security/
block/     Documentation/   init/       lib/          net/       sound/
certs/     drivers/         ipc/        LICENSES      README     tools/
COPYING    firmware/        Kbuild      MAINTAINERS   samples/   usr/
CREDITS    fs/              Kconfig     Makefile      scripts/   virt/
$
```

Figure 2.3 – The root of the 5.4 Linux kernel source tree

Great! How big is it? A quick `du -m .` in the root of the kernel source tree reveals that this particular kernel source tree (recall, it's version 5.4) is a little over 1,000 MB in size – almost a gigabyte!

> FYI, the Linux kernel has grown to be big and is getting bigger in terms of **Source Lines Of Code** (**SLOCs**). Current estimates are well over 20 million SLOCs. Of course, do realize that not *all* of this code will get compiled when building a kernel.

How do we know which version exactly of the Linux kernel this code is by just looking at the source? That's easy, one quick way is to just check out the first few lines of the project's Makefile. Incidentally, the kernel uses Makefile's all over the place; most directories have one. We will refer to this Makefile, the one at the root of the kernel source tree, as the *top-level Makefile*:

```
$ head Makefile
# SPDX-License-Identifier: GPL-2.0
VERSION = 5
PATCHLEVEL = 4
SUBLEVEL = 0
EXTRAVERSION =
NAME = Kleptomaniac Octopus

# *DOCUMENTATION*
# To see a list of typical targets execute "make help"
# More info can be located in ./README
$
```

Clearly, it's the source of the 5.4.0 kernel.

Let's get for ourselves a zoomed-out 10,000-foot view of the kernel source tree. The following table summarizes the broad categorization and purpose of the (more) important files and directories within the root of the Linux kernel source tree:

File or directory name	Purpose
Top-level files	
README	The project's README file. It informs us as to where the kernel documentation is kept – spoiler, it's in the directory called Documentation – and how to begin using it. The documentation is really important; it's the authentic thing, written by the kernel developers themselves.
COPYING	The license terms under which the kernel source is released. The vast majority are released under the well-known GNU GPL v2 (written as GPL-2.0) license [1].
MAINTAINERS	*FAQ: something's wrong in XYZ, who do I contact to get some support?* That is precisely what this file provides – the list of all kernel subsystems, indeed down to the level of individual components (such as a particular driver), its status, who is currently maintaining it, the mailing list, website, and so on. Very helpful! There's even a helper script to find the person or team to talk to: scripts/get_maintainer.pl [2].

Makefile	This is the kernel's top-level Makefile; the `kbuild` kernel build system as well as kernel modules use this Makefile (at least initially) for the build.
Major subsystem directories	
`kernel/`	Core kernel subsystem: the code here deals with process/thread life cycle, CPU scheduling, locking, cgroups, timers, interrupts, signaling, modules, tracing, and more.
`mm/`	The bulk of the **memory management** (**mm**) code lives here. We will cover a little of this in `Chapter 6`, *Kernel Internals Essentials – Processes and Threads*, and some related coverage in `Chapter 7`, *Memory Management Internals – Essentials*, and `Chapter 8`, *Kernel Memory Allocation for Module Authors – Part 1*, as well.
`fs/`	The code here implements two key filesystem features: the abstraction layer – the kernel **Virtual Filesystem Switch** (**VFS**), and the individual filesystem drivers (for example, `ext[2|4]`, `btrfs`, `nfs`, `ntfs`, `overlayfs`, `squashfs`, `jffs2`, `fat`, `f2fs`, and so on).
`block/`	The underlying (to the VFS/FS) block I/O code path. It includes the code implementing the page cache, a generic block IO layer, IO schedulers, and so on.
`net/`	Complete (to the letter of the **Request For Comments** (**RFCs**)—`https://whatis.techtarget.com/definition/Request-for-Comments-RFC`) implementation of the network protocol stack. Includes a high-quality implementation of TCP, UDP, IP, and many more networking protocols.
`ipc/`	The **Inter-Process Communication** (**IPC**) subsystem code; covers IPC mechanisms such as (both SysV and POSIX) message queues, shared memory, semaphores, and so on.
`sound/`	The audio subsystem code, also known as **Advanced Linux Sound Architecture** (**ALSA**).
`virt/`	The *virtualization* (hypervisor) code; the popular and powerful **Kernel Virtual Machine** (**KVM**) is implemented here.
Infrastructure/misc	

Chapter 2

`arch/`	The arch-specific code lives here (by the word arch, we mean CPU). Linux started as a small hobby project for the i386. It is now probably the most ported OS (see the arch ports in *step 3* of the list that follows after this table).
`crypto/`	This directory contains the kernel-level implementation of ciphers (encryption/decryption algorithms, aka transformations) and kernel APIs to serve consumers that require cryptographic services.
`include/`	This directory contains the arch-independent kernel headers (there are also some arch-specific ones under `arch/<cpu>/include/...`).
`init/`	The arch-independent kernel initialization code; perhaps the closest we get to the kernel's main function (remember, the kernel is not an application) is here: `init/main.c:start_kernel()`, with the `start_kernel()` function within it considered the early C entry point during kernel initialization.
`lib/`	The closest equivalent to a library for the kernel. It's important to understand that the kernel does *not* support shared libraries as userspace apps do. The code here is auto-linked into the kernel image file and hence available to the kernel at runtime (various useful components exist within `/lib`: [un]compression, checksum, bitmap, math, string routines, tree algos, and so on).
`scripts/`	Various scripts are housed here, some of which are used during kernel build, many for other purposes (like static/dynamic analysis, and so on; mostly Bash and Perl).
`security/`	Houses the kernel's **Linux Security Module** (**LSM**), a **Mandatory Access Control** (**MAC**) framework that aims at imposing stricter access control of user apps to kernel space than the default kernel does (the default model is called **Discretionary Access Control** (**DAC**)). Currently, Linux supports several LSMs; well-known ones are SELinux, AppArmor, Smack, Tomoyo, Integrity, and Yama (note that LSMs are "off" by default).
`tools/`	Various tools are housed here, mostly userspace applications (or scripts) that have a "tight coupling" with the kernel (*perf*, the modern profiling tool, serves as an excellent example).

Table 2.2 – Layout of the Linux kernel source tree

Building the 5.x Linux Kernel from Source - Part 1

The following are some important explanations from the table:

1. **Kernel licensing**: Without getting stuck in the legal details, here's the pragmatic essence of the thing: as the kernel is released under the GNU GPL-2.0 license (**GNU GPL** is the **GNU General Public License**), any project that directly uses the kernel code base (even a tiny bit of it!), automatically falls under this license (the "derivative work" property of the GPL-2.0). These projects or products must release their kernels under the same license terms. Practically speaking, the situation on the ground is a good deal hazier; many commercial products that run on the Linux kernel do have proprietary user- and/or kernel-space code within them. They typically do so by refactoring kernel (most often, device driver) work in **Loadable Kernel Module (LKM)** format. It is possible to release the kernel module (LKM) under a *dual license* model (for example, as dual BSD/GPL; the LKM is the subject matter of Chapter 4, *Writing your First Kernel Module – LKMs Part 1*, and Chapter 5, *Writing your First Kernel Module – LKMs Part 2*, and we cover some information on the licensing of kernel modules there). Some folks, preferring proprietary licenses, manage to release their kernel code within a kernel module that is not licensed under GPL-2.0 terms; technically, this is perhaps possible, but is (at the very least) considered as being anti-social (and can even cross the line to being illegal). The interested among you can find more links on licensing in the *Further reading* document for this chapter.

2. MAINTAINERS: An example of running the get_maintainer.pl Perl script (note: it is meant to run on a Git tree only):

```
$ scripts/get_maintainer.pl -f drivers/android/
Greg Kroah-Hartman <gregkh@linuxfoundation.org>
(supporter:ANDROID DRIVERS)
"Arve Hjønnevåg" <arve@android.com> (supporter:ANDROID
DRIVERS)
Todd Kjos <tkjos@android.com> (supporter:ANDROID DRIVERS)
Martijn Coenen <maco@android.com> (supporter:ANDROID DRIVERS)
Joel Fernandes <joel@joelfernandes.org> (supporter:ANDROID
DRIVERS)
Christian Brauner <christian@brauner.io> (supporter:ANDROID
DRIVERS)
devel@driverdev.osuosl.org (open list:ANDROID DRIVERS)
linux-kernel@vger.kernel.org (open list)
$
```

3. Linux `arch` (CPU) ports:

```
$ cd ${LLKD_KSRC} ; ls arch/
alpha/   arm64/  h8300/     Kconfig      mips/    openrisc/  riscv/
sparc/   x86/
arc/     c6x/    hexagon/   m68k/        nds32/   parisc/    s390/   um/
xtensa/
arm/     csky/   ia64/      microblaze/  nios2/   powerpc/   sh/
unicore32/
```

> **TIP**
> As a kernel or driver developer, browsing the kernel source tree is something you will have to get quite used to (and even enjoy!). Searching for a particular function or variable can be a daunting task when the code is in the ballpark of 20 million SLOCs! Do use efficient code browser tools. I suggest the `ctags(1)` and `cscope(1)` **Free and Open Source Software** (**FOSS**) tools. In fact, the kernel's top-level Makefile has targets for precisely these:
>
> `make tags ; make cscope`

We have now completed *step 2*, the extraction of the kernel source tree! As a bonus, you also learned the basics regarding the layout of the kernel source. Let's now move on to *step 3* of the process and learn how to *configure* the Linux kernel prior to building it.

Step 3 – configuring the Linux kernel

Configuring the new kernel is perhaps *the most* critical step in the kernel build process. One of the many reasons Linux is a critically acclaimed OS is its versatility. It's a common misconception to think that there is a separate Linux kernel code base for an (enterprise-class) server, a data center, a workstation, and a tiny embedded Linux device – no, *they all use the very same unified Linux kernel source!* Thus, carefully *configuring* the kernel for a particular use case (server, desktop, embedded, or hybrid/custom) is a powerful feature and a requirement. This is precisely what we are delving into here.

Building the 5.x Linux Kernel from Source - Part 1

> **TIP**
> Do carry out this kernel configuration step regardless. Even if you feel you do not require any changes to the existing (or default) config, it's very important to run this step at least once as part of the build process. Otherwise, certain headers that are auto-generated here will be missing and cause issues. At the very least, `make oldconfig` should be carried out. This will set up the kernel config to that of the existing system with config options being requested from the user only for any new options.

First though, let's cover some required background on the **kernel build** (**kbuild**) system.

Understanding the kbuild build system

The infrastructure that the Linux kernel uses to configure and build the kernel is known as the **kbuild** system. Without delving into the gory details, the kbuild system ties together the complex kernel configuration and build process via four key components:

- The `CONFIG_FOO` symbols
- The menu specification file(s), called `Kconfig`
- The Makefile(s)
- The overall kernel config file itself

The purpose of these components is summarized as follows:

Kbuild component	Purpose in brief
Config symbol: `CONFIG_FOO`	Every kernel configurable `FOO` is represented by a `CONFIG_FOO` macro. Depending on the user's choice, the macro will resolve to one of y, m, or n: - y=yes: Implying to build the feature into the kernel image itself - m=module: Implying to build it as a separate object, a kernel module - n=no: Implying not to build the feature Note that `CONFIG_FOO` is an alphanumeric string (as we will soon see, you can look up the precise config option name by using the `make menuconfig` option, navigating to a config option, and selecting the < Help > button).

[64]

`Kconfig` files	This is where the `CONFIG_FOO` symbol is defined. The kbuild syntax specifies its type (Boolean, tristate, [alpha]numeric, and so on) and dependency tree. Furthermore, for the menu-based config UI (invoked via one of `make [menu|g|x]config`), it specifies the menu entries themselves. We will, of course, make use of this feature later.
Makefile(s)	The kbuild system uses a *recursive* Makefile approach. The Makefile under the kernel source tree root folder is called the *top-level* Makefile, with a Makefile within each sub-folder to build the source there. The 5.4 vanilla kernel source has over 2,500 Makefiles in all!
The `.config` file	Ultimately, the essence of it – the actual kernel configuration – is generated and stored within the kernel source tree root folder in an ASCII text file called `.config`. Keep this file safe, it's a key part of your product.

Table 2.3 – Major components of the Kbuild build system

The key thing is to get ourselves a working `.config` file. How can we do so? We do this iteratively. We begin with a "default" configuration – the topic of the following section – and carefully work our way up to a custom config as required.

Arriving at a default configuration

So, how do you decide the initial kernel configuration to begin with? Several techniques exist; a few common ones are as follows:

- Don't specify anything; the kbuild system will pull in a default kernel configuration.
- Use the existing distribution's kernel configuration.
- Build a custom configuration based on the kernel modules currently loaded in memory.

The first approach has the benefit of simplicity. The kernel will handle the details, giving you a default configuration. The downside is that the default config is really pretty large (here, we mean with reference to building Linux for an x86-based desktop or server-type system) – a huge number of options are turned on, just in case, which can make the build time very long and kernel image size very large. Of course, you are then expected to manually configure the kernel to the desired settings.

This brings up the question, *where is the default kernel config stored*? The kbuild system uses a priority list fallback scheme to retrieve a default configuration. The priority list and its order (first being highest priority) are specified within `init/Kconfig:DEFCONFIG_LIST`:

```
$ cat init/Kconfig
config DEFCONFIG_LIST
    string
    depends on !UML
    option defconfig_list
    default "/lib/modules/$(shell,uname -r)/.config"
    default "/etc/kernel-config"
    default "/boot/config-$(shell,uname -r)"
    default ARCH_DEFCONFIG
    default "arch/$(ARCH)/defconfig"
config CC_IS_GCC
[...]
```

FYI, the kernel documentation on `Kconfig` (found here: https://www.kernel.org/doc/Documentation/kbuild/kconfig-language.txt) documents what `defconfig_list` is:

```
"defconfig_list"
    This declares a list of default entries which can be used when
    looking for the default configuration (which is used when the main
    .config doesn't exists yet.)
```

From the list, you can see that the kbuild system first checks for the presence of a `.config` file in the `/lib/modules/$(uname -r)` folder. If found, the values there will be used as the defaults. If not found, it next checks for the presence of a `/etc/kernel-config` file. If found, the values there will be used as defaults, and if not found it moves on to the next option in the preceding priority list, and so on. Note, though, that the presence of a `.config` file in the root of the kernel source tree overrides all of this!

Obtaining a good starting point for kernel configuration

This brings us to a **really important point**: playing around with the kernel configuration is okay to do as a learning exercise (as we do here), but for a production system, it's really critical that you use a proven – known, tested, and working – kernel configuration.

Here, to help you understand the nuances of selecting a valid starting point for kernel configuration, we will see three approaches to obtaining a starting point for kernel configuration that (we hope) are typical:

- First, the approach to follow for a typical small embedded Linux system
- Next, an approach where you emulate the distribution's configuration
- Finally, an approach where you base the kernel configuration on the existing (or another) system's kernel modules (the `localmodconfig` approach)

Let's examine each of these approaches in a bit more detail.

Kernel config for typical embedded Linux systems

The typical target system for using this approach is a small embedded Linux system. The goal here is to begin with a proven – a known, tested, and working – kernel configuration for our embedded Linux project. Well, how exactly can we achieve this?

Interestingly, the kernel code base itself provides known, tested, and working kernel configuration files for various hardware platforms. We merely have to select the one that matches (or is the nearest match to) our embedded target board. These kernel config files are present within the kernel source tree in the `arch/<arch>/configs/` directory. The config files are in the format `<platform-name>_defconfig`. A quick peek is in order; see the following screenshot showing the command `ls arch/arm/configs` being performed on the v5.4 Linux kernel code base:

Figure 2.4 – The contents of arch/arm/configs on the 5.4 Linux kernel

[67]

Thus, for example, if you find yourself configuring the Linux kernel for a hardware platform having, say, a Samsung Exynos **System on Chip** (**SoC**) on it, please don't start with an x86-64 kernel config file as the default (or simply attempt to use it). It won't work. Even if you manage it, the kernel will not build/work cleanly. Pick the appropriate kernel config file: for our example here, the `arch/arm/configs/exynos_defconfig` file would be a good starting point. You can copy this file into `.config` in the root of your kernel source tree and then proceed to fine-tune it to your project-specific needs.

As another example, the Raspberry Pi (https://www.raspberrypi.org/) is a popular hobbyist platform. The kernel config file – within its kernel source tree – used (as a base) is this one: `arch/arm/configs/bcm2835_defconfig`. The filename reflects the fact that Raspberry Pi boards use a Broadcom 2835-based SoC. You can find details regarding kernel compilation for the Raspberry Pi here: https://www.raspberrypi.org/documentation/linux/kernel/building.md. Hang on, though, we will be covering at least some of this in `Chapter 3`, *Building the 5.x Linux Kernel from Source – Part 2*, in the *Kernel build for the Raspberry Pi* section.

> **TIP**: An easy way to see exactly which configuration file is good for which platform is to simply perform `make help` on the target platform itself. The latter part of the output displays the config files under the *Architecture specific targets* heading (note though that this is meant for foreign CPUs and doesn't work for the x86[-64]).

The careful tweaking and setup of the kernel config for a product is an important part of the work typically carried out by the engineers working within the *platform* or **Board Support Package** (**BSP**) team.

Kernel config using distribution config as a starting point

The typical target system for using this approach is a desktop or server Linux system.

Moving along, this second approach is also quick:

```
cp /boot/config-5.0.0-36-generic ${LLKD_KSRC}/.config
```

Chapter 2

Here, we simply copy the existing Linux distribution's (here, it's our Ubuntu 18.04.3 LTS guest VM) config file into the `.config` file in the root of the kernel source tree, of course, thereby making the distribution config the starting point, which can then be further edited (a more generic command: `cp /boot/config-$(uname -r) ${LLKD_KSRC}/.config`).

Tuned kernel config via the localmodconfig approach

The typical target system for using this approach is a desktop or server Linux system.

This third approach we consider is a good one to use when the goal is to begin with a kernel config that is based on your existing system and is thus (usually) relatively compact compared to the typical default config on a desktop or server Linux system. Here, we provide the kbuild system with a snapshot of the kernel modules currently running on the system by simply redirecting the output of `lsmod(8)` into a temporary file, and then providing that file to the build. This can be achieved as follows:

```
lsmod > /tmp/lsmod.now
cd ${LLKD_KSRC}
make LSMOD=/tmp/lsmod.now localmodconfig
```

The `lsmod(8)` utility simply lists all the kernel modules currently residing in system (kernel) memory. We will see (a lot) more on this in Chapter 4, *Writing Your First Kernel Module – LKMs Part 1*. We save its output in a temporary file, which we pass within the `LSMOD` environment variable to the Makefile's `localmodconfig` target. The job of this target is to configure the kernel in a manner as to only include the base functionality plus the functionality provided by these kernel modules and leave out the rest, in effect giving us a reasonable facsimile of the current kernel (or of whichever kernel the `lsmod` output represents). We use precisely this technique to configure our 5.4 kernel in the following *Getting started with the localmodconfig approach* section.

Right, this concludes the three approaches to setting up a starting point for kernel configuration. As a matter of fact, we have just scratched the surface. Many more techniques to explicitly generate the kernel configuration in a given manner are encoded into the kbuild system itself! How? Via configuration targets to `make`. See them under the `Configuration targets` heading:

```
$ cd ${LKDC_KSRC}        # root of the kernel source tree
$ make help
```

```
Cleaning targets:
  clean            - Remove most generated files but keep the config and
                     enough build support to build external modules
  mrproper         - Remove all generated files + config + various backup
                     files
  distclean        - mrproper + remove editor backup and patch files

Configuration targets:
  config           - Update current config utilising a line-oriented
                     program
  nconfig          - Update current config utilising a ncurses menu based
                     program
  menuconfig       - Update current config utilising a menu based program
  xconfig          - Update current config utilising a Qt based front-end
  gconfig          - Update current config utilising a GTK+ based front-end
  oldconfig        - Update current config utilising a provided .config as
                     base
  localmodconfig   - Update current config disabling modules not loaded
  localyesconfig   - Update current config converting local mods to core
  defconfig        - New config with default from ARCH supplied defconfig
  savedefconfig    - Save current config as ./defconfig (minimal config)
  allnoconfig      - New config where all options are answered with no
  allyesconfig     - New config where all options are accepted with yes
  allmodconfig     - New config selecting modules when possible
  alldefconfig     - New config with all symbols set to default
  randconfig       - New config with random answer to all options
  listnewconfig    - List new options
  olddefconfig     - Same as oldconfig but sets new symbols to their
                     default value without prompting
  kvmconfig        - Enable additional options for kvm guest kernel support
  xenconfig        - Enable additional options for xen dom0 and guest
                     kernel support
  tinyconfig       - Configure the tiniest possible kernel
  testconfig       - Run Kconfig unit tests (requires python3 and pytest)

Other generic targets:
```

```
    all              - Build all targets marked with [*]
[...]
$
```

A quick but very useful point: to ensure a clean slate, use the `mrproper` target first. We will show a summary of all the steps carried out next, so don't worry for now.

Getting started with the localmodconfig approach

Now, let's quickly get started on creating a base kernel configuration for our new kernel by using the third approach we discussed previously – the `localmodconfig` technique. As mentioned, this existing kernel modules-only approach is a good one when the goal is to obtain a starting point for kernel config on an x86-based system by keeping it relatively small and thus make the build quicker as well.

> Don't forget: the kernel configuration being performed right now is appropriate for your typical x86-based desktop/server systems. For embedded targets, the approach is different (as seen in the *Kernel config for typical embedded Linux systems* section). We further cover this practically in Chapter 3, *Building the 5.x Linux Kernel from Source - Part 2*, under the *Kernel build for the Raspberry Pi* section.

As described previously, first obtain a snapshot of the currently loaded kernel modules, and then have the kbuild system operate upon it by specifying the `localmodconfig` target, like so:

```
lsmod > /tmp/lsmod.now
cd ${LLKD_KSRC} ; make LSMOD=/tmp/lsmod.now localmodconfig
```

Now, something to understand: when we perform the actual `make [...] localmodconfig` command, it's entirely possible, indeed even probable, that there will be a difference in the configuration options between the kernel you are currently building (version 5.4) and the kernel you are currently actually running the build on ($(uname -r) = 5.0.0-36-generic, here). In these cases, the kbuild system will display every single new config option and the available values you can set it to, on the console (terminal) window. Then, it will prompt the user to select the value of any new config options it encounters in the kernel being built. You will see this as a series of questions and a prompt to answer them on the command line.

> **TIP:** The prompt will be suffixed with (NEW), in effect telling you that this is a *new* kernel config option and it wants your answer as to how to configure it.

Here, at least, we will take the easy way out: just press the [Enter] key to accept the default selection, as follows:

```
$ uname -r
5.0.0-36-generic
$ make LSMOD=/tmp/lsmod.now localmodconfig
using config: '/boot/config-5.0.0-36-generic'
vboxsf config not found!!
module vboxguest did not have configs CONFIG_VBOXGUEST
*
* Restart config...
*
*
* General setup
*
Compile also drivers which will not load (COMPILE_TEST) [N/y/?] n
Local version - append to kernel release (LOCALVERSION) []
Automatically append version information to the version string
(LOCALVERSION_AUTO) [N/y/?] n
Build ID Salt (BUILD_SALT) [] (NEW) [Enter]
Kernel compression mode
> 1. Gzip (KERNEL_GZIP)
  2. Bzip2 (KERNEL_BZIP2)
  3. LZMA (KERNEL_LZMA)
  4. XZ (KERNEL_XZ)
  5. LZO (KERNEL_LZO)
  6. LZ4 (KERNEL_LZ4)
choice[1-6?]: 1
Default hostname (DEFAULT_HOSTNAME) [(none)] (none)
Support for paging of anonymous memory (swap) (SWAP) [Y/n/?] y
System V IPC (SYSVIPC) [Y/n/?] y
[...]
Enable userfaultfd() system call (USERFAULTFD) [Y/n/?] y
Enable rseq() system call (RSEQ) [Y/n/?] (NEW)
[...]
  Test static keys (TEST_STATIC_KEYS) [N/m/?] n
  kmod stress tester (TEST_KMOD) [N/m/?] n
  Test memcat_p() helper function (TEST_MEMCAT_P) [N/m/y/?] (NEW)
#
# configuration written to .config
#
$ ls -la .config
```

```
-rw-r--r-- 1 llkd llkd  140764 Mar  7 17:31 .config
$
```

After pressing the `[Enter]` key many times, the interrogation mercifully finishes and the kbuild system writes the newly generated configuration to the `.config` file in the current working directory (we truncated the previous output as it's simply too voluminous, and unnecessary, to reproduce fully).

The preceding two steps take care of generating the `.config` file via the `localmodconfig` approach. Before we conclude this section, here are some key points to note:

- To ensure a completely clean slate, run `make mrproper` or `make distclean` in the root of the kernel source tree (useful when you want to restart from scratch; rest assured, it will happen one day! Note that doing this deletes the kernel configuration file(s) too).
- Here, in this chapter, all the kernel configuration steps and the screenshots pertaining to it have been performed on an Ubuntu 18.04.3 LTS x86-64 guest VM, which we use as the host to build a brand spanking new 5.4 Linux kernel. The precise names, the presence and content of the menu items, as well as the look and feel of the menu system (the UI) can and do vary based on (a) the architecture (CPU) and (b) the kernel version.
- As mentioned earlier, on a production system or project, the platform or **Board Support Package** (**BSP**) team, or indeed the embedded Linux BSP vendor company if you have partnered with one, will provide a good known, working, and tested kernel config file. Do use this as a starting point by copying it onto the `.config` file in the root of the kernel source tree.

As you gain experience with building the kernel, you will realize that the effort in setting up the kernel configuration correctly the first time (critical!) is higher; and, of course, the time required for the very first build is a lengthy one. Once done correctly, though, the process typically becomes much simpler – a recipe to run over and over again.

Now, let's learn how to use a useful and intuitive UI to tune our kernel configuration.

Building the 5.x Linux Kernel from Source - Part 1

Tuning our kernel configuration via the make menuconfig UI

Okay, great, we now have an initial kernel config file (.config) generated for us via the localmodconfig Makefile target, as shown in detail in the previous section, which is a good starting point. Now, we want to further examine and fine-tune our kernel's configuration. One way to do this – in fact, the recommended way – is via the menuconfig Makefile target. This target has the kbuild system generate a pretty sophisticated (C-based) program executable (scripts/kconfig/mconf), which presents to the end user a neat menu-based UI. In the following code block, when we invoke the command for the first time, the kbuild system builds the mconf executable and invokes it:

```
$ make menuconfig
  UPD     scripts/kconfig/.mconf-cfg
  HOSTCC  scripts/kconfig/mconf.o
  HOSTCC  scripts/kconfig/lxdialog/checklist.o
  HOSTCC  scripts/kconfig/lxdialog/inputbox.o
  HOSTCC  scripts/kconfig/lxdialog/menubox.o
  HOSTCC  scripts/kconfig/lxdialog/textbox.o
  HOSTCC  scripts/kconfig/lxdialog/util.o
  HOSTCC  scripts/kconfig/lxdialog/yesno.o
  HOSTLD  scripts/kconfig/mconf
scripts/kconfig/mconf Kconfig
...
```

Of course, a picture is no doubt worth a thousand words, so here's what the menuconfig UI looks like:

[74]

Chapter 2

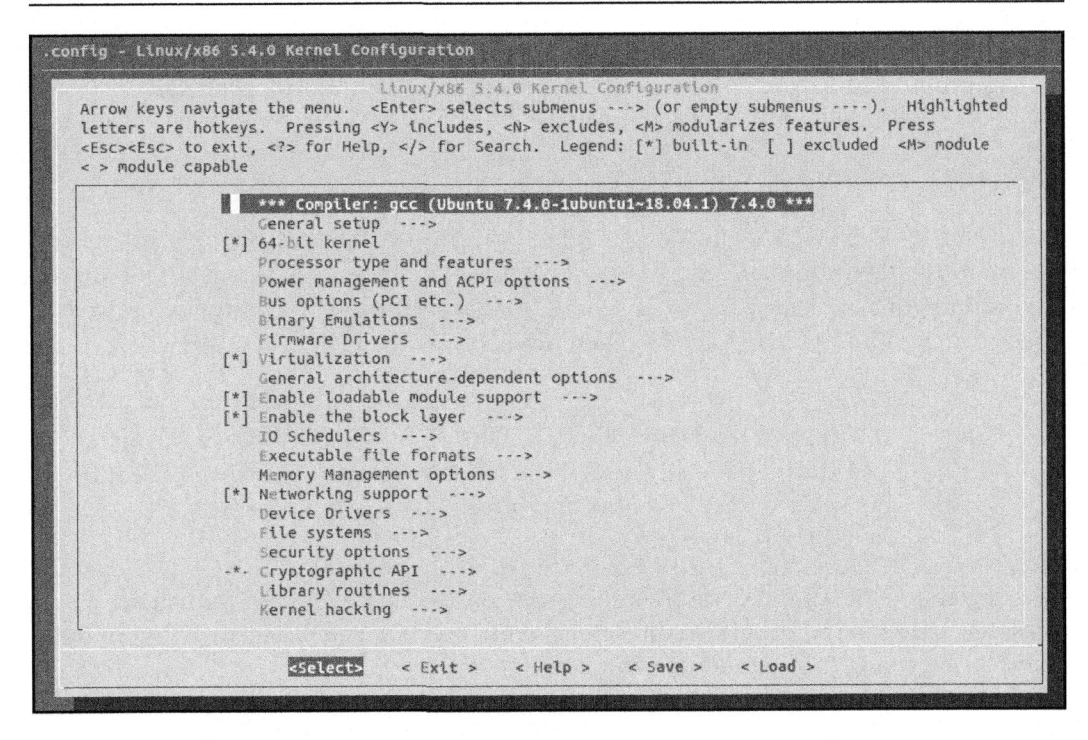

```
.config - Linux/x86 5.4.0 Kernel Configuration
                        Linux/x86 5.4.0 Kernel Configuration
  Arrow keys navigate the menu.  <Enter> selects submenus --->  (or empty submenus ----).  Highlighted
  letters are hotkeys.  Pressing <Y> includes, <N> excludes, <M> modularizes features.  Press
  <Esc><Esc> to exit, <?> for Help, </> for Search.  Legend: [*] built-in  [ ] excluded  <M> module
  < > module capable

            *** Compiler: gcc (Ubuntu 7.4.0-1ubuntu1~18.04.1) 7.4.0 ***
                General setup  --->
            [*] 64-bit kernel
                Processor type and features  --->
                Power management and ACPI options  --->
                Bus options (PCI etc.)  --->
                Binary Emulations  --->
                Firmware Drivers  --->
            [*] Virtualization  --->
                General architecture-dependent options  --->
            [*] Enable loadable module support  --->
            [*] Enable the block layer  --->
                IO Schedulers  --->
                Executable file formats  --->
                Memory Management options  --->
            [*] Networking support  --->
                Device Drivers  --->
                File systems  --->
                Security options  --->
            -*- Cryptographic API  --->
                Library routines  --->
                Kernel hacking  --->

                    <Select>    < Exit >    < Help >    < Save >    < Load >
```

Figure 2.5 – The main menu of kernel configuration via make menuconfig (on x86-64)

As experienced developers, or indeed anyone who has sufficiently used a computer, well know, things can and do go wrong. Take, for example, the following scenario – running `make menuconfig` for the first time on a freshly installed Ubuntu system:

```
$ make menuconfig
 UPD     scripts/kconfig/.mconf-cfg
 HOSTCC  scripts/kconfig/mconf.o
 YACC    scripts/kconfig/zconf.tab.c
/bin/sh: 1: bison: not found
scripts/Makefile.lib:196: recipe for target
'scripts/kconfig/zconf.tab.c' failed
make[1]: *** [scripts/kconfig/zconf.tab.c] Error 127
Makefile:539: recipe for target 'menuconfig' failed
make: *** [menuconfig] Error 2
$
```

Hang on, don't panic (yet). Read the failure message(s) carefully. The line after `YACC [...]` provides the clue: `/bin/sh: 1: bison: not found`. Ah, so install `bison(1)` with the following command:

`sudo apt install bison`

Now, all should be well. Well, almost; again, on a freshly baked Ubuntu guest, `make menuconfig` then complains that `flex(1)` was not installed. So, we install it (you guessed it: via `sudo apt install flex`). Also, specifically on Ubuntu, you need the `libncurses5-dev` package installed (on Fedora, do `sudo dnf install ncurses-devel`).

> If you have read and followed `Chapter 1`, *Kernel Workspace Setup*, you would have all these prerequisite packages already installed. If not, please refer to it now and install all required packages. Remember, *as ye sow...*

Moving along, the kbuild open source framework (reused in a whole bunch of projects, incidentally) provides some clues to the user via its UI. The meaning of the symbols prefixing the menu entries are as follows:

- `[.]`: In-kernel feature, Boolean option (it's either on or off):
    - `[*]`: On, feature compiled and built in (compiled in) to the kernel image (y)
    - `[ ]`: Off, not built at all (n)
- `<.>`: A feature that could be in one of three states (tristate):
    - `<*>`: On, feature compiled and built in (compiled in) the kernel image (y)
    - `<M>`: Module, feature compiled and built as a kernel module (an LKM) (m)
    - `< >`: Off, not built at all (n)
- `{.}`: A dependency exists for this config option; hence, it's required to be built (compiled) as either a module (m) or built in (compiled in) to the kernel image (y).
- `-*-`: A dependency requires this item to be compiled in (y).
- `(...)`: Prompt: an alphanumeric input is required (press the `[Enter]` key while on this option and a prompt appears).

- `<Menu entry>    --->`: A sub-menu follows (press `[Enter]` on this item to navigate to the sub-menu).

Again, the empirical approach is key. Let's actually experiment with the `make menuconfig` UI to see how it works. This is the topic of the next section.

Sample usage of the make menuconfig UI

To get a feel for using the kbuild menu system via the convenient `menuconfig` target, let's step through the process to navigate to the tristate menu item called `Kernel .config support`. It will be off by default, so let's turn it on; that is, let's make it `y`, built into the kernel image. We can find it under the `General Setup` main menu item on the home screen.

What exactly does turning this feature on achieve? When turned on to `y` (or, of course, if made to `M`, then a kernel module will become available, and once it's loaded up), then the currently running kernel's configuration settings can be looked up at any time in two ways:

- By running the `scripts/extract-ikconfig` script
- By directly reading the content of the `/proc/config.gz` pseudo-file (of course, it's `gzip(1)`-compressed; first uncompress it, and then read it)

As a learning exercise, we will now learn how to configure our 5.4 Linux kernel (for the x86-64 architecture) for the kernel config options with the values shown in the following table. For now, don't stress regarding the meaning of each of these options; it's just to get some practice with the kernel config system:

Feature	Effect and location in the make menuconfig UI	Select the < Help > button to see the precise CONFIG_<FOO> option	Value: original -> new value
Local version	Sets the -EXTRAVERSION component of the kernel release/version (seen with `uname -r`); `General Setup / Local version - append to kernel release`	CONFIG_LOCALVERSION	(none) -> -llkd01
Kernel config file support	Allows you to see the current kernel configuration details; `General Setup / Kernel .config support`	CONFIG_IKCONFIG	n -> y

[77]

Building the 5.x Linux Kernel from Source - Part 1

The same as the preceding plus access via procfs	Allows you to see the current kernel configuration details via **proc filesystem (procfs)**; `General Setup / Enable access to .config through /proc/config.gz`	`CONFIG_IKCONFIG_PROC`	n -> y
Kernel profiling	Kernel profiling support; `General Setup / Profiling support`	`CONFIG_PROFILING`	y -> n
HAM radio	Support for HAM radio; `Networking support / Amateur Radio support`	`CONFIG_HAMRADIO`	y -> n
VirtualBox support	(Para)virtualization support for VirtualBox; `Device Drivers / Virtualization drivers / Virtual Box Guest integration support`	`CONFIG_VBOXGUEST`	n -> m
Userspace IO Drivers (UIO)	UIO support; `Device Drivers / Userspace I/O Drivers`	`CONFIG_UIO`	n -> m
The preceding plus the UIO platform driver with generic IRQ handling	UIO platform driver with generic IRQ handling; `Device Drivers / Userspace I/O Drivers / Userspace I/O platform driver with generic IRQ handling`	`CONFIG_UIO_PDRV_GENIRQ`	n -> m
MS-DOS filesystem support	`File systems / DOS/FAT/NT Filesystems / MSDOS fs support`	`CONFIG_MSDOS_FS`	n -> m
Security: LSMs	Turn *off* kernel LSMs; `Security options / Enable different security models` (*NOTE: it's typically, safer to keep this ON for production systems!*)	`CONFIG_SECURITY`	y -> n
Kernel debug: stack utilization info	`Kernel hacking / Memory Debugging / Stack utilization instrumentation`	`CONFIG_DEBUG_STACK_USAGE`	n -> y

Table 2.4 – Items to configure

How exactly do you interpret this table? Let's take the first row as an example; we go over it column by column:

- **The first column** specifies the kernel *feature* we are wanting to modify (edit/enable/disable). Here, it's the last part of the kernel version string (as it shows up in the output of `uname -r`). It's called the `-EXTRAVERSION` component of the release (see the *Kernel release nomenclature* section for details).

Chapter 2

- **The second column** specifies two things:
    - One, what we're attempting to do. Here, we want to *set* the `-EXTRAVERSION` component of the kernel release string.
    - Two, the location of this kernel config option within the `menuconfig` UI is shown. Here, it's within the `General Setup` sub-menu, and under that it's the menu item called `Local version - append to kernel release`. We write it as `General Setup / Local version - append to kernel release`.
- **The third column** specifies the kernel config option's name as `CONFIG_<FOO>`. You can search for this within the menu system if required. In this example, it's called `CONFIG_LOCALVERSION`.
- **The fourth column** shows the original *value* of this kernel config option and the value we'd like you to change it to (the "new" value). It's shown in the format *original value -> new value*. In our example, it's `(none) -> -llkd01`, implying that the original value of the `-EXTRAVERSION` string component was empty and we would like you to modify it, changing it to the value `-llkd01`.

On the other hand, for several items we show, it may not be immediately apparent – say `n -> m`; what does this mean? `n -> m` implies that you should change the original value from `n` (not selected) to `m` (selected to be built as a kernel module). Similarly, the `y -> n` string means change the config option from on to off.

> **TIP**
> You can *search* for kernel config options within the `menuconfig` system UI by pressing the / key (just as with vi; we show more on this in the section that follows).

Then (in the following chapter, actually), we will build the kernel (and modules) with these new config options, boot from it, and verify that the preceding kernel config options were set as we wanted.

But right now, you are expected to do your bit: fire up the menu UI (with the usual `make menuconfig`), then navigate the menu system, finding the relevant kernel config options described previously, and edit it as required, to whatever the fourth column in the preceding table shows.

> **TIP:** Note that, depending on the Linux distribution you're currently running and its kernel modules (we used `lsmod(8)` to generate an initial config, remember?), the actual values and defaults you see when configuring the kernel might differ from that of the *Ubuntu 18.04.3 LTS* distribution (running the 5.0.0-36-generic kernel), as we have used and shown previously.

Here, to keep the discussion sane and compact, we will only show the complete detailed steps in setting up the second and third of the kernel config options shown in the preceding table (the `Kernel .config support` ones). It's up to you to edit the remainder. Let's get going:

1. Change directory to the root of your kernel source tree (wherever you extracted it on your disk):

   ```
   cd ${LLKD_KSRC}
   ```

2. Set up an initial kernel configuration file, based on the third approach described previously (in the *Tuned kernel config via the localmodconfig approach* section):

   ```
   lsmod > /tmp/lsmod.now
   make LSMOD=/tmp/lsmod.now localmodconfig
   ```

3. Run the UI:

   ```
   make menuconfig
   ```

4. Once the `menuconfig` UI loads up, go to the `General Setup` menu item. Usually, it's the second item on x86-64. Navigate to it using the keyboard arrow keys and enter into it by pressing the *Enter* key.

5. You are now within the `General Setup` menu item. Scroll down the menu items by pressing the down arrow key a few times. We scroll down to the menu of interest for us – `Kernel .config support` – and highlight it; the screen should look (something) like this:

Chapter 2

```
.config - Linux/x86 5.4.0 Kernel Configuration
> General setup
                                   General setup
  Arrow keys navigate the menu.  <Enter> selects submenus ---> (or empty submenus ----).
  Highlighted letters are hotkeys.  Pressing <Y> includes, <N> excludes, <M> modularizes
  features.  Press <Esc><Esc> to exit, <?> for Help, </> for Search.  Legend: [*] built-in
  [ ] excluded   <M> module   < > module capable

             [ ] Automatically append version information to the version string
             ()  Build ID Salt
                 Kernel compression mode (Gzip)  --->
             ((none)) Default hostname
             [*] Support for paging of anonymous memory (swap)
             [*] System V IPC
             [*] POSIX Message Queues
             [*] Enable process_vm_readv/writev syscalls
             [*] uselib syscall
             -*- Auditing support
                 IRQ subsystem  --->
                 Timers subsystem  --->
                 Preemption Model (Voluntary Kernel Preemption (Desktop))  --->
                 CPU/Task time and stats accounting  --->
             [*] CPU isolation
                 RCU Subsystem  --->
             <M> Kernel .config support
             [ ]   Enable access to .config through /proc/config.gz
             < > Enable kernel headers through /sys/kernel/kheaders.tar.xz


                    <Select>    < Exit >    < Help >    < Save >    < Load >
```

Figure 2.6 – Kernel configuration via make menuconfig: General setup / Kernel .config support

> **TIP**
> For the 5.4.0 vanilla Linux kernel on the x86-64, `General Setup / Kernel .config support` is the 20th menu item from the top of the `General Setup` menu.

6. Once on the `Kernel .config support` menu item, we can see (in the preceding screenshot) from its `<M>` prefix that it's a tristate menu item that's set to the choice `<M>` for module, to begin with.

[81]

Building the 5.x Linux Kernel from Source - Part 1

7. Keeping this item (`Kernel .config support`) highlighted, use the right arrow key to navigate to the `< Help >` button on the bottom toolbar and press the *Enter* key while on the `< Help >` button. The screen should now look (something) like this:

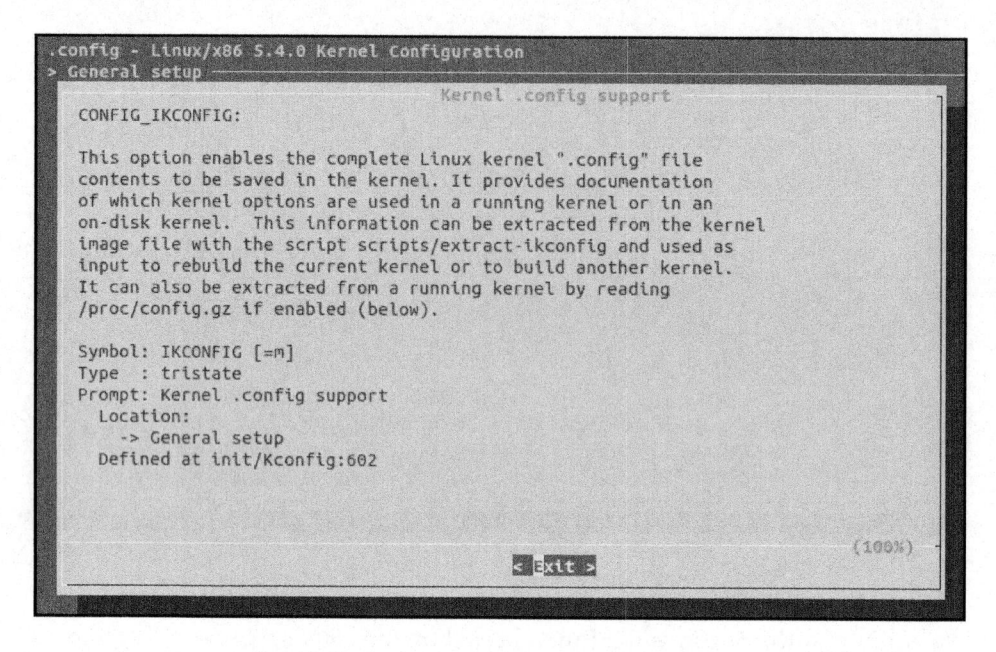

```
.config - Linux/x86 5.4.0 Kernel Configuration
> General setup
                            Kernel .config support
   CONFIG_IKCONFIG:

   This option enables the complete Linux kernel ".config" file
   contents to be saved in the kernel. It provides documentation
   of which kernel options are used in a running kernel or in an
   on-disk kernel.  This information can be extracted from the kernel
   image file with the script scripts/extract-ikconfig and used as
   input to rebuild the current kernel or to build another kernel.
   It can also be extracted from a running kernel by reading
   /proc/config.gz if enabled (below).

   Symbol: IKCONFIG [=m]
   Type  : tristate
   Prompt: Kernel .config support
     Location:
       -> General setup
     Defined at init/Kconfig:602

                                                              (100%)
                                < Exit >
```

Figure 2.7 – Kernel configuration via make menuconfig: an example help screen

The help screen is quite informative. Indeed, several of the kernel config help screens are very well populated and actually helpful. Unfortunately, some just aren't.

8. Okay, next, press *Enter* on the `< Exit >` button so that we go back to the previous screen.
9. Then, toggle the `Kernel .config support` menu item by pressing the space bar (assuming it's initially like this: <M>; that is, set to module). Pressing the space bar once makes the UI items appear like this:

```
<*> Kernel .config support
[ ]   Enable access to .config through /proc/config.gz (NEW)
```

Notice how it's become <*>, implying that this feature will be built into the kernel image itself (in effect, it will be *always on*). For now, let's do it this way (of course, pressing the space bar again makes it toggle to the off state, < >, and then back to the original <M> state).

10. Now, with the item in the <*> (yes) state, scroll down to the next menu item, `[*] Enable access to .config through /proc/config.gz`, and enable it (again, by pressing the space bar); the screen should now appear (something) like this (we've zoomed in to the relevant portion only):

```
    RCU Subsystem   --->
<*> Kernel .config support
[*]     Enable access to .config through /proc/config.gz
(18) Kernel log buffer size (16 => 64KB, 17 => 128KB)
(12) CPU kernel log buffer size contribution (13 => 8 KB, 17
```

Figure 2.8 – Kernel configuration via make menuconfig: toggling a Boolean config option to the on state

> **TIP**
> You can always use the right arrow key to go to < Help > and view the help screen for this item as well.

Here, we will not explore the remaining kernel config menus; I will leave that to you to find and set as shown in the preceding table.

11. Back in the main menu (the home screen), use the right arrow key to navigate to the < Exit > button and press *Enter* on it. A dialog pops up:

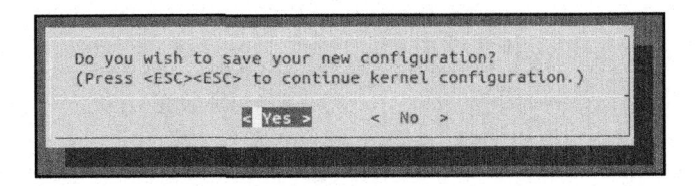

```
Do you wish to save your new configuration?
(Press <ESC><ESC> to continue kernel configuration.)
             < Yes >      < No >
```

Figure 2.9 – Kernel configuration via make menuconfig: save dialog

It's quite straightforward, isn't it? Press *Enter* on the < Yes > button to save and exit. If you select the < No > button, you lose all your configuration changes (made during this session). Or, you can press the *Esc* key *twice* to get rid of this dialog and continue working on the kernel config.

12. **Save and exit.** Press *Enter* while on the < Yes > button. The menu system UI now saves the new kernel configuration and the process exits; we're back on the console (a shell or terminal window) prompt.

But where's the new kernel configuration saved? This is important: the kernel configuration is written into a simple ASCII text file in the root of the kernel source tree, named .config. That is, it's saved in ${LLKD_KSRC}/.config.

As mentioned earlier, every single kernel config option is associated with a config variable of the form CONFIG_<FOO>, where <FOO>, of course, is replaced with an appropriate name. Internally, these become *macros* that the build system and indeed the kernel source code uses. For example, consider this for the Kernel .config support option:

```
$ grep IKCONFIG .config
CONFIG_IKCONFIG=y
CONFIG_IKCONFIG_PROC=y
$
```

Aha! The configuration now reflects the fact that we have done the following:

- Turned on the CONFIG_IKCONFIG kernel feature (=y indicates that it is on and will be built into the kernel image).
- The /proc/config.gz (pseudo) file will now be available, as CONFIG_IKCONFIG_PROC=y.

> *Caution:* it's best to NOT attempt to edit the .config file manually ("by hand"). There are several inter-dependencies you may not be aware of; always use the kbuild menu system (we suggest via make menuconfig) to edit it.

In reality, during our quick adventure with the kbuild system so far, quite a lot has occurred under the hood. The next section examines a little bit to do with this, searching within the menu system and cleanly visualizing the differences between the original (or older) and new kernel configuration files.

More on kbuild

The creation of, or edits to, the `.config` file within the root of the kernel source tree via `make menuconfig` or other methods is not the final step in how the kbuild system works with the configuration. No, it now proceeds to internally invoke a target called `syncconfig`, which was earlier (mis)named `silentoldconfig`. This target has kbuild generate a few header files that are further used in the setup to build the kernel. These files include some meta headers under `include/config`, as well as the `include/generated/autoconf.h` header file, which stores the kernel config as C macros, thus enabling both the kernel Makefile(s) and kernel code to make decisions based on whether or not a kernel feature is available.

Moving along, what if you are looking for a particular kernel configuration option but are having difficulty spotting it? No problem, the `menuconfig` UI system has a `Search Configuration Parameter` feature. Just as with the famous `vi(1)` editor, press the / (forward slash) key to have a search dialog pop up, then enter your search term with or without `CONFIG_` preceding it, and select the `< Ok >` button to have it go on its way.

The following couple of screenshots show the search dialog and the result dialog (as an example, we searched for the term `vbox`):

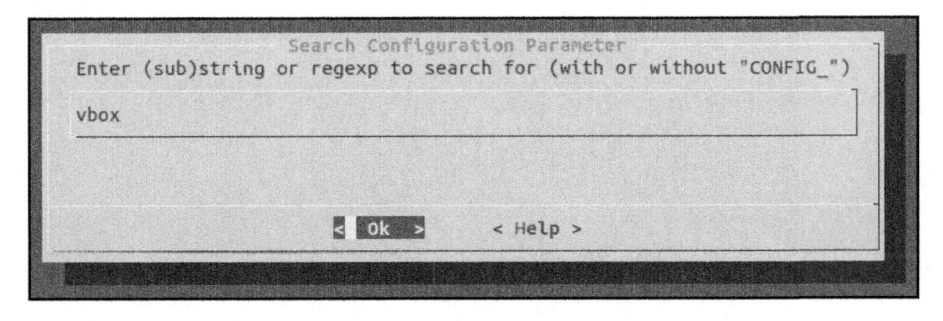

Figure 2.10 – Kernel configuration via make menuconfig: searching for a config parameter

The result dialog for the preceding search is interesting. It reveals several pieces of information regarding the configuration option(s):

- The config directive (just prefix `CONFIG_` onto whatever it shows in `Symbol:`)
- The type of config (Boolean, tristate, alphanumeric, and so on)

- The prompt string
- Importantly, its location in the menu system (so you can find it)
- Its internal dependencies, if any
- Any config option it auto-selects (turns on) if it itself is selected

The following is a screenshot of the result dialog:

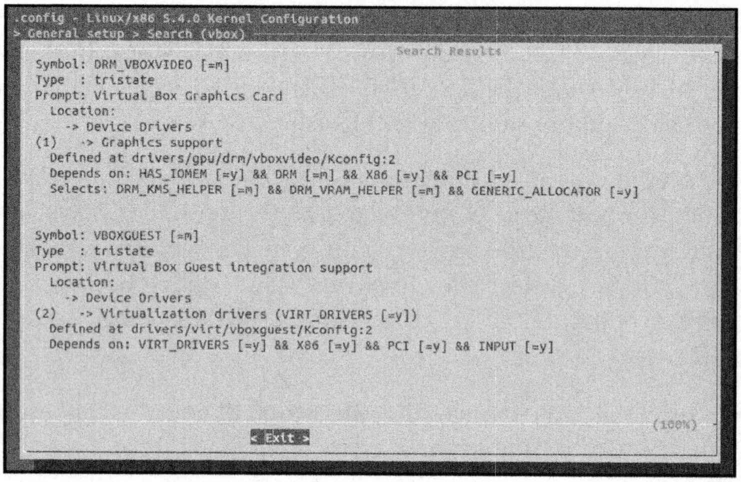

Figure 2.11 – Kernel configuration via make menuconfig: the result dialog from the preceding search

All this information is present in an ASCII text file used by the kbuild system to build the menu system UI – this file is called `Kconfig` (there are several of them, actually). Its location, too, is shown (in the `Defined at ...` line).

Looking up the differences in configuration

The moment the `.config` kernel configuration file is to be written to, the kbuild system checks whether it already exists, and if so, it backs it up with the name `.config.old`. Knowing this, we can always differentiate the two to see the changes we have wrought. However, using your typical `diff(1)` utility to do so makes the differences quite hard to interpret. The kernel helpfully provides a better way, a console-based script that specializes in doing precisely this. The `scripts/diffconfig` script (within the kernel source tree) is really useful for this. To see why, let's just run its help screen first:

```
$ scripts/diffconfig --help
Usage: diffconfig [-h] [-m] [<config1> <config2>]
```

[86]

```
Diffconfig is a simple utility for comparing two .config files.
Using standard diff to compare .config files often includes extraneous
and
distracting information. This utility produces sorted output with only
the
changes in configuration values between the two files.

Added and removed items are shown with a leading plus or minus,
respectively.
Changed items show the old and new values on a single line.
[...]
```

Now, we try it out:

```
$ scripts/diffconfig .config.old .config
-AX25 n
-DEFAULT_SECURITY_APPARMOR y
-DEFAULT_SECURITY_SELINUX n
-DEFAULT_SECURITY_SMACK n
[...]
-SIGNATURE y
 DEBUG_STACK_USAGE n -> y
 DEFAULT_SECURITY_DAC n -> y
 FS_DAX y -> n
 HAMRADIO y -> n
 IKCONFIG m -> y
 IKCONFIG_PROC n -> y
 LOCALVERSION "" -> "-llkd01"
 MSDOS_FS n -> m
 PROFILING y -> n
 SECURITY y -> n
 UIO n -> m
+UIO_AEC n
 VBOXGUEST n -> m
[...]
$
```

If you modified the kernel configuration changes as shown in the preceding table, you should see an output similar to that shown in the preceding code block via the kernel's `diffconfig` script. It clearly shows us exactly which kernel config options we changed and how.

Before we finish, a quick note on something critical: *kernel security*. While userspace security hardening technologies have vastly grown, kernel-space security hardening technologies are actually playing catch-up. Careful configuration of the kernel's config options does play a key role in determining the security posture of a given Linux kernel; the trouble is, there are so many options (and indeed opinions) that it's often hard to (cross) check what's a good idea security-wise and what isn't. Alexander Popov has written a very useful Python script named `kconfig-hardened-check`; it can be run to check and compare a given kernel configuration (via the usual config file) to a set of predetermined hardening preferences (from various Linux kernel security projects: the well known **Kernel Self Protection Project (KSPP)**, the last public grsecurity patch, the CLIP OS and the security lockdown LSM). Lookup the `kconfig-hardened-check` GitHub repository at `https://github.com/a13xp0p0v/kconfig-hardened-check` and try it out!

Alright! You have now completed the first three steps of the Linux kernel build, quite a thing. (Of course, we will complete the remaining four steps in the build process in the following chapter.) We will end this chapter with a final section on learning a useful skill – how to customize the kernel UI menu.

Customizing the kernel menu – adding our own menu item

So, let's say you have developed a device driver, an experimental new scheduling class, a custom `debugfs` (debug filesystem) callback, or some other cool kernel feature. How will you let others on the team – or for that matter, your customer – know that this fantastic new kernel feature exists and allow them to select it (as either a built-in or as a kernel module) and thus build and make use of it? The answer is to insert *a new menu item* at an appropriate place in the kernel configuration menu.

To do so, it's useful to first understand a little more about the various `Kconfig*` files and where they reside. Let's find out.

The Kconfig* files

The `Kconfig` file at the root of the kernel source tree is used to fill in the initial screen of the `menuconfig` UI. Take a look at it if you wish. It works by sourcing various other `Kconfig` files in different folders of the kernel source tree. The following table summarizes the more important `Kconfig*` files and which menu they serve in the kbuild UI:

Menu	Kconfig file location for it
The main menu, the initial screen	`Kconfig`
General setup + Enable loadable module support	`init/Kconfig`
Processor types and features + **Bus options** + **Binary Emulations** (arch-specific; above the menu title is for x86; in general, the Kconfig file is here: `arch/<arch>/Kconfig`)	`arch/<arch>/Kconfig`
Power management	`kernel/power/Kconfig`
Firmware drivers	`drivers/firmware/Kconfig`
Virtualization	`arch/<arch>/kvm/Kconfig`
General architecture-dependent options	`arch/Kconfig`
Enable the block layer + **IO Schedulers**	`block/Kconfig`
Executable file formats	`fs/Kconfig.binfmt`
Memory Management options	`mm/Kconfig`
Networking support	`net/Kconfig, net/*/Kconfig`
Device Drivers	`drivers/Kconfig, drivers/*/Kconfig`
File systems	`fs/Kconfig, fs/*/Kconfig`
Security options	`security/Kconfig, security/*/Kconfig*`
Cryptographic API	`crypto/Kconfig, crypto/*/Kconfig`
Library routines	`lib/Kconfig, lib/*/Kconfig`
Kernel hacking	`lib/Kconfig.debug, lib/Kconfig.*`

Table 2.5 – Kernel config menu items and the corresponding Kconfig* file defining them

Typically, a single `Kconfig` file drives a single menu. Now, let's move on to actually adding a menu item.

Creating a new menu item in the Kconfig file

As a trivial example, let's add our own Boolean dummy config option within the `General Setup` menu. We want the config name to be `CONFIG_LLKD_OPTION1`. As can be seen from the preceding table, the relevant `Kconfig` file to edit is the `init/Kconfig` one as this is the menu meta file that defines the `General Setup` menu.

Let's get to it:

1. To be safe, always make a backup copy:

    `cp init/Kconfig init/Kconfig.orig`

2. Now, edit the `init/Kconfig` file:

    `vi init/Kconfig`

Scroll down to an appropriate location within the file; here, we choose to insert our menu entry just after the `CONFIG_LOCALVERSION_AUTO` one. The following screenshot shows our new entry:

```
166         which is done within the script "scripts/setlocalversion".)
167
168 config LLKD_OPTION1
169         bool "Test case for LLKD book/Ch 2: creating a new menu item in kernel config"
170         default n
171         help
172           This option is merely a dummy 'test'; it's simply to have readers of our book
173           - 'Learn Linux Kernel Development', Kaiwan NB, Packt - try out the creation of
174           a few menu items within the kernel config.
175
176           Try setting this option to 'Y' (true), save and exit, and see the effect this
177           has by doing:
178             grep "CONFIG_LLKD_OPTION1" .config
179
180           If unsure, say N
181
182 config BUILD_SALT
183         string "Build ID Salt"
184         default ""
```

Figure 2.12 – Editing init/Kconfig and inserting our own menu entry

[90]

Chapter 2

> 💡 **TIP**: We have provided the preceding text as a patch to the original `init/Kconfig` file in our book's *GitHub* source tree. Find it under `ch2/Kconfig.patch`.

The new item starts with the `config` keyword followed by the `FOO` part of your new `CONFIG_LLKD_OPTION1` config variable. For now, just read the statements we have made in the `Kconfig` file regarding this entry. More details on the `Kconfig` language/syntax are in the *A few details on the Kconfig language* section that follows.

3. Save the file and exit the editor.
4. (Re)configure the kernel. Navigate to our new menu item and turn the feature on (notice how, in the following clipped screenshot, it's highlighted and *off* by default):

```
make menuconfig
[...]
```

Here's the output:

```
.config - Linux/x86 5.4.0 Kernel Configuration
 > General setup
 ──────────────────────────────── General setup ────────────────────────────────
   Arrow keys navigate the menu.  <Enter> selects submenus ---> (or empty submenus ----).  Highlighted letters
   are hotkeys.  Pressing <Y> includes, <N> excludes, <M> modularizes features.  Press <Esc><Esc> to exit, <?>
   for Help, </> for Search.  Legend: [*] built-in  [ ] excluded  <M> module  < > module capable
  ┌─────────────────────────────────────────────────────────────────────────────┐
  │            [ ] Compile also drivers which will not load                     │
  │            [ ] Compile test headers that should be standalone compilable    │
  │            (-llkd01) Local version - append to kernel release               │
  │            [ ] Automatically append version information to the version string│
  │            [ ] Test case for LLKD book/Ch 2: creating a new menu item in kernel config│
  │            ()  Build ID Salt                                                │
  │                Kernel compression mode (Gzip)  --->                         │
  └─────────────────────────────────────────────────────────────────────────────┘
```

Figure 2.13 – Kernel configuration via make menuconfig showing our new menu entry

5. Turn it *on* (toggle it with the space bar), then save and exit the menu system.

> **TIP**: While there, try pressing the < Help > button. You should see the "help" we provided within the `Kconfig` file.

6. Check whether our feature has been selected:

```
$ grep "LLKD_OPTION1" .config
CONFIG_LLKD_OPTION1=y
$ grep "LLKD_OPTION1" include/generated/autoconf.h
$
```

We find that indeed it has been set to *on* within our `.config` file, but is not (yet!) within the kernel's internal auto-generated header file. This will happen when we build the kernel.

7. Build the kernel (worry not; the full details on building the kernel are found in the next chapter. You could always first cover Chapter 3, *Building the 5.x Linux Kernel from Source – Part 2*, and then come back to this point, if you so wish...):

```
make -j4
```

8. Once done, recheck the `autoconf.h` header for the presence of our new config option:

```
$ grep "LLKD_OPTION1" include/generated/autoconf.h
#define CONFIG_LLKD_OPTION1 1
```

It worked! Yes, but when working on an actual project (or product), we would typically require a further step, setting up our config entry within the Makefile relevant to the code that uses this config option.

Here's a quick example of how this might look. In the kernel's top-level (or whichever) Makefile, the following line will ensure that our own code (the following is within the `llkd_option1.c` source file) gets compiled into the kernel at build time. Add this line to the end of the relevant Makefile:

```
obj-${CONFIG_LLKD_OPTION1}   +=   llkd_option1.o
```

> Don't stress about the fairly weird kernel Makefile syntax for now. The next few chapters will shed some light on this.

Also, you should realize that the very same config can be used as a normal C macro within a piece of kernel code; for example, we could do things like this:

```
#ifdef CONFIG_LLKD_OPTION1
    do_our_thing();
#endif
```

However, it's very much worth noting that the Linux kernel community has devised and strictly adheres to certain rigorous coding style guidelines. In this context, the guidelines state that conditional compilation should be avoided whenever possible, and if it is required to use a `Kconfig` symbol as a conditional, then please do it this way:

```
if (IS_ENABLED(CONFIG_LLKD_OPTION1)) {
    do_our_thing();
}
```

> The Linux kernel *coding style guidelines* can be found here: https://www.kernel.org/doc/html/latest/process/coding-style.html. I urge you to refer to them often, and, of course, to follow them!

A few details on the Kconfig language

Our usage of the `Kconfig` language so far is just the tip of the proverbial iceberg. The fact is, the kbuild system uses the `Kconfig` language (or syntax) to express and create menus using simple ASCII text directives. The language includes menu entries, attributes, (reverse) dependencies, visibility constraints, help text, and so on.

> The kernel documents the `Kconfig` language constructs and syntax here: https://www.kernel.org/doc/Documentation/kbuild/kconfig-language.txt. Do refer to this document for complete details.

Building the 5.x Linux Kernel from Source - Part 1

A brief (and incomplete) mention of the more common `Kconfig` constructs is given in the following table:

Construct	Meaning
`config <FOO>`	Specifies the menu entry name (of the form `CONFIG_FOO`) here; just put the `FOO` part.
Menu attributes	
`bool ["<description>"]`	Specifies the config option as a *Boolean*; its value in `.config` will be either `Y` (built into the kernel image) or will not exist (will show up as a commented-out entry).
`tristate ["<description>"]`	Specifies the config option as *tristate*; its value in `.config` will be either `Y`, `M` (built as a kernel module), or will not exist (will show up as a commented-out entry)
`int ["<description>"]`	Specifies the config option as taking an *integer* value.
`range x-y`	The integer range is from `x` to `y`.
`default <value>`	Specifies the default value; use `y`, `m`, `n`, or another, as required.
`prompt "<description>"`	A sentence describing the kernel config.
`depends on "expr"`	Defines a dependency for the menu item; can have several with the `depends on FOO1 && FOO2 && (FOO3 || FOO4)` type of syntax.
`select <config> [if "expr"]`	Defines a reverse dependency.
`help "help-text"`	Text to display when the `< Help >` button is selected.

Table 2.6 – Kconfig, a few constructs

To help understand the syntax, a few examples from `lib/Kconfig.debug` (the file that describes the menu items for the `Kernel Hacking` - kernel debugging, really - section of the UI) follow:

1. We will start with a simple one (the `CONFIG_DEBUG_INFO` option):

```
config DEBUG_INFO
    bool "Compile the kernel with debug info"
    depends on DEBUG_KERNEL && !COMPILE_TEST
    help
      If you say Y here the resulting kernel image will include
        debugging info resulting in a larger kernel image. [...]
```

[94]

2. Next, let's look at the `CONFIG_FRAME_WARN` option. Notice range and the conditional default value syntax, as follows:

```
config FRAME_WARN
    int "Warn for stack frames larger than (needs gcc 4.4)"
    range 0 8192
    default 3072 if KASAN_EXTRA
    default 2048 if GCC_PLUGIN_LATENT_ENTROPY
    default 1280 if (!64BIT && PARISC)
    default 1024 if (!64BIT && !PARISC)
    default 2048 if 64BIT
    help
      Tell gcc to warn at build time for stack frames larger
than this.
        Setting this too low will cause a lot of warnings.
        Setting it to 0 disables the warning.
        Requires gcc 4.4
```

3. Next, the `CONFIG_HAVE_DEBUG_STACKOVERFLOW` option is a simple Boolean; it's either on or off. The `CONFIG_DEBUG_STACKOVERFLOW` option is also a Boolean. Notice how it depends on two other options, separated with a Boolean AND (`&&`) operator:

```
config HAVE_DEBUG_STACKOVERFLOW
        bool

config DEBUG_STACKOVERFLOW
        bool "Check for stack overflows"
        depends on DEBUG_KERNEL && HAVE_DEBUG_STACKOVERFLOW
        ---help---
          Say Y here if you want to check for overflows of
kernel, IRQ
          and exception stacks (if your architecture uses
them). This
          option will show detailed messages if free stack
space drops
          below a certain limit. [...]
```

Alright! This completes our coverage for creating (or editing) a custom menu entry in the kernel config, and indeed this chapter.

Summary

In this chapter, you first learned how to obtain for yourself a Linux kernel source tree. You then understood its release (or version) nomenclature, the various types of Linux kernels (-next trees, -rc/mainline trees, stable, LTS, SLTS and distributions), and the basic kernel development workflow. Along the way, you even got a quick tour of the kernel source tree so that its layout is clearer. Next, you saw how to extract the compressed kernel source tree to disk and, critically, how to configure the kernel – a key step in the process. Furthermore, you learned how to customize the kernel menu, adding your own entries to it, and a bit about the kbuild system and the associated Kconfig files it uses, among others.

Knowing how to fetch and configure the Linux kernel is a useful skill to possess. We have just begun this long and exciting journey. You will realize that with more experience and knowledge of kernel internals, drivers, and the target system hardware, your ability to fine-tune the kernel to your project's purpose will only get better.

We're halfway there; I suggest you first digest this material, and, importantly - try out the steps in this chapter, work on the questions/exercises, and browse through the *Further reading* section. Then, in the next chapter, let's actually build the 5.4.0 kernel and verify it!

Questions

As we conclude, here is a list of questions for you to test your knowledge regarding this chapter's material: https://github.com/PacktPublishing/Linux-Kernel-Programming/tree/master/questions. You will find some of the questions answered in the book's GitHub repo: https://github.com/PacktPublishing/Linux-Kernel-Programming/tree/master/solutions_to_assgn.

Further reading

To help you delve deeper into the subject with useful materials, we provide a rather detailed list of online references and links (and at times, even books) in a Further reading document in this book's GitHub repository. The *Further reading* document is available here: https://github.com/PacktPublishing/Linux-Kernel-Programming/blob/master/Further_Reading.md.

3
Building the 5.x Linux Kernel from Source - Part 2

This chapter continues where the previous chapter left off. In the previous chapter, in the *Steps to build the kernel from source* section, we covered the first three steps of building our kernel. There, you learned how to download and extract the kernel source tree or even `git clone` one (*steps 1* and *2*). We then proceeded to understand the kernel source tree layout, and, very importantly, the various approaches to correctly arrive at a starting point to configure the kernel (*step 3*). We even added a custom menu item to the kernel config menu.

In this chapter, we continue our quest to build the kernel, by, well, covering the remaining four steps to actually build it. First, of course, we build it (*step 4*). You will then see how to properly install the kernel modules that get generated as part of the build (*step 5*). Next, we run a simple command that sets up the GRUB bootloader and generates the `initramfs` (or `initrd`) image (*step 6*). The motivation for using an `initramfs` image and how it's used are discussed as well. Some details on configuring the GRUB bootloader (for x86) are then covered (*step 7*).

By the end of the chapter, we'll boot the system with our new kernel image and verify that it's built as expected. We'll then finish off by learning how to *cross-compile* a Linux kernel for a foreign architecture (that is, ARM, the board in question being the well-known Raspberry Pi).

Briefly, these are the areas covered:

- Step 4 – building the kernel image and modules
- Step 5 – installing the kernel modules
- Step 6 – generating the initramfs image and bootloader setup
- Understanding the initramfs framework
- Step 7 – customizing the GRUB bootloader

- Verifying our new kernel's configuration
- Kernel build for the Raspberry Pi
- Miscellaneous tips on the kernel build

Technical requirements

Before we begin, I assume that you have downloaded, extracted (if required), and configured the kernel, thus having a .config file ready. If you haven't already, please refer to the previous chapter for the details on how exactly this is done. We can now proceed to build it.

Step 4 – building the kernel image and modules

Performing the build from the end user point of view is actually quite simple. In its simplest form, just ensure you're in the root of the configured kernel source tree and type make. That's it – the kernel image and any kernel modules (and, on an embedded system, possibly a **Device Tree Blob (DTB)** binary) will get built. Grab a coffee! The first time around, it could take a while.

Of course, there are various Makefile targets we can pass to make. A quick make help command issued on the command line reveals quite a bit. Remember, we used this earlier, in fact, to see all possible configuration targets. Here, we use it to see what gets built by default with the all target:

```
$ cd ${LLKD_KSRC}      # the env var LLKD_KSRC holds the 'root' of our
                       # 5.4 kernel source tree
$ make help
[...]
Other generic targets:
  all             - Build all targets marked with [*]
* vmlinux        - Build the bare kernel
* modules        - Build all modules
[...]
Architecture specific targets (x86):
* bzImage       - Compressed kernel image (arch/x86/boot/bzImage)
[...]
$
```

Okay, so performing `make all` will get us the preceding three targets, the ones prefixed with *; what do they mean?

- `vmlinux` actually matches the name of the uncompressed kernel image.
- The `modules` target implies that all kernel config options marked as m (for module) will be built as kernel modules (.ko files) within the kernel source tree (details on what exactly a kernel module is and how to program one are the subject matter of the following two chapters).
- `bzImage` is architecture-specific. On an x86[-64] system, this is the name of the compressed kernel image – the one the bootloader will actually load into RAM, uncompress in memory, and boot into; in effect, the kernel image file.

So, an FAQ: if `bzImage` is the actual kernel that we use to boot and initialize the system, then what's `vmlinux` for? Notice that `vmlinux` is the uncompressed kernel image. It can be large (even very large, in the presence of kernel symbols generated during a debug build). While we never boot via `vmlinux`, it's nevertheless important. Do keep it around for kernel debugging purposes (which are unfortunately beyond the scope of this book).

> **TIP:** With the kbuild system, just running a `make` command equates to `make all`.

The kernel code base is enormous. Current estimates are in the region of 20 million **source lines of code** (SLOC), thus, building the kernel is indeed *a very memory- and CPU-intensive job*. Indeed, some folks use the kernel build as a stress test! The modern `make(1)` utility is powerful and multi-process capable. We can request it to spawn multiple processes to handle different (unrelated) parts of the build in parallel, leading to higher throughput and thus shorter build times. The relevant option is -j'n', where n is the upper limit on the number of tasks to spawn and run in parallel. A heuristic (rule of thumb) used to determine this is as follows:

```
n = num-CPU-cores * factor;
```

Here, `factor` is 2 (or 1.5 on very high-end systems with hundreds of CPU cores). Also, technically, we require the cores to be internally "threaded" or using **Simultaneous Multi-Threading** (**SMT**) – what Intel calls *Hyper-Threading* – for this heuristic to be useful.

> **TIP:** More details on parallelized `make` and how it works can be found in the man page of `make(1)` (invoked with `man 1 make`) in the `PARALLEL MAKE AND THE JOBSERVER` section.

Another FAQ: how many CPU cores *are* there on your system? There are several ways to determine this, an easy one being to use the `nproc(1)` utility:

```
$ nproc
2
```

> **TIP:** A quick word regarding `nproc(1)` and related utilities:
> a) Performing `strace(1)` on `nproc(1)` reveals that it works by essentially using the `sched_getaffinity(2)` system call. We shall mention more on this and related system calls in Chapter 9, *The CPU Scheduler – Part 1*, and Chapter 10, *The CPU Scheduler – Part 2*, on CPU scheduling.
> b) FYI, the `lscpu(1)` utility yields the number of cores as well as additional useful CPU info. For example, it shows whether it's running on a **Virtual Machine (VM)** (as does the `virt-what` script). Try it out on your Linux system.

Clearly, our guest VM has been configured with two CPU cores, so let's keep n=2*2=4. So, off we go and build the kernel. The following output is from our trusty x86_64 Ubuntu 18.04 LTS guest system configured to have 2 GB of RAM and two CPU cores.

> Remember, the kernel must first be *configured*. For details, refer to Chapter 2, *Building the 5.x Linux Kernel from Source – Part 1*.

Again, when you begin, it's entirely possible that the kernel build emits a warning, although non-fatal in this case:

```
$ time make -j4
scripts/kconfig/conf --syncconfig Kconfig
  UPD     include/config/kernel.release
warning: Cannot use CONFIG_STACK_VALIDATION=y, please install libelf-dev, libelf-devel or elfutils-libelf-devel
[...]
```

Chapter 3

So, to address this, we break off the build with *Ctrl + C*, then follow the output's advice and install the `libelf-dev` package. On our Ubuntu box, `sudo apt install libelf-dev` is sufficient. If you followed the detailed setup in Chapter 1, *Kernel Workspace Setup*, this will not happen. Retry, and it now works! To give you a feel of this, we've show the following tiny snippets of the build output. Really though, it's best to just try it out yourself:

> **TIP**: Precisely because the kernel build is very CPU- and RAM-intensive, carrying this out on a guest VM is going to be a lot slower than on a native Linux system. It helps to conserve RAM by at least booting your guest at run-level 3 (multiuser with networking, no GUI): https://www.if-not-true-then-false.com/2012/howto-change-runlevel-on-grub2/.

```
$ cd ${LLKD_KSRC}
$ time make -j4
scripts/kconfig/conf --syncconfig Kconfig
  SYSHDR  arch/x86/include/generated/asm/unistd_32_ia32.h
  SYSTBL  arch/x86/include/generated/asm/syscalls_32.h
[...]
  DESCEND objtool
  HOSTCC  /home/llkd/kernels/linux-5.4/tools/objtool/fixdep.o
  HOSTLD  /home/llkd/kernels/linux-5.4/tools/objtool/fixdep-in.o
  LINK    /home/llkd/kernels/linux-5.4/tools/objtool/fixdep
[...]

[...]
  LD      vmlinux.o
  MODPOST vmlinux.o
  MODINFO modules.builtin.modinfo
  LD      .tmp_vmlinux1
  KSYM    .tmp_kallsyms1.o
  LD      .tmp_vmlinux2
  KSYM    .tmp_kallsyms2.o
  LD      vmlinux
  SORTEX  vmlinux
  SYSMAP  System.map
  Building modules, stage 2.
  MODPOST 59 modules
  CC      arch/x86/boot/a20.o
[...]
  LD      arch/x86/boot/setup.elf
  OBJCOPY arch/x86/boot/setup.bin
  BUILD   arch/x86/boot/bzImage
Setup is 17724 bytes (padded to 17920 bytes).
System is 8385 kB
```

```
    CRC 6f010e63
      CC [M]  drivers/hid/hid.mod.o
    Kernel: arch/x86/boot/bzImage is ready  (#1)
```

Okay, the kernel image (here, it's called `bzImage`) and the `vmlinux` file have successfully been built by stitching together the various object files generated, as can be seen in the preceding output – the last line in the preceding block confirms this fact. But hang on, the build isn't done yet. The kbuild system now proceeds to finish building all kernel modules; the last portion of the output is shown as follows:

```
[...]
  CC [M]  drivers/hid/usbhid/usbhid.mod.o
  CC [M]  drivers/i2c/algos/i2c-algo-bit.mod.o
[...]
  LD [M]  sound/pci/snd-intel8x0.ko
  LD [M]  sound/soundcore.ko

real    17m31.980s
user    23m58.451s
sys     3m22.280s
$
```

The entire process seems to have taken a total of around 17.5 minutes. The `time(1)` utility gives us a (very) coarse-grained idea of the time taken by the command that follows it.

> If you'd like accurate CPU profiling, learn to use the powerful `perf(1)` utility. Here, you can try it out with the `perf stat make -j4` command. I suggest you try this out on a distro kernel as otherwise, `perf` itself will have to be manually built for your custom kernel.

Also, in the previous output, `Kernel: arch/x86/boot/bzImage is ready (#1)`, `#1` implies it's the very first build of this kernel. This number will auto-increment on subsequent builds and show up when you boot into the new kernel and then execute `uname -a`.

> As we're doing a parallelized build (via `make -j4`, implying four processes performing the build in parallel), all the build processes still write to the same `stdout` location – the terminal window. Hence, it can happen that the output is out of order or mixed up.

Chapter 3

The build should run cleanly, without any errors or warnings. Well, at times compiler warnings are seen, but we shall blithely ignore them. What if you encounter compiler errors and thus a failed build during this step? How can we put this politely? Oh well, we cannot – it's very likely your fault, not the kernel community's. Please check and re-check every step, redoing it from scratch with a `make mrproper` command if all else fails! Very often, a failure to build the kernel implies either kernel configuration errors (randomly selected configs that might conflict), outdated versions of the toolchain, or incorrect patching, among other things.

Assuming it goes off well, as indeed it should, by the time this step terminates, three key files (among many) have been generated by the kbuild system.

In the root of the kernel source tree, we have the following:

- The uncompressed kernel image file, `vmlinux` (only for debugging)
- The symbol-address mapping file, `System.map`
- The compressed bootable kernel image file, `bzImage` (see the following output)

Let's check them out! We make the output (specifically the file size) more human-readable by passing the `-h` option to `ls(1)`:

```
$ ls -lh vmlinux System.map
-rw-rw-r-- 1 llkd llkd 4.1M Jan 17 12:27 System.map
-rwxrwxr-x 1 llkd llkd 591M Jan 17 12:27 vmlinux
$ file ./vmlinux
./vmlinux: ELF 64-bit LSB executable, x86-64, version 1 (SYSV),
statically linked, BuildID[sha1]=<...>, with debug_info, not stripped
```

As you can see, the `vmlinux` file is pretty huge. This is because it contains all the kernel symbols as well as extra debug information encoded into it. (FYI, the `vmlinux` and `System.map` files are used in the kernel debug context; keep them around.) The useful `file(1)` utility shows us more detail regarding this image file. The actual kernel image file that the bootloader loads up and boots into will always be in the generic location of `arch/<arch>/boot/`; hence, for the x86 architecture, we have the following:

```
$ ls -l arch/x86/boot/bzImage
-rw-rw-r-- 1 llkd llkd 8604032 Jan 17 12:27 arch/x86/boot/bzImage
$ file arch/x86/boot/bzImage
arch/x86/boot/bzImage: Linux kernel x86 boot executable bzImage,
version 5.4.0-llkd01 (llkd@llkd-vbox) #1 SMP Thu [...], RO-rootFS,
swap_dev 0x8, Normal VGA
```

Building the 5.x Linux Kernel from Source - Part 2

The compressed kernel image version 5.4.0-llkd01 for the x86_64 is a little over 8 MB in size. The file(1) utility again clearly reveals that indeed it is a Linux kernel boot image for the x86 architecture.

> The kernel documents several tweaks and switches that can be performed during the kernel build by setting various environment variables. This documentation can be found within the kernel source tree at Documentation/kbuild/kbuild.rst. We shall in fact use the INSTALL_MOD_PATH, ARCH, and CROSS_COMPILE environment variables in the material that follows.

Great! Our kernel image and modules are ready! Read on as we install the kernel modules as part of our next step.

Step 5 – installing the kernel modules

In the previous step, all the kernel config options that were marked as m have actually now been built. As you shall learn, that's not quite enough: they must now be installed into a known location on the system. This section covers these details.

Locating the kernel modules within the kernel source

To see the kernel modules just generated by the previous step – the kernel build – let's perform a quick find(1) command within the kernel source folder. Understand the naming convention used, where kernel module filenames end in .ko:

```
$ cd ${LLKD_KSRC}
$ find . -name "*.ko"
./arch/x86/events/intel/intel-rapl-perf.ko
./arch/x86/crypto/crc32-pclmul.ko
./arch/x86/crypto/ghash-clmulni-intel.ko
[...]
./net/ipv4/netfilter/ip_tables.ko
./net/sched/sch_fq_codel.ko
$ find . -name "*.ko" | wc -l
59
```

We can see from the preceding output that, in this particular build, a total of 59 kernel modules have happened to be built (the actual `find` output is truncated in the preceding block for brevity).

Now, recall the exercise I asked you to work on in Chapter 2, *Building the 5.x Linux Kernel from Source – Part 1*, in the *Sample usage of the make menuconfig UI* section. There, in *Table 2.4*, the last column specifies the type of change we made. Look for the `n -> m` (or `y -> m`) changes, implying we are configuring that particular feature to be built as a kernel module. There, we can see that this includes the following features:

- VirtualBox support, `n -> m`
- **Userspace I/O (UIO)** drivers, `n -> m`; and a UIO platform driver with generic IRQ handling, `n -> m`
- MS-DOS filesystem support, `n -> m`

As these features have been asked to be built as modules, they will not be encoded within the `vmlinux` or `bzImage` kernel image files. No, they will exist as standalone (well, kind of) *kernel modules*. Let's hunt for the kernel modules for the preceding features within the kernel source tree (showing their pathname and sizes with a bit of scripting foo):

```
$ find . -name "*.ko" -ls | egrep -i "vbox|msdos|uio" | awk '{printf "%-40s %9d\n", $11, $7}'
./fs/fat/msdos.ko                          361896
./drivers/virt/vboxguest/vboxguest.ko      948752
./drivers/gpu/drm/vboxvideo/vboxvideo.ko  3279528
./drivers/uio/uio.ko                       408136
./drivers/uio/uio_pdrv_genirq.ko           324568
$
```

Okay, great, the binary kernel modules have indeed been generated within the kernel source tree. But this alone is not enough. Why? They need to be *installed* into a well-known location within the root filesystem so that, at boot, the system *can actually find and load them* into kernel memory. This is why we need to *install* the kernel modules. The "well-known location within the root filesystem" is `/lib/modules/$(uname -r)/`, where `$(uname -r)` yields the kernel version number, of course.

Getting the kernel modules installed

Performing the kernel module installation is simple; (after the build step) just invoke the `modules_install` Makefile target. Let's do so:

```
$ cd ${LLKD_KSRC}
$ sudo make modules_install
[sudo] password for llkd:
  INSTALL arch/x86/crypto/aesni-intel.ko
  INSTALL arch/x86/crypto/crc32-pclmul.ko
  INSTALL arch/x86/crypto/crct10dif-pclmul.ko
[...]
  INSTALL sound/pci/snd-intel8x0.ko
  INSTALL sound/soundcore.ko
  DEPMOD 5.4.0-llkd01
$
```

Notice that we use `sudo(8)` to perform the installation *as root* (superuser). This is required as the default install location (under `/lib/modules/`) is only root-writeable. Once the kernel modules have been prepared and copied across (the work that shows up in the preceding output block as `INSTALL`), the kbuild system runs a utility called `depmod(8)`. Its job essentially is to resolve dependencies between kernel modules and encode them (if they exist) into some metafiles (refer to the man page on `depmod(8)` for more details: https://linux.die.net/man/8/depmod).

Now let's see the result of the module installation step:

```
$ uname -r
5.0.0-36-generic       # this is the 'distro' kernel (for Ubuntu
18.04.3 LTS) we're running on
$ ls /lib/modules/
5.0.0-23-generic 5.0.0-36-generic 5.4.0-llkd01
$
```

In the preceding code, we can see that for each (Linux) kernel we can boot the system into, there is a folder under `/lib/modules/`, whose name is the kernel release, as expected. Let's look within the folder of interest – our new kernel's (`5.4.0-llkd01`). There, under the `kernel/` sub-directory – within various directories – live the just-installed kernel modules:

```
$ ls /lib/modules/5.4.0-llkd01/kernel/
arch/   crypto/   drivers/   fs/   net/   sound/
```

> Incidentally, the `/lib/modules/<kernel-ver>/modules.builtin` file has the list of all installed kernel modules (under `/lib/modules/<kernel-ver>/kernel/`).

Let's search here for the kernel modules that we mentioned earlier:

```
$ find /lib/modules/5.4.0-llkd01/kernel/ -name "*.ko" | egrep
"vboxguest|msdos|uio"
/lib/modules/5.4.0-llkd01/kernel/fs/fat/msdos.ko
/lib/modules/5.4.0-llkd01/kernel/drivers/virt/vboxguest/vboxguest.ko
/lib/modules/5.4.0-llkd01/kernel/drivers/uio/uio.ko
/lib/modules/5.4.0-llkd01/kernel/drivers/uio/uio_pdrv_genirq.ko
$
```

They all show up. Excellent!

A final key point: during the kernel build, we can install the kernel modules into a location that *we* specify, overriding the (default) `/lib/modules/<kernel-ver>` location. This is done by setting the environment variable of `INSTALL_MOD_PATH` to the required location; for example, doing the following:

```
export STG_MYKMODS=../staging/rootfs/my_kernel_modules
make INSTALL_MOD_PATH=${STG_MYKMODS} modules_install
```

With this, we have all our kernel modules installed into the `${STG_MYKMODS}/` folder. Note how, perhaps, `sudo` is not required if `INSTALL_MOD_PATH` refers to a location that does not require *root* for writing.

> This technique – overriding the *kernel modules' install location* – can be especially useful when building a Linux kernel and kernel modules for an embedded target. Clearly, we must definitely *not* overwrite the host system's kernel modules with that of the embedded target's; that could be disastrous!

The next step is to generate the so-called `initramfs` (or `initrd`) image and set up the bootloader. We also need to clearly understand what exactly this `initramfs` image is and the motivation behind using it. The section after the following one delves into these details.

Step 6 – generating the initramfs image and bootloader setup

Firstly, please note that this discussion is highly biased toward the x86[_64] architecture. For the typical x86 desktop or server kernel build procedure, this step is internally divided into two distinct parts:

- Generating the `initramfs` (formerly called `initrd`) image
- (GRUB) bootloader setup for the new kernel image

The reason it's encapsulated into a single step in this recipe for the kernel build process here is that, on the x86 architecture, convenience scripts perform both tasks, giving the appearance of a single step.

> **TIP**: Wondering what exactly this `initramfs` (or `initrd`) image file is? Please see the following *Understanding the initramfs framework* section for details. We'll get there soon.

For now, let's just go ahead and generate the **initramfs** (short for **initial ram filesystem**) image file as well as update the bootloader. Performing this on x86[_64] Ubuntu is easily done in one simple step:

```
$ sudo make install
sh ./arch/x86/boot/install.sh 5.4.0-llkd01 arch/x86/boot/bzImage \
   System.map "/boot"
run-parts: executing /etc/kernel/postinst.d/apt-auto-removal 5.4.0-
llkd01 /boot/vmlinuz-5.4.0-llkd01
run-parts: executing /etc/kernel/postinst.d/initramfs-tools 5.4.0-
llkd01 /boot/vmlinuz-5.4.0-llkd01
update-initramfs: Generating /boot/initrd.img-5.4.0-llkd01
[...]
run-parts: executing /etc/kernel/postinst.d/zz-update-grub 5.4.0-
llkd01 /boot/vmlinuz-5.4.0-llkd01
Sourcing file `/etc/default/grub'
Generating grub configuration file ...
Found linux image: /boot/vmlinuz-5.4.0-llkd01
Found initrd image: /boot/initrd.img-5.4.0-llkd01
[...]
Found linux image: /boot/vmlinuz-5.0.0-36-generic
Found initrd image: /boot/initrd.img-5.0.0-36-generic
[...]
done
$
```

Notice that, again, we prefix the `make install` command with `sudo(8)`. Quite obviously, this is as we require *root* permission to write the concerned files and folders.

So that's it, we are done: a brand new 5.4 kernel, along with all requested kernel modules and the `initramfs` image, have been generated, and the (GRUB) bootloader has been updated. All that remains is to reboot the system, select the new kernel image on boot (from the bootloader menu screen), boot up, log in, and verify that all is okay.

Generating the initramfs image on Fedora 30 and above

Unfortunately, on Fedora 30 and above, generating the `initramfs` image does not appear to work as easily as with Ubuntu in the preceding section. Some folks suggest explicitly specifying the architecture via the `ARCH` environment variable. Take a look:

```
$ sudo make ARCH=x86_64 install
sh ./arch/x86/boot/install.sh 5.4.0-llkd01 arch/x86/boot/bzImage \
System.map "/boot"
Cannot find LILO.
$
```

It fails! Want to know why? I won't go into the details here, but this link should help you out: https://discussion.fedoraproject.org/t/installing-manually-builded-kernel-in-system-with-grub2/1895. To help set this situation right, here's what I did on my Fedora 31 VM (and, yes, it worked!):

1. Manually create the `initramfs` image:

    sudo mkinitrd /boot/initramfs-5.4.0-llkd01.img 5.4.0-llkd01

2. Ensure that the `grubby` package is installed:

    sudo dnf install grubby-deprecated-8.40-36.fc31.x86_64

    > 💡 Pressing the *Tab* key twice after typing `grubby-` results in the full package name being auto-completed.

3. (Re)run the `make install` command:

```
$ sudo make ARCH=x86_64 install
 sh ./arch/x86/boot/install.sh 5.4.0-llkd01
arch/x86/boot/bzImage \
 System.map "/boot"
 grubby fatal error: unable to find a suitable template
 grubby fatal error: unable to find a suitable template
 grubby: doing this would leave no kernel entries. Not writing
out new config.
 $
```

Though the `make install` command appears to fail, it has sufficiently succeeded. Let's peek at the content of the `/boot` directory to verify this:

```
$ ls -lht /boot
total 204M
-rw-------. 1 root root   44M Mar 26 13:08 initramfs-5.4.0-llkd01.img
lrwxrwxrwx. 1 root root   29 Mar 26 13:07 System.map ->
/boot/System.map-5.4.0-llkd01
lrwxrwxrwx. 1 root root   26 Mar 26 13:07 vmlinuz ->
/boot/vmlinuz-5.4.0-llkd01
-rw-r--r--. 1 root root 4.1M Mar 26 13:07 System.map-5.4.0-llkd01
-rw-r--r--. 1 root root 9.0M Mar 26 13:07 vmlinuz-5.4.0-llkd01
[...]
```

Indeed, the `initramfs` image, the `System.map` file, and `vmlinuz` (along with the required symbolic links) seem to be set up! Reboot, select the new kernel from the GRUB menu, and verify that it works.

In this step, we generated the `initramfs` image. The question is, what did the *kbuild* system perform under the hood when we did this? Read on to find out.

Generating the initramfs image – under the hood

Recall from the previous section what you will first see when the `sudo make install` command executes (reproduced as follows for your convenience):

```
$ sudo make install
sh ./arch/x86/boot/install.sh 5.4.0-llkd01 arch/x86/boot/bzImage \
 System.map "/boot"
```

Clearly, it's (`install.sh`) a script being executed. Internally, as part of its work, it copies the following files into the `/boot` folder, with the name format typically being `<filename>-$(uname -r)`:

```
System.map-5.4.0-llkd01, initrd.img-5.4.0-llkd01, vmlinuz-5.4.0-
llkd01, config-5.4.0-llkd01
```

The `initramfs` image is built as well. A shell script named `update-initramfs` performs this task (which is itself a convenience wrapper over another script called `mkinitramfs(8)` that performs the actual work). Once built, the `initramfs` image is also copied into the `/boot` directory, seen as `initrd.img-5.4.0-llkd01` in the preceding output snippet.

If at all a file being copied into `/boot` already exists, it is backed up as `<filename>-$(uname -r).old`. The file named `vmlinuz-<kernel-ver>` is a copy of the `arch/x86/boot/bzImage` file. In other words, it is the compressed kernel image – the image file that the bootloader will be configured to load into RAM, uncompress, and jump to its entry point, thus handing over control to the kernel!

> Why the names `vmlinux` (recall, this is the uncompressed kernel image file stored in the root of the kernel source tree) and `vmlinuz`? It's an old Unix convention that the Linux OS is quite happy to follow: on many Unix flavors, the kernel was called `vmunix`, so Linux calls it `vmlinux` and the compressed one `vmlinuz`; the z in `vmlinuz` is to hint at the (by default) `gzip(1)` compression.

As well, the GRUB bootloader configuration file located at `/boot/grub/grub.cfg` is updated to reflect the fact that a new kernel is now available for boot.

Again, it's worth emphasizing the fact that all this is *very architecture-specific*. The preceding discussion is with respect to building the kernel on an Ubuntu Linux x86[-64] system. While conceptually similar, the details of the kernel image filenames, their locations, and especially the bootloader, vary on different architectures.

You can skip ahead to the *Customizing the GRUB bootloader* section if you wish. If you are curious (I'm hoping so), read on. In the following section, we describe in some more detail the *hows* and *whys* of the `initramfs/inird` framework.

Understanding the initramfs framework

A bit of a mystery remains! What exactly *is* this `initramfs` or `initrd` image for? Why is it there?

Firstly, using this feature is a choice – the config directive is called `CONFIG_BLK_DEV_INITRD`. It's on and hence set to `y` by default. In brief, for systems that either do not know in advance certain things such as the boot disk host adapter or controller type (SCSI, RAID, and so on), the exact filesystem type that the root filesystem is formatted as (is it `ext2`, `ext3`, `ext4`, `btrfs`, `reiserfs`, `f2fs`, or another?), or for those systems where these functionalities are always built as kernel modules, we require the `initramfs` capability. Why exactly will become clear in a moment. Also, as mentioned earlier, `initrd` is now considered an older term. Nowadays, we more often use the term `initramfs` in its place.

Why the initramfs framework?

The `initramfs` framework is essentially a kind of middle-man between the early kernel boot and usermode. It allows us to run user space applications (or scripts) before the actual root filesystem has been mounted. This is useful in many circumstances, a couple of which are detailed in the following list. The key point is that `initramfs` allows us to run user mode apps that the kernel cannot normally run during boot time.

Practically speaking, among various uses, this framework allows us to do things including the following:

- Set up a console font.
- Customize keyboard layout settings.
- Print a custom welcome message on the console device.
- Accept a password (for encrypted disks).
- Load up kernel modules as required.
- Spawn a "rescue" shell if something fails.
- And many more!

Imagine for a moment that you are in the business of building and maintaining a new Linux distribution. Now, at installation time, the end user of your distribution might decide to format their SCSI disk with the `reiserfs` filesystem (FYI, it's the earliest general-purpose journaled filesystem in the kernel). The thing is, you cannot know in advance what choice exactly the end user will make – it could be one of any number of filesystems. So, you decide to pre-build and supply a large variety of kernel modules that will fulfill almost every possibility. Fine, when the installation is complete and the user's system boots up, the kernel will, in this scenario, require the `reiserfs.ko` kernel module in order to successfully mount the root filesystem and thus proceed with system boot-up.

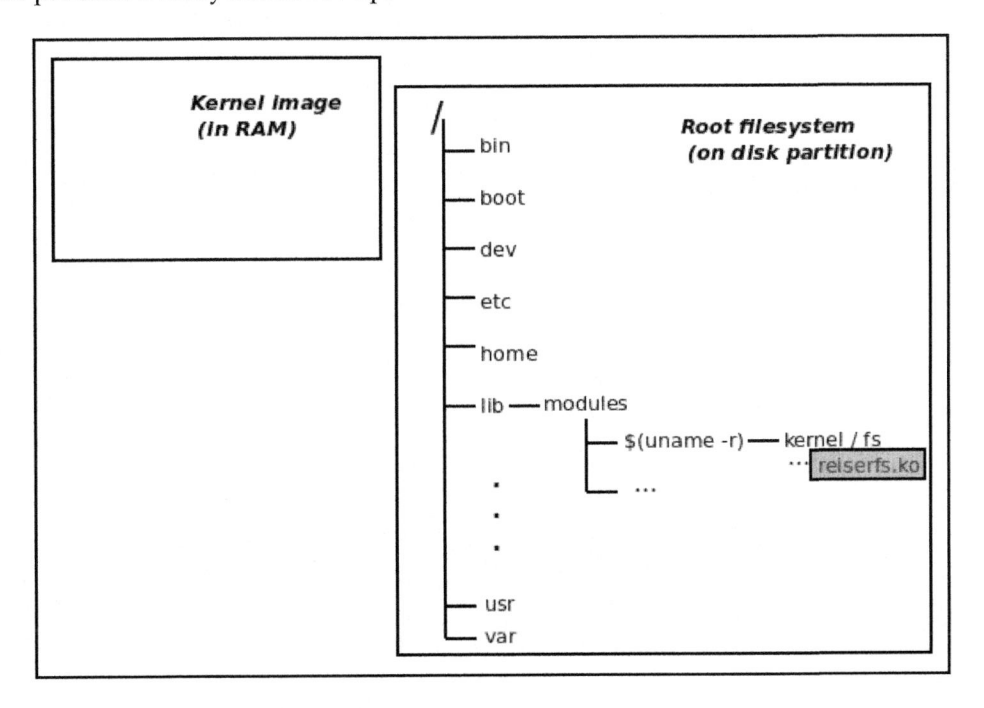

Figure 3.1 – The root filesystem's on the disk and yet to be mounted, kernel image is in RAM

But wait, think about this, we now have a classic *chicken-and-egg problem*: in order for the kernel to mount the root filesystem, it requires the `reiserfs.ko` kernel module file to be loaded into RAM (as it contains the necessary code to be able to work with the filesystem). *But,* that file is itself embedded inside the `reiserfs` root filesystem; to be precise, within the `/lib/modules/<kernel-ver>/kernel/fs/reiserfs/` directory! (see Figure 3.1). One of the primary purposes of the `initramfs` framework is to solve this chicken-and-egg problem.

Building the 5.x Linux Kernel from Source - Part 2

The `initramfs` image file is a compressed `cpio` archive (`cpio` is a flat file format used by `tar(1)`). As we saw in the previous section, the `update-initramfs` script internally invokes the `mkinitramfs` script (on Ubuntu at least, this is the case). These scripts build a minimal root filesystem containing the kernel modules as well as supporting infrastructure such as the `/etc` and `/lib` folders in a simple `cpio` file format, which is then usually gzip-compressed. This now forms the so-called `initramfs` (or `initrd`) image file and as we saw earlier, it will be placed in `/boot/initrd.img-<kernel-ver>`. Well, so how does that help?

At boot, if we are using the `initramfs` feature, the bootloader will, as part of its work, load the `initramfs` image file in RAM. Next, when the kernel itself runs on the system, it detects the presence of an `initramfs` image, uncompresses it, and using its content (via scripts), loads up the required kernel modules into RAM (Figure 3.2):

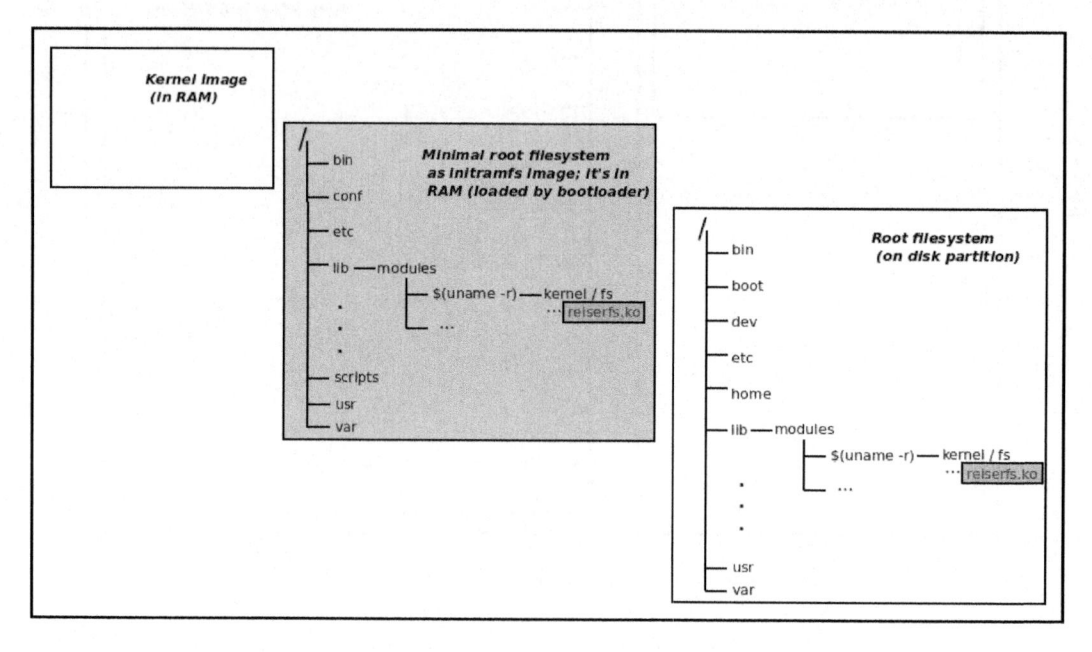

Figure 3.2 – The initramfs image serves as a middle-man between early kernel and actual root filesystem availability

Some more details on both the boot process (on x86) and the initramfs image can be found in the following sections.

[114]

Understanding the basics of the boot process on the x86

In the following list, we provide a brief overview of the typical boot process on an x86[_64] desktop (or laptop), workstation, or server:

1. Early boot, POST, BIOS initialization – the **BIOS** (short for **Basic Input Output System**; essentially, the *firmware* on the x86) loads up the first sector of the first bootable disk into RAM and jumps to its entry point. This forms what is often referred to as the *stage one* bootloader, whose main job is to load the *stage two (larger) bootloader* code into memory and jump to it.
2. Now the stage two bootloader code takes control. Its main job is to *load the actual (stage three) GRUB bootloader* into memory and jump to its entry point (GRUB is typically the bootloader employed on x86[-64] systems)
3. The (GRUB) bootloader will be passed both the compressed kernel image file (`/boot/vmlinuz-<kernel-ver>`) as well as the compressed `initramfs` image file (`/boot/initrd.img-<kernel-ver>`) as parameters. The bootloader will (simplistically) do the following:

    - Perform low-level hardware initialization.
    - Load these images into RAM, uncompressing the kernel image to a certain extent.
    - It will *jump to the kernel entry point*.

4. The Linux kernel, now having control of the machine, will initialize the hardware and software environment. It makes no assumptions regarding the earlier work performed by the bootloader.
5. Upon completing the majority of hardware and software initialization, it notices that the `initramfs` feature is turned on (`CONFIG_BLK_DEV_INITRD=y`). It will thus locate (and if required, uncompress) the `initramfs` (`initrd`) image in RAM (see Figure 3.2).
6. It will then *mount it* as a temporary root filesystem in RAM itself, within a `RAMdisk`.
7. We now have a base, minimal root filesystem set up in memory. Thus, the `initrd` startup scripts now run, performing, among other tasks, the loading of the required kernel modules into RAM (in effect, loading the root filesystem drivers, including, in our scenario, the `reiserfs.ko` kernel module; again, see Figure 3.2).

[115]

8. The kernel then performs a *pivot-root*, *un-mounting* the temporary `initrd` root filesystem, freeing its memory, and *mounting the real root filesystem*; it's now possible because the kernel module providing that filesystem support is indeed available.
9. Once the (actual) root filesystem is successfully mounted, system initialization can proceed. The kernel continues, ultimately invoking the first user space process, typically `/sbin/init` PID 1.
10. The *SysV init* framework now proceeds to initialize the system, bringing up system services as configured.

> A couple of things to note:
> (a) On modern Linux systems, the traditional (read: old) SysV *init* framework has largely been replaced with a modern optimized framework called **systemd**. Thus, on many (if not most) modern Linux systems, including embedded ones, the traditional `/sbin/init` has been replaced with `systemd` (or is a symbolic link to its executable file). Find out more about *systemd* in the *Further reading* section at the end of this chapter.
>
> (b) FYI, the generation of the root filesystem itself is not covered in this book; as one simple example, I suggest you look at the code of the SEALS project (at `https://github.com/kaiwan/seals`) that I mentioned in `Chapter 1`, *Kernel Workspace Setup*; it has script that generates a very minimal, or "skeleton", root filesystem from scratch.

Now that you understand the motivation behind `initrd/initramfs`, we'll complete this section by providing a bit of a deeper look into `initramfs` in the following section. Do read on!

More on the initramfs framework

Another place where the `initramfs` framework helps is in bringing up computers whose disks are *encrypted*. Quite early in the boot process, the kernel will have to query the user for the password, and if correct, proceed with mounting the disks, and so on. But, think about this: how can we run a C program executable that is, say, requesting a password without having a C runtime environment in place – a root filesystem containing libraries, the loader program, required kernel modules (for the crypto support perhaps), and so on?

Remember, the kernel *itself* hasn't yet completed initialization; how can user space apps run? Again, the `initramfs` framework solves this issue by indeed setting up a temporary user space runtime environment complete with the required root filesystem containing libraries, the loader, kernel modules, and so on, in memory.

Can we verify this? Yes we can! Let's take a peek into the `initramfs` image file. The `lsinitramfs(8)` script on Ubuntu serves exactly this purpose (on Fedora the equivalent is called `lsinitrd` instead):

```
$ lsinitramfs /boot/initrd.img-5.4.0-llkd01 | wc -l
334
$ lsinitramfs /boot/initrd.img-5.4.0-llkd01
.
kernel
kernel/x86
[...]
lib
lib/systemd
lib/systemd/network
lib/systemd/network/99-default.link
lib/systemd/systemd-udevd
[...]
lib/modules/5.4.0-
llkd01/kernel/drivers/net/ethernet/intel/e1000/e1000.ko
lib/modules/5.4.0-llkd01/modules.dep
[...]
lib/x86_64-linux-gnu/libc-2.27.so
[...]
lib/x86_64-linux-gnu/libaudit.so.1
lib/x86_64-linux-gnu/ld-2.27.so
lib/x86_64-linux-gnu/libpthread.so.0
[...]
etc/udev/udev.conf
etc/fstab
etc/modprobe.d
[...]
bin/dmesg
bin/date
bin/udevadm
bin/reboot
[...]
sbin/fsck.ext4
sbin/dmsetup
sbin/blkid
sbin/modprobe
[...]
scripts/local-premount/resume
```

Building the 5.x Linux Kernel from Source - Part 2

```
scripts/local-premount/ntfs_3g
$
```

There's quite a bit in there: we truncate the output to show a few select snippets. Clearly, we can see a *minimal* root filesystem with support for the required runtime libraries, kernel modules, /etc, /bin, and /sbin directories, along with their utilities.

> **TIP**
> The details of constructing the initramfs (or initrd) image goes beyond what we wish to cover here. I suggest you peek into these scripts to reveal their inner workings (on Ubuntu): /usr/sbin/update-initramfs, a wrapper script over the /usr/sbin/mkinitramfs shell script. Do see the *Further reading* section for more.

Also, modern systems feature what is sometimes referred to as hybrid initramfs: an initramfs image that consists of an early ramfs image prepended to the regular or main ramfs image. The reality is that we require special tools to unpack/pack (uncompress/compress) these images. Ubuntu provides the unmkinitramfs(8) and mkinitramfs(8) scripts, respectively, to perform these operations.

As a quick experiment, let's unpack our brand-new initramfs image (the one generated in the previous section) into a temporary directory. Again, this has been performed on our Ubuntu 18.04 LTS guest VM. View its output truncated for readability with tree(1):

```
$ TMPDIR=$(mktemp -d)
$ unmkinitramfs /boot/initrd.img-5.4.0-llkd01 ${TMPDIR}
$ tree ${TMPDIR} | less
/tmp/tmp.T53zY3gR91
├── early
│   └── kernel
│       └── x86
│           └── microcode
│               └── AuthenticAMD.bin
└── main
    ├── bin
    │   ├── [
    │   ├── [[
    │   ├── acpid
    │   ├── ash
    │   ├── awk
[...]
    ├── etc
    │   ├── console-setup
```

```
           |       |       ├── cached_UTF-8_del.kmap.gz
[...]
           ├── init
           ├── lib
[...]
           |       ├── modules
           |       |     └── 5.4.0-llkd01
           |       |          ├── kernel
           |       |          |    └── drivers
[...]
           ├── scripts
           |       ├── functions
           |       ├── init-bottom
[...]
           └── var
                 └── lib
                      └── dhcp
$
```

This concludes our (rather lengthy!) discussion on the `initramfs` framework and the basics of the boot process on the x86. The good news is that now, armed with this knowledge, you can further customize your product by tweaking the `initramfs` image as required – an important skill!

As an example (and as mentioned earlier), with *security* being a key factor on modern systems, being able to encrypt a disk at the block level is a powerful security feature; doing this very much involves tweaking the `initramfs` image. (Again, as this goes beyond the scope of this book, do refer to the *Further reading* section at the end of this chapter for useful links to articles on this and other aspects.)

Now let's complete the kernel build with some simple customization of the (x86) GRUB bootloader's boot script.

Step 7 – customizing the GRUB bootloader

We have now completed *steps 1 to 6* as outlined in Chapter 2, *Building the 5.x Linux Kernel from Source – Part 1*, in the *Steps to build the kernel from source* section). We can reboot the system; of course, do first close all your apps and files. By default, though, the modern **GRUB (GRand Unified Bootloader)** bootloader does not even show us any menu on reboot; it will by default boot into the newly built kernel (do remember that here, we're describing this process *only* for x86[_64] systems running Ubuntu).

> **TIP:** On x86[_64] you can always get to the GRUB menu during early system boot. Just ensure you keep the *Shift* key pressed down during boot.

What if we would like to see and customize the GRUB menu every time we boot the system, thus allowing us to possibly select an alternate kernel/OS to boot from? This is often very useful during development, so let's find out how we can do this.

Customizing GRUB – the basics

Customizing GRUB is quite easy to do. Do note the following:

- The following steps are to be carried out on the "target" system itself (not on the host); in our case, the Ubuntu 18.04 guest VM.
- This has been tested and verified on our Ubuntu 18.04 LTS guest system only.

Here's a quick series of steps for our customization:

1. Let's be safe and keep a backup copy of the GRUB bootloader config file:

   `sudo cp /etc/default/grub /etc/default/grub.orig`

   > **TIP:** The `/etc/default/grub` file is the user-configuration file in question. Before editing it, we make a backup to be safe. This is always a good idea.

2. Edit it. You can use `vi(1)` or your editor of choice:

   `sudo vi /etc/default/grub`

3. To always show the GRUB prompt at boot, insert this line:

   `GRUB_HIDDEN_TIMEOUT_QUIET=false`

   > **TIP:** On some Linux distros, you might instead have the `GRUB_TIMEOUT_STYLE=hidden` directive; simply change it to `GRUB_TIMEOUT_STYLE=menu` to achieve the same effect.

4. Set the timeout to boot the default OS (in seconds) as required; the default is `10` seconds; see the following example:

   ```
   GRUB_TIMEOUT=3
   ```

   Setting the preceding timeout value to the following values will produce the following outcomes:

   - `0`: Boot the system immediately without displaying the menu.
   - `-1`: Wait indefinitely.

   Furthermore, if a `GRUB_HIDDEN_TIMEOUT` directive is present, just comment it out:

   ```
   #GRUB_HIDDEN_TIMEOUT=1
   ```

5. Finally, run the `update-grub(8)` program as *root* to have your changes take effect:

   sudo update-grub

The preceding command will typically cause the `initramfs` image to be refreshed (regenerated). Once done, you're ready to reboot the system. Hang on a second though! The following section shows you how you can modify GRUB's configuration to boot by default into a kernel of your choice.

Selecting the default kernel to boot into

The GRUB default kernel is preset to be the number zero (via the `GRUB_DEFAULT=0` directive). This will ensure that the "first kernel" – the most recently added one – boots by default (upon timeout). This may not be what we want; as a real example, on our Ubuntu 18.04.3 LTS guest VM, we set it to the default Ubuntu *distro kernel* by, as earlier, editing the `/etc/default/grub` file (as root, of course) like so:

```
GRUB_DEFAULT="Advanced options for Ubuntu>Ubuntu, with Linux 5.0.0-36-generic"
```

> Of course, this implies that if your distro is updated or upgraded, you must again manually change the preceding line to reflect the new distro kernel that you wish to boot into by default, and then run `sudo update-grub`.

Right, our freshly edited GRUB configuration file is shown as follows:

```
$ cat /etc/default/grub
[...]
#GRUB_DEFAULT=0
GRUB_DEFAULT="Advanced options for Ubuntu>Ubuntu, with Linux 5.0.0-36-generic"
#GRUB_TIMEOUT_STYLE=hidden
GRUB_HIDDEN_TIMEOUT_QUIET=false
GRUB_TIMEOUT=3
GRUB_DISTRIBUTOR=`lsb_release -i -s 2> /dev/null || echo Debian`
GRUB_CMDLINE_LINUX_DEFAULT="quiet splash"
GRUB_CMDLINE_LINUX=""
[...]
```

As in the previous section, don't forget: if you make any changes here, run the `sudo update-grub` command to have your changes take effect.

> Additional points to note:
> a) In addition, you can add "pretty" tweaks, such as changing the background image (or color) via the `BACKGROUND_IMAGE="<img_file>"` directive.
> b) On Fedora, the GRUB bootloader config file is a bit different; run this command to show the GRUB menu at every boot: `sudo grub2-editenv - unset menu_auto_hide`
> The details can be found in the *Fedora wiki: Changes/HiddenGrubMenu*: `https://fedoraproject.org/wiki/Changes/HiddenGrubMenu`.
> c) Unfortunately, GRUB2 (the latest version is now 2) seems to be implemented differently on pretty much every Linux distro, leading to incompatibilities when trying to tune it in one given manner.

Now let's reboot the guest system, get into the GRUB menu, and boot our new kernel.

All done! Let's (finally!) reboot the system:

```
$ sudo reboot
[sudo] password for llkd:
```

Once the system completes its shutdown procedure and reboots, you should soon see the GRUB bootloader menu (the following section shows several screenshots too). Be sure to interrupt it by pressing any keyboard key!

> Though always possible, I recommend you don't delete the original distro kernel image(s) (and associated `initrd`, `System.map` files, and so on). What if your brand-new kernel fails to boot? (*If it can happen to the Titanic...*) By keeping our original images, we thus have a fallback option: boot from the original distro kernel, fix our issue(s), and retry.
>
> As a worst-case scenario, what if all other kernels/`initrd` images have been deleted and your single new kernel fails to boot successfully? Well, you can always boot into a *recovery mode* Linux via a USB pen drive; a bit of googling regarding this will yield many links and video tutorials.

Booting our VM via the GNU GRUB bootloader

Now our guest VM (using the *Oracle VirtualBox hypervisor*) is about to come up; once its (emulated) BIOS routines are done, the GNU GRUB bootloader screen shows up first. This happens because we quite intentionally changed the `GRUB_HIDDEN_TIMEOUT_QUIET` GRUB configuration directive to the value of `false`. See the following screenshot (Figure 3.3). The particular styling seen in the screenshot is how it's customized to appear by the Ubuntu distro:

```
                      GNU GRUB  version 2.02

 ┌────────────────────────────────────────────────────────────────────┐
 │ Ubuntu                                                             │
 │*Advanced options for Ubuntu                                        │
 │ Memory test (memtest86+)                                           │
 │ Memory test (memtest86+, serial console 115200)                    │
 │                                                                    │
 │                                                                    │
 │                                                                    │
 │                                                                    │
 │                                                                    │
 │                                                                    │
 │                                                                    │
 │                                                                    │
 └────────────────────────────────────────────────────────────────────┘

       Use the ↑ and ↓ keys to select which entry is highlighted.
       Press enter to boot the selected OS, `e' to edit the commands
       before booting or `c' for a command-line.
```

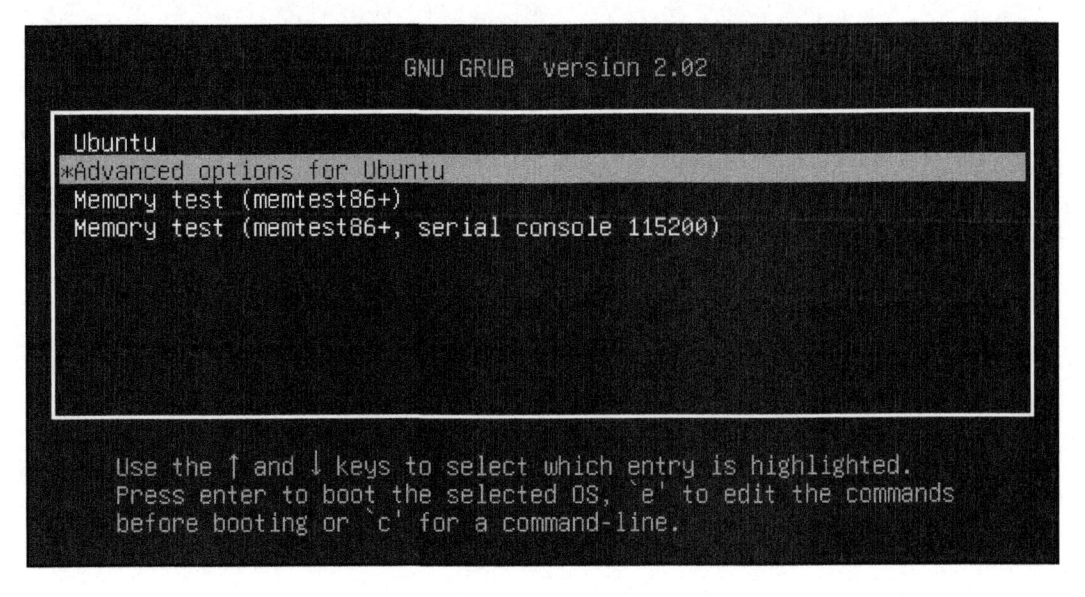

Figure 3.3 – The GRUB2 bootloader – paused on system startup

Building the 5.x Linux Kernel from Source - Part 2

Now let's go straight into booting our VM:

1. Press any keyboard key (besides *Enter*) to ensure the default kernel is not booted once the timeout (recall, we set it to 3 seconds) expires.
2. If not already there, scroll to the `Advanced options for Ubuntu` menu, highlighting it, and press *Enter*.
3. Now you'll see a menu similar, but likely not identical, to the following screenshot (Figure 3.4). For each kernel that GRUB has detected and can boot into, there are two lines shown – one for the kernel itself and one for the special **recovery mode** boot option into the same kernel:

```
                    GNU GRUB  version 2.02

 Ubuntu, with Linux 5.4.0-llkd01
 Ubuntu, with Linux 5.4.0-llkd01 (recovery mode)
 Ubuntu, with Linux 5.3.0-26-generic
 Ubuntu, with Linux 5.3.0-26-generic (recovery mode)
 Ubuntu, with Linux 5.0.0-37-generic
 Ubuntu, with Linux 5.0.0-37-generic (recovery mode)
*Ubuntu, with Linux 5.0.0-36-generic
 Ubuntu, with Linux 5.0.0-36-generic (recovery mode)


    Use the ↑ and ↓ keys to select which entry is highlighted.
    Press enter to boot the selected OS, `e' to edit the commands
    before booting or `c' for a command-line. ESC to return previous
    menu.
```

Figure 3.4 – The GRUB2 bootloader showing available kernels to boot from

Notice how the kernel that will boot by default – in our case, the `5.0.0-36-generic` kernel – is highlighted by default with an asterisk (*).

> The preceding screenshot shows a few "extra" line items. This is because, at the time of taking this screenshot, I had updated the VM and hence a few newer kernels were installed as well. We can spot the `5.0.0-37-generic` and `5.3.0-26-generic` kernels. No matter; we ignore them here.

[124]

Chapter 3

4. Whatever the case, simply scroll to the entry of interest, that is, the `5.4.0-llkd01` kernel entry. Here, it's the very first line of the GRUB menu (as it's the most recent addition to the GRUB menu of bootable OSes): `Ubuntu, with Linux 5.4.0-llkd01`.
5. Once you have highlighted the preceding menu item, press *Enter* and voilà! The bootloader will proceed to do its job, uncompressing and loading the kernel image and `initrd` image into RAM, and jumping to the Linux kernel's entry point, thus handing over control to Linux!

Right, if all goes well, as it should, you will have booted into your brand-new freshly built 5.4.0 Linux kernel! Congratulations on a task well done. Then again, you could always do more – the following section shows you how you can further edit and customize GRUB's config at runtime (boot time). Again, this skill comes in handy every now and then – for example, *forgot the root password?* Yes indeed, you can actually *bypass it* using this technique! Read on to find out how.

Experimenting with the GRUB prompt

You could experiment further; instead of merely pressing *Enter* while on the `Ubuntu, with Linux 5.4.0-llkd01` kernel's menu entry, ensure that this line is highlighted and press the e key (for edit). We shall now enter GRUB's *edit screen*, wherein we are free to change any value we like. Here's a screenshot after pressing the *e* key:

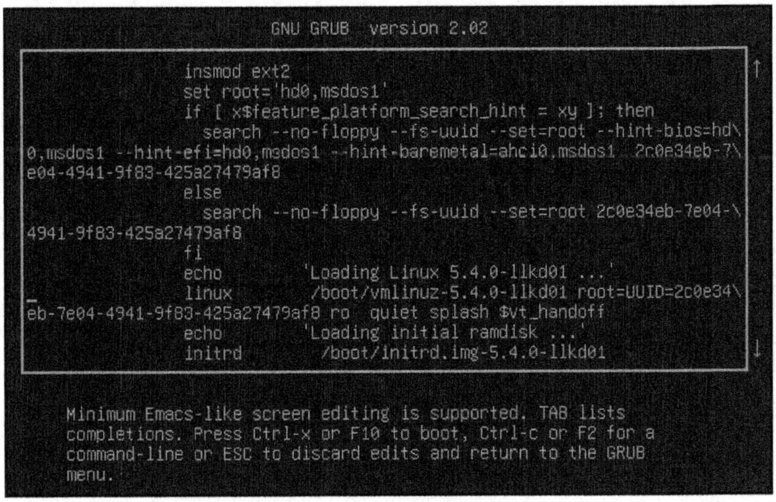

Figure 3.5 – The GRUB2 bootloader – detail on the custom 5.4.0-llkd01 kernel

[125]

Building the 5.x Linux Kernel from Source - Part 2

The screenshot has been taken after scrolling down a few lines; look carefully, you can spot the cursor (an underscore-like one, "_") at the very beginning of the third line from the bottom of the edit box. This is the crucial line; it starts with the suitably indented keyword `linux`. It specifies the list of *kernel parameters* being passed via the GRUB bootloader to the Linux kernel.

Try experimenting a bit here. As a simple example, delete the words `quiet` and `splash` from this entry, then press *Ctrl + X* or *F10* to boot. This time, the pretty Ubuntu splash screen does not appear; you are directly in the console seeing all kernel messages as they flash past.

A common question: what if we forget our password and thus cannot log in? Well, there are several approaches to tackle this. One is via the bootloader: boot into the GRUB menu as we have done, go to the relevant menu entry, press *e* to edit it, scroll down to the line beginning with the word `linux`, and append the word `single` (or just the number 1) at the end of this entry, such that it looks like this:

```
            linux       /boot/vmlinuz-5.0.0-36-generic \
root=UUID=<...> ro quiet splash single
```

Now, when you boot, the kernel boots into single-user mode and gives you, the eternally grateful user, *a shell with root access*. Just run the `passwd <username>` command to change your password.

> **TIP**: The precise procedure to boot into single-user mode varies with the distro. Exactly what to edit in the GRUB2 menu is a bit different on Red Hat/Fedora/CentOS. See the *Further reading* section for a link on how to set it for these systems.

This teaches us something regarding *security*, doesn't it? A system is considered insecure when access to the bootloader menu (and even to the BIOS) is possible without a password! In fact, in highly secured environments, even physical access to the console device must be restricted.

Now you have learned how to customize the GRUB bootloader, and, I expect, have booted into your fresh 5.4 Linux kernel! Let's not just assume things; let's verify that the kernel is indeed configured as per our plan.

Verifying our new kernel's configuration

Okay, so back to our discussion: we have now booted into our newly built kernel. But hang on, let's not blindly assume things, let's actually verify that all has gone according to plan. The *empirical approach* is always best:

```
$ uname -r
5.4.0-llkd01
```

Indeed, we are now running Ubuntu 18.04.3 LTS on our just-built **5.4.0** Linux kernel!

Recall our table of kernel configs to edit from Chapter 2, *Building the 5.x Linux Kernel from Source – Part 1*, in *Table 2.4*. We should check row by row that each configuration we have changed has actually taken effect. Let's list some of them, starting with the concerned CONFIG_'FOO' name, as follows:

- CONFIG_LOCALVERSION: The preceding output of uname -r clearly shows the localversion (or -EXTRAVERSION) part of the kernel version has been set to what we wanted: the -llkd01 string.
- CONFIG_IKCONFIG: Allows us to see the current kernel configuration details. Let's check. Recall that you are to set the LLKD_KSRC environment variable to the root location of your 5.4 kernel source tree directory:

    ```
    $ ${LLKD_KSRC}/scripts/extract-ikconfig /boot/vmlinuz-5.4.0-llkd01
    #
    # Automatically generated file; DO NOT EDIT.
    # Linux/x86 5.4.0 Kernel Configuration
    [...]
    CONFIG_IRQ_WORK=y
    [...]
    ```

It works! We can see the entire kernel configuration via the `scripts/extract-ikconfig` script. We shall use this very script to `grep(1)` the remainder of the config directives that we changed in the aforementioned *Table 2.4*:

```
$ scripts/extract-ikconfig /boot/vmlinuz-5.4.0-llkd01 | egrep
"IKCONFIG|HAMRADIO|PROFILING|VBOXGUEST|UIO|MSDOS_FS|SECURITY|DEBUG_STA
CK_USAGE"
CONFIG_IKCONFIG=y
CONFIG_IKCONFIG_PROC=y
# CONFIG_PROFILING is not set
# CONFIG_HAMRADIO is not set
CONFIG_UIO=m
# CONFIG_UIO_CIF is not set
CONFIG_UIO_PDRV_GENIRQ=m
# CONFIG_UIO_DMEM_GENIRQ is not set
[...]
CONFIG_VBOXGUEST=m
CONFIG_EXT4_FS_SECURITY=y
CONFIG_MSDOS_FS=m
# CONFIG_SECURITY_DMESG_RESTRICT is not set
# CONFIG_SECURITY is not set
CONFIG_SECURITYFS=y
CONFIG_DEFAULT_SECURITY_DAC=y
CONFIG_DEBUG_STACK_USAGE=y
$
```

Carefully looking through the preceding output, we can see that we got precisely what we wanted. Our new kernel's configuration settings match precisely the settings expected in Chapter 2, *Building the 5.x Linux Kernel from Source – Part 1*, *Table 2.4*; perfect.

Alternatively, as we have enabled the `CONFIG_IKCONFIG_PROC` option, we could have achieved the same verification by looking up the kernel config via the (compressed) `proc` filesystem entry, `/proc/config.gz`, like this:

```
gunzip -c /proc/config.gz | egrep \
"IKCONFIG|HAMRADIO|PROFILING|VBOXGUEST|UIO|MSDOS_FS|SECURITY|DEBUG_STA
CK_USAGE"
```

So, the kernel build is done! Fantastic. I urge you to refer back to Chapter 2, *Building the 5.x Linux Kernel from Source – Part 1*, in the *Steps to build the kernel from source* section, to again see the high-level overview of steps for the entire process. We round off this chapter with an interesting *cross-compile* of the Raspberry Pi device kernel and a few remaining tips.

Kernel build for the Raspberry Pi

A popular and relatively inexpensive **Single-Board Computer** (**SBC**) to experiment and prototype with is the ARM-based Raspberry Pi. Hobbyists and tinkerers find it very useful to try out and learn how to work with embedded Linux, especially as it has a strong community backing (with many Q&A forums) and good support:

Figure 3.6 – A Raspberry Pi 3 Model B+ device (note that the USB-to-serial cable seen in the photo does not come with it)

There are two ways in which you can build a kernel for the target device:

- Build the kernel on a powerful host system, typically an Intel/AMD x86_64 (or Mac) desktop or laptop running a Linux distro.
- Perform the build on the target device itself.

We shall follow the first method – it's a lot faster and is considered the right way to perform embedded Linux development.

We shall assume (as usual) that we are running on our Ubuntu 18.04 LTS guest VM. So, think about it; now, the host system is actually the guest Linux VM! Also, we're targeting building the kernel for ARM 32-bit architecture, not 64-bit.

> **TIP:** Performing large downloads and kernel build operations on a guest VM isn't really ideal. Depending on the power and RAM of the host and guest, it will take a while. It could end up being twice as slow as building on a native Linux box. Nevertheless, assuming you have set aside sufficient disk space in the guest (and of course the host actually has this space available), this procedure works.

We will have to use an *x86_64-to-ARM (32-bit) cross-compiler* to build the kernel, or any component for that matter, for the Raspberry Pi target. This implies installing an appropriate **cross-toolchain** as well to perform the build.

In the following few sections, we divide the work up into three discrete steps:

1. Getting ourselves a kernel source tree appropriate for the device
2. Learning how to install an appropriate cross toolchain
3. Configuring and building the kernel

So let's begin!

Step 1 – cloning the kernel source tree

We arbitrarily select a *staging folder* (the place where the build happens) for the kernel source tree and the cross-toolchain, and assign it to an environment variable (so as to avoid hard-coding it):

1. Set up your workspace. We set an environment variable as `RPI_STG` (it's not required to use exactly this name for the environment variable; just pick a reasonable-sounding name and stick to it) to the staging folder's location – the place where we shall perform the work. Feel free to use a value appropriate to your system:

   ```
   export RPI_STG=~/rpi_work
   mkdir -p ${RPI_STG}/kernel_rpi ${RPI_STG}/rpi_tools
   ```

Chapter 3

> **TIP**: Do ensure you have sufficient disk space available: the kernel source tree takes approximately 900 MB, and the toolchain around 1.5 GB. You'll require at least another gigabyte for working space.

2. Download the Raspberry Pi kernel source tree (we clone it from the official source, the Raspberry Pi GitHub repository for the kernel tree, here: https://github.com/raspberrypi/linux/):

```
cd ${RPI_STG}/kernel_rpi
git clone --depth=1 --branch rpi-5.4.y
https://github.com/raspberrypi/linux.git
```

The kernel source tree gets cloned under a directory called linux/ (that is, under ${RPI_WORK}/kernel_rpi/linux). Notice how, in the preceding code, we have the following:

- The particular Raspberry Pi kernel tree branch we have selected is *not* the very latest one (at the time of writing, the very latest is the 5.11 series), it's the 5.4 kernel; that's perfectly okay (it's an LTS kernel and matches our x86 one as well!).
- We pass the --depth parameter set to 1 to git clone to reduce the download and uncompress loads.

Now the Raspberry Pi kernel source is installed. Let's briefly verify this:

```
$ cd ${RPI_STG}/kernel_rpi/linux ; head -n5 Makefile
# SPDX-License-Identifier: GPL-2.0
VERSION = 5
PATCHLEVEL = 4
SUBLEVEL = 51
EXTRAVERSION =
```

Okay, it's the 5.4.51 Raspberry Pi kernel port (the kernel version we use on the x86_64 is the 5.4.0 one; the slight variation is fine).

Step 2 – installing a cross-toolchain

Now it's time to install a *cross-toolchain* on your host system that's appropriate for performing the actual build. The thing is, there are several working toolchains available... Here, I shall show two ways of obtaining and installing a toolchain. The first is the simplest and typically sufficient, while the second way installs a more elaborate version.

First method – package install via apt

This is really simple and works well; do use this method routinely:

```
sudo apt install crossbuild-essential-armhf
```

The tools are typically installed under `/usr/bin/` and are therefore already part of your `PATH`; you can simply use them. For example, check out the ARM-32 `gcc` compiler's location and version as follows:

```
$ which arm-linux-gnueabihf-gcc
/usr/bin/arm-linux-gnueabihf-gcc
$ arm-linux-gnueabihf-gcc --version |head -n1
arm-linux-gnueabihf-gcc (Ubuntu 9.3.0-17ubuntu1~20.04) 9.3.0
```

Also, do keep in mind: this toolchain is appropriate for building the kernel for ARM 32-bit architecture, not for 64-bit. If that's your intention (building for 64-bit, which we don't cover here), you will need to install a x86_64-to-ARM64 toolchain with `sudo apt install crossbuild-essential-arm64`.

Second method – installation via the source repo

This is a more elaborate method. Here, we clone the toolchain from the Raspberry Pi's GitHub repo:

1. Download the toolchain. Let's place it under the folder called `rpi_tools` within our Raspberry Pi staging directory:

   ```
   cd ${RPI_STG}/rpi_tools
   git clone https://github.com/raspberrypi/tools
   ```

2. Update the `PATH` environment variable so that it contains the toolchain binaries:

   ```
   export PATH=${PATH}:${RPI_STG}/rpi_tools/tools/arm-bcm2708/arm-linux-gnueabihf/bin/
   ```

   > **TIP:** Setting the `PATH` environment variable (as shown in the preceding code) is required. However, it's only valid for the current shell session. Make it permanent by putting the preceding line into a startup script (typically your `${HOME}/.bashrc` file or equivalent).

As mentioned earlier, alternate toolchains can be used as well. For example, several toolchains for ARM development (for A-profile processors) are available on the ARM developer site at https://developer.arm.com/tools-and-software/open-source-software/developer-tools/gnu-toolchain/gnu-a/downloads.

Step 3 – configuring and building the kernel

Let's configure the kernel (for the Raspberry Pi 2, Pi 3, and Pi 3[B]+). Before we begin, it's *very important* to keep the following in mind:

- The ARCH environment variable is to be set to the CPU (architecture) for which the software is to be cross-compiled (that is, the compiled code will run on that CPU). The value to set ARCH to is the name of the directory under the arch/ directory in the kernel source tree. For example, set ARCH to arm for ARM32, to arm64 for the ARM64, to powerpc for the PowerPC, and to openrisc for the OpenRISC processor.

- The CROSS_COMPILE environment variable is to be set to the cross compiler (toolchain) prefix. Essentially, it's the first few common letters that precede every utility in the toolchain. In our following example, all the toolchain utilities (the C compiler gcc, linker, C++, objdump, and so on) begin with arm-linux-gnueabihf-, so that's what we set CROSS_COMPILE to. The Makefile will always invoke the utilities as ${CROSS_COMPILE}<utility>, hence invoking the correct toolchain executable. This does imply that the toolchain directory should be within the PATH variable (as we mentioned in the preceding section).

Okay, let's build the kernel:

```
cd ${RPI_STG}/kernel_rpi/linux
make mrproper
KERNEL=kernel7
make ARCH=arm CROSS_COMPILE=arm-linux-gnueabihf- bcm2709_defconfig
```

[133]

A quick explanation regarding the configuration target, `bcm2709_defconfig`: this key point was mentioned in Chapter 2, *Building the 5.x Linux Kernel from Source – Part 1*. We must ensure that we use an appropriate board-specific kernel config file as a starting point. Here, this is the correct kernel config file for the Broadcom SoC on the Raspberry Pi 2, Pi 3, Pi 3+ and Compute Module 3 devices. The `bcm2709_defconfig` config target specified results in parsing in the content of the `arch/arm/configs/bcm2709_defconfig` file. (The Raspberry Pi website documents this as `bcm2709_defconfig` for Raspberry Pi 2, Pi 3, Pi 3+, and Compute Module 3 default build configuration. Important: if you are building the kernel for another type of Raspberry Pi device, please see https://www.raspberrypi.org/documentation/linux/kernel/building.md.)

FYI, the `kernel7` value is as such because the processor is ARMv7-based (actually, from the Raspberry Pi 3 onward, the SoC is a 64-bit ARMv8, which is compatible with running in 32-bit ARMv7 mode; here, as we're building a 32-bit kernel for ARM32 (AArch32), we specify `KERNEL=kernel7`).

> **TIP**: The variety of SoCs, their packaging, and their resulting naming creates a good deal of confusion; this link might help: https://raspberrypi.stackexchange.com/questions/840/why-is-the-cpu-sometimes-referred-to-as-bcm2708-sometimes-bcm2835.

If any further customization of the kernel config is required, you could always do so with the following:

```
make ARCH=arm menuconfig
```

If not, just skip this step and proceed. Build (cross-compile) the kernel, the kernel modules, and the DTBs with the following:

```
make -j4 ARCH=arm CROSS_COMPILE=arm-linux-gnueabihf- zImage modules dtbs
```

(Adjust the `-jn` appropriately for your build host). Once the build is successfully completed, we can see the following files have been generated:

```
$ ls -lh vmlinux System.map arch/arm/boot/zImage
-rwxrwxr-x 1 llkd llkd  5.3M Jul 23 12:58 arch/arm/boot/zImage
-rw-rw-r-- 1 llkd llkd  2.5M Jul 23 12:58 System.map
-rwxrwxr-x 1 llkd llkd   16M Jul 23 12:58 vmlinux
$
```

Here, our purpose is just to show how a Linux kernel can be configured and built for an architecture other than the host system it's compiled upon, or in other words, cross-compiled. The gory details of placing the kernel image (and DTB file) on the microSD card and so on are not delved into. I refer you to the complete documentation for the Raspberry Pi kernel build, which can be found here: https://www.raspberrypi.org/documentation/linux/kernel/building.md.

Nevertheless, here's a quick tip to try out your new kernel on the Raspberry Pi 3[B+]:

1. Mount the microSD card. It will typically have a Raspbian distro on it and two partitions, `boot` and `rootfs`, corresponding to the `mmcblk0p1` and `mmcblk0p2` partitions respectively.

2. **The bootloader and associated binaries**: It's key to get the low-level startup binaries, which includes the bootloader itself, onto the SD card's boot partition; this includes the `bootcode.bin` (the actual bootloader), `fixup*.dat`, and `start*.elf` binaries; the content of the `/boot` folder is explained here: https://www.raspberrypi.org/documentation/configuration/boot_folder.md. (If you're unsure of how to get these binaries, it's perhaps easiest to simply install a stock version of Raspberry Pi OS onto an SD card; these binaries will get installed within its boot partition. The stock Raspberry Pi OS images can be obtained from https://www.raspberrypi.org/downloads/; also, FYI, the newer Raspberry Pi Imager app (for Windows, macOS, Linux) makes it really easy to perform the first-time installation).

3. If it exists, back up and then replace the `kernel7.img` file within the `/boot` partition on the microSD card with the `zImage` file that we just built, naming it `kernel7.img`.

4. Install the just-built kernel modules; ensure you specify the location as the microSD card's root filesystem with the `INSTALL_MOD_PATH` environment variable! (Failing to do so means it might overwrite your host's modules, which would be disastrous!) Here, we imagine that the microSD card's second partition (which contains the root filesystem) is mounted under `/media/${USER}/rootfs`; then, do the following (all in one line):

   ```
   sudo env PATH=$PATH make ARCH=arm CROSS_COMPILE=arm-linux-gnueabihf-  INSTALL_MOD_PATH=/media/${USER}/rootfs modules_install
   ```

5. Install the DTBs (and overlays) that we just generated on the SD card as well:

   ```
   sudo cp arch/arm/boot/dts/*.dtb /media/${USER}/boot
   sudo cp arch/arm/boot/dts/overlays/*.dtb*
   arch/arm/boot/dts/overlays/README /media/${USER}/boot/overlays
   sync
   ```

6. Unmount the SD card, re-insert it into the device, and try it out.

> **TIP**
> Again, to ensure it works, please refer to the official documentation (available at `https://www.raspberrypi.org/documentation/linux/kernel/building.md`). We have not covered the details regarding the generation and copying of kernel modules and DTBs to the microSD card.
>
> Also, FYI, we again discuss kernel configuration and build for the Raspberry Pi in `Chapter 11`, *The CPU Scheduler – Part 2*.

This completes our brief coverage on experimenting with a kernel cross-compilation for the Raspberry Pi. We'll end this chapter with a few miscellaneous but nevertheless useful tips.

Miscellaneous tips on the kernel build

We complete this chapter on building the Linux kernel from source with a few tips. Each of the following subsections encapsulates a tip for you to take note of.

Often a point of confusion for folks new to this: once we configure, build, and boot from a new Linux kernel, we notice that the root filesystem and any other mounted filesystems remain identical to what was on the original (distro or custom) system. Only the kernel itself has changed. This is entirely intentional, due to the Unix paradigm of having *a loose coupling* between the kernel and the root filesystem. Since it's the root filesystem that holds all the applications, system tools, and utilities, including libraries, in effect, we can have several kernels, to suit different product flavors perhaps, for the same base system.

Minimum version requirements

To successfully build the kernel, you have to ensure that your build system has the documented *bare minimum* versions of the various software pieces of the toolchain (and other miscellaneous tools and utilities). This very information is clearly within the kernel documentation in the *Minimal requirements to compile the kernel* section, available at https://github.com/torvalds/linux/blob/master/Documentation/process/changes.rst#minimal-requirements-to-compile-the-kernel.

For example, as of the time of writing, the recommended minimum version of gcc is 4.9 and that of make is 3.81.

Building a kernel for another site

In our kernel build walk-through in this book, we built a Linux kernel on a certain system (here, it was an x86_64 guest) and booted the newly built kernel off the very same system. What if this isn't the case, as will often happen when you are building a kernel for another site or customer premises? While it's always possible to manually put the pieces in place on the remote system, there's a far easier and more correct way to do it – build the kernel and associated meta-work bundled along with it (the initrd image, the kernel modules collection, the kernel headers, and so on) into a well-known **package format** (Debian's deb, Red Hat's rpm, and so on)! A quick help command on the kernel's top-level Makefile reveals these package targets:

```
$ make help
[ ... ]
Kernel packaging:
  rpm-pkg         - Build both source and binary RPM kernel packages
  binrpm-pkg      - Build only the binary kernel RPM package
  deb-pkg         - Build both source and binary deb kernel packages
  bindeb-pkg      - Build only the binary kernel deb package
  snap-pkg        - Build only the binary kernel snap package (will connect to external hosts)
  tar-pkg         - Build the kernel as an uncompressed tarball
  targz-pkg       - Build the kernel as a gzip compressed tarball
  tarbz2-pkg      - Build the kernel as a bzip2 compressed tarball
  tarxz-pkg       - Build the kernel as a xz compressed tarball
[ ... ]
```

So, for example, to build the kernel and its associated files as Debian packages, simply do the following:

```
$ make -j8 bindeb-pkg
scripts/kconfig/conf --syncconfig Kconfig
sh ./scripts/package/mkdebian
dpkg-buildpackage -r"fakeroot -u" -a$(cat debian/arch) -b -nc -uc
dpkg-buildpackage: info: source package linux-5.4.0-min1
dpkg-buildpackage: info: source version 5.4.0-min1-1
dpkg-buildpackage: info: source distribution bionic
[ ... ]
```

The actual packages are written into the directory immediately above the kernel source directory. For example, from the command we just ran, here are the `deb` packages that were generated:

```
$ ls -l ../*.deb
-rw-r--r-- 1 kaiwan kaiwan 11106860 Feb 19 17:05 ../linux-headers-5.4.0-min1_5.4.0-min1-1_amd64.deb
-rw-r--r-- 1 kaiwan kaiwan 8206880 Feb 19 17:05 ../linux-image-5.4.0-min1_5.4.0-min1-1_amd64.deb
-rw-r--r-- 1 kaiwan kaiwan 1066996 Feb 19 17:05 ../linux-libc-dev_5.4.0-min1-1_amd64.deb
```

This is indeed very convenient! Now, you can literally install the packages on any other matching (in terms of CPU and Linux flavor) system with a simple `dpkg -i <package-name>` command.

Watching the kernel build run

To see details (the `gcc(1)` compiler flags, and so on) while the kernel build runs, pass the `V=1` verbose option switch to `make(1)`. The following is a bit of sample output when building the Raspberry Pi 3 kernel with the verbose switch set to *on*:

```
$ make V=1 ARCH=arm CROSS_COMPILE=arm-linux-gnueabihf- zImage modules dtbs
[...]
make -f ./scripts/Makefile.build obj=kernel/sched
arm-linux-gnueabihf-gcc -Wp,-MD,kernel/sched/.core.o.d
 -nostdinc
 -isystem <...>/gcc-linaro-7.3.1-2018.05-x86_64_arm-linux-gnueabihf/bin/../lib/gcc/arm-linux-gnueabihf/7.3.1/include
 -I./arch/arm/include -I./arch/arm/include/generated/uapi
 -I./arch/arm/include/generated -I./include
 -I./arch/arm/include/uapi -I./include/uapi
```

```
-I./include/generated/uapi -include ./include/linux/kconfig.h
-D__KERNEL__ -mlittle-endian -Wall -Wundef -Wstrict-prototypes
-Wno-trigraphs -fno-strict-aliasing -fno-common
-Werror-implicit-function-declaration -Wno-format-security
-std=gnu89 -fno-PIE -fno-dwarf2-cfi-asm -fno-omit-frame-pointer
-mapcs -mno-sched-prolog -fno-ipa-sra -mabi=aapcs-linux
-mno-thumb-interwork -mfpu=vfp -funwind-tables -marm
-D__LINUX_ARM_ARCH__=7 -march=armv7-a -msoft-float -Uarm
-fno-delete-null-pointer-checks -Wno-frame-address
-Wno-format-truncation -Wno-format-overflow
-Wno-int-in-bool-context -O2 --param=allow-store-data-races=0
-DCC_HAVE_ASM_GOTO -Wframe-larger-than=1024 -fno-stack-protector
-Wno-unused-but-set-variable -Wno-unused-const-variable
-fno-omit-frame-pointer -fno-optimize-sibling-calls
-fno-var-tracking-assignments -pg -Wdeclaration-after-statement
-Wno-pointer-sign -fno-strict-overflow -fno-stack-check
-fconserve-stack -Werror=implicit-int -Werror=strict-prototypes
-Werror=date-time -Werror=incompatible-pointer-types
-fno-omit-frame-pointer -DKBUILD_BASENAME='"core"'
-DKBUILD_MODNAME='"core"' -c -o kernel/sched/.tmp_core.o
kernel/sched/core.c
[...]
```

Note that we have made the preceding output a bit more human-readable by inserting new lines and highlighting some switches. This level of detail can help debug situations where the build fails.

A shortcut shell syntax to the build procedure

A shortcut shell (Bash, typically) syntax to the build procedure (assuming the kernel configuration step is done) could be something like the following example, to be used in non-interactive build scripts, perhaps:

```
time make -j4 [ARCH=<...> CROSS_COMPILE=<...>] all && sudo make modules_install && sudo make install
```

In the preceding code, the && and || elements are the shell's (Bash's) convenience conditional list syntax:

- cmd1 && cmd2 implies : run cmd2 only if cmd1 succeeds.
- cmd1 || cmd2 implies : run cmd2 only if cmd1 fails.

Dealing with compiler switch issues

A while back, in October 2016, when attempting to build an (older 3.x) kernel for the x86_64, I got the following error:

```
$ make
[...]
CC scripts/mod/empty.o
scripts/mod/empty.c:1:0: error: code model kernel does not support PIC mode
/* empty file to figure out endianness / word size */
[...]
```

It turns out that it's not a kernel issue at all. Rather, it's a compiler switch issue on Ubuntu 16.10: `gcc(1)` insists on using the `-fPIE` (where **PIE** is short for **Position Independent Executable**) flag by default. In the Makefile of older kernels, we need to turn this off. It's been fixed since.

This Q&A on the *AskUbuntu* website, on the topic of *Kernel doesn't support PIC mode for compiling?*, describes how this can be done: https://askubuntu.com/questions/851433/kernel-doesnt-support-pic-mode-for-compiling.

(Interestingly, in the preceding *Watching the kernel build run* section, with a recent kernel, notice how the build does use the `-fno-PIE` compiler switch.)

Dealing with missing OpenSSL development headers

In one instance, the kernel build on x86_64 on an Ubuntu box failed with the following error:

```
[...] fatal error: openssl/opensslv.h: No such file or directory
```

This is just a case of missing OpenSSL development headers; this is clearly mentioned in the *Minimal requirements to compile the kernel* document here: https://github.com/torvalds/linux/blob/master/Documentation/process/changes.rst#openssl. Specifically, it mentions that from v4.3 and higher, the `openssl` development packages are required.

FYI, this Q&A too shows how the installation of the `openssl-devel` package (or equivalent; for example, on the Raspberry Pi, the `libssl-dev` package needs to be installed) solves the issue: *OpenSSL missing during ./configure. How to fix?*, available at https://superuser.com/questions/371901/openssl-missing-during-configure-how-to-fix.

In fact, exactly this error occurred on a vanilla x86_64 *Fedora 29* distro as well:

```
make -j4
[...]
HOSTCC scripts/sign-file
scripts/sign-file.c:25:10: fatal error: openssl/opensslv.h: No such file or directory
 #include <openssl/opensslv.h>
          ^~~~~~~~~~~~~~~~~~~~
compilation terminated.
make[1]: *** [scripts/Makefile.host:90: scripts/sign-file] Error 1
make[1]: *** Waiting for unfinished jobs....
make: *** [Makefile:1067: scripts] Error 2
make: *** Waiting for unfinished jobs....
```

The fix here is as follows:

```
sudo dnf install openssl-devel-1:1.1.1-3.fc29
```

Finally, remember an almost guaranteed way to succeed: when you get those build and/or boot errors that you *just cannot fix*: copy the exact error message into the clipboard, go to Google (or another search engine), and type something akin to `linux kernel build <ver ...> fails with <paste-your-error-message-here>`. You might be surprised at how often this helps. If not, diligently do your research, and if you really cannot find any relevant/correct answers, do post your (well-thought-out) question on an appropriate forum.

> Several Linux "builder" projects exist, which are elaborate frameworks for building a Linux system or distribution in its entirety (typically used for embedded Linux projects). As of the time of writing, **Yocto** (https://www.yoctoproject.org/) is considered the industry standard Linux-builder project, with **Buildroot** (https://buildroot.org/) being an older but very much supported one; they are indeed well worth checking out.

Summary

This chapter, along with the previous one, covered in a lot of detail how to build the Linux kernel from source. We began with the actual kernel (and kernel modules') build process. Once built, we showed how the kernel modules are to be installed onto the system. We then moved on to both the practicalities of generating the `initramfs` (or `initrd`) image and went on to explain the motivation behind it. The final step in the kernel build was the (simple) customization of the bootloader (here, we focused only on x86 GRUB). We then showed how to boot the system via the newly baked kernel and verify that its configuration is as we expect. As a useful add-on, we then showed (the basics) of how we can even cross-compile the Linux kernel for another processor (ARM, in this instance). Finally, we shared some additional tips to help you with the kernel build.

Again, if you haven't done so already, we urge you to carefully review and try out the procedures mentioned here and build your own custom Linux kernel.

So, congratulations on completing a Linux kernel build from scratch! You might well find that on an actual project (or product), you may *not* have to actually carry out each and every step of the kernel build procedure as we have tried hard to carefully show. Why? Well, one reason is that there might be a separate BSP team that works on this aspect; another reason – increasingly likely, especially on embedded Linux projects – is that a Linux-builder framework such as *Yocto* (or *Buildroot*) is being used. Yocto will typically take care of the mechanical aspects of the build. *However*, it is really important for you to be able to *configure* the kernel as required by the project; that still requires the knowledge and understanding gained here.

The next two chapters will take you squarely into the world of Linux kernel development, showing you how to write your first kernel module.

Questions

As we conclude, here is a list of questions for you to test your knowledge regarding this chapter's material: https://github.com/PacktPublishing/Linux-Kernel-Programming/tree/master/questions. You will find some of the questions answered in the book's GitHub repo: https://github.com/PacktPublishing/Linux-Kernel-Programming/tree/master/solutions_to_assgn.

Further reading

To help you delve deeper into the subject with useful materials, we provide a rather detailed list of online references and links (and at times, even books) in a Further reading document in this book's GitHub repository. The *Further reading* document is available here: `https://github.com/PacktPublishing/Linux-Kernel-Programming/blob/master/Further_Reading.md`.

4
Writing Your First Kernel Module - LKMs Part 1

Welcome to your journey of learning about a fundamental aspect of Linux kernel development – the **Loadable Kernel Module (LKM)** framework – and how it is to be used by the *module user* or *module author*, who is typically a kernel or device driver programmer. This topic is rather vast and hence is split into two chapters – this one and the next.

In this chapter, we'll begin by taking a quick look at the basics of the Linux kernel architecture, which will help us to understand the LKM framework. Then, we'll look into why kernel modules are useful and write our own simple *Hello, world* LKM, build and run it. We'll see how messages are written to the kernel log and understand and make use of the LKM Makefile. By the end of this chapter, you will have learned the basics of Linux kernel architecture and the LKM framework, applying it to write a simple yet complete piece of kernel code.

In this chapter, we cover the following recipes:

- Understanding the kernel architecture – part I
- Exploring LKMs
- Writing our very first kernel module
- Common operations on kernel modules
- Understanding kernel logging and printk
- Understanding the basics of a kernel module Makefile

Technical requirements

If you have already carefully followed `Chapter 1`, *Kernel Workspace Setup*, the technical prerequisites that follow will already be taken care of. (The chapter also mentions various useful open source tools and projects; I definitely recommend that you browse through it at least once.) For your convenience, we summarize some key points here.

To build and use a kernel module on a Linux distribution (or custom system), you need, at minimum, the following two components to be installed:

- **A toolchain**: This includes the compiler, assembler, linker/loader, C library, and various other bits and pieces. If building for the local system, as we assume for now, then any modern Linux distribution will have a native toolchain pre-installed. If not, simply installing the `gcc` package for your distribution should be sufficient; on an Ubuntu- or Debian-based Linux system, use this:

  ```
  sudo apt install gcc
  ```

- **Kernel headers**: These headers will be used during compilation. In reality, you install a package geared to not only install the kernel headers but also other required bits and pieces (such as the kernel Makefile) onto the system. Again, any modern Linux distribution will/should have the kernel header pre-installed. If not (you can check using `dpkg(1)`, as shown here), simply install the package for your distribution; on an Ubuntu- or Debian-based Linux system, use this:

  ```
  $ sudo apt install linux-headers-generic
  $ dpkg -l | grep linux-headers | awk '{print $1, $2}'
  ii linux-headers-5.3.0-28
  ii linux-headers-5.3.0-28-generic
  ii linux-headers-5.3.0-40
  ii linux-headers-5.3.0-40-generic
  ii linux-headers-generic-hwe-18.04
  $
  ```

  Here, the second command using the `dpkg(1)` utility is simply used to verify that the `linux-headers` packages are indeed installed.

  > **TIP**: This package may be named `kernel-headers-<ver#>` on some distributions. Also, for development directly on a Raspberry Pi, install the relevant kernel headers package named `raspberrypi-kernel-headers`.

The entire source tree for this book is available in its GitHub repository at https://github.com/PacktPublishing/Linux-Kernel-Programming, and the code for this chapter under the `ch4` directory. We definitely expect you to clone it:

```
git clone
https://github.com/PacktPublishing/Linux-Kernel-Programming.git
```

The code for this chapter is under its directory namesake, `chn` (where `n` is the chapter number; so here, it's under `ch4/`).

Understanding kernel architecture – part 1

In this section, we begin to deepen our understanding of the kernel. More specifically, here we delve into what user and kernel spaces are and the major subsystems and various components that make up the Linux kernel. This information is dealt with at a higher level of abstraction for now and is deliberately kept brief. We shall delve a lot deeper into understanding the fabric of the kernel in Chapter 6, *Kernel Internals Essentials - Processes and Threads*.

User space and kernel space

Modern microprocessors support a minimum of two privilege levels. As a real-world example, the Intel/AMD x86[-64] family supports four privilege levels (they call them *ring levels*), and the ARM (32-bit) microprocessor family supports up to seven (ARM calls them *execution modes*; six are privileged and one is non-privileged).

The key point here is that for security and stability on the platform, all modern operating systems running on these processors will make use of (at least) two of the privilege levels (or modes):

- **User space**: For *applications* to run in *unprivileged user mode*
- **Kernel space**: For the *kernel* (and all its components) to run in privileged mode – *kernel mode*

The following figure shows this basic architecture:

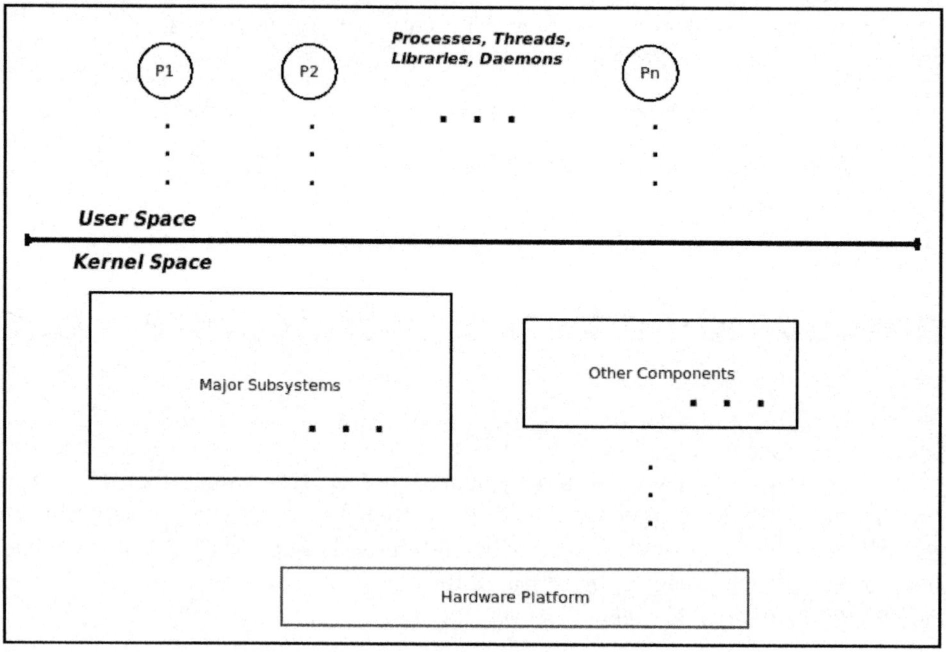

Figure 4.1 – Basic architecture – two privilege modes

A few details on the Linux system architecture follow; do read on.

Library and system call APIs

User space applications often rely on **Application Programming Interfaces (APIs)** to perform their work. A *library* is essentially a collection or archive of APIs, allowing you to use a standardized, well-written, and well-tested interface (and leverage the usual benefits: not having to reinvent the wheel, portability, standardization, and so on). Linux systems have several libraries; even hundreds on enterprise-class systems is not uncommon. Of these, *all* usermode Linux applications (executables) are "auto-linked" into one important, always-used library: `glibc` – *the GNU standard C library*, as you shall learn. However, libraries are only ever available in user mode; the kernel does not have libraries (more on this in the following chapter).

Examples of library APIs are the well-known `printf(3)` (recall, from Chapter 1, *Kernel Workspace Setup*, the section of the man pages where this API can be found), `scanf(3)`, `strcmp(3)`, `malloc(3)`, and `free(3)`.

Now, a key point: if user and kernel are separate address spaces and at differing privilege levels, how can a user process *access* the kernel? The short answer is *via system calls*. A **system call** is a special API, in the sense that it is the only legal (synchronous) way for user space processes to access the kernel. In other words, system calls are the only legal *entry point* into the kernel space. They have the ability to *switch* from non-privileged user mode to privileged kernel mode (more on this and the monolithic design in `Chapter 6`, *Kernel Internals Essentials – Processes and Threads*, under the *Process and interrupt contexts* section). Examples of system calls include `fork(2)`, `execve(2)`, `open(2)`, `read(2)`, `write(2)`, `socket(2)`, `accept(2)`, `chmod(2)`, and so on.

> **TIP**
> Look up all library and system call APIs in the man pages online:
> - Library APIs, man section 3: `https://linux.die.net/man/3/`
> - System call APIs, man section 2: `https://linux.die.net/man/2/`

The point being stressed here is that it's really only via system calls that user applications and the kernel communicate; that is the interface. In this book, we do not delve further into these details. If you are interested in knowing more, please refer to the book *Hands-On System Programming with Linux*, by Packt (specifically *Chapter 1, Linux System Architecture*).

Kernel space components

This book focuses entirely on the kernel space, of course. The Linux kernel today is a rather large and complex beast. Internally, it consists of a few major subsystems and several components. A broad enumeration of kernel subsystems and components yields the following list:

- **Core kernel**: This code handles the typical core work of any modern operating system, including (user and kernel) process and thread creation/destruction, CPU scheduling, synchronization primitives, signaling, timers, interrupt handling, namespaces, cgroups, module support, crypto, and more.
- **Memory Management (MM)**: This handles all memory-related work, including the setup and maintenance of kernel and process **Virtual Address Spaces (VASes)**.

- **VFS (for filesystem support)**: The **Virtual Filesystem Switch** (**VFS**) is an abstraction layer over the actual filesystems implemented within the Linux kernel (for example, `ext[2|4]`, `vfat`, `reiserfs`, `ntfs`, `msdos`, `iso9660`, JFFS2, and UFS).
- **Block IO**: The code paths implementing the actual file I/O, from the VFS right down to the block device driver and everything in between (really, quite a lot!), is encompassed here.
- **Network protocol stack**: Linux is well known for its precise, to-the-letter-of-the-RFC, high-quality implementation of the well-known (and not-so-well-known) network protocols at all layers of the model, with TCP/IP being perhaps the most famous.
- **Inter-Process Communication (IPC) support**: The implementation of IPC mechanisms is done here; Linux supports message queues, shared memory, semaphores (both the older SysV and the newer POSIX ones), and other IPC mechanisms.
- **Sound support**: All the code that implements audio is here, from the firmware to drivers and codecs.
- **Virtualization support**: Linux has become extremely popular with large and small cloud providers alike, a big reason being its high-quality, low-footprint virtualization engine, **Kernel-based Virtual Machine** (**KVM**).

All this forms the major kernel subsystems; in addition, we have these:

- Arch-specific (meaning CPU-specific) code
- Kernel initialization
- Security frameworks
- Many types of device drivers

> **TIP**
> Recall that in `Chapter 2`, *Building the 5.x Linux Kernel from Source – Part 1*, the *A brief tour of the kernel source tree* section gave the kernel source tree (code) layout corresponding to the major subsystems and other components.

It is a well-known fact that the Linux kernel follows the **monolithic kernel architecture**. Essentially, a monolithic design is one in which *all* kernel components (that we mentioned in this section) live in and share the kernel address space (or kernel *segment*). This can be clearly seen in the following diagram:

Chapter 4

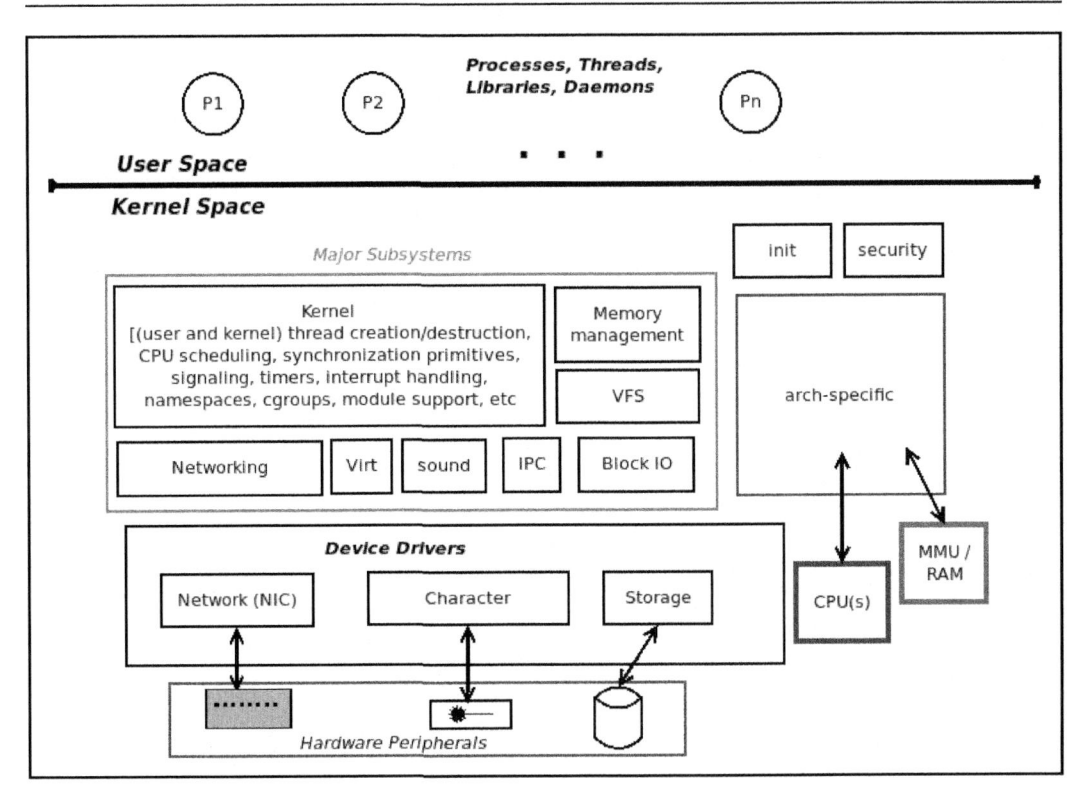

Figure 4.2 – Linux kernel space - major subsystems and blocks

Another fact you should be aware of is that these address spaces are of course *virtual* address spaces and not physical. The kernel will (leveraging hardware such as the MMU/TLB/caches) *map*, at the page granularity level, virtual pages to physical page frames. It does this by using a *master* kernel paging table to map kernel virtual pages to physical frames, and, for every single process that is alive, it maps the process's virtual pages to physical page frames via individual paging tables for each process.

> More in-depth coverage of the essentials of the kernel and memory management architecture and internals awaits you in `Chapter 6`, *Kernel Internals Essentials – Processes and Threads* (and more chapters that follow).

Now that we have a basic understanding of the user and kernel spaces, let's move on and begin our journey into the LKM framework.

[151]

Exploring LKMs

Simply put, a kernel module is a means to provide kernel-level functionality without resorting to working within the kernel source tree.

Visualize a scenario where you have to add a support feature to the Linux kernel – perhaps a new device driver in order to use a certain hardware peripheral chip, a new filesystem, or a new I/O scheduler. One way to do this is pretty obvious: update the kernel source tree with the new code, build it, and test it.

Though this may seem straightforward, it's actually a lot of work – every change in the code that we write, no matter how minor, will require us to rebuild the kernel image and then reboot the system in order to test it. There must be a cleaner, easier way; indeed there is – *the LKM framework*!

The LKM framework

The LKM framework is a means to compile a piece of kernel code *outside of* the kernel source tree, often referred to as "out-of-tree" code, keeping it independent from the kernel in a limited sense, and then insert it into or *plug it into* kernel memory, have it run and perform its job, and then remove it (or *unplug* it) from kernel memory.

The kernel module's source code, typically consisting of one or more C source files, header files, and a Makefile, is built (via `make(1)`, of course) into a *kernel module*. The kernel module itself is merely a binary object file and not a binary executable. In Linux 2.4 and earlier, the kernel module's filename had a `.o` suffix; on modern 2.6 Linux and later, it instead has a `.ko` (**k**ernel **o**bject) suffix. Once built, you can insert this `.ko` file – the kernel module – into the live kernel at runtime, effectively making it a part of the kernel.

> Note that not *all* kernel functionality can be provided via the LKM framework. Several core features, such as the core CPU scheduler code, memory manage the signaling, timer, interrupt management code paths, and so on, can only be developed within the kernel itself. Similarly, a kernel module is only allowed access to a subset of the full kernel API; more on this later.

You might ask: how do I *insert* an object into the kernel? Let's keep it simple – the answer is: via the `insmod(8)` utility. For now, let's skip the details (these will be explained in the upcoming *Running the kernel module* section). The following figure provides an overview of first building and then inserting a kernel module into kernel memory:

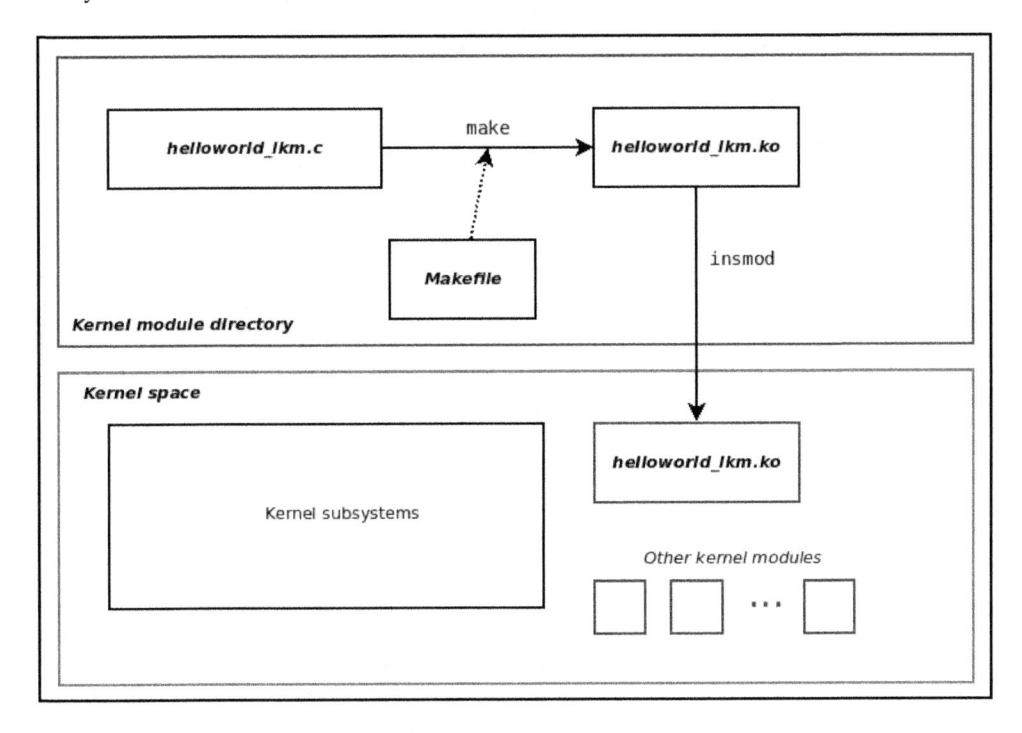

Figure 4.3 – Building and then inserting a kernel module into kernel memory

> **TIP**
> Worry not: the actual code for both the kernel module C source as well as its Makefile is dealt with in detail in an upcoming section; for now, we want to gain a conceptual understanding only.

The kernel module is loaded into and lives in kernel memory, that is, the kernel VAS (the bottom half of *Figure 4.3*) in an area of space allocated for it by the kernel. Make no mistake, *it is kernel code and runs with kernel privileges*. This way, you, the kernel (or driver) developer does not have to reconfigure, rebuild, and reboot the system each time. All you have to do is edit the code of the kernel module, rebuild it, remove the old copy from memory (if it exists), and insert the new version. It saves time, and it increases productivity.

One reason that kernel modules are advantageous is that they lend themselves to dynamic product configuration. For example, kernel modules can be designed to provide different features at differing price points; a script generating the final image for an embedded product could install a given set of kernel modules depending on the price the customer is willing to pay. Here's another example of how this technology is leveraged in a *debug* or troubleshooting scenario: a kernel module could be used to dynamically generate diagnostics and debug logs on an existing product. Technologies such as kprobes and the like allow just this.

In effect, the LKM framework gives us a means of dynamically extending kernel functionality by allowing us to insert and remove live code from kernel memory. This ability to plug in and unplug kernel functionality at our whim makes us realize that the Linux kernel is not purely monolithic, it is also *modular*.

Kernel modules within the kernel source tree

In fact, the kernel module object isn't completely unfamiliar to us. In Chapter 3, *Building the 5.x Linux Kernel from Source - Part 2*, we built kernel modules as part of the kernel build process and had them installed.

Recall that these kernel modules are part of the kernel source and have been configured as modules by selecting M in the tristate kernel menuconfig prompt. They get installed into directories under /lib/modules/$(uname -r)/. So, to see a little bit regarding the kernel modules installed under our currently running an Ubuntu 18.04.3 LTS guest kernel, we can do this:

```
$ lsb_release -a 2>/dev/null |grep Description
Description:    Ubuntu 18.04.3 LTS
$ uname -r
5.0.0-36-generic
$ find /lib/modules/$(uname -r)/ -name "*.ko" | wc -l
5359
```

Okay, the folks at Canonical and elsewhere have been busy! Over five thousand kernel modules... Think about it – it makes sense: distributors cannot know in advance exactly what hardware peripherals a user will end up using (especially on generic computers like x86-based systems). Kernel modules serve as a convenient means to support huge amounts of hardware without insanely bloating the kernel image file (bzImage or zImage, for example).

The installed kernel modules for our Ubuntu Linux system live within the `/lib/modules/$(uname -r)/kernel` directory, as seen here:

```
$ ls /lib/modules/5.0.0-36-generic/kernel/
arch/    block/   crypto/   drivers/   fs/    kernel/   lib/   mm/   net/
samples/ sound/   spl/      ubuntu/    virt/  zfs/
$ ls /lib/modules/5.4.0-llkd01/kernel/
arch/    crypto/  drivers/  fs/   net/   sound/
$
```

Here, looking at the top level of the `kernel/` directory under `/lib/modules/$(uname -r)` for the distro kernel (Ubuntu 18.04.3 LTS running the `5.0.0-36-generic` kernel), we see that there are many sub folders and literally a few thousand kernel modules packed within. By contrast, for the kernel we built (refer to Chapter 2, *Building the 5.x Linux Kernel from Source – Part 1*, and Chapter 3, *Building the 5.x Linux Kernel from Source – Part 2*, for the details), there are much fewer. You will recall from our discussions in Chapter 2, *Building the 5.x Linux Kernel from Source – Part 1*, that we deliberately used the `localmodconfig` target to keep the build small and fast. Thus, here, our custom 5.4.0 kernel has just some 60-odd kernel modules built against it.

One area that sees pretty heavy usage of kernel modules is that of *device drivers*. As an example, let's look at a network device driver that is architected as a kernel module. You can find several (with familiar brands too!) under the distro kernel's `kernel/drivers/net/ethernet` folder:

```
llkd ~ $ ls /lib/modules/5.0.0-36-generic/kernel/drivers/net/ethernet/
3com/         amd/           chelsio/     ethoc.ko     mellanox/     ni/              samsung/     tehuti/
8390/         aquantia/      cirrus/      fealnx.ko    micrel/       nvidia/          sfc/         ti/
adaptec/      atheros/       cisco/       fujitsu/     microchip/    packetengines/   silan/       via/
agere/        aurora/        dec/         hp/          mscc/         qlogic/          sis/         wiznet/
alacritech/   broadcom/      dlink/       huawei/      myricom/      qualcomm/        smsc/        xircom/
alteon/       brocade/       dnet.ko      intel/       natsemi/      rdc/             stmicro/
altera/       cadence/       ec_bhf.ko    jme.ko       neterion/     realtek/         sun/
amazon/       cavium/        emulex/      marvell/     netronome/    rocker/          synopsys/
llkd ~ $
```

Figure 4.4 – Content of our distro kernel's ethernet network drivers (kernel modules)

Popular on many Intel-based laptops is the Intel 1GbE **Network Interface Card** (**NIC**) ethernet adapter. The network device driver that drives it is called the `e1000` driver. Our x86-64 Ubuntu 18.04.3 guest (running on an x86-64 host laptop) shows that it indeed uses this driver:

```
$ lsmod | grep e1000
e1000                  139264  0
```

We shall cover the `lsmod(8)` ('list modules') utility in more detail soon. More importantly for us, we can see that it's a kernel module! How about obtaining some more information on this particular kernel module? That's quite easily done by leveraging the `modinfo(8)` utility (for readability, we truncate its verbose output here):

```
$ ls -l /lib/modules/5.0.0-36-generic/kernel/drivers/net/ethernet/intel/e1000
total 220
-rw-r--r-- 1 root root 221729 Nov 12 16:16 e1000.ko
$ modinfo /lib/modules/5.0.0-36-generic/kernel/drivers/net/ethernet/intel/e1000/e1000.ko
filename:       /lib/modules/5.0.0-36-generic/kernel/drivers/net/ethernet/intel/e1000/e1000.ko
version:        7.3.21-k8-NAPI
license:        GPL v2
description:    Intel(R) PRO/1000 Network Driver
author:         Intel Corporation, <linux.nics@intel.com>
srcversion:     C521B82214E3F5A010A9383
alias:          pci:v00008086d00002E6Esv*sd*bc*sc*i*
[...]
name:           e1000
vermagic:       5.0.0-36-generic SMP mod_unload
[...]
parm:           copybreak:Maximum size of packet that is copied to a new
                buffer on receive (uint)
parm:           debug:Debug level (0=none,...,16=all) (int)
$
```

The `modinfo(8)` utility allows us to peek into a kernel module's binary image and extract some details regarding it; more on using `modinfo` in the next section.

> **TIP:** Another way to gain useful information on the system, including information on kernel modules that are currently loaded up, is via the `systool(1)` utility. For an installed kernel module (details on *installing* a kernel module follow in the next chapter in the *Auto-loading modules on system boot* section), doing `systool -m <module-name> -v` reveals information about it. Look up the `systool(1)` man page for usage details.

The bottom line is that kernel modules have come to be *the* pragmatic way to build and distribute some types of kernel components, with *device drivers* being the most frequent use case for them. Other uses include but aren't limited to filesystems, network firewalls, packet sniffers, and custom kernel code.

Chapter 4

So, if you would like to learn how to write a Linux device driver, a filesystem, or a firewall, you must first learn how to write a kernel module, thus leveraging the kernel's powerful LKM framework. That's precisely what we will be doing next.

Writing our very first kernel module

When introducing a new programming language or topic, it has become a widely accepted computer programming tradition to mimic the original *K&R Hello, world* program as the very first piece of code. I'm happy to follow this venerated tradition to introduce the powerful LKM framework. In this section, you will learn the steps to code a simple LKM. We explain the code in detail.

Introducing our Hello, world LKM C code

Without further ado, here is some simple *Hello, world* C code, implemented to abide by the Linux kernel's LKM framework:

> For reasons of readability and space constraints, only the key parts of the source code are displayed here. To view the complete source code, build it, and run it, the entire source tree for this book is available in it's GitHub repository here: https://github.com/PacktPublishing/Linux-Kernel-Programming. We definitely expect you to clone it:
> git clone https://github.com/PacktPublishing/Linux-Kernel-Programming.git

```
// ch4/helloworld_lkm/hellowworld_lkm.c
#include <linux/init.h>
#include <linux/kernel.h>
#include <linux/module.h>

MODULE_AUTHOR("<insert your name here>");
MODULE_DESCRIPTION("LLKD book:ch4/helloworld_lkm: hello, world, our first LKM");
MODULE_LICENSE("Dual MIT/GPL");
MODULE_VERSION("0.1");

static int __init helloworld_lkm_init(void)
{
    printk(KERN_INFO "Hello, world\n");
    return 0;     /* success */
```

[157]

```
}

static void __exit helloworld_lkm_exit(void)
{
    printk(KERN_INFO "Goodbye, world\n");
}

module_init(helloworld_lkm_init);
module_exit(helloworld_lkm_exit);
```

You can try out this simple *Hello, world* kernel module right away! Just `cd` to the correct source directory as shown here and get our helper `lkm` script to build and run it:

```
$ cd <...>/ch4/helloworld_lkm
$ ../../lkm helloworld_lkm
Version info:
Distro:     Ubuntu 18.04.3 LTS
Kernel: 5.0.0-36-generic
[...]
dmesg
[ 5399.230367] Hello, world
$
```

The *hows and whys* are explained in a lot of detail shortly. Though tiny, the code of this, our very first kernel module, requires careful perusal and understanding. Do read on.

Breaking it down

The following subsections explain pretty much each line of the preceding *Hello, world* C code. Remember that although the program appears very small and trivial, there is a lot to be understood regarding it and the surrounding LKM framework. The rest of this chapter focuses on this and goes into great detail. I highly recommend that you take the time to read through and understand these fundamentals first. This will help you immensely in later, possibly difficult-to-debug situations.

Kernel headers

We use `#include` for a few header files. Unlike in user space 'C' application development, these are *kernel headers* (as mentioned in the *Technical requirements* section). Recall from Chapter 3, *Building the 5.x Linux Kernel from Source – Part 2*, that kernel modules were installed under a specific root-writeable branch. Let's check it out again (here, we're running on our guest x86_64 Ubuntu VM with the 5.0.0-36-generic distro kernel):

```
$ ls -l /lib/modules/$(uname -r)/
total 5552
lrwxrwxrwx  1 root root      39 Nov 12 16:16 build -> /usr/src/linux-headers-5.0.0-36-generic/
drwxr-xr-x  2 root root    4096 Nov 28 08:49 initrd/
[...]
```

Notice the symbolic or soft link named `build`. It points to the location of the kernel headers on the system. In the preceding code, it's under `/usr/src/linux-headers-5.0.0-36-generic/`! As you shall see, we will supply this information to the Makefile used to build our kernel module. (Also, some systems have a similar soft link called `source`).

> The `kernel-headers` or `linux-headers` package unpacks a limited kernel source tree onto the system, typically under `/usr/src/`.... This code, however, isn't complete, hence our use of the phrase *limited* source tree. This is because the complete kernel source tree isn't required for the purpose of building modules – just the required components (the headers, the Makefiles, and so on) are what's packaged and extracted.

The first line of code in our *Hello, world* kernel module is `#include <linux/init.h>`.

The compiler resolves this by searching for the previously mentioned kernel header file under `/lib/modules/$(uname -r)/build/include/`. Thus, by following the `build` soft link, we can see that it ultimately picks up this header file:

```
$ ls -l /usr/src/linux-headers-5.0.0-36-generic/include/linux/init.h
-rw-r--r-- 1 root root 9704 Mar  4  2019 /usr/src/linux-headers-5.0.0-36-generic/include/linux/init.h
```

The same follows for the other kernel headers included in the kernel module's source code.

Module macros

Next, we have a few module macros of the form `MODULE_FOO()`; most are quite intuitive:

- `MODULE_AUTHOR()`: Specifies the author(s) of the kernel module
- `MODULE_DESCRIPTION()`: Briefly describes the function of this LKM
- `MODULE_LICENSE()`: Specifies the license(s) under which this kernel module is released
- `MODULE_VERSION()`: Specifies the (local) version of the kernel module

In the absence of the source code, how will this information be conveyed to the end user (or customer)? Ah, the `modinfo(8)` utility does precisely that! These macros and their information might seem trivial, but they are important in projects and products. This information is relied upon, for example, by a vendor establishing the (open source) licenses that code is running under by using `grep` on the `modinfo` output on all installed kernel modules.

Entry and exit points

Never forget, kernel modules are, after all, *kernel code running with kernel privileges*. It's *not* an application and thus does not have it's entry point as the familiar `main()` function (that we know well and love). This, of course, begs the question: what are the entry and exit points of the kernel module? Notice, at the bottom of our simple kernel module, the following lines:

```
module_init(helloworld_lkm_init);
module_exit(helloworld_lkm_exit);
```

The `module_[init|exit]()` code is macros specifying the entry and exit points, respectively. The parameter to each is a function pointer. With modern C compilers, we can just specify the name of the function. Thus, in our code, the following applies:

- The `helloworld_lkm_init()` function is the entry point.
- The `helloworld_lkm_exit()` function is the exit point.

You can almost think of these entry and exit points as a *constructor/destructor* pair for a kernel module. Technically, it's not the case, of course, as this isn't object-oriented C++ code, it's plain C. Nevertheless, it's a useful analogy.

Return values

Notice the signature of the `init` and `exit` functions is as follows:

```
static int   __init <modulename>_init(void);
static void  __exit <modulename>_exit(void);
```

As a good coding practice, we have used the naming format for the functions as `<modulename>__[init|exit]()`, where `<modulename>` is replaced with the name of the kernel module. You will realize that this naming convention is just that - it's merely a convention that is, technically speaking, unnecessary, but it is intuitive and thus helpful. Clearly, neither routine receives any parameter.

Marking both functions with the `static` qualifier implies that they are private to this kernel module. That is what we want.

Now let's move along to the important convention that is followed for a kernel module's `init` function's return value.

The 0/-E return convention

The kernel module's `init` function is to return a value of type `int`; this is a key aspect. The Linux kernel has evolved a *style* or convention, if you will, with regard to returning values from it (meaning from the kernel space to the user space process). The LKM framework follows what is colloquially referred to as the `0/-E` convention:

- Upon success, return integer value `0`.
- Upon failure, return the negative of the value you would like the user space global uninitialized integer `errno` to be set to.

Writing Your First Kernel Module - LKMs Part 1

> Be aware that `errno` is a global residing in a user process VAS within the uninitialized data segment. With very few exceptions, whenever a Linux system call fails, `-1` is returned and `errno` is set to a positive value, representing the failure code; this work is carried out by `glibc` "glue" code on the `syscall` return path.
>
> Furthermore, the `errno` value is actually an index into a global table of English error messages (`const char * const sys_errlist[]`); this is really how routines such as `perror(3)`, `strerror[_r](3)` and the like can print out failure diagnostics.
>
> By the way, you can look up the **complete list of error codes** available to you from within these (kernel source tree) header files: `include/uapi/asm-generic/errno-base.h` and `include/uapi/asm-generic/errno.h`.

A quick example of how to return from a kernel module's `init` function will help make this clear: say our kernel module's `init` function is attempting to dynamically allocate some kernel memory (details on the `kmalloc()` API and so on will be covered in later chapters of course; please ignore it for now). Then, we could code it like so:

```
[...]
ptr = kmalloc(87, GFP_KERNEL);
if (!ptr) {
    pr_warning("%s:%s:%d: kmalloc failed!\n", __FILE__, __func__,
__LINE__);
    return -ENOMEM;
}
[...]
return 0;    /* success */
```

If the memory allocation does fail (very unlikely, but hey, it can happen!), we do the following:

1. First, we emit a warning `printk`. Actually, in this particular case – "out of memory" – it's pedantic and unnecessary. The kernel will certainly emit sufficient diagnostic information if a kernel-space memory allocation ever fails! See this link for more details: https://lkml.org/lkml/2014/6/10/382; we do so here merely as it's early in the discussion and for reader continuity.

2. Return the `-ENOMEM` value:
    - The layer to which this value will be returned in user space is actually `glibc`; it has some "glue" code that multiplies this value by `-1` and sets the global integer `errno` to it.
    - Now, the `[f]init_module(2)` system call will return `-1`, indicating failure (this is because `insmod(8)` actually invokes this system call, as you will soon see).
    - `errno` will be set to `ENOMEM`, reflecting the fact that the kernel module insertion failed due to a failure to allocate memory.

Conversely, the framework *expects* the `init` function to return the value `0` upon success. In fact, in older kernel versions, failure to return `0` upon success would cause the kernel module to be abruptly unloaded from kernel memory. Nowadays, this removal of the kernel module does not happen but the kernel emits a warning message regarding the fact that a *suspicious* non-zero value has been returned.

There's not much to be said for the cleanup routine. It receives no parameters and returns nothing (`void`). Its job is to perform any and all required cleanup before the kernel module is unloaded from kernel memory.

> *Not* including the `module_exit()` macro in your kernel module makes it impossible to ever unload it (notwithstanding a system shutdown or reboot, of course). Interesting... (I suggest you try this out as a small exercise!).
>
> Of course, it's never that simple: this behavior preventing the unload is guaranteed only if the kernel is built with the `CONFIG_MODULE_FORCE_UNLOAD` flag set to `Disabled` (the default).

The ERR_PTR and PTR_ERR macros

On the discussion of return values, you now understand that the kernel module's `init` routine must return an integer. What if you wish to return a pointer instead? The `ERR_PTR()` inline function comes to our rescue, allowing us to return a pointer *disguised* as an integer simply by typecasting it as `void *`. It actually gets better: you can check for an error using the `IS_ERR()` inline function (which really just figures out whether the value is in the range [-1 to -4095]), *encodes* a negative error value into a pointer via the `ERR_PTR()` inline function, and *retrieves* this value from the pointer using the converse routine `PTR_ERR()`.

As a simple example, see the callee code given here. This time, we have the (sample) function `myfunc()` return a pointer (to a structure named `mystruct`) and not an integer:

```
struct mystruct * myfunc(void)
{
    struct mystruct *mys = NULL;
    mys = kzalloc(sizeof(struct mystruct), GFP_KERNEL);
    if (!mys)
        return ERR_PTR(-ENOMEM);
    [...]
    return mys;
}
```

The caller code is as follows:

```
[...]
gmys = myfunc();
if (IS_ERR(gmys)) {
    pr_warn("%s: myfunc alloc failed, aborting...\n", OURMODNAME);
    stat = PTR_ERR(gmys); /* sets 'stat' to the value -ENOMEM */
    goto out_fail_1;
}
[...]
return stat;
out_fail_1:
    return stat;
}
```

FYI, the inline `ERR_PTR()`, `PTR_ERR()`, and `IS_ERR()` functions all live within the (kernel header) `include/linux/err.h` file. The kernel documentation (https://kernel.readthedocs.io/en/sphinx-samples/kernel-hacking.html#return-conventions) talks about kernel function return conventions. Also, you can find example usage for these functions under the `crypto/api-samples` code within the kernel source tree: https://www.kernel.org/doc/html/v4.17/crypto/api-samples.html.

The __init and __exit keywords

A niggling leftover: what exactly are the __init and __exit macros we see within the preceding function signatures? These are merely memory optimization attributes inserted by the linker.

The `__init` macro defines an `init.text` section for code. Similarly, any data declared with the `__initdata` attribute goes into an `init.data` section. The whole point here is the code and data in the `init` function is used exactly once during initialization. Once it's invoked, it will never be called again; so, once called, it is then freed up (via `free_initmem()`).

The deal is similar with the `__exit` macro, though, of course, this only makes sense with kernel modules. Once the `cleanup` function is called, all the memory is freed. If the code were instead part of the static kernel image (or if module support were disabled), this macro would have no effect.

Fine, but so far, we have still not explained some practicalities: how exactly can you get the kernel module object into kernel memory, have it execute, and then unload it, plus several other operations you might wish to perform. Let's discuss these in the following section.

Common operations on kernel modules

Now let's delve into how exactly you can build, load, and unload a kernel module. Besides this, we'll also walk through the basics regarding the tremendously useful `printk()` kernel API, details on listing the currently loaded kernel modules with `lsmod(8)`, and a convenience script for automating some common tasks during kernel module development. So, let's begin!

Building the kernel module

> We definitely urge you to try out our simple *Hello, world* kernel module exercise (if you haven't already done so)! To do so, we assume you have cloned this book's GitHub repository (https://github.com/PacktPublishing/Linux-Kernel-Programming) already. If not, please do so now (refer to the *Technical requirements* section for details).

Writing Your First Kernel Module - LKMs Part 1

Here, we show step by step how exactly you can build and then insert our first kernel module into kernel memory. Again, a quick reminder: we have performed these steps on an x86-64 Linux guest VM (under Oracle VirtualBox 6.1) running the Ubuntu 18.04.3 LTS distribution:

1. Change to this books' source code chapter directory and sub-directory. Our very first kernel module lives in its own folder (as it should!) called `helloworld_lkm`:

   ```
   cd <book-code-dir>/ch4/helloworld_lkm
   ```

   > **TIP**: `<book-code-dir>` is, of course, the folder into which you cloned this book's GitHub repository; here (see the screenshot, Figure 4.5), you can see that it's `/home/llkd/book_llkd/Linux-Kernel-Programming/`.

2. Now verify the code base:

   ```
   $ pwd
   <book-code-dir>/ch4/helloworld_lkm
   $ ls -l
   total 8
   -rw-rw-r-- 1 llkd llkd 1211 Jan 24 13:01 helloworld_lkm.c
   -rw-rw-r-- 1 llkd llkd  333 Jan 24 13:01 Makefile
   $
   ```

3. Build it with `make`:

```
$ ls -l
total 8
-rw-rw-r-- 1 llkd llkd 1211 Jan 24 13:05 helloworld_lkm.c
-rw-rw-r-- 1 llkd llkd  333 Jan 24 13:05 Makefile
$ make
make -C /lib/modules/5.4.0-llkd01/build/ M=/home/llkd/llkd_book/Learn-Linux-Kernel-Development/ch4/helloworld_lkm modules
make[1]: Entering directory '/home/llkd/kernels/linux-5.4'
  CC [M]  /home/llkd/llkd_book/Learn-Linux-Kernel-Development/ch4/helloworld_lkm/helloworld_lkm.o
  Building modules, stage 2.
  MODPOST 1 modules
  CC [M]  /home/llkd/llkd_book/Learn-Linux-Kernel-Development/ch4/helloworld_lkm/helloworld_lkm.mod.o
  LD [M]  /home/llkd/llkd_book/Learn-Linux-Kernel-Development/ch4/helloworld_lkm/helloworld_lkm.ko
make[1]: Leaving directory '/home/llkd/kernels/linux-5.4'
$ ls -l helloworld_lkm.ko
-rw-rw-r-- 1 llkd llkd 217224 Mar 17 17:29 helloworld_lkm.ko
$
```

Figure 4.5 – Listing and building our very first *Hello, world* kernel module

The preceding screenshot shows that the kernel module has been successfully built. It's the `./helloworld_lkm.ko` file. (Also, note that we booted from, and thus have built the kernel module against, our custom 5.4.0 kernel, built in earlier chapters.)

[166]

Running the kernel module

In order to have the kernel module run, you need to first load it into kernel memory space, of course. This is known as *inserting* the module into kernel memory.

Getting the kernel module into the Linux kernel segment can be done in a few ways, which all ultimately boil down to invoking one of the `[f]init_module(2)` system calls. For convenience, several wrapper utilities exist that will do so (or you can always write one). We will use the popular `insmod(8)` (read it as "**ins**ert **mod**ule") utility below; the parameter for `insmod` is the pathname to the kernel module to insert:

```
$ insmod ./helloworld_lkm.ko
insmod: ERROR: could not insert module ./helloworld_lkm.ko: Operation not permitted
$
```

It fails! In fact, it should be pretty obvious why. Think about it: inserting code into the kernel is, in a very real sense, even superior to being *root* (superuser) on the system - again, I remind you: *it's kernel code and will run with kernel privilege*. If any and every user is allowed to insert or remove kernel modules, hackers would have a field day! Deploying malicious code would become a fairly trivial affair. So, for security reasons, **only with root access can you insert or remove kernel modules**.

> Technically, being *root* implies that the process' (or thread's) **Real** and/or **Effective UID (RUID/EUID)** value is the special value *zero*. Not just that, but the modern kernel "sees" a thread as having certain **capabilities** (via the modern and superior POSIX Capabilities model); only a process/thread with the `CAP_SYS_MODULE` capability can (un)load kernel modules. We refer the reader to the man page on `capabilities(7)` for more details.

So, let's again attempt to insert our kernel module into memory, this time with *root* privileges via `sudo(8)`:

```
$ sudo insmod ./helloworld_lkm.ko
[sudo] password for llkd:
$ echo $?
0
```

[167]

Now it works! As alluded to earlier, the `insmod(8)` utility works by invoking the `[f]init_module(2)` system call. When might the `insmod(8)` utility (in effect, internally the `[f]init_module(2)` system calls) *fail*?

There are a few cases:

- **Permissions**: Not run as root or lack of the `CAP_SYS_MODULE` capability (`errno <- EPERM`).
- The kernel tunable within the `proc` filesystem, `/proc/sys/kernel/modules_disabled`, is set to `1` (it defaults to `0`).
- A kernel module with the same name is already in kernel memory (`errno <- EEXISTS`).

Okay, all looks good. The `$?` result being `0` implies that the previous shell command was successful. That's great, but where is our *Hello, world* message? Read on!

A quick first look at the kernel printk()

To emit a message, the user space C developer will often use the trusty `printf(3)` glibc API (or perhaps the `cout` when writing C++ code). However, it's important to understand that in kernel space, *there are no libraries*. Hence, we simply do *not* have access to the good old `printf()` API. Instead, it has essentially been re-implemented *within* the kernel as the `printk()` kernel API (curious as to where its code is? its here within the kernel source tree: `kernel/printk/printk.c:printk()`).

Emitting a message via the `printk()` API is simple and very much similar to doing so with `printf(3)`. In our simple kernel module, here's where the action occurs:

```
printk(KERN_INFO "Hello, world\n");
```

Though very similar to `printf` at first glance, `printk` is really quite different. In terms of similarities, the API receives a format string as its parameter. The format string is pretty much identical to that of `printf`.

But the similarities end there. The key difference between `printf` and `printk` is this: the user space `printf(3)` library API works by formatting a text string as requested and invoking the `write(2)` system call, which in turn actually performs a write to the `stdout` *device*, which, by default, is the Terminal window (or console device). The kernel `printk` API also formats its text string as requested, but its *output destination* differs. It writes to at least one place – the first one in the following list – and possibly to a few more:

- A kernel log buffer in RAM (volatile)
- A log file, the kernel log file (non-volatile)
- The console device

> For now, we shall skip the inner details regarding the workings of `printk`. Also, please ignore the `KERN_INFO` token within the `printk` API; we shall cover all this soon enough.

When you emit a message via `printk`, it's guaranteed that the output goes into a log buffer in kernel memory (RAM). This, in effect, constitutes the **kernel log**. It's important to note that you will never see the `printk` output directly when working in graphical mode with an X server process running (the default environment when working on a typical Linux distro). So, the obvious question here is: how do you see the kernel log buffer content? There are a few ways. For now, let's just make use of the quick and easy way.

Use the `dmesg(1)` utility! By default, `dmesg` will dump the entire kernel log buffer content to stdout. Here, we look up the last two lines of the kernel log buffer with it:

```
$ dmesg | tail -n2
[ 2912.880797] hello: loading out-of-tree module taints kernel.
[ 2912.881098] Hello, world
$
```

There it is, finally: our *Hello, world* message!

> You can simply ignore the `loading out-of-tree module taints kernel.` message for now. For security reasons, most modern Linux distros will mark the kernel as *tainted* (literally, "contaminated" or "polluted") if a third party "out-of-tree" (or non-signed) kernel module is inserted. (Well, it's really more of a pseudo-legal cover-up along the lines of: *"if something goes wrong from this point in time onward, we are not responsible, and so on..."*; you get the idea).

For a bit of variety, here is a screenshot of our *Hello, world* kernel module being inserted and removed (details follow) on an x86-64 CentOS 8 guest running the 5.4 Linux LTS kernel (that we custom-built as shown in detail in the first and second chapters):

```
$ lsb_release -a|grep Description
Description:    CentOS Linux release 8.0.1905 (Core)
$ uname -r
5.4.0-llkd01
$ ls
helloworld_lkm.c  Makefile
$ make
make -C /lib/modules/5.4.0-llkd01/build/ M=/home/llkd/bookwork/Learn-Linux-Kernel-Development/ch4/helloworld_lkm modules
make[1]: Entering directory '/home/llkd/bookwork/linux-5.4'
  CC [M]  /home/llkd/bookwork/Learn-Linux-Kernel-Development/ch4/helloworld_lkm/helloworld_lkm.o
  Building modules, stage 2.
  MODPOST 1 modules
  CC [M]  /home/llkd/bookwork/Learn-Linux-Kernel-Development/ch4/helloworld_lkm/helloworld_lkm.mod.o
  LD [M]  /home/llkd/bookwork/Learn-Linux-Kernel-Development/ch4/helloworld_lkm/helloworld_lkm.ko
make[1]: Leaving directory '/home/llkd/bookwork/linux-5.4'
$ ls -l ./helloworld_lkm.ko
-rw-rw-r-- 1 llkd llkd 202592 Nov 27 18:24 ./helloworld_lkm.ko
$ sudo insmod ./helloworld_lkm.ko
$ dmesg |tail -n1
[ 4731.967653] Hello, world
$ lsmod |grep helloworld_lkm
helloworld_lkm          16384  0
$ sudo rmmod helloworld_lkm
$ dmesg |tail -n2
[ 4731.967653] Hello, world
[ 4767.651584] Goodbye, world
$
```

Figure 4.6 – Screenshot showing our working with the *Hello, world* kernel module on a CentOS 8 x86-64 guest

Within the kernel log, as displayed by the `dmesg(1)` utility, the numbers in the leftmost column are a simple timestamp, in `[seconds.microseconds]` format, of time elapsed since system boot (it is not recommended to treat it as being perfectly accurate, though). By the way, this timestamp is a `Kconfig` variable – a kernel config option – named `CONFIG_PRINTK_TIME`; it can be overridden by the `printk.time` kernel parameter.

Listing the live kernel modules

Back to our kernel module: so far, we have built it, loaded it into the kernel, and verified that its entry point, the `helloworld_lkm_init()` function, got invoked, thus executing the `printk` API. So now, what does it do? Well, nothing really; the kernel module merely (happily?) sits in kernel memory doing absolutely nothing. We can in fact easily look it up with the `lsmod(8)` utility:

```
$ lsmod | head
Module                  Size  Used by
helloworld_lkm         16384  0
isofs                  32768  0
fuse                  139264  3
tun                    57344  0
[...]
e1000                 155648  0
dm_mirror              28672  0
dm_region_hash         20480  1 dm_mirror
dm_log                 20480  2 dm_region_hash,dm_mirror
dm_mod                151552  11 dm_log,dm_mirror
$
```

`lsmod` shows all kernel modules currently residing (or *live*) in kernel memory, sorted in reverse chronological order. Its output is column formatted, with three columns and an optional fourth one. Let's look at each column separately:

- The first column displays the *name* of the kernel module.
- The second column is the (static) *size* in bytes that it's taking in the kernel.
- The third column is the module *usage count*.
- The optional fourth column (and more that may follow) is explained in the next chapter (in the *Understanding module stacking* section. Also, on recent x86-64 Linux kernels, a minimum of 16 KB of kernel memory seems to be taken up by a kernel module.)

So, great: by now you've successfully built, loaded and run your first kernel module into kernel memory and it basically works: what next? Well, nothing much really with this one! We simply learn how to unload it in the following section. There's a lot more to come of course... keep going!

Unloading the module from kernel memory

To unload the kernel module, we use the convenience utility `rmmod(8)` (*remove module*):

```
$ rmmod
rmmod: ERROR: missing module name.
$ rmmod helloworld_lkm
rmmod: ERROR: could not remove 'helloworld_lkm': Operation not
permitted
rmmod: ERROR: could not remove module helloworld_lkm: Operation not
permitted
$ sudo rmmod helloworld_lkm
[sudo] password for llkd:
$ dmesg |tail -n2
[ 2912.881098] Hello, world
[ 5551.863410] Goodbye, world
$
```

The parameter to `rmmod(8)` is the *name* of the kernel module (as shown in the first column of `lsmod(8)`), not the pathname. Clearly, just as with `insmod(8)`, we need to run the `rmmod(8)` utility as the *root* user for it to succeed.

Here, we can also see that, because of our `rmmod`, the exit routine (or "destructor") `helloworld_lkm_exit()` function of the kernel module got invoked. It in turn invoked `printk`, which emitted the *Goodbye, world* message (which we looked up with `dmesg`).

When could `rmmod` (note that internally, it becomes the `delete_module(2)` system call) *fail*? Here are some cases:

- **Permissions**: If it is not run as root or there is a lack of the `CAP_SYS_MODULE` capability (`errno <- EPERM`).
- If the kernel module's code and/or data is being used by another module (if a dependency exists; this is covered in detail in the next chapter's *Module stacking* section) or the module is currently in use by a process (or thread), then the module usage count will be positive and `rmmod` will fail (`errno <- EBUSY`).
- The kernel module did not specify an exit routine (or destructor) with the `module_exit()` macro *and* the `CONFIG_MODULE_FORCE_UNLOAD` kernel config option is disabled.

Several convenience utilities concerned with module management are nothing but symbolic (soft) links to the single kmod(8) utility (analogous to what the popular *busybox* utility does). The wrappers are lsmod(8), rmmod(8), insmod(8), modinfo(8), modprobe(8), and depmod(8). Take a look at a few of them:

```
$ ls -l $(which insmod) ; ls -l $(which lsmod) ; ls -l $(which rmmod)
lrwxrwxrwx 1 root root 9 Oct 24 04:50 /sbin/insmod -> /bin/kmod
lrwxrwxrwx 1 root root 9 Oct 24 04:50 /sbin/lsmod -> /bin/kmod
lrwxrwxrwx 1 root root 9 Oct 24 04:50 /sbin/rmmod -> /bin/kmod
$
```

Note that the precise location of these utilities (/bin, /sbin, or /usr/sbin) can vary with the distribution.

Our lkm convenience script

Let's round off this *first kernel module* discussion with a simple yet useful custom Bash script called lkm that helps you out by automating the kernel module build, load, dmesg, and unload workflow. Here it is (the complete code is in the root of the book source tree):

```
#!/bin/bash
# lkm : a silly kernel module dev - build, load, unload - helper
wrapper script
[...]
unset ARCH
unset CROSS_COMPILE
name=$(basename "${0}")

# Display and run the provided command.
# Parameter(s) : the command to run
runcmd()
{
    local SEP="-------------------------------"
    [ $# -eq 0 ] && return
    echo "${SEP}
$*
${SEP}"
    eval "$@"
    [ $? -ne 0 ] && echo " ^--[FAILED]"
}

### "main" here
[ $# -ne 1 ] && {
  echo "Usage: ${name} name-of-kernel-module-file (without the .c)"
```

Writing Your First Kernel Module - LKMs Part 1

```
    exit 1
}
[[ "${1}" = *"."* ]] && {
  echo "Usage: ${name} name-of-kernel-module-file ONLY (do NOT put any extension)."
  exit 1
}
echo "Version info:"
which lsb_release >/dev/null 2>&1 && {
  echo -n "Distro: "
  lsb_release -a 2>/dev/null |grep "Description" |awk -F':' '{print $2}'
}
echo -n "Kernel: " ; uname -r
runcmd "sudo rmmod $1 2> /dev/null"
runcmd "make clean"
runcmd "sudo dmesg -c > /dev/null"
runcmd "make || exit 1"
[ ! -f "$1".ko ] && {
  echo "[!] ${name}: $1.ko has not been built, aborting..."
  exit 1
}
runcmd "sudo insmod ./$1.ko && lsmod|grep $1"
runcmd dmesg
exit 0
```

Given the name of the kernel module as a parameter – without any extension part (such as `.c`) – the `lkm` script performs some validity checks, displays some version information, and then uses a wrapper `runcmd()` bash function to display the name of and run a given command, in effect getting the `clean/build/load/lsmod/dmesg` workflow done painlessly. Let's try it out on our first kernel module:

```
$ pwd
<...>/ch4/helloworld_lkm
$ ../../lkm
Usage: lkm name-of-kernel-module-file (without the .c)
$ ../../lkm helloworld_lkm
Version info:
Distro:         Ubuntu 18.04.3 LTS
Kernel: 5.0.0-36-generic
------------------------------
sudo rmmod helloworld_lkm 2> /dev/null
------------------------------
[sudo] password for llkd:
------------------------------
sudo dmesg -C
------------------------------
```

Chapter 4

```
---------------------------------
make || exit 1
---------------------------------
make -C /lib/modules/5.0.0-36-generic/build/
M=/home/llkd/book_llkd/Learn-Linux-Kernel-
Development/ch4/helloworld_lkm modules
make[1]: Entering directory '/usr/src/linux-headers-5.0.0-36-generic'
  CC [M]  /home/llkd/book_llkd/Learn-Linux-Kernel-
Development/ch4/helloworld_lkm/helloworld_lkm.o
  Building modules, stage 2.
  MODPOST 1 modules
  CC      /home/llkd/book_llkd/Learn-Linux-Kernel-
Development/ch4/helloworld_lkm/helloworld_lkm.mod.o
  LD [M]  /home/llkd/book_llkd/Learn-Linux-Kernel-
Development/ch4/helloworld_lkm/helloworld_lkm.ko
make[1]: Leaving directory '/usr/src/linux-headers-5.0.0-36-generic'
---------------------------------
sudo insmod ./helloworld_lkm.ko && lsmod|grep helloworld_lkm
---------------------------------
helloworld_lkm         16384  0
---------------------------------
dmesg
---------------------------------
[ 8132.596795] Hello, world
$
```

All done! Remember to unload the kernel module with `rmmod(8)`.

Congratulations! You have now learned how to write and try out a simple *Hello, world* kernel module. Much work remains, though, before you rest on your laurels; the next section delves into more key details regarding kernel logging and the versatile printk API.

Understanding kernel logging and printk

There is still a lot to cover regarding the logging of kernel messages via the printk kernel API. This section delves into some of the details. It's important for a budding kernel developer like you to clearly understand these.

In this section, we delve into more detail regarding kernel logging. We come to understand how exactly printk output is dealt with, looking at its pros and cons. We discuss the printk log levels, how modern systems log messages via the systemd journal, and how output can be directed to the console device. We round off this discussion with a note on rate-limiting printk and user-generated prints, generating printk's from user space and standardizing the printk output format.

We saw earlier, in the *A quick first look at the kernel printk* section, the essentials of using the kernel printk API's functionality. Here, we explore a lot more with respect to the `printk()` API's usage. In our simple kernel module, here's the line of code that emits the "*Hello, world*" message:

```
printk(KERN_INFO "Hello, world\n");
```

Again, `printk` is similar to `printf` in terms of the *format string* and how that works – but the similarities end there. For emphasis, we repeat: a key difference between `printf` and `printk` is that `printf(3)` is a *user space library* API that works by invoking the `write(2)` system call, which writes to the *stdout device,* which by default is usually the Terminal window (or console device). The printk, on the other hand, is a *kernel space* API whose output instead goes to at least one place, the first one shown in the list below, and possibly to more places:

- A kernel log buffer (in RAM; volatile)
- A kernel log file (non-volatile)
- The console device

Let's examine the kernel log buffer in more detail.

Using the kernel memory ring buffer

The kernel log buffer is simply a memory buffer within a kernel address space where the printk output is saved (logged). More technically, it's the global `__log_buf[]` variable. Its definition in the kernel source is as follows:

```
kernel/printk/printk.c:
#define __LOG_BUF_LEN (1 << CONFIG_LOG_BUF_SHIFT)
static char __log_buf[__LOG_BUF_LEN] __aligned(LOG_ALIGN);
```

It's architected as a *ring buffer*; it has a finite size (`__LOG_BUF_LEN` bytes), and once it's full, it gets overwritten from byte zero. Hence, it's called a "ring" or circular, buffer). Here, we can see that the size is based on the `Kconfig` variable `CONFIG_LOG_BUF_SHIFT` (`1 << n` in C implies `2^n`). This value is shown and can be overridden as part of the kernel `(menu)config` here: `General Setup > Kernel log buffer size`.

It's an integer value with a range of `12 - 25` (we can always search `init/Kconfig` and see its spec), with a default value of `18`. So, the size of the log buffer = 2^{18} = 256 KB. However, the actual runtime size is affected by other config directives as well, notably `LOG_CPU_MAX_BUF_SHIFT`, which makes the size a function of the number of CPUs on the system. Furthermore, the relevant `Kconfig` file says, *"Also this option is ignored when the log_buf_len kernel parameter is used as it forces an exact (power of two) size of the ring buffer."* So, that's interesting; we can often override defaults by passing a *kernel parameter* (via the bootloader)!

Kernel parameters are useful, many, and varied, and are well worth checking out. See the official documentation here: `https://www.kernel.org/doc/html/latest/admin-guide/kernel-parameters.html`. A snippet from the Linux kernel documentation on the `log_buf_len` kernel parameter reveals the details:

```
    log_buf_len=n[KMG]      Sets the size of the printk ring buffer,
                            in bytes. n must be a power of two and greater
                            than the minimal size. The minimal size is
    defined
                            by LOG_BUF_SHIFT kernel config parameter. There
    is
                            also CONFIG_LOG_CPU_MAX_BUF_SHIFT config
    parameter
                            that allows to increase the default size
    depending
                            on the number of CPUs. See init/Kconfig for more
                            details.
```

Whatever the size of the kernel log buffer, two issues when dealing with the printk API become obvious:

- Its messages are being logged in *volatile* memory (RAM); if the system crashes or power cycles in any manner, we will lose the precious kernel log (often eliminating our ability to debug).
- The log buffer isn't very large by default, typically just 256 KB; voluminous prints will overwhelm the ring buffer, making it wrap around, thus losing information.

How can we fix this? Read on...

Kernel logging and systemd's journalctl

An obvious solution to the previously mentioned issues is to write (append) the kernel printk to a file. This is precisely how most modern Linux distributions are set up. The location of the log file varies with the distro: conventionally, the Red Hat-based ones write into the `/var/log/messages` file and the Debian-based ones into `/var/log/syslog`. Traditionally, the kernel printk would hook into the user space *system logger daemon* (`syslogd`) to perform file logging, thus automatically getting the benefit of more sophisticated features, such as log rotation, compression, and archival.

Over the past several years, though, system logging has been completely taken over by a useful and powerful new framework for system initialization called **systemd** (it replaces, or often works in addition to, the old SysV init framework). Indeed, systemd is now routinely used on even embedded Linux devices. Within the systemd framework, logging is performed by a daemon process called `systemd-journal`, and the `journalctl(1)` utility is the user interface to it.

> The detailed coverage of systemd and its associated utilities is beyond the scope of this book. Please refer to the *Further reading* section of this chapter for links to (a lot) more on it.

One key advantage of using the journal to retrieve and interpret logs is that **all logs** from applications, libraries, system daemons, the kernel, drivers, and so on are written (merged) here. This way, we can see a (reverse) chronological timeline of events without having to manually piece together different logs into a timeline. The man page on the `journalctl(1)` utility covers its various options in detail. Here, we present some (hopefully) convenient aliases based on this utility:

```
#--- a few journalctl(1) aliases
# jlog: current (from most recent) boot only, everything
alias jlog='/bin/journalctl -b --all --catalog --no-pager'
# jlogr: current (from most recent) boot only, everything,
#   in *reverse* chronological order
alias jlogr='/bin/journalctl -b --all --catalog --no-pager --reverse'
# jlogall: *everything*, all time; --merge => _all_ logs merged
alias jlogall='/bin/journalctl --all --catalog --merge --no-pager'
# jlogf: *watch* log, akin to 'tail -f' mode;
#   very useful to 'watch live' logs
alias jlogf='/bin/journalctl -f'
```

```
# jlogk: only kernel messages, this (from most recent) boot
alias jlogk='/bin/journalctl -b -k --no-pager'
```

> Note that the -b option current boot implies that the journal is displayed from the most recent system boot date at the present moment. A numbered listing of stored system (re)boots can be seen with `journalctl --list-boots`.

We deliberately use the `--no-pager` option as it allows us to further filter the output with `[e]grep(1)`, `awk(1)`, `sort(1)`, and so on, as required. A simple example of using `journalctl(1)` follows:

```
$ journalctl -k |tail -n2
Mar 17 17:33:16 llkd-vbox kernel: Hello, world
Mar 17 17:47:26 llkd-vbox kernel: Goodbye, world
$
```

Notice the default log format of the journal:

```
[timestamp] [hostname] [source]: [... log message ...]
```

Here `[source]` is `kernel` for kernel messages, or the name of the particular application or service that writes the message.

It's useful to see a couple of usage examples from the man page on `journalctl(1)`:

```
Show all kernel logs from previous boot:
    journalctl -k -b -1

Show a live log display from a system service apache.service:
    journalctl -f -u apache
```

The non-volatile logging of kernel messages into files is very useful, of course. Note, though, that there exist circumstances, often dictated by hardware constraints, that might render it impossible. For example, a tiny, highly resource-constrained embedded Linux device might use a small internal flash chip as its storage medium. Now, not only is it small and all the space is pretty much used up by the apps, libraries, kernel, and bootloader, it is also a fact that flash-based chips have an effective limit on the number of erase-write cycles they can sustain before wearing out. Thus, writing to it a few million times might finish it off! So, sometimes, system designers deliberately and/or additionally use cheaper external flash memory such as (micro)SD/MMC cards (for non-critical data) to mitigate this impact, as they're easily replaceable.

Let's move on to understanding printk log levels.

Using printk log levels

To understand and use printk log levels, let's begin by reproducing that single line of code – the first printk from our `helloworld_lkm` kernel module:

```
printk(KERN_INFO "Hello, world\n");
```

Let's now address the elephant in the room: what exactly does `KERN_INFO` mean? Firstly, be careful now: it's *not* what your knee-jerk reaction says it is – a parameter. No! Notice that there is no comma character between it and the format string; just white space. `KERN_INFO` is merely one of **eight log levels** that a kernel printk gets logged at. A key thing to understand right away is that this log level is *not* a priority of any sort; its presence allows us *to filter messages* based on log level. The kernel defines eight possible log levels for printk; here they are:

```
// include/linux/kern_levels.h
#ifndef __KERN_LEVELS_H__
#define __KERN_LEVELS_H__

#define KERN_SOH        "\001"          /* ASCII Start Of Header */
#define KERN_SOH_ASCII  '\001'

#define KERN_EMERG      KERN_SOH "0"    /* system is unusable */
#define KERN_ALERT      KERN_SOH "1"    /* action must be taken
                                           immediately */
#define KERN_CRIT       KERN_SOH "2"    /* critical conditions */
#define KERN_ERR        KERN_SOH "3"    /* error conditions */
#define KERN_WARNING    KERN_SOH "4"    /* warning conditions */
#define KERN_NOTICE     KERN_SOH "5"    /* normal but significant
                                           condition */
#define KERN_INFO       KERN_SOH "6"    /* informational */
#define KERN_DEBUG      KERN_SOH "7"    /* debug-level messages */

#define KERN_DEFAULT    KERN_SOH "d"    /* the default kernel
loglevel */
```

So, now we see that the `KERN_<FOO>` log levels are merely strings (`"0"`, `"1"`, ..., `"7"`) that get prefixed to the kernel message being emitted by printk; nothing more. This gives us the useful ability to filter messages based on log level. The comment on the right of each of them clearly shows the developer when to use which log level.

> What's `KERN_SOH`? That's the ASCII **Start Of Header (SOH)** value `\001`. See the man page on `ascii(7)`; the `ascii(1)` utility dumps the ASCII table in various numerical bases. From here, we can clearly see that numeric 1 (or `\001`) is the `SOH` character, a convention that is followed here.

Let's quickly look at a couple of actual examples from within the Linux kernel source tree. When the kernel's `hangcheck-timer` device driver (somewhat akin to a software watchdog) determines that a certain timer expiry (60 seconds by default) was delayed for over a certain threshold (by default, 180 seconds), it restarts the system! Here we show the relevant kernel code – the place where the `hangcheck-timer` driver emits printk in this regard:

```
// drivers/char/hangcheck-timer.c
[...]
if (hangcheck_reboot) {
  printk(KERN_CRIT "Hangcheck: hangcheck is restarting the machine.\n");
  emergency_restart();
} else {
[...]
```

Check out how the printk API was called with log level set to `KERN_CRIT`.

On the other hand, squeaking out an informational message might be just what the doctor ordered: here, we see the generic parallel printer driver politely informing all concerned that the printer is on fire (rather understated, yes?):

```
// drivers/char/lp.c
[...]
  if (last != LP_PERRORP) {
      last = LP_PERRORP;
      printk(KERN_INFO "lp%d on fire\n", minor);
  }
```

You'd think a device being on fire will qualify the printk to be emitted at the "emergency" logging level... well, at least the `arch/x86/kernel/cpu/mce/p5.c:pentium_machine_check()` function adheres to this:

```
// arch/x86/kernel/cpu/mce/p5.c
[...]
    pr_emerg("CPU#%d: Machine Check Exception: 0x%8X (type 0x%8X).\n",
        smp_processor_id(), loaddr, lotype);

    if (lotype & (1<<5)) {
```

Writing Your First Kernel Module - LKMs Part 1

```
            pr_emerg("CPU#%d: Possible thermal failure (CPU on fire
?).\n",
                smp_processor_id());
        }
[...]
```

(The `pr_<foo>()` convenience macros are covered next).

An FAQ: if, within the `printk()`, the log level is *not* specified, what log level is the print emitted at? It's 4 by default, that is, `KERN_WARNING` (the *Writing to the console* section reveals why exactly this is). Note, though, that you are expected to always specify a suitable log level when using printk.

There's an easy way to specify the kernel message log level. This is what we delve into next.

The pr_<foo> convenience macros

The convenience `pr_<foo>()` macros given here ease coding pain. The clunky `printk(KERN_FOO "<format-str>");` is replaced with the elegant `pr_foo("<format-str>");`, where `<foo>` is the log level; their use is encouraged:

```
// include/linux/printk.h:
[...]
/*
 * These can be used to print at the various log levels.
 * All of these will print unconditionally, although note that pr_debug()
 * and other debug macros are compiled out unless either DEBUG is defined
 * or CONFIG_DYNAMIC_DEBUG is set.
 */
#define pr_emerg(fmt, ...) \
        printk(KERN_EMERG pr_fmt(fmt), ##__VA_ARGS__)
#define pr_alert(fmt, ...) \
        printk(KERN_ALERT pr_fmt(fmt), ##__VA_ARGS__)
#define pr_crit(fmt, ...) \
        printk(KERN_CRIT pr_fmt(fmt), ##__VA_ARGS__)
#define pr_err(fmt, ...) \
        printk(KERN_ERR pr_fmt(fmt), ##__VA_ARGS__)
#define pr_warning(fmt, ...) \
        printk(KERN_WARNING pr_fmt(fmt), ##__VA_ARGS__)
#define pr_warn pr_warning
#define pr_notice(fmt, ...) \
        printk(KERN_NOTICE pr_fmt(fmt), ##__VA_ARGS__)
#define pr_info(fmt, ...) \
```

```
            printk(KERN_INFO pr_fmt(fmt), ##__VA_ARGS__)
[...]
/* pr_devel() should produce zero code unless DEBUG is defined */
#ifdef DEBUG
#define pr_devel(fmt, ...) \
    printk(KERN_DEBUG pr_fmt(fmt), ##__VA_ARGS__)
#else
#define pr_devel(fmt, ...) \
    no_printk(KERN_DEBUG pr_fmt(fmt), ##__VA_ARGS__)
#endif
```

> **TIP**
> The kernel allows us to pass `loglevel=n` as a kernel command-line parameter, where n is an integer between 0 and 7, corresponding to the eight log levels mentioned previously. As expected (as you shall soon learn), all printk instances with a log level less than that which was passed will be directed to the console device as well.

Writing a kernel message directly to the console device is at times very useful; the next section deals with the details on how we can achieve this.

Wiring to the console

Recall that the printk output might go to up to three locations:

- The first being the kernel memory log buffer (always)
- The second being non-volatile log files
- The last one (that we'll address here): the *console device*

Traditionally, the console device is a pure kernel feature, the initial Terminal window that the superuser logs into (`/dev/console`) in a non-graphical environment. Interestingly, on Linux, we can define several consoles – a **teletype terminal** (**tty**) window (such as `/dev/console`), a text-mode VGA, a framebuffer, or even a serial port served over USB (this being common on embedded systems during development; see more on Linux consoles in the *Further reading* section of this chapter).

Writing Your First Kernel Module - LKMs Part 1

For example, when we connect a Raspberry Pi to an x86-64 laptop via a USB-to-RS232 TTL UART (USB-to-serial) cable (see the *Further reading* section of this chapter for a blog article on this very useful accessory and how to set it up on the Raspberry Pi!) and then use `minicom(1)` (or `screen(1)`) to get a serial console, this is what shows up as the `tty` device – it's the serial port:

```
rpi # tty
/dev/ttyS0
```

The point here is that the console is often the target of *important-enough* log messages, including those originating from deep within the kernel. Linux's printk uses a `proc`-based mechanism for conditionally delivering its data to the console device. To understand this better, let's first check out the relevant `proc` pseudo-file:

```
$ cat /proc/sys/kernel/printk
4       4       1       7
$
```

We interpret the preceding four numbers as printk log levels (with 0 being the highest and 7 the lowest in terms of "urgency"). The preceding four-integer sequence's meaning is this:

- The current (console) log level
  - *The implication being that all messages less than this value will appear on the console device!*
- The default level for messages that lack an explicit log level
- The minimum allowed log level
- The boot-time default log level

From this, we can see that log level 4 corresponds to `KERN_WARNING`. Thus, with the first number being 4 (indeed, the typical default on a Linux distro), *all printk instances lower than log level 4 will appear on the console device,* as well as being logged to a file, of course – in effect, all messages at the following log levels: `KERN_EMERG`, `KERN_ALERT`, `KERN_CRIT`, and `KERN_ERR`.

> Kernel messages at log level 0 `[KERN_EMERG]` are *always* printed to the console, and indeed to all Terminal windows and the kernel log file, regardless of any settings.

Chapter 4

It's worth noting that very often, when working on embedded Linux or any kernel development, you will work *on* the console device, as is the case with the Raspberry Pi example just given. Setting the `proc printk` pseudo-file's first integer value to 8 will *guarantee that all printk instances appear directly on the console,* **thus making printk behave like a regular printf would!** Here, we show how the root user can easily set this up:

```
# echo "8 4 1 7" > /proc/sys/kernel/printk
```

(Of course, this would have to be done as root.) This can be very convenient during development and test.

> **TIP**
> On my Raspberry Pi, I keep a startup script that contains the following line:
> `[ $(id -u) -eq 0 ] && echo "8 4 1 7" > /proc/sys/kernel/printk`
> Thus, when running it as root, this takes effect and all printk instances now directly appear on the `minicom(1)` console, just as `printf` would.

Talking about the versatile Raspberry Pi, the next section demonstrates running a kernel module on one.

Writing output to the Raspberry Pi console

On to our second kernel module! Here, we shall emit nine printk instances, one at each of the eight log levels, plus one via the `pr_devel()` macro (which is really nothing but the `KERN_DEBUG` log level). Let's check out the relevant code:

```c
// ch4/printk_loglvl/printk_loglvl.c
static int __init printk_loglvl_init(void)
{
    pr_emerg ("Hello, world @ log-level KERN_EMERG    [0]\n");
    pr_alert ("Hello, world @ log-level KERN_ALERT    [1]\n");
    pr_crit  ("Hello, world @ log-level KERN_CRIT     [2]\n");
    pr_err   ("Hello, world @ log-level KERN_ERR      [3]\n");
    pr_warn  ("Hello, world @ log-level KERN_WARNING  [4]\n");
    pr_notice("Hello, world @ log-level KERN_NOTICE   [5]\n");
    pr_info  ("Hello, world @ log-level KERN_INFO     [6]\n");
    pr_debug ("Hello, world @ log-level KERN_DEBUG    [7]\n");
    pr_devel("Hello, world via the pr_devel() macro"
        " (eff @KERN_DEBUG) [7]\n");
    return 0; /* success */
}
```

Writing Your First Kernel Module - LKMs Part 1

```
static void __exit printk_loglvl_exit(void)
{
    pr_info("Goodbye, world @ log-level KERN_INFO [6]\n");
}
module_init(printk_loglvl_init);
module_exit(printk_loglvl_exit);
```

> Now, we will discuss the output when running the preceding `printk_loglvl` kernel module on a Raspberry Pi device. If you don't possess one or it's not handy, that's not a problem; please go ahead and try it out on an x86-64 guest VM.

On the Raspberry Pi device (here I used the Raspberry Pi 3B+ model running the default Raspberry Pi OS), we log in and get ourselves a root shell via a simple `sudo -s`. We then build the kernel module. If you have installed the default Raspberry Pi image on the Raspberry Pi, all required development tools, kernel headers, and more will be pre-installed! Figure 4.7 is a screenshot of running our `printk_loglvl` kernel module on a Raspberry Pi board. Also, it's important to realize that we're running **on the console device** as we are using the aforementioned USB-to-serial cable over the `minicom(1)` Terminal emulator app (and *not* simply over an SSH connection):

```
rpi #
rpi # cat /proc/sys/kernel/printk
3       4       1       3
rpi #
rpi # insmod ./printk_loglvl.ko
[  257.712077] Hello, world @ log-level KERN_EMERG   [0]
[  257.719735] Hello, world @ log-level KERN_ALERT   [1]
[  257.727371] Hello, world @ log-level KERN_CRIT    [2]
rpi #
Message from syslogd@raspberrypi at Dec 17 05:36:01 ...
 kernel:[  257.712077] Hello, world @ log-level KERN_EMERG   [0]

CTRL-A Z for help | 115200 8N1 | NOR | Minicom 2.7.1 | VT102 | Online 3:5 | ttyUSB0
```

Figure 4.7 – The minicom Terminal emulator app window – the console – with the printk_loglvl kernel module output

Notice something a bit different from the x86-64 environment: here, by default, the first integer in the output of `/proc/sys/kernel/printk` – the current console log level – is 3 (not 4). Okay, so this implies that all kernel printk instances at log level *less than log level 3* will appear directly on the console device. Look at the screenshot: this is indeed the case! Furthermore, and as expected, the printk instance at the "emergency" log level (0) always appears on the console, indeed on every open Terminal window.

Now for the interesting part: let's set (as root, of course) the current console log level (remember, it's the first integer in the output of /proc/sys/kernel/printk) to the value 8. This way, all printk instances should appear directly on the console. We test precisely this here:

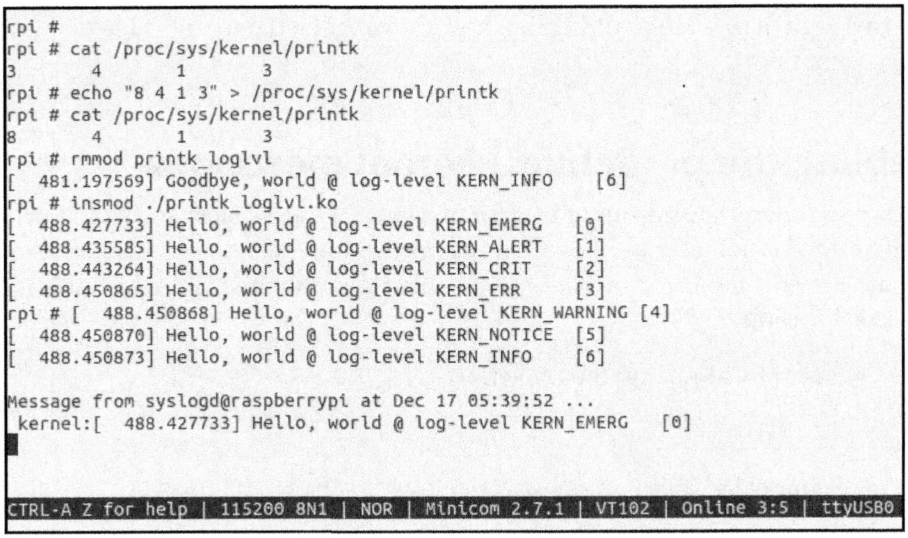

```
rpi #
rpi # cat /proc/sys/kernel/printk
3       4       1       3
rpi # echo "8 4 1 3" > /proc/sys/kernel/printk
rpi # cat /proc/sys/kernel/printk
8       4       1       3
rpi # rmmod printk_loglvl
[  481.197569] Goodbye, world @ log-level KERN_INFO      [6]
rpi # insmod ./printk_loglvl.ko
[  488.427733] Hello, world @ log-level KERN_EMERG      [0]
[  488.435585] Hello, world @ log-level KERN_ALERT      [1]
[  488.443264] Hello, world @ log-level KERN_CRIT       [2]
[  488.450865] Hello, world @ log-level KERN_ERR        [3]
rpi # [  488.450868] Hello, world @ log-level KERN_WARNING [4]
[  488.450870] Hello, world @ log-level KERN_NOTICE     [5]
[  488.450873] Hello, world @ log-level KERN_INFO       [6]

Message from syslogd@raspberrypi at Dec 17 05:39:52 ...
 kernel:[  488.427733] Hello, world @ log-level KERN_EMERG      [0]


CTRL-A Z for help | 115200 8N1 | NOR | Minicom 2.7.1 | VT102 | Online 3:5 | ttyUSB0
```

Figure 4.8 – The minicom Terminal – in effect, the console – window, with the console log level set to 8

Indeed, as expected, we see *all* the printk instances on the console device itself obviating the need to use dmesg.

Hang on a moment, though: whatever happened to the pr_debug() and pr_devel() macros emitting a kernel message at log level KERN_DEBUG (that is, integer value 7)? It has *not* appeared here, nor in the following dmesg output? We explain this shortly; please read on.

With dmesg(1), of course, all kernel messages – well, at least those still in the kernel log buffer in RAM – will be revealed. We see this to be the case here:

```
rpi # rmmod printk_loglvl
rpi # dmesg
[...]
[ 1408.603812] Hello, world @ log-level KERN_EMERG      [0]
[ 1408.611335] Hello, world @ log-level KERN_ALERT      [1]
[ 1408.618625] Hello, world @ log-level KERN_CRIT       [2]
[ 1408.625778] Hello, world @ log-level KERN_ERR        [3]
[ 1408.625781] Hello, world @ log-level KERN_WARNING    [4]
```

```
[ 1408.625784] Hello, world @ log-level KERN_NOTICE   [5]
[ 1408.625787] Hello, world @ log-level KERN_INFO     [6]
[ 1762.985496] Goodbye, world @ log-level KERN_INFO   [6]
rpi #
```

All printk's instances – except the `KERN_DEBUG` ones – are seen as we are looking at the kernel log via the `dmesg` utility. So, how do we get a debug message displayed? That's covered next.

Enabling the pr_debug() kernel messages

Ah yes, `pr_debug()` turns out to be a bit of a special case: unless the `DEBUG` symbol is *defined* for the kernel module, a `printk` instance at log level `KERN_DEBUG` does not show up. We edit the kernel module's Makefile to enable this. There are (at least) two ways to set this up:

- Insert this line into the Makefile:

  `CFLAGS_printk_loglvl.o := -DDEBUG`

  Generically, it's `CFLAGS_<filename>.o := -DDEBUG`.

- We could also just insert this statement into the Makefile:

  `EXTRA_CFLAGS += -DDEBUG`

In our Makefile, we have deliberately kept the `-DDEBUG` commented out, to begin with. Now, to try it out, un-comment one of the following commented-out lines:

```
# Enable the pr_debug() as well (rm the comment from one of the lines
below)
#EXTRA_CFLAGS += -DDEBUG
#CFLAGS_printk_loglvl.o := -DDEBUG
```

Once done, we remove the old stale kernel module from memory, rebuild it, and insert it using our `lkm` script. The output reveals that `pr_debug()` now does take effect:

```
# exit                         << exit from the previous root shell >>
$ ../../lkm printk_loglvl
Version info:
Distro:      Ubuntu 18.04.3 LTS
Kernel: 5.4.0-llkd01
------------------------------
sudo rmmod printk_loglvl 2> /dev/null
------------------------------
```

Chapter 4

```
[...]
sudo insmod ./printk_loglvl.ko && lsmod|grep printk_loglvl
-----------------------------
printk_loglvl             16384   0
-----------------------------
dmesg
-----------------------------
[  975.271766] Hello, world @ log-level KERN_EMERG [0]
[  975.277729] Hello, world @ log-level KERN_ALERT [1]
[  975.283662] Hello, world @ log-level KERN_CRIT [2]
[  975.289561] Hello, world @ log-level KERN_ERR [3]
[  975.295394] Hello, world @ log-level KERN_WARNING [4]
[  975.301176] Hello, world @ log-level KERN_NOTICE [5]
[  975.306907] Hello, world @ log-level KERN_INFO [6]
[  975.312625] Hello, world @ log-level KERN_DEBUG [7]
[  975.312628] Hello, world via the pr_devel() macro (eff @KERN_DEBUG)
[7]
$
```

A partial screenshot (Figure 4.9) of the `lkm` script's output clearly reveals the `dmesg` color-coding, with KERN_ALERT / KERN_CRIT / KERN_ERR background highlighted in red/in bold red typeface/in red foreground color, respectively, and KERN_WARNING in bold black typeface, helping us humans quickly spot important kernel messages:

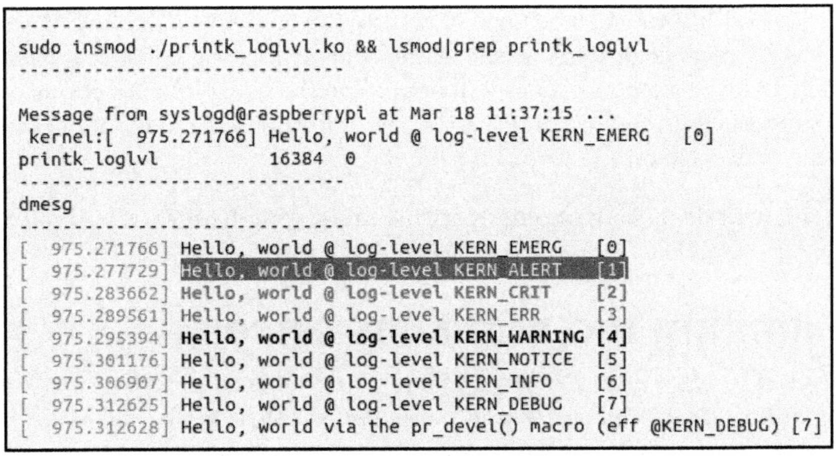

Figure 4.9 – Partial screenshot of lkm script's output

Note that the behavior of `pr_debug()` is not identical when the dynamic debug feature (`CONFIG_DYNAMIC_DEBUG=y`) is enabled.

> **TIP**: Device driver authors should note that for the purpose of emitting debug `printk` instances, they should avoid using `pr_debug()`. Instead, it is recommended that a device driver uses the `dev_dbg()` macro (additionally passing along a parameter to the device in question). Also, `pr_devel()` is meant to be used for kernel-internal debug `printk` instances whose output should never be visible in production systems.

Now, back to the section on console output. So, for perhaps the purpose of kernel debugging (if nothing else), is there a guaranteed way to ensure that *all* printk instances are directed to the console? Yes, indeed – just pass the kernel (boot-time) parameter called `ignore_level`. For more details on this, do look up the description in the official kernel documentation: https://www.kernel.org/doc/html/latest/admin-guide/kernel-parameters.html. Toggling the ignoring of the printk log level is also possible: as mentioned there, you can turn on the ignoring of printk log levels by doing this, thus allowing all printk's to appear on the console device (and conversely, turn it off by echoing N into the same pseudo-file):

```
sudo bash -c "echo Y > /sys/module/printk/parameters/ignore_loglevel"
```

The `dmesg(1)` utility can also be used to control the enabling/disabling of kernel messages to the console device, as well as the console logging level (that is, the level numerically below which messages will appear on the console) via various option switches (in particular, the `--console-level` option). I leave it to you to browse through the man page on `dmesg(1)` for the details.

The next segment deals with another very useful logging feature: rate-limiting.

Rate limiting the printk instances

When we emit `printk` instances from a code path that is executed very often, the sheer amount of `printk` instances might quickly overflow the kernel log buffer (in RAM; remember that it's a circular buffer), thus overwriting what might well be key information. Besides that, ever-growing non-volatile log files that then repeat pretty much the same `printk` instances (almost) ad infinitum are not a great idea either and waste disk space, or worse, flash space. For example, think of a large-ish printk in an interrupt handler code path. What if the hardware interrupt is invoked at a frequency of, say, 100 Hz, that is, 100 times every single second!

To mitigate these issues, the kernel provides an interesting alternative: the *rate-limited* printk. The `printk_ratelimited()` macro has identical syntax to the regular printk; the key point is that it effectively *suppresses* regular prints when certain conditions are fulfilled. The kernel provides two control files named `printk_ratelimit` and `printk_ratelimit_burst` via the `proc` filesystem for this purpose. Here, we directly reproduce the `sysctl` documentation (from https://www.kernel.org/doc/Documentation/sysctl/kernel.txt) that explains the precise meaning of these two (pseudo) files:

```
printk_ratelimit:
Some warning messages are rate limited. printk_ratelimit specifies
the minimum length of time between these messages (in jiffies), by
default we allow one every 5 seconds.
A value of 0 will disable rate limiting.
==============================================================
printk_ratelimit_burst:
While long term we enforce one message per printk_ratelimit
seconds, we do allow a burst of messages to pass through.
printk_ratelimit_burst specifies the number of messages we can
send before ratelimiting kicks in.
```

On our Ubuntu 18.04.3 LTS guest system, we find that their (default) values are as follows:

```
$ cat /proc/sys/kernel/printk_ratelimit
/proc/sys/kernel/printk_ratelimit_burst
5
10
$
```

This implies that by default, up to 10 instances of the same message occurring within a 5-second time interval can make it through before rate limiting kicks in.

The printk rate limiter, when it does suppress kernel `printk` instances, emits a helpful message mentioning exactly how many earlier printk callbacks were suppressed. As an example, we have a custom kernel module that makes use of the `Kprobes` framework to emit a `printk` instance prior to every call to `schedule()`, the kernel's core scheduling routine.

> A **kprobe** is essentially an instrumentation framework often leveraged for production system troubleshooting; using it, you can specify a function that can be set to execute before or after a given kernel routine. The details are beyond the scope of this book.

Now, as scheduling occurs often, a regular printk would cause the kernel log buffer to quickly overflow. Precisely this sort of situation warrants the use of the rate-limited printk. Here, we see some sample output from our example kernel module (we don't show it's code here) using the `printk_ratelimited()` API via a `kprobe` that sets up a *pre-handler* function called `handle_pre_schedule()`:

```
[ 1000.154763] kprobe schedule pre_handler: intr ctx = 0 :process systemd-journal:237
[ 1005.162183] handler_pre_schedule: 5860 callbacks suppressed
[ 1005.162185] kprobe schedule pre_handler: intr ctx = 0 :process dndX11:1071
```

A code-level example of using the rate-limited printk is seen in the interrupt handler code of the Linux kernel's **Real-Time Clock (RTC)** driver here: `drivers/char/rtc.c`:

```
static void rtc_dropped_irq(struct timer_list *unused)
{
[...]
    spin_unlock_irq(&rtc_lock);
    printk_ratelimited(KERN_WARNING "rtc: lost some interrupts at %ldHz.\n", freq);
    /* Now we have new data */
    wake_up_interruptible(&rtc_wait);
[...]
}
```

> **TIP**: Don't mix up the `printk_ratelimited()` macro with the older (and now deprecated) `printk_ratelimit()` macro. Also, the actual rate-limiting code is in `lib/ratelimit.c:___ratelimit()`.

Also, just as with the `pr_<foo>` macros we saw earlier, the kernel also provides the equivalent `pr_<foo>_ratelimited` macros for generating a kernel printk at log level `<foo>` with rate limiting enabled. Here's a quick list of them:

```
pr_emerg_ratelimited(fmt, ...)
pr_alert_ratelimited(fmt, ...)
pr_crit_ratelimited(fmt, ...)
pr_err_ratelimited(fmt, ...)
pr_warn_ratelimited(fmt, ...)
pr_notice_ratelimited(fmt, ...)
pr_info_ratelimited(fmt, ...)
```

Can we generate kernel-level messages from user space? Sounds interesting; that's our next sub-topic.

Generating kernel messages from the user space

A popular debug technique that we programmers use is to sprinkle prints at various points in the code, often allowing us to narrow down the source of an issue. This is indeed a useful debugging technique and is called **instrumenting** the code. Kernel developers often use the venerable printk API for just this purpose.

So, imagine you have written a kernel module and are in the process of debugging it (by adding several printk's). Your kernel code now emits several printk instances, which, of course, you can see at runtime via `dmesg` or some other means. That's fine, but what if, especially because you're running some automated user space test script, you'd like to see the point at which the script initiated some action within our kernel module, by printing out a certain message. As a concrete example, say we want the log to look something like this:

```
test_script: msg 1 ; kernel_module: msg n, msg n+1, ..., msg n+m ;
test_script: msg 2 ; ...
```

We can have our user space test script write a message into the kernel log buffer, just like a kernel printk would, by writing said message into the special `/dev/kmsg` device file:

```
echo "test_script: msg 1" > /dev/kmsg
```

Well, hang on – doing so requires running with root access, of course. However, notice here that a simple `sudo(8)` before `echo` just doesn't work:

```
$ sudo echo "test_script: msg 1" > /dev/kmsg
bash: /dev/kmsg: Permission denied
$ sudo bash -c "echo \"test_script: msg 1\" > /dev/kmsg"
[sudo] password for llkd:
$ dmesg |tail -n1
[55527.523756] test_script: msg 1
$
```

The syntax used in the second attempt works, but it's just simpler to get yourself a root shell and carry out tasks such as this.

Writing Your First Kernel Module - LKMs Part 1

One more thing: the `dmesg(1)` utility has several options designed to make the output more human-readable; we show some of them via our sample alias to `dmesg` here, after which we use it:

```
$ alias dmesg='/bin/dmesg --decode --nopager --color --ctime'
$ dmesg | tail -n1
user :warn : [Sat Dec 14 17:21:50 2019] test_script: msg 1
$
```

The message written to the kernel log via the special `/dev/kmsg` device file will be *printed* at the current default log level, typically, 4 : KERN_WARNING. We can override this by actually prefixing the message with the required log level (as a number in string format). For example, to write from the user space into the kernel log at log level 6 : KERN_INFO, use this:

```
$ sudo bash -c "echo \"<6>test_script: test msg at KERN_INFO\"  \
    > /dev/kmsg"
$ dmesg | tail -n2
user :warn : [Fri Dec 14 17:21:50 2018] test_script: msg 1
user :info : [Fri Dec 14 17:31:48 2018] test_script: test msg at
KERN_INFO
```

We can see that our latter message is emitted at log level 6, as specified within `echo`.

There is really no way to distinguish between a user-generated kernel message and a kernel `printk()`-generated one; they look identical. So, of course, it could be as simple as inserting some special signature byte or string within the message, such as `@user@`, in order to help you distinguish these user-generated prints from the kernel ones.

Standardizing printk output via the pr_fmt macro

A last but important point regarding the kernel printk; pretty often, to give context to your `printk()` output (*where exactly did it occur?*), you might write the code like this, taking advantage of various gcc macros (like __FILE__, __func__, and __LINE__):

```
pr_warning("%s:%s():%d: kmalloc failed!\n", OURMODNAME,  __func__,
   __LINE__);
```

[194]

This is fine; the problem is, if there are a lot of printk's in your project, it can be fairly painful to guarantee a standard printk format (for example, first displaying the module name followed by the function name and possibly the line number, as seen here) is always followed by everyone working on the project.

Enter the `pr_fmt` macro; defining this macro right at the beginning of your code (it must be even before the first `#include`), guarantees that every single subsequent printk in your code *will be prefixed with the format specified by this macro*. Lets take an example (we show a snippet of code from the next chapter; worry not, it's really very simple, and serves as a template for your future kernel modules):

```
// ch5/lkm_template/lkm_template.c
[ ... ]
 */
#define pr_fmt(fmt) "%s:%s(): " fmt, KBUILD_MODNAME, __func__

#include <linux/init.h>
#include <linux/module.h>
#include <linux/kernel.h>
[ ... ]
static int __init lkm_template_init(void)
{
    pr_info("inserted\n");
    [ ... ]
```

The `pr_fmt()` macro is highlighted in bold font; it uses the pre-defined `KBUILD_MODNAME` macro to substitute the name of your kernel module, and the gcc `__func__` specifier to display the name of the function we're currently running! (You can even add a `%d` matched by the corresponding `__LINE__` macro to display the line number). So, bottom line: the `pr_info()` we emit in the init function of this LKM will display like this in the kernel log:

```
[381534.391966] lkm_template:lkm_template_init(): inserted
```

Notice how the LKM name and the function name are automatically prefixed. This is very useful and indeed very common; in the kernel, literally hundreds of source files begin with the `pr_fmt()`. (A quick search on the 5.4 kernel code base revealed over 2,000 instances of this macro in the code base! We too shall follow this convention, though not in all our demo kernel modules).

> **TIP**: The `pr_fmt()` also takes effect on the recommended printk usage for driver authors - via the `dev_<foo>()` functions.

Portability and the printk format specifiers

There's a question to ponder regarding the versatile printk kernel API, how will you ensure that your printk output looks correct (is correctly formatted) and works equally well on any CPU regardless of bit width? The portability issue raises its head here; the good news is that getting familiar with the various format specifiers provided will help you a great deal in this regard, in effect allowing you to write arch-independent printks.

> It's important to realize that the `size_t` - pronounced *size type* - is a `typedef` for an unsigned integer; similarly, `ssize_t` (*signed size type*) is a `typedef` for a signed integer.

Here's a few top-of-mind common printk format specifiers to keep in mind when writing portable code:

- For `size_t, ssize_t` (signed and unsigned) integers : use `%zd` and `%zu` respectively
- Kernel pointers: use `%pK` for security (hashed values), `%px` for actual pointers (don't use this in production!), additionally, use `%pa` for physical addresses (must pass it by reference)
- Raw buffer as a string of hex characters : `%*ph` (where * is replaced by the number of characters; use for buffers within 64 characters, use the `print_hex_dump_bytes()` routine for more); variations are available (see the kernel doc, link follows)
- IPv4 addresses with `%pI4`, IPv6 addresses with `%pI6` (variations too)

An exhaustive list of printk format specifiers, which to use when (with examples) is part of the official kernel documentation here: https://www.kernel.org/doc/Documentation/printk-formats.txt. The kernel also explicitly documents the fact that using the unadorned `%p` in a `printk()` statement can lead to security issues (link: https://www.kernel.org/doc/html/latest/process/deprecated.html#p-format-specifier). I urge you to browse through it!

Okay! Let's move towards completing this chapter by learning the basics of how the Makefile for your kernel module builds the kernel.

Understanding the basics of a kernel module Makefile

You will have noticed that we tend to follow a *one-kernel-module-per-directory* rule of sorts. Yes, that definitely helps keep things organized. So, let's take our second kernel module, the `ch4/printk_loglvl` one. To build it, we just `cd` to its folder, type `make`, and (fingers crossed!) voilà, it's done. We have the `printk_loglevel.ko` kernel module object freshly generated (which we can then `insmod(8)`/`rmmod(8)`). But how exactly did it get built when we typed `make`? Ah, explaining this is the purpose of this section.

> As this is our very first chapter that deals with the LKM framework and its corresponding Makefile, we will keep things nice and simple, especially with regard to the Makefile here. However, early in the following chapter, we shall introduce a more sophisticated, simply *better* Makefile (that is still quite simple to understand). We shall then use this better Makefile in all subsequent code; do look out for it and use it!

As you will know, the `make` command will by default look for a file named `Makefile` in the current directory; if it exists, it will parse it and execute command sequences as specified within it. Here's our Makefile for the kernel module `printk_loglevel` project:

```
// ch4/printk_loglvl/Makefile
PWD         := $(shell pwd)
obj-m       += printk_loglvl.o

# Enable the pr_debug() as well (rm the comment from the line below)
#EXTRA_CFLAGS += -DDEBUG
#CFLAGS_printk_loglvl.o := -DDEBUG

all:
	make -C /lib/modules/$(shell uname -r)/build/ M=$(PWD) modules
install:
	make -C /lib/modules/$(shell uname -r)/build/ M=$(PWD) modules_install
clean:
	make -C /lib/modules/$(shell uname -r)/build/ M=$(PWD) clean
```

It should go without saying that the Unix Makefile syntax basically demands this:

```
target: [dependent-source-file(s)]
	rule(s)
```

The `rule(s)` instances are always prefixed with a `[Tab]` character, *not* white space.

Let's gather the basics regarding how this Makefile works. First off, a key point is this: the kernel's `Kbuild` system (which we've been mentioning and using since Chapter 2, *Building the 5.x Linux Kernel from Source – Part 1*), primarily uses two variable strings of software to build, chained up within the two `obj-y` and `obj-m` variables.

The `obj-y` string has the concatenated list of all objects to build and merge into the final kernel image files - the uncompressed `vmlinux` and the compressed (bootable) `[b]zImage` images. Think about it – it makes sense: the y in `obj-y` stands for *Yes*. All kernel built-ins and `Kconfig` options that were set to Y during the kernel configuration process (or are Y by default) are chained together via this item, built, and ultimately woven into the final kernel image files by the `Kbuild` build system.

On the other hand, it's now easy to see that the `obj-m` string is a concatenated list of all kernel objects to build *separately, as kernel modules*! This is precisely why our Makefile has this all-important line:

```
obj-m += printk_loglvl.o
```

In effect, it tells the `Kbuild` system to include our code; more correctly, it tells it to implicitly compile the `printk_loglvl.c` source code into the `printk_loglvl.o` binary object, and then add this object to the `obj-m` list. Next, the default rule for `make` being the `all` rule, it is processed:

```
all:
        make -C /lib/modules/$(shell uname -r)/build/ M=$(PWD) modules
```

The processing of this single statement is quite involved; here's what transpires:

1. The `-C` option switch to `make` has the `make` process *change directory* (via the `chdir(2)` system call) to the directory name that follows `-C`. Thus, it changes directory to the kernel `build` folder (which, as we covered earlier, is the location of the 'limited' kernel source tree that got installed via the `kernel-headers` package).

2. Once there, it *parses in* the content of the *kernel's top-level* Makefile – that is, the Makefile that resides there, in the root of this limited kernel source tree. This is a key point. This way, it's guaranteed that all kernel modules are tightly coupled to the kernel that they are being built against (more on this a bit later). This also guarantees that kernel modules are built with the exact same set of rules, that is, the compiler/linker configurations (the `CFLAGS` options, the compiler option switches, and so on), as the kernel image itself is. All this is required for binary compatibility.
3. Next, you can see the initialization of the variable named `M`, and that the target specified is `modules`; hence, the `make` process now changes directory to that specified by the `M` variable, which you can see is set to `$(PWD)` – the very folder we started from (the present working directory; the `PWD := $(shell pwd)` in the Makefile initializes it to the correct value)!

So, interestingly, it's a recursive build: the build process, having (very importantly) parsed the kernel top-level Makefile, now switches back to the kernel module's directory and builds the module(s) therein.

Did you notice that when a kernel module is built, a fair number of intermediate working files are generated as well? Among them are `modules.order`, `<file>.mod.c`, `<file>.o`, `Module.symvers`, `<file>.mod.o`, `.<file>.o.cmd`, `.<file>.ko.cmd`, a folder called `.tmp_versions/`, and, of course, the kernel module binary object itself, `<file>.ko` – the whole point of the build exercise. Getting rid of all these objects, including the kernel module object itself, is easy: just perform `make clean`. The `clean` rule cleans it all up. (We shall delve into the `install` target in the following chapter.)

> You can look up what the `modules.order` and `modules.builtin` files (and other files) are meant for within the kernel documentation here: `Documentation/kbuild/kbuild.rst`.
>
> Also as mentioned previously, we shall, in the following chapter, introduce and use a more sophisticated Makefile variant - **a 'better' Makefile**; it is designed to help you, the kernel module/driver developer, improve code quality by running targets related to kernel coding style checks, static analysis, simple packaging, and (a dummy target) for dynamic analysis.

With that, we conclude this chapter. Well done – you are now well on your way to learning Linux kernel development!

Summary

In this chapter, we covered the basics of Linux kernel architecture and the LKM framework. You learned what a kernel module is and why it's useful. We then wrote a simple yet complete kernel module, a very basic *Hello, world*. The material then delved further into how it works, along with how to load it, see the module listing, and unload it. Kernel logging with printk was covered in some detail, along with rate limiting printk, generating kernel messages from the user space, standardizing it's output format, and understanding the basics of the kernel module Makefile.

That ends this chapter; I urge you to work on the sample code (via the book's GitHub repository), work on the *Questions*/assignments, and then proceed on to the next chapter, continuing our coverage of writing a Linux kernel module.

Questions

As we conclude, here is a list of questions for you to test your knowledge regarding this chapter's material: https://github.com/PacktPublishing/Linux-Kernel-Programming/tree/master/questions. You will find some of the questions answered in the book's GitHub repo: https://github.com/PacktPublishing/Linux-Kernel-Programming/tree/master/solutions_to_assgn.

Further reading

To help you delve deeper into the subject with useful materials, we provide a rather detailed list of online references and links (and at times, even books) in a *Further reading* document in this book's GitHub repository. The *Further reading* document is available here: https://github.com/PacktPublishing/Linux-Kernel-Programming/blob/master/Further_Reading.md.

5
Writing Your First Kernel Module - LKMs Part 2

This chapter is the second half of our coverage regarding the **Loadable Kernel Module (LKM)** framework and how to write kernel modules using it. To get the most out of it, I expect you to complete the previous chapter and try out the code and questions there before tackling this one.

In this chapter, we continue from the point where we left off in the previous one. Here, we cover making use of a 'better' Makefile for LKMs, cross-compiling a kernel module for the ARM platform (as a typical example), what module stacking is and how to do it, and how to set up and use module parameters. Along the way, among several other things, you will learn about the kernel API/ABI stability (or rather, the lack thereof!), the key differences between writing userspace and kernel code, auto-loading a kernel module at system boot, and security concerns and how they can be addressed. We end with information on the kernel documentation (including coding style) and contributing to mainline.

In brief, we will cover the following topics in this chapter:

- A "better" Makefile template for your kernel modules
- Cross-compiling a kernel module
- Gathering minimal system information
- Licensing kernel modules
- Emulating "library-like" features for kernel modules
- Passing parameters to a kernel module
- Floating point not allowed in the kernel
- Auto-loading modules on system boot
- Kernel modules and security - an overview
- Coding style guidelines for kernel developers
- Contributing to the mainline kernel

Technical requirements

The technical requirements – the software packages required – for this chapter are identical to what was shown in the *Technical requirements* section in Chapter 4, *Writing Your First Kernel Module – LKMs Part 1*; please refer to it. As always, you can find the source code for this chapter in this book's GitHub repository. Clone it with the following:

```
git clone https://github.com/PacktPublishing/Linux-Kernel-Programming
```

The code displayed in the book is often just a relevant snippet. Follow along with the full source code from the repository. For this chapter (and those that follow), more on the technical requirements is found in the following section.

A "better" Makefile template for your kernel modules

The preceding chapter introduced you to the Makefile used to generate the kernel module from source, to install and clean it up. However, as we briefly mentioned there, I will now introduce what is, in my opinion, a superior, a "better" Makefile, and explain how it's better.

Ultimately, we all have to write better and more secure code – both user and kernel-space. The good news is, there are several tools that help improve your code's robustness and security posture, static and dynamic analyzers being among them (as several have already been mentioned in Chapter 1, *Kernel Workspace Setup*, I won't repeat them here).

I have devised a simple yet useful Makefile "template" of sorts for kernel modules that includes several targets that help you run these tools. These targets allow you to perform valuable checks and analysis very easily; *stuff you might otherwise forget or ignore or put off for ever!* These targets include the following:

- The "usual" ones – the `build`, `install`, and `clean` targets.
- Kernel coding style generation and checking (via `indent(1)` and the kernel's `checkpatch.pl` script, respectively).
- Kernel static analysis targets (`sparse`, `gcc`, and `flawfinder`), with a mention of **Coccinelle**.

- A couple of "dummy" kernel dynamic analysis targets (KASAN and LOCKDEP / CONFIG_PROVE_LOCKING), encouraging you to configure, build, and use a "debug" kernel for all your test cases.
- A simple tarxz-pkg target that tars and compresses the source files into the preceding directory. This enables you to transfer the compressed tar-xz file to any other Linux system, and extract and build the LKM there.
- A "dummy" dynamic analysis target, pointing out how you should invest time in configuring and building a "debug" kernel and using it to catch bugs! (More on this follows shortly.)

You can find the code (along with a README file as well) in the ch5/lkm_template directory. To help you understand its use and power and to help you get started, the following figure simply shows a screenshot of the output the code produces when run with its help target:

```
lkm_template $ make
all             clean          help           install        sa_cppcheck    sa_gcc         tarxz-pkg
checkpatch      code-style     indent         sa             sa_flawfinder  sa_sparse
lkm_template $ make help
=== Makefile Help : additional targets available ===

TIP: type make <tab><tab> to show all valid targets

--- usual kernel LKM targets ---
typing "make" or "all" target : builds the kernel module object (the .ko)
install      : installs the kernel module(s) to INSTALL_MOD_PATH (default here: /lib/modules/5.4.0-58-generic/)
clean        : cleanup - remove all kernel objects, temp files/dirs, etc

--- kernel code style targets ---
code-style : "wrapper" target over the following kernel code style targets
  indent     : run the indent utility on source file(s) to indent them as per the kernel code style
  checkpatch : run the kernel code style checker tool on source file(s)

--- kernel static analyzer targets ---
sa           : "wrapper" target over the following kernel static analyzer targets
  sa_sparse    : run the static analysis sparse tool on the source file(s)
  sa_gcc       : run gcc with option -W1 ("Generally useful warnings") on the source file(s)
  sa_flawfinder : run the static analysis flawfinder tool on the source file(s)
  sa_cppcheck  : run the static analysis cppcheck tool on the source file(s)
TIP: use coccinelle as well (requires spatch): https://www.kernel.org/doc/html/v4.15/dev-tools/coccinelle.html

--- kernel dynamic analysis targets ---
da_kasan   : DUMMY target: this is to remind you to run your code with the dynamic analysis KASAN tool enabled; requires conf
iguring the kernel with CONFIG_KASAN On, rebuild and boot it
da_lockdep : DUMMY target: this is to remind you to run your code with the dynamic analysis LOCKDEP tool (for deep locking is
sues analysis) enabled; requires configuring the kernel with CONFIG_PROVE_LOCKING On, rebuild and boot it
TIP: best to build a debug kernel with several kernel debug config options turned On, boot via it and run all your test cases

--- misc targets ---
tarxz-pkg  : tar and compress the LKM source files as a tar.xz into the dir above; allows one to transfer and build the modul
e on another system
 Tip: when extracting, to extract into a dir of the same name as the tar file,
  do: tar -xvf lkm_template.tar.xz --one-top-level
help         : this help target
lkm_template $
```

Figure 5.1 – The output of the help target from our "better" Makefile

In *Figure 5.1*, we first do `make`, followed by pressing the *Tab* key twice, thus having it display all available targets. Do study this carefully and use it! For example, running `make sa` will cause it to run all its **static analysis** (`sa`) targets on your code!

It's also important to note that using this Makefile will require you to have installed a few packages/ apps on the system; these include (for a base Ubuntu system) `indent(1)`, `linux-headers-$(uname -r)`, `sparse(1)`, `flawfinder(1)`, `cppcheck(1)`, and `tar(1)`. (`Chapter 1`, *Kernel Workspace Setup*, already specified that these should be installed.)

Also, note that the so-called **dynamic analysis** (`da`) targets mentioned in the Makefile are merely dummy targets that don't do anything other than print a message. They are there *to remind you* to thoroughly test your code by running it on an appropriately configured "debug" kernel!

Speaking of a 'debug' kernel, the next section shows you how to configure one.

Configuring a "debug" kernel

(For details on configuring and building the kernel, look back to `Chapter 2`, *Building the 5.x Linux Kernel from Source - Part 1*, and `Chapter 3`, *Building the 5.x Linux Kernel from Source - Part 2*).

Running your code on a *debug kernel* can help you uncover hard-to-spot bugs and issues. I highly recommend doing so, typically during development and testing! Here, I minimally expect you to configure your custom 5.4 kernel to have the following kernel debug config options turned on (within the `make menuconfig` UI, you will find most of them under the `Kernel Hacking` sub-menu; the following list is with respect to Linux 5.4.0):

- `CONFIG_DEBUG_INFO`
- `CONFIG_DEBUG_FS` (the `debugfs` pseudo filesystem)
- `CONFIG_MAGIC_SYSRQ` (the Magic SysRq hotkeys feature)
- `CONFIG_DEBUG_KERNEL`
- `CONFIG_DEBUG_MISC`
- Memory debugging:
    - `CONFIG_SLUB_DEBUG`.
    - `CONFIG_DEBUG_MEMORY_INIT`.

- `CONFIG_KASAN`: this is the **Kernel Address Sanitizer** port; however, as of the time of writing, it only works on 64-bit systems.
- `CONFIG_DEBUG_SHIRQ`
- `CONFIG_SCHED_STACK_END_CHECK`
- Lock debugging:
- `CONFIG_PROVE_LOCKING`: the very powerful `lockdep` feature to catch locking bugs! This turns on several other lock debug configs as well, explained in Chapter 13, *Kernel Synchronization - Part 2*.
- `CONFIG_LOCK_STAT`
- `CONFIG_DEBUG_ATOMIC_SLEEP`
- `CONFIG_STACKTRACE`
- `CONFIG_DEBUG_BUGVERBOSE`
- `CONFIG_FTRACE` (`ftrace`: within its sub-menu, turn on at least a couple of "tracers")
- `CONFIG_BUG_ON_DATA_CORRUPTION`
- `CONFIG_KGDB` (kernel GDB; optional)
- `CONFIG_UBSAN`
- `CONFIG_EARLY_PRINTK`
- `CONFIG_DEBUG_BOOT_PARAMS`
- `CONFIG_UNWINDER_FRAME_POINTER` (selects `FRAME_POINTER` and `CONFIG_STACK_VALIDATION`)

> **TIP**
> A couple of things to note:
> a) Don't worry too much right now if you don't get what all the previously mentioned kernel debug config options do; by the time you're done with this book, most of them will be clear.
> b) Turning on some Ftrace tracers (or plugins), such as `CONFIG_IRQSOFF_TRACER`, would be useful as we actually make use of it in our *Linux Kernel Programming (Part 2)* book in the *Handling Hardware Interrupts* chapter; (note that though Ftrace itself may be enabled by default, all its tracers aren't).

Note that turning on these config options *does* entail a performance hit, but that's okay. We're running a "debug" kernel of this sort for the express purpose of *catching errors and bugs* (especially the hard-to-uncover kind!). It can indeed be a life-saver! On your project, *your workflow should involve your code being tested and run on both of the following*:

- The *debug* kernel system, where all required kernel debug config options are turned on (as previously shown minimally)
- The *production* kernel system (where all or most of the preceding kernel debug options will be turned off)

Needless to say, we will be using the preceding Makefile style in all the subsequent LKM code in this book.

Alright, now that you're all set, let's dive into an interesting and practical scenario – compiling your kernel module(s) for another target (typically ARM).

Cross-compiling a kernel module

In `Chapter 3`, *Building the 5.x Linux Kernel from Source - Part 2*, in the *Kernel build for the Raspberry Pi* section, we showed how you can cross-compile the Linux kernel for a "foreign" target architecture (such as ARM, PowerPC, MIPS, and so on). Essentially, the same can be done for a kernel module as well; you can easily cross-compile a kernel module by setting up the "special" `ARCH` and `CROSS_COMPILE` environment variables appropriately.

For example, let's imagine we are working on an embedded Linux product; the target device on which our code will run has an AArch32 (ARM-32) CPU. Why not take an actual example. Let's cross-compile our *Hello, world* kernel module for the Raspberry Pi 3 **Single-Board Computer (SBC)**!

This is interesting. You will find that although it appears simple and straightforward, we will end up taking four iterations before we succeed. Why? Read on to find out.

Setting up the system for cross-compilation

The prerequisites to cross-compile a kernel module are quite clear:

- We need the *kernel source tree for the target system* installed as part of the workspace on our host system, typically an x86_64 desktop (for our example, using the Raspberry Pi as a target, please refer to the official Raspberry Pi documentation here: `https://www.raspberrypi.org/documentation/linux/kernel/building.md`).
- We now need a cross toolchain. Typically, the host system is an x86_64 and here, as the target is an ARM-32, we will need an *x86_64-to-ARM32 cross toolchain*. Again, as is clearly mentioned in `Chapter 3`, *Building the 5.x Linux Kernel from Source - Part 2*, *Kernel Build for the Raspberry Pi*, you must download and install the Raspberry Pi-specific x86_64-to-ARM toolchain as part of the host system workspace (refer to `Chapter 3`, *Building the 5.x Linux Kernel from Source - Part 2*, to learn how to install the toolchain).

Okay, from this point on, I will assume that you have an x86_64-to-ARM cross toolchain installed. I will also assume the *toolchain prefix* is `arm-linux-gnueabihf-`; we can quickly check that the toolchain is installed and its binaries added to the path by trying to invoke the `gcc` cross-compiler:

```
$ arm-linux-gnueabihf-gcc
arm-linux-gnueabihf-gcc: fatal error: no input files
compilation terminated.
$
```

It works – it's just that we have not passed any C program as a parameter to compile, hence it complains.

> **TIP**: You can certainly look up the compiler version as well with the `arm-linux-gnueabihf-gcc --version` command.

Attempt 1 – setting the "special" environment variables

Actually, cross-compiling the kernel module is very easy (or so we think!). Just ensure that you set the "special" ARCH and CROSS_COMPILE environment variables appropriately. Follow along with the following steps:

1. Let's re-build our very first *Hello, world* kernel module for the Raspberry Pi target. Here's how to build it:

   > To do so without corrupting the original code, we make a new folder called cross with a copy of the (helloworld_lkm) code from Chapter 4, *Writing your First Kernel Module - LKMs Part 1*, to begin with.

   `cd <dest-dir>/ch5/cross`

   Here, <dest-dir> is the root of the book's GitHub source tree.

2. Now, run the following command:

   `make ARCH=arm CROSS_COMPILE=arm-linux-gnueabihf-`

But it doesn't work (or it may work; please see the following info box) straight off the bat. We get compile failures, as seen here:

```
$ make ARCH=arm CROSS_COMPILE=arm-linux-gnueabihf-
make -C /lib/modules/5.4.0-llkd01/build/ M=/home/llkd/book_llkd/Linux-Kernel-Programming/ch5/cross modules
make[1]: Entering directory '/home/llkd/kernels/linux-5.4'
  CC [M]  /home/llkd/book_llkd/Linux-Kernel-Programming/ch5/cross/helloworld_lkm.o
arm-linux-gnueabihf-gcc: error: unrecognized command line option '-fstack-protector-strong'
scripts/Makefile.build:265: recipe for target '/home/llkd/book_llkd/Linux-Kernel-Programming/ch5/cross/helloworld_lkm.o' failed
[...]
make: *** [all] Error 2
$
```

Why did it fail?

[208]

> Assuming all tools are set up as per the technical requirements discussed earlier, the cross-compile should work. This is because the `Makefile` provided in the book's repository is a proper working one, the Raspberry Pi kernel has been correctly configured and built, the device is booted off this kernel, and the kernel module is compiled against it. The purpose here, in this book, is to explain the details; thus, we begin with no assumptions, and guide you through the process of correctly performing the cross-compilation.

The clue as to why the preceding cross-compilation attempt failed lies in the fact that it is attempting to use – *build against* – the kernel source of the current *host system* and not the target's kernel source tree. So, *we need to modify the Makefile to point it to the correct kernel source tree for the target*. It's really quite easy to do so. In the following code, we see the typical way that the (corrected) Makefile code is written:

```
# ch5/cross/Makefile:
# To support cross-compiling for kernel modules:
# For architecture (cpu) 'arch', invoke make as:
# make ARCH=<arch> CROSS_COMPILE=<cross-compiler-prefix>
ifeq ($(ARCH),arm)
  # *UPDATE* 'KDIR' below to point to the ARM Linux kernel source tree on
  # your box
  KDIR ?= ~/rpi_work/kernel_rpi/linux
else ifeq ($(ARCH),arm64)
  # *UPDATE* 'KDIR' below to point to the ARM64 (Aarch64) Linux kernel
  # source tree on your box
  KDIR ?= ~/kernel/linux-4.14
else ifeq ($(ARCH),powerpc)
  # *UPDATE* 'KDIR' below to point to the PPC64 Linux kernel source tree
  # on your box
  KDIR ?= ~/kernel/linux-4.9.1
else
  # 'KDIR' is the Linux 'kernel headers' package on your host system; this
  # is usually an x86_64, but could be anything, really (f.e. building
  # directly on a Raspberry Pi implies that it's the host)
  KDIR ?= /lib/modules/$(shell uname -r)/build
endif

PWD            := $(shell pwd)
obj-m          += helloworld_lkm.o
EXTRA_CFLAGS   += -DDEBUG

all:
```

Writing Your First Kernel Module - LKMs Part 2

```
        @echo
        @echo '--- Building : KDIR=${KDIR} ARCH=${ARCH}
CROSS_COMPILE=${CROSS_COMPILE} EXTRA_CFLAGS=${EXTRA_CFLAGS} ---'
        @echo
        make -C $(KDIR) M=$(PWD) modules
[...]
```

Look carefully at the (new and "better," as explained in the preceding section) Makefile and you will see how it works:

- Most importantly, we conditionally set the `KDIR` variable to point to the correct kernel source tree, depending on the value of the `ARCH` environment variable (of course, I've used some pathname to kernel source trees for the ARM[64] and PowerPC as examples; do substitute the pathname with the actual path to your kernel source trees).
- As usual, we set `obj-m += <module-name>.o`.
- We also set `CFLAGS_EXTRA` to add the `DEBUG` symbol (so that the `DEBUG` symbol is defined in our LKM and even the `pr_debug()`/`pr_devel()` macros work).
- The `@echo '<...>'` line is equivalent to the shell's `echo` command; it just emits some useful information while building (the `@` prefix hides the echo statement itself from displaying).
- Finally, we have the "usual" Makefile targets: `all`, `install`, and `clean` – these are the same as earlier *except for* this important change: **we make it change directory** (via the `-C` switch) to the value of `KDIR`!
- Though not shown in the preceding code, this "better" Makefile has several additional useful targets. You should definitely take the time to explore and use them (as explained in the preceding section; to start, simply type `make help`, study the output and try things out).

Having done all this, let's retry the cross-compile with this version and see how it goes.

[210]

Attempt 2 – pointing the Makefile to the correct kernel source tree for the target

So now, with the *enhanced* Makefile described in the previous section, it *should* work. In our new directory where we will try this out – `cross` (as we're cross-compiling, not that we're angry!) – follow along with these steps:

1. Attempt the build (for a second time) with the `make` command appropriate for cross-compilation:

    ```
    $ make ARCH=arm CROSS_COMPILE=arm-linux-gnueabihf-

    --- Building : KDIR=~/rpi_work/kernel_rpi/linux ARCH=arm
    CROSS_COMPILE=arm-linux-gnueabihf- EXTRA_CFLAGS=-DDEBUG ---

    make -C ~/rpi_work/kernel_rpi/linux
    M=/home/llkd/booksrc/ch5/cross modules
    make[1]: Entering directory
    '/home/llkd/rpi_work/kernel_rpi/linux'
    ```

    ERROR: Kernel configuration is invalid.
    ```
      include/generated/autoconf.h or include/config/auto.conf are
    missing.
      Run 'make oldconfig && make prepare' on kernel src to fix it.


     WARNING: Symbol version dump ./Module.symvers
     is missing; modules will have no dependencies and
    modversions.
    [...]
    make: *** [all] Error 2
    $
    ```

The actual reason it failed is that the Raspberry Pi kernel that we're compiling our kernel module against is still in a "virgin" state. It does not even have the `.config` file present (among other required headers, as the preceding output informs us) in its root directory, which it requires to (at least) be configured.

2. To fix this, switch to the root of your Raspberry Pi kernel source tree and follow these steps:

```
$ cd ~/rpi-work/kernel_rpi/linux
$ make ARCH=arm bcmrpi_defconfig
#
# configuration written to .config
#
$ make ARCH=arm CROSS_COMPILE=arm-linux-gnueabihf- oldconfig
scripts/kconfig/conf --oldconfig Kconfig
#
# configuration written to .config
#
$ make ARCH=arm CROSS_COMPILE=arm-linux-gnueabihf- prepare
scripts/kconfig/conf --silentoldconfig Kconfig
  CHK     include/config/kernel.release
  UPD     include/config/kernel.release
  WRAP    arch/arm/include/generated/asm/bitsperlong.h
  WRAP    arch/arm/include/generated/asm/clkdev.h
  [...]
$ make ARCH=arm CROSS_COMPILE=arm-linux-gnueabihf-
  CHK     include/config/kernel.release
  CHK     include/generated/uapi/linux/version.h
  CHK     include/generated/utsrelease.h
  [...]
  HOSTCC  scripts/recordmcount
  HOSTCC  scripts/sortextable
  [...]
$
```

Notice that these steps are really quite equivalent to performing a partial build of the Raspberry Pi kernel! Indeed, if you have already built (cross-compiled) this kernel as explained earlier in Chapter 3, *Building the 5.x Linux Kernel from Source - Part 2*, then the kernel module cross-compilation should just work without the intervening steps seen here.

Chapter 5

Attempt 3 – cross-compiling our kernel module

Now that we have a configured Raspberry Pi kernel source tree (on the host system) and the enhanced Makefile (see the *Attempt 2 – pointing the Makefile to the correct kernel source tree for the target* section), it *should* work. Let's retry:

1. We (again) attempt to build (cross-compile) the kernel. Issue the `make` command, passing along the `ARCH` and `CROSS_COMPILE` environment variables as usual:

```
$ ls -l
total 12
-rw-rw-r-- 1 llkd llkd 1456 Mar 18 17:48 helloworld_lkm.c
-rw-rw-r-- 1 llkd llkd 6470 Jul  6 17:30 Makefile
$ make ARCH=arm CROSS_COMPILE=arm-linux-gnueabihf-

--- Building : KDIR=~/rpi_work/kernel_rpi/linux ARCH=arm
CROSS_COMPILE=arm-linux-gnueabihf- EXTRA_CFLAGS=-DDEBUG ---

make -C ~/rpi_work/kernel_rpi/linux
M=/home/llkd/booksrc/ch5/cross modules
make[1]: Entering directory
'/home/llkd/rpi_work/kernel_rpi/linux'

  WARNING: Symbol version dump ./Module.symvers
  is missing; modules will have no dependencies and
modversions.

Building for: ARCH=arm CROSS_COMPILE=arm-linux-gnueabihf-
EXTRA_CFLAGS= -DDEBUG
  CC [M] /home/llkd/book_llkd/Linux-Kernel-
Programming/ch5/cross/helloworld_lkm.o
  Building modules, stage 2.
  MODPOST 1 modules
  CC /home/llkd/booksrc/ch5/cross/helloworld_lkm.mod.o
  LD [M] /home/llkd/booksrc/ch5/cross/helloworld_lkm.ko
make[1]: Leaving directory
'/home/llkd/rpi_work/kernel_rpi/linux'
$ file ./helloworld_lkm.ko
./helloworld_lkm.ko: ELF 32-bit LSB relocatable, ARM, EABI5
version 1 (SYSV), BuildID[sha1]=17...e, not stripped
$
```

[213]

Writing Your First Kernel Module - LKMs Part 2

The build is successful! The `helloworld_lkm.ko` kernel module has indeed been cross-compiled for the ARM architecture (using the Raspberry Pi cross toolchain and kernel source tree).

> We can ignore the preceding warning regarding the `Module.symvers` file for now. It isn't present as (here) the entire Raspberry Pi kernel hasn't been built.
>
> Also, FYI, on recent hosts running GCC 9.x or later and kernel versions 4.9 or later, there are some compiler attribute warnings emitted. When I tried cross-compiling this kernel module using `arm-linux-gnueabihf-gcc` version 9.3.0 and the Raspberry Pi kernel version 4.14.114, warnings such as this were emitted:
>
> ```
> ./include/linux/module.h:131:6: warning: 'init_module' specifies less restrictive attribute than its target 'helloworld_lkm_init': 'cold' [-Wmissing-attributes]
> ```
>
> Miguel Ojeda points this out (`https://lore.kernel.org/lkml/CANiq72=T8nH3HHkYvWF+vPMscgwXki1Ugiq6C9PhVHJUHAwDYw@mail.gmail.com/`) and has even generated a patch to handle this issue (`https://github.com/ojeda/linux/commits/compiler-attributes-backport`). As of the time of writing, the patch is applied in the kernel mainline and in *recent* Raspberry Pi kernels (so, the `rpi-5.4.y` branch works fine but earlier ones such as the `rpi-4.9.y` branch don't seem to have it)! Hence the compiler warnings... effectively, if you do see these warnings, update the Raspberry Pi branch to `rpi-5.4.y` or later (or, for now, just ignore them).

2. The proof of the pudding is in the eating though. So, we fire up our Raspberry Pi, `scp(1)` across our cross-compiled kernel module object file to it, and, as follows (within an `ssh(1)` session on the Raspberry Pi), try it out (the following output is directly from the device):

   ```
   $ sudo insmod ./helloworld_lkm.ko
   insmod: ERROR: could not insert module ./helloworld_lkm.ko: Invalid module format
   $
   ```

   Clearly, `insmod(8)` in the preceding code fails! *It's important to understand why.*

[214]

It's really to do with a *mismatch in the kernel version* that we're attempting to load the module on and the kernel version the module has been compiled against.

3. While logged in to the Raspberry Pi, print out the current Raspberry Pi kernel version we're running on and use the modinfo(8) utility to print out details regarding the kernel module itself:

```
rpi ~ $ cat /proc/version
Linux version 4.19.75-v7+ (dom@buildbot) (gcc version 4.9.3
(crosstool-NG crosstool-ng-1.22.0-88-g8460611)) #1270 SMP Tue
Sep 24 18:45:11 BST 2019
rpi ~ $ modinfo ./helloworld_lkm.ko
filename: /home/pi/./helloworld_lkm.ko
version: 0.1
license: Dual MIT/GPL
description: LLKD book:ch5/cross: hello, world, our first
Raspberry Pi LKM
author: Kaiwan N Billimoria
srcversion: 7DDCE78A55CF6EDEEE783FF
depends:
name: helloworld_lkm
vermagic: 5.4.51-v7+ SMP mod_unload modversions ARMv7 p2v8
rpi ~ $
```

From the preceding output, clearly, here we're running the 4.19.75-v7+ kernel on the Raspberry Pi. This, in fact, is the kernel I inherited when I installed the *default* Raspbian OS on the device's microSD card (it's a deliberate scenario introduced here, at first *not* using the 5.4 kernel we built earlier for the Raspberry Pi). The kernel module, on the other hand, reveals that it's been compiled against the 5.4.51-v7+ Linux kernel (the vermagic string from modinfo(8) reveals this). *Clearly, there's a mismatch.* Well, so what?

The Linux kernel has a rule, part of the *kernel* **Application Binary Interface (ABI): it will only ever insert a kernel module into kernel memory if that kernel module has been built against it** – the precise kernel version, build flags, and even the kernel configuration options matter!

> **TIP:** The *built against* kernel is the kernel whose source location you specified in the Makefile (we did so via the KDIR variable previously).

Writing Your First Kernel Module - LKMs Part 2

In other words, kernel modules are **not binary-compatible with kernels other than the one they have been built against**. For example, if we build a kernel module on, say, an Ubuntu 18.04 LTS box, then it will *only work on a system running this precise environment* (libraries, kernel, or toolchain)! It will *not* work on a Fedora 29 or an RHEL 7.x, a Raspberry Pi, and so on. Now – and again, think about this – this does not mean that kernel modules are completely incompatible. No, they are *source-compatible across different architectures* (at least they can or *should* be written that way). So, assuming you have the source code, you can always *rebuild* a kernel module on a given system and then it will work on that system. It's just that the *binary image* (the .ko file) is incompatible with kernels other than the precise one it's built against.

Relax, this issue is actually easy to spot. Look up the kernel log:

```
$ dmesg |tail -n2
[ 296.130074] helloworld_lkm: no symbol version for module_layout
[ 296.130093] helloworld_lkm: version magic '5.4.51-v7+ mod_unload modversions ARMv6 p2v8 ' should be '4.19.75-v7+ SMP mod_unload modversions ARMv7 p2v8 '
$
```

On the device, the currently running kernel is this: 4.19.75-v7+. The kernel literally tells us that our kernel module has been built against the 5.4.51-v7+ kernel version (it also shows some of the expected kernel config) and what it should be. There is a mismatch! Hence the failure to insert the kernel module.

Though we don't use this approach here, there is a way to ensure the successful build and deployment of third-party out-of-tree kernel modules (as long as their source code is available), via a framework called **DKMS (Dynamic Kernel Module Support)**. The following is a quote directly from it:

Dynamic Kernel Module Support (DKMS) is a program/framework that enables generating Linux kernel modules whose sources generally reside outside the kernel source tree. The concept is to have DKMS modules automatically rebuilt when a new kernel is installed.

As an example of DKMS usage, the Oracle VirtualBox hypervisor (when running on a Linux host) uses DKMS to auto-build and keep up to date its kernel modules.

Attempt 4 – cross-compiling our kernel module

So, now that we understand the issue, there are two possible solutions:

- We must use the required custom configured kernel for the product and build all our kernel modules against it.
- Alternatively, we could rebuild the kernel module to match the current kernel the device happens to be running.

Now, in typical embedded Linux projects, you will almost certainly have a custom configured kernel for the target device, one that you must work with. All kernel modules for the product will/must be built against it. Thus, we follow the first approach – we must boot the device with our custom configured and built (5.4!) kernel, and since our kernel module is built against it, it should certainly work now.

> **TIP**: We (briefly) covered the kernel build for the Raspberry Pi in Chapter 3, *Building the 5.x Linux Kernel from Source - Part 2*. Refer back there for the details if required.

Okay, I will have to assume that you've followed the steps (covered in Chapter 3, *Building the 5.x Linux Kernel from Source - Part 2*) and have by now configured and built a 5.4 kernel for the Raspberry Pi. The nitty-gritty details regarding how to copy our custom zImage onto the microSD card of the device and so on is not covered here. I refer you to the official Raspberry Pi documentation here: https://www.raspberrypi.org/documentation/linux/kernel/building.md.

Nevertheless, we will point out a convenient way to switch between kernels on the device (here, I assume the device is a Raspberry Pi 3B+ running a 32-bit kernel):

1. Copy your custom-built zImage kernel binary into the device's microSD card's /boot partition. Save the original Raspberry Pi kernel image – the Raspbian one – as kernel7.img.orig.
2. Copy (scp) the just-cross-compiled kernel module (helloworld_lkm.ko for ARM, done in the previous section) from your host system onto the microSD card (typically into /home/pi).

Writing Your First Kernel Module - LKMs Part 2

3. Next, again on the device's microSD card, edit the `/boot/config.txt` file, setting the kernel to boot via the `kernel=xxx` line. A snippet from this file on the device shows this:

   ```
   rpi $ cat /boot/config.txt
   [...]
   # KNB: enable the UART (for the adapter cable: USB To RS232
   TTL UART
   # PL2303HX Converter USB to COM)
   enable_uart=1
   # KNB: select the kernel to boot from via kernel=xxx
   #kernel=kernel7.img.orig
   kernel=zImage
   rpi $
   ```

4. Once saved and rebooted, we log in to the device and retry our kernel module. Figure 5.2 is a screenshot showing the just-cross-compiled `helloworld_lkm.ko` LKM being used on the Raspberry Pi device:

   ```
   rpi $ cat /proc/version
   Linux version 5.4.51-v7+ (kaiwan@kaiwan-T460) (gcc version 4.8.3 20140303 (prerelease) (crosstool-NG
   linaro-1.13.1+bzr2650 - Linaro GCC 2014.03)) #1 SMP Thu Jul 23 12:36:25 IST 2020
   rpi $
   rpi $ modinfo ./helloworld_lkm.ko
   filename:       /home/pi/booksrc/ch5/cross/./helloworld_lkm.ko
   version:        0.1
   license:        Dual MIT/GPL
   description:    LLKD book:ch5/cross: hello, world, our first Raspberry Pi LKM
   author:         Kaiwan N Billimoria
   srcversion:     7DDCE78A55CF6EDEEE783FF
   depends:
   name:           helloworld_lkm
   vermagic:       5.4.51-v7+ SMP mod_unload modversions ARMv7 p2v8
   rpi $ sudo dmesg -C
   rpi $ sudo rmmod helloworld_lkm 2>/dev/null
   rpi $ sudo insmod ./helloworld_lkm.ko
   rpi $ dmesg
   [ 3302.148946] Hello, Raspberry Pi world
   rpi $ lsmod |grep helloworld_lkm
   helloworld_lkm         16384  0
   rpi $ sudo rmmod helloworld_lkm 2>/dev/null
   rpi $ dmesg
   [ 3302.148946] Hello, Raspberry Pi world
   [ 3312.406669] Goodbye, Raspberry Pi world
   rpi $
   ```

   Figure 5.2 – The cross-compiled LKM being used on a Raspberry Pi

Ah, it worked! Notice how, this time, the current kernel version (`5.4.51-v7+`) precisely matches that of the kernel the module was built against – in the `modinfo(8)` output, we can see that the `vermagic` string shows it's `5.4.51-v7+`.

> If you do see an issue with `rmmod(8)` throwing a non-fatal error (though the cleanup hook is still called), the reason is that you haven't yet fully set up the newly built kernel on the device. You will have to copy in all the kernel modules (under `/lib/modules/<kernel-ver>`) and run the `depmod(8)` utility there. Here, we will not delve further into these details – as mentioned before, the official documentation for the Raspberry Pi covers all these steps.
>
> Of course, the Raspberry Pi is a pretty powerful system; you can install the (default) Raspbian OS along with development tools and kernel headers and thus compile kernel modules on the board itself! (No cross-compile required.) Here, though, we have followed the cross-compile approach as this is typical when working on embedded Linux projects.

The LKM framework is a rather large piece of work. Plenty more remains to be explored. Let's get to it. In the next section, we will examine how you can obtain some minimal system information from within a kernel module.

Gathering minimal system information

In our simple demo from the previous section (`ch5/cross/helloworld_lkm.c`), we have hard-coded a `printk()` to emit a "`Hello/Goodbye, Raspberry Pi world\n`" string, regardless of whether or not the kernel module actually runs on a Raspberry Pi device. For a better, though still quite simplistic, way to "detect" some system details (such as the CPU or OS), we refer you to our sample `ch5/min_sysinfo/min_sysinfo.c` kernel module. In the following code snippet, we show only the relevant function:

```
// ch5/min_sysinfo/min_sysinfo.c
[ ... ]
void llkd_sysinfo(void)
{
    char msg[128];

    memset(msg, 0, strlen(msg));
    snprintf(msg, 47, "%s(): minimal Platform Info:\nCPU: ",
__func__);

    /* Strictly speaking, all this #if... is considered ugly and should be
```

[219]

Writing Your First Kernel Module - LKMs Part 2

```c
         * isolated as far as is possible */
#ifdef CONFIG_X86
#if(BITS_PER_LONG == 32)
    strncat(msg, "x86-32, ", 9);
#else
    strncat(msg, "x86_64, ", 9);
#endif
#endif
#ifdef CONFIG_ARM
    strncat(msg, "ARM-32, ", 9);
#endif
#ifdef CONFIG_ARM64
    strncat(msg, "Aarch64, ", 10);
#endif
#ifdef CONFIG_MIPS
    strncat(msg, "MIPS, ", 7);
#endif
#ifdef CONFIG_PPC
    strncat(msg, "PowerPC, ", 10);
#endif
#ifdef CONFIG_S390
    strncat(msg, "IBM S390, ", 11);
#endif

#ifdef __BIG_ENDIAN
    strncat(msg, "big-endian; ", 13);
#else
    strncat(msg, "little-endian; ", 16);
#endif

#if(BITS_PER_LONG == 32)
    strncat(msg, "32-bit OS.\n", 12);
#elif(BITS_PER_LONG == 64)
    strncat(msg, "64-bit OS.\n", 12);
#endif
    pr_info("%s", msg);

  show_sizeof();
 /* Word ranges: min & max: defines are in include/linux/limits.h */
  [ ... ]
}
EXPORT_SYMBOL(lkdc_sysinfo);
```

(Additional details that this LKM shows you - like the size of various primitive data types plus word ranges - is not shown here; please do refer to the source code from our GitHub repository and try it out for yourself.) The preceding kernel module code is instructive as it helps demonstrate how you can write portable code. Remember, the kernel module itself is a binary non-portable object file, but its source code could (perhaps, should, depending on your project) be written in such a manner so that it's portable across various architectures. A simple build on (or for) the target architecture would then have it ready for deployment.

> For now, please ignore the EXPORT_SYMBOL() macro used here. We will cover its usage shortly.

Building and running it on our now familiar x86_64 Ubuntu 18.04 LTS guest, we get this output:

```
$ cd ch5/min_sysinfo
$ make
[...]
$ sudo insmod ./min_sysinfo.ko
$ dmesg
[...]
[29626.257341] min_sysinfo: inserted
[29626.257352] llkd_sysinfo(): minimal Platform Info:
               CPU: x86_64, little-endian; 64-bit OS.
$
```

Great! Similarly (as demonstrated earlier), we can *cross-compile* this kernel module for ARM-32 (Raspberry Pi), then transfer (scp(1)) the cross-compiled kernel module to our Raspberry Pi target and run it there (the following output is from a Raspberry Pi 3B+ running the 32-bit Raspbian OS):

```
$ sudo insmod ./min_sysinfo.ko
$ dmesg
[...]
[   80.428363] min_sysinfo: inserted
[   80.428370] llkd_sysinfo(): minimal Platform Info:
               CPU: ARM-32, little-endian; 32-bit OS.
$
```

This, in fact, reveals something interesting; the Raspberry Pi 3B+ has a native *64-bit CPU*, but by default (as of the time of writing) runs a 32-bit OS, hence the preceding output. We will leave it to you to install a 64-bit Linux OS on a Raspberry Pi (or other) device and re-run this kernel module.

[221]

> The powerful *Yocto Project* (https://www.yoctoproject.org/) is one (industry-standard) way to generate a 64-bit OS for the Raspberry Pi. Alternatively (and much easier to quickly try), Ubuntu provides a custom Ubuntu 64-bit kernel and root filesystem for the device (https://wiki.ubuntu.com/ARM/RaspberryPi).

Being a bit more security-aware

Security, of course, is a key concern these days. Professional developers are expected to write secure code. In recent years, there have been many known exploits against the Linux kernel (see the *Further reading* section for more on this). In parallel, many efforts toward improving Linux kernel security are in place.

In our preceding kernel module (`ch5/min_sysinfo/min_sysinfo.c`), be wary of using older-style routines (like the `sprintf`, `strlen`, and so on; yes, they're present within the kernel)! *Static analyzers* can greatly aid in catching potential security-related and other bugs; we highly recommend you use them. `Chapter 1`, *Kernel Workspace Setup*, mentions several useful static analysis tools for the kernel. In the following code, we use one of the `sa` targets within our our "better" Makefile to run a relatively simple static analyzer: `flawfinder(1)` (written by David Wheeler):

```
$ make [tab][tab]
all          clean       help         install      sa_cppcheck    sa_gcc
tarxz-pkg    checkpatch  code-style   indent       sa
sa_flawfinder sa_sparse
$ make sa_flawfinder
make clean
make[1]: Entering directory '/home/llkd/llkd_book/Linux-Kernel-
Programming/ch5/min_sysinfo'

--- cleaning ---

[...]

--- static analysis with flawfinder ---

flawfinder *.c
Flawfinder version 1.31, (C) 2001-2014 David A. Wheeler.
Number of rules (primarily dangerous function names) in C/C++ ruleset:
169
Examining min_sysinfo.c

FINAL RESULTS:
```

```
min_sysinfo.c:60:  [2] (buffer) char:
  Statically-sized arrays can be improperly restricted, leading to
potential overflows or other issues (CWE-119:CWE-120). Perform bounds
checking, use functions that limit length, or ensure that the size is
larger than the maximum possible length.

[...]

min_sysinfo.c:138:  [1] (buffer) strlen:
  Does not handle strings that are not \0-terminated; if given one it
may
  perform an over-read (it could cause a crash if unprotected)
(CWE-126).
[...]
```

Look carefully at the warning emitted by `flawfinder(1)` regarding the `strlen()` function (among the many it generates!). It is indeed the case we face here! Remember, uninitialized local variables (such as our `msg` buffer) have *random content* when declared. Thus, the `strlen()` function may or may not yield the value we expect.

> **TIP**
> The output of `flawfinder` even mentions the **CWE** number (here, CWE-126) of the *generalized class* of security issue that is being seen here; (do google it and you will see the details. In this instance, CWE-126 represents the buffer over-read issue: https://cwe.mitre.org/data/definitions/126.html).

Similarly, we avoid the use of `strncat()` and replace it with the `strlcat()` function. So, taking security concerns into account, we rewrite the code of the `llkd_sysinfo()` function as `llkd_sysinfo2()`.

We also add a few lines of code to show the *range* (min, max) of both unsigned and signed variables on the platform (in both base 10 and 16). We leave it to you to read through. As a simple assignment, run this kernel module on your Linux box(es) and verify the output.

Now, let's move on to discuss a little bit regarding the licensing of the Linux kernel and kernel module code.

Licensing kernel modules

As is well known, the Linux kernel code base itself is licensed under the GNU GPL v2 (aka GPL-2.0; **GPL** stands for **General Public License**), and as far as most people are concerned, will remain that way. As briefly mentioned before, in `Chapter 4`, *Writing Your First Kernel Module – LKMs Part 1*, licensing your kernel code is required and important. Essentially, what the discussion, at least for our purposes, boils down to is this: if your intention is to directly use kernel code and/or contribute your code upstream into the mainline kernel (a few notes on this follow), you *must* release the code under the same license that the Linux kernel is released under: the GNU GPL-2.0. For a kernel module, the situation is still a bit "fluid," shall we say. No matter, to engage the kernel community and have them help (a huge plus), you should, or are expected to, release the code under the GNU GPL-2.0 license (though dual-licensing is certainly possible and acceptable).

The license(s) is specified using the `MODULE_LICENSE()` macro. The following comment reproduced from the `include/linux/module.h` kernel header clearly shows what license "idents" are acceptable (notice the dual-licensing). Obviously, the kernel community would highly recommend releasing your kernel module under the GPL-2.0 (GPL v2) and/or another, such as BSD/MIT/MPL. If you are intending to contribute code upstream to the kernel mainline, it goes without saying that the GPL-2.0 alone *is* the license to release under:

```
// include/linux/module.h
[...]
/*
 * The following license idents are currently accepted as indicating free
 * software modules
 *
 *  "GPL"                           [GNU Public License v2 or later]
 *  "GPL v2"                        [GNU Public License v2]
 *  "GPL and additional rights"     [GNU Public License v2 rights and more]
 *  "Dual BSD/GPL"                  [GNU Public License v2
 *                                   or BSD license choice]
 *  "Dual MIT/GPL"                  [GNU Public License v2
 *                                   or MIT license choice]
 *  "Dual MPL/GPL"                  [GNU Public License v2
 *                                   or Mozilla license choice]
 *
 * The following other idents are available
 *
 *  "Proprietary"  [Non free products]
 *
```

```
 * There are dual licensed components, but when running with Linux it
is the GPL that is relevant so this is a non issue. Similarly LGPL
linked with GPL is a GPL combined work.
 *
 * This exists for several reasons
 * 1. So modinfo can show license info for users wanting to vet their
setup is free
 * 2. So the community can ignore bug reports including proprietary
modules
 * 3. So vendors can do likewise based on their own policies
 */
#define MODULE_LICENSE(_license) MODULE_INFO(license, _license)
[...]
```

FYI, the kernel source tree has a LICENSES/ directory under which you will find detailed information on licenses; a quick ls on this folder reveals the sub-folders therein:

$ ls <...>/linux-5.4/LICENSES/
deprecated/ dual/ exceptions/ preferred/

We'll leave it to you to take a look, and with this, will leave the discussion on licensing at that; the reality is that it's a complex topic requiring legal knowledge. You would be well advised to consult specialist legal staff (lawyers) within your company (or hire them) with regard to getting the legal angle right for your product or service.

While on the topic, in order to be consistent, recent kernels have a rule: every single source file's first line must be an SPDX license identifier (see https://spdx.org/ for details). Of course, scripts will require the first line to specify the interpreter. Also, some answers to FAQs on the GPL license are addressed here: https://www.gnu.org/licenses/gpl-faq.html.

More on licensing models, not abusing the MODULE_LICENSE macro, and particularly the multi-licensing/dual-licensing one, can be found at the link provided in the *Further reading* section of this chapter. Now, let's get back to the technical stuff. The next section explains how you can effectively emulate a library-like feature in kernel space.

Emulating "library-like" features for kernel modules

One of the major differences between user-mode and kernel-mode programming is the complete absence of the familiar "library" concept in the latter. Libraries are essentially a collection or archive of APIs, conveniently allowing developers to meet the important goals, typically: *do not reinvent the wheel, software reuse, modularity,* and the like. But within the Linux kernel, libraries just do not exist.

The good news, though, is that broadly speaking, there are two techniques by which you can achieve a "library-like" functionality in kernel space for our kernel modules:

- The first technique: explicitly "link in" multiple source files – including the "library" code – to your kernel module object.
- The second is called module stacking.

Do read on as we discuss these techniques in more detail. A spoiler, perhaps, but useful to know right away: the first of the preceding techniques is often superior to the second. Then again, it does depend on the project. Do read the details in the next section; we list out some pros and cons as we go along.

Performing library emulation via multiple source files

So far, we have dealt with very simple kernel modules that have had exactly one C source file. What about the (quite typical) real-world situation where there is *more than one C source file for a single kernel module*? All source files will have to be compiled and then linked together as a single .ko binary object.

For example, say we're building a kernel module project called projx. It consists of three C source files: prj1.c, prj2.c, and prj3.c. We want the final kernel module to be called projx.ko. The Makefile is where you specify these relationships, as shown:

```
obj-m      := projx.o
projx-objs := prj1.o prj2.o prj3.o
```

In the preceding code, note how the `projx` label has been used after the `obj-m` directive *and* as the prefix for the
`-objs` directive on the next line. Of course, you can use any label. Our preceding example will have the kernel build system compile the three individual C source files into individual object (`.o`) files, and will then *link them all together to form the final binary kernel module object file*, `projx.ko`, just as we desire.

We can leverage this mechanism in building a small "library" of routines within our book's source tree (the source files for this 'kernel library' are in the root of the source tree here: `klib_llkd.h` and `klib_llkd.c`). The idea is that other kernel modules can use the functions within here by linking into them! For example, in the upcoming `Chapter 7`, *Memory Management Internals - Essentials*, we have our `ch7/lowlevel_mem/lowlevel_mem.c` kernel module code invoke a function that resides in our library code, `../../klib_llkd.c`. The "linking into" our so-called "library" code is achieved by putting the following into the `lowlevel_mem` kernel module's Makefile:

```
obj-m                    += lowlevel_mem_lib.o
lowlevel_mem_lib-objs    := lowlevel_mem.o ../../klib_llkd.o
```

The second line specifies the source files to build (into object files); they are the code of the `lowlevel_mem.c` kernel module and the `../../klib_llkd` library code. Then, it *links* both into a single binary kernel module, `lowlevel_mem_lib.ko`, achieving our objective. (Why not work on the assignment 5.1 specified in the *Questions* section at the end of this chapter.)

Understanding function and variable scope in a kernel module

Before delving further, a quick re-look at some basics is a good idea. When programming with C, you should understand the following:

- Variables declared locally within a function are obviously local to it and only have scope within that function.
- Variables and functions prefixed with the `static` qualifier have scope only within the current "unit"; effectively, the file they have been declared within. This is good as it helps reduce namespace pollution. Static (and global) data variables retain their value within that function.

Prior to 2.6 Linux (that is, <= 2.4.x, ancient history now), kernel module static and global variables, as well as all functions, were automatically visible throughout the kernel. This was, in retrospect, obviously not a great idea. The decision was reversed from 2.5 (and thus 2.6 onward, modern Linux): **all kernel module variables (static and global data) and functions are by default scoped to be private to their kernel module only, and are thus invisible outside it**. So, if two kernel modules, `lkmA` and `lkmB` have a global named `maya`, it's unique to each of them; there is no clash.

To change the scope, the LKM framework provides the `EXPORT_SYMBOL()` macro. Using it, you can declare a data item or function to be *global* in scope – in effect, visible to all other kernel modules as well as to the kernel core.

Let's take a simple example. We have a kernel module called `prj_core` that contains a global and a function:

```
static int my_glob = 5;
static long my_foo(int key)
{ [...] 
}
```

Though both are usable within this kernel module itself, neither can be seen outside it. This is intentional. To make them visible outside this kernel module, we can *export* them:

```
int my_glob = 5;
EXPORT_SYMBOL(my_glob);

long my_foo(int key)
{ [...] 
}
EXPORT_SYMBOL(my_foo);
```

Now, both have scope outside this kernel module (notice how, in the preceding code block, the `static` keyword has been deliberately removed). *Other kernel modules (as well as the core kernel) can now "see" and use them*. Precisely, this idea is leveraged in two broad ways:

- First, the kernel exports a well-thought-out subset of global variables and functions that form a part of its core functionality, as well as that of other subsystems. Now, these globals and functions are visible and thus usable from kernel modules! We will see some sample uses shortly.

- Second, kernel module authors (often device drivers) use this very notion to export certain data and/or functionality so that other kernel modules, at a higher abstraction level, perhaps, can leverage this design and use this data and/or functionality – this concept is called *module stacking* and we will delve into it shortly with an example.

With the first use case, for example, a device driver author might want to handle a hardware interrupt from a peripheral device. A common way to do so is via the `request_irq()` API, which, in fact, is nothing but a thin (inline) wrapper over this API:

```
// kernel/irq/manage.c
int request_threaded_irq(unsigned int irq, irq_handler_t handler,
                 irq_handler_t thread_fn, unsigned long irqflags,
                         const char *devname, void *dev_id)
{
    struct irqaction *action;
[...]
    return retval;
}
EXPORT_SYMBOL(request_threaded_irq);
```

Precisely because the `request_threaded_irq()` function is *exported*, it can be called from within a device driver, which is very often written as a kernel module. Similarly, developers often require some "convenience" routines – for example, string processing ones. The Linux kernel, in `lib/string.c`, provides an implementation of several common string processing functions (that you expect to be present): `str[n]casecmp, str[n|l|s]cpy, str[n|l]cat, str[n]cmp, strchr[null], str[n|r]chr, str[n]len`, and so on. Of course, these are all *exported* via the `EXPORT_SYMBOL()` macro so as to make them visible and thus available to module authors.

> Here, we used the `str[n|l|s]cpy` notation to imply that the kernel provides the four functions: `strcpy, strncpy, strlcpy,` and `strscpy`. Note that some interfaces may be deprecated (`strcpy(), strncpy(),` and `strlcpy()`). In general, always avoid using deprecated stuff documented here: *Deprecated Interfaces, Language Features, Attributes, and Conventions* (https://www.kernel.org/doc/html/latest/process/deprecated.html#deprecated-interfaces-language-features-attributes-and-conventions).

On the other hand, let's glance at a (tiny) bit of the core **CFS (Completely Fair Scheduler**) scheduling code deep within the kernel core. Here, the `pick_next_task_fair()` function is the one invoked by the scheduling code when we need to find another task to context-switch to:

```
// kernel/sched/fair.c
static struct task_struct *
pick_next_task_fair(struct rq *rq, struct task_struct *prev, struct rq_flags *rf)
{
        struct cfs_rq *cfs_rq = &rq->cfs;
[...]
        if (new_tasks > 0)
                goto again;
        return NULL;
}
```

We don't really want to study scheduling here (Chapter 10, *The CPU Scheduler - Part 1*, and Chapter 11, *The CPU Scheduler - Part 2*, take care of it), the point here is this: as the preceding function is *not* marked with the `EXPORT_SYMBOL()` macro, it cannot ever be invoked by a kernel module. It remains *private* to the core kernel.

You can also mark data structures as exported with the same macro. Also, it should be obvious that only globally scoped data – not local variables – can be marked as exported.

> If you want to see how the `EXPORT_SYMBOL()` macro works, please refer to the *Further reading* section of this chapter, which links to the book's GitHub repository.

Recall our brief discussion on the licensing of kernel modules. The Linux kernel has a, shall we say, interesting, proposition: there is also a macro called `EXPORT_SYMBOL_GPL()`. It's just like its cousin, the `EXPORT_SYMBOL()` macro, except that, yes, the data item or function exported will only be visible to those kernel modules that include the word `GPL` within their `MODULE_LICENSE()` macro! Ah, the sweet revenge of the kernel community. It is indeed used in several places in the kernel code base. (I'll leave this as an exercise to you to find occurrences of this macro in the code; on the 5.4.0 kernel, a quick search with `cscope(1)` revealed "just" 14,000 odd usage instances!)

> **TIP:** To view all exported symbols, navigate to the root of your kernel source tree and issue the `make export_report` command. Note though that this works only upon a kernel tree that has been configured and built.

Let's now look at another key approach to realizing a library-like kernel feature: module stacking.

Understanding module stacking

The second important idea here – *module stacking* – is what we will now delve further into.

Module stacking is a concept that provides a "library-like" feature to kernel module authors, to a degree. Here, we typically architect our project or product design in such a manner that we have one or more "core" kernel modules, whose job is to act as a library of sorts. It will include the data structures and functionality (functions/APIs) that will be *exported* to other kernel modules (the preceding section discussed the exporting of symbols).

To better understand this, let's look at a couple of real examples. To begin with, on my host system, an Ubuntu 18.04.3 LTS native Linux system, I ran a guest VM(s) over the *Oracle VirtualBox 6.1* hypervisor application. Okay, performing a quick `lsmod(8)` on the host system while filtering for the string `vbox` reveals the following:

```
$ lsmod | grep vbox
vboxnetadp             28672  0
vboxnetflt             28672  1
vboxdrv               479232  3 vboxnetadp,vboxnetflt
$
```

Recall from our earlier discussion that the third column is the *usage count*. It's 0 in the first row but has a value of 3 in the third row. Not only that, but also the `vboxdrv` kernel module has two kernel modules listed to its right (after the usage count column). If any kernel modules show up after the third column, they represent **dependencies**; read it this way: the kernel modules displayed on the right *depend on* the kernel module on the left.

Writing Your First Kernel Module - LKMs Part 2

So, in the preceding example, the `vboxnetadp` and `vboxnetflt` kernel modules depend on the `vboxdrv` kernel module. *Depend on it* in what way? They use data structures and/or functions (APIs) within the `vboxdrv` core kernel module, of course! In general, kernel modules showing up on the right of the third column imply they are using one or more data structures and/or functions of the kernel module on the left (leading to an increment in the usage count; this usage count is a good example of a *reference counter* (here, it's actually a 32-bit atomic variable), something we delve into in the last chapter). In effect, the `vboxdrv` kernel module is akin to a "library" (in a limited sense, with none of the usual userspace connotations associated with user-mode libraries except that it provides modular functionality). You can see that, in this snapshot, its usage count is 3 and the kernel modules that depend on it are stacked on top of it – literally! (You can see them in the preceding two lines of `lsmod(1)` output.) Also, notice that the `vboxnetflt` kernel module has a positive usage count (1) but no kernel modules show up on its right; this still implies that something is using it at the moment, typically a process or thread.

> **TIP** FYI, the **Oracle VirtualBox** kernel modules we see in this example are actually the implementation of the **VirtualBox Guest Additions**. They are essentially a para-virtualization construct, helping to accelerate the working of the guest VM. Oracle VirtualBox provides similar functionality for Windows and macOS hosts as well (as do all the major virtualization vendors).

Another example of module stacking, as promised: running the powerful **LTTng** (**Linux Tracing Toolkit next generation**) framework enables you to perform detailed system profiling. The LTTng project installs and uses a fairly large number of kernel modules (typically 40 or more). Several of these kernel modules are "stacked," allowing the project to leverage precisely the "library-like" feature we have been discussing here.

In the following figure (having installed LTTng on a Ubuntu 18.04.4 LTS system), see a partial screenshot of the `lsmod | grep --color=auto "^lttng"` output pertaining to its kernel modules:

```
lttng_probe_irq              16384  0
lttng_probe_gpio             16384  0
lttng_probe_compaction       16384  0
lttng_probe_block            36864  0
lttng_probe_asoc             24576  0
lttng_ring_buffer_metadata_mmap_client    16384  0
lttng_ring_buffer_client_mmap_overwrite   20480  0
lttng_ring_buffer_client_mmap_discard     20480  0
lttng_ring_buffer_metadata_client         16384  0
lttng_ring_buffer_client_overwrite        20480  0
lttng_ring_buffer_client_discard          20480  0
lttng_tracer       1523712  35 lttng_probe_udp,lttng_probe_scsi,lttng_probe_sched,lttng_probe_compaction,lt
tng_probe_net,lttng_probe_vmscan,lttng_probe_writeback,lttng_probe_power,lttng_probe_rcu,lttng_probe_module,l
ttng_ring_buffer_client_mmap_overwrite,lttng_probe_statedump,lttng_ring_buffer_client_discard,lttng_probe_pri
ntk,lttng_probe_sock,lttng_probe_asoc,lttng_probe_irq,lttng_ring_buffer_client_mmap_discard,lttng_probe_kvm,l
ttng_probe_random,lttng_probe_timer,lttng_probe_workqueue,lttng_probe_jbd2,lttng_probe_v4l2,lttng_probe_signa
l,lttng_probe_skb,lttng_probe_block,lttng_probe_napi,lttng_ring_buffer_metadata_client,lttng_probe_kmem,lttng
_ring_buffer_metadata_mmap_client,lttng_probe_gpio,lttng_ring_buffer_client_overwrite,lttng_probe_regulator,l
ttng_probe_sunrpc
lttng_statedump    737280   1 lttng_tracer
lttng_kprobes      16384    1 lttng_tracer
lttng_clock        16384    5 lttng_ring_buffer_client_mmap_overwrite,lttng_ring_buffer_client_discard,lttn
g_tracer,lttng_ring_buffer_client_mmap_discard,lttng_ring_buffer_client_overwrite
lttng_lib_ring_buffer   57344  23 lttng_probe_scsi,lttng_probe_sched,lttng_probe_net,lttng_probe_power,lttng
_probe_rcu,lttng_probe_module,lttng_ring_buffer_client_mmap_overwrite,lttng_probe_statedump,lttng_ring_buffer
_client_discard,lttng_probe_printk,lttng_probe_sock,lttng_tracer,lttng_probe_asoc,lttng_probe_irq,lttng_ring_
buffer_client_mmap_discard,lttng_probe_kvm,lttng_probe_random,lttng_probe_napi,lttng_ring_buffer_metadata_cli
ent,lttng_ring_buffer_metadata_mmap_client,lttng_ring_buffer_client_overwrite,lttng_probe_regulator,lttng_pro
be_sunrpc
lttng_kretprobes   16384    1 lttng_tracer
~ $
```

Figure 5.3 – Heavy module stacking within the LTTng product

As can be seen, the `lttng_tracer` kernel module has 35 kernel modules on its right side, indicating that they are "stacked" upon it, using functionality that it provides (similarly, the `lttng_lib_ring_buffer` kernel module has 23 kernel modules that "depend" on it).

Here's some quick scripting magic to see all kernel modules whose usage count is non-zero (they often – but not always – have some dependent kernel modules show up on their right):

```
lsmod | awk '$3 > 0 {print $0}'
```

An implication of module stacking: you can only successfully `rmmod(8)` a kernel module if its usage count is 0; that is, it is not in use. Thus, for the preceding first example, we can only remove the `vboxdrv` kernel module after removing the two dependent kernel modules that are stacked on it (thus getting the usage count down to 0).

Trying out module stacking

Let's architect a very simple proof-of-concept code for module stacking. To do so, we will build two kernel modules:

- The first we will call `core_lkm`; its job is to act as a "library" of sorts, making available to the kernel and other modules a couple of functions (APIs).
- Our second kernel module, `user_lkm`, is the 'user' (or consumer) of the 'library'; it will simply invoke the functions (and use some data) residing within the first.

To do so, our pair of kernel modules will need to do the following:

- The core kernel module must use the `EXPORT_SYMBOL()` macro to mark some data and functions as being *exported*.
- The user kernel module must declare the data and/or functions that it expects to use as being external to it, via the C `extern` keyword (remember, exporting data or functionality merely sets up the appropriate linkage; the compiler still needs to know about the data and/or functions being invoked).
- With recent toolchains, marking the exported function(s) and data items as `static` is allowed. A warning results, though; we don't use the `static` keyword for exported symbols.
- Edit the custom Makefile to build both kernel modules.

The code follows; first, the core or library kernel module. To (hopefully) make this more interesting, we will copy the code of one of our previous module's functions – `ch5/min_sysinfo/min_sysinfo.c:llkd_sysinfo2()` – into this kernel module and *export* it, thus making it visible to our second "user" LKM, which will invoke that function:

> Here, we do not show the full code; you can refer to the book's GitHub repo for it.

```
// ch5/modstacking/core_lkm.c
#define pr_fmt(fmt) "%s:%s(): " fmt, KBUILD_MODNAME, __func__
#include <linux/init.h>
#include <linux/module.h>

#define MODNAME     "core_lkm"
```

```
#define THE_ONE     0xfedface
MODULE_LICENSE("Dual MIT/GPL");

int exp_int = 200;
EXPORT_SYMBOL_GPL(exp_int);

/* Functions to be called from other LKMs */
void llkd_sysinfo2(void)
{
[...]
}
EXPORT_SYMBOL(llkd_sysinfo2);

#if(BITS_PER_LONG == 32)
u32 get_skey(int p)
#else // 64-bit
u64 get_skey(int p)
#endif
{
#if(BITS_PER_LONG == 32)
    u32 secret = 0x567def;
#else // 64-bit
    u64 secret = 0x123abc567def;
#endif
    if (p == THE_ONE)
        return secret;
    return 0;
}
EXPORT_SYMBOL(get_skey);
[...]
```

Next is the `user_lkm` kernel module, the one "stacked" on top of the `core_lkm` kernel module:

```
// ch5/modstacking/user_lkm.c
#define pr_fmt(fmt) "%s:%s(): " fmt, KBUILD_MODNAME, __func__
#define MODNAME "user_lkm"

#if 1
MODULE_LICENSE("Dual MIT/GPL");
#else
MODULE_LICENSE("MIT");
#endif

extern void llkd_sysinfo2(void);
extern long get_skey(int);
extern int exp_int;
```

```c
/* Call some functions within the 'core' module */
static int __init user_lkm_init(void)
{
#define THE_ONE 0xfedface
    pr_info("%s: inserted\n", MODNAME);
    u64 sk = get_skey(THE_ONE);
    pr_debug("%s: Called get_skey(), ret = 0x%llx = %llu\n",
            MODNAME, sk, sk);
    pr_debug("%s: exp_int = %d\n", MODNAME, exp_int);
    llkd_sysinfo2();
    return 0;
}

static void __exit user_lkm_exit(void)
{
    pr_info("%s: bids you adieu\n", MODNAME);
}
module_init(user_lkm_init);
module_exit(user_lkm_exit);
```

The Makefile remains largely identical to our earlier kernel modules, except that this time we need two kernel module objects to be built, as follows:

```
obj-m       := core_lkm.o
obj-m       += user_lkm.o
```

Okay, let's try it out:

1. First, build the kernel modules:

    ```
    $ make

    --- Building : KDIR=/lib/modules/5.4.0-llkd02-kasan/build
    ARCH= CROSS_COMPILE= EXTRA_CFLAGS=-DDEBUG ---

    make -C /lib/modules/5.4.0-llkd02-kasan/build
    M=/home/llkd/booksrc/ch5/modstacking modules
    make[1]: Entering directory '/home/llkd/kernels/linux-5.4'
      CC [M]  /home/llkd/booksrc/ch5/modstacking/core_lkm.o
      CC [M]  /home/llkd/booksrc/ch5/modstacking/user_lkm.o
      [...]
      Building modules, stage 2.
      MODPOST 2 modules
      CC [M]  /home/llkd/booksrc/ch5/modstacking/core_lkm.mod.o
      LD [M]  /home/llkd/booksrc/ch5/modstacking/core_lkm.ko
      CC [M]  /home/llkd/booksrc/ch5/modstacking/user_lkm.mod.o
      LD [M]  /home/llkd/booksrc/ch5/modstacking/user_lkm.ko
    make[1]: Leaving directory '/home/llkd/kernels/linux-5.4'
    ```

```
$ ls *.ko
core_lkm.ko  user_lkm.ko
$
```

> Note that we're building our kernel modules against our custom 5.4.0 kernel. Do notice its full version is 5.4.0-llkd02-kasan; this is deliberate. This is the "debug kernel" that I have built and am using as a test-bed!

2. Now, let's perform a quick series of tests to demonstrate the *module stacking* proof of concept. Let's first do it *wrongly*: we will first attempt to insert the user_lkm kernel module before inserting the core_lkm module.

   This will fail – why? You will realize that the exported functionality (and data) that the user_lkm kernel module depends on is not (yet) available within the kernel. More technically, the symbols will not be located within the kernel's symbol table as the core_lkm kernel module that has them hasn't been inserted yet:

   ```
   $ sudo dmesg -C
   $ sudo insmod ./user_lkm.ko
   insmod: ERROR: could not insert module ./user_lkm.ko: Unknown symbol in module
   $ dmesg
   [13204.476455] user_lkm: Unknown symbol exp_int (err -2)
   [13204.476493] user_lkm: Unknown symbol get_skey (err -2)
   [13204.476531] user_lkm: Unknown symbol llkd_sysinfo2 (err -2)
   $
   ```

   As expected, as the required (to-be-exported) symbols are unavailable, insmod(8) fails (the precise error message you see in the kernel log may vary slightly depending on the kernel version and debug config options set).

3. Now, let's do it right:

   ```
   $ sudo insmod ./core_lkm.ko
   $ dmesg
   [...]
   [19221.183494] core_lkm: inserted
   $ sudo insmod ./user_lkm.ko
   $ dmesg
   [...]
   [19221.183494] core_lkm:core_lkm_init(): inserted
   [19242.669208] core_lkm:core_lkm_init():
   /home/llkd/book_llkd/Linux-Kernel-
   ```

```
Programming/ch5/modstacking/core_lkm.c:get_skey():100: I've
been called
[19242.669212] user_lkm:user_lkm_init(): inserted
[19242.669217] user_lkm:user_lkm:user_lkm_init(): Called
get_skey(), ret = 0x123abc567def = 20043477188079
[19242.669219] user_lkm:user_lkm_init(): exp_int = 200
[19242.669223] core_lkm:llkd_sysinfo2(): minimal Platform
Info:
             CPU: x86_64, little-endian; 64-bit OS.
$
```

4. It works as expected! Check out the modules listing with `lsmod(8)`:

```
$ lsmod | egrep "core_lkm|user_lkm"
user_lkm                20480  0
core_lkm                16384  1 user_lkm
$
```

Notice how, for the `core_lkm` kernel module, the usage count column has incremented to 1 *and* we can now see that the `user_lkm` kernel module depends on the `core_lkm` one. Recall that the kernel module(s) displayed in the extreme-right columns of `lsmod`'s output depend on the one in the extreme-left column.

5. Now, let's remove the kernel modules. Removing the kernel modules has an *ordering dependency* as well (just as with insertion). Attempting to remove the `core_lkm` one first fails, as obviously, there is another module still in kernel memory relying upon its code/data; in other words, it's still in use:

```
$ sudo rmmod core_lkm
rmmod: ERROR: Module core_lkm is in use by: user_lkm
$
```

> **TIP**: Note that if the modules are *installed* onto the system, then you could use the `modprobe -r <modules...>` command to remove all related modules; we cover this topic in the *Auto-loading modules on system boot* section.

6. The preceding `rmmod(8)` failure message is self-explanatory. So, let's do it right:

```
$ sudo rmmod user_lkm core_lkm
$ dmesg
[...]
 CPU: x86_64, little-endian; 64-bit OS.
```

[238]

```
[19489.717265] user_lkm:user_lkm_exit(): bids you adieu
[19489.732018] core_lkm:core_lkm_exit(): bids you adieu
$
```

There, done!

You will notice that in the code of the `user_lkm` kernel module, the license we release it under is in a conditional `#if` statement:

```
#if 1
MODULE_LICENSE("Dual MIT/GPL");
#else
MODULE_LICENSE("MIT");
#endif
```

We can see that it's released (by default) under the *Dual MIT/GPL* license; well, so what? Think about it: in the code of the `core_lkm` kernel module, we have the following:

```
int exp_int = 200;
EXPORT_SYMBOL_GPL(exp_int);
```

The `exp_int` integer is *only visible to those kernel modules that run under a GPL license*. So, try this out: change the `#if 1` statement in `core_lkm` to `#if 0`, thus now releasing it under an MIT-only license. Now, rebuild and retry. It *fails* at the build stage itself:

```
$ make
[...]
Building for: kver=5.4.0-llkd01 ARCH=x86 CROSS_COMPILE= EXTRA_CFLAGS=-DDEBUG
  Building modules, stage 2.
  MODPOST 2 modules
FATAL: modpost: GPL-incompatible module user_lkm.ko uses GPL-only symbol 'exp_int'
[...]
$
```

The license does matter! Before we wind up this section, here's a quick list of things that can go wrong with module stacking; that is, things to check:

- The wrong order of kernel modules specified at insertion/at removal
- Attempting to insert an exported routine that is already in kernel memory – a namespace collision issue:

    ```
    $ sudo insmod ./min_sysinfo.ko
    [...]
    ```

Writing Your First Kernel Module - LKMs Part 2

```
$ cd ../modstacking ; sudo insmod ./core_lkm.ko
insmod: ERROR: could not insert module ./core_lkm.ko: Invalid
module format
$ dmesg
[...]
[32077.823472] core_lkm: exports duplicate symbol
llkd_sysinfo2 (owned by min_sysinfo)
$ sudo rmmod min_sysinfo
$ sudo insmod ./core_lkm.ko     # now it's ok
```

- License issues caused by the usage of the `EXPORT_SYMBOL_GPL()` macro

> **TIP**
> Always look up the kernel log (with `dmesg(1)` or `journalctl(1)`). It often helps to show what actually went awry.

So, let's summarize: for emulating a library-like feature within the kernel module space, we explored two techniques:

- The first technique we used works by *linking multiple source files together into a single kernel module*.
- This is as opposed to the *module stacking* technique, where we actually build multiple kernel modules and "stack" them on top of each other.

Not only does the first technique work well, it also has these advantages:

- We do *not* have to explicitly mark (via `EXPORT_SYMBOL()`) every data/function symbol that we use as exported.
- The functions are only available to the kernel module to which it is actually linked to (and not the *entire kernel, including other modules*). This is a good thing! All this at the cost of slightly tweaking the Makefile – well worth it.

A downside to the "linking" approach: when linking multiple files, the size of the kernel module can grow to be large.

This concludes your learning a powerful feature of kernel programming – the ability to link multiple source files together to form one kernel module, and/or leveraging the module stacking design, both allowing you to develop more sophisticated kernel projects.

In the following section, we dive into the details of how you can pass parameters to a kernel module.

Passing parameters to a kernel module

A common debugging technique is to *instrument* your code; that is, insert prints at appropriate points such that you can follow the path the code takes. Within a kernel module, of course, we would use the versatile `printk` function for this purpose. So, let's say we do something like the following (pseudo-code):

```
#define pr_fmt(fmt) "%s:%s():%d: " fmt, KBUILD_MODNAME, __func__, \
__LINE__
[ ... ]
func_x() {
    pr_debug("At 1\n");
    [...]
    while (<cond>) {
        pr_debug("At 2: j=0x%x\n", j);
        [...]
    }
    [...]
}
```

Okay, great. But we don't want the debug prints to appear in a production (or release) version. That's precisely why we're using the `pr_debug()` : it emits a printk only when the symbol `DEBUG` is defined! Indeed, but what if, interestingly, our customer is an engineering customer and wants to *dynamically turn on or turn off these debug prints*? There are several approaches you might take; one is as in the following pseudo-code:

```
static int debug_level;     /* will be init to zero */
func_x() {
    if (debug_level >= 1)
        pr_debug("At 1\n");
    [...]
    while (<cond>) {
        if (debug_level >= 2)
            pr_debug("At 2: j=0x%x\n", j);
        [...]
    }
    [...]
}
```

Ah, that's nice. So, what we're getting at really is this: *what if we can make the* `debug_level` *module variable a parameter to our kernel module?* Then, a powerful thing, the user of your kernel module has control over which debug messages appear or not.

Declaring and using module parameters

Module parameters are passed to a kernel module as *name=value* pairs at module insertion (`insmod`) time. For example, assume we have a *module parameter* named `mp_debug_level`; then, we could pass its value at `insmod(8)` time, like this:

```
sudo insmod modparams1.ko mp_debug_level=2
```

> Here, the `mp` prefix stands for module parameter. It's not required to name it that way, of course, it is pedantic, but might just makes it a bit more intuitive.

That would be powerful. Now, the end user can decide at exactly what *verbosity* they want the *debug-level* messages. We can even easily arrange for the default value to be 0.

You might wonder: kernel modules have no `main()` function and hence no conventional (`argc, argv`) parameter list, so how exactly, then, do you pass parameters along? The fact is, it's a bit of linker trickery; just do this: declare your intended module parameter as a global (`static`) variable, then specify to the build system that it's to be treated as a module parameter by employing the `module_param()` macro.

This is easy to see with our first module parameter's demo kernel module (as usual, the full source code and Makefile can be found in the book's GitHub repo):

```
// ch5/modparams/modparams1/modparams1.c
[ ... ]
/* Module parameters */
static int mp_debug_level;
module_param(mp_debug_level, int, 0660);
MODULE_PARM_DESC(mp_debug_level,
"Debug level [0-2]; 0 => no debug messages, 2 => high verbosity");

static char *mp_strparam = "My string param";
module_param(mp_strparam, charp, 0660);
MODULE_PARM_DESC(mp_strparam, "A demo string parameter");
```

In the `static int mp_debug_level;` statement, there is no harm in changing it to `static int mp_debug_level = 0;` , thus explicitly initializing the variable to 0, right? Well, no: the kernel's `scripts/checkpatch.pl` script output reveals that this is not considered good coding style by the kernel community:

```
ERROR: do not initialise statics to 0
#28: FILE: modparams1.c:28:
+static int mp_debug_level = 0;
```

In the preceding code block, we have declared two variables to be module parameters via the `module_param()` macro. The `module_param()` macro takes three parameters:

- The first parameter: the variable name (which we would like treated as a module parameter). This should be declared using the `static` qualifier.
- The second parameter: its data type.
- The third parameter: permissions (really, its visibility via `sysfs`; this is explained as follows).

The `MODULE_PARM_DESC()` macro allows us to "describe" what the parameter represents. Think about it, this is how you inform the end user of the kernel module (or driver) and what parameters are actually available. The lookup is performed via the `modinfo(8)` utility. Furthermore, you can specifically print only the information on parameters to a module by using the `-p` option switch, as shown:

```
cd <booksrc>/ch5/modparams/modparams1
make
$ modinfo -p ./modparams1.ko
parm:           mp_debug_level:Debug level [0-2]; 0 => no debug
messages, 2 => high verbosity (int)
parm:           mp_strparam:A demo string parameter (charp)
$
```

The `modinfo(8)` output displays available module parameters, if any. Here, we can see that our `modparams1.ko` kernel module has two parameters, their name, description, and data type (within parentheses; `charp` is character pointer, a string) is shown. Right, let's now give our demo kernel module a quick spin:

```
sudo dmesg -C
sudo insmod ./modparams1.ko
dmesg
[42724.936349] modparams1: inserted
[42724.936354] module parameters passed: mp_debug_level=0
mp_strparam=My string param
```

Here, we see from the `dmesg(1)` output that, as we did not explicitly pass any kernel module parameters, the module variables obviously retain their default (original) values. Let's redo this, this time passing explicit values to the module parameters:

```
sudo rmmod modparams1
sudo insmod ./modparams1.ko mp_debug_level=2 mp_strparam=\"Hello modparams1\"
$ dmesg
[...]
[42734.162840] modparams1: removed
[42766.146876] modparams1: inserted
[42766.146880] module parameters passed: mp_debug_level=2
mp_strparam=Hello modparams1
$
```

It works as expected. Now that we've seen how to declare and pass along some parameters to a kernel module, let's look at retrieving or even modifying them at runtime.

Getting/setting module parameters after insertion

Let's look carefully at the `module_param()` macro usage in our preceding `modparams1.c` source file again:

```
module_param(mp_debug_level, int, 0660);
```

[244]

Chapter 5

Notice the third parameter, the *permissions* (or *mode*): it's 0660 (which, of course, is an *octal* number, implying read-write access for the owner and group and no access for others). It's a bit confusing until you realize that if the permissions parameter is specified as non-zero, pseudo-file(s) get created under the sysfs filesystem, representing the kernel module parameter(s), here: /sys/module/<module-name>/parameters/:

> sysfs is usually mounted under /sys. Also, by default, all pseudo-files will have the owner and group as root.

1. So, for our modparams1 kernel module (assuming it's loaded into kernel memory), let's look them up:

   ```
   $ ls /sys/module/modparams1/
   coresize    holders/    initsize   initstate   notes/
   parameters/  refcnt  sections/   srcversion   taint       uevent
   version
   $ ls -l /sys/module/modparams1/parameters/
   total 0
   -rw-rw---- 1 root root 4096 Jan  1 17:39 mp_debug_level
   -rw-rw---- 1 root root 4096 Jan  1 17:39 mp_strparam
   $
   ```

   Indeed, there they are! Not only that, the real beauty of it is that these "parameters" can now be read and written at will, at any time (though only with root permission, of course)!

2. Check it out:

   ```
   $ cat /sys/module/modparams1/parameters/mp_debug_level
   cat: /sys/module/modparams1/parameters/mp_debug_level:
   Permission denied
   $ sudo cat /sys/module/modparams1/parameters/mp_debug_level
   [sudo] password for llkd:
   2
   ```

   Yes, the current value of our mp_debug_level kernel module parameter is indeed 2.

[245]

3. Let's dynamically change it to 0, implying that no "debug" messages will be emitted by the `modparams1` kernel module:

```
$ sudo bash -c "echo 0 >
/sys/module/modparams1/parameters/mp_debug_level"
$ sudo cat /sys/module/modparams1/parameters/mp_debug_level
0
```

Voilà, done. You can similarly get and/or set the `mp_strparam` parameter; we will leave it to you to try this as a simple exercise. This is powerful stuff: you could write simple scripts to control a device (or whatever) behavior via kernel module parameters, get (or cut off) debug info, and so on; the possibilities are quite endless.

Actually, coding the third parameter to `module_param()` as a literal octal number (such as `0660`) is not considered best programming practice in some circles. Specify the permissions of the `sysfs` pseudo-file via appropriate macros (specified in `include/uapi/linux/stat.h`), for example:

```
module_param(mp_debug_level, int, S_IRUSR|S_IWUSR|S_IRGRP|S_IWGRP);
```

However, having said this, our "better" Makefile's *checkpatch* target (which, of course, invokes the kernel's `scripts/checkpatch.pl` "coding-style" Perl script checker) politely informs us that simply using octal permissions is better:

```
$ make checkpatch
[ ... ]
checkpatch.pl: /lib/modules/<ver>/build//scripts/checkpatch.pl --no-tree -f *.[ch]
[ ... ]
WARNING: Symbolic permissions 'S_IRUSR|S_IWUSR|S_IRGRP|S_IWGRP' are not preferred. Consider using octal permissions '0660'.
 #29: FILE: modparams1.c:29:
 +module_param(mp_debug_level, int, S_IRUSR|S_IWUSR|S_IRGRP|S_IWGRP);
```

So, the kernel community disagrees. Hence, we will just use the "usual" octal number notation of `0660`.

Module parameter data types and validation

In our preceding simple kernel module, we set up two parameters of the integer and string data types (`charp`). What other data types can be used? Several, as it turns out: the `moduleparam.h` include file reveals all (within a comment, duplicated as follows):

```
// include/linux/moduleparam.h
[...]
 * Standard types are:
 * byte, short, ushort, int, uint, long, ulong
 * charp: a character pointer
 * bool: a bool, values 0/1, y/n, Y/N.
 * invbool: the above, only sense-reversed (N = true).
```

You can even define your own data types, if required. Usually, though, the standard types more than suffice.

Validating kernel module parameters

All kernel module parameters are *optional* by default; the user may or may not explicitly pass them. But what if our project requires that the user *must explicitly pass* a value for a given kernel module parameter? We address this here: let's enhance our previous kernel module, creating another (`ch5/modparams/modparams2`), the key difference being that we set up an additional parameter called `control_freak`. Now, we *require* that the user *must* pass this parameter along at module insertion time:

1. Let's set up the new module parameter in code:

    ```
    static int control_freak;
    module_param(control_freak, int, 0660);
    MODULE_PARM_DESC(control_freak, "Set to the project's control
    level [1-5]. MANDATORY");
    ```

2. How can we achieve this "mandatory passing"? Well, it's a bit of a hack really: just check at insertion time whether the value is the default (0, here). If so, then abort with an appropriate message (we also do a simple validity check to ensure that the integer passed is within a given range). Here's the init code of `ch5/modparams/modparams2/modparams2.c`:

    ```
    static int __init modparams2_init(void)
    {
        pr_info("%s: inserted\n", OUR_MODNAME);
        if (mp_debug_level > 0)
    ```

Writing Your First Kernel Module - LKMs Part 2

```
            pr_info("module parameters passed: "
                "mp_debug_level=%d mp_strparam=%s\n   control_freak=%d\n",
                mp_debug_level, mp_strparam, control_freak);

    /* param 'control_freak': if it hasn't been passed (implicit guess),
     * or is the same old value, or isn't within the right range,
     * it's Unacceptable!  :-)
     */
    if ((control_freak < 1) || (control_freak > 5)) {
        pr_warn("%s: Must pass along module parameter"
            " 'control_freak', value in the range [1-5]; aborting...\n",
            OUR_MODNAME);
        return -EINVAL;
    }
    return 0; /* success */
}
```

3. Also, as a quick demo, notice how we emit a printk, showing the module parameter values only if `mp_debug_level` is positive.
4. Finally, on this topic, the kernel framework provides a more rigorous way to "get/set" kernel (module) parameters and perform validity checking on them via the `module_parm_cb()` macro (`cb` for callbacks). We will not delve into this here; I refer you to a blog article mentioned in the *Further reading* document for details on using it.

Now, let's move on to how (and why) we can override a module parameter's name.

Overriding the module parameter's name

To explain this feature, let's take an example from the (5.4.0) kernel source tree: the direct mapping buffered I/O library driver, `drivers/md/dm-bufio.c`, has a need to use the `dm_bufio_current_allocated` variable as a module parameter. However, this name is really that of an *internal variable* and is not highly intuitive to a user of this driver. The authors of this driver would much prefer to use another name – `current_allocated_bytes` – as an *alias* or *name override*. Precisely this can be achieved via the `module_param_named()` macro, overriding and completely equivalent to the internal variable name, as follows:

```
// drivers/md/dm-bufio.c
[...]
```

[248]

```
module_param_named(current_allocated_bytes,
dm_bufio_current_allocated, ulong, S_IRUGO);
MODULE_PARM_DESC(current_allocated_bytes, "Memory currently used by
the cache");
```

So, when the user performs `insmod` on this driver, they can do stuff like the following:

```
sudo insmod <path/to/>dm-bufio.ko current_allocated_bytes=4096 ...
```

Internally, the actual variable, `dm_bufio_current_allocated`, will be assigned the value `4096`.

Hardware-related kernel parameters

For security reasons, module or kernel parameters that specify hardware-specific values have a separate macro – `module_param_hw[_named|array]()`. David Howells submitted a patch series for these new hardware parameters kernel support on 1 December 2016. The patch email [https://lwn.net/Articles/708274/] mentions the following:

```
Provided an annotation for module parameters that specify hardware
parameters (such as io ports, iomem addresses, irqs, dma channels,
fixed
dma buffers and other types).

This will enable such parameters to be locked down in the core
parameter
parser for secure boot support.  [...]
```

That concludes our discussion on kernel module parameters. Let's move on to a peculiar aspect – that of floating-point usage within the kernel.

Floating point not allowed in the kernel

Years ago, when working on a temperature sensor device driver, I had an amusing experience (though it wasn't quite so amusing at the time). Attempting to express a temperature value in millidegrees Celsius as a "regular" temperature value in degrees Celsius, I did something like the following:

```
double temp;
[... processing ...]
temp = temp / 1000.0;
printk(KERN_INFO "temperature is %.3f degrees C\n", temp);
```

It all went bad from there!

The venerable LDD (*Linux Device Drivers*, by *Corbet, Rubini, and G-K-Hartman*) book pointed out my error – **floating-point** (FP) arithmetic is not allowed in kernel space! It's a conscious design decision – saving processor (FP) state, turning on the FP unit, working on and then turning off and restoring the FP state is just not considered a worthwhile thing to do while in the kernel. The kernel (or driver) developer is well advised *to* just not attempt performing FP work while in kernel space.

Well, then, you ask, how can you do the (in my example) temperature conversion? Simple: pass the *integer* millidegrees Celsius value *to userspace* and perform the FP work there!

Having said that, there is apparently a way to force the kernel to perform FP: put your floating-point code between the `kernel_fpu_begin()` and `kernel_fpu_end()` macros. There are a few places where precisely this technique is used within the kernel code base (typically, some code paths covering crypto/AES, CRC, and so on). Regardless, the recommendation is that the typical module (or driver) developer *performs only integer arithmetic within the kernel*.

Nevertheless, to test this whole scenario (always remember, *the empirical approach – actually trying things out – is the only realistic way forward!*), we write a simple kernel module that attempts to perform some FP work. The key part of the code is shown here:

```
// ch5/fp_in_kernel/fp_in_kernel.c
static double num = 22.0, den = 7.0, mypi;
static int __init fp_in_lkm_init(void)
{
    [...]
    kernel_fpu_begin();
```

```
        mypi = num/den;
        kernel_fpu_end();
#if 1
        pr_info("%s: PI = %.4f = %.4f\n", OURMODNAME, mypi, num/den);
#endif
        return 0;       /* success */
}
```

It actually works, *until we attempt to display the FP value via* `printk()`! At that point, it goes quite berserk. See the following screenshot:

```
dmesg
--------------------
[ 5732.199769] fp_in_lkm: inserted
[ 5732.200659] fp_in_lkm: PI =
[ 5732.200666] ------------[ cut here ]------------
[ 5732.200667] Please remove unsupported %f in format string
[ 5732.200667] WARNING: CPU: 1 PID: 3524 at lib/vsprintf.c:2366 format_decode+0x3f4/0x400
[ 5732.200668] Modules linked in: fp_in_lkm(OE+) vboxsf(OE) vboxvideo(OE) vmwgfx drm_kms_helper syscopyarea snd_intel8x0 sysfillrect snd_ac97_
codec crct10dif_pclmul sysimgblt crc32_pclmul fb_sys_fops ac97_bus ghash_clmulni_intel ttm snd_pcm aesni_intel glue_helper drm snd_seq crypto_
simd joydev cryptd snd_timer snd_seq_device input_leds intel_rapl_perf snd serio_raw soundcore vboxguest(OE) video mac_hid sch_fq_codel nls_sy
sinfo(O) parport_pc ppdev lp parport ip_tables x_tables autofs4 hid_generic usbhid hid ahci e1000 psmouse libahci i2c_piix4 pata_acpi
[ 5732.200683] CPU: 1 PID: 3524 Comm: insmod Tainted: G           OE     5.4.0-llkd01 #1
[ 5732.200683] Hardware name: innotek GmbH VirtualBox/VirtualBox, BIOS VirtualBox 12/01/2006
[ 5732.200683] RIP: 0010:format_decode+0x3f4/0x400
[ 5732.200685] Code: ff ff 48 8d 42 02 b9 4c 00 00 00 48 89 45 e8 e9 cd fc ff ff 0f be f2 48 c7 c7 68 e3 3b a0 c6 05 5e 4b c1 00 01 e8 2c 95 6
d ff <0f> 0b 48 8b 45 e8 e9 ff fe ff ff 90 89 f0 c1 e0 08 c1 f8 08 89 c2
[ 5732.200685] RSP: 0018:ffffb57fc1ae3a70 EFLAGS: 00010086
[ 5732.200686] RAX: 0000000000000000 RBX: ffffb57fc1ae3ab0 RCX: 0000000000000000
[ 5732.200687] RDX: 0000000000000003 RSI: ffffffffa03be398 RDI: ffff987dfdb19488
[ 5732.200687] RBP: ffffb57fc1ae3a88 R08: 0000000000000000 R09: ffffffffa0b30600
[ 5732.200688] R10: 00000000a0b30221 R11: 00000000ffffffff R12: ffffffffc0600047
[ 5732.200689] R13: 00000000000003e0 R14: ffffffffc0600047 R15: ffffffffc0600047
[ 5732.200689] FS:  00007fa67a2ce540(0000) GS:ffff987dfdb00000(0000) knlGS:0000000000000000
[ 5732.200690] CS:  0010 DS: 0000 ES: 0000 CR0: 0000000080050033
[ 5732.200690] CR2: 0000560751f8f788 CR3: 000000085f560005 CR4: 00000000000606e0
[ 5732.200690] Call Trace:
[ 5732.200691]  vsnprintf+0x66/0x510
[ 5732.200691]  vscnprintf+0xd/0x30
[ 5732.200692]  vprintk_store+0x3e/0x220
[ 5732.200692]  ? vprintk_func+0x47/0xc0
[ 5732.200692]  vprintk_emit+0xa9/0x2d0
[ 5732.200692]  ? 0xffffffffc0605000
[ 5732.200693]  vprintk_default+0x29/0x50
[ 5732.200694]  vprintk_func+0x47/0xc0
[ 5732.200694]  printk+0x52/0x6e
[ 5732.200694]  fp_in_lkm_init+0x5e/0x1000 [fp_in_lkm]
[ 5732.200695]  do_one_initcall+0x4a/0x1fa
```

Figure 5.4 – The output of WARN_ONCE() when we try and print an FP number in kernel space

The key line is `Please remove unsupported %f in format string`.

This tells us the story. The system does not actually crash or panic as this is a mere WARNING, spat out to the kernel log via the `WARN_ONCE()` macro. Do realize, though, that on a production system, the `/proc/sys/kernel/panic_on_warn` pseudo-file will, in all probability, be set to the value 1, causing the kernel to (quite rightly) panic.

Writing Your First Kernel Module - LKMs Part 2

> **TIP**
> The section in the preceding screenshot (Figure 5.3) beginning with `Call Trace:` is, of course, a peek into the current state of the *kernel-mode stack* of the process or thread that was "caught" in the preceding `WARN_ONCE()` code path (hang on, you will learn key details regarding the user- and kernel-mode stacks and so on in Chapter 6, *Kernel Internals Essentials – Processes and Threads*).
> Interpret the kernel stack by reading it in a bottom-up fashion; so here, the `do_one_initcall` function called `fp_in_lkm_init` (which belongs to the kernel module in square brackets, `[fp_in_lkm_init]`), which then calls `printk()`, which then ends up causing all kinds of trouble as it attempts to print a FP (floating point) quantity!

The moral is clear: *avoid using floating-point math within kernel space*. Let's now move on to the topic of how you can install and auto-load kernel modules on system startup.

Auto-loading modules on system boot

Until now, we have written simple "out-of-tree" kernel modules that reside in their own private directories and have to be manually loaded up, typically via the `insmod(8)` or `modprobe(8)` utilities. In most real-world projects and products, you will require your out-of-tree kernel module(s) *to be auto-loaded at boot*. This section covers how you can achieve this.

Consider we have a kernel module named `foo.ko`. We assume we have access to the source code and Makefile. In order to have it *auto-load* on system boot, you need to first *install* the kernel module to a known location on the system. To do so, we expect that the Makefile for the module contains an `install` target, typically:

```
install:
        make -C $(KDIR) M=$(PWD) modules_install
```

This is not something new; we have been placing the `install` target within the `Makefile`'s of our demo kernel modules.

To demonstrate this "auto-load" procedure, we have shown the set of steps to follow in order to actually *install and auto-load on boot* our `ch5/min_sysinfo` kernel module:

1. First, change directory to the module's source directory:

    ```
    cd <...>/ch5/min_sysinfo
    ```

2. Next, it's important to first build the kernel module (with `make`), and, on success, install it (as you'll soon see, our 'better' Makefile makes the process simpler by guaranteeing that the build is done first, followed by the install and the `depmod`):

   `make && sudo make install`

   Assuming it builds, the `sudo make install` command then *installs* the kernel module here, `/lib/modules/<kernel-ver>/extra/`, as expected (do see the following info box and tips as well):

   ```
   $ cd <...>/ch5/min_sysinfo
   $ make                   <-- ensure it's first built 'locally'
                       generating the min_sysinfo.ko kernel module
   object
   [...]
   $ sudo make install
   Building for: KREL= ARCH= CROSS_COMPILE= EXTRA_CFLAGS=-DDEBUG
   make -C /lib/modules/5.4.0-llkd01/build
   M=<...>/ch5/min_sysinfo modules_install
   make[1]: Entering directory '/home/llkd/kernels/linux-5.4'
     INSTALL <...>/ch5/min_sysinfo/min_sysinfo.ko
     DEPMOD  5.4.0-llkd01
   make[1]: Leaving directory '/home/llkd/kernels/linux-5.4'
   $ ls -l /lib/modules/5.4.0-llkd01/extra/
   total 228
   -rw-r--r-- 1 root root 232513 Dec 30 16:23 min_sysinfo.ko
   $
   ```

   > During `sudo make install`, it's possible you might see (non-fatal) errors regarding SSL; they can be safely ignored. They indicate that the system failed to "sign" the kernel module. More on this in the note on security coming up.
   >
   > Also, just in case you find that `sudo make install` fails, try the following approaches:
   >
   > a) Switch to a root shell (`sudo -s`) and within it, run the `make ; make install` commands.
   >
   > b) A useful reference: *Makefile: installing external Linux kernel module, StackOverflow, June 2016* (https://unix.stackexchange.com/questions/288540/makefile-installing-external-linux-kernel-module).

3. Another module utility, called `depmod(8)`, is then typically invoked by default within `sudo make install` (as can be seen from the preceding output). Just in case (for whatever reason) this has not occurred, you can always manually invoke `depmod`: its job is essentially to resolve module dependencies (see its man page for details): `sudo depmod`. Once you install the kernel module, you can see the effect of `depmod(8)` with its `--dry-run` option switch:

```
$ sudo depmod --dry-run | grep min_sysinfo
extra/min_sysinfo.ko:
alias symbol:lkdc_sysinfo2 min_sysinfo
alias symbol:lkdc_sysinfo min_sysinfo
$
```

4. Auto-load the kernel module on boot: One way is create the `/etc/modules-load.d/<foo>.conf` config file (of course, you will need root access to create this file); the simple case: just put the kernel module's `foo` name inside, that's it. Any line starting with a `#` character is treated as a comment and ignored. For our `min_sysinfo` example, we have the following:

```
$ cat /etc/modules-load.d/min_sysinfo.conf
# Auto load kernel module for LLKD book: ch5/min_sysinfo
min_sysinfo
$
```

> **TIP**
> FYI, another (even simpler) way to inform systemd to load up our kernel module is to enter the *name* of the module into the (preexisting) `/etc/modules-load.d/modules.conf` file.

5. Reboot the system with `sync; sudo reboot`.

Once the system is up, use `lsmod(8)` and look up the kernel log (with `dmesg(1)`, perhaps). You should see relevant info pertaining to the kernel module loading up (in our example, `min_sysinfo`):

```
[... system boots up ...]

$ lsmod | grep min_sysinfo
min_sysinfo           16384  0
$ dmesg | grep -C2 min_sysinfo
[...]
[ 2.395649] min_sysinfo: loading out-of-tree module taints kernel.
[ 2.395667] min_sysinfo: module verification failed: signature and/or
```

```
required key missing - tainting kernel
[ 2.395814] min_sysinfo: inserted
[ 2.395815] lkdc_sysinfo(): minimal Platform Info:
            CPU: x86_64, little-endian; 64-bit OS.
$
```

There, it's done: our `min_sysinfo` kernel module has indeed been auto-loaded into kernel space on boot!

As you just learned, you must first build your kernel module and then perform the install; to help automate this, our 'better' Makefile has the following in it's module installation `install` target:

```
// ch5/min_sysinfo/Makefile
[ ... ]
install:
    @echo
    @echo "--- installing ---"
    @echo " [First, invoke the 'make' ]"
    make
    @echo
    @echo " [Now for the 'sudo make install' ]"
    sudo make -C $(KDIR) M=$(PWD) modules_install
    sudo depmod
```

It ensures that, first, the build is done, followed by the install and (explicitly) the `depmod(8)`.

What if your auto-loaded kernel module requires some (module) parameters passed at load time? There are two ways to assure that this happens: via a so-called modprobe config file (under `/etc/modprobe.d/`) or, if the module's built-in to the kernel, via the kernel command line.

Here we show the first way: simply setup your modprobe configuration file (as an example here, we use the name `mykmod` as the name of our LKM; again, you require root access to create this file): `/etc/modprobe.d/mykmod.conf`; in it, you can pass parameters like this:

```
options <module-name> <parameter-name>=<value>
```

As an example, the `/etc/modprobe.d/alsa-base.conf` modprobe config file on my x86_64 Ubuntu 20.04 LTS system contains the lines (among several others):

```
# Ubuntu #62691, enable MPU for snd-cmipci
options snd-cmipci mpu_port=0x330 fm_port=0x388
```

A few more points on kernel module auto-loading related items follow.

Module auto-loading – additional details

Once a kernel module has been installed on a system (via `sudo make install`, as shown previously), you can also insert it into the kernel interactively (or via a script) simply by using a "smarter" version of the `insmod(8)` utility, called `modprobe(8)`. For our example, we could first `rmmod(8)` the module and then do the following:

```
sudo modprobe min_sysinfo
```

As an interesting aside, consider the following. In cases where there are several kernel module objects to load (for example, the *module stacking* design), how does `modprobe` know the *order* in which to load up kernel modules? When performing a build locally, the build process generates a file called `modules.order`. It tells utilities such as `modprobe` the order in which to load up kernel modules such that all dependencies are resolved. When kernel modules are *installed* into the kernel (that is, into the `/lib/modules/$(uname -r)/extra/`, or similar, location), the `depmod(8)` utility generates a `/lib/modules/$(uname -r)/modules.dep` file. This contains the dependency information – it specifies whether a kernel module depends on another. Using this information, modprobe then loads them up in the required order. To flesh this out, let's install our module stacking example:

```
$ cd <...>/ch5/modstacking
$ make && sudo make install
[...]
$ ls -l /lib/modules/5.4.0-llkd01/extra/
total 668K
-rw-r--r-- 1 root root 218K Jan 31 08:41 core_lkm.ko
-rw-r--r-- 1 root root 228K Dec 30 16:23 min_sysinfo.ko
-rw-r--r-- 1 root root 217K Jan 31 08:41 user_lkm.ko
$
```

Clearly, the two kernel modules from our module stacking example (`core_lkm.ko` and `user_lkm.ko`) are now installed under the expected location, `/lib/modules/$(uname -r)/extra/`. Now, check this out:

```
$ grep user_lkm /lib/modules/5.4.0-llkd01/* 2>/dev/null
/lib/modules/5.4.0-llkd01/modules.dep:extra/user_lkm.ko:
extra/core_lkm.ko
Binary file /lib/modules/5.4.0-llkd01/modules.dep.bin matches
$
```

Chapter 5

The first line of output after `grep` is relevant: `depmod` has arranged for the `modules.dep` file to show that the `extra/user_lkm.ko` kernel module depends on the `extra/core_lkm.ko` kernel module (via the `<k1.ko>: <k2.ko>...` notation, implying that the `k1.ko` module depends on the `k2.ko` module). Thus, modprobe, seeing this, loads them in the required order, avoiding any issues.

(FYI, while on this topic, the generated `Module.symvers` file has information on all exported symbols.)

Next, recall the new(ish) `init` framework on Linux, *systemd*. The fact is, on modern Linux systems, it's actually systemd that takes care of auto-loading kernel modules at system boot, by parsing the content of files such as `/etc/modules-load.d/*` (the systemd service responsible for this is `systemd-modules-load.service(8)`. For details, refer to the man page on `modules-load.d(5)`).

Conversely, sometimes you might find that a certain auto-loaded kernel module is misbehaving – causing lockups or delays, or it simply doesn't work – and so you want to definitely disable loading it. This can be done by *blacklisting* the module. You can specify this either on the kernel command line (convenient when all else fails!) or within the (previously mentioned) `/etc/modules-load.d/<foo>.conf` config file. On the kernel command line, via `module_blacklist=mod1,mod2,...`, the kernel docs shows us the syntax/explanation:

```
module_blacklist=   [KNL] Do not load a comma-separated list of
                    modules.  Useful for debugging problem
modules.
```

> **TIP**
> You can look up the current kernel command line by doing `cat /proc/cmdline`.

While on the topic of the kernel command line, several other useful options exist, enabling us to use the kernel's help for debugging issues concerned with kernel initialization. As an example, among several others, the kernel provides the following parameters in this regard (source: https://www.kernel.org/doc/html/latest/admin-guide/kernel-parameters.html):

```
debug           [KNL] Enable kernel debugging (events log level).
[...]
initcall_debug  [KNL] Trace initcalls as they are executed. Useful
                      for working out where the kernel is dying during
                      startup.
[...]
```

Writing Your First Kernel Module - LKMs Part 2

```
ignore_loglevel [KNL] Ignore loglevel setting - this will print /all/
                kernel messages to the console. Useful for
                debugging. We also add it as printk module
                parameter, so users could change it dynamically,
                usually by
/sys/module/printk/parameters/ignore_loglevel.
```

FYI, and as mentioned earlier in this chapter, there is an alternate framework for third-party kernel module auto-rebuilding, called **Dynamic Kernel Module Support (DKMS)**.

The *Further reading* document for this chapter also provides some helpful links. In conclusion, auto-loading kernel modules into memory on system startup is a useful and often required functionality in a product. Building high-quality products requires a keen understanding of, and the knowledge to build in, *security*; that's the topic of the next section.

Kernel modules and security – an overview

An ironic reality is that enormous efforts spent on improving *user space* security considerations have resulted in a pretty large payoff over recent years. A malicious user performing a viable **Buffer Overflow** (**BoF**) attack was well within the realms of possibility a couple of decades back, but today is really hard to do. Why? Because there are many layers of beefed-up security mechanisms to prevent many of these attack classes.

> To quickly name a few countermeasures: compiler protections (`-fstack-protector[...]`, `-Wformat-security`, `-D_FORTIFY_SOURCE=2`, partial/full RELRO, better sanity and security checker tools (`checksec.sh`, the address sanitizers, paxtest, static analysis tools, and so on), secure libraries, hardware-level protection mechanisms (NX, SMEP, SMAP, and so on), [K]ASLR, better testing (fuzzing), and so on.

The irony is that *kernel-space* attacks have become increasingly common over the last few years! It has been demonstrated that revealing even a single valid kernel (virtual) address (and it's corresponding symbol) to a clever attacker can allow her to figure the location of some key internal kernel structures, paving the way to carry out all kinds of **privilege escalation** (**privesc**) attacks. Thus, even revealing a single innocent-looking piece of kernel information (such as a kernel address and the symbol it's associated with) is a potential **information leak** (or info-leak) and must be prevented on production systems. Coming up, we will enumerate and briefly describe a few security features that the Linux kernel provides. However, ultimately, the kernel developer – you! – have a large role to play: writing secure code, to begin with! Using our 'better' Makefile is a great way to get started - several targets within it are concerned with security (all the static analysis ones, for example).

Proc filesystem tunables affecting the system log

We directly refer you to the man page on `proc(5)` – very valuable! – to glean information on these two security-related tunables:

- dmesg_restrict
- kptr_restrict

First, `dmesg_restrict`:

```
dmesg_restrict
/proc/sys/kernel/dmesg_restrict (since Linux 2.6.37)
  The value in this file determines who can see kernel syslog contents.
A  value of 0 in this file imposes no restrictions. If the value is 1,
only privileged users can read the kernel syslog. (See syslog(2) for
more details.) Since Linux 3.4, only users with the CAP_SYS_ADMIN
capability may change the value in this file.
```

The default (on both our Ubuntu and Fedora platforms) is 0:

```
$ cat /proc/sys/kernel/dmesg_restrict
0
```

Linux kernels use the powerful fine-granularity POSIX *capabilities* model. The `CAP_SYS_ADMIN` capability essentially is a catch-all for what is traditionally *root* (*superuser/sysadmin*) access. The `CAP_SYSLOG` capability gives the process (or thread) the capability to perform privileged `syslog(2)` operations.

Writing Your First Kernel Module - LKMs Part 2

As already mentioned, "leaking" a kernel address and the symbol it's associated with might result in an info-leak-based attack. To help prevent these, kernel and module authors are advised to always print kernel addresses using a new `printf`-style format: instead of the familiar `%p` or `%px` to print a kernel address, you should use the newer `%pK` format specifier for printing an address. (Using the `%px` format specifier ensures the actual address is printed; you'll want to avoid this in production). How does this help? Read on...

The `kptr_restrict` tunable (2.6.38 onward) affects the `printk()` output when printing kernel addresses; doing `printk("&var = %pK\n", &var);` and not the good old `printk("&var = %p\n", &var);` is considered a security best practice. Understanding how exactly the `kptr_restrict` tunable works is key to this:

```
kptr_restrict
/proc/sys/kernel/kptr_restrict (since Linux 2.6.38)
  The value in this file determines whether kernel addresses are
exposed via /proc files and other interfaces. A value of 0 in this
file imposes no restrictions. If the value is 1, kernel pointers
printed using the %pK format specifier will be replaced with zeros
unless the user has the CAP_SYSLOG capability. If the value is 2,
kernel pointers printed using the %pK format specifier will be
replaced with zeros regardless of the user's capabilities. The initial
default value for this file was 1, but the default was changed to 0 in
Linux 2.6.39. Since Linux 3.4, only users with the CAP_SYS_ADMIN
capability can change the value in this file.
```

The default (on both our recent-enough Ubuntu and Fedora platforms) is 1:

```
$ cat /proc/sys/kernel/kptr_restrict
1
```

You can – rather, *must* – change these tunables on production systems to a secure value (1 or 2) for security. Of course, security measures only work when developers make use of them; as of the 5.4.0 Linux kernel, there is a total of (just!) 14 uses of the `%pK` format specifier in the entire Linux kernel code base (out of a total of about 5,200-odd uses of printk employing the `%p`, and around 230 explicitly employing the `%px` format specifier).

> a) As `procfs` is, of course, a volatile filesystem, you can always make the changes permanent by using the `sysctl(8)` utility with the `-w` option switch (or by directly updating the `/etc/sysctl.conf` file).
> b) For the purpose of debugging, if you must print an actual kernel (unmodified) address, you're advised to use the `%px` format specifier; do remove these prints on production systems!
> c) Detailed kernel documentation on `printk` format specifiers can be found at https://www.kernel.org/doc/html/latest/core-api/printk-formats.html#how-to-get-printk-format-specifiers-right; do browse through it.

With the advent of hardware-level defects in early 2018 (the now well-known *Meltdown*, *Spectre*, and other processor speculation security issues), there was a sense of renewed urgency in *detecting information leakage*, thus enabling developers and administrators to block them off.

> A useful Perl script, `scripts/leaking_addresses.pl`, was released in mainline in 4.14 (in November 2017; I am happy to have lent a hand in this important work: https://github.com/torvalds/linux/commit/1410fe4eea22959bd31c05e4c1846f1718300bde), with more checks being made for detecting leaking kernel addresses.

The cryptographic signing of kernel modules

Once a malicious attacker gets a foothold on a system, they will typically attempt some kind of privesc vector in order to gain root access. Once this is achieved, the typical next step is to install a *rootkit*: essentially, a collection of scripts and kernel modules that will pretty much take over the system (by "hijacking" system calls, setting up backdoors and keyloggers, and so on).

Of course, it's not easy – the security posture of a modern production quality Linux system, replete with **Linux Security Modules** (**LSMs**), and so on, means it's not at all a trivial thing to do, but for a skilled and motivated attacker, anything's possible. Assuming they have a sufficiently sophisticated rootkit installed, the system is now considered compromised.

Writing Your First Kernel Module - LKMs Part 2

An interesting idea is this: even with root access, do not allow `insmod(8)` (or `modprobe(8)`, or even the underlying `[f]init_module(2)` system calls) to insert kernel modules into kernel address space **unless they are cryptographically signed with a security key** that is in the kernel's keyring. This powerful security feature was introduced with the 3.7 kernel (the relevant commit is here: https://git.kernel.org/pub/scm/linux/kernel/git/torvalds/linux.git/commit/?id=106a4ee258d14818467829bf0e12aeae14c16cd7).

> The details on performing cryptographic signing of kernel modules is beyond the scope of this book; you can refer to the official kernel documentation here: https://www.kernel.org/doc/html/latest/admin-guide/module-signing.html.

A few relevant kernel configuration options concerned with this feature are `CONFIG_MODULE_SIG`, `CONFIG_MODULE_SIG_FORCE`, `CONFIG_MODULE_SIG_ALL`, and so on. To help understand what exactly this means, see the `Kconfig 'help'` section for the first of them, as follows (from `init/Kconfig`):

```
config MODULE_SIG
  bool "Module signature verification"
  depends on MODULES
  select SYSTEM_DATA_VERIFICATION
  help
    Check modules for valid signatures upon load: the signature is simply
    appended to the module. For more information see
    <file:Documentation/admin-guide/module-signing.rst>. Note that this
    option adds the OpenSSL development packages as a kernel build
    dependency so that the signing tool can use its crypto library.

    !!!WARNING!!! If you enable this option, you MUST make sure that the
    module DOES NOT get stripped after being signed. This includes the
    debuginfo strip done by some packagers (such as rpmbuild) and
    inclusion into an initramfs that wants the module size reduced
```

The `MODULE_SIG_FORCE` kernel config is a Boolean value (defaults to n). It only comes into play if `MODULE_SIG` is turned on. If `MODULE_SIG_FORCE` is set to y, then kernel modules *must* have a valid signature in order to be loaded. If not, loading will fail. If its value is left as n, this implies that even kernel modules that aren't signed will be loaded into the kernel, but the kernel will be marked as tainted. This tends to be the default on a typical modern Linux distribution. In the following code block, we look up these kernel configs on our x86_64 Ubuntu 20.04.1 LTS guest VM:

```
$ grep MODULE_SIG /boot/config-5.4.0-58-generic
CONFIG_MODULE_SIG_FORMAT=y
```

```
CONFIG_MODULE_SIG=y
# CONFIG_MODULE_SIG_FORCE is not set
CONFIG_MODULE_SIG_ALL=y
[ ... ]
```

The cryptographic signing of kernel modules is encouraged on production systems (in recent years, with (I)IoT edge devices becoming more prevalent, security is a key concern).

Disabling kernel modules altogether

Paranoid folks might want to completely disable the loading (and unloading) of kernel modules. Rather drastic, but hey, this way you can completely lock down the kernel space of a system (as well as render any rootkits pretty much harmless). This can be achieved in two broad ways:

- First, by setting the `CONFIG_MODULES` kernel config to off (it's on, of course, by default) during kernel config prior to building. Doing this is pretty drastic – it makes the decision a permanent one!
- Second, assuming `CONFIG_MODULES` is turned on, module loading can be dynamically turned off at runtime via the `modules_disabled` `sysctl` tunable; take a look at this:

    ```
    $ cat /proc/sys/kernel/modules_disabled
    0
    ```

It's *off* (0) by default, of course. As usual, the man page on `proc(5)` tells us the story:

```
/proc/sys/kernel/modules_disabled (since Linux 2.6.31)
   A toggle value indicating if modules are allowed to be loaded in an
   otherwise modular kernel. This toggle defaults to off (0), but can be
   set true (1). Once true, modules can be neither loaded nor unloaded,
   and the toggle cannot be set back to false. The file is present only
   if the kernel is built with the CONFIG_MODULES option enabled.
```

In conclusion, of course, kernel security hardening and malicious attacks are a cat-and-mouse game. For example, (K)ASLR (we talk about what (K)ASLR means in the chapters to come on Linux memory management) is quite regularly defeated. Also, see this article – *Effectively bypassing kptr_restrict on Android*: http://bits-please.blogspot.com/2015/08/effectively-bypassing-kptrrestrict-on.html. Security is not easy; it's always a work in progress. It (almost) goes without saying: developers – in both user and kernel space – *must* write code that is security-aware and use tools and testing on a continuous basis.

Let's complete this chapter with topics on coding style guidelines for the Linux kernel, accessing kernel documentation, and how you can go about contributing to the mainline kernel.

Coding style guidelines for kernel developers

Many large projects specify their own set of coding guidelines; so does the Linux kernel community. Adhering to the Linux kernel *coding style* guidelines is a really good idea. You can find them officially documented here: `https://www.kernel.org/doc/html/latest/process/coding-style.html` **(please do read it!)**.

Furthermore, as part of the (quite exhaustive) code-submission checklist(s) for developers like you wanting to upstream your code, you are expected to run your patch through a Perl script that checks your code for congruence with the Linux kernel coding style: `scripts/checkpatch.pl`.

By default, this script only runs on a well-formatted `git` patch. It's possible to run it against standalone C code (as in your out-of-tree kernel module code), as follows (as our 'better' Makefile indeed does):

```
<kernel-src>/scripts/checkpatch.pl --no-tree -f <filename>.c
```

Doing this as a habit on your kernel code is helpful, enabling you to catch those annoying little issues – plus more serious ones! – that might otherwise hold your patch up. Again, we remind you: our "better" Makefile's `indent` and `checkpatch` targets are geared toward this.

Besides coding style guidelines, you will find that every now and then, you need to dig into the elaborate and useful kernel documentation. A gentle reminder: we covered locating and using the kernel documentation in `Chapter 1`, *Kernel Workspace Setup*, under the *Locating and Using the Linux Kernel Documentation* section.

We will now complete this chapter by making a brief mention of how you can get started on a noble objective: contributing code to the mainline Linux kernel project.

Chapter 5

Contributing to the mainline kernel

In this book, we typically perform kernel development *outside* the kernel source tree, via the LKM framework. What if you are writing code *within* the kernel tree, with the explicit goal of *upstreaming* your code to the kernel mainline? This is a laudable goal indeed – the whole basis of open source stems from the community's willingness to put in work and contribute it upstream to the project.

Getting started with contributing to the kernel

The most frequently asked question, of course, is *how do I get started*? To help with precisely this, a long and very detailed answer lies within the kernel documentation here: *HOWTO do Linux kernel development*: `https://www.kernel.org/doc/html/latest/process/howto.html#howto-do-linux-kernel-development`.

As a matter of fact, you can generate the full Linux kernel documentation (via the `make pdfdocs` command, in the root of the kernel source tree); once successful, you will find this PDF document here: `<root-of-kernel-source-tree>/Documentation/output/latex/development-process.pdf`.

It is a very detailed guide to the Linux kernel development process, including guidelines for code submission. A cropped screenshot of this document is shown here:

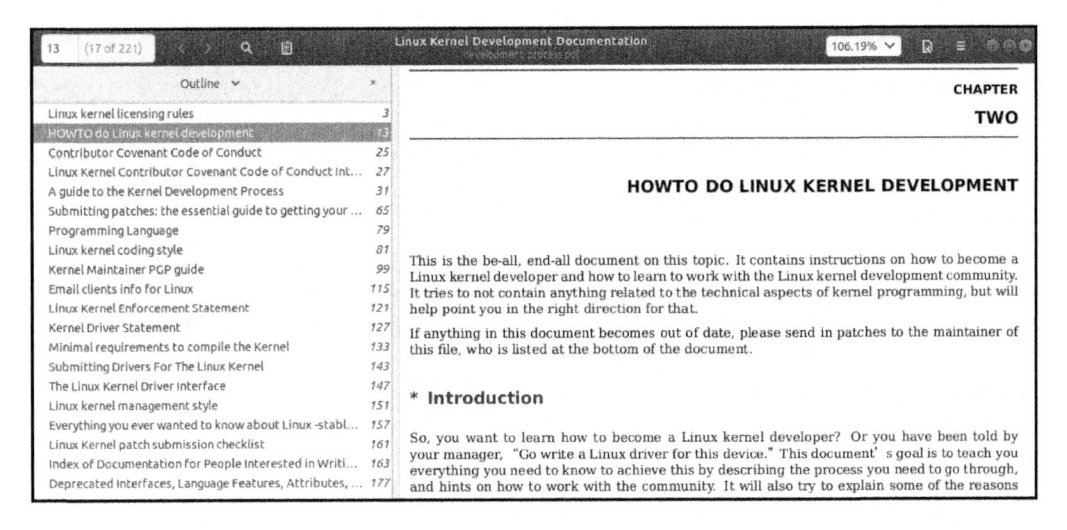

Figure 5.5 – (Partial) screenshot of the kernel development docs just generated

As part of this kernel development process, to maintain quality standards, a rigorous and *must-be-followed* checklist – a long recipe of sorts! – is very much part of the kernel patch submission process. The official checklist resides here: *Linux Kernel patch submission checklist*: `https://www.kernel.org/doc/html/latest/process/submit-checklist.html#linux-kernel-patch-submission-checklist`.

Though it may seem an onerous task for a kernel newbie, carefully following this checklist lends both rigor and credibility to your work and ultimately results in superior code. I strongly encourage you to read through the kernel patch submission checklist and try out the procedures mentioned therein.

> Is there a really practical hands-on tip, an almost guaranteed way to become a kernel hacker? Of course, keep reading this book! Ha ha, yes, besides, do partake in the simply awesome **Eudyptula Challenge** (`http://www.eudyptula-challenge.org/`) Oh, hang on, it's – very unfortunately, and as of the time of writing – closed down.
>
> Fear not; here's a site with all the challenges (and solutions, but don't cheat!) posted. Do check it out and try the challenges. This will greatly accelerate your kernel hacking skills: `https://github.com/agelastic/eudyptula`.

Summary

In this chapter, the second of two on writing a kernel module using the LKM framework, we covered several (remaining) areas pertaining to this important topic: among them, using a "better" Makefile for your kernel module, tips on configuring a debug kernel (it's very important!), cross-compiling a kernel module, gathering some minimal platform information from within a kernel module, and even a bit on the licensing of kernel modules. We also looked at emulating library-like features with two different approaches (one - preferred - the linking approach, and two, the module stacking approach), using module parameters, avoiding floating-point, the auto-loading of your kernel modules, and so on. Security concerns and how they can be addressed are important. Finally, we wrapped up this chapter by covering kernel coding style guidelines, kernel documentation, and how you can get started with contributing to the mainline kernel. So, congratulations! You now know how to develop a kernel module and can even get started on the journey to kernel upstream contribution.

In the next chapter, we will delve into an interesting and necessary topic. We will begin our exploration in some depth into the *internals* of both the Linux kernel and its memory management subsystem.

Questions

As we conclude, here is a list of questions for you to test your knowledge regarding this chapter's material: `https://github.com/PacktPublishing/Linux-Kernel-Programming/tree/master/questions`. You will find some of the questions answered in the book's GitHub repo: `https://github.com/PacktPublishing/Linux-Kernel-Programming/tree/master/solutions_to_assgn`.

Further reading

To aid you in delving deeper into the subject with useful materials, we provide a rather detailed list of online references and links (and at times even books) in a *Further reading* markdown document – organized by chapter – in this book's GitHub repository. The *Further reading* document is available here: `https://github.com/PacktPublishing/Linux-Kernel-Programming/blob/master/Further_Reading.md`.

Section 2: Understanding and Working with the Kernel

A key reason why many struggle with kernel development is a lack of understanding of its internals. Here, some essentials of kernel architecture, memory management, and scheduling are covered.

This section comprises the following chapters:

- Chapter 6, *Kernel Internals Essentials – Processes and Threads*
- Chapter 7, *Memory Management Internals – Essentials*
- Chapter 8, *Kernel Memory Allocation for Module Authors, Part 1*
- Chapter 9, *Kernel Memory Allocation for Module Authors, Part 2*

6
Kernel Internals Essentials - Processes and Threads

Kernel internals, and especially those concerning memory management, are a vast and complex topic. In this book, we do not intend to delve deep into the gory details of kernel and memory internals. At the same time, I would like to provide sufficient, and definitely requisite, background knowledge for a budding kernel or device driver developer like you to successfully tackle the key topics necessary to understand the kernel architecture in terms of how processes, threads, and their stacks are managed. You'll also be able to correctly and efficiently manage dynamic kernel memory (with the focus on writing kernel or driver code using the **Loadable Kernel Module (LKM)** framework). As a side benefit, armed with this knowledge, you will find yourself becoming more proficient at *debugging* both user and kernel space code.

I have divided the discussion on essential internals into two chapters, this one and the next. This chapter covers key aspects of the architecture of Linux kernel internals, especially with respect to how processes and threads are managed within the kernel. The following chapter will focus on memory management internals, another critical aspect of understanding and working with the Linux kernel. Of course, the reality is that all of these things do not really get covered in a chapter or two but are spread out across this book (for example, details on the CPU scheduling of processes/threads will be found in later chapters; similarly for memory internals, hardware interrupts, synchronization, and so on).

Briefly, these are the topics covered in this chapter:

- Understanding process and interrupt contexts
- Understanding the basics of the process VAS (virtual address space)
- Organizing processes, threads, and their stacks – user and kernel space
- Understanding and accessing the kernel task structure
- Working with the task structure via current
- Iterating over the kernel's task lists

Technical requirements

I assume that you have gone through `Chapter 1`, *Kernel Workspace Setup*, and have appropriately prepared a guest **Virtual Machine** (**VM**) running Ubuntu 18.04 LTS (or a later stable release) and installed all the required packages. If not, I recommend you do this first.

To get the most out of this book, I strongly recommend you first set up the workspace environment, including cloning this book's GitHub repository for the code (found here: `https://github.com/PacktPublishing/Linux-Kernel-Programming`) and work on it in a hands-on fashion.

I do assume that you are familiar with basic virtual memory concepts, the user-mode process **Virtual Address Space** (**VAS**) layout of segments, the stack, and so on. Nevertheless, we do devote a few pages to explaining these basics (in the *Understanding the basics of the process VAS* section that soon follows).

Understanding process and interrupt contexts

In `Chapter 4`, *Writing Your First Kernel Module – LKMs, Part 1*, we presented a brief section entitled *Kernel architecture I* (if you haven't read it yet, I suggest you do so before continuing). We will now expand on this discussion.

It's critical to understand that most modern OSes are **monolithic** in design. The word *monolithic* literally means a *single large piece of stone*. We shall defer a little later to how exactly this applies to our favorite OS! For now, we understand *monolithic* as meaning this: when a process or thread issues a system call, it switches to (privileged) kernel mode and executes kernel code, and possibly works on kernel data. Yes, there is no kernel or kernel thread executing code on its behalf; the process (or thread) *itself* executes kernel code. Thus, we say that kernel code executes within the context of a user space process or thread – we call this the **process context**. Think about it, significant portions of the kernel execute precisely this way, including a large portion of the code of device drivers.

Well, you may ask, now that you understand this, how else – besides process context – can kernel code execute? There is another way: when a hardware interrupt (from a peripheral device – the keyboard, a network card, a disk, and so on) fires, the CPU's control unit saves the current context and immediately re-vectors the CPU to run the code of the interrupt handler (the **interrupt service routine—ISR**). Now this code runs in kernel (privileged) mode too – in effect, this is another, asynchronous, way to switch to kernel mode! The interrupt code path of many device drivers are executed like this; we say that the kernel code being executed in this manner is executing in **interrupt context**.

So, any and every piece of kernel code is entered by and executes in one of two contexts:

- **Process context**: The kernel is entered from a system call or processor *exception* (such as a page fault) and kernel code is executed, kernel data worked upon; it's synchronous (top down).
- **Interrupt context**: The is kernel entered from a peripheral chip's hardware interrupt and kernel code is executed, kernel data worked upon; it's asynchronous (bottom up).

Figure 6.1 shows the conceptual view: user-mode processes and threads execute in unprivileged user context; the user mode thread can switch to privileged kernel mode by issuing a *system call*. The diagram also shows us that pure *kernel threads* exist as well within Linux; they're very similar to user-mode threads, with the key difference that they only execute in kernel space; they cannot even *see* the user VAS. A synchronous switch to kernel mode via a system call (or processor exception) has the task now running kernel code in *process context*. (Kernel threads too run kernel code in process context.) Hardware interrupts, though, are a different ball game – they cause execution to asynchronously enter the kernel; the code they execute (typically a device driver's interrupt handler) runs in the so-called *interrupt context*.

Kernel Internals Essentials - Processes and Threads

Figure 6.1 shows more details – interrupt context top and bottom halves, kernel threads and workqueues; we request you to have some patience, we'll cover all this and much more in later chapters:

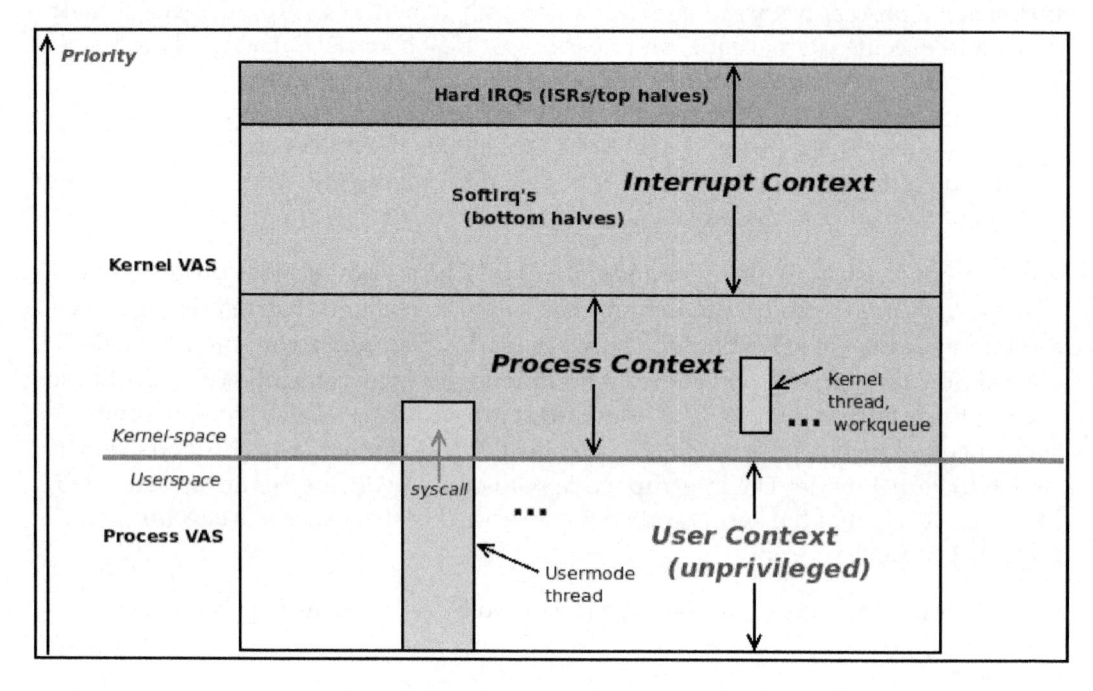

Figure 6.1 – Conceptual diagram showing unprivileged user-mode execution and privileged kernel-mode execution with both process and interrupt contexts

Further on in the book, we shall show you how exactly you can check *in which context* your kernel code is currently running. Read on!

Understanding the basics of the process VAS

A fundamental 'rule' of virtual memory is this: all potentially addressable memory is in a box; that is, it's *sandboxed*. We think of this 'box' as the *process image* or the process VAS. Looking outside the box is disallowed.

> Here, we provide only a quick overview of the process user VAS. For details, please refer to the *Further reading* section at the end of this chapter.

The user VAS is divided into homogeneous memory regions called *segments* or, more technically, *mappings*. Every Linux process has at least these mappings (or segments):

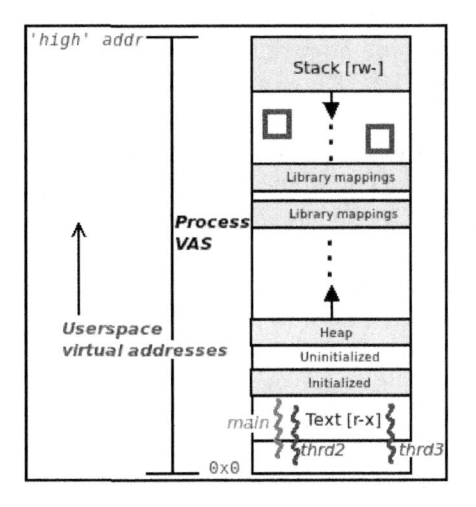

Figure 6.2 – Process VAS

Let's go over a quick breakdown of these segments or mappings:

- **Text segment**: This is where the machine code is stored; static (mode: r-x).
- **Data segment(s)**: This is where the global and static data variables are stored (mode: rw-). It is internally divided into three distinct segments:
    - **Initialized data segment**: Pre-initialized variables are stored here; static.
    - **Uninitialized data segment**: Uninitialized variables are stored here (they are auto-initialized to 0 at runtime; this region is sometimes called the *bss*); static.
    - **Heap segment**: The *library APIs* for memory allocation and freeing (the familiar malloc(3) family of routines) get memory from here. That's also not completely true. On modern systems, only malloc() instances below MMAP_THRESHOLD (128 KB by default) get their memory from the heap. Any higher and it's allocated as a separate 'mapping' in the process VAS (via the powerful mmap(2) system call). It is a dynamic segment (it can grow/shrink). The last legally reference-able location on the heap is referred to as the *program break*.

[275]

- **Libraries (text, data)**: All shared libraries that a process dynamically links into are mapped (at runtime, via the loader) into the process VAS (mode: `r-x`/`rw-`).
- **Stack**: A region of memory that uses the **Last In, First Out** (LIFO) semantics; the stack is used for the purpose of *implementing a high-level language's function-calling* mechanism. It includes parameter passing, local variable instantiation (and destruction), and return value propagation. It is a dynamic segment. On all modern processors (including the x86 and ARM families), *the stack 'grows' toward lower addresses* (called a fully descending stack). Every time a function is called, a *stack frame* is allocated and initialized as required; the precise layout of a stack frame is very CPU dependent (you must refer to the respective CPU **Application Binary Interface** (**ABI**) document for this; see the *Further reading* section for references). The SP register (or equivalent) always points to the current frame, the top of the stack; as stacks grow towards lower (virtual) addresses, the top of the stack is actually the lowest (virtual) address! It's non-intuitive but true (mode: `rw-`).

Of course, you will understand that processes must contain at least one *thread* of execution (a thread is an execution path within a process); that one thread typically being the `main()` function. In *Figure 6.2*, as an example, we show three threads of execution – `main`, `thrd2`, and `thrd3`. Also, as expected, every thread shares everything in the VAS *except* for the stack; as you'll know, every thread has its own private stack. The stack of `main` is shown at the very top of the process (user) VAS; the stacks of the `thrd2` and `thrd3` threads are shown as being between the library mappings and the stack of `main` and is illustrated with the two (blue) squares.

> **TIP**: I have designed and implemented what I feel is a pretty useful learning/teaching and debugging utility called *procmap* (https://github.com/kaiwan/procmap); it's a console-based process VAS visualization utility. It can actually show you the process VAS (in quite a bit of detail); we shall commence using it in the next chapter. Don't let that stop you from trying it out right away though; do clone it and give it a spin on your Linux system.

Now that you understand the basics of the process VAS, it's time to delve quite a bit deeper into the kernel internals regarding the process VAS, the user and kernel address spaces, and their threads and stacks.

Organizing processes, threads, and their stacks – user and kernel space

The traditional **UNIX process model** – *Everything is a process; if it's not a process, it's a file* – has a lot going for it. The very fact that it is still *the* model followed by operating systems after a span of nearly five decades amply validates this. Of course, nowadays, the **thread** is important; *a thread is merely an execution path within a process*. Threads *share all* process resources, including the user VAS, *except for the stack*. Every thread has its own private stack region (this makes perfect sense; if not, how could threads truly run in parallel, as it's the stack that holds execution context).

The other reason we focus on the *thread* and not the process is made clearer in Chapter 10, *The CPU Scheduler, Part 1*. For now, we shall just say this: *the thread, not the process, is the kernel schedulable entity* (also known as the KSE). This is actually a fallout of a key aspect of the Linux OS architecture. On the Linux OS, every thread – including kernel threads – maps to a kernel metadata structure called the **task structure**. The task structure (also known as the *process descriptor*) is essentially a large kernel data structure that the kernel uses as an attribute structure. For every *thread* alive, the kernel maintains a corresponding *task structure* (see *Figure 6.3*, and worry not, we shall cover more on the task structure in the coming sections).

The next really key point to grasp: we *require one stack per thread per privilege level supported by the CPU*. On modern OSes such as Linux, we support two privilege levels – *the unprivileged user mode (or user space) and the privileged kernel mode (or kernel space)*. Thus, on Linux, *every user space thread alive has two stacks*:

- **A user space stack**: This stack is in play when the thread executes user-mode code paths.
- **A kernel space stack**: This stack is in play when the thread switches to kernel mode (via a system call or processor exception) and executes kernel code paths (in process context).

> Of course, every good rule has an exception: *kernel threads* are threads that live purely within the kernel and thus have a "view" of *only* kernel (virtual) address space; they cannot "see" userland. Hence, as they will only ever execute kernel space code paths, they have **just one stack** – a kernel space stack.

Kernel Internals Essentials - Processes and Threads

Figure 6.3 divides up the address space into two – user space and kernel space. In the upper part of the diagram – user space – you can see several processes and their *user VASes*. In the bottom part – kernel space – you can see, corresponding to every user-mode thread, a kernel metadata structure (struct `task_struct`, which we shall cover a bit later in detail) and the kernel-mode stack of that thread. In addition, we see (at the very bottom) three kernel threads (labeled `kthrd1`, `kthrd2`, and `kthrdn`); as expected, they too have a `task_struct` metadata structure representing their innards (attributes) and a kernel-mode stack:

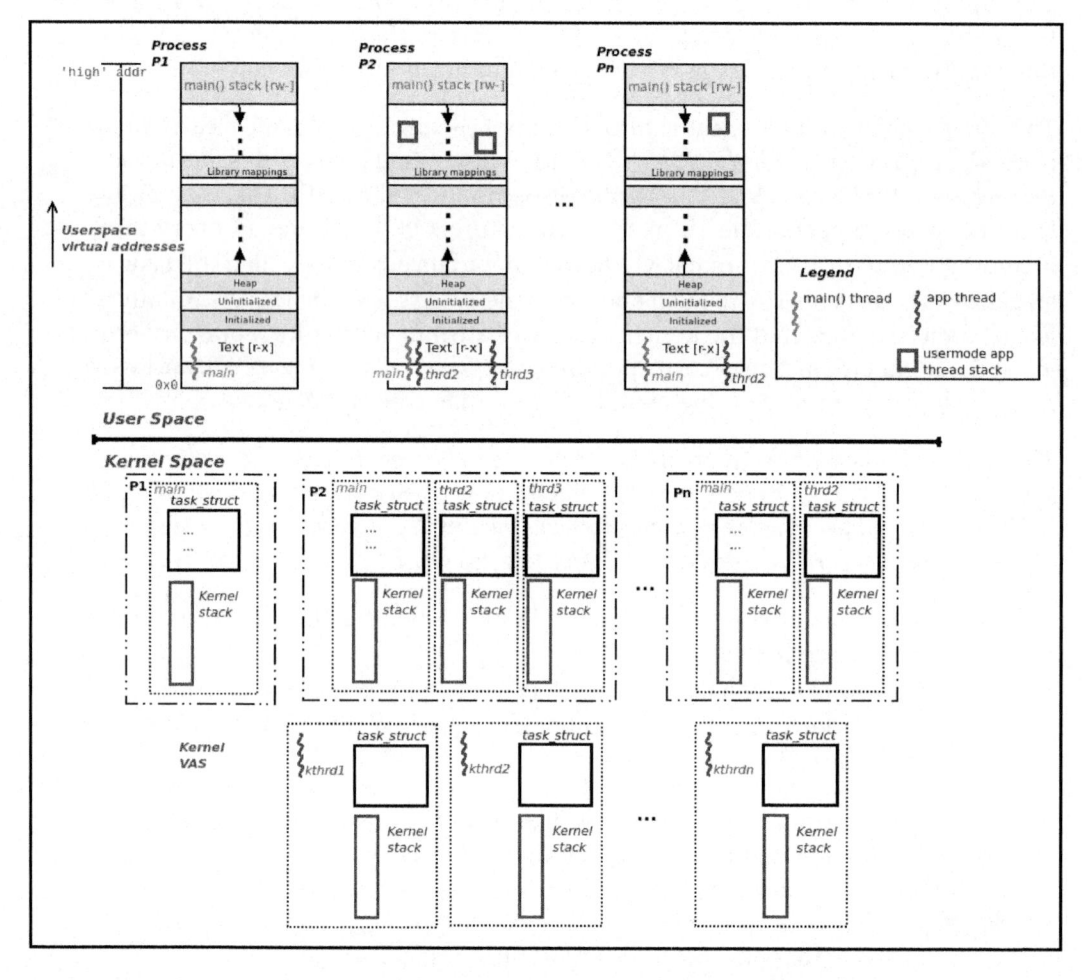

Figure 6.3 – Processes, threads, stacks, and task structures – user and kernel VAS

[278]

Chapter 6

To help make this discussion practical, let's execute a simple Bash script (`ch6/countem.sh`) that counts the number of processes and threads currently alive. I did this on my native x86_64 Ubuntu 18.04 LTS box; see the following resulting output:

```
$ cd <booksrc>/ch6
$ ./countem.sh
System release info:
Distributor ID: Ubuntu
Description:    Ubuntu 18.04.4 LTS
Release:        18.04
Codename:       bionic

Total # of processes alive                  =      362
Total # of threads alive                    =     1234
Total # of kernel threads alive             =      181
Thus, total # of user-mode threads alive    =     1053
$
```

I'll leave it to you to look up the code of this simple script here: `ch6/countem.sh`. Study the preceding output and understand it. You will realize, of course, that this is a snapshot of the situation at a certain point in time. It can and does change.

In the following sections, we divide up the discussion into two parts (corresponding to the two address spaces) – that of what we see in Figure 6.3 in user space and what is seen in Figure 6.3 in kernel space. Let's begin with the user space components.

User space organization

With reference to the `countem.sh` Bash script that we ran in the preceding section, we will now break it down and discuss some key points, confining ourselves to the *user space portion* of the VAS for now. Please take care to read and understand this (the numbers we refer to in the following discussion are with reference to our sample run of our `countem.sh` script in the preceding section). For the sake of better understanding, I have placed the user space portion of the diagram here:

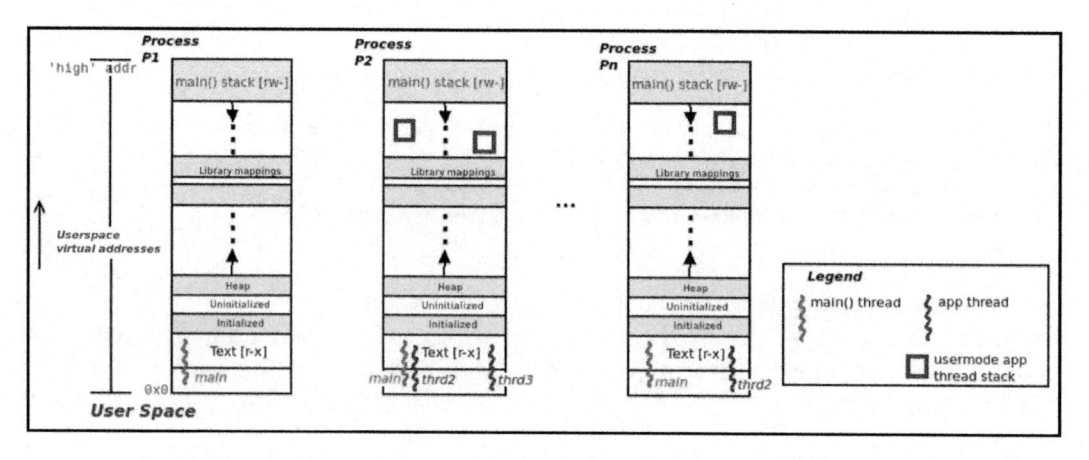

Figure 6.4 – User space portion of overall picture seen in Figure 6.3

Here (Figure 6.4) you can see three individual processes. Every process has at least one thread of execution (the `main()` thread). In the preceding example, we show three processes `P1`, `P2`, and `Pn`, with one, three, and two threads in them respectively, including `main()`. From our preceding sample run of the `countem.sh` script, `Pn` would have *n*=362.

> Do note that these diagrams are purely conceptual. In reality, the 'process' with PID 2 is typically a single-threaded kernel thread called `kthreadd`.

Each process consists of several segments (technically, *mappings*). Broadly, the user-mode segments (mappings) are as follows:

- **Text**: Code; `r-x`
- **Data segments**: `rw-`; consists of three distinct mappings – the initialized data segment, the uninitialized data segment (or `bss`), and an 'upward-growing' heap

- **Library mappings**: For the text and data of each shared library the process dynamically links to
- **Downward-growing stack(s)**

Regarding these stacks, we saw from our preceding sample run that there are 1,053 user-mode threads currently alive on the system. This implies that there are 1,053 user space stacks as well, as there will exist one user mode stack for every user-mode thread alive. Of these user space thread stacks, we can say the following:

- One user space stack is always present for the `main()` thread, it will be located close to the very top – the high end – of the user VAS; if the process is single-threaded (only a `main()` thread), then it will have just one user-mode stack; the `P1` process in *Figure 6.4* shows this case.
- If the process is multithreaded, it will have one user-mode thread stack per thread alive (including `main()`); processes `P2` and `Pn` in *Figure 6.4* illustrate this case. The stacks are allocated either at the time of calling `fork(2)` (for `main()`) or `pthread_create(3)` (for the remaining threads within the process), which results in this code path being executed in process context within the kernel:

    ```
    sys_fork() --> do_fork() --> _do_fork()
    ```

- FYI, the `pthread_create(3)` library API on Linux invokes the (very Linux-specific) `clone(2)` system call; this system call ends up calling `_do_fork()`; the `clone_flags` parameter passed along informs the kernel as to how exactly to create the 'custom process'; in other words, a thread!
- These user space stacks are of course dynamic; they can grow/shrink up to the stack size resource limit (`RLIMIT_STACK`, typically 8 MB; you can use the `prlimit(1)` utility to look it up).

Having seen and understood the user space portion, now let's delve into the kernel space side of things.

Kernel Internals Essentials - Processes and Threads

Kernel space organization

Continuing our discussion with reference to the `countem.sh` Bash script that we ran in the previous section, we will now break it down and discuss some key points, confining ourselves to the *kernel space portion* of the VAS. Please take care to carefully read and understand this (while reading the numbers that were output in our preceding sample run of the `countem.sh` script). For the sake of better understanding I have placed the kernel space portion of the diagram here (Figure 6.5):

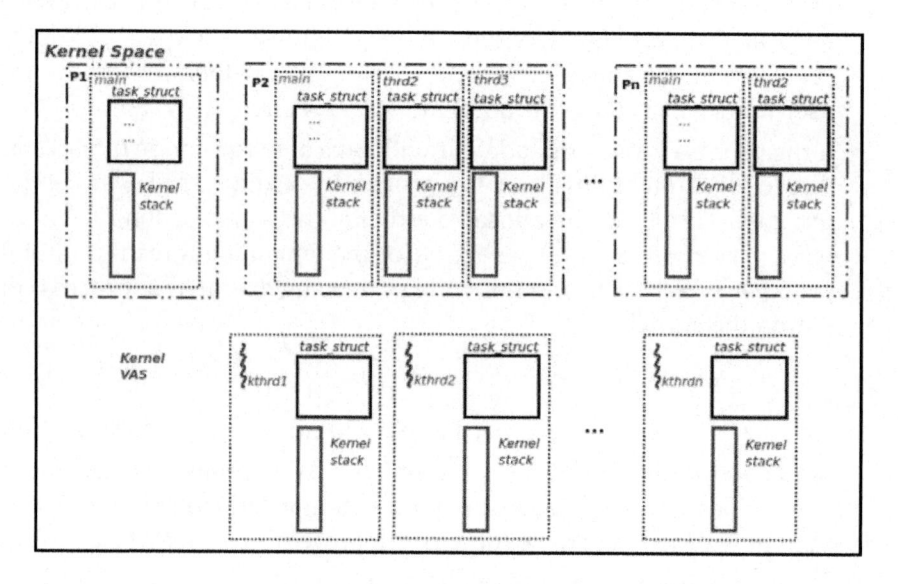

Figure 6.5 – Kernel space portion of overall picture seen in Figure 6.3

Again, from our preceding sample run, you can see that there are 1,053 user-mode threads and 181 kernel threads currently alive on the system. This yields a total of 1,234 kernel space stacks. How? As mentioned earlier, every user-mode thread has two stacks – one user-mode stack and one kernel-mode stack. Thus, we'll have 1,053 kernel-mode stacks for each of the user-mode threads, plus 181 kernel-mode stacks for the (pure) kernel threads (recall, kernel threads have *only* a kernel-mode stack; they cannot 'see' user space at all). Let's list a few characteristics of kernel-mode stacks:

- There will be one kernel-mode stack for each application (user-mode) thread alive, including `main()`.

[282]

- **Kernel-mode stacks are *fixed in size (static) and are quite small*.**
  Practically speaking, their size is 2 pages on 32-bit and 4 pages on 64-bit OSes (with a page typically being 4 KB in size).
- They are allocated at thread creation time (usually boils down to `_do_fork()`).

Again, let's be crystal clear on this: each user-mode thread has two stacks – a user-mode stack and a kernel-mode stack. The exception to this rule is kernel threads; they only have a kernel-mode stack (as they possess no user mapping and thus no user space 'segments'). In the lower part of *Figure 6.5*, we show three *kernel threads* – `kthrd1`, `kthrd2`, and `kthrdn` (in our preceding sample run, `kthrdn` would have $n=181$). Further, each kernel thread has a task structure and a kernel-mode stack allocated to it at creation time.

A kernel-mode stack is similar in most respects to its user-mode counterpart – every time a function is called, a *stack frame* is set up (the frame layout is particular to the architecture and forms a part of the CPU ABI document; see the *Further reading* section for more on these details); the CPU has a register to track the current location of the stack (usually called a **Stack Pointer** (**SP**)), and the stack "grows" toward *lower* virtual addresses. But, unlike the dynamic user-mode stack, *the kernel-mode stack is fixed in size and small*.

> *An important implication of the pretty small (two-page or four-page) kernel-mode stack size for the kernel / driver developer – be very careful to not overflow your kernel stack by performing stack-intensive work (such as recursion).*

> *There exists a kernel configurable to warn you about high (kernel) stack usage at compile time; here's the text from the* `lib/Kconfig.debug` *file:*
> `CONFIG_FRAME_WARN`:
> Tell gcc to warn at build time for stack frames larger than this.
> Setting this too low will cause a lot of warnings.
> Setting it to 0 disables the warning.
> Requires gcc 4.4

Summarizing the current situation

Okay, great, let's now summarize our learning and findings from our preceding sample run of the `countem.sh` script:

- **Task structures**:
    - Every thread alive (user or kernel) has a corresponding task structure (`struct task_struct`) in the kernel; this is how the kernel tracks it and all its attributes are stored here (you'll learn more in the *Understanding and accessing the kernel task structure* section)
    - With respect to our sample run of our `ch6/countem.sh` script:
        - As there are a total of 1,234 threads (both user and kernel) alive on the system, this implies a total of 1,234 *task (metadata) structures* in kernel memory (in the code, `struct task_struct`), of which we can say the following:
        - 1,053 of these task structures represent user threads.
        - The remaining 181 task structures represent kernel threads.
- **Stacks**:
    - Every user space thread has two stacks:
        - A user mode stack (is in play when the thread executes user-mode code paths)
        - A kernel mode stack (is in play when the thread executes kernel-mode code paths)
    - A pure kernel thread has only one stack - a kernel mode stack

- With respect to our sample run of
  our `ch6/countem.sh` script:
  - 1,053 user space stacks (in user land).
  - 1,053 kernel space stacks (in kernel memory).
  - 181 kernel space stacks (for the 181 kernel threads that are alive).
  - This comes together for a grand total of 1053+1053+181 = 2,287 stacks!

While discussing user and kernel-mode stacks, we should also briefly mention this point: many architectures (including x86 and ARM64) support a separate per-CPU stack for *interrupt handling*. When an external hardware interrupt occurs, the CPU's control unit immediately re-vectors control to, ultimately, the interrupt handling code (perhaps within a device driver). A separate per-CPU interrupt stack is used to hold the stack frame(s) for the interrupt code path(s); this helps avoid putting too much pressure on the existing (small) kernel-mode stack of the process/thread that got interrupted.

Okay, now that you understand the overall organization of the user and kernel spaces in terms of processes/threads and their stacks, let's move on to seeing how you can actually 'view' the content of both the kernel and user space stacks. Besides being useful for learning purposes, this knowledge can greatly aid you in debugging situations.

Viewing the user and kernel stacks

The *stack* is often the key to a debug session. It is the stack, of course, that holds the *current execution context* of the process or thread – where it is now – which allows us to infer what it's doing. More importantly, being able to see and interpret the thread's *call stack (or call chain/backtrace)* crucially allows us to understand how exactly we got here. All this precious information resides in the stack. But wait, there are two stacks for every thread – the user space and the kernel space stack. How do we view them?

Kernel Internals Essentials - Processes and Threads

Here, we shall show two broad ways of viewing the kernel and user-mode stacks of a given process or thread, firstly via the 'traditional' approach, and then a more recent modern approach (via [e]BPF). Do read on.

Traditional approach to viewing the stacks

Let's first learn to view both the kernel and user-mode stacks of a given process or thread using what we shall call the 'traditional' approach. Let's begin with the kernel-mode stack.

Viewing the kernel space stack of a given thread or process

Good news; this is really easy. The Linux kernel makes the stack visible via the usual mechanism to expose kernel internals to user space – the powerful `proc` filesystem interfaces. Just peek under `/proc/<pid>/stack`.

So, okay, let's look up the kernel-mode stack of our *Bash* process. Let's say that, on our x86_64 Ubuntu guest (running the 5.4 kernel), our Bash process' PID is 3085:

> On modern kernels, to avoid *information leakage*, viewing the kernel-mode stack of a process or thread requires *root* access as a security requirement.

```
$ sudo cat /proc/3085/stack
[<0>] do_wait+0x1cb/0x230
[<0>] kernel_wait4+0x89/0x130
[<0>] __do_sys_wait4+0x95/0xa0
[<0>] __x64_sys_wait4+0x1e/0x20
[<0>] do_syscall_64+0x5a/0x120
[<0>] entry_SYSCALL_64_after_hwframe+0x44/0xa9
$
```

In the preceding output, each line represents a *call frame* on the stack. To help decipher a kernel stack backtrace, it's worth knowing the following points:

- It should be read in a bottom-up fashion (from bottom to top).
- Each line of output represents a *call frame*; in effect, a function in the call chain.
- A function name appearing as ?? implies that the kernel cannot reliably interpret the stack. Ignore it, it's the kernel saying that it's an invalid stack frame (a 'blip' left behind); the kernel backtrace code is usually right!

[286]

Chapter 6

- On Linux, any `foo()` system call will typically become a `SyS_foo()` function within the kernel. Also, very often but not always, `SyS_foo()` is a wrapper that invokes the 'real' code `do_foo()`. A detail: in the kernel code, you might see macros of the type `SYSCALL_DEFINEn(foo, ...);` the macro becomes the `SyS_foo()` routine; the number appended, n, is in the range [0, 6]; it's the number of parameters being passed to the kernel from user space for the system call.

Now look again at the preceding output; it should be quite clear: our *Bash* process is currently executing the `do_wait()` function; it got there via a system call, the `wait4()` system call! This is quite right; the shell works by forking off a child process and then waiting for its demise via the `wait4(2)` system call.

> Curious readers (you!) should note that the `[<0>]` in the leftmost column of each stack frame displayed in the preceding snippet are the placeholders for the *text (code) address* of that function. Again, for *security* reasons (to prevent information leakage), it is zeroed out on modern kernels. (Another security measure related to the kernel and process layout is discussed in *Chapter 7, Memory Management Internals – Essentials*, in the *Randomizing the memory layout – KASLR* and *User-mode ASLR* sections).

Viewing the user space stack of a given thread or process

Ironically, viewing the *user space stack* of a process or thread seems harder to do on a typical Linux distro (as opposed to viewing the kernel-mode stack, as we just saw in the previous section). There is a utility to do so: `gstack(1)`. In reality, it's just a simple wrapper over a script that invokes `gdb(1)` in batch mode, getting `gdb` to invoke its `backtrace` command.

> Unfortunately, on Ubuntu (18.04 LTS at least), there seems to be an issue; the `gstack` program was not found in any native package. (Ubuntu does have a `pstack(1)` utility, but, at least on my test VM, it failed to work well.) A workaround is to simply use `gdb` directly (you can always `attach <PID>` and issue the `[thread apply all] bt` command to view the user mode stack(s)).

On my x86_64 Fedora 29 guest system, though, the `gstack(1)` utility cleanly installs and runs well; an example is as follows (our Bash process' PID here happens to be `12696`):

```
$ gstack 12696
#0  0x00007fa6f60754eb in waitpid () from /lib64/libc.so.6
#1  0x0000556f26c03629 in ?? ()
#2  0x0000556f26c04cc3 in wait_for ()
#3  0x0000556f26bf375c in execute_command_internal ()
#4  0x0000556f26bf39b6 in execute_command ()
#5  0x0000556f26bdb389 in reader_loop ()
#6  0x0000556f26bd9b69 in main ()
$
```

Again, each line represents a call frame. Read it bottom-up. Clearly, *Bash* executes a command and ends up invoking the `waitpid()` system call (in reality on modern Linux systems, `waitpid()` is just a `glibc` wrapper over the actual `wait4(2)` system call! Again, simply ignore any call frames labeled `??`).

> **TIP**: Being able to peek into the kernel and user space stacks (as shown in the preceding snippets), and using utilities including `strace(1)` and `ltrace(1)` for tracing system and library calls of a process/thread respectively, can be a tremendous aid when debugging! Don't ignore them.

Now for a 'modern' approach to this question.

[e]BPF – the modern approach to viewing both stacks

Now – a lot more exciting! – let's learn (the very basics) of using a powerful modern approach, leveraging (as of the time of writing) very recent technology – called the **extended Berkeley Packet Filter** (**eBPF**; or simply, BPF. We did mention the [e]BPF project in Chapter 1, *Kernel Workspace Setup*, under the *Additional useful projects* section.) The older BPF has been around a long time and has been used for network packet tracing; [e]BPF is a recent innovation, available only as of 4.x Linux kernels (which of course implies that you will need to be on a 4.x or more recent Linux system to use this approach).

Directly using the underlying kernel-level BPF bytecode technology is (extremely) difficult to do; thus, the good news is that there are several easy-to-use frontends (tools and scripts) to this technology. (A diagram showing the current BCC performance analysis tools can be found at http://www.brendangregg.com/BPF/bcc_tracing_tools_early2019.png; a list of the [e]BPF frontends can be found at http://www.brendangregg.com/ebpf.html#frontends; these links are from *Brendan Gregg's* blog.) Among the frontends, **BCC** and **bpftrace** are considered very useful. Here, we shall simply provide a quick demonstration using a BCC tool called stackcount (well, on Ubuntu at least it's named stackcount-bpfcc(8)). Another advantage: using this tool allows you to see both the kernel and user-mode stacks at once; there's no need for separate tools.

> **TIP**
> You can install the BCC tools for your *host* Linux distro by reading the installation instructions here: https://github.com/iovisor/bcc/blob/master/INSTALL.md. Why not on our guest Linux VM? You can, *when running a distro kernel* (such as an Ubuntu- or Fedora-supplied kernel). The reason: the installation of the BCC toolset includes the installation of the linux-headers-$(uname -r) package; the latter exists only for distro kernels (and not for our custom 5.4 kernel that we're running on the guest).

In the following example, we use the stackcount BCC tool (on my x86_64 Ubuntu 18.04 LTS host system) to look up the stacks of our VirtualBox Fedora31 guest process (the virtual machine is, after all, a process on the host system!). For this tool, you have to specify a function (or functions) of interest (interestingly, you can specify either a user space or kernel space function and also use 'wildcards' or a regular expression when doing so!); only when those function(s) are invoked will the stacks be traced and reported. As an example, we select any function containing the name malloc:

```
$ sudo stackcount-bpfcc -p 29819 -r ".*malloc.*" -v -d
Tracing 73 functions for ".*malloc.*"... Hit Ctrl-C to end.
^C
  ffffffff99a56811 __kmalloc_reserve.isra.43
  ffffffff99a59436 alloc_skb_with_frags
  ffffffff99a51f72 sock_alloc_send_pskb
  ffffffff99b2e986 unix_stream_sendmsg
  ffffffff99a4d43e sock_sendmsg
  ffffffff99a4d4e3 sock_write_iter
  ffffffff9947f59a do_iter_readv_writev
  ffffffff99480cf6 do_iter_write
  ffffffff99480ed8 vfs_writev
  ffffffff99480fb8 do_writev
  ffffffff99482810 sys_writev
  ffffffff99203bb3 do_syscall_64
```

```
ffffffff99c00081 entry_SYSCALL_64_after_hwframe
  --
7fd0cc31b6e7     __GI___writev
12bc             [unknown]
600000195        [unknown]
1
[...]
```

> **TIP**: [e]BPF programs might fail due to the new *kernel lockdown* feature being merged into the mainline 5.4 kernel (it's disabled by default though). It's a **Linux Security Module (LSM)** that enables an extra 'hard' level of security on Linux systems. Of course, security is a double-edged sword; having a very secure system implicitly means that certain things will not work as expected, and this includes some [e]BPF programs. Do refer to the *Further reading* section for more on kernel lockdown.

The -d option switch passed prints the delimiter --; it denotes the boundary between the kernel-mode and the user-mode stack of the process. (Unfortunately, as most production user-mode apps will have their symbolic information stripped, most user-mode stack frames simply show up as "[unknown]".) On this system at least, the kernel stack frames are very clear though; even the virtual address of the text (code) function in question is printed on the left. (To help you better understand the stack trace: firstly, read it bottom-up; next, as mentioned already, on
Linux, any foo() system call will typically become the SyS_foo() function within the kernel, and often SyS_foo() is a wrapper around do_foo(), the actual worker function.)

Note that the stackcount-bpfcc tool works only with Linux 4.6+, and requires root access. Do see its man page for details.

As a second simpler example, we write a simple *Hello, world* program (with the caveat that it's in an infinite loop, so that we can capture the underlying `write(2)` system calls as they occur), build it with symbolic info enabled (that is, with `gcc -g ...`), and use a simple Bash script to perform the same job as previously: tracing the kernel and user-mode stacks as it executes. (You will find the code in `ch6/ebpf_stacktrace_eg/`.) A screenshot showing a sample run (okay, here's an exception: I've run the script on an x86_64 Ubuntu 20.04 LTS host) looks as follows:

```
$ make
gcc -Wall -UDEBUG helloworld.c -o helloworld
strip --strip-all helloworld
gcc -g -ggdb -gdwarf-4 -O0 -Wall -Wextra -DDEBUG helloworld.c -o helloworld_dbg
$ ls
helloworld*  helloworld.c  helloworld_dbg*  Makefile  runit.sh*
$ ./runit.sh
sudo stackcount-bpfcc -p 1497640 -r .*sys_write.* -v -d
Tracing 10 functions for ".*sys_write.*"... Hit Ctrl-C to end.
^C
  ffffffffb24dde21 b'__x64_sys_write'
  ffffffffb2e0008c b'entry_SYSCALL_64_after_hwframe'
    --
  7f856dbe0057     b'[unknown]'
  49502021646c726f b'[unknown]'
    1

  ffffffffb24ddd41 b'ksys_write'
  ffffffffb22044c7 b'do_syscall_64'
  ffffffffb2e0008c b'entry_SYSCALL_64_after_hwframe'
    --
  7f856dbe0057     b'[unknown]'
  49502021646c726f b'[unknown]'
    1

Detaching...
$
```

Figure 6.6 – A sample run using the stackcount-bpfcc BCC tool to trace both kernel and user-mode stacks for the write() of our Hello, world process

> **TIP**
> We have merely scratched the surface here; [e]BPF tools such as BCC and `bpftrace` really are the modern, powerful approach to system, app tracing and performance analysis on the Linux OS. Do take the time to learn how to use these powerful tools! (Each BCC tool also has a dedicated man page *with examples*.) We refer you to the *Further reading* section for links on [e]BPF, BCC and `bpftrace`.

Let's conclude this section by zooming out and looking at an overview of what you have learned so far!

[291]

The 10,000-foot view of the process VAS

Before we conclude this section, it's important to take a step back and see the complete VASes of each process and how it looks for the system as a whole; in other words, to zoom out and see the "10,000-foot view" of the complete system address space. This is what we attempt to do with the following rather large and detailed diagram (*Figure 6.7*), an extension or superset of our earlier *Figure 6.3*.

> **TIP**
> For those of you reading a hard copy of the book, I'd definitely recommend you view the book's figures in full color from this PDF document at `https://static.packt-cdn.com/downloads/9781789953435_ColorImages.pdf`.

Besides what you have learned about and seen just now – the process user space segments, the (user and kernel) threads, and the kernel-mode stacks – don't forget that there is a lot of other metadata within the kernel: the task structures, the kernel threads, the memory descriptor metadata structures, and so on. They all are very much a part of the *kernel VAS,* which is often called the *kernel segment.* There's more to the kernel segment than tasks and stacks. It also contains (obviously!) the static kernel (core) code and data, in effect, all the major (and minor) *subsystems* of the kernel, the arch-specific code, and so on (that we spoke about in `Chapter 4`, *Writing Your First Kernel Module – LKMs Part 1,* under the *Kernel space components* section).

As just mentioned, the following diagram presents an attempt to sum up and present all (well, much) of this information in one place:

Chapter 6

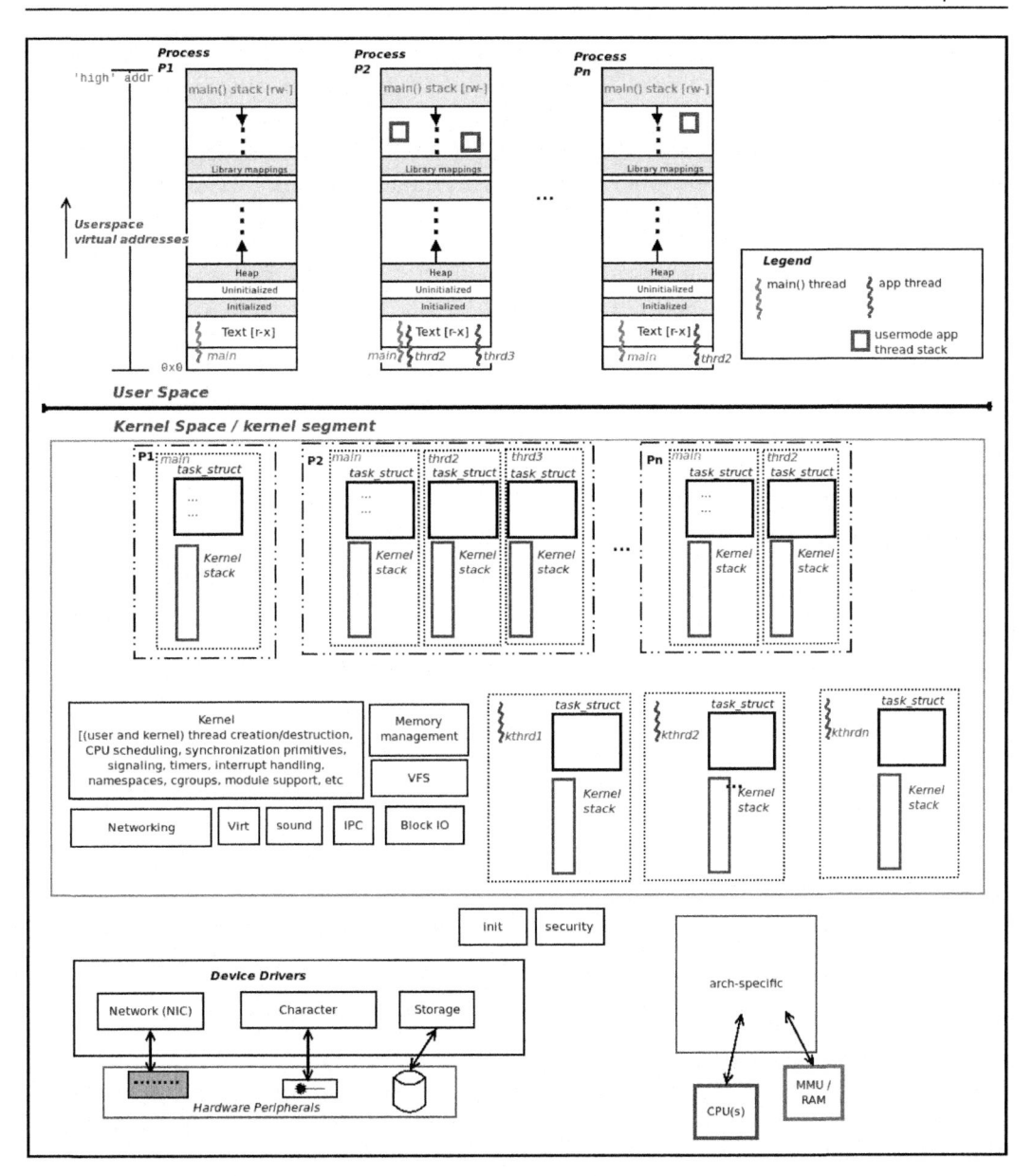

Figure 6.7 – The 10,000-foot view of the processes, threads, stacks, and task structures of the user and kernel VASes

Whew, quite a thing, isn't it? The red box in the kernel segment of the preceding diagram encompasses the *core kernel code and data* – the major kernel subsystems, and shows the task structures and kernel-mode stacks. The rest of it is considered non-core stuff; this includes device drivers. (The arch-specific code can arguably be viewed as core code; we just show it separately here.) Also, don't let the preceding information overwhelm you; just focus on what we're here for right now – the processes, threads, their task structures, and stacks. If you're still unclear about it, be sure to re-read the preceding material.

Now, let's move on to actually understanding and learning how to reference the key or 'root' metadata structure for every single thread alive – the *task structure*.

Understanding and accessing the kernel task structure

As you have learned by now, every single user and kernel space thread is internally represented within the Linux kernel by a metadata structure containing all its attributes – the **task structure**. The task structure is represented in kernel code as `include/linux/sched.h:struct task_struct`.

It's often, unfortunately, referred to as the "process descriptor," causing no end of confusion! Thankfully, the phrase *task structure* is so much better; it represents a runnable task, in effect, a *thread*.

So there we have it: in the Linux design, every process consists of one or more threads and *each thread maps to a kernel data structure called a task structure* (`struct task_struct`).

The task structure is the "root" metadata structure for the thread – it encapsulates all the information required by the OS for that thread. This includes information on its memory (segments, paging tables, usage info, and more), CPU scheduling details, any files it currently has open, its credentials, capability bitmasks, timers, locks, **Asynchronous I/O** (**AIO**) contexts, hardware context, signaling, IPC objects, resource limits, (optional) audit, security and profiling info, and many more such details.

Figure 6.8 is a conceptual representation of the Linux kernel *task structure* and most of the information (metadata) it contains:

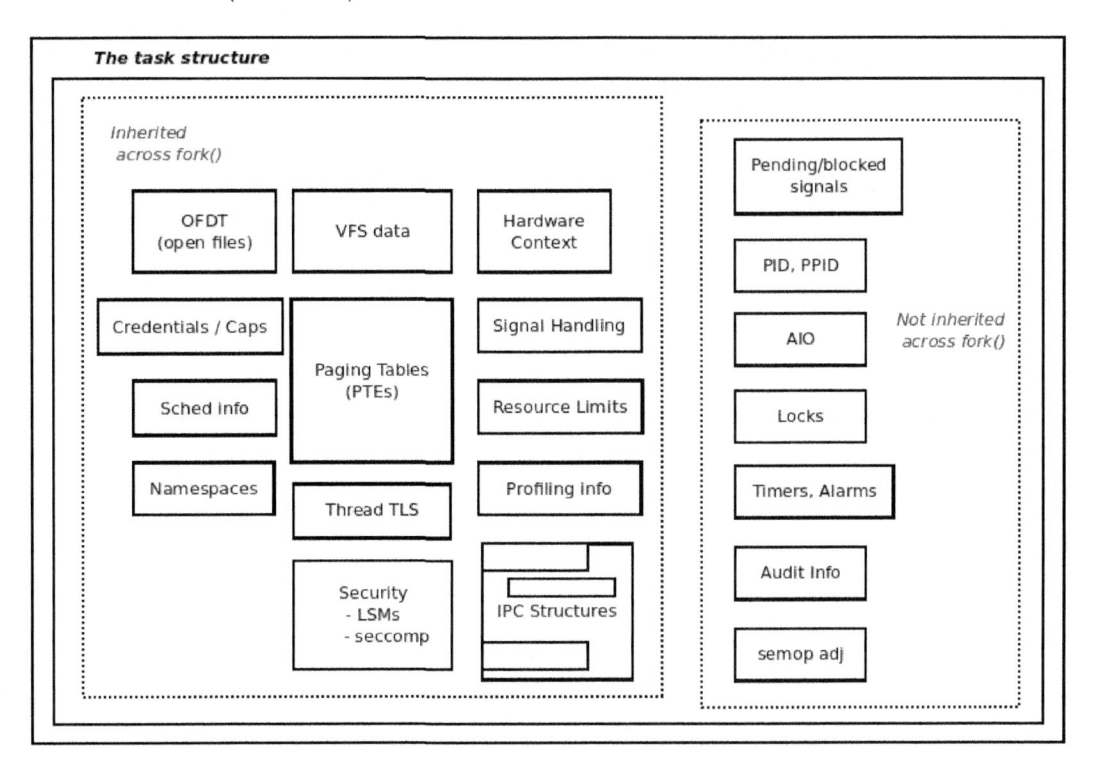

Figure 6.8 – Linux kernel task structure: struct task_struct

As can be seen from *Figure 6.8*, the task structure holds a huge quantity of information regarding every single task (process/thread) alive on the system (again, I reiterate: this includes kernel threads as well). We show – in a compartmentalized conceptual format in Figure 6.8 – the different kinds of attributes encapsulated within this data structure. Also, as can be seen, certain attributes will be *inherited* by a child process or thread upon `fork(2)` (or `pthread_create(3)`); certain attributes will not be inherited and will be merely reset. (The kernel-mode stack for

For now, at least, suffice it to say that the kernel 'understands' whether a task is a process or a thread. We'll later demonstrate a kernel module (`ch6/foreach/thrd_showall`) that reveals exactly how we can determine this (hang on, we'll get there!).

Now let's start to understand in more detail some of the more important members of the huge task structure; read on!

> Here, I only intend to give you a 'feel' for the kernel task structure; we do not delve deep into the details as it's not required for now. You will find that in later parts of this book, we delve into specific areas as required.

Looking into the task structure

Firstly, recall that the task structure is essentially the 'root' data structure of the process or thread – it holds all attributes of the task (as we saw earlier). Thus, it's rather large; the powerful `crash(8)` utility (used to analyze Linux crash dump data or investigate a live system) reports its size on x86_64 to be 9,088 bytes, as does the `sizeof` operator.

The task structure is defined in the `include/linux/sched.h` kernel header (it's a rather key header). In the following code, we show its definition with the caveat that we display only a few of its many members. (Also, the annotations in `<< angle brackets like this >>` are used to very briefly explain the member(s)):

```
// include/linux/sched.h
struct task_struct {
#ifdef CONFIG_THREAD_INFO_IN_TASK
    /*
     * For reasons of header soup (see current_thread_info()), this
     * must be the first element of task_struct.
     */
    struct thread_info      thread_info;    << important flags and status bits >>
#endif
    /* -1 unrunnable, 0 runnable, >0 stopped: */
    volatile long           state;
    [...]
    void                    *stack; << the location of the kernel-mode stack >>
    [...]
    /* Current CPU: */
    unsigned int            cpu;
    [...]
<< the members that follow are to do with CPU scheduling; some of them are discussed in Ch 9 & 10 on CPU Scheduling >>
    int on_rq;
    int prio;
    int static_prio;
    int normal_prio;
    unsigned int rt_priority;
```

```
    const struct sched_class *sched_class;
    struct sched_entity se;
    struct sched_rt_entity rt;
    [...]
```

Continuing with the task structure in the following code block, see the members relating to memory management (mm), the PID and TGID values, the credentials structure, open files, signal handling, and many more. Again, it's not the intention to delve into (all of) them in detail; where appropriate, in later sections of this chapter, and possibly in other chapters of this book, we shall revisit them:

```
    [...]
    struct mm_struct *mm;         << memory management info >>
    struct mm_struct *active_mm;
    [...]
    pid_t pid;        << task PID and TGID values; explained below >>
    pid_t tgid;
    [...]
    /* Context switch counts: */
    unsigned long nvcsw;
    unsigned long nivcsw;
    [...]
    /* Effective (overridable) subjective task credentials (COW): */
    const struct cred __rcu *cred;
    [...]
    char comm[TASK_COMM_LEN];              << task name >>
    [...]
     /* Open file information: */
    struct files_struct *files;    << pointer to the 'open files' ds
>>
    [...]
     /* Signal handlers: */
    struct signal_struct *signal;
    struct sighand_struct *sighand;
    sigset_t blocked;
    sigset_t real_blocked;
    [...]
#ifdef CONFIG_VMAP_STACK
    struct vm_struct *stack_vm_area;
#endif
    [...]
#ifdef CONFIG_SECURITY
    /* Used by LSM modules for access restriction: */
    void *security;
#endif
    [...]
    /* CPU-specific state of this task: */
```

```
       struct thread_struct thread;       << task hardware context detail
>>
       [...]
};
```

> Note that the `struct task_struct` members in the preceding code are shown with respect to the 5.4.0 kernel source; on other kernel versions, the members can and do change! Of course, it should go without saying, this is true of the entire book – all code/data is presented with regard to the 5.4.0 LTS Linux kernel (which will be maintained up to December 2025).

Okay, now that you have a better idea of the members within the task structure, how exactly do you access it and its various members? Read on.

Accessing the task structure with current

You will recall, in our sample run of the preceding `countem.sh` script (in the *Organizing processes, threads, and their stacks – user and kernel space* section), we found that there are a total of 1,234 threads (both user and kernel) alive on the system. This implies that there will be a total of 1,234 task structure objects in the kernel memory.

They need to be organized in a way that the kernel can easily access them as and when required. Thus, all the task structure objects in kernel memory are chained up on a *circular doubly linked list* called the **task list**. This kind of organization is required in order for various kernel code paths to iterate over them (commonly the `procfs` code, among others). Even so, think on this: when a process or thread is running kernel code (in process context), how can it find out which `task_struct` belongs to it among the perhaps hundreds or thousands that exist in kernel memory? This turns out to be a non-trivial task. The kernel developers have evolved a way to guarantee you can find the particular task structure representing the thread currently running the kernel code. It's achieved via a macro called `current`. Think of it this way:

- Looking up `current` yields the pointer to `task_struct` of the thread that is running the kernel code right now, in other words, *the process context running right now on some particular processor core.*
- `current` is analogous (but of course, not exactly) to what object-oriented languages call the `this` pointer.

Chapter 6

The implementation of the `current` macro is very architecture-specific. Here, we do not delve into the gory details. Suffice it to say that the implementation is carefully engineered to be fast (typically via an *O(1)* algorithm). For example, on some **Reduced Instruction Set Computer (RISC)** architectures with many general-purpose registers (such as the PowerPC and Aarch64 processors), a register is dedicated to holding the value of `current`!

> I urge you to browse the kernel source tree and see the implementation details of `current` (under `arch/<arch>/asm/current.h`). On the ARM32, an *O(1)* calculation yields the result; on AArch64 and PowerPC it's stored in a register (and thus the lookup is blazing fast). On x86_64 architectures, the implementation uses a `per-cpu` *variable* to hold `current` (avoiding the use of costly locking). Including the `<linux/sched.h>` header is required to include the definition of `current` in your code.

We can use `current` to dereference the task structure and cull information from within it; for example, the process (or thread) PID and name can be looked up as follows:

```
#include <linux/sched.h>
current->pid, current->comm
```

In the next section, you will see a full-fledged kernel module that iterates over the task list, printing out some details from each task structure it encounters along the way.

Determining the context

As you now know, kernel code runs in one of two contexts:

- Process (or task) context
- Interrupt (or atomic) context

They are mutually exclusive – kernel code runs in either the process or atomic/interrupt context at any given point in time.

Kernel Internals Essentials - Processes and Threads

Often, when writing kernel or driver code, it is imperative for you to first figure out *what context* the code that you're working on is running in. One way to learn this is by employing the following macro:

```
#include <linux/preempt.h>
    in_task()
```

It returns a Boolean: `True` if your code is running in process (or task) context, where it's – usually – safe to sleep; returning `False` implies you are in some kind of atomic or interrupt context where it is never safe to sleep.

> **TIP**
> You might have come across the usage of the `in_interrupt()` macro; if it returns `True`, your code is within an interrupt context, if `False`, it isn't. However, the recommendation for modern code is to *not* rely on this macro (due to the fact that **Bottom Half (BH)** disabling can interfere with this). Hence, we recommend using `in_task()` instead.

Hang on though! It can get a bit tricky: while `in_task()` returning `True` does imply that your code is in process context, this fact by itself does *not* guarantee that it's currently *safe to sleep*. Sleeping really implies invoking the scheduler code and a subsequent context switch (we cover this in detail in `Chapter 10`, *The CPU Scheduler – Part 1*, and `Chapter 11`, *The CPU Scheduler – Part 2*). For example, you could be in process context but holding a spinlock (a very common lock used within the kernel); the code between the lock and unlock – the so-called *critical section* – must run atomically! This implies that though your code may be in process (or task) context, it still will cause a bug if it attempts to issue any blocking (sleeping) APIs!

Also, be careful: `current` is only considered valid when running in *process context*.

Right; by now you have learned useful background information on the task structure, how it can be accessed via the `current` macro, and the caveats to doing so – such as figuring out the context that your kernel or driver code is currently running in. So now, let's actually write some kernel module code to examine a bit of the kernel task structure.

[300]

Working with the task structure via current

Here, we will write a simple kernel module to show a few members of the task structure and reveal the *process context* that its *init* and *cleanup* code paths run in. To do so, we cook up a `show_ctx()` function that uses `current` to access a few members of the task structure and display their values. It's invoked from both the *init* as well as the *cleanup* methods, as follows:

> For reasons of readability and space constraints, only key parts of the source code are displayed here. The entire source tree for this book is available in its GitHub repository; we expect you to clone and use it: `git clone https://github.com/PacktPublishing/Linux-Kernel-Programming.git`.

```
/* code: ch6/current_affairs/current_affairs.c */
[ ... ]
#include <linux/sched.h>      /* current */
#include <linux/cred.h>       /* current_{e}{u,g}id() */
#include <linux/uidgid.h>     /* {from,make}_kuid() */
[...]
#define OURMODNAME    "current_affairs"
[ ... ]

static void show_ctx(char *nm)
{
    /* Extract the task UID and EUID using helper methods provided */
    unsigned int uid = from_kuid(&init_user_ns, current_uid());
    unsigned int euid = from_kuid(&init_user_ns, current_euid());

    pr_info("%s:%s():%d ", nm, __func__, __LINE__);
    if (likely(in_task())) {
            pr_info(
            "%s: in process context ::\n"
            " PID         : %6d\n"
            " TGID        : %6d\n"
            " UID         : %6u\n"
            " EUID        : %6u (%s root)\n"
            " name        : %s\n"
            " current (ptr to our process context's task_struct)    :\n"
            "              0x%pK (0x%px)\n"
            " stack start : 0x%pK (0x%px)\n",
                    nm,
```

[301]

```
                    /* always better to use the helper methods provided */
                    task_pid_nr(current), task_tgid_nr(current),
                    /* ... rather than the 'usual' direct lookups:
                        current->pid, current->tgid, */
                    uid, euid,
                    (euid == 0?"have":"don't have"),
                    current->comm,
                    current, current,
                    current->stack, current->stack);
        } else
            pr_alert("%s: in interrupt context [Should NOT Happen here!]\n",
    nm);
    }
```

As is highlighted in bold in the preceding snippet, you can see that (for some members) we can simply dereference the `current` pointer to gain access to various `task_struct` members and display them (via the kernel log buffer).

Great! The preceding code snippet does indeed show you how to gain access to a few `task_struct` members directly via `current`; not all members, though, can or should be accessed directly. Rather, the kernel provides some helper methods to access them; let's get into this next.

Built-in kernel helper methods and optimizations

In the preceding code, we made use of a few of the kernel's *built-in helper methods* to extract various members of the task structure. This is the recommended approach; for example, we use `task_pid_nr()` to peek at the PID member instead of directly via `current->pid`. Similarly, the process credentials within the task structure (such as the `EUID` members we showed in the preceding code) are abstracted within `struct cred` and access to them is provided via helper routines, just like with `from_kuid()`, which we used in the preceding code. In a similar fashion, there are several other helper methods; look them up in `include/linux/sched.h` just below the `struct task_struct` definition.

> Why is this the case? Why not simply access task structure members directly via `current-><member-name>`? Well, there are various real reasons; one, perhaps the access requires a *lock* to be taken (we cover details on the key topic of locking and synchronization in the last two chapters of this book). Two, perhaps there's a more optimal way to access them; read on to see more on this...

Also, as shown in the preceding code, we can easily figure out whether the kernel code (of our kernel module) is running in the process or interrupt context by employing the `in_task()` macro – it returns `True` if in the process (or task) context, and `False` if otherwise.

Interestingly, we also use the `likely()` macro (it becomes a compiler `__built-in_expect` attribute) to give a hint to the compiler's branch prediction setup and optimize the instruction sequence being fed into the CPU pipeline, thus keeping our code on the "fast path" (more on this micro-optimization with the `likely()`/`unlikely()` macros can be found in the *Further reading* section for this chapter). You will see kernel code often employing the `likely()`/`unlikely()` macros in situations where the developer "knows" whether the code path is likely or unlikely, respectively.

> The preceding `[un]likely()` macros are a good example of micro-optimization, of how the Linux kernel leverages the `gcc(1)` compiler. In fact, until recently, the Linux kernel could *only* be compiled with `gcc`; recently, patches are slowly making compilation with `clang(1)` a reality. (FYI, the modern **Android Open Source Project** (**AOSP**) is compiled with `clang`.)

Okay, now that we have understood the workings of our kernel module's `show_ctx()` function, let's try it out.

Trying out the kernel module to print process context info

We build our `current_affair.ko` kernel module (we don't show the build output here) and then insert it into kernel space (via `insmod(8)` as usual). Now let's view the kernel log with `dmesg(1)`, then `rmmod(8)` it and use `dmesg(1)` again. The following screenshot shows this:

```
$ uname -r
5.4.0-llkd01
$ sudo insmod ./current_affairs.ko ; dmesg
[ 7605.102692] current_affairs: inserted
[ 7605.109628] current_affairs:show_ctx():39
[ 7605.109639] current_affairs: in process context ::
                PID      :   2205
                TGID     :   2205
                UID      :   0
                EUID     :   0 (have root)
                name     :   insmod
                current (ptr to our process context's task_struct) :
                             0xffff8f4ae5d116c0 (0xffff8f4ae5d116c0)
                stack start : 0xffff9da3c16d8000 (0xffff9da3c16d8000)
$ sudo rmmod current_affairs ; dmesg | tail
[ 7616.002865] current_affairs: in process context ::
                PID      :   2209
                TGID     :   2209
                UID      :   0
                EUID     :   0 (have root)
                name     :   rmmod
                current (ptr to our process context's task_struct) :
                             0xffff8f4af023ad80 (0xffff8f4af023ad80)
                stack start : 0xffff9da3c061c000 (0xffff9da3c061c000)
[ 7616.043353] current_affairs: removed
$
```

Figure 6.9 – The output of the current_affairs.ko kernel module

Clearly, as can be seen from the preceding screenshot, the *process context* – the process (or thread) running the kernel code of `current_affairs.ko:current_affairs_init()` – is the `insmod` process (see the output: 'name   :   insmod'), and the `current_affairs.ko:current_affairs_exit()` process context executing the cleanup code is the `rmmod` process!

> **TIP**
> Notice how the timestamps in the left column ([sec.usec]) in the preceding figure help us understand that `rmmod` was called close to 11 seconds after `insmod`.

There's more to this small demo kernel module than first meets the eye. It's actually very helpful in understanding Linux kernel architecture. The following section explains how this is so.

Seeing that the Linux OS is monolithic

Besides the exercise of using the `current` macro, a key point behind this kernel module (`ch6/current_affairs`) is to clearly show you the *monolithic nature of the Linux OS*. In the preceding code, we saw that when we performed the `insmod(8)` process on our kernel module file (`current_affairs.ko`), it got inserted into the kernel and its *init* code path ran; *who ran it?* Ah, that question is answered by checking the output: the `insmod` process itself ran it in process context, thus proving the monolithic nature of the Linux kernel! (Ditto with the `rmmod(8)` process and the *cleanup* code path; it was run by the `rmmod` process in process context.)

> Note carefully and clearly: there is no "kernel" (or kernel thread) that executes the code of the kernel module, it's the user space process (or thread) *itself* that, by issuing system calls (recall that both the `insmod(8)` and `rmmod(8)` utilities issue system calls), switches into kernel space and executes the code of the kernel module. This is how it is with a monolithic kernel.

Of course, this type of execution of kernel code is what we refer to as *running in process context*, as opposed to running in *interrupt context*. The Linux kernel, though, isn't considered to be purely monolithic; if so, it would be a single hard-coded piece of memory. Instead, like all modern OSes, Linux supports *modularization* (via the LKM framework).

> As an aside, do note that you can create and run *kernel threads* within kernel space; they still execute kernel code in process context when scheduled.

Coding for security with printk

In our previous kernel module demo (`ch6/current_affairs/current_affairs.c`), you noticed, I hope, the usage of `printk` with the 'special' `%pK` format specifier. We repeat the relevant code snippet here:

```
pr_info(
[...]
    " current (ptr to our process context's task_struct) :\n"
    " 0x%pK (0x%px)\n"
    " stack start : 0x%pK (0x%px)\n",
[...]
```

Kernel Internals Essentials - Processes and Threads

```
                current, (long unsigned)current,
                current->stack, (long unsigned)current->stack); [...]
```

Recall from our discussion in Chapter 5, *Writing Your First Kernel Module – LKMs Part 2*, in the *Proc filesystem tunables affecting the system log* section, that when printing an address (firstly, you really shouldn't be printing addresses in production) I urged you to not use the usual `%p` (or `%px`) but the `%pK` format specifier instead. That's what we've done in the preceding code; *this is for security, to prevent a kernel information leak*. With a well-tuned (for security) system, `%pK` will result in a mere hashed value and not the actual address being displayed. To show this, we also display the actual kernel address via the `0x%px` format specifier just for contrast.

Interestingly enough, `%pK` seems to have no effect on a default desktop Ubuntu 18.04 LTS system. Both formats – the `%pK` and the `0x%px` – turn out to print identical values (as can be seen in Figure 6.9); this is *not* what's expected. On my x86_64 Fedora 31 VM, though, it does work as expected, yielding a mere hashed (incorrect) value with `%pK` and the correct kernel address with `0x%px`. Here's the relevant output on my Fedora 31 VM:

```
$ sudo insmod ./current_affairs.ko
[...]
$ dmesg
[...]
name : insmod
 current (ptr to our process context's task_struct) :
           0x0000000049ee4bd2 (0xffff9bd6770fa700)
 stack start : 0x00000000c3f1cd84 (0xffffb42280c68000)
[...]
```

In the preceding output, we can clearly see the difference.

> **TIP**
> On production systems (embedded or otherwise) be safe: set `kernel.kptr_restrict` to 1 (or even better, to 2), thus sanitizing pointers,
> and set `kernel.dmesg_restrict` to 1 (allowing only privileged users to read the kernel log).

Now, let's move on to something more interesting: in the following section, you will learn how to iterate over the Linux kernel's *task lists*, thus in effect learning how to obtain kernel-level information on every single process and/or thread alive on the system.

Iterating over the kernel's task lists

As mentioned earlier, all the task structures are organized in kernel memory in a linked list called the *task list* (allowing them to be iterated over). The list data structure has evolved to become the very commonly used *circular doubly linked list*. In fact, the core kernel code to work with these lists has been factored out into a header called `list.h`; it's well known and expected to be used for any list-based work.

> The `include/linux/types.h:list_head` data structure forms the essential doubly linked circular list; as expected, it consists of two pointers, one to the `prev` member on the list and one to the `next` member.

You can easily iterate over various lists concerned with tasks via conveniently provided macros in the `include/linux/sched/signal.h` header file for versions >= 4.11; note that for kernels 4.10 and older, the macros are in `include/linux/sched.h`.

Now, let's make this discussion empirical and hands-on. In the following sections we will write kernel modules to iterate over the kernel task list in two ways:

- **One**: Iterate over the kernel task list and display all *processes* alive.
- **Two**: Iterate over the kernel task list and display all *threads* alive.

We show the detailed code view for the latter case. Read on and be sure to try it out yourself!

Iterating over the task list I – displaying all processes

The kernel provides a convenient routine, the `for_each_process()` macro, which lets you easily iterate over every *process* in the task list:

```
// include/linux/sched/signal.h:
#define for_each_process(p) \
    for (p = &init_task ; (p = next_task(p)) != &init_task ; )
```

Clearly, the macro expands to a `for` loop, allowing us to loop over the circular list. `init_task` is a convenient 'head' or starting pointer – it points to the task structure of the very first user space process, traditionally `init(1)`, now `systemd(1)`.

Kernel Internals Essentials - Processes and Threads

> Note that the `for_each_process()` macro is expressly designed to only iterate over the `main()` thread of every *process* and not the ('child' or peer) threads.

A brief snippet of our `ch6/foreach/prcs_showall` kernel module's output is shown here (when run on our x86_64 Ubuntu 18.04 LTS guest system):

```
$ cd ch6/foreach/prcs_showall; ../../../lkm prcs_showall
[...]
[ 111.657574] prcs_showall: inserted
[ 111.658820]         Name    |  TGID  |  PID  |  RUID  |  EUID
[ 111.659619] systemd         |     1|     1|      0|      0
[ 111.660330] kthreadd        |     2|     2|      0|      0
[...]
[ 111.778937] kworker/0:5     |  1123| 1123|      0|      0
[ 111.779833] lkm             |  1143| 1143|   1000|   1000
[ 111.780835] sudo            |  1536| 1536|      0|      0
[ 111.781819] insmod          |  1537| 1537|      0|      0
```

> **TIP**: Notice how, in the preceding snippet, the TGID and PID of each process are always equal, 'proving' that the `for_each_process()` macro only iterates over the *main* thread of every process (and not every thread). We explain the details in the following section.

We'll leave the studying and trying out of the sample kernel module at `ch6/foreach/prcs_showall` as an exercise for you.

Iterating over the task list II – displaying all threads

To iterate over each *thread* that's alive and well on the system, we could use the `do_each_thread() { ... } while_each_thread()` *pair* of macros; we write a sample kernel module to do just this (here: `ch6/foreach/thrd_showall/`).

[308]

Chapter 6

Before diving into the code, let's build it, `insmod` it (on our x86_64 Ubuntu 18.04 LTS guest), and see the bottom part of the output it emits via `dmesg(1)`. As displaying the complete output isn't really possible here – it's far too large – I've shown only the lower part of the output in the following screenshot. Also, we've reproduced the header (Figure 6.9) so that you can make sense of what each column represents:

```
    Threads       TGID   PID    Current            Stack-start        Thread Name    MT?#
[10287.419993]    881    881    0xffff9b09b65f8000 0xffffbaffc0998000    kerneloops
[10287.421278]    912    912    0xffff9b09e58c2d80 0xffffbaffc0a48000    VBoxClient
[10287.422776]    913    913    0xffff9b09e99e0000 0xffffbaffc0a94000    VBoxClient
[10287.424430]    938    938    0xffff9b09e99edb00 0xffffbaffc0b0c000    VBoxService    9
[10287.425889]    938    940    0xffff9b09e98496c0 0xffffbaffc0b14000       RTThrdPP
[10287.427307]    938    941    0xffff9b09fc30c440 0xffffbaffc0ad4000        control
[10287.428704]    938    942    0xffff9b09fcc596c0 0xffffbaffc0a8c000       timesync
[10287.430202]    938    943    0xffff9b09fcc5ad80 0xffffbaffc0b1c000         vminfo
[10287.431569]    938    944    0xffff9b09e99e4440 0xffffbaffc0b24000      cpuhotplug
[10287.432960]    938    945    0xffff9b09e99e16c0 0xffffbaffc0b2c000      memballoon
[10287.434417]    938    946    0xffff9b09b65fad80 0xffffbaffc0b34000        vmstats
[10287.435852]    938    947    0xffff9b09b6ae2d80 0xffffbaffc0b3c000      automount
[10287.437194]    979    979    0xffff9b09e5aadb00 0xffffbaffc06e0000           sshd
[10287.438539]    981    981    0xffff9b09e984ad80 0xffffbaffc0af4000        systemd
[10287.439832]    982    982    0xffff9b09e9848000 0xffffbaffc08f4000        (sd-pam)
[10287.441266]    1082   1082   0xffff9b09f0354440 0xffffbaffc0920000           sshd
[10287.442807]    1083   1083   0xffff9b09f03516c0 0xffffbaffc081c000           bash
[10287.444219]    1427   1427   0xffff9b09fc30d000 0xffffbaffc10dc000      packagekitd    3
[10287.445680]    1427   1428   0xffff9b09fc30ad80 0xffffbaffc10e4000          gmain
[10287.446959]    1427   1429   0xffff9b09fc3096c0 0xffffbaffc10ec000          gdbus
[10287.448340]    1748   1748   0xffff9b09b640ad80 0xffffbaffc0a08000          cupsd
[10287.449635]    1750   1750   0xffff9b09fae916c0 0xffffbaffc14f0000   cups-browsed    3
[10287.451182]    1750   1759   0xffff9b09e9b7ad80 0xffffbaffc0ae4000          gmain
[10287.452580]    1750   1760   0xffff9b09e9b7db00 0xffffbaffc1528000          gdbus
[10287.454007]    1844   1844   0xffff9b09fd5cc440 0xffffbaffc17c0000 [   kworker/u4:0]
[10287.455235]    1873   1873   0xffff9b09a34d4440 0xffffbaffc1820000 [    kworker/0:1]
[10287.456450]    1878   1878   0xffff9b09a34d16c0 0xffffbaffc1888000 [    kworker/1:1]
[10287.457668]    1879   1879   0xffff9b09a34d2d80 0xffffbaffc1810000 [   kworker/u4:2]
[10287.459160]    1882   1882   0xffff9b09a34d5b00 0xffffbaffc1768000 [   kworker/u4:1]
[10287.460920]    1887   1887   0xffff9b09fd5c96c0 0xffffbaffc18a0000            lkm
[10287.462270]    2280   2280   0xffff9b09e99ead80 0xffffbaffc1ac8000           sudo
[10287.463463]    2281   2281   0xffff9b09f0212d80 0xffffbaffc1a48000          insmod
[10287.464738] thrd_showall: total # of threads on the system: 159
```

Figure 6.10 – Output from our thrd_showall.ko kernel module

[309]

> **TIP**
> In Figure 6.9, notice how all the (kernel-mode) stack start addresses (the fifth column) end in zeroes:
> `0xffff .... .... .000`, implying that the stack region is *always aligned on a page boundary* (as `0x1000` is `4096` in decimal). This will be the case as kernel-mode stacks are always fixed in size and a multiple of the system page size (typically 4 KB).

Following convention, in our kernel module, we arrange that if the thread is a *kernel thread*, its name shows up within square brackets.

Before continuing on to the code, we first need to examine in a bit of detail the TGID and PID members of the task structure.

Differentiating between the process and thread – the TGID and the PID

Think about this: as the Linux kernel uses a unique task structure (`struct task_struct`) to represent every thread, and as the unique member within it has a PID, this implies that, within the Linux kernel, *every thread has a unique PID*. This gives rise to an issue: how can multiple threads of the same process share a common PID? This violates the POSIX.1b standard (*pthreads*; indeed, for a while Linux was non-compliant with the standard, creating porting issues, among other things).

To fix this annoying user space standards issue, Ingo Molnar (of Red Hat) proposed and mainlined a patch way back, in the 2.5 kernel series. A new member called the **Thread Group IDentifier** or TGID was slipped into the task structure. This is how it works: if the process is single-threaded, the `tgid` and `pid` values are equal. If it's a multithreaded process, then the `tgid` value of the *main* thread is equal to its `pid` value; other threads of the process will inherit the *main* thread's `tgid` value but will retain their own unique `pid` values.

To understand this better, let's take an actual example from the previous screenshot. In Figure 6.9, notice how, if a positive integer appears in the last column on the right, it represents the number of threads in the multithreaded process to its immediate left.

So, check out the `VBoxService` process seen in Figure 6.9; for your convenience, we have duplicated that snippet as follows (note that we: eliminated the first column, the `dmesg` timestamp, and added the header line, for better readability): it has PID and TGID values of 938 representing its *main* thread (called `VBoxService`; for clarity, we've shown it in bold font), and a total of *nine threads*:

PID	TGID	current	stack-start	Thread Name	MT?#
938	**938**	**0xffff9b09e99edb00**	**0xffffbaffc0b0c000**	**VBoxService**	**9**
938	940	0xffff9b09e98496c0	0xffffbaffc0b14000	RTThrdPP	
938	941	0xffff9b09fc30c440	0xffffbaffc0ad4000	control	
938	942	0xffff9b09fcc596c0	0xffffbaffc0a8c000	timesync	
938	943	0xffff9b09fcc5ad80	0xffffbaffc0b1c000	vminfo	
938	944	0xffff9b09e99e4440	0xffffbaffc0b24000	cpuhotplug	
938	945	0xffff9b09e99e16c0	0xffffbaffc0b2c000	memballoon	
938	946	0xffff9b09b65fad80	0xffffbaffc0b34000	vmstats	
938	947	0xffff9b09b6ae2d80	0xffffbaffc0b3c000	automount	

What are the nine threads? First, of course, the *main* thread is `VBoxService`, and the eight displayed below it are, by name: `RTThrdPP`, `control`, `timesync`, `vminfo`, `cpuhotplug`, `memballoon`, `vmstats`, and `automount`. How do we know this for sure? It's easy: look carefully at the first and second columns in the preceding code block that represent the TGID and PID respectively: if they are the same, it's the main thread of the process; *if the TGID repeats, the process is multithreaded* and the PID value represents the unique IDs of the 'child' threads.

As a matter of fact, it's entirely possible to see the kernel's TGID/PID representation in user space via the ubiquitous GNU `ps(1)` command, by using its `-LA` options (among other ways to do so):

```
$ ps -LA
    PID    LWP TTY          TIME CMD
      1      1 ?        00:00:02 systemd
      2      2 ?        00:00:00 kthreadd
      3      3 ?        00:00:00 rcu_gp
[...]
    938    938 ?        00:00:00 VBoxService
    938    940 ?        00:00:00 RTThrdPP
    938    941 ?        00:00:00 control
    938    942 ?        00:00:00 timesync
    938    943 ?        00:00:03 vminfo
    938    944 ?        00:00:00 cpuhotplug
    938    945 ?        00:00:00 memballoon
    938    946 ?        00:00:00 vmstats
    938    947 ?        00:00:00 automount
[...]
```

The ps(1) labels are as follows:

- The first column is PID – this is actually representative of the tgid member of the task structure within the kernel for this task
- The second column is LWP (LightWeight Process or thread!) – this is actually representative of the pid member of the task structure within the kernel for this task.

> **TIP**
> Note that only with the ps(1) GNU can you pass parameters (like -LA) and see the threads; this isn't possible with a lightweight implementation of ps like that of *busybox*. It isn't a problem though: you can always look up the same by looking under procfs; in this example, under /proc/938/task, you'll see sub-folders representing the child threads. Guess what: this is actually how GNU ps works as well!

Okay, on to the code now...

Iterating over the task list III – the code

Now let's see the (relevant) code of our thrd_showall kernel module:

```
// ch6/foreach/thrd_showall/thrd_showall.c */
[...]
#include <linux/sched.h>    /* current */
#include <linux/version.h>
#if LINUX_VERSION_CODE > KERNEL_VERSION(4, 10, 0)
#include <linux/sched/signal.h>
#endif
[...]

static int showthrds(void)
{
    struct task_struct *g, *t;      // 'g' : process ptr; 't': thread ptr
    [...]
#if 0
    /* the tasklist_lock reader-writer spinlock for the task list 'should'
     * be used here, but, it's not exported, hence unavailable to our
     * kernel module */
    read_lock(&tasklist_lock);
#endif
    disp_idle_thread();
```

[312]

A few points to note regarding the preceding code:

- We use the `LINUX_VERSION_CODE()` macro to conditionally include a header, as required.
- Please ignore the *locking* work for now – usage (or the lack thereof) of the `tasklist_lock()` and `task_[un]lock()` APIs.
- Don't forget the CPU idle thread! Every CPU core has a dedicated idle thread (named `swapper/n`) that runs when no other thread wants to (n being the core number, starting with 0). The `do .. while` loop we run does not start at this thread (nor does `ps(1)` ever show it). We include a small routine to display it, making use of the fact that the hard-coded task structure for the idle thread is available and exported at `init_task` (a detail: `init_task` always refers to the first CPU's – core # 0 – idle thread).

Let's continue: in order to iterate over every thread alive, we need to use a *pair* of macros, forming a loop: the `do_each_thread() { ... } while_each_thread()` pair of macros do precisely this, allowing us to iterate over every *thread* alive on the system. The following code shows this:

```
do_each_thread(g, t) {
    task_lock(t);
    snprintf(buf, BUFMAX-1, "%6d %6d ", g->tgid, t->pid);

    /* task_struct addr and kernel-mode stack addr */
    snprintf(tmp, TMPMAX-1, " 0x%px", t);
    strncat(buf, tmp, TMPMAX);
    snprintf(tmp, TMPMAX-1, " 0x%px", t->stack);
    strncat(buf, tmp, TMPMAX);

    [...]                  << see notes below >>

    total++;
    memset(buf, 0, sizeof(buf));      << cleanup >>
    memset(tmp, 0, sizeof(tmp));
    task_unlock(t);
} while_each_thread(g, t);
#if 0
    /* <same as above, reg the reader-writer spinlock for the task list> */
    read_unlock(&tasklist_lock);
#endif
    return total;
}
```

[313]

Kernel Internals Essentials - Processes and Threads

Referring to the preceding code, the `do_each_thread() { ... } while_each_thread()` pair of macros form a loop, allowing us to iterate over every *thread* alive on the system:

- We follow a strategy of using a temporary variable (named `tmp`) to fetch a data item, which we then append to a 'result' buffer, `buf`, which we print once on every loop iteration.
- Obtaining the `TGID`, `PID`, `task_struct`, and `stack` start addresses is trivial – here, keeping it simple, we just use `current` to dereference them (of course, you could use the more sophisticated kernel helper methods we saw earlier in this chapter to do so as well; here, we wish to keep it simple). Also notice that here we deliberately do *not* use the (safer) `%pK` printk format specifier but rather the generic `%px` specifier in order to display the *actual* kernel virtual addresses of the task structure and the kernel-mode stack .
- Clean up as required before looping over (increment a counter of total threads, `memset()` the temporary buffers to `NULL`, and so on).
- On completion, we return the total number of threads we have iterated across.

In the following code block, we cover the portion of code that was deliberately left out in the preceding block. We retrieve the thread's name and print it within square brackets if it's a kernel thread. We also query the number of threads within the process. The explanation follows the code:

```
if (!g->mm) {    // kernel thread
/* One might question why we don't use the get_task_comm() to
 * obtain the task's name here; the short reason: it causes a
 * deadlock! We shall explore this (and how to avoid it) in
 * some detail in the chapters on Synchronization. For now, we
 * just do it the simple way ...
 */
    snprintf(tmp, TMPMAX-1, " [%16s]", t->comm);
} else {
    snprintf(tmp, TMPMAX-1, "  %16s ", t->comm);
}
strncat(buf, tmp, TMPMAX);
/* Is this the "main" thread of a multithreaded process?
 * We check by seeing if (a) it's a user space thread,
 * (b) its TGID == its PID, and (c), there are >1 threads in
 * the process.
 * If so, display the number of threads in the overall process
 * to the right..
 */
```

```
            nr_thrds = get_nr_threads(g);
            if (g->mm && (g->tgid == t->pid) && (nr_thrds > 1)) {
                snprintf(tmp, TMPMAX-1, " %3d", nr_thrds);
                strncat(buf, tmp, TMPMAX);
            }
```

On the preceding code, we can say the following:

- A *kernel thread* has no user space mapping. The `main()` thread's `current->mm` is a pointer to a structure of type `mm_struct` and represents the entire process' *user space* mapping; if `NULL`, it stands to reason that this is a kernel thread (as kernel threads have no user space mappings); we check and print the name accordingly.
- We print the name of the thread as well (by looking up the `comm` member of the task structure). You might question why we don't use the `get_task_comm()` routine to obtain the task's name here; the short reason: it causes a *deadlock*! We shall explore this (and how to avoid it) in detail in the later chapters on kernel synchronization. For now, again, we just do it the simple way.
- We fetch the number of threads in a given process conveniently via the `get_nr_threads()` macro; the rest is explained clearly in the code comment above the macro in the preceding block.

Great! With this, we complete our discussion (for now) on Linux kernel internals and architecture with a primary focus on processes, threads, and their stacks.

Summary

In this chapter, we covered the key aspects of kernel internals that will help you as a kernel module or device driver author to better and more deeply understand the internal workings of the OS. You examined in some detail the organization of and relationships between the process and its threads and stacks (in both user and kernel space). We examined the kernel `task_struct` data structure and learned how to iterate over the *task list* in different ways via kernel modules.

Though it may not be obvious, the fact is that understanding these kernel internal details is a necessary and required step in your journey to becoming a seasoned kernel (and/or device driver) developer. The content of this chapter will help you debug many system programming scenarios and lays the foundation for our deeper exploration into the Linux kernel, particularly that of memory management.

The next chapter and the couple that follow it are critical indeed: we'll cover what you need to understand regarding the deep and complex topic of memory management internals. I suggest you digest the content of this chapter first, browse through the Further reading links of interest, work on the exercises (*Questions* section), and then, get to the next chapter!

Questions

As we conclude, here is a list of questions for you to test your knowledge regarding this chapter's material: `https://github.com/PacktPublishing/Linux-Kernel-Programming/tree/master/questions`. You will find some of the questions answered in the book's GitHub repo: `https://github.com/PacktPublishing/Linux-Kernel-Programming/tree/master/solutions_to_assgn`.

Further reading

To help you delve deeper into the subject with useful materials, we provide a rather detailed list of online references and links (and at times, even books) in a Further reading document in this book's GitHub repository. The *Further reading* document is available here: `https://github.com/PacktPublishing/Linux-Kernel-Programming/blob/master/Further_Reading.md`.

7
Memory Management Internals - Essentials

Kernel internals, especially regarding memory management, is a vast and complex topic. In this book, I do not intend to delve into the deep, gory details of kernel memory internals. At the same time, I would like to provide sufficient – and definitely required – background knowledge for a budding kernel or device driver developer like you to successfully tackle this key topic.

Accordingly, this chapter will help you understand to sufficient depth the internals of how memory management is performed on the Linux OS; this includes delving into the **Virtual Memory** (**VM**) split, examining both the user-mode and kernel segment of the process to a good level of depth, and covering the basics of how the kernel manages physical memory. In effect, you will come to understand the memory maps – both virtual and physical – of the process and the system.

This background knowledge will go a long way in helping you correctly and efficiently manage dynamic kernel memory (with a focus on writing kernel or driver code using the **Loadable Kernel Module** (**LKM**) framework; this aspect - dynamic memory management - in a practical fashion is the focal point of the next two chapters in the book). As an important side benefit, armed with this knowledge, you will find yourself becoming more proficient at the debugging of both user and kernel-space code. (The importance of this cannot be overstated! Debugging code is both an art and a science, as well as a reality.)

In this chapter, the areas we will cover include the following:

- Understanding the VM split
- Examining the process VAS
- Examining the kernel segment
- Randomizing the memory layout – [K]ASLR
- Physical memory

Technical requirements

I assume that you have gone through `Chapter 1`, *Kernel Workspace Setup*, and have appropriately prepared a guest VM running Ubuntu 18.04 LTS (or a later stable release) and installed all the required packages. If not, I recommend you do this first. To get the most out of this book, I strongly recommend you first set up the workspace environment, including cloning this book's GitHub repository for the code (`https://github.com/PacktPublishing/Linux-Kernel-Programming`), and work on it in a hands-on fashion.

I assume that you are familiar with basic virtual memory concepts, the user-mode process **Virtual Address Space** (**VAS**) layout of segments, user-and kernel-mode stacks, the task structure, and so on. If you're unsure on this footing, I strongly suggest you read the preceding chapter first.

Understanding the VM split

In this chapter, we will broadly be looking at how the Linux kernel manages memory in two ways:

- The virtual memory-based approach, where memory is virtualized (the usual case)
- A view of how the kernel actually organizes physical memory (RAM pages)

First, let's begin with the virtual memory view, and then discuss physical memory organization later in the chapter.

As we saw earlier in the previous chapter, in the *Understanding the basics of the process Virtual Address Space (VAS)* section, a key property of the process, VAS, is that it is completely self-contained, a sandbox. You cannot look outside the box. In `Chapter 6`, *Kernel Internals Essentials – Processes and Threads*, Figure 6.2, we saw that the process VAS ranges from virtual address 0 to what we simply termed the high address. What is the actual value of this high address? Obviously, it's the highest extent of the VAS and thus depends on the number of bits used for addressing:

- On a Linux OS running on a 32-bit processor (or compiled for 32-bit), the highest virtual address will be 2^{32} = 4 GB.

- On a Linux OS running on (and compiled for) a 64-bit processor, the highest virtual address will be 2^{64} = *16 EB*. (EB is short for exabyte. Believe me, it's an enormous quantity. 16 EB is equivalent to the number *16 x 10^{18}*.)

For simplicity, to keep the numbers manageable, let's focus for now on the 32-bit address space (we will certainly cover 64-bit addressing as well). So, according to our discussions, on a 32-bit system, the process VAS is from 0 to 4 GB – this region consists of empty space (unused regions, called **sparse regions** or **holes**) and valid regions of memory commonly termed **segments** (or more correctly, **mappings**) – text, data, library, and stack (all of this having been covered in some detail in Chapter 6, *Kernel Internals Essentials – Processes and Threads*).

On our journey to understanding virtual memory, it's useful to take up the well-known Hello, world C program and understand its inner workings on a Linux system; this is what the next section covers!

Looking under the hood – the Hello, world C program

Right, is there anyone here who knows how to code the canonical Hello, world C program? Okay, very amusing, let's check out the one meaningful line therein:

```
printf("Hello, world.\n");
```

The process is calling the printf(3) function. Have you written the code of the printf()? "No, of course not," you say, "it's within the standard libc C library, typically glibc (GNU libc) on Linux." But hang on, unless the code and data of printf (and similarly all other library APIs) is actually within the process VAS, how can we ever access it? (Recall, you can't look *outside the box*!) For that, the code (and data) of printf(3) (in fact, of the glibc library) must be mapped within the process *box* – the process VAS. It is indeed mapped within the process VAS, in the library segments or mappings (as we saw in Chapter 6, *Kernel Internals Essentials – Processes and Threads, Figure 6.1*). How did this happen?

The reality is that on application startup, as part of the C runtime environment setup, there is a small **Executable and Linkable Format** (**ELF**) binary (embedded into your `a.out` binary executable file) called the **loader** (`ld.so` or `ld-linux.so`). It is given control early. It detects all required shared libraries and memory maps all of them – the library text (code) and data segments – into the process VAS by opening the library file(s) and issuing the `mmap(2)` system call. So, now, once the code and data of the library are mapped within the process VAS, the process can indeed access it, and thus – wait for it – the `printf()` API can be successfully invoked! (We've skipped the gory details of memory mapping and linkage here).

Further verifying this, the `ldd(1)` script (the following output is from an x86_64 system) reveals that this is indeed the case:

```
$ gcc helloworld.c -o helloworld
$ ./helloworld
Hello, world
$ ldd ./helloworld
        linux-vdso.so.1 (0x00007fffcfce3000)
        libc.so.6 => /lib/x86_64-linux-gnu/libc.so.6
(0x00007feb7b85b000)
        /lib64/ld-linux-x86-64.so.2 (0x00007feb7be4e000)
$
```

A few quick points to note:

- Every single Linux process – automatically and by default – links to a minimum of two objects: the `glibc` shared library and the program loader (no explicit linker switch is required).
- The name of the loader program varies with the architecture. Here, on our x86_64 system, it's `ld-linux-x86-64.so.2`.
- In the preceding `ldd` output, the address within parentheses on the right is the virtual address of the location of the mapping. For example, in the preceding output, `glibc` is mapped into our process VAS at the **User Virtual Address** (**UVA**), which equals `0x00007feb7b85b000`. Note that it's runtime dependent (it also varies due to **Address Space Layout Randomization** (**ASLR**) semantics (seen later)).
- For security reasons (and on architectures besides x86), it's considered better to use the `objdump(1)` utility to look up details like these.

> **TIP**: Try performing strace(1) on the Hello, world binary executable and you will see numerous mmap() system calls, mapping in glibc (and other) segments!

Let's further examine our simple Hello, world application more deeply.

Going beyond the printf() API

As you will know, the printf(3) API translates to the write(2) system call, which of course writes the "Hello, world" string to stdout (by default, the terminal window or the console device).

We also understand that as write(2) is a system call, this implies that the current process running this code – the process context – must now switch to kernel mode and run the kernel code of write(2) (monolithic kernel architecture)! Indeed it does. But hang on a second: the kernel code of write(2) is in kernel VAS (refer to Chapter 6, *Kernel Internals Essentials – Processes and Threads*, Figure 6.1). The point here is if the kernel VAS is outside the box, then how in the world are we going to call it?

Well, it could be done by placing the kernel in a separate 4 GB VAS, but this approach results in very slow context switching, so it's simply not done.

The way it is engineered is like this: both user and kernel VASes live in the same 'box' – the available VAS. How exactly? By *splitting* the available address space between the user and kernel in some User:Kernel :: u:k ratio. This is called the **VM split** (the ratio u:k being typically expressed in gigabytes, terabytes, or even petabytes).

Memory Management Internals - Essentials

The following diagram is representative of a 32-bit Linux process having a *2:2* VM split (in gigabytes); that is, the total 4 GB process VAS is split into 2 GB of user space and 2 GB of kernel-space. This is often the typical VM split on an ARM-32 system running the Linux OS:

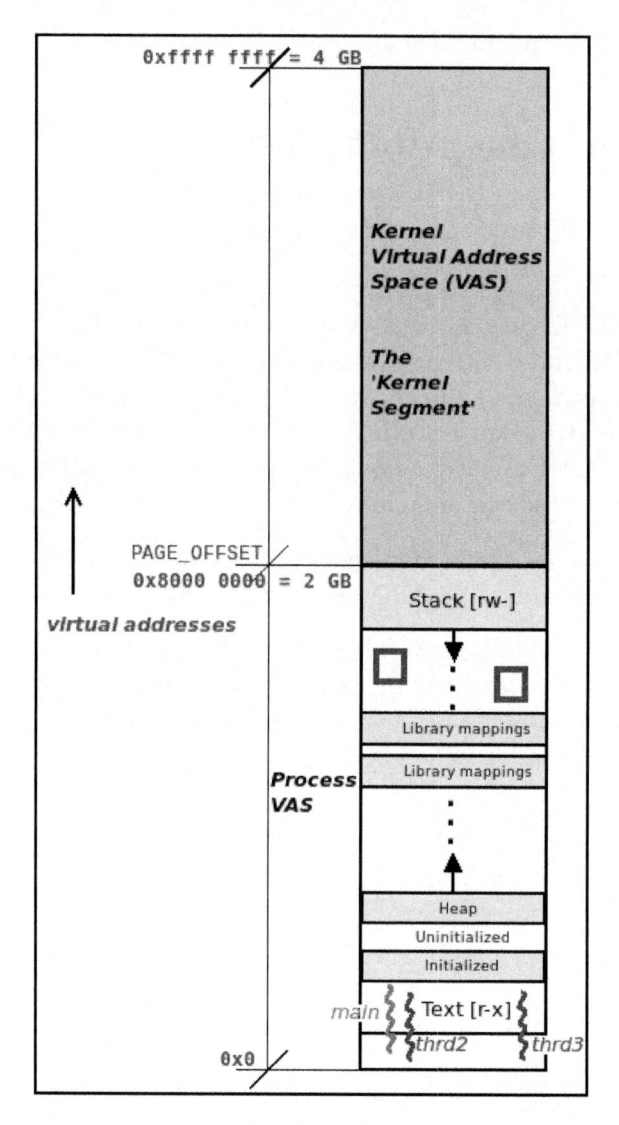

Figure 7.1 – User:Kernel :: 2:2 GB VM split on an ARM-32 system running Linux

So, now that the kernel VAS is within the box, it's suddenly clear and critical to understand this: when a user-mode process or thread issues a system call, there is a context switch to the kernel's 2 GB VAS (various CPU registers, including the stack pointer, get updated) within the very same process's VAS. The thread issuing the system call now runs its kernel code in process context in privileged kernel mode (and works on kernel-space data). When done, it returns from the system call, context switching back into unprivileged user mode, and is now running user-mode code within the first 2 GB VAS.

The exact virtual address where the kernel VAS – also known as the **kernel segment** – begins is typically represented via the PAGE_OFFSET macro within the kernel. We will examine this, and some other key macros as well, in the *Macros and variables describing the kernel segment layout* section.

Where is this decision regarding the precise location and size of the VM split taken? Ah, on 32-bit Linux, it's a kernel build-time configurable. It's done within the kernel build as part of the make [ARCH=xxx] menuconfig procedure – for example, when configuring the kernel for a Broadcom BCM2835 (or the BCM2837) **System on Chip** (**SoC**) (the Raspberry Pi being a popular board with this very SoC). Here's a snippet from the official kernel configuration file (the output is from the Raspberry Pi console):

```
$ uname -r
5.4.51-v7+
$ sudo modprobe configs       << gain access to /proc/config.gz via
this LKM >>
$ zcat /proc/config.gz | grep -C3 VMSPLIT
[...]
# CONFIG_BIG_LITTLE is not set
# CONFIG_VMSPLIT_3G is not set
# CONFIG_VMSPLIT_3G_OPT is not set
CONFIG_VMSPLIT_2G=y
# CONFIG_VMSPLIT_1G is not set
CONFIG_PAGE_OFFSET=0x80000000
CONFIG_NR_CPUS=4
[...]
```

As seen in the preceding snippet, the CONFIG_VMSPLIT_2G kernel config option is set to y implying that the default VM split is user:kernel :: 2:2. For 32-bit architectures, the VM split location is **tunable** (as can be seen in the preceding snippet, CONFIG_VMSPLIT_[1|2|3]G; CONFIG_PAGE_OFFSET gets set accordingly). With a 2:2 VM split, PAGE_OFFSET is literally halfway, at the virtual address 0x8000 0000 (2 GB)!

Memory Management Internals - Essentials

The default VM split for the IA-32 processor (the Intel x86-32) is 3:1 (GB). Interestingly, the (ancient) Windows 3.x OS running on the IA-32 had the same VM split, showing that these concepts are essentially OS-agnostic. Later in this chapter, we will cover several more architectures and their VM split, in addition to other details.

Configuring the VM split is not directly possible for 64-bit architectures. So, now that we understand the VM split on 32-bit systems, let's now move on to examining how it's done on 64-bit systems.

VM split on 64-bit Linux systems

First off, it is worth noting that on 64-bit systems, all 64 bits are not used for addressing. On a standard or typical Linux OS configuration for the x86_64 with a (typical) 4 KB page size, we use (the **Least Significant Bit** (**LSB**)) 48 bits for addressing. Why not the full 64 bits? It's simply too much! No existing computer comes close to having even half of the full 2^{64} = *18,446,744,073,709,551,616* bytes, which is equivalent to 16 EB (that's 16,384 petabytes) of RAM!

> **TIP**
> "Why," you might well wonder, "do we equate this with RAM?". Please read on – more material needs to be covered before this becomes clear. The *Examining the kernel segment* section is where you will understand this fully.

Virtual addressing and address translation

Before diving further into these details, it's very important to clearly understand a few key points.

Consider a small and typical code snippet from a C program:

```
int i = 5;
printf("address of i is 0x%x\n", &i);
```

[324]

The address you see the `printf()` emit is a virtual address and not a physical one. We distinguish between two kinds of virtual addresses:

- If you run this code in a user space process, the address of variable `i` that you will see is a UVA.
- If you run this code within the kernel, or a kernel module (of course, you'd then use the `printk()` API), the address of variable `i` you will see is a **Kernel Virtual Address (KVA)**.

Next, a virtual address is not an absolute value (an offset from 0); it's actually a *bitmask*:

- On a 32-bit Linux OS, the 32 available bits are divided into what's called the **Page Global Directory (PGD)** value, the **Page Table (PT)** value, and the offset.
- These become indices via which the **MMU** (the **Memory Management Unit** that's within the silicon of modern microprocessors), with access to the kernel page tables for the current process context, performs address translation.

> We do not intend on covering the deep details on MMU-level address translation here. It's also very arch-specific. Do refer to the *Further reading* section for useful links on this topic.

- As might be expected, on a 64-bit system, even with 48-bit addressing, there will be more fields within the virtual address bitmask.

Okay, if this 48-bit addressing is the typical case on the x86_64 processor, then how are the bits in a 64-bit virtual address laid out? What happens to the unused 16 MSB bits? The following figure answers the question; it's a representation of the breakup of a virtual address on an x86_64 Linux system:

63			48 47		39 38		30 29		21 20		12 11		0
K va: 1111 ...	<unused>	1111		PGD		PUD		PMD		PTE		offset	
U va: 0000 ...	<unused>	0000											
	16 bits			9 bits		9 bits		9 bits		9 bits		12 bits	

Figure 7.2 – Breakup of a 64-bit virtual address on the Intel x86_64 processor with 4 KB pages

Essentially, with 48-bit addressing, we use bits 0 to 47 (the LSB 48 bits) and ignore the **Most Significant Bit (MSB)** 16 bits, treating it much as a sign extension. Not so fast though; the value of the unused sign-extended MSB 16 bits varies with the address space you are in:

- **Kernel VAS**: MSB 16 bits are always set to 1.
- **User VAS**: MSB 16 bits are always set to 0.

This is useful information! Knowing this, by merely looking at a (full 64-bit) virtual address, you can therefore tell whether it's a KVA or a UVA:

- KVAs on a 64-bit Linux system always follow the format 0xffff ....
- UVAs always have the format 0x0000 ....

> **A word of caution**: the preceding format holds true only for processors (MMUs, really) that self-define virtual addresses as being KVAs or UVAs; the x86 and ARM family of processors do fall in this bracket.

As can now be seen (and I reiterate here), the reality is that virtual addresses are not absolute addresses (absolute offsets from zero, as you might have mistakenly imagined) but are actually bitmasks. The fact is that memory management is a complex area where the work is shared: **the OS is in charge of creating and manipulating the paging tables of each process, the toolchain (compiler) generates virtual addresses, and it's the processor MMU that actually performs runtime address translation, translating a given (user or kernel) virtual address to a physical (RAM) address!**

We will not delve into further details regarding hardware paging (and various hardware acceleration technologies, such as the **Translation Lookaside Buffer** (TLB) and CPU caches) in this book. This particular topic is well covered by various other excellent books and reference sites that are mentioned in the *Further reading* section of this chapter.

Back to the VAS on a 64-bit processor. The available VAS on a 64-bit system is a simply gigantic 2^{64} = *16 EB (16 x 10^{18}* bytes!). The story goes that when AMD engineers were first porting the Linux kernel to the x86_64 (or AMD64) 64-bit processor, they would have had to decide how to lay out the process and kernel segments within this enormous VAS. The decision reached has more or less remained identical, even on today's x86_64 Linux OS. This enormous 64-bit VAS is split as follows. Here, we assume 48-bit addressing with a 4 KB page size:

- Canonical lower half, for 128 TB: User VAS and virtual address ranges from `0x0` to `0x0000 7fff ffff ffff`
- Canonical upper half, for 128 TB: Kernel VAS and virtual address ranges from `0xffff 8000 0000 0000` to `0xffff ffff ffff ffff`

> The word *canonical* effectively means *as per the law* or as *per common convention*.

This 64-bit VM split on an x86_64 platform can be seen in the following figure:

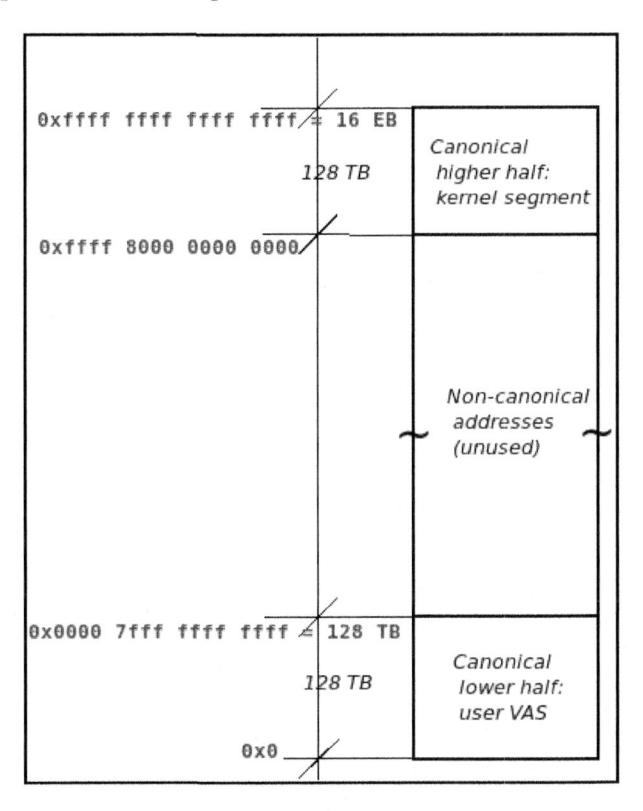

```
0xffff ffff ffff ffff ― 16 EB
                      128 TB      Canonical
                                  higher half:
                                  kernel segment
0xffff 8000 0000 0000

                                  Non-canonical
                                  addresses
                                  (unused)

0x0000 7fff ffff ffff ― 128 TB
                      128 TB      Canonical
                                  lower half:
                                  user VAS
                      0x0
```

Figure 7.3 – The Intel x86_64 (or AMD64) 16 EB VAS layout (48-bit addressing): VM split is User : Kernel :: 128 TB : 128 TB

In the preceding figure, the in-between unused region – a hole or sparse region – is also called the **non-canonical addresses** region. Interestingly, with the 48-bit addressing scheme, the vast majority of the VAS is left unused. This is why we term the VAS as being very sparse.

Memory Management Internals - Essentials

> The preceding figure is certainly not drawn to scale! Always keep in mind that this is all *virtual* memory space, not physical.

To round off our discussion on the VM split, some common `user:kernel` VM split ratios for different CPU architectures are shown in the following figure (we assume an MMU page size of 4 KB):

With standard 4 KB Page size				Userspace		Kernel-space	
Arch	N-Level	Addr Bits	VM "Split"	Start vaddr	End vaddr	Start vaddr	End vaddr
IA-32	2	32	3 GB : 1 GB	0x0	0xbfff ffff	0xc000 0000	0xffff ffff
ARM	2	32	2 GB : 2 GB	0x0	0x7fff ffff	0x8000 0000	0xffff ffff
x86_64	4	48	128 TB : 128 TB	0x0	0x0000 7fff ffff ffff	0xffff 8000 0000 0000	0xffff ffff ffff ffff
	5*	56	64 **PB** : 64 **PB**	0x0	0x00ff ffff ffff ffff	0xff00 0000 0000 0000	0xffff ffff ffff ffff
Aarch64	3	39	512 GB : 512 GB	0x0	0x0000 007f ffff ffff	0xffff ff800 0000 000	0xffff ffff ffff ffff
	4	48	256 TB : 256 TB	0x0	0x0000 ffff ffff ffff	0xffff 0000 0000 0000	0xffff ffff ffff ffff

* >= 4.14 Linux

Figure 7.4 – Common user:kernel VM split ratios for different CPU architectures (for 4 KB page size)

We highlight the third row in bold red as it's considered the common case: running Linux on the x86_64 (or AMD64) architecture, with a `user:kernel :: 128 TB:128 TB` VM split. Also, be careful when reading the table: the numbers in the sixth and eighth columns, **End vaddr**, are single 64-bit quantities each and not two numbers. The number may have simply wrapped around. So, for example, in the x86_64 row, column 6, it's the *single* number `0x0000 7fff ffff ffff` and not two numbers.

The third column, **Addr Bits**, shows us that, on 64-bit processors, no real-world processor actually uses all 64 bits for addressing.

Under the x86_64, there are two VM splits shown in the preceding table:

- The first one, **128 TB : 128 TB** (4-level paging) is the typical VM split being used on Linux x86_64-bit systems as of today (embedded laptops, PCs, workstations, and servers). It limits the physical address space to 64 TB (of RAM).
- The second one, **64 PB : 64 PB**, is, as of the time of writing at least, still purely theoretical; it comes with support for what is called 5-level paging from 4.14 Linux; the assigned VASes (56-bit addressing; a total of 128 petabytes of VAS and 4 PB of physical address space!) is so enormous that, as of the time of writing, no actual computer is (yet) using it.

Note that the two rows for the AArch64 (ARM-64) architecture running on Linux are merely representative. The BSP vendor or platform team working on the product could well use differing splits. As an interesting aside, the VM split on the (old) Windows 32-bit OS is 2:2 (GB).

What's actually residing within the kernel VAS, or as it's commonly called, the kernel segment? All kernel code, data structures (including the task structures, the lists, the kernel-mode stacks, paging tables, and so on), device drivers, kernel modules, and so on are within here (as the lower half of *Figure 6.7* in `Chapter 6`, *Kernel Internals Essentials – Processes and Threads*, showed; we cover precisely this in some detail in the *Understanding the kernel segment* section).

> It's important to realize that, as a performance optimization on Linux, kernel memory is always non-swappable; that is, kernel memory can never be paged out to a swap partition. User space memory pages are always candidates for paging, unless locked (see the `mlock[all](2)` system calls).

With this background, you're now in a position to understand the full process VAS layout. Read on.

The process VAS – the full view

Once again, refer to *Figure 7.1*; it shows the actual process VAS layout for a single 32-bit process. The reality, of course – and this is key – is that **all processes alive on the system have their own unique user-mode VAS but share the same kernel segment**. For some contrast from *Figure 7.1*, which showed a 2:2 (GB) VM split, the following figure shows the actual situation for a typical IA-32 system, with a 3:1 (GB) VM split:

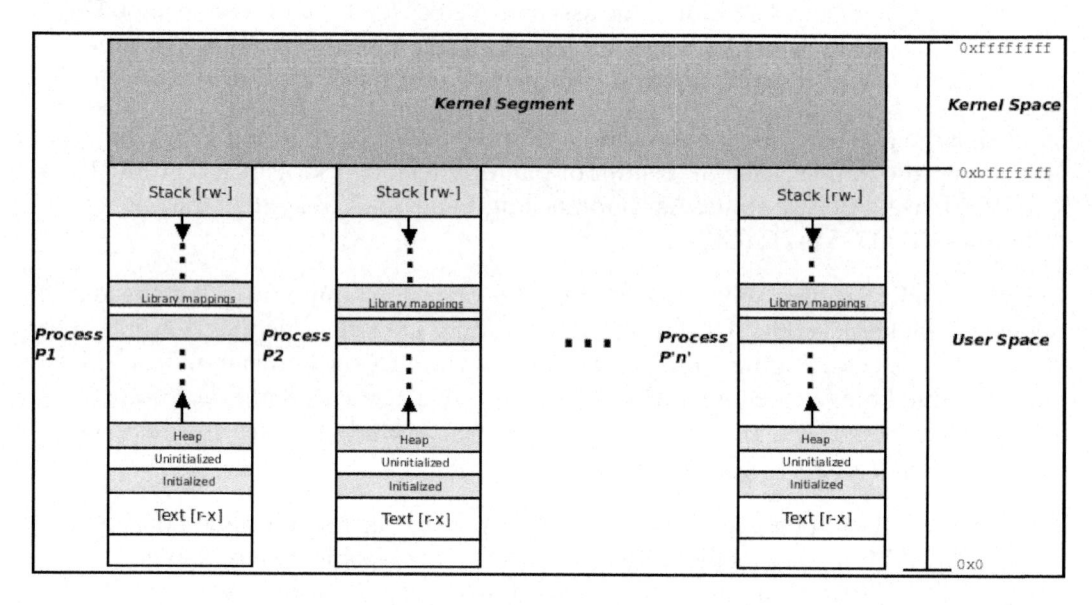

Figure 7.5 – Processes have a unique user VAS but share the kernel segment (32-bit OS); IA-32 with a 3:1 VM split

Notice in the preceding figure how the address space reflects a 3:1 (GB) VM split. The user address space extends from 0 to `0xbfff ffff` (`0xc000 0000` is the 3 GB mark; this is what the `PAGE_OFFSET` macro is set to), and the kernel VAS extends from `0xc000 0000` (3 GB) to `0xffff ffff` (4 GB).

Later in this chapter, we will cover the usage of a useful utility called `procmap`. It will help you literally visualize the VASes, both kernel and user VASes, in detail, similar to how our preceding diagrams have been showing.

A few things to note:

- For the example shown in Figure 7.5, the value of `PAGE_OFFSET` is `0xc000 0000`.
- The figures and numbers we have shown here are not absolute and binding across all architectures; they tend to be very arch-specific and many highly vendor-customized Linux systems may change them.
- *Figure 7.5* details the VM layout on a 32-bit Linux OS. On 64-bit Linux, the *concepts* remain identical, it's just the numbers that (significantly) change. As shown in some detail in the preceding sections, the VM split on an x86_64 (with 48-bit addressing) Linux system becomes `User : Kernel :: 128 TB : 128 TB`.

Now that the fundamentals of the virtual memory layout of a process are understood, you will find that it greatly helps in deciphering and making progress in difficult-to-debug situations. As usual, there's still more to it; sections follow on the user space and kernel-space memory map (the kernel segment), and some coverage on the physical memory map as well. Read on!

Examining the process VAS

We have already covered the layout – the segments or mappings – that every process's VAS is made up of (see the *Understanding the basics of the process Virtual Address Space (VAS)* section in `Chapter 6`, *Kernel Internals Essentials – Processes and Threads*). We learned that the process VAS consists of various mappings or segments, and among them are text (code), data segments, library mappings, and at least one stack. Here, we expand greatly on that discussion.

Being able to dive deep into the kernel and see various runtime values is an important skill for a developer like you, as well as the user, QA, sysadmin, DevOps, and so on. The Linux kernel provides us with an amazing interface to do precisely this – it's, you guessed it, the `proc` filesystem (`procfs`).

Memory Management Internals - Essentials

This is always present on Linux (at least it should be) and is mounted under `/proc`. The `procfs` system has two primary jobs:

- To provide a unified set of (pseudo or virtual) files and directories, enabling you to look deep into the kernel and hardware internal details.
- To provide a unified set of root-writeable files, allowing the sysad to modify key kernel parameters. These are present under `/proc/sys/` and are termed `sysctl` – they are the tuning knobs of the Linux kernel.

Familiarity with the `proc` filesystem is indeed a must. I urge you to check it out, and read the excellent man page on `proc(5)` as well. For example, simply doing `cat /proc/PID/status` (where `PID` is, of course, the unique process identifier of a given process or thread) yields a whole bunch of useful details from the process or thread's task structure!

> **TIP:** Conceptually similar to `procfs` is the `sysfs` filesystem, mounted under `/sys` (and under it `debugfs`, typically mounted at `/sys/kernel/debug`). `sysfs` is a representation of 2.6 Linux's new device and driver model; it exposes a tree of all devices on the system, as well as several kernel-tuning knobs.

Examining the user VAS in detail

Let's begin by checking out the user VAS of any given process. A pretty detailed map of the user VAS is made available via `procfs`, particularly via the `/proc/PID/maps` pseudo-file. Let's learn how to use this interface to peek into a process's user space memory map. We will see two ways:

- Directly via the `procfs` interface's `/proc/PID/maps` pseudo-file
- Using a few useful frontends (making the output more human-digestible)

Let's start with the first one.

[332]

Directly viewing the process memory map using procfs

Looking up the internal process details of any arbitrary process does require root access, whereas looking up details of a process under your ownership (including the caller process itself) does not. So, as a simple example, we will look up the calling process's VAS by using the `self` keyword in place of the PID. The following screenshot shows this (on an x86_64 Ubuntu 18.04 LTS guest):

```
$ cat /proc/self/maps
555d83b65000-555d83b6d000 r-xp 00000000 08:01 524313      /bin/cat
555d83d6c000-555d83d6d000 r--p 00007000 08:01 524313      /bin/cat
555d83d6d000-555d83d6e000 rw-p 00008000 08:01 524313      /bin/cat
555d840a7000-555d840c8000 rw-p 00000000 00:00 0           [heap]
7f7d1e7e0000-7f7d1f1af000 r--p 00000000 08:01 1186501     /usr/lib/locale/locale-archive
7f7d1f1af000-7f7d1f396000 r-xp 00000000 08:01 2102698     /lib/x86_64-linux-gnu/libc-2.27.so
7f7d1f396000-7f7d1f596000 ---p 001e7000 08:01 2102698     /lib/x86_64-linux-gnu/libc-2.27.so
7f7d1f596000-7f7d1f59a000 r--p 001e7000 08:01 2102698     /lib/x86_64-linux-gnu/libc-2.27.so
7f7d1f59a000-7f7d1f59c000 rw-p 001eb000 08:01 2102698     /lib/x86_64-linux-gnu/libc-2.27.so
7f7d1f59c000-7f7d1f5a0000 rw-p 00000000 00:00 0
7f7d1f5a0000-7f7d1f5c7000 r--p 00000000 08:01 2102670     /lib/x86_64-linux-gnu/ld-2.27.so
7f7d1f78c000-7f7d1f7b0000 rw-p 00000000 00:00 0
7f7d1f7c7000-7f7d1f7c8000 r--p 00027000 08:01 2102670     /lib/x86_64-linux-gnu/ld-2.27.so
7f7d1f7c8000-7f7d1f7c9000 rw-p 00028000 08:01 2102670     /lib/x86_64-linux-gnu/ld-2.27.so
7f7d1f7c9000-7f7d1f7ca000 rw-p 00000000 00:00 0
7fffee9ea000-7fffeea0b000 rw-p 00000000 00:00 0           [stack]
7fffeea43000-7fffeea46000 r--p 00000000 00:00 0           [vvar]
7fffeea46000-7fffeea48000 r-xp 00000000 00:00 0           [vdso]
ffffffffff600000-ffffffffff601000 r-xp 00000000 00:00 0   [vsyscall]
$
```

Figure 7.6 – Output of the cat /proc/self/maps command

In the preceding screenshot, you can actually see the user VAS of the `cat` process – a veritable memory map of the user VAS of that process! Also, notice that the preceding `procfs` output is sorted in ascending order by (user) virtual address (UVA).

> **TIP**: Familiarity with using the powerful `mmap(2)` system call will help greatly in understanding further discussions. Do (at least) browse through its man page.

Interpreting the /proc/PID/maps output

To interpret the output of Figure 7.6, read it one line at a time. **Each line represents a segment or mapping of the user-mode VAS** of the process in question (in the preceding example, it's of the `cat` process). Each line consists of the following fields.

Memory Management Internals - Essentials

To make it easier, I will show just a single line of output whose fields we will label and refer to in the following notes:

```
start_uva   -   end_uva     mode,mapping   start-off    mj:mn inode# image-
name
555d83b65000-555d83b6d000       r-xp        00000000    08:01 524313
/bin/cat
```

Here, the entire line represents a segment, or more correctly, a *mapping* within the process (user) VAS. `uva` is the user virtual address. `start_uva` and `end_uva` for each segment are displayed as the first two fields (or columns). Thus, the length of the mapping (segment) is easily calculated (`end_uva`−`start_uva` bytes). Thus, in the preceding line, `start_uva` is `0x555d83b65000` and `end_uva` is `0x555d83b6d000` (and the length can be calculated to be 32 KB); but, what is this segment? Do read on...

The third field, `r-xp`, is actually a combination of two pieces of information:

- The first three letters represent the mode (permissions) of the segment (in the usual `rwx` notation).
- The next letter represents whether the mapping is a private one (`p`) or a shared one (`s`). Internally, this is set up by the fourth parameter to the `mmap(2)` system call, `flags`; it's really **the `mmap(2)` system call that is internally responsible for creating every segment or mapping within a process!**
- So, for the preceding sample segment shown, the third field being the value `r-xp`, we can now tell it's a text (code) segment and is a private mapping (as expected).

The fourth field `start-off` (here, it's the value 0) is the start offset from the beginning of the file whose contents has been mapped into the process VAS. Obviously, this value is only valid for file mappings. You can tell whether the current segment is a file mapping by glancing at the penultimate (sixth) field. For mappings that are not file-mapped – called **anonymous mappings** – it's always 0 (examples would be the mappings representing the heap or stack segments). In our preceding example line, it's a file mapping (that of `/bin/cat`) and the offset from the beginning of that file is 0 bytes (the length of the mapping, as we calculated in the preceding paragraph, is 32 KB).

The fifth field (08:01) is of the form `mj:mn`, where `mj` is the major number and `mn` is the minor number of the device file where the image resides. Similar to the fourth field, it's only valid for file mappings, else it's simply shown as 00:00; in our preceding example line, it's a file mapping (that of /bin/cat), and the major and minor numbers (of the *device* that the file resides on) are 8 and 1, respectively.

The sixth field (524313) represents the inode number of the image file – the file whose contents are being mapped into the process VAS. The inode is the key data structure of the **VFS (Virtual FileSystem)**; it holds all metadata of the file object, everything except for its name (which is in the directory file). Again, this value is only valid for file mappings and simply shows as 0 otherwise. This is, in fact, a quick way to tell whether the mapping is file-mapped or an anonymous mapping! In our preceding example mapping, clearly it's a file mapping (that of /bin/cat), and the inode number is 524313. Indeed, we can confirm this:

```
ls -i /bin/cat
524313 /bin/cat
```

The seventh and last field represents the pathname of the file whose contents are being mapped into the user VAS. Here, as we're viewing the memory map of the cat(1) process, the pathname (for the file-mapped segments) is /bin/cat, of course. If the mapping represents a file, the file's inode number (the sixth field) shows up as a positive quantity; if not – meaning it's a pure memory or anonymous mapping with no backing store – the inode number shows up as 0 and this field will be empty.

It should by now be obvious, but we will point this out nevertheless – it is a key point: all the preceding addresses seen are virtual, not physical. Furthermore, they only belong to user space, hence they are termed UVAs and are always accessed (and translated) via the unique paging tables for that process. Also, the preceding screenshot was taken on a 64-bit (x86_64) Linux guest. Hence, here, we see 64-bit virtual addresses.

> Though the way the virtual addresses are displayed isn't as a full 64-bit number – for example, as 0x555d83b65000 and not as 0x0000555d83b65000 – I want you to notice how, because it's a **user virtual address** (a **UVA**), the MSB 16 bits are zero!

Right, that covers how to interpret a particular segment or mapping, but there seems to be a few strange ones – the vvar, vdso, and vsyscall mappings. Let's see what they mean.

Memory Management Internals - Essentials

The vsyscall page

Did you notice something a tad unusual in the output of Figure 7.6? The very last line there – the so-called `vsyscall` entry – maps a kernel page (by now, you know how we can tell: the MSB 16 bits of its start and end virtual addresses are set). Here, we just mention the fact that this is an (old) optimization for performing system calls. It works by alleviating the need to actually switch to kernel mode for a small subset of syscalls that don't really need to.

Currently, on the x86, these include the `gettimeofday(2)`, `time(2)`, and `getcpu(2)` system calls. Indeed, the `vvar` and `vdso` (aka vDSO) mappings above it are (slightly) modern variations on the same theme. If you are interested in finding out more about this, visit the *Further reading* section for this chapter.

So, you've now seen how to examine the user space memory map of any given process by directly reading and interpreting the output of the `/proc/PID/maps` (pseudo) file for the process with PID. There are other convenient frontends to do so; we'll now check out a few.

Frontends to view the process memory map

Besides the raw or direct format via `/proc/PID/maps` (which we saw how to interpret in the previous section), there are some wrapper utilities that help us more easily interpret the user-mode VAS. Among them are the additional (raw) `/proc/PID/smaps` pseudo-file, the `pmap(1)` and `smem(8)` utilities, and my own simple utility (christened `procmap`).

The kernel provides detailed information on each segment or mapping via the `/proc/PID/smaps` pseudo-file under `proc`. Do try `cat /proc/self/smaps` to see this for yourself. You will notice that for each segment (mapping), a good amount of detail information is provided on it. The man page on `proc(5)` helps explain the many fields seen.

For both the `pmap(1)` and `smem(8)` utilities, I refer you to the man pages on them for details. For example, with `pmap(1)`, the man page informs us of the more verbose -X and -XX options:

```
-X Show even more details than the -x option. WARNING: format changes
   according to /proc/PID/smaps
-XX Show everything the kernel provides
```

[336]

Regarding the `smem(8)` utility, the fact is that it does *not* show you the process VAS; rather, it's more about answering an FAQ: namely, ascertaining which process is taking up the most physical memory. It uses metrics such as **Resident Set Size (RSS)**, **Proportional Set Size (PSS)**, and **Unique Set Size (USS)** to throw up a clearer picture. I will leave the further exploration of these utilities as an exercise to you, dear reader!

Now, let's move on to exploring how we can use a useful utility – `procmap` – to view in quite a bit of detail both the kernel and user memory map of any given process.

The procmap process VAS visualization utility

As a small learning and teaching (and helpful during debug!) project, I have authored and hosted a small project on GitHub going by the name of `procmap`, available here: `https://github.com/kaiwan/procmap` (do `git clone` it). A snippet from its `README.md` file helps explain its purpose:

> ```
> procmap is designed to be a console/CLI utility to visualize the
> complete memory map of a Linux process, in effect, to visualize the
> memory mappings of both the kernel and user mode Virtual Address Space
> (VAS).
> ```
>
> ```
> It outputs a simple visualization, in a vertically-tiled format
> ordered by descending virtual address, of the complete memory map of a
> given process (see screenshots below). The script has the intelligence
> to show kernel and user space mappings as well as calculate and show
> the sparse memory regions that will be present. Also, each segment or
> mapping is scaled by relative size (and color-coded for readability).
> On 64-bit systems, it also shows the so-called non-canonical sparse
> region or 'hole' (typically close to 16,384 PB on the x86_64).
> ```

Memory Management Internals - Essentials

An aside: at the time of writing this material (April/May 2020), the COVID-19 pandemic is in full swing across most of the globe. Similar to the earlier *SETI@home* project (`https://setiathome.berkeley.edu/`), the *Folding@home* project (`https://foldingathome.org/category/covid-19/`) is a distributed computing project that leverages internet-connected home (or any) computers to help simulate and solve problems related to COVID-19 treatments (among finding cures for several other serious diseases that affect us). You can download the software from `https://foldingathome.org/start-folding/` (install it, and it runs during your system's idle cycles). I did just this; here's the FAH viewer (a nice GUI showing protein molecules!) process running on my (native) Ubuntu Linux system:

```
$ ps -e|grep -i FAH
6190 ?        00:00:13 FAHViewer
```

Alright, let's interrogate its VAS using the `procmap` utility. How do we invoke it? Simple, see what follows (due to a lack of space, I won't show all the information, caveats, and more here; do try it out yourself):

```
$ git clone https://github.com/kaiwan/procmap
$ cd procmap
$ ./procmap
Options:
  --only-user   : show ONLY the user mode mappings or segments
  --only-kernel : show ONLY the kernel-space mappings or segments
  [default is to show BOTH]
  --export-maps=filename
      write all map information gleaned to the file you specify in CSV
  --export-kernel=filename
      write kernel information gleaned to the file you specify in CSV
  --verbose : verbose mode (try it! see below for details)
  --debug : run in debug mode
  --version|--ver : display version info.
See the config file as well.
[...]
```

Do note that this `procmap` utility is not the same as the `procmap` utility provided by BSD Unix. Also, it depends upon the `bc(1)` and `smem(8)` utilities; please ensure they're installed.

Chapter 7

When I run the `procmap` utility with only `--pid=<PID>`, it will display both the kernel and user space VASes of the given process. Now, as we have not yet covered the details regarding the kernel VAS (or segment), I won't show the kernel-space detailed output here; let's defer that to the upcoming section, *Examining the kernel segment*. As we proceed, you will find partial screenshots of only the user VAS output from the `procmap` utility. The complete output can be quite lengthy, depending, of course, on the process in question; do try it out for yourself.

As you'll see, it attempts to provide a basic visualization of the complete process memory map – both kernel and user space VAS in a vertically tiled format (as mentioned, here we just display truncated screenshots):

```
kaiwan $ procmap --pid=$(pgrep FAHViewer)
[i] will display memory map for process PID=6190
Detected machine type: x86_64, 64-bit system & OS

[==================---     P R O C M A P    ---==================]
Process Virtual Address Space (VAS) Visualization utility
https://github.com/kaiwan/procmap

Sun Aug  2 14:59:40 IST 2020
[=====---  Start memory map for 6190:FAHViewer  ---=====]
[Pathname: /usr/bin/FAHViewer ]
+------------------ K E R N E L   V A S    end kva ----------------+ ffffffffffffffff
|<... K sparse region ...> [   8.00 MB,--- ]                       |
|                                                                  |
```

Figure 7.7 – Partial screenshot: the first line of the kernel VAS output from the procmap utility

Notice, from the preceding (partial) screenshot, a few things:

- The `procmap` (Bash) script auto-detects that we're running on an x86_64 64-bit system.
- Though we're not focused on it right now, the output of the kernel VAS appears first; this is natural as we show the output ordered by descending virtual address (Figures 7.1, 7.3 and 7.5 reiterate this)
- You can see that the very first line (after the `KERNEL VAS` header) corresponds to a KVA at the very top of the VAS – the value `0xffff ffff ffff ffff` (as we're on 64-bit).

[339]

Memory Management Internals - Essentials

Moving on to the next part of the `procmap` output, let's look at a truncated view of the upper end of the user VAS of the `FAHViewer` process:

```
+-------------------    U S E R   V A S    end uva -----------------+ 00007ffffffffffff
| /usr/bin/FAHViewer [   4.33 MB,r-x,p,0x5f000]                     |
|                                                                   |
|                                                                   |
+-------------------------------------------------------------------+ 00007ffffffffffff
|<... Sparse Region ...> [  13.01 GB,---,-,0x0]                     |
|                                                                   |
|                                                                   |
|                                                                   |
|                                                                   |
|                                                                   |
|                                                                   |
|                                                                   |
|                                                                   |
+-------------------------------------------------------------------+ 00007ffcbed81000
|              [vdso]  [   4 KB,r-x,p,0x0]                          |
+-------------------------------------------------------------------+ 00007ffcbed80000
|              [vvar]  [  12 KB,r--,p,0x0]                          |
+-------------------------------------------------------------------+ 00007ffcbed7d000
|<... Sparse Region ...> [ 740 KB,---,-,0x0]                        |
|                                                                   |
+-------------------------------------------------------------------+ 00007ffcbecc4000
|             [stack]  [ 132 KB,rw-,p,0x0]                          |
|                                                                   |
+-------------------------------------------------------------------+ 00007ffcbeca3000
|<... Sparse Region ...> [  92.71 GB,---,-,0x0]                     |
|                                                                   |
|                                                                   |
|                                                                   |
|                                                                   |
|                                                                   |
|                                                                   |
+-------------------------------------------------------------------+ 00007fe591422000
|         [-unnamed-]  [   4 KB,rw-,p,0x0]                          |
+-------------------------------------------------------------------+ 00007fe591421000
|/usr/lib/x86_64-linux-gnu/ld-2.31.so [   4 KB,rw-,p,0x2d000]       |
+-------------------------------------------------------------------+ 00007fe591420000
|/usr/lib/x86_64-linux-gnu/ld-2.31.so [   4 KB,r--,p,0x2c000]       |
+-------------------------------------------------------------------+ 00007fe59141f000
|       /dev/nvidiactl [   4 KB,rw-,s,0x0]                          |
+-------------------------------------------------------------------+ 00007fe59141e000
|/usr/lib/x86_64-linux-gnu/ld-2.31.so [  32 KB,r--,p,0x24000]       |
+-------------------------------------------------------------------+ 00007fe591416000
```

Figure 7.8 – Partial screenshot: first few lines (high end) of the user VAS output from the procmap utility

Figure 7.8 is a partial screenshot of the `procmap` output, and shows the user space VAS; at the very top of it, you can see the (high) end UVA.

Chapter 7

On our x86_64 system (recall, this is arch-dependent), the (high) `end_uva` value is `0x0000 7fff ffff ffff` and `start_uva` is, of course, `0x0`. How does `procmap` figure out the precise address values? Ah, it's fairly sophisticated: for the kernel-space memory information, it uses a kernel module (an LKM!) to query the kernel and sets up a config file depending on the system architecture; user space details, of course, come from the `/proc/PID/maps` direct `procfs` pseudo-file.

> As an aside, the kernel component of `procmap`, a kernel module, sets up a way to interface with user space – the `procmap` scripts – by creating and setting up a `debugfs` (pseudo) file.

The following screenshot shows a partial screenshot of the low end of the user mode VAS for the process, right down to the lowest UVA, `0x0`:

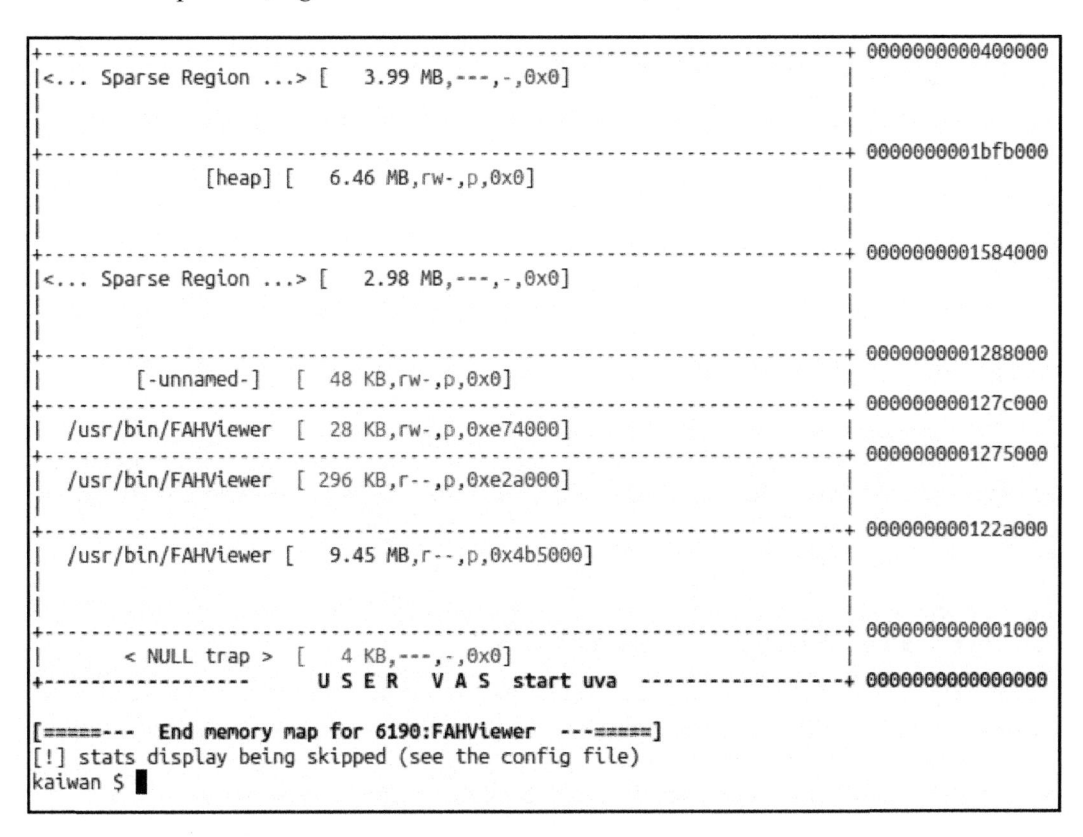

```
+-------------------------------------------------------+ 0000000000400000
|<... Sparse Region ...> [   3.99 MB,---,-,0x0]         |
|                                                       |
|                                                       |
+-------------------------------------------------------+ 0000000001bfb000
|           [heap] [   6.46 MB,rw-,p,0x0]               |
|                                                       |
|                                                       |
+-------------------------------------------------------+ 0000000001584000
|<... Sparse Region ...> [   2.98 MB,---,-,0x0]         |
|                                                       |
|                                                       |
+-------------------------------------------------------+ 0000000001288000
|       [-unnamed-]  [   48 KB,rw-,p,0x0]               |
+-------------------------------------------------------+ 000000000127c000
| /usr/bin/FAHViewer  [   28 KB,rw-,p,0xe74000]         |
+-------------------------------------------------------+ 0000000001275000
| /usr/bin/FAHViewer  [  296 KB,r--,p,0xe2a000]         |
|                                                       |
+-------------------------------------------------------+ 000000000122a000
| /usr/bin/FAHViewer  [   9.45 MB,r--,p,0x4b5000]       |
|                                                       |
|                                                       |
+-------------------------------------------------------+ 0000000000001000
|       < NULL trap >  [    4 KB,---,-,0x0]             |
+---------------------    U S E R   V A S  start uva ---+ 0000000000000000
[=====--- End memory map for 6190:FAHViewer  ---=====]
[!] stats display being skipped (see the config file)
kaiwan $ ▮
```

Figure 7.9 – Partial screenshot: last few lines (low end) of the user VAS output from the procmap utility

Memory Management Internals - Essentials

The last mapping, a single page, is, as expected, the null trap page (from UVA `0x1000` to `0x0`; we will explain its purpose in the upcoming *The null trap page* section).

The `procmap` utility, then, if enabled in its config file, calculates and displays a few statistics; this includes the sizes of both the kernel and user-mode VASes, the amount of user space memory taken up by sparse regions (on 64-bit, as in the preceding example, it's usually the vast majority of the space!) as an absolute number and a percentage, the amount of physical RAM reported, and finally, the memory usage details for this particular process as reported by the `ps(1)` and `smem(8)` utilities.

You will find, in general, on a 64-bit system (see Figure 7.3), that the *sparse* (empty) memory regions of the process VAS take up close to 100% of the available address space! (It's often a number such as 127.99[...] TB of VAS out of the 128 TB available.) This implies that 99.99[...]% of the memory space is sparse (empty)! This is the reality of the simply enormous VAS on a 64-bit system. Only a tiny fraction of the gigantic 128 TB of VAS (as this is the case on the x86_64) is actually in use. Of course, the actual amounts of sparse and used VAS depend on the size of the particular application process.

Being able to clearly visualize the process VAS can aid greatly when debugging or analyzing issues at a deeper level.

> **TIP**
> If you're reading this book in its hardcopy format, be sure to download the full-color PDF of diagrams/figures from the publisher's website: `https://static.packt-cdn.com/downloads/9781789953435_ColorImages.pdf`.

You will also see that the statistics printed out at the end of the output (if enabled) show the number of **Virtual Memory Areas** (**VMAs**) set up for the target process. The following section briefly explains what a VMA is. Let's get to it!

Understanding VMA basics

In the output of `/proc/PID/maps`, each line of the output is actually extrapolated from a kernel metadata structure called a VMA. It's quite straightforward, really: the kernel uses the VMA data structure to abstract what we have been calling a segment or mapping. Thus, for every single segment in the user VAS, there is a VMA object maintained by the OS. Please realize that only user space segments or mappings are governed by the kernel metadata structure called the VMA; the kernel segment itself has no VMAs.

So, how many VMAs will a given process have? Well, it's equal to the number of mappings (segments) in its user VAS. In our example with the *FAHViewer* process, it happened to have 206 segments or mappings, implying that there are 206 VMA metadata objects – representing the 206 user space segments or mappings – for this process in kernel memory.

Programmatically speaking, the kernel maintains a VMA "chain" (which is actually a red-black tree data structure for efficiency reasons) via the task structure rooted at `current->mm->mmap`. Why is the pointer called `mmap`? It's very deliberate: every time an `mmap(2)` system call – that is, a memory mapping operation – is performed, the kernel generates a mapping (or "segment") within the calling process's (that is, within `current` instances) VAS and a VMA object representing it.

The VMA metadata structure is akin to an umbrella encompassing the mapping and includes all required information for the kernel to perform various kinds of memory management: servicing page faults (very common), caching the contents of a file during I/O into (or out of) the kernel page cache, and so on.

> Page fault handling is a very important OS activity, whose algorithm makes up quite a bit of usage of the kernel VMA objects; in this book, though, we don't delve into these details as it's largely transparent to kernel module/driver authors.

Just to give you a feel for it, we will show a few members of the kernel VMA data structure in the following snippet; the comments alongside help explain their purpose:

```
// include/linux/mm_types.h
struct vm_area_struct {
    /* The first cache line has the info for VMA tree walking. */
    unsigned long vm_start;     /* Our start address within vm_mm. */
    unsigned long vm_end;       /* The first byte after our end address
    within vm_mm. */
    /* linked list of VM areas per task, sorted by address */
    struct vm_area_struct *vm_next, *vm_prev;
    struct rb_node vm_rb;
    [...]
    struct mm_struct *vm_mm;    /* The address space we belong to. */
    pgprot_t vm_page_prot;      /* Access permissions of this VMA. */
    unsigned long vm_flags;     /* Flags, see mm.h. */
    [...]
    /* Function pointers to deal with this struct. */
    const struct vm_operations_struct *vm_ops;
    /* Information about our backing store: */
```

```
        unsigned long vm_pgoff;/* Offset (within vm_file) in PAGE_SIZE
units */
        struct file * vm_file;        /* File we map to (can be NULL). */
        [...]
} __randomize_layout
```

It should now be clearer as to how `cat /proc/PID/maps` really works under the hood: when the user space does, say, `cat /proc/self/maps`, a `read(2)` system call is issued by `cat`; this results in the `cat` process switching to kernel mode and running the `read(2)` system call code within the kernel with kernel privileges. Here, the kernel **Virtual Filesystem Switch (VFS)** redirects control to the appropriate `procfs` callback handler (function). This code iterates (loops) over every VMA metadata structures (for `current`, which is our `cat` process, of course), sending relevant information back to user space. The `cat` process then faithfully dumps the data received via the read to `stdout`, and thus we see it: all the segments or mappings of the process – in effect, the memory map of the user-mode VAS!

Right, with this, we conclude this section, where we have covered details on examining the process user VAS. This knowledge helps not only with understanding the precise layout of user-mode VAS but also with debugging user space memory issues!

Now, let's move on to understanding another critical aspect of memory management – the detailed layout of the kernel VAS, in other words, the kernel segment.

Examining the kernel segment

As we have talked about in the preceding chapter, and as seen in *Figure 7.5*, it's really critical to understand that all processes have their own unique user VAS but share the kernel space – what we call the kernel segment or kernel VAS. Let's begin this section by starting to examine some common (arch-independent) regions of the kernel segment.

The kernel segment's memory layout is very arch (CPU)-dependent. Nevertheless, all architectures share some commonalities. The following basic diagram represents both the user VAS and the kernel segment (in a horizontally tiled format), as seen on an x86_32 with a 3:1 VM split:

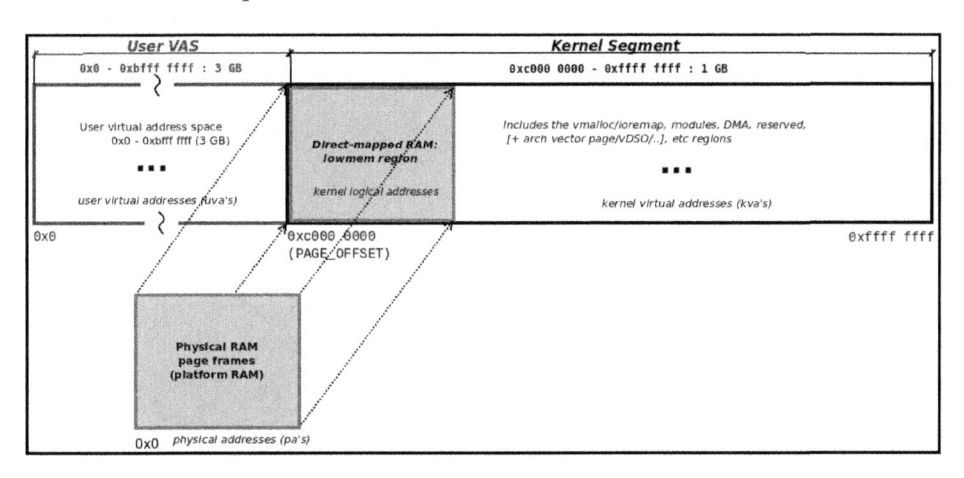

Figure 7.10 – User and kernel VASes on an x86_32 with a 3:1 VM split with focus on the lowmem region

Let's go over each region one by one:

- **The user mode VAS**: This is the user VAS; we have covered it in detail in the preceding chapter as well as earlier sections in this chapter; in this particular example, it takes 3 GB of VAS (UVAs from `0x0` to `0xbfff ffff`).
- All that follows belongs to kernel VAS or the kernel segment; in this particular example, it takes 1 GB of VAS (KVAs from `0xc000 0000` to `0xffff ffff`); let's examine individual portions of it now.
- **The lowmem region**: This is where platform (system) RAM direct-maps into the kernel. (We will cover this key topic in more detail in the *Direct-mapped RAM and address translation* section. If you feel it helps, you can read that section first and then return here). Skipping a bit ahead for now, let's just understand that the base location in the kernel segment where platform RAM is mapped is specified by a kernel macro called `PAGE_OFFSET`. The precise value of this macro is very arch-dependent; we will leave this discussion to a later section. For now, we ask you to just take it on faith that on the IA-32 with a 3:1 (GB) VM split, the value of `PAGE_OFFSET` is `0xc000 0000`.

The length or size of the kernel lowmem region is equal to the amount of RAM on the system. (Well, at least the amount of RAM as seen by the kernel; enabling the kdump facility, for example, has the OS reserve some RAM early). The virtual addresses that make up this region are termed **kernel logical addresses** as they are at a fixed offset from their physical counterparts. The core kernel and device drivers can allocate (physically contiguous!) memory from this region via various APIs (we cover precisely these APIs in detail in the following two chapters). The kernel static text (code), data, and BSS (uninitialized data) memory also resides within this lowmem region.

- **The kernel vmalloc region**: This is a region of the kernel VAS that is completely virtual. Core kernel and/or device driver code can allocate virtually contiguous memory from this region using the `vmalloc()` (and friends) API. Again, we will cover this in detail in Chapter 8, *Kernel Memory Allocation for Module Authors Part 1*, and Chapter 9, *Kernel Memory Allocation for Module Authors Part 2*. This is also the so-called `ioremap` space.
- **The kernel modules space**: A region of kernel VAS is set aside for memory taken up by the static text and data of **Loadable Kernel Modules (LKMs)**. When you perform `insmod(8)`, the underlying kernel code of the resulting `[f]init_module(2)` system call allocates memory from this region (typically via the `vmalloc()` API) and loads the kernel module's (static) code and data there.

The preceding figure (Figure 7.10) is deliberately left simplistic and even a bit vague as the exact kernel virtual memory layout is very arch-dependent. We'll put off the temptation to draw a detailed diagram for a bit. Instead, to make this discussion less pedantic and more practical and useful, we'll present, in a soon-to-come section, a kernel module that queries and prints relevant information regarding the kernel segment layout. Only then, once we have actual values for various regions of the kernel segment for a particular architecture, will we present a detailed diagram depicting this.

> Pedantically (as can be seen in Figure 7.10), the addresses belonging to the lowmem region are termed kernel logical addresses (they're at a fixed offset from their physical counterparts), whereas the addresses for the remainder of the kernel segment are termed KVAs. Though this distinction is made here, please realize that, for all practical purposes, it's a rather pedantic one: we will often simply refer to all addresses within the kernel segment as KVAs.

Before that, there are several other pieces of information to cover. Let's begin with another peculiarity, mostly brought about by the limitations of a 32-bit architecture: the so-called high memory region of the kernel segment.

High memory on 32-bit systems

Regarding the kernel lowmem region that we briefly discussed previously, an interesting observation ensues. On a 32-bit system with, say, a 3:1 (GB) VM split (just as Figure 7.10 depicts), a system with (say) 512 MB of RAM will have its 512 MB RAM direct-mapped into the kernel starting at PAGE_OFFSET (3 GB or KVA 0xc000 0000). This is quite clear.

But think about it: what would happen if the system has a lot more RAM, say, 2 GB? Now, it's obvious that we cannot direct-map the whole of the RAM into the lowmem region. It just cannot fit (as, in this example, the entire available kernel VAS is just a gigabyte and RAM is 2 gigabytes)! So, on a 32-bit Linux OS, a certain amount of memory (typically 768 MB on the IA-32) is allowed to be direct-mapped and thus falls into the lowmem region. The remaining RAM is *indirectly mapped* into another memory zone called ZONE_HIGHMEM (we think of it as a high-memory region or *zone* as opposed to lowmem; more on memory zones follows in a later section, *Zones*). More correctly, as the kernel now finds it impossible to direct-map all physical memory at once, it sets up a (virtual) region where it can set up and use temporary virtual mappings of that RAM. This is the so-called high-memory region.

> **TIP**
> Don't get confused by the phrase "high memory"; one, it's not necessarily placed "high" in the kernel segment, and two, this is not what the high_memory global variable represents – it (high_memory) represents the upper bound of the kernel's lowmem region. More on this follows in a later section, *Macros and variables describing the kernel segment layout*.

Nowadays, though (and especially with 32-bit systems being used more and more infrequently), these concerns completely disappear on 64-bit Linux. Think about it: on 64-bit Linux, the kernel segment size is a whopping 128 TB (!) on the x86_64. No single system in existence has anywhere close to this much RAM. Hence, all platform RAM can indeed (easily) be direct-mapped into the kernel segment and the need for ZONE_HIGHMEM (or equivalent) disappears.

Memory Management Internals - Essentials

Again, the kernel documentation provides details on this "high-memory" region. Take a look if interested: `https://www.kernel.org/doc/Documentation/vm/highmem.txt`.

Okay, let's now tackle the thing we've been waiting to do – writing a kernel module (an LKM) to delve into some details regarding the kernel segment.

Writing a kernel module to show information about the kernel segment

As we have learned, the kernel segment consists of various regions. Some are common to all architectures (arch-independent): they include the lowmem region (which contains, among other things, the uncompressed kernel image – its code, data, BSS), the kernel modules region, `vmalloc/ioremap` regions, and so on.

The precise location within the kernel segment where these regions lie, and indeed which regions may be present, is very arch (CPU)-dependent. To help understand and pin it down for any given system, let's develop a kernel module that queries and prints various details regarding the kernel segment (in fact, if asked to, it also prints some useful user space memory details).

Viewing the kernel segment on a Raspberry Pi via dmesg

Before jumping into and analyzing the code for such a kernel module, the fact is that something pretty similar to what we're attempting here – printing the location and size of various interesting regions within the kernel segment/VAS – is already performed at early boot on the popular Raspberry Pi (ARM) Linux kernel. In the following snippet, we show the relevant output from the kernel log when the Raspberry Pi 3 B+ (running the stock (default) 32-bit Raspberry Pi OS) boots:

```
rpi $ uname -r
4.19.97-v7+
rpi $ journalctl -b -k
[...]
Apr 02 14:32:48 raspberrypi kernel: Virtual kernel memory layout:
                vector  : 0xffff0000 - 0xffff1000   (    4 kB)
                fixmap  : 0xffc00000 - 0xfff00000   ( 3072 kB)
                vmalloc : 0xbb800000 - 0xff800000   ( 1088 MB)
                lowmem  : 0x80000000 - 0xbb400000   (  948 MB)
                modules : 0x7f000000 - 0x80000000   (   16 MB)
```

```
             .text : 0x(ptrval) - 0x(ptrval)    (9184 kB)
             .init : 0x(ptrval) - 0x(ptrval)    (1024 kB)
             .data : 0x(ptrval) - 0x(ptrval)    ( 654 kB)
              .bss : 0x(ptrval) - 0x(ptrval)    ( 823 kB)
[...]
```

It's important to note that these preceding prints are very specific to the OS and device. The default Raspberry Pi 32-bit OS prints this information out, while others may not: **YMMV (Your Mileage May Vary**!). For example, with the standard 5.4 kernel for Raspberry Pi that I built and ran on the device, these informative prints weren't present. On recent kernels (as seen in the preceding logs on the 4.19.97-v7+ Raspberry Pi OS kernel), for security reasons – that of preventing kernel information leakage – many early `printk` functions will not display a "real" kernel address (pointer) value; you might simply see it prints the `0x(ptrval)` string.

This `0x(ptrval)` output implies that the kernel is deliberately not showing even a hashed printk (recall the `%pK` format specifier from `Chapter 5`, *Writing Your First Kernel Module – LKMs Part 2*) as the system entropy is not yet high enough. If you insist on seeing a (weakly) hashed printk, you can always pass the `debug_boot_weak_hash` kernel parameter at boot (look up details on kernel boot parameters here: https://www.kernel.org/doc/html/latest/admin-guide/kernel-parameters.html).

Interestingly, (as mentioned in the preceding information box), the code that prints this `Virtual kernel memory layout :` information is very specific to the Raspberry Pi kernel patches! It can be found in the Raspberry Pi kernel source tree here: https://github.com/raspberrypi/linux/blob/rpi-5.4.y/arch/arm/mm/init.c.

Now, in order for you to query and print similar information, you must first get familiar with some key kernel macros and globals.; let's do so in the next section.

Memory Management Internals - Essentials

Macros and variables describing the kernel segment layout

To write a kernel module that displays relevant kernel segment information, we need to know how exactly to interrogate the kernel with regard to these details. In this section, we will briefly describe a few key macros and variables within the kernel representing the memory of the kernel segment (on most architectures, in descending order by KVA):

- **The vector table** is a common OS data structure – it's an array of function pointers (aka a switching or jump table). It is arch-specific: ARM-32 uses it to initialize its vectors such that when a processor exception or mode change (such as an interrupt, syscall, page fault, MMU abort, and so on) occurs, the processor knows what code to run:

Macro or variable	Interpretation
VECTORS_BASE	Typically ARM-32 only; start KVA of a kernel vector table spanning 1 page

- **The fix map region** is a range of compile-time special or reserved virtual addresses; they are employed at boot time to fix, into the kernel segment, required kernel elements that must have memory available for them. Typical examples include the setup of initial kernel page tables, early `ioremap` and `vmalloc` regions, and so on. Again, it's an arch-dependent region and is thus used differently on different CPUs:

Macro or variable	Interpretation
FIXADDR_START	Start KVA of the kernel fixmap region spanning FIXADDR_SIZE bytes

- **Kernel modules** are allocated memory – for their static text and data – within a specific range in the kernel segment. The precise location of the kernel module region varies with the architecture. On ARM 32-bit systems, in fact, it's placed just above the user VAS; while on 64-bit, it's usually higher up in the kernel segment:

Kernel modules (LKMs) region	Memory allocated from here for static code + data of LKMs
MODULES_VADDR	Start KVA of the kernel modules region
MODULES_END	End KVA of kernel modules region; size is MODULES_END - MODULES_VADDR

- **KASAN**: The modern kernel (4.0 onward for x86_64, 4.4 for ARM64) employs a powerful mechanism to detect and report memory issues. It's based on the user space **Address SANitizer** *(ASAN)* code base and is thus called **Kernel Address SANitizer (KASAN)**. Its power lies in ably (via compile-time instrumentation) detecting memory issues such as **Use After Free (UAF)** and **Out Of Bounds (OOB)** access (including buffer over/under flows). It, however, works *only on 64-bit Linux* and requires a rather large **shadow memory region** (of a size that is one-eighth that of the kernel VAS, whose extents we show if it's enabled). It's a kernel configuration feature (`CONFIG_KASAN`) and is typically enabled only for debug purposes (but it's really crucial to keep it enabled during debug and testing!):

KASAN shadow memory region (only 64-bit)	[Optional] (only on 64-bit and only if CONFIG_KASAN is defined; see more as follows)
`KASAN_SHADOW_START`	Start KVA of the KASAN region
`KASAN_SHADOW_END`	End KVA of the KASAN region; size is `KASAN_SHADOW_END - KASAN_SHADOW_START`

- **The vmalloc region** is the space from where memory for the `vmalloc()` (and friends) APIs are allocated; we will cover various memory allocation APIs in detail in the next two chapters:

The vmalloc region	For memory allocated via vmalloc() and friends
`VMALLOC_START`	Start KVA of the `vmalloc` region
`VMALLOC_END`	End KVA of the `vmalloc` region; size is `VMALLOC_END - VMALLOC_START`

- **The lowmem region** – direct-mapped RAM into the kernel segment on a `1:1 :: physical page frame:kernel page` basis – is in fact the region where the Linux kernel maps and manages (typically) all RAM. Also, it's often set up as `ZONE_NORMAL` within the kernel (we will cover zones as well, a bit later):

Lowmem region	Direct-mapped memory region
`PAGE_OFFSET`	Start KVA of the lowmem region; also represents the start of the kernel segment on some architectures and is (often) the VM split value on 32-bit.
`high_memory`	End KVA of the lowmem region, upper bound of direct-mapped memory; in effect, this value minus `PAGE_OFFSET` is the amount of (platform) RAM on the system (careful, this is not necessarily the case on all arches though); not to be confused with `ZONE_HIGHMEM`.

Memory Management Internals - Essentials

- **The highmem region** or zone is an optional region. It might exist on some 32-bit systems (typically, where the amount of RAM present is greater than the size of the kernel segment itself). It's often set up as `ZONE_HIGHMEM` in this case (we will cover zones a bit later. Also, you can refer back to more on this highmem region in the earlier section entitled *High memory on 32-bit systems*):

Highmem region (only possible on 32-bit)	[Optional] HIGHMEM may be present on some 32-bit systems
`PKMAP_BASE`	Start KVA of the highmem region, runs until `LAST_PKMAP` pages; represents the kernel mapping of so-called high-memory pages (older, only possible on 32-bit)

- The (uncompressed) **kernel image** itself – its code, `init`, and data regions – are private symbols and thus unavailable to kernel modules; we don't attempt to print them:

Kernel (static) image	The content of the uncompressed kernel image (see the following); not exported and thus unavailable to modules
`_text, _etext`	Start and end KVAs (respectively) of the kernel text (code) region
`__init_begin, __init_end`	Start and end KVAs (respectively) of the kernel `init` section region
`_sdata, _edata`	Start and end KVAs (respectively) of the kernel static data region
`__bss_start, __bss_stop`	Start and end KVAs (respectively) of the kernel BSS (uninitialized data) region

- **The user VAS**: The last item, of course, is the process user VAS. It's below the kernel segment (when ordered by descending virtual address), and is of size `TASK_SIZE` bytes. It was discussed in detail earlier in this chapter:

User VAS	User Virtual Address Space (VAS)
(User-mode VAS follows) `TASK_SIZE`	(Examined in detail earlier via `procfs` or our `procmap` utility script); the kernel macro `TASK_SIZE` represents the size of the user VAS (bytes).

Well, that's that; we've seen several kernel macros and variables that, in effect, describe the kernel VAS.

[352]

Moving on to the code of our kernel module, you'll soon see that its `init` method calls two functions (that matter):

- `show_kernelseg_info()`, which prints relevant kernel segment details
- `show_userspace_info()`, which prints relevant user VAS details (it's optional, decided via a kernel parameter)

We will start by describing the kernel segment function and seeing its output. Also, the way the Makefile is set up, it links into the object file of our kernel library code, `klib_llkd.c`, and generates a kernel module object called `show_kernel_seg.ko`.

Trying it out – viewing kernel segment details

For clarity, we will show only relevant parts of the source code in this section. Do clone and use the complete code from this book's GitHub repository. Also, recall the `procmap` utility mentioned earlier; it has a kernel component, an LKM, which indeed does a similar job to this one – making kernel-level information available to user space. With it being more sophisticated, we won't delve into its code here; seeing the code of the following demo kernel module `show_kernel_seg` is more than sufficient here:

```
// ch7/show_kernel_seg/kernel_seg.c
[...]
static void show_kernelseg_info(void)
{
    pr_info("\nSome Kernel Details [by decreasing address]\n"
    "+------------------------------------------------------------
+\n");
#ifdef CONFIG_ARM
    /* On ARM, the definition of VECTORS_BASE turns up only in kernels
>= 4.11 */
#if LINUX_VERSION_CODE > KERNEL_VERSION(4, 11, 0)
    pr_info("|vector table: "
        " %px - %px | [%4ld KB]\n",
        SHOW_DELTA_K(VECTORS_BASE, VECTORS_BASE + PAGE_SIZE));
#endif
#endif
```

The preceding code snippet displays the extents of the ARM vector table. Of course, it's conditional. The output only occurs on an ARM-32 – hence the `#ifdef CONFIG_ARM` preprocessor directive. (Also, our use of the `%px` printk format specifier ensures the code is portable.)

Memory Management Internals - Essentials

The `SHOW_DELTA_*()` macros used here in this demo kernel module are defined in our `convenient.h` header and are helpers that enable us to easily display the low and high values passed to it, calculate the delta (the difference) between the two quantities passed, and display it; here's the relevant code:

```
// convenient.h
[...]
/* SHOW_DELTA_*(low, hi) :
 * Show the low val, high val and the delta (hi-low) in either
bytes/KB/MB/GB, as required.
 * Inspired from raspberry pi kernel src: arch/arm/mm/init.c:MLM()
 */
#define SHOW_DELTA_b(low, hi)  (low), (hi), ((hi) - (low))
#define SHOW_DELTA_K(low, hi)  (low), (hi), (((hi) - (low)) >> 10)
#define SHOW_DELTA_M(low, hi)  (low), (hi), (((hi) - (low)) >> 20)
#define SHOW_DELTA_G(low, hi)  (low), (hi), (((hi) - (low)) >> 30)
#define SHOW_DELTA_MG(low, hi) (low), (hi), (((hi) - (low)) >> 20), \
(((hi) - (low)) >> 30)
```

In the following code, we show the code snippet that emits `printk` functions describing the following region extents:

- Kernel module region
- (Optional) KASAN region
- The vmalloc region
- The lowmem, and a possible highmem, region

Regarding the kernel modules region, as explained in the detailed comment in the following source, we try and keep the order as by descending KVAs:

```
// ch7/show_kernel_seg/kernel_seg.c
[...]
/* kernel module region
 * For the modules region, it's high in the kernel segment on typical 64-
 * bit systems, but the other way around on many 32-bit systems
 * (particularly ARM-32); so we rearrange the order in which it's shown
 * depending on the arch, thus trying to maintain a 'by descending
address' ordering. */
#if (BITS_PER_LONG == 64)
  pr_info("|module region: "
    " %px - %px | [%4ld MB]\n",
      SHOW_DELTA_M(MODULES_VADDR, MODULES_END));
#endif
```

[354]

```c
#ifdef CONFIG_KASAN        // KASAN region: Kernel Address SANitizer
  pr_info("|KASAN shadow:   "
    " %px - %px | [%21d GB]\n",
    SHOW_DELTA_G(KASAN_SHADOW_START, KASAN_SHADOW_END));
#endif

  /* vmalloc region */
  pr_info("|vmalloc region: "
    " %px - %px | [%4ld MB = %2ld GB]\n",
    SHOW_DELTA_MG(VMALLOC_START, VMALLOC_END));

  /* lowmem region */
  pr_info("|lowmem region:  "
    " %px - %px | [%4ld MB = %2ld GB]\n"
#if (BITS_PER_LONG == 32)
    "|                 (above:PAGE_OFFSET - highmem)          |\n",
#else
    "|                      (above:PAGE_OFFSET - highmem) |\n",
#endif
    SHOW_DELTA_MG((unsigned long)PAGE_OFFSET, (unsigned long)high_memory));

  /* (possible) highmem region; may be present on some 32-bit systems */
#ifdef CONFIG_HIGHMEM
  pr_info("|HIGHMEM region: "
    " %px - %px | [%4ld MB]\n",
    SHOW_DELTA_M(PKMAP_BASE, (PKMAP_BASE) + (LAST_PKMAP * PAGE_SIZE)));
#endif
[ ... ]
#if (BITS_PER_LONG == 32) /* modules region: see the comment above reg this */
  pr_info("|module region:  "
    " %px - %px | [%4ld MB]\n",
    SHOW_DELTA_M(MODULES_VADDR, MODULES_END));
#endif
  pr_info(ELLPS);
}
```

Memory Management Internals - Essentials

Let's build and insert our LKM on the ARM-32 Raspberry Pi 3 B+; the following screenshot shows it being set up and then the kernel log:

```
rpi $ sudo rmmod show_kernel_seg 2>/dev/null ; sudo dmesg -C
rpi $ sudo insmod ./show_kernel_seg.ko ; dmesg |grep -v "Journal effective setting"
[ 9930.611526] show_kernel_seg: inserted
[ 9930.617597] llkd_minsysinfo(): minimal platform info:
                CPU: ARM-32, little-endian; 32-bit OS.
[ 9930.650276]
                Some Kernel Details [by decreasing address]
                +------------------------------------------------------------+
[ 9930.650291] |vector table:       ffff0000 - ffff1000 | [    4 KB]
[ 9930.689147] |                         [ . . . ]                          |
               |fixmap region:      ffc00000 - fff00000   | [    3 MB]
[ 9930.689166] |vmalloc region:     bb800000 - ff800000   | [1088 MB =  1 GB]
[ 9930.715765] |lowmem region:      80000000 - bb400000   | [ 948 MB =  0 GB]
               |                (above:PAGE_OFFSET - highmem)               |
[ 9930.715776] |module region:      7f000000 - 80000000 | [   16 MB]
[ 9930.715786] |                         [ . . . ]                          |
[ 9930.715800] +------------------------------------------------------------+
[ 9930.749197] show_kernel_seg: skipping show userspace...
rpi $
```

Figure 7.11 – Output from the show_kernel_seg.ko LKM on a Raspberry Pi 3B+ running stock Raspberry Pi 32-bit Linux

As expected, the output we receive regarding the kernel segment perfectly matches what the stock Raspberry Pi kernel itself prints at boot (you can refer back to the *Viewing the kernel segment on a Raspberry Pi via dmesg* section to verify this). As can be deciphered from the value of `PAGE_OFFSET` (the KVA `0x8000 0000` in Figure 7.11), our Raspberry Pi's kernel's VM split is configured as 2:2 (GB) (as the hexadecimal value `0x8000 0000` is 2 GB in decimal base. Interestingly, the default Raspberry Pi 32-bit OS on the more recent Raspberry Pi 4 Model B device is configured with a 3:1 (GB) VM split).

> Technically, on ARM-32 systems, at least, user space is slightly under 2 GB (*2 GB – 16 MB = 2,032 MB*) as this 16 MB is taken as the *kernel module region* just below `PAGE_OFFSET`; indeed, exactly this can be seen in Figure 7.11 (the kernel module region here spans from `0x7f00 0000` to `0x8000 0000` for 16 MB). Also, as you'll soon see, the value of the `TASK_SIZE` macro – the size of the user VAS – reflects this fact as well.

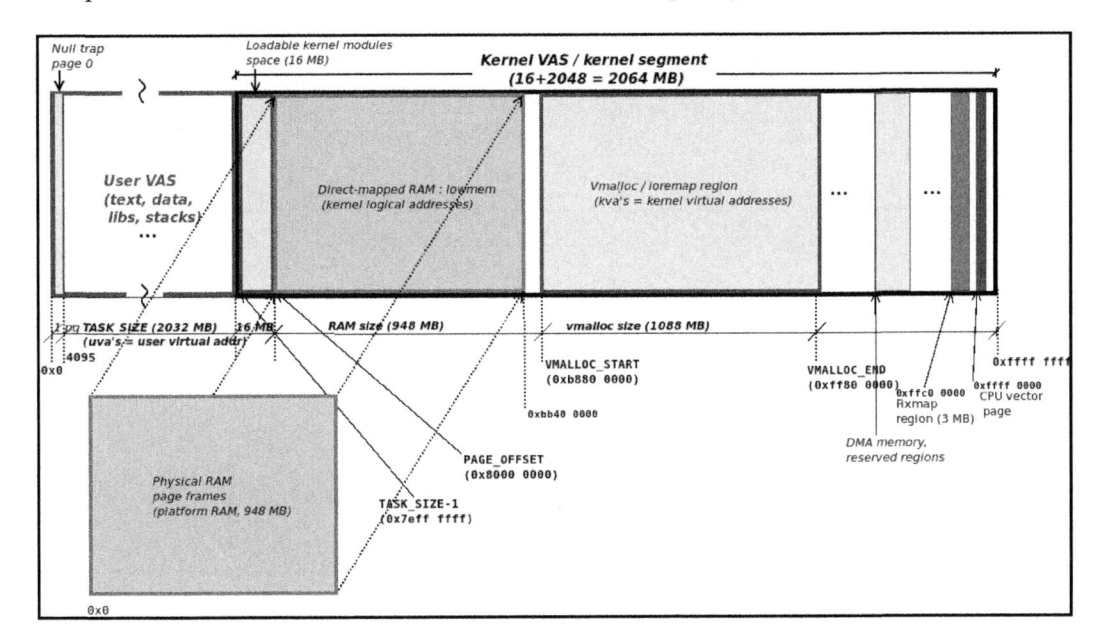

We present much of this information in the following diagram:

Figure 7.12 – The complete VAS of a process on ARM-32 (Raspberry Pi 3B+) with a 2:2 GB VM split

> Do note that due to variations in differing models, the amount of usable RAM, or even the device tree, the layout shown in Figure 7.12 may not precisely match that on the Raspberry Pi you have.

Okay, now you know how to print relevant kernel segment macros and variables within a kernel module, helping you understand the kernel VM layout on any Linux system! In the following section, we will attempt to "see" (visualize) the kernel VAS, this time via our `procmap` utility.

The kernel VAS via procmap

Okay, this is interesting: the view of the memory map layout seen in some detail in the preceding figure is exactly what our aforementioned `procmap` utility provides! As promised earlier, let's now see screenshots of the kernel VAS when running `procmap` (earlier, we showed screenshots of the user VAS).

Memory Management Internals - Essentials

To keep in sync with the immediate discussion, we will now show screenshots of `procmap` providing a "visual" view of the kernel VAS on the very same Raspberry Pi 3B+ system (we could specify the `--only-kernel` switch to show only the kernel VAS; we don't do so here, though). As we have to run `procmap` on some process, we arbitrarily choose *systemd* PID 1; we also use the `--verbose` option switch. However, it seems to fail:

```
rpi $ ./procmap --pid=1 --verbose
[i] will display memory map for process PID=1
[i] running in VERBOSE mode
[v] kernel: init kernel LKM and get details:
[v]   debugfs location verfied
[i] kernel: building the procmap LKM now...
FatalError :: procmap: suitable build env for kernel modules is missing! Pl install the Linux
kernel headers (via the appropriate package)
 Stack Call-trace:
    [frame #1] ./err_common.sh:cli_handle_error:116      <-- top of stack
    [frame #2] ./err_common.sh:FatalError:178
    [frame #3] ./lib_procmap.sh:build_lkm:209
    [frame #4] ./lib_procmap.sh:init_kernel_lkm_get_details:317
    [frame #5] ./procmap:main:0
./lib_procmap.sh: line 521: /tmp/procmap/arch_dtl: No such file or directory
```

Figure 7.13 – Truncated screenshot showing the procmap kernel module build failing

Why did it fail to build the kernel module (that's part of the `procmap` project)? I mention this in the project's `README.md` file (https://github.com/kaiwan/procmap/blob/master/README.md#procmap):

> [...]to build a kernel module on the target system, you will require
> it to have a kernel development environment setup; this boils down to
> having the compiler, make and - key here - the 'kernel headers'
> package installed for the kernel version it's currently running upon.
> [...]

The kernel headers package for our *custom* 5.4 kernel (for the Raspberry Pi) isn't available, hence it fails. While you can conceivably copy in the entire 5.4 Raspberry Pi kernel source tree onto the device and set up the `/lib/module/<kver>/build` symbolic link, this isn't considered the right way to do so. So, what is? *Cross-compiling* the `procmap` kernel module for the Raspberry Pi from your host, of course! We have covered the details on cross-compiling the kernel itself for the Raspberry Pi here in Chapter 3, *Building the 5.x Linux Kernel from Source - Part 2*, in the *Kernel Build for the Raspberry Pi* section; it, of course, applies to cross-compiling kernel modules as well.

> I want to stress this point: the `procmap` kernel module build on the Raspberry Pi only fails due to the lack of a Raspberry Pi-supplied kernel headers package when running a custom kernel. If you are happy to work with the stock (default) Raspberry Pi kernel (earlier called Raspbian OS), the kernel headers package is certainly installable (or already installed) and everything will work. Similarly, on your typical x86_64 Linux distribution, the `procmap.ko` kernel module gets cleanly built and inserted at runtime. Do read the `procmap` project's `README.md` file in detail; within it, the section labeled *IMPORTANT: Running procmap on systems other than x86_64* details how to cross-compile the `procmap` kernel module.

Once you successfully cross-compile the `procmap` kernel module on your host system, copy across the `procmap.ko` kernel module (via `scp(1)`, perhaps) to the device and place it under the `procmap/procmap_kernel` directory; now you're ready to go!

Here's the copied-in kernel module (on the Raspberry Pi):

```
cd <...>/procmap/procmap_kernel
ls -l procmap.ko
-rw-r--r-- 1 pi pi 7909 Jul 31 07:45 procmap.ko
```

(You can also run the `modinfo(8)` utility on it to verify that it's built for ARM.)

Memory Management Internals - Essentials

With this in place, let's retry our `procmap` run to display the kernel VAS details:

```
rpi $ ./procmap --pid=1 --verbose
[i] will display memory map for process PID=1
[i] running in VERBOSE mode
[v] kernel: init kernel LKM and get details:
[v]   debugfs location verfied
[v]   LKM inserted into kernel
[v]   debugfs file present
[v]   Parsing in various kernel variables as required
[v] set config for Aarch32:
Detected machine type: ARM-32, 32-bit OS
--------------------------------------------------------
[v] System details detected ::
--------------------------------------------------------
VECTORS_BASE = ffff0000
MODULES_VADDR = 7f000000
MODULES_END = 80000000
VMALLOC_START = bb800000
VMALLOC_END = ff800000
PAGE_OFFSET = 80000000
high_memory = bb400000
TASK_SIZE = 7f000000
ARCH = Aarch32
IS_64_BIT = 0
PAGE_SIZE = 4096
KERNEL_VAS_SIZE = 2164260864
USER_VAS_SIZE = 2130706432
HIGHEST_KVA = 0xffffffff
START_KVA = 7f000000
START_KVA_DEC = 2130706432
END_UVA = 7effffff
END_UVA_DEC = 2130706431
START_UVA = 0x0
--------------------------------------------------------
```

Figure 7.14 – Truncated screenshot showing the procmap kernel module successfully inserted and various system details

It does work now! As we've specified the `verbose` option to `procmap`, you get to see its detailed progress, as well as – quite usefully – various kernel variables/macros of interest and their current value.

[360]

Chapter 7

Okay, let's continue and view what we're really after – the "visual map" of the kernel VAS on the Raspberry Pi 3B+, in descending order by KVA; the following screenshot captures this output from `procmap`:

```
[=================---    P R O C M A P    ---=================]
Process Virtual Address Space (VAS) Visualization utility
https://github.com/kaiwan/procmap

Mon Aug  3 05:18:15 BST 2020
[=====---   Start memory map for 1:systemd   ---=====]
[Pathname: /lib/systemd/systemd ]
VAS mappings:   name     [ size,perms,u:maptype,u:0xfile-offset]
+------------------  K E R N E L   V A S    end kva ------------------+ ffffffff
|<... K sparse region ...> [    59 KB, --- ]                          |
+---------------------------------------------------------------------+ ffff1000
|            vector table  [    4 KB, r-- ]                           |
+---------------------------------------------------------------------+ ffff0000   <-- VECTORS_BASE
|<... K sparse region ...> [   7.93 MB, --- ]                         |
|                                                                     |
+---------------------------------------------------------------------+ ff800000   <-- VMALLOC_END
|          vmalloc region  [   1.06 GB, rw- ]                         |
|                                                                     |
|                                                                     |
|                                                                     |
|                                                                     |
|                                                                     |
+---------------------------------------------------------------------+ bb800000   <-- VMALLOC_START
|<... K sparse region ...> [   4.00 MB, --- ]                         |
|                                                                     |
+---------------------------------------------------------------------+ bb400000   <-- high_memory
|           lowmem region  [ 948.00 MB, rwx ]                         |
|                                                                     |
|                                                                     |
|                                                                     |
|                                                                     |
|   [-------------------------------------------------------]  | 80e784b7
|              Kernel data [   1.46 MB, ... ]                         |
|                                                                     |
|   [-------------------------------------------------------]  | 80bfffff
|              Kernel code [  11.96 MB, ... ]                         |
|                                                                     |
|                                                                     |
|                                                                     |
+---------------------------------------------------------------------+ 80000000   <-- MODULES_END/PAGE_OFFSET
|          module region:  [  16.00 MB, rwx ]                         |
|                                                                     |
|                                                                     |
+------------------  K E R N E L   V A S   start kva -----------------+ 7f000000
+------------------  U S E R     V A S     end uva  ------------------+ 7effffff
|<... Sparse Region ...>   [   1.30 MB, ---,-,0x0]                    |
|                                                                     |
+---------------------------------------------------------------------+ 7eeb1000
|               [vdso]     [    4 KB, r-x,p,0x0]                      |
+---------------------------------------------------------------------+ 7eeb0000
|               [vvar]     [    4 KB, r--,p,0x0]                      |
+---------------------------------------------------------------------+ 7eeaf000
```

Figure 7.15 – Partial screenshot of our procmap utility's output showing the complete kernel VAS (Raspberry Pi 3B+ with 32-bit Linux)

[361]

Memory Management Internals - Essentials

The complete kernel VAS – from `end_kva` (value `0xffff ffff`) right to the start of the kernel, `start_kva` (`0x7f00 0000`, which, as you can see, is the kernel module region) – is displayed. Notice (in green color) the label on the right of certain key addresses denoting what they are! For completeness, we also included in the preceding screenshot the kernel-user boundary (and the upper portion of the user VAS below the kernel segment, just as we have been saying all along!). As the preceding output is on a 32-bit system, the user VAS immediately follows the kernel segment. On a 64-bit system though, there is an (enormous!) "non-canonical" sparse region between the start of the kernel segment and the top of the user VAS. On the x86_64 (as we have already discussed), it spans the vast majority of the VAS: 16,383.75 petabytes (out of a total VAS of 16,384 petabytes)!

I will leave it as an exercise to you to run this `procmap` project and carefully study the output (on your x86_64 or whichever box or VM). It also works well on a BeagleBone Black embedded board with a 3:1 VM split, showing details as expected. FYI, this forms an assignment.

> I also provide a solution in the form of three (large, stitched-together) screenshots of `procmap`'s output on a native x86_64 system, a BeagleBone Black (AArch32) board, and the Raspberry Pi running a 64-bit OS (AArch64) here: `solutions_to_assgn/ch7`. Studying the code of `procmap`, and, especially relevant here, its kernel module component, will certainly help. It's open source, after all!

Let's finish this section by glancing at the user segment view that our earlier demo kernel module – `ch7/show_kernel_seg` – provides.

Trying it out – the user segment

Now, let's go back to our `ch7/show_kernel_seg` LKM demo program. We have provided a kernel module parameter named `show_uservas`(defaulting to the value 0); when set to 1, some details regarding the process context's *user space* are displayed as well. Here's the definition of the module parameter:

```
static int show_uservas;
module_param(show_uservas, int, 0660);
MODULE_PARM_DESC(show_uservas,
"Show some user space VAS details; 0 = no (default), 1 = show");
```

Right, on the same device (our Raspberry Pi 3 B+), let's again run our `show_kernel_seg` kernel module, this time requesting it to display user space details as well (via the aforementioned parameter). The following screenshot shows the complete output:

```
rpi $ uname -r
5.4.51-v7+
rpi $ sudo rmmod show_kernel_seg 2>/dev/null ; sudo dmesg -C
rpi $ sudo insmod ./show_kernel_seg.ko show_uservas=1 ; dmesg |grep -v "Journal effective setting"
[10224.062806] Voltage normalised (0x00000000)
[10235.740208] show_kernel_seg: inserted
[10235.744027] llkd_minsysinfo(): minimal platform info:
                CPU: ARM-32, little-endian; 32-bit OS.
[10235.771252]
                Some Kernel Details [by decreasing address]
                +-------------------------------------------------------------+
[10235.810117]  |vector table:      ffff0000 - ffff1000 | [   4 KB]           |
[10235.810130]  |                        [ . . . ]                            |
                |fixmap region:     ffc00000 - fff00000  | [   3 MB]          |
[10235.810142]  |vmalloc region:    bb800000 - ff800000  | [1088 MB =  1 GB]  |
[10235.836752]  |lowmem region:     80000000 - bb400000  | [ 948 MB =  0 GB]  |
                |                   (above:PAGE_OFFSET - highmem)             |
[10235.836763]  |module region:     7f000000 - 80000000 | [  16 MB]           |
[10235.870125]  |                        [ . . . ]                            |
[10235.870159]  +----------- Above is kernel-seg; below, user VAS ----------+
                |                        [ . . . ]                            |
                |Process environment 7ec9a8df - 7ec9afef | [ 1808 bytes]      |
                |          arguments 7ec9a8b4 - 7ec9a8df | [   43 bytes]      |
                |        stack start 7ec9a7a0                                  |
                |       heap segment 01a60000 - 01a81000 | [  132 KB]         |
                |static data segment 0003fc48 - 00040038 | [ 1008 bytes]      |
                |       text segment 00010000 - 0002f430 | [  125 KB]         |
                |                        [ . . . ]                            |
                +-------------------------------------------------------------+
[10235.909717] Above: TASK_SIZE        = 2130706432 size of userland  [ 2032 MB]
                # userspace memory regions (VMAs) = 40
                Above statistics are wrt 'current' thread (see below):
[10235.909736] 003)   insmod :3989   |  .N.0   /* show_userspace_info() */
rpi $
```

Figure 7.16 – Screenshot of our show_kernel_seg.ko LKM's output showing both kernel and user VAS details when running on a Raspberry Pi 3B+ with the stock Raspberry Pi 32-bit Linux OS

This is useful; we can now literally see a (more or less) complete memory map of the process – both the so-called "upper (canonical) half" kernel-space as well as the "lower (canonical) half" user space – in one shot (yes, that's right, even though the `procmap` project shows this better and in more detail).

Memory Management Internals - Essentials

I will leave it as an exercise to you to run this kernel module and carefully study the output on your x86_64, or whichever box or VM. Do carefully go through the code as well. We printed the user space details that you see in the preceding screenshot, such as the segment start and end addresses, by dereferencing the `mm_struct` structure (the task structure member named mm) from `current`. Recall, mm is the abstraction of the user mapping of the process. A small snippet of the code that does this is as follows:

```c
// ch7/show_kernel_seg/kernel_seg.c
[ ... ]
static void show_userspace_info(void)
{
    pr_info (
    "+------------ Above is kernel-seg; below, user VAS   ----------+\n"
    ELLPS
    "|Process environment "
    " %px - %px | [ %4zd bytes]\n"
    "| arguments "
    " %px - %px | [ %4zd bytes]\n"
    "| stack start %px\n"
    [...],
        SHOW_DELTA_b(current->mm->env_start, current->mm->env_end),
        SHOW_DELTA_b(current->mm->arg_start, current->mm->arg_end),
        current->mm->start_stack,
    [...]
```

Remember the so-called null trap page at the very beginning of the user VAS? (Again, `procmap`'s output – see *Figure 7.9* – shows the null trap page.) Let's see what it's for in the following section.

The null trap page

Did you notice how the preceding diagrams (Figure 7.9) and, in and Figure 7.12, at the extreme left edge (albeit very small!), a single page at the very beginning of the user space, named the **null trap** page? What is it? That's easy: virtual page 0 is given no permissions (at the hardware MMU/PTE level). Thus, any access to this page, be it r, w, or x (read/write/execute), will result in the MMU raising what is called a fault or exception. This will have the processor jump to an OS handler routine (the fault handler). It runs, killing the culprit trying to access a memory region with no permissions!

It's very interesting indeed: the OS handler mentioned previously runs in process context, and guess what `current` is: why, it's the process (or thread) that initiated this bad `NULL` pointer lookup! Within the fault handler code, the `SIGSEGV` signal is delivered to the faulting process (`current`), causing it to die (via a segfault). In a nutshell, this is how the well-known `NULL` pointer dereference bug is caught by the OS.

Viewing kernel documentation on the memory layout

Back to the kernel segment; obviously, with a 64-bit VAS, the kernel segment is *much* larger than on 32-bit. As we saw earlier, it's typically 128 TB on the x86_64. Study again the VM split table shown previously (Figure 7.4 in the section *VM split on 64-bit Linux systems*); there, the fourth column is the VM split for different architectures. You can see how on the 64-bit Intel/AMD and AArch64 (ARM64), the numbers are much larger than for their 32-bit counterparts. For arch-specific details, we refer you to the 'official' kernel documentation on the process virtual memory layout here:

Architecture	Documentation location in kernel source tree
ARM-32	`Documentation/arm/memory.txt`.
AArch64	`Documentation/arm64/memory.txt`.
x86_64	`Documentation/x86/x86_64/mm.txt` Note: this document's readability was vastly improved recently (as of the time of writing) with commit `32b8976` for Linux 4.20: `https://github.com/torvalds/linux/commit/32b89760ddf4477da436c272be2abc016e169031`. I recommend you browse through this file: `https://www.kernel.org/doc/Documentation/x86/x86_64/mm.txt`.

> **TIP**: At the risk of repetition, I urge you to try out this `show_kernel_seg` kernel module – and, even better, the `procmap` project (`https://github.com/kaiwan/procmap`) – on different Linux systems and study the output. You can then literally see the "memory map" – the complete process VAS – of any given process, which includes the kernel segment! This understanding is critical when working with and/or debugging issues at the system layer.

Again, at the risk of overstating it, the previous two sections – covering the detailed examination of the *user and kernel VASes* – are very important indeed. Do take the time required to go over them and work on the sample code and assignments. Great going!

Moving along on our journey through the Linux kernel's memory management, let's now check out another interesting topic – that of the [K]ASLR protection-via-memory-layout-randomization feature. Read on!

Randomizing the memory layout – KASLR

In infosec circles, it's a well-known fact that, with **proc filesystem (procfs)** and various powerful tools at their disposal, a malicious user, knowing in advance the precise location (virtual addresses) of various functions and/or globals with a process's VAS, could devise an attack to exploit and ultimately compromise a given system. Thus, for security, to make it impossible (or at least difficult) for attackers to rely on "known" virtual addresses, user space as well as kernel space supports **ASLR (Address Space Layout Randomization)** and **KASLR (Kernel ASLR)** techniques (often pronounced *Ass-ler / Kass-ler*).

The keyword here is *randomization:* this feature, when enabled, *changes the location* of portions of the process (and kernel) memory layout in terms of absolute numbers as it *offsets portions of memory* from a given base address by a random (page-aligned) quantity. What "portions of memory" exactly are we talking about? With respect to user space mappings (we will talk about KASLR later), the starting addresses of shared libraries (their load address), `mmap(2)`-based allocations (remember, any `malloc()` function (`/calloc/realloc`) above 128 KB becomes an `mmap`-based allocation, not off the heap), stack start, the heap, and the vDSO page; all of these can be randomized at process run (launch) time.

Hence, an attacker cannot depend on, say, a `glibc` function (such as `system(3)`) being mapped at a particular fixed UVA in any given process; not only that, the location will vary every time the process runs! Before ASLR, and on systems where ASLR is unsupported or turned off, the location of symbols can be ascertained in advance for a given architecture and software version (procfs plus utilities like `objdump`, `readelf`, `nm`, and so on make this quite easy).

It's key to realize that [K]ASLR is merely a statistical protection. In fact, typically, not many bits are available for randomization and thus the entropy isn't very good. This implies that the page-sized offsets are not too many, even on 64-bit systems, thus leading to a possibly weakened implementation.

Let's now briefly look at a few more details regarding both user mode and kernel-mode ASLR (the latter being referred to as KASLR); the following sections cover these areas, respectively.

User-mode ASLR

User-mode ASLR is usually what is meant by the term ASLR. It being enabled implies this protection to be available on the user space mapping of every process. Effectively, ASLR being enabled implies that the absolute memory map of user-mode processes will vary every time they're run.

ASLR has been supported on Linux for a very long time (since 2005 on 2.6.12). The kernel has a tunable pseudo-file within procfs, to query and set (as root) the ASLR status; here it is: `/proc/sys/kernel/randomize_va_space`.

It can have three possible values; the three values and their meaning are shown in the following table:

Tunable value	Interpretation of this value in `/proc/sys/kernel/randomize_va_space`
0	(User mode) ASLR turned OFF; or can be turned off by passing the kernel parameter `norandmaps` at boot.
1	(User mode) ASLR is ON: `mmap(2)` based allocations, the stack, and the vDSO page is randomized. It also implies that shared library load locations and shared memory segments are randomized.
2	(User mode) ASLR is ON: all of the preceding (value 1) *plus* the heap location is randomized (since 2.6.25); this is the OS value by default.

(As noted in an earlier section, *The vsyscall page*, the vDSO page is a system call optimization, allowing some frequently issued system calls (`gettimeofday(2)` being a typical one) to be invoked with less overhead. If interested, you can look up more details on the man page on vDSO(7) here: https://man7.org/linux/man-pages/man7/vdso.7.html.)

User-mode ASLR can be turned *off* at boot by passing the `norandmaps` parameter to the kernel (via the bootloader).

Memory Management Internals - Essentials

KASLR

Similar to (user) ASLR – and, more recently, from the 3.14 kernel onward – even *kernel* VAS can be randomized (to some extent) by having KASLR enabled. Here, the base location of the kernel and module code within the kernel segment will be randomized by a page-aligned random offset from the base of RAM. This remains in effect for that session; that is, until a power cycle or reboot.

Several kernel configuration variables exist, enabling the platform developer to enable or disable these randomization options. As an example specific to the x86, the following is quoted directly from `Documentation/x86/x86_64/mm.txt`:

> "Note that if CONFIG_RANDOMIZE_MEMORY is enabled, the direct mapping of all physical memory, vmalloc/ioremap space and virtual memory map are randomized. Their order is preserved but their base will be offset early at boot time."

KASLR can be controlled at boot time by passing a parameter to the kernel (via the bootloader):

- Explicitly turned *off* by passing the `nokaslr` parameter
- Explicitly turned *on* by passing the `kaslr` parameter

So, what is the current setting on your Linux system? And can we change it? Yes, of course (provided we have *root* access); the next section shows you how to do so via a Bash script.

Querying/setting KASLR status with a script

We provide a simple Bash script at `<book-source>/ch7/ASLR_check.sh`. It checks for the presence of both (user-mode) ASLR as well as KASLR, printing (color-coded!) status information about them. It also allows you to change the ASLR value.

Let's give it a spin on our x86_64 Ubuntu 18.04 guest. As our script is programmed to be color-coded, we show a screenshot of its output here:

```
$ sudo ./ASLR_check.sh
++++++++++++++++++++++++++++++++++++++++++++++++++++++++++++++++++++++++++++
Simple [Kernel] Address Space Layout Randomization / [K]ASLR checks:
Usage: ASLR_check.sh [ASLR_value] ; where 'ASLR_value' is one of:
 0 = turn OFF ASLR
 1 = turn ON ASLR only for stack, VDSO, shmem regions
 2 = turn ON ASLR for stack, VDSO, shmem regions and data segments [OS default]

The 'ASLR_value' parameter, setting the ASLR value, is optional; in any case,
I shall run the checks... thanks and visit again!
++++++++++++++++++++++++++++++++++++++++++++++++++++++++++++++++++++++++++++
[+] Checking for (usermode) ASLR support now ...
 (in /proc/sys/kernel/randomize_va_space)
 Current (usermode) ASLR setting = 2
 => (usermode) ASLR ON: mmap(2)-based allocations, stack, vDSO page,
   shlib, shmem locations and heap are randomized on startup
++++++++++++++++++++++++++++++++++++++++++++++++++++++++++++++++++++++++++++
[+] Checking for kernel ASLR (KASLR) support now ...
 (this kernel is ver 5.4.0-llkd01, need >= 3.14)
 Kernel ASLR (KASLR) is On [default]
++++++++++++++++++++++++++++++++++++++++++++++++++++++++++++++++++++++++++++
ASLR quick test:
Doing
 egrep "heap|stack" /proc/self/maps
twice:

560915f82000-560915fa3000 rw-p 00000000 00:00 0                      [heap]
7ffdb94d5000-7ffdb94f6000 rw-p 00000000 00:00 0                      [stack]

55852f9f1000-55852fa12000 rw-p 00000000 00:00 0                      [heap]
7ffc8cc04000-7ffc8cc25000 rw-p 00000000 00:00 0                      [stack]

With ASLR:
  enabled: the uva's (user virtual addresses) should differ in each run
  disabled: the uva's (user virtual addresses) should be the same in each run.
```

Figure 7.17 – Screenshot showing the output when our ch7/ASLR_check.sh Bash script runs on an x86_64 Ubuntu guest

It runs, showing you that (at least on this box) both the user mode as well as KASLR are indeed turned on. Not only that, we write a small "test" routine to see ASLR functioning. It's very simple: it runs the following command twice:

```
grep -E "heap|stack" /proc/self/maps
```

From what you learned in an earlier section, *Interpreting the /proc/PID/maps output*, you can now see in Figure 7.17, that the UVAs for the heap and stack segments are *different in each run*, thus proving that the ASLR feature indeed works! For example, look at the starting heap UVA: in the first run, it's `0x5609 15f8 2000`, and in the second run, it's `0x5585 2f9f 1000`.

[369]

Memory Management Internals - Essentials

Next, we will perform a sample run where we pass the parameter 0 to the script, thus turning ASLR off; the following screenshot shows the (expected) output:

```
$ sudo ./ASLR_check.sh 0
++++++++++++++++++++++++++++++++++++++++++++++++++++++++++++++++++++++++
Simple [Kernel] Address Space Layout Randomization / [K]ASLR checks:
Usage: ASLR_check.sh [ASLR_value] ; where 'ASLR_value' is one of:
 0 = turn OFF ASLR
 1 = turn ON ASLR only for stack, VDSO, shmem regions
 2 = turn ON ASLR for stack, VDSO, shmem regions and data segments [OS default]

The 'ASLR_value' parameter, setting the ASLR value, is optional; in any case,
I shall run the checks... thanks and visit again!
++++++++++++++++++++++++++++++++++++++++++++++++++++++++++++++++++++++++
[+] Checking for (usermode) ASLR support now ...
 (in /proc/sys/kernel/randomize_va_space)
 Current (usermode) ASLR setting = 2
 => (usermode) ASLR ON: mmap(2)-based allocations, stack, vDSO page,
 shlib, shmem locations and heap are randomized on startup
++++++++++++++++++++++++++++++++++++++++++++++++++++++++++++++++++++++++
[+] Checking for kernel ASLR (KASLR) support now ...
 (this kernel is ver 5.4.0-llkd01, need >= 3.14)
 Kernel ASLR (KASLR) is On [default]
++++++++++++++++++++++++++++++++++++++++++++++++++++++++++++++++++++++++
[+] Setting (usermode) ASLR value to "0" now...
ASLR setting now is: 0
 => (usermode) ASLR is curently OFF
++++++++++++++++++++++++++++++++++++++++++++++++++++++++++++++++++++++++
ASLR quick test:
Doing
 egrep "heap|stack" /proc/self/maps
twice:

55555578a000-5555557ac000 rw-p 00000000 00:00 0                          [heap]
7fffffffde000-7fffffffff000 rw-p 00000000 00:00 0                        [stack]

55555578a000-5555557ac000 rw-p 00000000 00:00 0                          [heap]
7fffffffde000-7fffffffff000 rw-p 00000000 00:00 0                        [stack]

With ASLR:
  enabled: the uva's (user virtual addresses) should differ in each run
  disabled: the uva's (user virtual addresses) should be the same in each run.
```

Figure 7.18 – Screenshot showing how ASLR is turned off (via our ch7/ASLR_check.sh script on an x86_64 Ubuntu guest)

This time, we can see that ASLR was on by default, but we turned it off. This is clearly highlighted in bold font and red in the preceding screenshot. (Do remember to turn it on again.) Also, as expected, as it's off, the UVAs of both the heap and stack (respectively) remain the same in both test runs, which is insecure. I will leave it to you to browse through and understand the source code of the script.

> **TIP:** To take advantage of ASLR, applications must be compiled with the `-fPIE` and `-pie` GCC flags (**PIE** stands for **Position Independent Executable**).

Both ASLR and KASLR protect against some types of attack vectors, the return-to-libc, **Return-Oriented Programming** (ROP) ones being the typical cases. However, and unfortunately, white and black hat security being the cat-and-mouse game it is, defeating [K]ASLR and similar methodologies is something advanced exploits do quite well. Refer to this chapter's *Further reading* section (under the *Linux kernel security* heading) for more details.

> **TIP:** While on the topic of security, many useful tools exist to carry out vulnerability checks on your system. Check out the following:
>
> - The `checksec.sh` script (http://www.trapkit.de/tools/checksec.html) displays various "hardening" measures and their current status (for both individual files and processes): RELRO, stack canary, NX-enabled, PIE, RPATH, RUNPATH, presence of symbols, and compiler fortification.
> - grsecurity's PaX suite.
> - The `hardening-check` script (an alternative to checksec).
> - The `kconfig-hardened-check` Perl script (https://github.com/a13xp0p0v/kconfig-hardened-check) checks (and suggests) kernel config options for security against some predefined checklists.
> - Several others: Lynis, `linuxprivchecker.py`, memory, and so on.

So, the next time you see differing kernel or user virtual addresses on multiple runs or sessions, you will know it's probably due to the [K]ASLR protection feature. Now, let's complete this chapter by moving on to an exploration of how the Linux kernel organizes and works with physical memory.

Physical memory

Now that we have examined the *virtual memory* view, for both user and kernel VASes in some detail, let's turn to the topic of physical memory organization on the Linux OS.

Physical RAM organization

The Linux kernel, at boot, organizes and partitions physical RAM into a tree-like hierarchy consisting of nodes, zones, and page frames (page frames are physical pages of RAM) (see Figure 7.19 and Figure 7.20). Nodes are divided into zones, and zones consist of page frames. A node abstracts a physical "bank" of RAM, which will be associated with one or more processor (CPU) cores. At the hardware level, the microprocessors are connected to the RAM controller chip(s); any memory controller chip, and thus any RAM, can be reached from any CPU as well, across an interconnect. Now, obviously, being able to reach the RAM physically nearest the core on which a thread is allocating (kernel) memory will lead to performance enhancement. This very idea is leveraged by hardware and OSes that support the so-called NUMA model (the meaning is explained shortly).

Nodes

Essentially, *nodes* are data structures used to denote a physical RAM module on the system motherboard and its associated controller chipset. Yes, we're talking actual *hardware* here being abstracted via software metadata. It's always associated with a physical socket (or collection of processor cores) on the system motherboard. Two types of hierarchies exist:

- **Non-Uniform Memory Access (NUMA) systems**: Where the core on which a kernel allocation request occurs does matter (memory is treated *non* uniformly), leading to performance improvements
- **Uniform Memory Access (UMA) systems**: Where the core on which a kernel allocation request occurs doesn't matter (memory is treated uniformly)

True NUMA systems are those whose hardware is multicore (two or more CPU cores, SMP) *and* have two or more physical "banks" of RAM each of which is associated with a CPU (or CPUs). In other words, NUMA systems will always have two or more nodes, whereas UMA systems will have exactly one node (FYI, the data structure that abstracts a node is called `pg_data_t` and is defined here: `include/linux/mmzone.h:pg_data_t`).

Why all this complexity, you may wonder? Well, it's – what else – all about performance! NUMA systems (they typically tend to be rather expensive server-class machines) and the OSes they run (Linux/Unix/Windows, typically) are designed in such a way that when a process (or thread) on a particular CPU core wants to perform a kernel memory allocation, the software guarantees that it does so with high performance by taking the required memory (RAM) from the node closest to the core (hence the NUMA moniker!). No such benefits accrue to UMA systems (your typical embedded systems, smartphones, laptops, and desktops), nor do they matter. Enterprise-class server systems nowadays can have hundreds of processors and terabytes, even a few petabytes, of RAM! These are almost always architected as NUMA systems.

With the way that Linux is designed, though – and this is a key point – even regular UMA systems are treated as NUMA by the kernel (well, pseudo-NUMA). They will have *exactly one node;* so that's a quick way to check whether the system is NUMA or UMA – if there are two or more nodes, it's a true NUMA system; only one, and it's a "fake NUMA" or pseudo-NUMA box. How can you check? The `numactl(8)` utility is one way (try doing `numactl --hardware`). There are other ways to (via *procfs* itself). Hang on a bit, you'll get there...

So, a simpler way to visualize this: on a NUMA box, one or more CPU cores is associated with a "bank" (a hardware module) of physical RAM. Thus, a NUMA system is always a **Symmetric Multi Processor (SMP)** one.

To make this discussion practical, let's briefly visualize the micro-architecture of an actual server system – one running the AMD Epyc/Ryzen/Threadripper (and the older Bulldozer) CPUs. It has the following:

- A total of 32 CPU cores (as seen by the OS) within two physical sockets (P#0 and P#1) on the motherboard. Each socket consists of a package of 8x2 CPU cores (8x2, as there are actually 8 physical cores each of which is hyperthreaded; the OS sees even the hyperthreaded cores as usable cores).
- A total of 32 GB of RAM split up into four physical banks of 8 GB each.

Memory Management Internals - Essentials

Thus, the Linux memory management code, upon detecting this topography at boot, will set up *four nodes* to represent it. (We won't delve into the processor's various (L1/L2/L3/etc) caches here; see the *Tip* box after the following diagram for a way to see all of this.)

The following conceptual diagram shows an approximation of the four tree-like hierarchies – one for each node – formed on some AMD server systems running the Linux OS. Figure 7.19 conceptually shows the nodes/zones/page frames per physical RAM bank on the system coupled to different CPU cores:

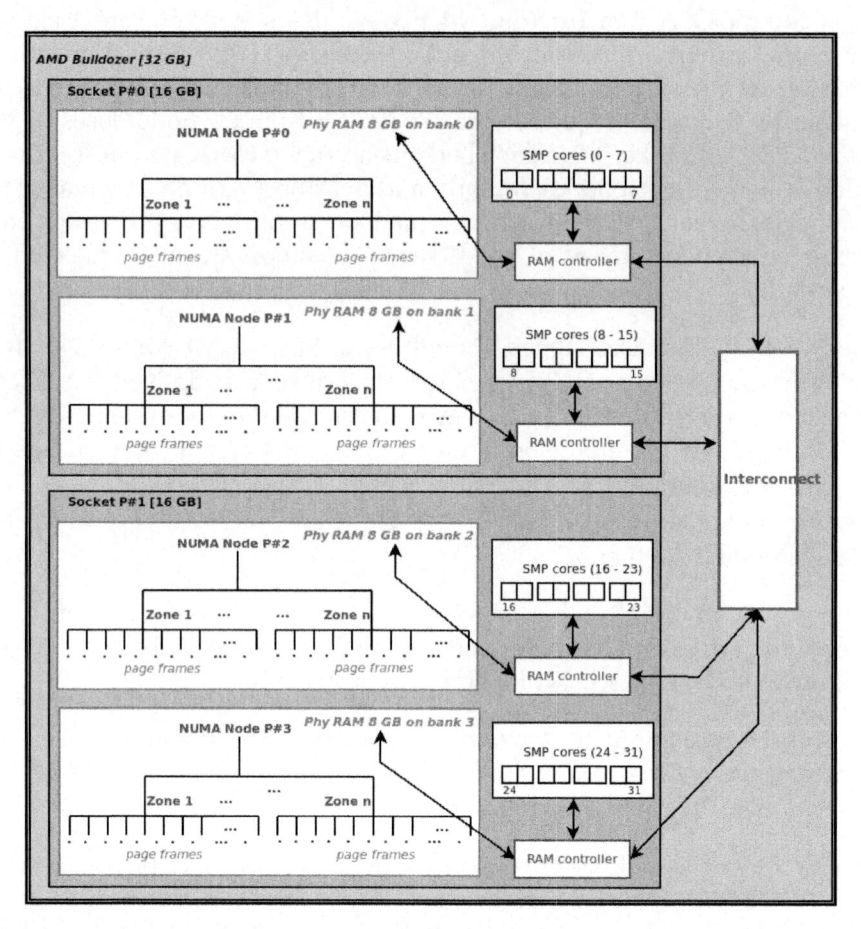

Figure 7.19 – (An approximate conceptual view of an) AMD server: physical memory hierarchy on Linux

> **TIP**: Use the powerful `lstopo(1)` utility (and its associated `hwloc-*` – hardware locality – utilities) to graphically view the hardware (CPU) topology of your system! (On Ubuntu, install it with `sudo apt install hwloc`). FYI, the hardware topography graphic of the previously mentioned AMD server system, generated by `lstopo(1)`, can be seen here: https://en.wikipedia.org/wiki/CPU_cache#/media/File:Hwloc.png.

To reassert the key point here: for performance (here with respect to Figure 7.19), a thread running some kernel or driver code in process context on, say, CPU #18 or above requests the kernel for some RAM. The kernel's MM layer, understanding NUMA, will have the request serviced (as first priority) from any free RAM page frames in any zone on NUMA node #2 (that is, from physical RAM bank #2) as it's "closest" to the processor core that the request was issued upon. Just in case there are no free page frames available in any zone within NUMA node #2, the kernel has an intelligent fallback system. It might now go across the interconnect and request RAM page frames from another **node:zone** (worry not, we cover these aspects in more detail in the following chapter).

Zones

Zones can be thought of as Linux's way of smoothing out and dealing with hardware quirks. These proliferate on the x86, where Linux "grew up," of course. They also deal with a few software difficulties (look up `ZONE_HIGHMEM` on the now mostly legacy 32-bit i386 architecture; we discussed this concept in an earlier section, *High memory on 32-bit systems*).

Memory Management Internals - Essentials

Zones consist of *page frames* – physical pages of RAM. More technically, a range of **Page Frame Numbers (PFNs)** are allocated to each zone within a node:

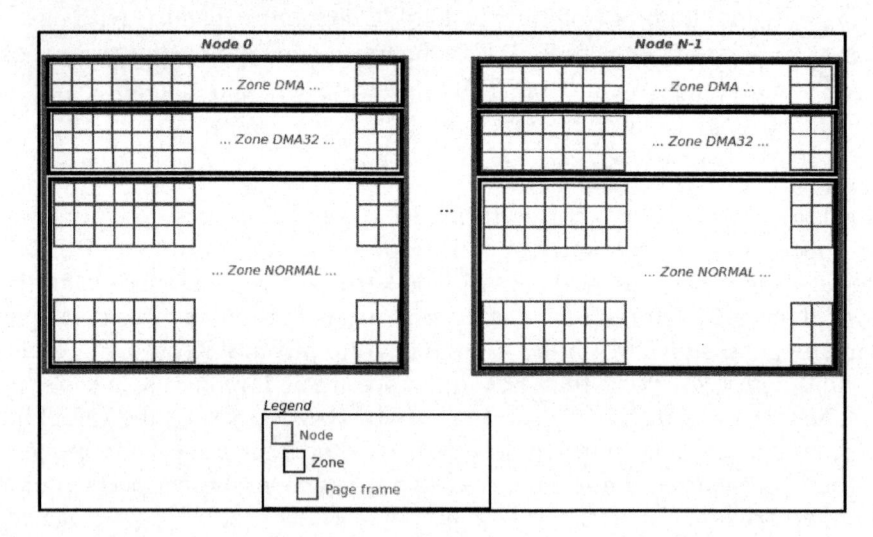

Figure 7.20 – Another view of the physical memory hierarchy on Linux – nodes, zones, and page frames

In Figure 7.10, you can see a generic (example) Linux system with N nodes (from 0 to $N-1$), each node consisting of (say) three zones, each zone being made up of physical pages of RAM – *page frames*. The number (and name) of zones per node is dynamically determined by the kernel at boot. You can check out the hierarchy on a Linux system by delving under *procfs*. In the following code, we take a peek into a native Linux x86_64 system with 16 GB of RAM:

```
$ cat /proc/buddyinfo
Node 0, zone      DMA      3      2      4      3      3      1      0      0      1      1      3
Node 0, zone    DMA32  31306  10918   1373    942    505    196     48     16      4      0      0
Node 0, zone   Normal  49135   7455   1917    535    237     89     19      3      0      0      0
$
```

The leftmost column reveals that we have exactly one node – `Node 0`. This tells us we're actually on an *UMA system*, though of course the Linux OS will treat it as a (pseudo/fake) NUMA system. This single node 0 is split into three zones, labeled `DMA`, `DMA32`, and `Normal`, and each zone, of course, consists of page frames. For now, ignore the numbers on the right; we will get to their meaning in the following chapter.

Another way to notice how Linux "fakes" a NUMA node on UMA systems is visible from the kernel log. We run the following command on the same native x86_64 system with 16 GB of RAM. For readability, I replaced the first few columns showing the timestamp and hostname with ellipses:

```
$ journalctl -b -k --no-pager | grep -A7 "NUMA"
 <...>: No NUMA configuration found
 <...>: Faking a node at [mem 0x0000000000000000-0x00000004427fffff]
 <...>: NODE_DATA(0) allocated [mem 0x4427d5000-0x4427fffff]
 <...>: Zone ranges:
   <...>:DMA      [mem 0x0000000000001000-0x0000000000ffffff]
 <...>:    DMA32    [mem 0x0000000001000000-0x00000000ffffffff]
 <...>:    Normal   [mem 0x0000000100000000-0x00000004427fffff]
 <...>:    Device   empty
$
```

We can clearly see that, as the system is detected as not NUMA (thus, UMA), the kernel fakes a node. The extents of the node are the total amount of RAM on the system (here, `0x0-0x00000004427fffff`, which is indeed 16 GB). We can also see that on this particular system, the kernel instantiates three zones – DMA, DMA32, and Normal – to organize the available physical page frames of RAM. This is fine and ties in with the /proc/buddyinfo output we saw previously. FYI, the data structure representing the *zone* on Linux is defined here: `include/linux/mmzone.h: struct zone`. We will have occasion to visit it later in the book.

To better understand how the Linux kernel organizes RAM, let's start at the very beginning – boot time.

Direct-mapped RAM and address translation

At boot, the Linux kernel "maps" all (usable) system RAM (aka *platform RAM*) directly into the kernel segment. So, we have the following:

- Physical page frame 0 maps to kernel virtual page 0.
- Physical page frame 1 maps to kernel virtual page 1.
- Physical page frame 2 maps to kernel virtual page 2, and so on.

Thus, we call this a 1:1 or direct mapping, identity-mapped RAM, or linear addresses. A key point is that all these kernel virtual pages are at a fixed offset from their physical counterparts (and, as already mentioned, these kernel addresses are referred to as kernel logical addresses). The fixed offset is the PAGE_OFFSET value (here, 0xc000 0000).

Memory Management Internals - Essentials

So, think of this. On a 32-bit system with a 3:1 (GB) VM split, physical address `0x0` = kernel logical address `0xc000 0000` (`PAGE_OFFSET`). As already mentioned, the terminology *kernel logical address* is applied to kernel addresses that are at a fixed offset from their physical counterparts. Thus, direct-mapped RAM maps to kernel logical addresses. This region of direct-mapped memory is often referred to as the *low-memory* (or simply, **lowmem**) region within the kernel segment.

We have already shown an almost identical diagram earlier, in Figure 7.10. In the following figure, it's slightly modified to actually show you how the first three (physical) page frames of RAM map to the first three kernel virtual pages (in the lowmem region of the kernel segment):

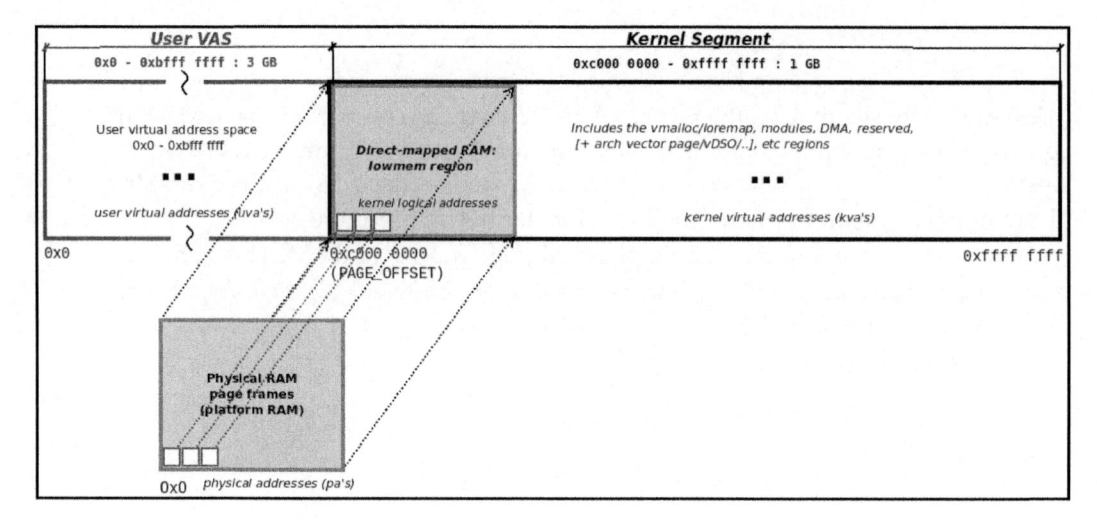

Figure 7.21 – Direct-mapped RAM – lowmem region, on 32-bit with a 3:1 (GB) VM split

As an example, Figure 7.21 shows a direct mapping of platform RAM to the kernel segment on a 32-bit system with a 3:1 (GB) VM split. The point where physical RAM address `0x0` maps into the kernel is the `PAGE_OFFSET` kernel macro (in the preceding figure, it's kernel logical address `0xc000 0000`). Notice how Figure 7.21 also shows the *user VAS* on the left side, ranging from `0x0` to `PAGE_OFFSET-1` (of size `TASK_SIZE` bytes). We have already covered details on the remainder of the kernel segment in the *Examining the kernel segment* section previously.

Understanding this mapping of physical-to-virtual pages might well tempt you into reaching these seemingly logical conclusions:

- Given a KVA, to calculate the corresponding **Physical Address (PA)** – that is, to perform a KVA-to-PA calculation – simply do this:

    ```
    pa = kva - PAGE_OFFSET
    ```

- Conversely, given a PA, to calculate the corresponding KVA – that is, to perform a PA-to-KVA calculation – simply do this:

    ```
    kva = pa + PAGE_OFFSET
    ```

Do refer to Figure 7.21 again. The direct mapping of RAM to the kernel segment (starting at PAGE_OFFSET) certainly predicates this conclusion. So, it is correct. But hang on, please pay careful attention here: **these address translation calculations work only for direct-mapped or linear addresses** – in other words, KVAs (technically, the kernel logical addresses) – **within the kernel's lowmem region, nothing else!** For all UVAs, and any and all KVAs *besides* the lowmem region (which includes module addresses, vmalloc/ioremap (MMIO) addresses, KASAN addresses, the (possible) highmem region addresses, DMA memory regions, and so on), it does *not* work!

As you will anticipate, the kernel does indeed provide APIs to perform these address conversions; of course, their implementation is arch-dependent. Here they are:

Kernel API	What it does
`phys_addr_t virt_to_phys(volatile void *address)`	Converts the given virtual address to its physical counterpart (return value)
`void *phys_to_virt(phys_addr_t address)`	Converts the given physical address to a virtual address (return value)

The `virt_to_phys()` API for the x86 has a comment above it clearly advocating that this API (and its ilk) are **not to be used by driver authors**; for clarity and completeness, we have reproduced the comment in the kernel source here:

```
// arch/x86/include/asm/io.h
[...]
/**
 * virt_to_phys     -   map virtual addresses to physical
 * @address: address to remap
 *
 * The returned physical address is the physical (CPU) mapping for
 * the memory address given. It is only valid to use this function on
```

[379]

Memory Management Internals - Essentials

```
 *    addresses directly mapped or allocated via kmalloc.
 *
 *    This function does not give bus mappings for DMA transfers. In
 *    almost all conceivable cases a device driver should not be using
 *    this function
 */
static inline phys_addr_t virt_to_phys(volatile void *address)
[...]
```

The preceding comment mentions the (very common) `kmalloc()` API. Worry not, it's covered in depth in the following two chapters. Of course, a similar comment to the preceding is in place for the `phys_to_virt()` API as well.

> So who – sparingly – uses these address conversion APIs (and the like)? The kernel internal *mm* code, of course! As a demo, we do actually use them in at least a couple of places in this book: in the following chapter, in an LKM called `ch8/lowlevel_mem` (well actually, its usage is within a function in our "kernel library" code, `klib_llkd.c`).
>
> FYI, the powerful `crash(8)` utility can indeed translate any given virtual address to a physical address via its `vtop` (virtual-to-physical) command (and vice versa, via its `ptov` command!).

Moving along, another key point: by mapping all physical RAM into it, do not get misled into thinking that the kernel is *reserving* RAM for itself. No, it isn't; it's merely *mapping* all of the available RAM, thus making it available for allocation to anyone who wants it – core kernel code, kernel threads, device drivers, or user space applications. This is part of the job of the OS; it is the system resource manager, after all. Of course, a certain portion of RAM will be taken up (allocated) – by the static kernel code, data, kernel page table, and so on – at boot, no doubt, but you should realize that this is quite small. As an example, on my guest VM with 1 GB RAM, the kernel code, data, and BSS typically take up a combined total of about 25 MB of RAM. All kernel memory comes to about 100 MB, whereas user space memory usage is in the region of 550 MB! It's almost always user space that is the memory hogger.

> **TIP:** You can try using the `smem(8)` utility with the `--system -p` option switches to see a summary of memory usage as percentages (also, use the `--realmem=` switch to pass the actual amount of RAM on the system).

Back to the point: we know that kernel page tables are set up early in the boot process. So, by the time applications start up, *the kernel has all RAM mapped and available*, ready for allocation! Thus, we understand that while the kernel *direct-maps* page frames into its VAS, user mode processes are not so lucky – they can only *indirectly map* page frames via the paging tables set up by the OS (at process creation – `fork(2)` – time) on a per-process basis. Again, it's interesting to realize that memory mapping via the powerful `mmap(2)` system call can provide the illusion of "direct mapping" files or anonymous pages into the user VAS.

> A few additional points to note:
>
> (a) For performance, kernel memory (kernel pages) can *never be swapped*, even if they aren't in use
>
> (b) Sometimes, you might think, it's quite obvious that *user space memory pages map to (physical) page frames (assuming the page is resident) via the paging tables set up by the OS on a per-process basis*. Yes, but what about kernel memory pages? Please be very clear on this point: *all kernel pages also map to page frames via the kernel "master" paging table. Kernel memory, too, is virtualized, just as user space memory is.*
>
> In this regard, for you, the interested reader, a QnA I initiated on Stack Overflow: *How exactly do kernel virtual addresses get translated to physical RAM?*: http://stackoverflow.com/questions/36639607/how-exactly-do-kernel-virtual-addresses-get-translated-to-physical-ram.
>
> (c) Several memory optimization techniques have been baked into the Linux kernel (well, many are configuration options); among them are **Transparent Huge Pages** (THPs) and, critical for cloud/virtualization workloads, **Kernel Samepage Merging** (KSM, aka memory de-duplication). I refer you to the *Further reading* section of this chapter for more information.

Alright, with this coverage on some aspects of physical RAM management behind us, we complete this chapter; excellent progress!

Summary

In this chapter, we delved – in quite some depth – into the big topic of kernel memory management in a level of detail sufficient for a kernel module or device driver author like you; also, there's more to come! A key piece of the puzzle – the VM split and how it's achieved on various architectures running the Linux OS – served as a starting point. We then moved into a deep examination of both regions of this split: first, user space (the process VAS) and then the kernel VAS (or kernel segment). Here, we covered many details and tools/utilities on how to examine it (notably, via the quite powerful `procmap` utility). We built a demo kernel module that can literally generate a pretty complete memory map of the kernel and the calling process. User and kernel memory layout randomization technology ([K]ASLR) was also briefly discussed. We closed the chapter by taking a look at the physical organization of RAM within Linux.

All of this information and the concepts learned within this chapter are actually *very useful*; not only for designing and writing better kernel/device driver code but very much also when you encounter system-level issues and bugs.

This chapter has been a long and indeed a critical one; great job on completing it! Next, in the following two chapters, you will move on to learning key and practical aspects of how exactly to allocate (and deallocate) kernel memory efficiently, along with related important concepts behind this common activity. On, on!

Questions

As we conclude, here is a list of questions for you to test your knowledge regarding this chapter's material: `https://github.com/PacktPublishing/Linux-Kernel-Programming/tree/master/questions`. You will find some of the questions answered in the book's GitHub repo: `https://github.com/PacktPublishing/Linux-Kernel-Programming/tree/master/solutions_to_assgn`.

Further reading

To help you delve deeper into the subject with useful materials, we provide a rather detailed list of online references and links (and at times, even books) in a Further reading document in this book's GitHub repository. The *Further reading* document is available here: `https://github.com/PacktPublishing/Linux-Kernel-Programming/blob/master/Further_Reading.md`.

8
Kernel Memory Allocation for Module Authors - Part 1

In the previous two chapters, one on kernel internal aspects and architecture and the other on the essentials of memory management internals, we covered key aspects that serve as required background information for this and the following chapter. In this and the next chapter, we will get down to the actual allocation and freeing of kernel memory by various means. We will demonstrate this via kernel modules that you can test and tweak, elaborate on the whys and hows of it, and provide many real-world tips and tricks to enable a kernel or driver developer like you to gain maximum efficiency when working with memory within your kernel module.

In this chapter, we will cover the kernel's two primary memory allocators – the **Page Allocator (PA)** (aka **Buddy System Allocator (BSA)**) and the slab allocator. We will delve into the nitty-gritty of working with their APIs within kernel modules. Actually, we will go well beyond simply seeing how to use the APIs, clearly demonstrating why all is not optimal in all cases, and how to overcome these situations. Chapter 9, *Kernel Memory Allocation for Module Authors – Part 2*, will continue our coverage of the kernel memory allocators, delving into a few more advanced areas.

In this chapter, we will cover the following topics:

- Introducing kernel memory allocators
- Understanding and using the kernel page allocator (or BSA)
- Understanding and using the kernel slab allocator
- Size limitations of the kmalloc API
- Slab allocator - a few additional details
- Caveats when using the slab allocator

Technical requirements

I assume that you have gone through `Chapter 1`, *Kernel Workspace Setup*, and have appropriately prepared a guest **Virtual Machine** (**VM**) running Ubuntu 18.04 LTS (or a later stable release) and installed all the required packages. If not, I highly recommend you do this first.

To get the most out of this book, I strongly recommend you first set up the workspace environment, including cloning this book's GitHub repository (`https://github.com/PacktPublishing/Linux-Kernel-Programming`) for the code, and work on it in a hands-on fashion.

Refer to *Hands-On System Programming with Linux*, Kaiwan N Billimoria, Packt (`https://www.packtpub.com/networking-and-servers/hands-system-programming-linux`) as a prerequisite to this chapter (essential reading, really):

- Chapter 1, *Linux System Architecture*
- Chapter 2, *Virtual Memory*

Introducing kernel memory allocators

The Linux kernel, like any other OS, requires a sturdy algorithm and implementation to perform a really key task – the allocation and subsequent deallocation of memory or page frames (RAM). The primary (de)allocator engine in the Linux OS is referred to as the PA, or the BSA. Internally, it uses a so-called buddy system algorithm to efficiently organize and parcel out free chunks of system RAM. We will find more on the algorithm in the *Understanding and using the kernel page allocator (or BSA)* section.

> **TIP**
> In this chapter and in this book, when we use the notation *(de)allocate*, please read it as both words: *allocate* and *deallocate*.

Of course, being imperfect, the page allocator is not the only or always the best way to obtain and subsequently release system memory. Other technologies exist within the Linux kernel to do so. High on the list of them is the kernel's **slab allocator** or **slab cache** system (we use the word *slab* here as the generic name for this type of allocator as it originated with this name; in practice, though, the internal implementation of the modern slab allocator used by the Linux kernel is called SLUB (the unqueued slab allocator); more on this later).

Think of it this way: the slab allocator solves some issues and optimizes performance with the page allocator. What issues exactly? We shall soon see. For now, though, it's really important to understand that the only way in which to actually (de)allocate physical memory is via the page allocator. The page allocator is the primary engine for memory (de)allocation on the Linux OS!

> To avoid confusion and repetition, we will from now on refer to this primary allocation engine as the page allocator. You will understand that it's also known as the BSA (derived from the name of the algorithm that drives it).

Thus, the slab allocator is layered upon (or above) the page allocator. Various core kernel subsystems, as well as non-core code within the kernel, such as device drivers, can allocate (and deallocate) memory either directly via the page allocator or indirectly via the slab allocator; the following diagram illustrates this:

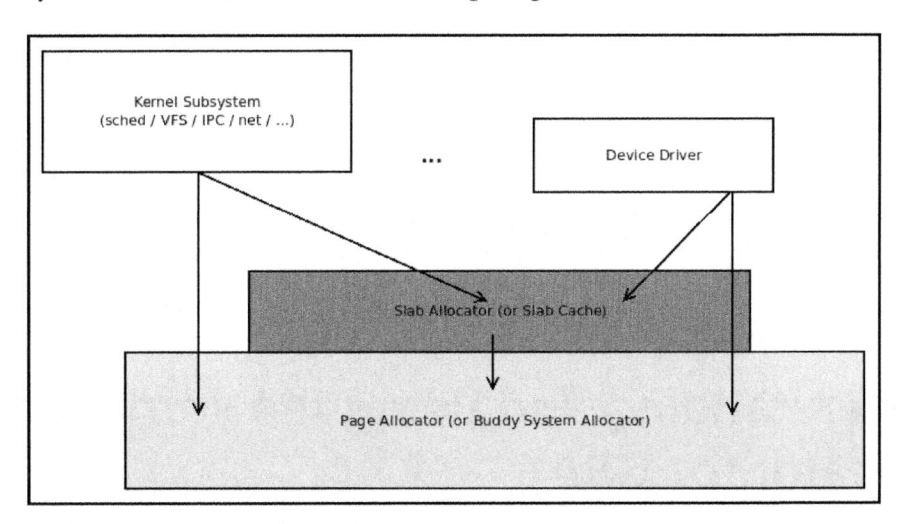

Figure 8.1 – Linux's page allocator engine with the slab allocator layered above it

A few things to be clear about at the outset:

- The entire Linux kernel and all of its core components and subsystems (excluding the memory management subsystem itself) ultimately use the page allocator (or BSA) for memory (de)allocation. This includes non-core stuff, such as kernel modules and device drivers.
- The preceding systems reside completely in kernel (virtual) address space and are not directly accessible from user space.

- The page frames (RAM) from where the page allocator gets memory is within the kernel lowmem region, or the direct-mapped RAM region of the kernel segment (we covered the kernel segment in detail in the previous chapter)
- The slab allocator is ultimately a user of the page allocator, and thus gets its memory from there itself (which again implies from the kernel lowmem region)
- User space dynamic memory allocation with the familiar `malloc` family of APIs does not directly map to the preceding layers (that is, calling `malloc(3)` in user space does *not* directly result in a call to the page or slab allocator). It does so indirectly. How exactly? You will learn how; patience! (This key coverage is found in two sections of the next chapter, in fact, involving demand paging; look out for it as you cover that chapter!)
- Also, to be clear, Linux kernel memory is non-swappable. It can never be swapped out to disk; this was decided in the early Linux days to keep performance high. User space memory pages are always swappable by default; this can be changed by the system programmer via the `mlock()`/`mlockall()` system calls.

Now, fasten your seatbelts! With this basic understanding of the page allocator and slab allocator, let's begin the journey on learning (the basics on) how the Linux kernel's memory allocators work and, more importantly, how to work well with them.

Understanding and using the kernel page allocator (or BSA)

In this section, you will learn about two aspects of the Linux kernel's primary (de)allocator engine:

- First, we will cover the fundamentals of the algorithm behind this software (called the buddy system).
- Then, we will cover the actual and practical usage of the APIs it exposes to the kernel or driver developer.

Understanding the basics of the algorithm behind the page allocator is important. You will then be able to understand the pros and cons of it, and thus, when and which APIs to use in which situation. Let's begin with its inner workings. Again, remember that the scope of this book with regard to the internal memory management details is limited. We will cover it to a depth deemed sufficient and no more.

The fundamental workings of the page allocator

We will break up this discussion into a few relevant parts. Let's begin with how the kernel's page allocator tracks free physical page frames via its freelist data structures.

Freelist organization

The key to the page allocator (buddy system) algorithm is its primary internal metadata structure. It's called the buddy system freelist and consists of an array of pointers to (the oh-so-common!) doubly linked circular lists. The index of this array of pointers is called the order of the list – it's the power to which to raise 2 to. The array length is from 0 to MAX_ORDER-1. The value of MAX_ORDER is arch-dependent. On the x86 and ARM, it's 11, whereas on a large-ish system such as the Itanium, it's 17. Thus, on the x86 and ARM, the order ranges from 2^0 to 2^{10}; that is, from 1 to 1,024. What does that mean? Do read on...

Each doubly linked circular list points to free physical contiguous page frames of size 2^{order}. Thus (assuming a 4 KB page size), we end up with lists of the following:

- 2^0 = 1 page = 4 KB chunks
- 2^1 = 2 pages = 8 KB chunks
- 2^2 = 4 pages = 16 KB chunks
- 2^3 = 8 pages = 32 KB chunks
- 2^{10} = 1024 pages = 1024*4 KB = 4 MB chunks

The following diagram is a simplified conceptual illustration of (a single instance of) the page allocator freelist:

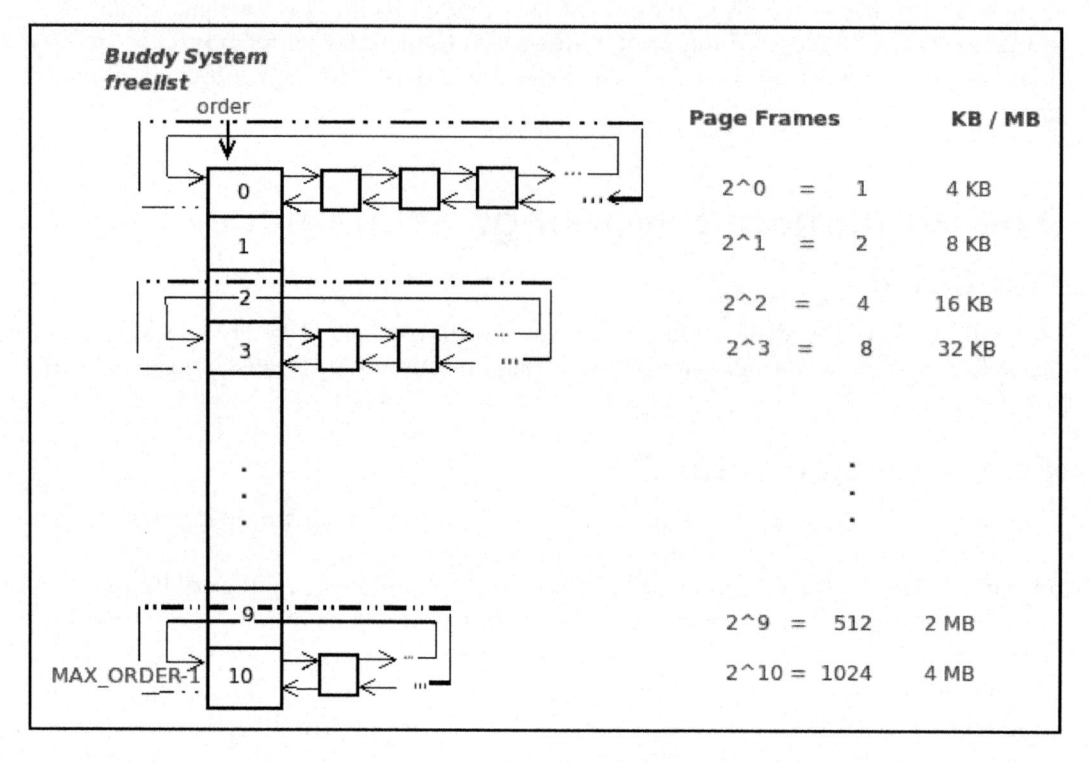

```
Buddy System
freelist
      order                              Page Frames           KB / MB

        0                                  2^0  =  1            4 KB
        1                                  2^1  =  2            8 KB
        2                                  2^2  =  4           16 KB
        3                                  2^3  =  8           32 KB
        .                                    .
        .                                    .
        .                                    .
        9                                  2^9  =  512          2 MB
MAX_ORDER-1  10                            2^10 =  1024         4 MB
```

Figure 8.2 – Buddy system/page allocator freelist on a system with 4 KB page size and MAX_ORDER of 11

In the preceding figure, each memory "chunk" is represented by a square box (to keep it simple, we use the same size in our diagram). Internally, of course, these aren't the actual memory pages; rather, the boxes represent metadata structures (struct page) that point to physical memory frames. On the right side of the figure, we show the size of each physically contiguous free memory chunk that could be enqueued on the list to the left.

The kernel gives us a convenient (summarized) view into the current state of the page allocator via the `proc` filesystem (on our Ubuntu guest VM with 1 GB RAM):

```
$ cat /proc/buddyinfo
Node 0, zone      DMA     35   24   37   28   13    5    4    1    0    0    0
Node 0, zone    DMA32   3173 1378  562  678  146   51   23    5    0    0    0
$
```

                    ↑   ↑   ↑
                    | | |
                 order 0 order 1   [...]   order 10

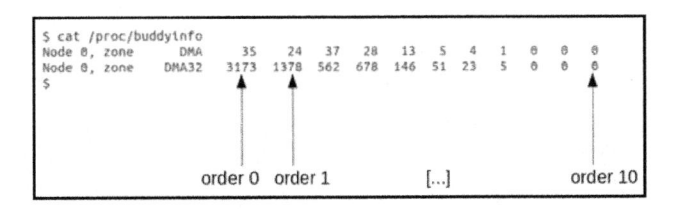

Figure 8.3 – Annotated screenshot of sample /proc/buddyinfo output

Our guest VM is a pseudo-NUMA box with one node (Node 0) and two zones (DMA and DMA32). The numbers following zone XXX are the number of free (physically contiguous!) page frames in order 0, order 1, order 2, right up to MAX_ORDER-1 (here, 11 − 1 = 10). So, let's take a couple of examples from the preceding output:

- There are 35 single-page free chunks of RAM in the order 0 list for node 0, zone DMA.
- In node 0, zone DMA32, order 3, the number shown in *Figure 8.3* here is **678**; now, take $2^{order} = 2^3 = 8$ *page frames = 32 KB* (assuming a page size of 4 KB); this implies that there are 678 32 KB physically contiguous free chunks of RAM on that list.

It is important to note that **each chunk is guaranteed to be physically contiguous RAM in and of itself**. Also, notice that the size of the memory chunks on a given order is always double that of the previous order (and half that of the next one). This is, of course, as they're all powers of 2.

> Note that MAX_ORDER can (and does) vary with the architecture. On regular x86 and ARM systems, it's 11, yielding a largest chunk size of 4 MB of physically contiguous RAM on order 10 of the freelists. On high-end enterprise server class systems running the Itanium (IA-64) processor, MAX_ORDER can be as high as 17 (implying a largest chunk size on order (17-1), thus of 2^{16} = *65,536 pages = 512 MB chunks* of physically contiguous RAM on order 16 of the freelists, for a 4 KB page size). The IA-64 MMU supports up to eight page sizes ranging from a mere 4 KB right up to 256 MB. As another example, with a page size of 16 MB, the order 16 list could potentially have physically contiguous RAM chunks of size *65,536 * 16 MB = 1 TB* each!

Another key point: the kernel keeps **multiple BSA freelists – one for every node:zone that is present on the system!** This lends a natural way to allocate memory on a NUMA system.

Kernel Memory Allocation for Module Authors - Part 1

The following diagram shows how the kernel instantiates multiple freelists – *one per node:zone present on the system* (diagram credit: *Professional Linux Kernel Architecture*, Mauerer, Wrox Press, Oct 2008):

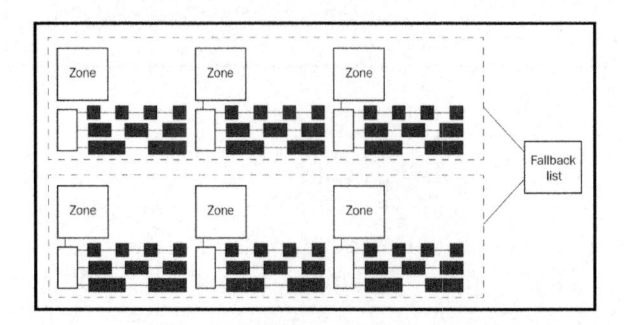

Figure 8.4 – Page allocator (BSA) "freelists," one per node:zone on the system; diagram credit: Professional Linux Kernel Architecture, Mauerer, Wrox Press, Oct 2008

Furthermore, as can be seen in Figure 8.5, when the kernel is called upon to allocate RAM via the page allocator, it picks the optimal freelist to allocate memory from – the one associated with the node upon which the thread asking the request is running (recall the NUMA architecture from the previous chapter). If this node is out of memory or cannot allocate it for whatever reason, the kernel then uses a fallback list to figure out which freelist to attempt to allocate memory from. (In reality, the real picture is even more complex; we provide a few more details in the *Page allocator internals – a few more details* section.)

Let's now understand (in a conceptual way) how all of this actually works.

The workings of the page allocator

The actual (de)allocation strategy can be explained by using a simple example. Let's say a device driver requests 128 KB of memory. To fulfill this request, the (simplified and conceptual) page allocator algorithm will do this:

1. The algorithm expresses the amount to be allocated (128 KB here) in pages. Thus, here, it's (assuming a page size of 4 KB) 128/4 = *32 pages*.
2. Next, it determines to what power 2 must be raised to get 32. That's $log_2 32$, which is 5 (as 2^5 is 32).
3. Now, it checks the list on order 5 of the appropriate *node:zone* page allocator freelist. If a memory chunk is available (it will be of size 2^5 *pages = 128 KB*), dequeue it from the list, update the list, and allocate it to the requester. Job done! Return to caller.

> Why do we say *of the appropriate node:zone page allocator freelist*? Does that mean there's more than one of them? Yes, indeed! We repeat: the reality is that there will be several freelist data structures, one each per *node:zone* on the system. (Also see more details in the section *Page allocator internals – a few more details*.)

4. If no memory chunk is available on the order 5 list (that is, if it's null), then it checks the list on the next order; that is, the order 6-linked list (if it's not empty, it will have 2^6 *pages* = 256 *KB* memory chunks enqueued on it, each chunk being double the size of what we want).
5. If the order 6 list is non-null, then it will take (dequeue) a chunk of memory from it (which will be 256 KB in size, double of what's required), and do the following:
    - Update the list to reflect the fact that one chunk is now removed.
    - Cut the chunk in half, thus obtaining two 128 KB halves or **buddies**! (Please see the following information box.)
    - Migrate (enqueue) one half (of size 128 KB) to the order 5 list.
    - Allocate the other half (of size 128 KB) to the requester.
    - Job done! Return to caller.
6. If the order 6 list is also empty, then it repeats the preceding process with the order 7 list, and so on, until it succeeds.
7. If all the remaining higher-order lists are empty (null), it will fail the request.

> We can cut or slice a memory chunk in half because every chunk on the list is guaranteed to be physically contiguous memory. Once cut, we have two halves; each is called a **buddy block**, hence the name of this algorithm. Pedantically, it's called the binary buddy system as we use power-of-2-sized memory chunks. A buddy block is defined as a block that is of the same size and physically adjacent to another.

You will understand that the preceding description is conceptual. The actual code implementation is certainly more complex and optimized. By the way, the code – the *heart of the zoned buddy allocator*, as its comment mentions, is here: `mm/page_alloc.c:__alloc_pages_nodemask()`. Being beyond the scope of this book, we won't attempt to delve into the code-level details of the allocator.

Working through a few scenarios

Now that we have the basics of the algorithm, let's consider a few scenarios: first, a simple straightforward case, and after that, a couple of more complex cases.

The simplest case

Let's say that a kernel-space device driver (or some core code) requests 128 KB and receives a memory chunk from the order 5 list of one of the freelist data structures. At some later point in time, it will necessarily free the memory chunk by employing one of the page allocator free APIs. Now, this API's algorithm calculates – via its order – that the just-freed chunk belongs on the order 5 list; thus, it enqueues it there.

A more complex case

Now, let's say that, unlike the previous simple case, when the device driver requests 128 KB, the order 5 list is null; thus, as per the page allocator algorithm, we go to the list on the next order, 6, and check it. Let's say it's non-null; the algorithm now dequeues a 256 KB chunk and splits (or cuts) it in half. Now, one half (of size 128 KB) goes to the requester, and the remaining half (again, of size 128 KB) is enqueued on to the order 5 list.

The really interesting property of the buddy system is what happens when the requester (the device driver), at some later point in time, frees the memory chunk. As expected, the algorithm calculates (via its order) that the just-freed chunk belongs on the order 5 list. But before blindly enqueuing it there, **it looks for its buddy block**, and in this case, it (possibly) finds it! It now merges the two buddy blocks into a single larger block (of size 256 KB) and places (enqueues) the merged block on the *order 6* list. This is fantastic – it has actually helped defragment memory!

The downfall case

Let's make it interesting now by not using a convenient rounded power-of-2 size as the requirement. This time, let's say that the device driver requests a memory chunk of size 132 KB. What will the buddy system allocator do? As, of course, it cannot allocate less memory than requested, it allocates more – you guessed it (see *Figure 8.2*), the next available memory chunk is on order 7, of size 256 KB. But the consumer (the driver) is only going to see and use the first 132 KB of the 256 KB chunk allocated to it. The remaining (124 KB) is wasted (think about it, that's close to 50% wastage!). This is called **internal fragmentation (or wastage)** and is the critical failing of the binary buddy system!

> **TIP:** You will learn, though, that there is indeed a mitigation to this: a patch was contributed to deal with similar scenarios (via the `alloc_pages_exact()` / `free_pages_exact()` APIs). We will cover the APIs to use the page allocator shortly.

Page allocator internals – a few more details

In this book, we do not intend to delve into code-level detail on the internals of the page allocator. Having said that, here's the thing: in terms of data structures, the `zone` structure contains an array of `free_area` structures. This makes sense; as you've learned, there can be (and usually are) multiple page allocator freelists on the system, one per node:zone:

```
// include/linux/mmzone.h
struct zone {
    [ ... ]
    /* free areas of different sizes */
    struct free_area free_area[MAX_ORDER];
    [ ... ]
};
```

The `free_area` structure is the implementation of the doubly-linked circular lists (of free memory page frames within that node:zone) along with the number of page frames that are currently free:

```
struct free_area {
    struct list_head free_list[MIGRATE_TYPES];
    unsigned long nr_free;
};
```

Kernel Memory Allocation for Module Authors - Part 1

Why is it an array of linked lists and not just one list? Without delving into the details, we'll mention that, in reality, the kernel layout for the buddy system freelists is more complex than let on until now: from the 2.6.24 kernel, each freelist we have seen is actually further broken up into multiple freelists to cater to different *page migration types*. This was required to deal with complications when trying to keep memory defragmented. Besides that, as mentioned earlier, these freelists exist per *node:zone* on the system. So, for example, on an actual NUMA system with 4 nodes and 3 zones per node, there will be 12 (4 x 3) freelists. Not just that, each freelist is actually further broken down into 6 freelists, one per migration type. Thus, on such a system, a total of *6 x 12 = 72* freelist data structures would exist system-wide!

> **TIP**
> If you are interested, dig into the details and check out the output of `/proc/buddyinfo` – a nice summary view of the state of the buddy system freelists (as Figure 8.3 shows). Next, for a more detailed and realistic view (of the type mentioned previously, showing *all* the freelists), look up `/proc/pagetypeinfo` (requires root access) – it shows all the freelists (broken up into page migration types as well).

The design of the page allocator (buddy system) algorithm is one of the best-fit class. It confers the major benefit of actually helping to defragment physical memory as the system runs. Briefly, its pros and cons are as follows.

The pros of the page allocator (buddy system) algorithm are as follows:

- Helps defragment memory (external fragmentation is prevented)
- Guarantees the allocation of a physically contiguous memory chunk
- Guarantees CPU cache line-aligned memory blocks
- Fast (well, fast enough; the algorithmic time complexity is $O(log\ n)$)

On the other hand, by far the biggest downside is that internal fragmentation or wastage can be much too high.

Okay, great! We have covered a good deal of background material on the internal workings of the page or buddy system allocator. Time to get hands on: let's now dive into actually understanding and using the page allocator APIs to allocate and free memory.

Learning how to use the page allocator APIs

The Linux kernel provides (exposes to the core and modules) a set of APIs to allocate and deallocate memory (RAM) via the page allocator. These are often referred to as the low-level (de)allocator routines. The following table summarizes the page allocation APIs; you'll notice that all the APIs or macros that have two parameters, the first parameter is called the *GFP flags or bitmask*; we shall explain it in detail shortly, please ignore it for now. The second parameters is the `order` - the order of the freelist, that is, the amount of memory to allocate is 2^{order} page frames. All prototypes can be found in `include/linux/gfp.h`:

API or macro name	Comments	API signature or macro
`__get_free_page()`	Allocates exactly one page frame. The allocated memory will have random content; it's a wrapper around the `__get_free_pages()` API. The return value is a pointer to the just-allocated memory's kernel logical address.	`#define __get_free_page(gfp_mask) \ __get_free_pages((gfp_mask), 0)`
`__get_free_pages()`	Allocates 2^{order} physically contiguous page frames. Allocated memory will have random content; the return value is a pointer to the just-allocated memory's kernel logical address.	`unsigned long __get_free_pages(gfp_t gfp_mask, unsigned int order);`
`get_zeroed_page()`	Allocates exactly one page frame; its contents are set to ASCII zero (NULL; that is, it's zeroed out); the return value is a pointer to the just-allocated memory's kernel logical address.	`unsigned long get_zeroed_page(gfp_t gfp_mask);`

Kernel Memory Allocation for Module Authors - Part 1

`alloc_page()`	Allocates exactly one page frame. The allocated memory will have random content; a wrapper over the `alloc_pages()` API; the return value is a pointer to the just-allocated memory's page metadata structure; can convert it into a kernel logical address via the `page_address()` function.	`#define alloc_page(gfp_mask) \` `alloc_pages(gfp_mask, 0)`

`alloc_pages()`	Allocates 2^{order} physically contiguous page frames. The allocated memory will have random content; the return value is a pointer to the start of the just-allocated memory's page metadata structure; can convert it into a kernel logical address via the `page_address()` function.	`struct page *`
		`alloc_pages(gfp_t gfp_mask,`
		`unsigned int order);`

Table 8.1 – Low-level (BSA/page) allocator – popular exported allocation APIs

All the preceding APIs are exported (via the `EXPORT_SYMBOL()` macro), and hence available to kernel module and device driver developers. Worry not, you will soon see a kernel module that demonstrates using them.

The Linux kernel considers it worthwhile to maintain a (small) metadata structure to track every single page frame of RAM. It's called the `page` structure. The point here is, be careful: unlike the usual semantics of returning a pointer (a virtual address) to the start of the newly allocated memory chunk, notice how both the `alloc_page()` and `alloc_pages()` APIs mentioned previously return a pointer to the start of the newly allocated memory's page structure, not the memory chunk itself (as the other APIs do). You must obtain the actual pointer to the start of the newly allocated memory by invoking the `page_address()` API on the page structure address that is returned. Example code in the *Writing a kernel module to demo using the page allocator APIs* section will illustrate the usage of all of the preceding APIs.

Before we can make use of the page allocator APIs mentioned here, though, it's imperative to understand at least the basics regarding the **Get Free Page (GFP)** flags, which are the topic of the section that follows.

[396]

Dealing with the GFP flags

You will notice that the first parameter to all the previous allocator APIs (or macros) is `gfp_t gfp_mask`. What does this mean? Essentially, these are GFP flags. These are flags (there are several of them) used by the kernel's internal memory management code layers. For all practical purposes, for the typical kernel module (or device driver) developer, just two GFP flags are crucial (as mentioned before, the rest are for internal usage). They are as follows:

- `GFP_KERNEL`
- `GFP_ATOMIC`

Deciding which of these to use when performing memory allocation via the page allocator APIs is important; a key rule to always remember is the following:

If in process context and it is safe to sleep, use the GFP_KERNEL flag. If it is unsafe to sleep (typically, when in any type of atomic or interrupt context), you must use the GFP_ATOMIC flag.

Following the preceding rule is critical. Getting this wrong can result in the entire machine freezing, kernel crashes, and/or random bad stuff happening. So, what exactly do the statements *safe/unsafe to sleep* really mean? For this and more, we defer to the *The GFP flags – digging deeper* section that follows. It *is* really important though, so I definitely recommend you read it.

[397]

Linux Driver Verification (LDV) project: back in Chapter 1, *Kernel Workspace Setup*, in the The LDV - Linux Driver Verification - project section, we mentioned that this project has useful "rules" with respect to various programming aspects of Linux modules (drivers, mostly) as well as the core kernel.

With regard to our current topic, here's one of the rules, a negative one, implying that you *cannot* do this: *"Using a blocking memory allocation when spinlock is held"* (http://linuxtesting.org/ldv/online?action=show_rulerule_id=0043). When holding a spinlock, you're not allowed to do anything that might block; this includes kernel-space memory allocations. Thus, very important, you must use the GFP_ATOMIC flag when performing a memory allocation in any kind of atomic or non-blocking context, like when holding a spinlock (you will learn that this isn't the case with the mutex lock; you are allowed to perform blocking activities while holding a mutex). Violating this rule leads to instability and even raises the possibility of (an implicit) deadlock. The LDV page mentions a device driver that was violating this very rule and the subsequent fix (https://git.kernel.org/pub/scm/linux/kernel/git/torvalds/linux.git/commit/?id=5b0691508aa99d309101a49b4b084dc16b3d7019). Take a look: the patch clearly shows (in the context of the kzalloc() API, which we shall soon cover) the GFP_KERNEL flag being replaced with the GFP_ATOMIC flag.

Another GFP flag commonly used is __GFP_ZERO. Its usage implies to the kernel that you want zeroed-out memory pages. It's often bitwise-ORed with GFP_KERNEL or GFP_ATOMIC flags in order to return memory initialized to zero.

> The kernel developers do take the trouble to document the GFP flags in detail. Take a look in include/linux/gfp.h. Within it, there's a long and detailed comment; it's headed DOC: Useful GFP flag combinations.

For now, and so that we get off the ground quickly, just understand that using the Linux kernel's memory allocation APIs with the GFP_KERNEL flag is indeed the common case for kernel-internal allocations.

Freeing pages with the page allocator

The flip side of allocating memory is freeing it, of course. Memory leakage in the kernel is definitely not something you'd like to contribute to. For the page allocator APIs shown in *Table 8.1*, here are the corresponding free APIs:

API or macro name	Comment	API signature or macro
free_page()	Free a (single) page that was allocated via the __get_free_page(), get_zeroed_page(), or alloc_page() APIs; it's a simple wrapper over the free_pages() API	#define free_page(addr) __free_pages((addr), 0)
free_pages()	Free multiple pages that were allocated via the __get_free_pages() or alloc_pages() APIs (it's actually a wrapper over __free_pages().)	void free_pages(unsigned long addr, unsigned int order)
__free_pages()	(*Same as the preceding row, plus*) it's the underlying routine where the work gets done; also, note that the first parameter is a pointer to the page metadata structure.	void __free_pages(struct page *page, unsigned int order)

Table 8.2 – Common free page(s) APIs to use with the page allocator

You can see that the actual underlying API in the preceding functions is free_pages(), which itself is just a wrapper over the mm/page_alloc.c:__free_pages() code. The first parameter to the free_pages() API is the pointer to the start of the memory chunk being freed; this, of course, being the return value from the allocation routine. However, the first parameter to the underlying API, __free_pages(), is the pointer to the *page* metadata structure of the start of the memory chunk being freed.

> **TIP**
> Generally speaking, unless you really know what you are doing, you're definitely advised to invoke the foo() wrapper routine and not its internal __foo() routine. One reason to do so is simply correctness (perhaps the wrapper uses some necessary synchronization mechanism - like a lock - prior to invoking the underlying routine). Another reason to do so is validity checking (which helps code remain robust and secure). Often, the __foo() routines bypass validity checks in favor of speed.

Kernel Memory Allocation for Module Authors - Part 1

As all experienced C/C++ application developers know, allocating and subsequently freeing memory is a rich source of bugs! This is primarily because C is an unmanaged language, as far as memory is concerned; hence, you can hit all sorts of memory bugs. These include the well-known memory leakage, buffer overflows/underflows for both read/write, double-free, and **Use After Free (UAF)** bugs.

Unfortunately, it's no different in kernel space; it's just that the consequences are (much) worse! Be extra careful! Please do take care to ensure the following:

- Favor routines that initialize the memory allocated to zero.
- Think about and use the appropriate GFP flag when performing an allocation – more on this in the *The GFP flags – digging deeper* section, but briefly, note the following:
    - When in process context where it's safe to sleep, use `GFP_KERNEL`.
    - When in an atomic context, such as when processing an interrupt, use `GFP_ATOMIC`.
- When using the page allocator (as we're doing now), try as much as possible to keep the allocation size as rounded power-of-2 pages (again, the rationale behind this and ways to mitigate this – when you don't require so much memory, the typical case – are covered in detail in the coming sections of this chapter).
- You only ever attempt to free memory that you allocated earlier; needless to say, don't miss freeing it, and don't double-free it.
- Keep the original memory chunk's pointer safe from reuse, manipulation (`ptr ++` or something similar), and corruption, so that you can correctly free it when done.
- Check (and recheck!) the parameters passed to APIs. Is a pointer to the previously allocated block required, or to its underlying `page` structure?

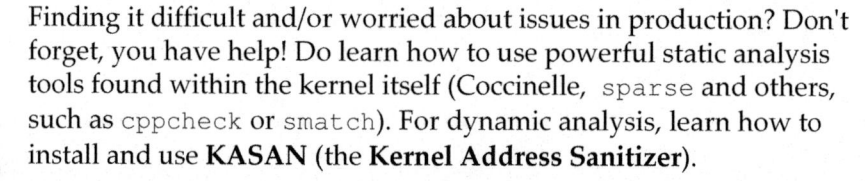

> **TIP**
>
> Finding it difficult and/or worried about issues in production? Don't forget, you have help! Do learn how to use powerful static analysis tools found within the kernel itself (Coccinelle, `sparse` and others, such as `cppcheck` or `smatch`). For dynamic analysis, learn how to install and use **KASAN** (the **Kernel Address Sanitizer**).
>
> Recall the Makefile template I provided in Chapter 5, *Writing Your First Kernel Module – LKMs Part 2*, in the *A better Makefile template* section. It contains targets that use several of these tools; please do use it!

[400]

Alright, now that we've covered both the (common) allocation and free APIs of the page allocator, it's time to put this learning to use. Let's write some code!

Writing a kernel module to demo using the page allocator APIs

Let's now get hands on with the low-level page allocator and free APIs that we've learned about so far. In this section, we will show relevant code snippets, followed by an explanation where warranted, from our demo kernel module (`ch8/lowlevel_mem/lowlevel_mem.c`).

In the primary worker routine, `bsa_alloc()`, of our small LKM, we highlighted (in bold font) the code comments that show what we are trying to achieve. A few points to note:

1. First, we do something very interesting: we use our small kernel "library" function `klib_llkd.c:show_phy_pages()` to literally show you how physical RAM page frames are identity mapped to kernel virtual pages in the kernel lowmem region! (The exact working of the `show_phy_pages()` routine is discussed very shortly):

   ```
   // ch8/lowlevel_mem/lowlevel_mem.c
   [...]
   static int bsa_alloc(void)
   {
       int stat = -ENOMEM;
       u64 numpg2alloc = 0;
       const struct page *pg_ptr1;

       /* 0. Show the identity mapping: physical RAM page frames
   to kernel virtual
        * addresses, from PAGE_OFFSET for 5 pages */
       pr_info("%s: 0. Show identity mapping: RAM page frames : kernel virtual pages :: 1:1\n", OURMODNAME);
       show_phy_pages((void *)PAGE_OFFSET, 5 * PAGE_SIZE, 1);
   ```

2. Next, we allocate one page of memory via the underlying `__get_free_page()` page allocator API (that we saw previously in *Table 8.1*):

   ```
   /* 1. Allocate one page with the __get_free_page() API */
   gptr1 = (void *) __get_free_page(GFP_KERNEL);
   if (!gptr1) {
       pr_warn("%s: __get_free_page() failed!\n",
   ```

[401]

Kernel Memory Allocation for Module Authors - Part 1

```
OURMODNAME);
        /* As per convention, we emit a printk above saying that the
         * allocation failed. In practice it isn't required; the kernel
         * will definitely emit many warning printk's if a memory alloc
         * request ever fails! Thus, we do this only once (here; could also
         * use the WARN_ONCE()); from now on we don't pedantically print any
         * error message on a memory allocation request failing. */
        goto out1;
    }
    pr_info("%s: 1. __get_free_page() alloc'ed 1 page from the BSA @ %pK (%px)\n",
        OURMODNAME, gptr1, gptr1);
```

Notice how we emit a `printk` function showing the kernel's logical address. Recall from the previous chapter that this is page allocator memory that lies very much in the direct-mapped RAM or lowmem region of the kernel segment/VAS.

> Now, for security, we should consistently, and only, use the `%pK` format specifier when printing kernel addresses so that a hashed value and not the real virtual address shows up in the kernel logs. However, here, in order to show you the actual kernel virtual address, we also use the `%px` format specifier (which, like the `%pK`, is portable as well; for security, please don't use the `%px` format specifier in production!).

Next, notice the detailed comment just after the first `__get_free_page()` API (in the preceding snippet) is issued. It mentions the fact that you don't really have to print an out-of-memory error or warning messages. (Curious? To find out why, visit https://lkml.org/lkml/2014/6/10/382.) In this example module (as with several earlier ones and more to follow), we code our printk's (or `pr_foo()` macro) instances for portability by using appropriate printk format specifiers (like the `%zd`, `%zu`, `%pK`, `%px`, and `%pa`).

Chapter 8

3. Let's move on to our second memory allocation using the page allocator; see the following code snippet:

```
/*2. Allocate 2^bsa_alloc_order pages with the
__get_free_pages() API */
    numpg2alloc = powerof(2, bsa_alloc_order); // returns
2^bsa_alloc_order
    gptr2 = (void *) __get_free_pages(GFP_KERNEL|__GFP_ZERO,
bsa_alloc_order);
    if (!gptr2) {
        /* no error/warning printk now; see above comment */
        goto out2;
    }
    pr_info("%s: 2. __get_free_pages() alloc'ed 2^%d = %lld
page(s) = %lld bytes\n"
        " from the BSA @ %pK (%px)\n",
        OURMODNAME, bsa_alloc_order, powerof(2,
bsa_alloc_order),
        numpg2alloc * PAGE_SIZE, gptr2, gptr2);
    pr_info(" (PAGE_SIZE = %ld bytes)\n", PAGE_SIZE);
```

In the preceding code snippet (see the code comments), we have allocated 2^3 – that is, 8 – pages of memory via the page allocator's `__get_free_pages()` API (as the default value of our module parameter, `bsa_alloc_order`, is 3).

> An aside: notice that we use the `GFP_KERNEL|__GFP_ZERO` GFP flags to ensure that the allocated memory is zeroed out, a best practice. Then again, zeroing out large memory chunks can result in a slight performance hit.

Now, we ask ourselves the question: is there a way to verify that the memory is really physically contiguous (as promised)? It turns out that yes, we can actually retrieve and print out the physical address of the start of each allocated page frame and retrieve its **Page Frame Number (PFN)** as well.

> The **PFN** is a simple concept: it's just the index or page number – for example, the PFN of physical address 8192 is 2 *(8192/4096)*. As we've shown how to (and importantly, when you can) translate kernel virtual addresses to their physical counterparts earlier (and vice versa; this coverage is in `Chapter 7`, *Memory Management Internals – Essentials*, in the *Direct-mapped RAM and address translation* section), we won't repeat it here.

Kernel Memory Allocation for Module Authors - Part 1

To do this work of translating virtual addresses to physical addresses and checking for contiguity, we write a small "library" function, which is kept in a separate C file in the root of this book's GitHub source tree, `klib_llkd.c`. Our intent is to modify our kernel module's Makefile to link in the code of this library file as well! (Doing this properly was covered back in Chapter 5, *Writing Your First Kernel Module – LKMs Part 2*, in the *Performing library emulation via multiple source files* section.) Here's our invocation of our library routine (just as was done in step 0):

```
show_phy_pages(gptr2, numpg2alloc * PAGE_SIZE, 1);
```

The following is the code of our library routine (in the `<booksrc>/klib_llkd.c` source file; again, for clarity, we won't show the entire code here):

```
// klib_llkd.c
[...]
/* show_phy_pages - show the virtual, physical addresses and
PFNs of the memory range provided on a per-page basis.
 * @kaddr: the starting kernel virtual address
 * @len: length of the memory piece (bytes)
 * @contiguity_check: if True, check for physical contiguity
of pages
 * 'Walk' the virtually contiguous 'array' of pages one by one
(that is, page by page),
 * printing the virt and physical address (and PFN- page frame
number). This way, we can see
 * if the memory really is *physically* contiguous or not
 */
void show_phy_pages(const void *kaddr, size_t len, bool
contiguity_check)
{
    [...]
    if (len % PAGE_SIZE)
        loops++;
    for (i = 0; i < len/PAGE_SIZE; i++) {
        pa = virt_to_phys(vaddr+(i*PAGE_SIZE));
        pfn = PHYS_PFN(pa);

        if (!!contiguity_check) {
        /* what's with the 'if !!(<cond>) ...' ??
         * a 'C' trick: ensures that the if condition always
evaluates
         * to a boolean - either 0 or 1 */
            if (i && pfn != prev_pfn + 1)
```

```
                    pr_notice(" *** physical NON-contiguity
detected ***\n");
        }
        pr_info("%05d 0x%px %pa %ld\n", i,
vaddr+(i*PAGE_SIZE), &pa, pfn);
        if (!!contiguity_check)
            prev_pfn = pfn;
    }
}
```

Study the preceding function. We walk through our given memory range, (virtual) page by (virtual) page, obtaining the physical address and PFN, which we then emit via printk (notice how we use the `%pa` format specifier to port-ably print a *physical address* - it requires it to be passed by reference though). Not only that, if the third parameter, `contiguity_check`, is 1, we check whether the PFNs are just a single digit apart, thus checking that the pages are indeed physically contiguous or not. (By the way, the simple `powerof()` function that we make use of is also within our library code.)

> Hang on, though, a key point: having kernel modules working with physical addresses is *highly discouraged*. Only the kernel's internal memory management code works directly with physical addresses. There are very few real-world cases of even hardware device drivers using physical memory directly (DMA is one, and using the `*ioremap*` APIs another).
>
> We only do so here to prove a point – that the memory allocated by the page allocator (with a single API call) is physically contiguous. Also, do realize that the `virt_to_phys()` (and friends) APIs that we employ are guaranteed to work *only* on direct-mapped memory (the kernel lowmem region) and nothing else (not the `vmalloc` range, the IO memory ranges, bus memory, DMA buffers, and so on).

4. Now, let's continue with the kernel module code:

```
    /* 3. Allocate and init one page with the
get_zeroed_page() API */
    gptr3 = (void *) get_zeroed_page(GFP_KERNEL);
    if (!gptr3)
        goto out3;
    pr_info("%s: 3. get_zeroed_page() alloc'ed 1 page from the
BSA @ %pK (%px)\n",
        OURMODNAME, gptr3, gptr3);
```

As seen in the preceding snippet, we allocate a single page of memory but ensure it's zeroed out by employing the PA `get_zeroed_page()` API. `pr_info()` shows the hashed and actual KVAs (using the `%pK` or `%px` has the addresses printed in a port-able fashion as well, irrespective of your running on a 32 or 64-bit system.)

5. Next, we allocate one page with the `alloc_page()` API. Careful! It does not return the pointer to the allocated page, but rather the pointer to the metadata structure `page` representing the allocated page; here's the function signature: `struct page * alloc_page(gfp_mask)`. Thus, we use the `page_address()` helper to convert it into a kernel logical (or virtual) address:

```
/* 4. Allocate one page with the alloc_page() API.
pg_ptr1 = alloc_page(GFP_KERNEL);
if (!pg_ptr1)
    goto out4;

gptr4 = page_address(pg_ptr1);
pr_info("%s: 4. alloc_page() alloc'ed 1 page from the BSA @ %pK (%px)\n"
        " (struct page addr=%pK (%px)\n)",
        OURMODNAME, (void *)gptr4, (void *)gptr4, pg_ptr1,
pg_ptr1);
```

In the preceding code snippet, we allocate one page of memory via the `alloc_page()` PA API. As explained, we need to convert the page metadata structure returned by it into a KVA (or kernel logical address) via the `page_address()` API.

6. Next, allocate and `init` 2^3 = 8 *pages* with the `alloc_pages()` API. The same warning as the preceding code snippet applies here too:

```
/* 5. Allocate and init 2^3 = 8 pages with the alloc_pages() API.
gptr5 = page_address(alloc_pages(GFP_KERNEL, 3));
if (!gptr5)
    goto out5;
pr_info("%s: 5. alloc_pages() alloc'ed %lld pages from the BSA @ %pK (%px)\n",
        OURMODNAME, powerof(2, 3), (void *)gptr5, (void *)gptr5);
```

In the preceding code snippet, we combine `alloc_pages()` wrapped within a `page_address()` API to allocate 2^3 = 8 pages of memory!

Interestingly, we use several local `goto` statements in the code (do peek at the code in the repo). Looking carefully at it, you will notice that it actually keeps error handling code paths clean and logical. This is indeed part of the Linux kernel coding style guidelines.

> Usage of the (sometimes controversial) `goto` is clearly documented right here: https://www.kernel.org/doc/html/v5.4/process/coding-style.html#centralized-exiting-of-functions. I urge you to check it out! Once you understand the usage pattern, you'll find that it helps reduce the all-too-typical memory leakage (and similar) cleanup errors!

7. Finally, in the cleanup method, prior to being removed from kernel memory, we free up all the memory chunks we just allocated in the cleanup code of the kernel module.

8. In order to link our library `klib_llkd` code with our `lowlevel_mem` kernel module, the Makefile changes to have the following (recall that we learned about compiling multiple source files into a single kernel module in Chapter 5, *Writing Your First Kernel Module – LKMs Part 2*, in the *Performing library emulation via multiple source files* section):

```
PWD                    := $(shell pwd)
obj-m                  += lowlevel_mem_lkm.o
lowlevel_mem_lkm-objs  := lowlevel_mem.o ../../klib_lkdc.o
EXTRA_CFLAGS           += -DDEBUG
```

Again, in this sample LKM we often used the `%px` printk format specifier so that we can see the actual virtual address and not a hashed value (kernel security feature). It's okay here, but don't do this in production.

Phew! That was quite a bit to cover. Do ensure you understand the code, and then read on to see it in action.

Deploying our lowlevel_mem_lkm kernel module

Okay, time to see our kernel module in action! Let's build and deploy it on both a Raspberry Pi 4 (running the default Raspberry Pi OS) and on an x86_64 VM (running Fedora 31).

Kernel Memory Allocation for Module Authors - Part 1

On the Raspberry Pi 4 Model B (here running Raspberry Pi kernel version 5.4.79-v7l+), we build and then `insmod(8)` our `lowlevel_mem_lkm` kernel module. The following screenshot shows the output:

```
rpi4 $ lsmod |grep lowlevel_mem_lkm
lowlevel_mem_lkm       16384  0
rpi4 $
rpi4 $ sudo rmmod lowlevel_mem_lkm ; dmesg
[ 7769.763984] lowlevel_mem: 0. Show identity mapping: RAM page frames : kernel virtual pages :: 1:1
[ 7769.764001] show_phy_pages(): start kaddr c0000000, len 20480, contiguity_check is on
[ 7769.764012]  -pg#-   ----va----      --------pa--------    -PFN-
[ 7769.764026]  00000   0xc0000000      0x0000000000000000    0
[ 7769.764039]  00001   0xc0001000      0x0000000000001000    1
[ 7769.764051]  00002   0xc0002000      0x0000000000002000    2
[ 7769.764063]  00003   0xc0003000      0x0000000000003000    3
[ 7769.764075]  00004   0xc0004000      0x0000000000004000    4
[ 7769.764093] lowlevel_mem: 1. __get_free_page() alloc'ed 1 page from the BSA @ 2b8441ff (d6350000)
[ 7769.764131] lowlevel_mem: 2. __get_free_pages() alloc'ed 2^3 = 8 page(s) = 32768 bytes
                 from the BSA @ b0a14090 (d73e8000)
[ 7769.764143]   (PAGE_SIZE = 4096 bytes)
[ 7769.764155] show_phy_pages(): start kaddr d73e8000, len 32768, contiguity_check is on
[ 7769.764166]  -pg#-   ----va----      --------pa--------    -PFN-
[ 7769.764178]  00000   0xd73e8000      0x00000000173e8000    95208
[ 7769.764190]  00001   0xd73e9000      0x00000000173e9000    95209
[ 7769.764202]  00002   0xd73ea000      0x00000000173ea000    95210
[ 7769.764213]  00003   0xd73eb000      0x00000000173eb000    95211
[ 7769.764225]  00004   0xd73ec000      0x00000000173ec000    95212
[ 7769.764237]  00005   0xd73ed000      0x00000000173ed000    95213
[ 7769.764249]  00006   0xd73ee000      0x00000000173ee000    95214
[ 7769.764260]  00007   0xd73ef000      0x00000000173ef000    95215
[ 7769.764278] lowlevel_mem: 3. get_zeroed_page() alloc'ed 1 page from the BSA @ a81b4775 (d63b2000)
[ 7769.764295] lowlevel_mem: 4. alloc_page() alloc'ed 1 page from the BSA @ 396e9eaf (d676e000)
                 (struct page addr=026b942c (dd8364a0))
[ 7769.764313] lowlevel_mem: 5. alloc_pages() alloc'ed 32 pages from the BSA @ 83cbb79d (d6200000)
[ 7791.066874] lowlevel_mem: free-ing up the BSA memory chunks...
[ 7791.066905] lowlevel_mem: removed
rpi4 $
```

Figure 8.5 – The lowlevel_mem_lkm kernel module's output on a Raspberry Pi 4 Model B

Check it out! In step 0 of the output in Figure 8.6 our `show_phy_pages()` library routine clearly shows that KVA `0xc000 0000` has PA `0x0`, KVA `0xc000 1000` has pa `0x1000`, and so on, for five pages (along with the PFN on the right); you can literally see the 1:1 identity mapping of physical RAM page frames to kernel virtual pages (in the lowmem region of the kernel segment)!

Next, the initial memory allocation with the `__get_free_page()` API goes through as expected. More interesting is our case 2. Here, we can clearly see that the physical address and PFN of each allocated page (from 0 to 7, for a total of 8 pages) are consecutive, showing that the memory pages allocated are indeed physically contiguous!

We build and run the same module on an x86_64 VM running Ubuntu 20.04 (running our custom 5.4 'debug' kernel). The following screenshot shows the output:

```
$ sudo rmmod lowlevel_mem_lkm 2>/dev/null ; sudo dmesg -C; sudo insmod ./lowlevel_mem_lkm.ko ; dmesg
[sudo] password for llkd:
[12747.967238] lowlevel_mem: 0. Show identity mapping: RAM page frames : kernel virtual pages :: 1:1
[12747.969619] show_phy_pages(): start kaddr ffff888000000000, len 20480, contiguity_check is on
[12747.971982]  -pg#-   -------va-------    --------pa--------   --PFN--
[12747.974140]  00000   0xffff888000000000   0x0000000000000000   0
[12747.976262]  00001   0xffff888000001000   0x0000000000001000   1
[12747.978384]  00002   0xffff888000002000   0x0000000000002000   2
[12747.980340]  00003   0xffff888000003000   0x0000000000003000   3
[12747.982356]  00004   0xffff888000004000   0x0000000000004000   4
[12747.984246] lowlevel_mem: 1. __get_free_page() alloc'ed 1 page from the BSA @ ffff88804e835000 (ffff88804e835000)
[12747.988101] lowlevel_mem: 2. __get_free_pages() alloc'ed 2^3 = 8 page(s) = 32768 bytes
               from the BSA @ ffff88805d820000 (ffff88805d820000)
[12747.992492]  (PAGE_SIZE = 4096 bytes)
[12747.994432] show_phy_pages(): start kaddr ffff88805d820000, len 32768, contiguity_check is on
[12747.996710]  -pg#-   -------va-------    --------pa--------   --PFN--
[12747.998893]  00000   0xffff88805d820000   0x000000005d820000   383008
[12748.001197]  00001   0xffff88805d821000   0x000000005d821000   383009
[12748.003358]  00002   0xffff88805d822000   0x000000005d822000   383010
[12748.005417]  00003   0xffff88805d823000   0x000000005d823000   383011
[12748.007451]  00004   0xffff88805d824000   0x000000005d824000   383012
[12748.009418]  00005   0xffff88805d825000   0x000000005d825000   383013
[12748.011368]  00006   0xffff88805d826000   0x000000005d826000   383014
[12748.013327]  00007   0xffff88805d827000   0x000000005d827000   383015
[12748.015712] lowlevel_mem: 3. get_zeroed_page() alloc'ed 1 page from the BSA @ ffff88804e2df000 (ffff88804e2df000)
[12748.019612] lowlevel_mem: 4. alloc_page() alloc'ed 1 page from the BSA @ ffff88804e2de000 (ffff88804e2de000)
               (struct page addr=ffffea000138b780 (ffffea000138b780))
[12748.025924] lowlevel_mem: 5. alloc_pages() alloc'ed 32 pages from the BSA @ ffff88800fe20000 (ffff88800fe20000)
$
```

Figure 8.6 – The lowlevel_mem_lkm kernel module's output on a x86_64 VM running Ubuntu 20.04

Kernel Memory Allocation for Module Authors - Part 1

This time (refer Figure 8.7), with the `PAGE_OFFSET` value being a 64-bit quantity (the value here is `0xffff 8880 0000 0000`), you can again clearly see the identity mapping of physical RAM frames to kernel virtual addresses (for 5 pages). Let's take a moment and look carefully at the kernel logical addresses returned by the page allocator APIs. In Figure 8.7, you can see that they are all in the range `0xffff 8880 .... .....` The following snippet is from the kernel source tree at `Documentation/x86/x86_64/mm.txt`, documenting (a part of) the virtual memory layout on the x86_64:

> If this all seems new and strange to you, please refer to Chapter 7, *Memory Management Internals – Essentials*, particularly the *Examining the kernel segment* and *Direct-mapped RAM and address translation* sections.

```
0000000000000000 - 00007fffffffffff (=47 bits) user space, different
per mm hole caused by [47:63] sign extension
ffff800000000000 - ffff87ffffffffff (=43 bits) guard hole, reserved
for hypervisor
ffff880000000000 - ffffc7ffffffffff (=64 TB) direct mapping of all
phys. memory
ffffc80000000000 - ffffc8ffffffffff (=40 bits) hole
ffffc90000000000 - ffffe8ffffffffff (=45 bits) vmalloc/ioremap space
```

It's quite clear, isn't it? The page allocator memory (the buddy system free lists) maps directly onto free physical RAM within the direct-mapped or lowmem region of the kernel VAS. Thus, it obviously returns memory from this region. You can see this region in the preceding documentation output (highlighted in bold font) – the kernel direct-mapped or lowmem region. Again, I emphasize the fact that the specific address range used is very arch-specific. In the preceding code, it's the (maximum possible) range on the x86_64.

Though tempting to claim that you're now done with the page allocator and its APIs, the reality is that this is (as usual) not quite the case. Do read on to see why – it's really important to understand these aspects.

The page allocator and internal fragmentation

Though all looks good and innocent on the surface, I urge you to delve a bit deeper. Just under the surface, a massive (unpleasant!) surprise might await you: the blissfully unaware kernel/driver developer. The APIs we covered previously regarding the page allocator (see *Table 8.1*) have the dubious distinction of being able to internally fragment – in simpler terms, **waste** – very significant portions of kernel memory!

To understand why this is the case, you must understand at least the basics of the page allocator algorithm and its freelist data structures. The section *The fundamental workings of the page allocator* covered this (just in case you haven't read it, please do so).

In the *Working through a few scenarios* section, you would have seen that when we make an allocation request of convenient, perfectly rounded power-of-two-size pages, it goes very smoothly. However, when this isn't the case – let's say the driver requests 132 KB of memory – then we end up with a major issue: the internal fragmentation or wastage is very high. This is a serious downside and must be addressed. We will see how, in two ways, in fact. Do read on!

The exact page allocator APIs

Realizing the vast potential for wastage within the default page allocator (or BSA), a developer from Freescale Semiconductor (see the information box) contributed a patch to the kernel page allocator that extends the API, adding a couple of new ones.

> In the 2.6.27-rc1 series, on 24 July 2008, Timur Tabi submitted a patch to mitigate the page allocator wastage issue. Here's the relevant commit: https://github.com/torvalds/linux/commit/2be0ffe2b29bd31d3debd0877797892ff2d91f4c.

Using these APIs leads to more efficient allocations for large-ish chunks (multiple pages) of memory **with far less wastage**. The new (well, it *was* new back in 2008, at least) pair of APIs to allocate and free memory are as follows:

```
#include <linux/gfp.h>
void *alloc_pages_exact(size_t size, gfp_t gfp_mask);
void free_pages_exact(void *virt, size_t size);
```

The first parameter to the `alloc_pages_exact()` API, `size`, is in bytes, the second is the "usual" GFP flags value discussed earlier (in the *Dealing with the GFP flags* section; `GFP_KERNEL` for the might-sleep process context cases, and `GFP_ATOMIC` for the never-sleep interrupt or atomic context cases).

Note that the memory allocated by this API is still guaranteed to be physically contiguous. Also, the amount that can be allocated at a time (with one function call) is limited by `MAX_ORDER`; in fact, this is true of all the other regular page allocation APIs that we have seen so far. We will discuss a lot more about this aspect in the upcoming section, *Size limitations of the kmalloc API*. There, you'll realize that the discussion is in fact not limited to the slab cache but to the page allocator as well!

The `free_pages_exact()` API must only be used to free memory allocated by its counterpart, `alloc_pages_exact()`. Also, note that the first parameter to the "free" routine is of course the value returned by the matching 'alloc' routine (the pointer to the newly allocated memory chunk).

The implementation of `alloc_pages_exact()` is simple and clever: it first allocates the entire memory chunk requested "as usual" via the `__get_free_pages()` API. Then, it loops – from the end of the memory to be used to the amount of actually allocated memory (which is typically far greater) – freeing up those unnecessary memory pages! So, in our example, if you allocate 132 KB via the `alloc_pages_exact()` API, it will actually first internally allocate 256 KB via `__get_free_pages()`, but will then free up memory from 132 KB to 256 KB!

Another example of the beauty of open source! A demo of using these APIs can be found here: `ch8/page_exact_loop`; we will leave it to you to try it out.

Before we began this section, we mentioned that there were two ways in which the wastage issue of the page allocator can be addressed. One is by using the more efficient `alloc_pages_exact()` and `free_pages_exact()` APIs, as we just learned; the other is by using a different layer to allocate memory – the *slab allocator*. We will soon cover it; until then, hang in there. Next, let's cover more, *crucial to understand*, details on the (typical) GFP flags and how you, the kernel module or driver author, are expected to use them.

The GFP flags – digging deeper

With regard to our discussions on the low-level page allocator APIs, the first parameter to every function is the so-called GFP mask. When discussing the APIs and their usage, we mentioned a *key rule*.

If in *process context and it is safe to sleep*, use the `GFP_KERNEL` flag. If it is *unsafe to sleep* (typically, when in any type of interrupt context or when holding some types of locks), you *must* use the `GFP_ATOMIC` flag.

We elaborate on this in the following sections.

Never sleep in interrupt or atomic contexts

What does the phrase *safe to sleep* actually mean? To answer this, think of blocking calls (APIs): a *blocking call* is one where the calling process (or thread) is put into a sleep state because it is waiting on something, an *event*, and the event it is waiting on has not occurred yet. Thus, it waits – it "sleeps." When, at some future point in time, the event it is waiting on occurs or arrives, it is woken up by the kernel and proceeds forward.

One example of a user space blocking API includes `sleep(3)`. Here, the event it is waiting on is the elapse of a certain amount of time. Another example is `read(2)` and its variants, where the event being waited on is storage or network data becoming available. With `wait4(2)`, the event being waited on is the death or stoppage/continuing of a child process, and so on.

So, any function that might possibly block can end up spending some time asleep (while asleep, it's certainly off the CPU run queues, and in a wait queue). Invoking this *possibly blocking* functionality when in kernel mode (which, of course, is the mode we are in when working on kernel modules) is *only allowed when in process context*. **It is a bug to invoke a blocking call of any sort in a context where it is unsafe to sleep, such as an interrupt or atomic context**. Think of this as a golden rule. This is also known as sleeping in an atomic context – it's wrong, it's buggy, and it must *never* happen.

Kernel Memory Allocation for Module Authors - Part 1

> **TIP**
> You might wonder, *how can I know in advance if my code will ever enter an atomic or interrupt context*? In one way, the kernel helps us out: when configuring the kernel (recall `make menuconfig` from Chapter 2, *Building the 5.x Linux Kernel from Source - Part 1*), under the `Kernel Hacking / Lock Debugging` menu, there is a Boolean tunable called `"Sleep inside atomic section checking"`. Turn it on! (The config option is named `CONFIG_DEBUG_ATOMIC_SLEEP`; you can always grep your kernel config file for it. Again, in Chapter 5, *Writing Your First Kernel Module - LKMs Part 2*, under the Configuring a "debug" kernel section, this is something you should definitely turn on.)

Another way to think of this situation is how exactly do you put a process or thread to sleep? The short answer is by having it invoke the scheduling code – the `schedule()` function. Thus, by implication of what we have just learned (as a corollary), `schedule()` must only be called from within a context where it's safe to sleep; process context usually is safe, interrupt context never is.

This is really important to keep in mind! (We briefly covered what process and interrupt context are in Chapter 4, *Writing Your First Kernel Module – LKMs Part 1*, in the *Process and interrupt contexts* section, and how the developer can use the `in_task()` macro to determine whether the code is currently running in a process or interrupt context.) Similarly, you can use the `in_atomic()` macro; if the code is an *atomic context* – where it must typically run to completion without interruption – it returns `True`; otherwise, `False`. You can be in process context but atomic at the same time – for example, when holding certain kinds of locks (spinlocks; we will, of course, cover this in the chapters on *synchronization* later); the converse cannot happen.

Besides the GFP flags we're focused upon - the `GFP_KERNEL` and `GFP_ATOMIC` ones - the kernel has several other `[__]GFP_*` flags that are used internally; several for the express purpose of reclaiming memory. These include (but are not limited to) `__GFP_IO`, `__GFP_FS`, `__GFP_DIRECT_RECLAIM`, `__GFP_KSWAPD_RECLAIM`, `__GFP_RECLAIM`, `__GFP_NORETRY`, and so on. In this book, we do not intend to delve into these details. I refer you to the detailed comment in `include/linux/gfp.h` that describes them (also see the *Further reading* section).

> **Linux Driver Verification (LDV)** project: back in Chapter 1, *Kernel Workspace Setup*, we mentioned that this project has useful "rules" with respect to various programming aspects of Linux modules (drivers, mostly) as well as the core kernel.
>
> With regard to our current topic, here's one of the rules, a negative one, implying that you *cannot* do this: *Not disabling IO during memory allocation while holding a USB device lock* (http://linuxtesting.org/ldv/online?action=show_rulerule_id=0077). Some quick background: when you specify the GFP_KERNEL flag, it implicitly means (among other things) that the kernel can start an IO (Input/Output; reads/writes) operation to reclaim memory. The trouble is, at times this can be problematic and should not be done; to get over this, you're expected use the GFP_NOIO flag as part of the GFP bitmask when allocating kernel memory.
>
> That's precisely the case that this LDV 'rule' is referring to: here, between the usb_lock_device() and usb_unlock_device() APIs, the GFP_KERNEL flag shouldn't be used and the GFP_NOIO flag should be used instead. (You can see several instances of this flag being used in this code: drivers/usb/core/message.c). The LDV page mentions the fact that a couple of USB-related code driver code source files were fixed to adhere to this rule.

All right, now that you're armed with a good amount of detail on the page allocator (it is, after all, the internal "engine" of RAM (de)allocation!), its APIs, and how to use them, let's move on to a very important topic – the motivation(s) behind the slab allocator, its APIs, and how to use them.

Understanding and using the kernel slab allocator

As seen in the first section of this chapter, *Introducing kernel memory allocators*, the *slab allocator* or *slab cache* is layered above the page allocator (or BSA; refer back to *Figure 8.1*). The slab allocator justifies its very existence with two primary ideas or purposes:

- **Object caching**: Here, it serves as a cache of common "objects," and the allocation (and subsequent freeing) of frequently allocated data structures within the Linux kernel, for high performance.

- Mitigate the high wastage (internal fragmentation) of the page allocator by providing small, conveniently sized caches, typically **fragments of a page**.

Let's now examine these ideas in a more detailed manner.

The object caching idea

Okay, we begin with the first of these design ideas – the notion of a cache of common objects. A long time ago, a SunOS developer, Jeff Bonwick, noticed that certain kernel objects – data structures, typically – were allocated and deallocated frequently within the OS. He thus had the idea of *pre-allocating* them in a cache of sorts. This evolved into what we call the *slab cache*.

Thus, on the Linux OS as well, the kernel (as part of the boot time initialization) pre-allocates a fairly large number of objects into several slab caches. The reason: performance! When core kernel code (or a device driver) requires memory for one of these objects, it directly requests the slab allocator. If cached, the allocation is almost immediate (the converse being true as well at deallocation). You might wonder, *is all this really necessary*? Indeed it is!

A good example of high performance being required is within the critical code paths of the network and block IO subsystems. Precisely for this reason, several network and block IO data structures (the network stack's socket buffer, `sk_buff`, the block layer's `biovec`, and, of course, the core `task_struct` data structures or objects, being a few good examples) are *auto-cached* (*pre-allocated*) by the kernel within the slab caches. Similarly, filesystem metadata structures (such as the `inode` and `dentry` structures, and so on), the memory descriptor (`struct mm_struct`), and several more are *pre-allocated* on slab caches. Can we see these cached objects? Yes, just a bit further down, we will do precisely this (via `/proc/slabinfo`).

The other reason that the slab (or, more correctly now, the SLUB) allocator has far superior performance is simply that traditional heap-based allocators tend to allocate and deallocate memory often, creating "holes" (fragmentation). Because the slab objects are allocated once (at boot) onto the caches, and freed back there (thus not really "freed" up), performance remains high. Of course, the modern kernel has the intelligence to, in a graceful manner, start freeing up the slab caches when the memory pressure gets too high.

The current state of the slab caches – the object caches, the number of objects in a cache, the number in use, the size of each object, and so on – can be looked up in several ways: a raw view via the `proc` and `sysfs` filesystems, or a more human-readable view via various frontend utilities, such as `slabtop(1)`, `vmstat(8)`, and `slabinfo`. In the following code snippet, on a native x86_64 (with 16 GB of RAM) running Ubuntu 18.04 LTS, we peek at the top 10 lines of output from `/proc/slabinfo`:

```
$ sudo head /proc/slabinfo
slabinfo - version: 2.1
# name            <active_objs> <num_objs> <objsize> <objperslab> <pagesperslab>
 : tunables <limit> <batchcount> <sharedfactor> : slabdata
<active_slabs> <num_slabs> <sharedavail>
lttng_event          0      0    280   29   2 : tunables 0 0 0 : slabdata 0 0 0
kvm_async_pf         0      0    136   30   1 : tunables 0 0 0 : slabdata 0 0 0
kvm_vcpu             0      0  24576    1   8 : tunables 0 0 0 : slabdata 0 0 0
kvm_mmu_page_header 0 0     168   24   1 : tunables 0 0 0 : slabdata 0 0 0
pte_list_desc        0      0     32  128   1 : tunables 0 0 0 : slabdata 0 0 0
i915_request       112    112    576   28   4 : tunables 0 0 0 : slabdata 4 4 0
ext4_groupinfo_4k 6482 6496    144   28   1 : tunables 0 0 0 : slabdata 232 232 0
scsi_sense_cache  325   416    128   32   1 : tunables 0 0 0 : slabdata 13 13 0
```

A few points to note:

- Even reading `/proc/slabinfo` requires root access (hence, we use `sudo(8)`).
- In the preceding output, the leftmost column is the name of the slab cache. It often, but not always, matches the name of the actual data structure within the kernel that it caches.
- Then follows, for each cache, information in this format: `<statistics>` : `<tunables>` : `<slabdata>`. The meaning of each of the fields shown in the header line is explained in the man page for `slabinfo(5)` (look it up with `man 5 slabinfo`).

Kernel Memory Allocation for Module Authors - Part 1

Incidentally, the `slabinfo` utility is one example of user space C code *within* the kernel source tree under the `tools/` directory (as are several others). It displays a bunch of slab layer statistics (try it with the `-X` switch). To build it, do the following:

```
cd <ksrc-tree>/tools/vm
make slabinfo
```

A question you might have at this point is, *how much memory in total is the slab cache currently using*? This is easily answered by grepping `/proc/meminfo` for the `Slab:` entry, as follows:

```
$ grep "^Slab:" /proc/meminfo
Slab:            1580772 kB
```

As is apparent, significant amounts of memory can be used by the slab caches! This, in fact, is a common feature on Linux that puzzles those new to it: the kernel can and will use RAM for cache purposes, thus greatly improving performance. It is, of course, designed to intelligently throttle down the amount of memory used for caching as the memory pressure increases. On a regular Linux system, a significant percentage of memory can go toward caching (especially the *page cache*; it's used to cache the content of files as IO is performed upon them). This is fine, *as long as memory pressure is low*. The `free(1)` utility clearly shows this (again, on my x86_64 Ubuntu box with 16 GB of RAM, in this example):

```
$ free -h
              total        used        free      shared  buff/cache   available
Mem:           15Gi       5.5Gi       1.4Gi       704Mi       8.6Gi       9.0Gi
Swap:         7.6Gi          0B       7.6Gi
$
```

The `buff/cache` column indicates two caches that the Linux kernel employs – the buffer and page caches. In reality, among the various caches that the kernel employs, the *page cache* is a key one and often accounts for a majority of memory usage.

> **TIP**: Look up `/proc/meminfo` for fine-granularity detail on system memory usage; the fields displayed are numerous. The man page on `proc(5)` describes them under the `/proc/meminfo` section.

Now that you understand the motivation behind the slab allocator (there's more on this too), let's dive into learning how to use the APIs it exposes for both the core kernel as well as module authors.

[418]

Learning how to use the slab allocator APIs

You may have noticed that, so far, we haven't explained the second "design idea" behind the slab allocator (cache), namely, *mitigate the high wastage (internal fragmentation) of the page allocator by providing small, conveniently sized caches, typically, fragments of a page*. We will see what exactly this means in a practical fashion, along with the kernel slab allocator APIs.

Allocating slab memory

Though several APIs to perform memory allocation and freeing exist within the slab layer, there are just a couple of really key ones, with the rest falling into a "convenience or helper" functions category (which we will of course mention later). The key slab allocation APIs for the kernel module or device driver author are as follows:

```
#include <linux/slab.h>
void *kmalloc(size_t size, gfp_t flags);
void *kzalloc(size_t size, gfp_t flags);
```

Be sure to include the `<linux/slab.h>` header file when using any slab allocator APIs.

The `kmalloc()` and `kzalloc()` routines tend to be the **most frequently used APIs for memory allocation** within the kernel. A quick check – we're not aiming to be perfectly precise – with the very useful `cscope(1)` code browsing utility on the 5.4.0 Linux kernel source tree reveals the (approximate) frequency of usage: `kmalloc()` is called around 4,600 times and `kzalloc()` is called over 11,000 times!

Both functions have two parameters: the first parameter to pass is the size of the memory allocation required in bytes, while the second is the type of memory to allocate, specified via the now familiar GFP flags (we already covered this topic in earlier sections, namely, *Dealing with the GFP flags* and *The GFP flags – digging deeper*. If you're not familiar with them, I suggest you read those sections first).

> To mitigate the risk of **Integer Overflow (IoF)** bugs, you should avoid dynamically calculating the size of memory to allocate (the first parameter). The kernel documentation warns us regarding precisely this (link: `https://www.kernel.org/doc/html/latest/process/deprecated.html#open-coded-arithmetic-in-allocator-arguments`).
>
> In general, always avoid using deprecated stuff documented here: *Deprecated Interfaces, Language Features, Attributes, and Conventions* (link: `https://www.kernel.org/doc/html/latest/process/deprecated.html#deprecated-interfaces-language-features-attributes-and-conventions`).

Upon successful allocation, the return value is a pointer, the *kernel logical address* (remember, it's still a virtual address, *not* physical) of the start of the memory chunk (or slab) just allocated. Indeed, you should notice that but for the second parameter, the `kmalloc()` and `kzalloc()` APIs closely resemble their user space counterpart, the all-too-familiar glibc `malloc(3)` (and friends) APIs. Don't get the wrong idea, though: they're completely different. `malloc()` returns a user space virtual address and, as mentioned earlier, there is no direct correlation between the user-mode `malloc(3)` and the kernel-mode `k[m|z]alloc()` (so no, a call to `malloc()` does *not* result in an immediate call to `kmalloc()`; more on this later!).

Next, it's important to understand that the memory returned by these slab allocator APIs **is guaranteed to be physically contiguous**. Furthermore, and another key benefit, the return address is guaranteed to be on a CPU cacheline boundary; that is, it will be **cacheline-aligned**. Both of these are important performance-enhancing benefits.

> Every CPU reads and writes data (from and to CPU caches <-> RAM) in an atomic unit called the **CPU cacheline**. The size of the cacheline varies with the CPU. You can look this up with the `getconf(1)` utility – for example, try doing `getconf -a | grep LINESIZE`. On modern CPUs, the cachelines for instructions and data are often separated out (as are the CPU caches themselves). A typical CPU cacheline size is 64 bytes.

The content of a memory chunk immediately after allocation by `kmalloc()` is random (again, like `malloc(3)`). Indeed, the reason why `kzalloc()` is the preferred and recommended API to use is that it *sets to zero* the allocated memory. Some developers argue that the initialization of the memory slab takes some time, thus reducing performance. Our counter argument is that unless the memory allocation code is in an extremely time-critical code path (which, you could reasonably argue, is not good design in the first place, but sometimes can't be helped), you should, as a best practice, *initialize your memory upon allocation*. A whole slew of memory bugs and security side effects can thereby be avoided.

> Many parts of the Linux kernel core code certainly use the slab layer for memory. Within these, there *are* time critical code paths – good examples can be found within the network and block IO subsystems. For maximizing performance, the slab (actually SLUB) layer code has been written to be *lockless* (via a lock-free technology called per-CPU variables). See more on the performance challenges and implementation details in the *Further reading* section.

Freeing slab memory

Of course, you must free the allocated slab memory you allocated at some point in the future (thus not leaking memory); the `kfree()` routine serves this purpose. Analogous to the user space `free(3)` API, `kfree()` takes a single parameter – the pointer to the memory chunk to free. It must be a valid kernel logical (or virtual) address and must have been initialized by, that is, the return value of, one of the slab layer APIs (`k[m|z]alloc()` or one of its helpers). Its API signature is simple:

```
void kfree(const void *);
```

Just as with `free(3)`, there is no return value. As mentioned before, take care to ensure that the parameter to `kfree()` is the precise value returned by `k[m|z]alloc()`. Passing an incorrect value will result in memory corruption, ultimately leading to an unstable system.

There are a few additional points to note.

Let's assume we have allocated some slab memory with `kzalloc()`:

```
static char *kptr = kzalloc(1024, GFP_KERNEL);
```

Later, after usage, we would like to free it, so we do the following:

```
if (kptr)
    kfree(kptr);
```

This code – checking that the value of `kptr` is not `NULL` before freeing it – *is unnecessary*; just perform `kfree(kptr);` and it's done.

Another example of *incorrect* code (pseudo-code) is shown as follows:

```
static char *kptr = NULL;
while (<some-condition-is-true>) {
    if (!kptr)
         kptr = kmalloc(num, GFP_KERNEL);
    [... work on the slab memory ...]
    kfree(kptr);
}
```

Interesting: here, from the second loop iteration onward, the programmer has *assumed* that the `kptr` pointer variable will be set to `NULL` upon being freed! This is definitely not the case (it would have been quite a nice semantic to have though; also, the same argument applies to the "usual" user space library APIs). Thus, we hit a dangerous bug: on the loop's second iteration, the `if` condition will likely turn out to be false, thus skipping the allocation. Then, we hit the `kfree()`, which, of course, will now corrupt memory (due to a double-free bug)! (We provide a demo of this very case in the LKM here: `ch8/slab2_buggy`).

With regard to *initializing* memory buffers after (or during) allocation, just as we mentioned with regard to allocations, the same holds true for freeing memory. You should realize that the `kfree()` API merely returns the just-freed slab to its corresponding cache, leaving the internal memory content exactly as it was! Thus, just prior to freeing up your memory chunk, a (slightly pedantic) best practice is to *wipe out (overwrite)* the memory content. This is especially true for security reasons (such as in the case of an "info-leak," where a malicious attacker could conceivably scan freed memory for "secrets"). The Linux kernel provides the `kzfree()` API for this express purpose (the signature is identical to that of `kfree()`).

Careful! In order to overwrite "secrets," a simple `memset()` of the target buffer might just not work. Why not? The compiler might well optimize away the code (as the buffer is no longer to be used). David Wheeler, in his excellent work *Secure Programming HOWTO* (https://dwheeler.com/secure-programs/), mentions this very fact and provides a solution: "One approach that seems to work on all platforms is to write your own implementation of memset with internal "volatilization" of the first argument." (This code is based on a workaround proposed by Michael Howard):

> ```
> void *guaranteed_memset(void *v,int c,size_t n)
> { volatile char *p=v; while (n--) *p++=c; return v; }
> ```
>
> "Then place this definition into an external file to force the function to be external (define the function in a corresponding .h file, and `#include` the file in the callers, as is usual). This approach appears to be safe at any optimization level (even if the function gets inlined)."
>
> The kernel's `kzfree()` API should work just fine. Take care when doing similar stuff in user space.

Data structures – a few design tips

Using the slab APIs for memory allocation in kernel space is highly recommended. For one, it guarantees both physically contiguous as well as cacheline-aligned memory. This is very good for performance; in addition, let's check out a few quick tips that can yield big returns.

CPU caching can provide tremendous performance gains. Thus, especially for time-critical code, take care to design your data structures for best performance:

- Keep the most important (frequently accessed, "hot") members together and at the top of the structure. To see why, imagine there are five important members (of a total size of say, 56 bytes) in your data structure; keep them all together and at the top of the structure. Say the CPU cacheline size is 64 bytes. Now, when your code accesses *any one* of these five important members (for anything, read/write), *all five members will be fetched into the CPU cache(s) as the CPU's memory read/writes work in an atomic unit of CPU cacheline size*; this optimizes performance (as working on the cache is typically multiple times faster than working on RAM).

[423]

- Try and align the structure members such that a single member does not "fall off a cacheline." Usually, the compiler helps in this regard, but you can even use compiler attributes to explicitly specify this.
- Accessing memory sequentially results in high performance due to effective CPU caching. However, we can't seriously push the case for making all our data structures arrays! Experienced designers and developers know that using linked lists is extremely common. But doesn't that actually hurt performance? Well, yes, to some extent. Thus, a suggestion: use linked lists. Keep the "node" of the list as a large data structure (with "hot" members at the top and together). This way, we try and maximize the best of both cases as the large structure is essentially an array. (Think about it, the list of task structures that we saw in Chapter 6, *Kernel Internals Essentials – Processes and Threads*, – the *task list* – is a perfect real-world example of a linked list with large data structures as nodes).

The upcoming section deals with a key aspect: we learn exactly which slab caches the kernel uses when allocating (slab) memory via the popular k[m|z]alloc() APIs.

The actual slab caches in use for kmalloc

We'll take a quick deviation – very important, though – before trying out a kernel module using the basic slab APIs. It's important to understand where exactly the memory allocated by the k[m|z]alloc() APIs is coming from. Well, it's from the slab caches, yes, but which ones exactly? A quick grep on the output of sudo vmstat -m reveals this for us (the following screenshot is on our x86_64 Ubuntu guest):

```
$ sudo vmstat -m|head -n1
Cache                        Num    Total    Size   Pages
$ sudo vmstat -m |grep --color=auto "^kmalloc"
kmalloc-8192                  45       54    8448       3
kmalloc-4096                3444     3542    4352       7
kmalloc-2048                 844      975    2176      15
kmalloc-1024                 891     1274    1152      14
kmalloc-512                 2303     2676     640      12
kmalloc-256                 1169     1248     320      12
kmalloc-192                 1198     1408     256      16
kmalloc-128                 1612     1617     192      21
kmalloc-96                  2080     3552     128      32
kmalloc-64                  5247     7014      96      42
kmalloc-32                  2967     3400      48      85
kmalloc-16                  5888     5888      32     128
kmalloc-8                   5333     6290      24     170
$
```

Figure 8.7 – Screenshot of sudo vmstat -m showing the kmalloc-n slab caches

That's very interesting! The kernel has a slew of dedicated slab caches for generic `kmalloc` memory of varying sizes, *ranging from 8,192 bytes down to a mere 8 bytes!* This tells us something – with the page allocator, if we had requested, say, 12 bytes of memory, it would have ended up giving us a whole page (4 KB) – the wastage is just too much. Here, with the slab allocator, an allocation request for 12 bytes ends up actually allocating just 16 bytes (from the second-to-last cache seen in Figure 8.8)! Fantastic.

Also, note the following:

- Upon `kfree()`, the memory is freed back into the appropriate slab cache.
- The precise sizing of the slab caches for `kmalloc` varies with the architecture. On our Raspberry Pi system (an ARM CPU, of course), the generic memory `kmalloc-N` caches ranged from 64 bytes to 8,192 bytes.
- The preceding screenshot also reveals a clue. Often, the demand is for small-to-tiny fragments of memory. As an example, in the preceding screenshot the column labelled Num represents the *Number of currently active objects*, the maximum number is from the 8- and 16-byte `kmalloc` slab caches (of course, this may not always be the case. Quick tip: use the `slabtop(1)` utility (you'll need to run it as root): the rows towards the top reveal the current frequently used slab caches.)

Linux keeps evolving, of course. As of the 5.0 mainline kernel, there is a newly introduced `kmalloc` cache type, called the reclaimable cache (the naming format is `kmalloc-rcl-N`). Thus, performing a grep as done previously on a 5.x kernel will also reveal these caches:

```
$ sudo vmstat -m | grep --color=auto "^kmalloc"
kmalloc-rcl-8k              0         0      8192       4
kmalloc-rcl-4k              0         0      4096       8
kmalloc-rcl-2k              0         0      2048      16
[...]
kmalloc-8k                 52        52      8192       4
kmalloc-4k                 99       120      4096       8
kmalloc-2k                521       560      2048      16
[...]
```

The new `kmalloc-rcl-N` caches help internally with more efficiencies (to reclaim pages under pressure and as an anti-fragmentation measure). However, a module author like you need not be concerned with these details. (The commit for this work can be viewed here: https://github.com/torvalds/linux/commit/1291523f2c1d631fea34102fd241fb54a4e8f7a0.)

Kernel Memory Allocation for Module Authors - Part 1

> **TIP**: `vmstat -m` is essentially a wrapper over the kernel's `/sys/kernel/slab` content (more on this follows). Deep internal details of the slab caches can be seen using utilities such as `slabtop(1)`, as well as the powerful `crash(1)` utility (on a "live" system, the relevant crash command is `kmem -s` (or `kmem -S`)).

Right! Time to again get hands on with some code to demonstrate the usage of the slab allocator APIs!

Writing a kernel module to use the basic slab APIs

In the following code snippet, take a look at the demo kernel module code (found at `ch8/slab1/`). In the `init` code, we merely perform a couple of slab layer allocations (via the `kmalloc()` and `kzalloc()` APIs), print some information, and free the buffers in the cleanup code path (of course, the full source code is accessible at this book's GitHub repository). Let's look at the relevant parts of the code step by step.

At the start of the `init` code of this kernel module, we initialize a global pointer (`gkptr`) by allocating 1,024 bytes to it (*remember: pointers have no memory!*) via the `kmalloc()` slab allocation API. Notice that, as we're certainly running in process context here, and it is thus "safe to sleep," we use the `GFP_KERNEL` flag for the second parameter (just in case you want to refer back, the earlier section, *The GFP flags – digging deeper*, has it covered):

```
// ch8/slab1/slab1.c
[...]
#include <linux/slab.h>
[...]
static char *gkptr;
struct myctx {
    u32 iarr[100];
    u64 uarr[100];
    char uname[128], passwd[16], config[16];
};
static struct myctx *ctx;

static int __init slab1_init(void)
{
    /* 1. Allocate slab memory for 1 KB using the kmalloc() */
    gkptr = kmalloc(1024, GFP_KERNEL);
    if (!gkptr) {
```

```
            WARN_ONCE(1, "%s: kmalloc() failed!\n", OURMODNAME);
            /* As mentioned earlier, there is really no need to print an
             * error msg when a memory alloc fails; the situation "shouldn't"
             * typically occur, and if it does, the kernel will emit a chain
             * of messages in any case. Here, we use the WARN_ONCE()
             * macro pedantically, and as this is a 'learning' program..
             */
            goto out_fail1;
        }
        pr_info("kmalloc() succeeds, (actual KVA) ret value = %px\n", gkptr);
        /* We use the %px format specifier here to show the actual KVA; in
           production, Don't! */
        print_hex_dump_bytes("gkptr before memset: ", DUMP_PREFIX_OFFSET, gkptr, 32);
        memset(gkptr, 'm', 1024);
        print_hex_dump_bytes(" gkptr after memset: ", DUMP_PREFIX_OFFSET, gkptr, 32);
```

In the preceding code, also notice that we use the `print_hex_dump_bytes()` kernel convenience routine as a convenient way to dump the buffer memory in a human-readable format. Its signature is:

```
void print_hex_dump_bytes(const char *prefix_str, int prefix_type,
    const void *buf, size_t len);
```

Where `prefix_str` is any string you would like to prefix to each line of the hex dump; `prefix_type` is one of `DUMP_PREFIX_OFFSET`, `DUMP_PREFIX_ADDRESS`, or `DUMP_PREFIX_NONE`, `buf` is the source buffer to hex-dump; and `len` is the number of bytes to dump.

Up next is a typical strategy (*a best practice*) followed by many device drivers: they keep all their required or context information in a single data structure, often termed the *driver context* structure. We mimic this by declaring a (silly/sample) data structure called `myctx`, as well as a global pointer to it called `ctx` (the structure and pointer definition is in the preceding code block):

```
        /* 2. Allocate memory for and initialize our 'context' structure */
        ctx = kzalloc(sizeof(struct myctx), GFP_KERNEL);
        if (!ctx)
            goto out_fail2;
        pr_info("%s: context struct alloc'ed and initialized (actual KVA ret = %px)\n",
            OURMODNAME, ctx);
```

Kernel Memory Allocation for Module Authors - Part 1

```
        print_hex_dump_bytes("ctx: ", DUMP_PREFIX_OFFSET, ctx, 32);

        return 0;           /* success */
out_fail2:
        kfree(gkptr);
out_fail1:
        return -ENOMEM;
}
```

After the data structure, we then allocate and initialize `ctx` to the size of the `myctx` data structure via the useful `kzalloc()` wrapper API. The subsequent *hexdump* will show that it is indeed initialized to all zeroes (for readability, we will only "dump" the first 32 bytes).

Do notice how we handle the error paths using `goto`; this has already been mentioned a few times earlier in this book, so we won't repeat ourselves here. Finally, in the cleanup code of the kernel module, we `kfree()` both buffers, preventing any memory leakage:

```
static void __exit slab1_exit(void)
{
    kfree(ctx);
    kfree(gkptr);
    pr_info("%s: freed slab memory, removed\n", OURMODNAME);
}
```

A screenshot of a sample run on my Raspberry Pi 4 follows. I used our `../../lkm` convenience script to build, load, and do `dmesg`:

```
-----------------------------------
sudo insmod ./slab1.ko && lsmod|grep slab1
-----------------------------------
slab1                  16384  0
-----------------------------------
dmesg
-----------------------------------
[19808.873995] kmalloc() succeeds, (actual KVA) ret value = d8af6800
[19808.874005] gkptr before memset: 00000000: 00 70 af d8 00 00 00 00 00 00 00 00 00 00 00 00  .p..............
[19808.874011] gkptr before memset: 00000010: 00 00 00 00 00 00 00 00 00 00 00 00 00 00 00 00  ................
[19808.874017]  gkptr after memset: 00000000: 6d 6d 6d 6d 6d 6d 6d 6d 6d 6d 6d 6d 6d 6d 6d 6d  mmmmmmmmmmmmmmmm
[19808.874023]  gkptr after memset: 00000010: 6d 6d 6d 6d 6d 6d 6d 6d 6d 6d 6d 6d 6d 6d 6d 6d  mmmmmmmmmmmmmmmm
[19808.874029] slab1: context struct alloc'ed and initialized (actual KVA ret = d8594000)
[19808.874035] ctx: 00000000: 00 00 00 00 00 00 00 00 00 00 00 00 00 00 00 00  ................
[19808.874041] ctx: 00000010: 00 00 00 00 00 00 00 00 00 00 00 00 00 00 00 00  ................
rpi4 slab1 $
```

Figure 8.8 – Partial screenshot of our slab1.ko kernel module in action on a Raspberry Pi 4

Okay, now that you have a grip on the basics of using the common slab allocator APIs, `kmalloc()`, `kzalloc()`, and `kfree()`, let's go further. In the next section, we will dive into a really key concern – the reality of size limitations on the memory you can obtain via the slab (and page) allocators. Read on!

Size limitations of the kmalloc API

One of the key advantages of both the page and slab allocators is that the memory chunk they provide upon allocation is not only virtually contiguous (obviously) but is also guaranteed to be *physically contiguous memory*. Now that is a big deal and will certainly help performance.

But (there's always a *but*, isn't there!), precisely because of this guarantee, it becomes impossible to serve up any given large size when performing an allocation. In other words, there is a definite limit to the amount of memory you can obtain from the slab allocator with a single call to our dear `k[m|z]alloc()` APIs. What is the limit? (This is indeed a really frequently asked question.)

Firstly, you should understand that, technically, the limit is determined by two factors:

- One, the system page size (determined by the `PAGE_SIZE` macro)
- Two, the number of "orders" (determined by the `MAX_ORDER` macro); that is, the number of lists in the page allocator (or BSA) freelist data structures (see Figure 8.2)

With a standard 4 KB page size and a MAX_ORDER value of 11, the maximum amount of memory that can be allocated with a single `kmalloc()` or `kzalloc()` API call is 4 MB. This is the case on both the x86_64 and ARM architectures.

You might wonder, *how exactly is this 4 MB limit arrived at*? Think about it: once a slab allocation request exceeds the maximum slab cache size that the kernel provides (often 8 KB), the kernel simply passes the request down to the page allocator. The page allocator's maximum allocable size is determined by MAX_ORDER. With it set to `11`, the maximum allocable buffer size is $2^{(MAX\_ORDER-1)} = 2^{10}$ *pages = 1024 pages = 1024 * 4K = 4 MB*!

Testing the limits – memory allocation with a single call

A really key thing for developers (and everyone else, for that matter) is to **be empirical** in your work! The English word *empirical* means based on what is experienced or seen, rather than on theory. This is a critical rule to always follow – do not simply assume things or take them at face value. Try them out for yourself and see.

Let's do something quite interesting: write a kernel module that allocates memory from the (generic) slab caches (via the `kmalloc()` API, of course). We will do so in a loop, allocating – and freeing – a (calculated) amount on each loop iteration. The key point here is that we will keep increasing the amount allocated by a given "step" size. The loop terminates when `kmalloc()` fails; this way, we can test just how much memory we can actually allocate with a single call to `kmalloc()` (you'll realize, of course, that `kzalloc()`, being a simple wrapper over `kmalloc()`, faces precisely the same limits).

In the following code snippet, we show the relevant code. The `test_maxallocsz()` function is called from the `init` code of the kernel module:

```
// ch8/slab3_maxsize/slab3_maxsize.c
[...]
static int stepsz = 200000;
module_param(stepsz, int, 0644);
MODULE_PARM_DESC(stepsz,
"Amount to increase allocation by on each loop iteration (default=200000");

static int test_maxallocsz(void)
{
    size_t size2alloc = 0;
    void *p;

    while (1) {
        p = kmalloc(size2alloc, GFP_KERNEL);
        if (!p) {
            pr_alert("kmalloc fail, size2alloc=%zu\n", size2alloc);
            return -ENOMEM;
        }
        pr_info("kmalloc(%7zu) = 0x%pK\n", size2alloc, p);
        kfree(p);
        size2alloc += stepsz;
    }
```

```
            return 0;
}
```

> **TIP:** By the way, notice how our `printk()` function uses the `%zu` format specifier for the `size_t` (essentially an unsigned integer) variable? `%zu` is a portability aid; it makes the variable format correct for both 32- and 64-bit systems!

Let's build (cross-compile on the host) and insert this kernel module on our Raspberry Pi device running our custom-built 5.4.51-v7+ kernel; almost immediately, upon `insmod(8)`, you will see an error message, `Cannot allocate memory`, printed by the `insmod` process; the following (truncated) screenshot shows this:

```
[  391.152433] slab3_maxsize: inserted
[  391.152450] kmalloc(      0) = 0xe021e872
[  391.152466] kmalloc( 200000) = 0x018a5208
[  391.152484] kmalloc( 400000) = 0xeef720d6
[  391.152504] kmalloc( 600000) = 0xc442a50c
[  391.152519] kmalloc( 800000) = 0xc442a50c
[  391.152534] kmalloc(1000000) = 0xc442a50c
[  391.152556] kmalloc(1200000) = 0xc442a50c
[  391.152576] kmalloc(1400000) = 0xc442a50c
[  391.152597] kmalloc(1600000) = 0xc442a50c
[  391.152617] kmalloc(1800000) = 0xc442a50c
[  391.152638] kmalloc(2000000) = 0xc442a50c
[  391.152685] kmalloc(2200000) = 0x4a074daa
[  391.152720] kmalloc(2400000) = 0x4a074daa
[  391.152753] kmalloc(2600000) = 0x4a074daa
[  391.152787] kmalloc(2800000) = 0x4a074daa
[  391.152820] kmalloc(3000000) = 0x4a074daa
[  391.152853] kmalloc(3200000) = 0x4a074daa
[  391.152886] kmalloc(3400000) = 0x4a074daa
[  391.152920] kmalloc(3600000) = 0x4a074daa
[  391.152953] kmalloc(3800000) = 0x4a074daa
[  391.152987] kmalloc(4000000) = 0x4a074daa
[  391.153005] ------------[ cut here ]------------
[  391.153025] WARNING: CPU: 2 PID: 1249 at mm/page_alloc.c:4731 __alloc_pages_nodemask+0x230/0xeb8
[  391.153029] Modules linked in: slab3_maxsize(O+) rfcomm cmac bnep hci_uart btbcm bluetooth ecdh_generic ec
c 8021q garp stp llc brcmfmac brcmutil sha256_generic libsha256 cfg80211 rfkill bcm2835_codec(C) bcm2835_isp(
C) v4l2_mem2mem bcm2835_v4l2(C) raspberrypi_hwmon bcm2835_mmal_vchiq(C) videobuf2_dma_contig videobuf2_vmallo
c videobuf2_memops videobuf2_v4l2 videobuf2_common snd_bcm2835(C) videodev snd_pcm mc snd_timer vc_sm_cma(C)
snd uio_pdrv_genirq uio fixed i2c_dev ip_tables x_tables ipv6 nf_defrag_ipv6 [last unloaded: slab1]
[  391.153130] CPU: 2 PID: 1249 Comm: insmod Tainted: G        C O      5.4.51-v7+ #1
[  391.153132] Hardware name: BCM2835
[  391.153135] Backtrace:
[  391.153147] [<8010cb68>] (dump_backtrace) from [<8010ce4c>] (show_stack+0x20/0x24)
[  391.153152]  r6:b5ea2000 r5:ffffffff r4:00000000 r3:eb02066f
[  391.153161] [<8010ce2c>] (show_stack) from [<8085f21c>] (dump_stack+0xd4/0x120)
[  391.153169] [<8085f148>] (dump_stack) from [<8011e9fc>] (__warn+0xe0/0x108)
[  391.153175]  r9:0000127b r8:802ab194 r7:00000009 r6:80ab4918 r5:00000000 r4:00000000
[  391.153181] [<8011e91c>] (__warn) from [<8011eab8>] (warn_slowpath_fmt+0x94/0xa0)
[  391.153187]  r9:0000000b r8:0000127b r7:00000009 r6:80ab4918 r5:802ab194 r4:00000000
[  391.153194] [<8011ea28>] (warn_slowpath_fmt) from [<802ab194>] (__alloc_pages_nodemask+0x230/0xeb8)
[  391.153199]  r8:802c004c r7:00000cc0 r6:00401640 r5:ad800000 r4:00000000
[  391.153209] [<802aaf64>] (__alloc_pages_nodemask) from [<80288e60>] (kmalloc_order+0x2c/0x84)
[  391.153215]  r10:7f1ac088 r9:0000000b r8:802c004c r7:00000cc0 r6:00401640 r5:ad800000
```

Figure 8.9 – The first insmod(8) of our slab3_maxsize.ko kernel module on a Raspberry Pi 3 running a custom 5.4.51 kernel

Kernel Memory Allocation for Module Authors - Part 1

This is expected! Think about it, the `init` function of our kernel module code has indeed failed with `ENOMEM` after all. Don't get thrown by this; looking up the kernel log reveals what actually transpired. The fact is that on the very first test run of this kernel module, you will find that at the place where `kmalloc()` fails, the kernel dumps some diagnostic information, including a pretty lengthy kernel stack trace. This is due to it invoking a `WARN()` macro.

So, our slab memory allocations worked, up to a point. To clearly see the failure point, simply scroll down in the kernel log (`dmesg`) display. The following screenshot shows this:

```
[  391.153320] [<801b40c4>] (sys_finit_module) from [<80101000>] (ret_fast_syscall+0x0/0x28)
[  391.153323] Exception stack(0xb5ea3fa8 to 0xb5ea3ff0)
[  391.153328] 3fa0:                   31fa8700 7ef117c4 00000003 0002d064 00000000 00000004
[  391.153334] 3fc0: 31fa8700 7ef117c4 0003fce8 0000017b 01b237e0 00000000 00000002 00000000
[  391.153338] 3fe0: 7ef115f8 7ef115e8 00022cb8 76c46af0
[  391.153343] r8:801011c4 r7:0000017b r6:0003fce8 r5:7ef117c4 r4:31fa8700
[  391.153347] ---[ end trace 95ab43fba62b2d3a ]---
[  391.153352] kmalloc fail, size2alloc=4200000
[  548.838970] slab3_maxsize: inserted
[  548.838988] kmalloc(       0) = 0xe021e872
[  548.839003] kmalloc(  200000) = 0xeef720d6
[  548.839020] kmalloc(  400000) = 0xeef720d6
[  548.839039] kmalloc(  600000) = 0xc442a50c
[  548.839054] kmalloc(  800000) = 0xc442a50c
[  548.839068] kmalloc( 1000000) = 0xc442a50c
[  548.839091] kmalloc( 1200000) = 0xc442a50c
[  548.839124] kmalloc( 1400000) = 0xc442a50c
[  548.839464] kmalloc( 1600000) = 0xc442a50c
[  548.839490] kmalloc( 1800000) = 0xc442a50c
[  548.839510] kmalloc( 2000000) = 0xc442a50c
[  548.839554] kmalloc( 2200000) = 0x4a074daa
[  548.839589] kmalloc( 2400000) = 0x4a074daa
[  548.839624] kmalloc( 2600000) = 0x4a074daa
[  548.839658] kmalloc( 2800000) = 0x4a074daa
[  548.839691] kmalloc( 3000000) = 0x4a074daa
[  548.839726] kmalloc( 3200000) = 0x4a074daa
[  548.839759] kmalloc( 3400000) = 0x4a074daa
[  548.839793] kmalloc( 3600000) = 0x4a074daa
[  548.839826] kmalloc( 3800000) = 0x4a074daa
[  548.839860] kmalloc( 4000000) = 0x4a074daa
[  548.839879] kmalloc fail, size2alloc=4200000
```

Figure 8.10 – Partial screenshot showing the lower part of the dmesg output (of our slab3_maxsize.ko kernel module) on a Raspberry Pi 3

Aha, look at the last line of output (Figure 8.11): the `kmalloc()` fails on an allocation above 4 MB (at 4,200,000 bytes), precisely as expected; until then, it succeeds.

As an interesting aside, notice that we have (quite deliberately) performed the very first allocation in the loop with size 0; it does not fail:

- `kmalloc(0, GFP_xxx);` returns the zero pointer; on x86[_64], it's the value `16` or `0x10` (see `include/linux/slab.h` for details). In effect, it's an invalid virtual address living in the page 0 NULL pointer trap. Accessing it will, of course, lead to a page fault (originating from the MMU).

- Similarly, attempting `kfree(NULL);` or `kfree()` of the zero pointer results in `kfree()` becoming a no-op.

Hang on, though – an extremely important point to note: in the *The actual slab caches in use for kmalloc* section, we saw that the slab caches that are used to allocate memory to the caller are the `kmalloc-n` slab caches, where n ranges from `64` to `8192` bytes (on the Raspberry Pi, and thus the ARM for this discussion). Also, FYI, you can perform a quick `sudo vmstat -m | grep -v "\-rcl\-" | grep --color=auto "^kmalloc"` to verify this.

But clearly, in the preceding kernel module code example, we have allocated via `kmalloc()` much larger quantities of memory (right from 0 bytes to 4 MB). The way it really works is that the `kmalloc()` API only uses the `kmalloc-'n'` slab caches for memory allocations less than or equal to 8,192 bytes (if available); any allocation request for larger memory chunks is then passed to the underlying page (or buddy system) allocator! Now, recall what we learned in the previous chapter: the page allocator uses the buddy system freelists (on a per *node:zone* basis) *and* the maximum size of memory chunks enqueued on the freelists are $2^{(MAX\_ORDER-1)} = 2^{10}$ *pages*, which, of course, is 4 MB (given a page size of 4 KB and `MAX_ORDER` of `11`). This neatly ties in with our theoretical discussions.

So, there we have it: both in theory and in practice, you can now see that (again, given a page size of 4 KB and `MAX_ORDER` of `11`), the maximum size of memory that can be allocated via a single call to `kmalloc()` (or `kzalloc()`) is 4 MB.

Checking via the /proc/buddyinfo pseudo-file

It's really important to realize that although we figured out that 4 MB of RAM is the maximum we can get at one shot, it definitely doesn't mean that you will always get that much. No, of course not. It completely depends upon the amount of free memory present within the particular freelist at the time of the memory request. Think about it: what if you are running on a Linux system that has been up for several days (or weeks). The likelihood of finding physically contiguous 4 MB chunks of free RAM is quite low (again, this depends upon the amount of RAM on the system and its workload).

Kernel Memory Allocation for Module Authors - Part 1

As a rule of thumb, if the preceding experiment did not yield a maximum allocation of what we have deemed to be the maximum size (that is, 4 MB), why not try it on a freshly booted guest system? Now, the chances of having physically contiguous 4 MB chunks of free RAM are a lot better. Unsure about this? Let's get empirical again and look up the content of `/proc/buddyinfo` – both on an in-use and a freshly booted system – to figure out whether the memory chunks are available. In the following code snippet, on our in-use x86_64 Ubuntu guest system with just 1 GB of RAM, we look it up:

```
$ cat /proc/buddyinfo
Node 0, zone      DMA    225  154   46   30   14    9    1    1    0    0
0
Node 0, zone    DMA32    314  861  326  291  138   50   27    2    5    0
0
    order --->            0    1    2    3    4    5    6    7    8    9
10
```

As we learned earlier (in the *Freelist organization* section), the numbers seen in the preceding code block are in the sequence order 0 to `MAX_ORDER-1` (typically, 0 to 11 – 1 = 10), and they represent the number of 2^{order} contiguous free page frames in that order.

In the preceding output, we can see that we do *not* have free blocks on the order 10 list (that is, the 4 MB chunks; it's zero). On a freshly booted Linux system, the chances are high that we will. In the following output, on the same system that's just been rebooted, we see that there are seven chunks of free physically contiguous 4 MB RAM available in node 0, zone DMA32:

```
$ cat /proc/buddyinfo
Node 0, zone      DMA     10    2    2    3    3    3    3    2    2    0
0
Node 0, zone    DMA32    276  143  349  189   99    3    6    3    6    4
7
    order --->            0    1    2    3    4    5    6    7    8    9
10
```

Reiterating this very point, on a Raspberry Pi that has been up for just about a half hour, we have the following:

```
rpi ~/ $ cat /proc/buddyinfo
Node 0, zone   Normal    82   32   11    6    5    3    3    3    4    4
160
```

Here, there are 160 4 MB chunks of physically contiguous RAM available (free).

Of course, there's more to explore. In the following section, we cover more on using the slab allocator – the resource-managed API alternative, additional slab helper APIs that are available, and a note on cgroups and memory in modern Linux kernels.

Slab allocator – a few additional details

A few more key points remain to be explored. First, some information on using the kernel's resource-managed versions of the memory allocator APIs, followed by a few additionally available slab helper routines within the kernel, and then a brief look at cgroups and memory. We definitely recommend you go through these sections as well. Please, do read on!

Using the kernel's resource-managed memory allocation APIs

Especially useful for device drivers, the kernel provides a few managed APIs for memory allocation. These are formally referred to as the device resource-managed or devres APIs (the link to kernel documentation on this is https://www.kernel.org/doc/Documentation/driver-model/devres.txt). They are all prefixed with `devm_`; though there are several of them, we will focus on only one common use case here – that of using these APIs in place of the usual `k[m|z]alloc()` ones. They are as follows:

- `void * devm_kmalloc(struct device *dev, size_t size, gfp_t gfp);`
- `void * devm_kzalloc(struct device *dev, size_t size, gfp_t gfp);`

The reason why these resource-managed APIs are useful is that there is *no need for the developer to explicitly free the memory allocated by them*. The kernel resource management framework guarantees that it will automatically free the memory buffer upon driver detach, or if a kernel module, when the module is removed (or the device is detached, whichever occurs first). This feature immediately enhances code robustness. Why? Simple, we're all human and make mistakes. Leaking memory (especially on error code paths) is indeed a pretty common bug!

A few relevant points regarding the usage of these APIs:

- A key point – please do not attempt to blindly replace `k[m|z]alloc()` with the corresponding `devm_k[m|z]alloc()`! These resource-managed allocations are really designed to be used only in the init and/or `probe()` methods of a device driver (all drivers that work with the kernel's unified device model will typically supply the `probe()` and `remove()` (or `disconnect()`) methods. We will not delve into these aspects here).
- `devm_kzalloc()` is usually preferred as it initializes the buffer as well. Internally (as with `kzalloc()`), it is merely a thin wrapper over the `devm_kmalloc()` API.
- The second and third parameters are the usual ones, as with the `k[m|z]alloc()` APIs – the number of bytes to allocate and the GFP flags to use. The first parameter, though, is a pointer to `struct device`. Quite obviously, it represents the *device* that your driver is driving.
- As the memory allocated by these APIs is auto-freed (on driver detach or module removal), you don't have to do anything. It can, though, be freed via the `devm_kfree()` API. You doing this, however, is usually an indication that the managed APIs are the wrong ones to use...
- Licensing: The managed APIs are exported (and thus available) only to modules licensed under the GPL (in addition to other possible licenses).

Additional slab helper APIs

There are several helper slab allocator APIs, friends of the `k[m|z]alloc()` API family. These include the `kcalloc()` and `kmalloc_array()` APIs for allocating memory for an array, as well as `krealloc()`, whose behavior is analogous to `realloc(3)`, the familiar user space API.

In conjunction with allocating memory for an array of elements, the `array_size()` and `struct_size()` kernel helper routines can be very helpful. In particular, `struct_size()` has been heavily used to prevent (and indeed fix) many integer overflow (and related) bugs when allocating an array of structures, a common task indeed. As a quick example, here's a small code snippet from `net/bluetooth/mgmt.c`:

```
rp = kmalloc(struct_size(rp, addr, i), GFP_KERNEL);
  if (!rp) {
     err = -ENOMEM; [...]
```

It's worth browsing through the `include/linux/overflow.h` kernel header file.

`kzfree()` is like `kfree()` but zeroes out the (possibly larger) memory region being freed. (Why larger? This will be explained in the next section.) Note that this is considered a security measure but might hurt performance.

The resource-managed versions of these APIs are also available: `devm_kcalloc()` and `devm_kmalloc_array()`.

Control groups and memory

The Linux kernel supports a very sophisticated resource management system called **cgroups** (**control groups**), which, in a nutshell, are used to hierarchically organize processes and perform resource management (more on cgroups, with an example of cgroups v2 CPU controller usage, can be found in Chapter 11, *The CPU Scheduler - Part 2*, on CPU scheduling).

Among the several resource controllers is one for memory bandwidth. By carefully configuring it, the sysadmin can effectively regulate the distribution of memory on the system. Memory protection is possible, both as (what is called) hard and best-effort protection via certain `memcg` (memory cgroup) pseudo-files (particularly, the `memory.min` and `memory.low` files). In a similar fashion, within a cgroup, the `memory.high` and `memory.max` pseudo-files are the main mechanism to control the memory usage of a cgroup. Of course, as there is a lot more to it than is mentioned here, I refer you to the kernel documentation on the new cgroups (v2) here: https://www.kernel.org/doc/html/latest/admin-guide/cgroup-v2.html.

Right, now that you have learned how to use the slab allocator APIs better, let's dive a bit deeper still. The reality is, there are still a few important caveats regarding the size of the memory chunks allocated by the slab allocator APIs. Do read on to find out what they are!

Caveats when using the slab allocator

We will split up this discussion into three parts. We will first re-examine some necessary background (which we covered earlier), then actually flesh out the problem with two use cases – the first being very simple, and the second a more real-world case of the issue at hand.

Background details and conclusions

So far, you have learned some key points:

- The *page* (or *buddy system*) *allocator* allocates power-of-2 pages to the caller. The power to raise 2 to is called the *order*; it typically ranges from 0 to 10 (on both x86[_64] and ARM).
- This is fine, except when it's not. When the amount of memory requested is very small, the *wastage* (or internal fragmentation) can be huge.
- Requests for fragments of a page (less than 4,096 bytes) are very common. Thus, the *slab allocator, layered upon the page allocator* (see Figure 8.1) is designed with object caches, as well as small generic memory caches, to efficiently fulfill requests for small amounts of memory.
- The page allocator guarantees physically contiguous page and cacheline-aligned memory.
- The slab allocator guarantees physically contiguous and cacheline-aligned memory.

So, fantastic – this leads us to conclude that when the amount of memory required is large-ish and a perfect (or close) power of 2, use the page allocator. When it's quite small (less than a page), use the slab allocator. Indeed, the kernel source code of kmalloc() has a comment that neatly sums up how the kmalloc() API should be used (reproduced in bold font as follows):

```
// include/linux/slab.h
[...]
 * kmalloc - allocate memory
 * @size: how many bytes of memory are required.
 * @flags: the type of memory to allocate.
 * kmalloc is the normal method of allocating memory
 * for objects smaller than page size in the kernel.
```

Sounds great, but there is still a problem! To see it, let's learn how to use another useful slab API, `ksize()`. Its signature is as follows:

```
size_t ksize(const void *);
```

The parameter to `ksize()` is a pointer to an existing slab cache (it must be a valid one). In other words, it's the return address from one of the slab allocator APIs (typically, `k[m|z]alloc()`). The return value is the actual number of bytes allocated.

Okay, now that you know what `ksize()` is for, let's use it in a more practical fashion, first with a simple use case and then with a better one!

Testing slab allocation with ksize() – case 1

To understand what we're getting at, consider a small example (for readability, we will not show essential validity checks. Also, as this is a tiny code snippet, we haven't provided it as a kernel module in the book's code base):

```
struct mysmallctx {
    int tx, rx;
    char passwd[8], config[4];
} *ctx;

pr_info("sizeof struct mysmallctx = %zd bytes\n", sizeof(struct mysmallctx));
ctx = kzalloc(sizeof(struct mysmallctx), GFP_KERNEL);
pr_info("(context structure allocated and initialized to zero)\n"
        "*actual* size allocated = %zu bytes\n", ksize(ctx));
```

The resulting output on my x86_64 Ubuntu guest system is as follows:

```
$ dmesg
[...]
sizeof struct mysmallctx = 20 bytes
(context structure allocated and initialized to zero)
*actual* size allocated = 32 bytes
```

So, we attempted to allocate 20 bytes with `kzalloc()`, but actually obtained 32 bytes (thus incurring a wastage of 12 bytes, or 60%!). This is expected. Recall the `kmalloc-n` slab caches – on x86, there is one for 16 bytes and another for 32 bytes (among the many others). So, when we ask for an amount in between the two, we obviously get memory from the higher of the two. (Incidentally, and FYI, on our ARM-based Raspberry Pi system, the smallest slab cache for `kmalloc` is 64 bytes, so, of course, we get 64 bytes when we ask for 20 bytes.)

> **TIP**
> Note that the `ksize()` API works only on allocated slab memory; you cannot use it on the return value from any of the page allocator APIs (which we saw in the *Understanding and using the kernel page allocator (or BSA)* section).

Now for the second, and more interesting, use case.

Testing slab allocation with ksize() – case 2

Okay, now, let's extend our previous kernel module (`ch8/slab3_maxsize`) to `ch8/slab4_actualsize`. Here, we will perform the same loop, allocating memory with `kmalloc()` and freeing it as before, but this time, we will also document the actual amount of memory allocated to us in each loop iteration by the slab layer, by invoking the `ksize()` API:

```
// ch8/slab4_actualsize/slab4_actualsize.c
static int test_maxallocsz(void)
{
    size_t size2alloc = 100, actual_alloced;
    void *p;

    pr_info("kmalloc(        n) :  Actual : Wastage : Waste %%\n");
    while (1) {
        p = kmalloc(size2alloc, GFP_KERNEL);
        if (!p) {
            pr_alert("kmalloc fail, size2alloc=%zu\n", size2alloc);
            return -ENOMEM;
        }
        actual_alloced = ksize(p);
        /* Print the size2alloc, the amount actually allocated,
         * the delta between the two, and the percentage of waste
         * (integer arithmetic, of course :-)  */
        pr_info("kmalloc(%7zu) : %7zu : %7zu : %3zu%%\n",
            size2alloc, actual_alloced, (actual_alloced-size2alloc),
            (((actual_alloced-size2alloc)*100)/size2alloc));
```

```
        kfree(p);
        size2alloc += stepsz;
    }
    return 0;
}
```

The output of this kernel module is indeed interesting to scan! In the following figure, we show a partial screenshot of the output I got on my x86_64 Ubuntu 18.04 LTS guest running our custom built 5.4.0 kernel:

```
[   92.257210] slab4_actualsize: inserted
[   92.259948] kmalloc(       n) :  Actual : Wastage : Waste %
[   92.261041] kmalloc(     100) :     128 :      28 :   28%
[   92.261826] kmalloc(  200100) :  262144 :   62044 :   31%
[   92.262615] kmalloc(  400100) :  524288 :  124188 :   31%
[   92.267690] kmalloc(  600100) : 1048576 :  448476 :   74%
[   92.269786] kmalloc(  800100) : 1048576 :  248476 :   31%
[   92.271410] kmalloc( 1000100) : 1048576 :   48476 :    4%
[   92.272284] kmalloc( 1200100) : 2097152 :  897052 :   74%
[   92.272994] kmalloc( 1400100) : 2097152 :  697052 :   49%
[   92.273695] kmalloc( 1600100) : 2097152 :  497052 :   31%
[   92.274337] kmalloc( 1800100) : 2097152 :  297052 :   16%
[   92.275292] kmalloc( 2000100) : 2097152 :   97052 :    4%
[   92.276297] kmalloc( 2200100) : 4194304 : 1994204 :   90%
[   92.277015] kmalloc( 2400100) : 4194304 : 1794204 :   74%
[   92.277698] kmalloc( 2600100) : 4194304 : 1594204 :   61%
[   92.278395] kmalloc( 2800100) : 4194304 : 1394204 :   49%
[   92.279326] kmalloc( 3000100) : 4194304 : 1194204 :   39%
[   92.280145] kmalloc( 3200100) : 4194304 :  994204 :   31%
[   92.280829] kmalloc( 3400100) : 4194304 :  794204 :   23%
[   92.281511] kmalloc( 3600100) : 4194304 :  594204 :   16%
[   92.282192] kmalloc( 3800100) : 4194304 :  394204 :   10%
[   92.282994] kmalloc( 4000100) : 4194304 :  194204 :    4%
[   92.283765] ------------[ cut here ]------------
[   92.284281] WARNING: CPU: 1 PID: 1525 at mm/page_alloc.c:4738 __alloc_pages_nodemask+0x40d/0x520
[   92.285225] Modules linked in: slab4_actualsize(OE+) vboxsf(OE) vboxvideo(OE) vmwgfx snd_intel8x0
m_kms_helper snd_timer aesni_intel glue_helper syscopyarea crypto_simd snd_seq_device cryptd sysfillr
video mac_hid vboxguest(OE) sch_fq_codel parport_pc ppdev lp parport ip_tables x_tables autofs4 hid_g
[   92.290634] CPU: 1 PID: 1525 Comm: insmod Tainted: G           OE     5.4.0-llkd02-kasan #4
[   92.291549] Hardware name: innotek GmbH VirtualBox/VirtualBox, BIOS VirtualBox 12/01/2006
[   92.292446] RIP: 0010:__alloc_pages_nodemask+0x40d/0x520
[   92.294196] Code: 0f 84 2a fe ff ff 80 ce 01 e9 22 fe ff ff 4c 89 ff e8 c7 21 fa ff 49 89 c7 e9 bb
4c 8b 3c 25 c0 fb 01
[   92.299994] RSP: 0018:ffff888035977728 EFLAGS: 00010246
```

Figure 8.11 – Partial screenshot of our slab4_actualsize.ko kernel module in action

The module's printk output can be clearly seen in the preceding screenshot. The remainder of the screen is diagnostic information from the kernel – this is emitted as a kernel-space memory allocation request failed. All this kernel diagnostic information is a result of the first invocation of the kernel calling the WARN_ONCE() macro, as the underlying page allocator code, mm/page_alloc.c:__alloc_pages_nodemask() – the "heart" of the buddy system allocator, as it's known - failed! This should typically never occur, hence the diagnostics (the details on the kernel diagnostics is beyond this book's scope, so we will leave this aside. Having said that, we do examine the kernel stack backtrace to some extent in coming chapters).

Interpreting the output from case 2

Look closely at the preceding screenshot (Figure 8.12; here, we will simply ignore the kernel diagnostics emitted by the `WARN()` macro, which got invoked because a kernel-level memory allocation failed!). The Figure 8.12 output has five columns, as follows:

- The timestamp from `dmesg(1)`; we ignore it.
- `kmalloc(n)`: The number of bytes requested by `kmalloc()` (where n is the required amount).
- The actual number of bytes allocated by the slab allocator (revealed via `ksize()`).
- The wastage (bytes): The difference between the actual and required bytes.
- The wastage as a percentage.

As an example, in the second allocation, we requested 200,100 bytes, but actually obtained 262,144 bytes (256 KB). This makes sense, as this is the precise size of one of the page allocator lists on a buddy system freelist (it's *order 6*, as $2^6 = 64\ pages = 64 \times 4 = 256\ KB$; see *Figure 8.2*). Hence, the delta, or wastage really, is *262,144 - 200,100 = 62,044 bytes*, which, when expressed as a percentage, is 31%.

It's like this: the closer the requested (or required) size gets to the kernel's available (or actual) size, the less the wastage will be; the converse is true as well. Let's look at another example from the preceding output (the snipped output is reproduced as follows for clarity):

```
[...]
[92.273695] kmalloc(1600100)  : 2097152 :  497052 : 31%
[92.274337] kmalloc(1800100)  : 2097152 :  297052 : 16%
[92.275292] kmalloc(2000100)  : 2097152 :   97052 :  4%
[92.276297] kmalloc(2200100)  : 4194304 : 1994204 : 90%
[92.277015] kmalloc(2400100)  : 4194304 : 1794204 : 74%
[92.277698] kmalloc(2600100)  : 4194304 : 1594204 : 61%
[...]
```

From the preceding output, you can see that when `kmalloc()` requests 1,600,100 bytes (around 1.5 MB), it actually gets 2,097,152 bytes (exactly 2 MB), and the wastage is 31%. The wastage then successively *reduces as we get closer to an allocation "boundary" or threshold* (the actual size of the kernel's slab cache or page allocator memory chunk) as it were: to 16%, then down to 4%. But look: with the next allocation, when we cross that threshold, asking for *just over* 2 MB (2,200,100 bytes), we actually get 4 MB, *a wastage of 90%*! Then, the wastage again drops as we move closer to the 4 MB memory size...

This is important! You might think you're being very efficient by mere use of the slab allocator APIs, but in reality, the slab layer invokes the page allocator when the amount of memory requested is above the maximum size that the slab layer can provide (typically, 8 KB, which is often the case in our preceding experiments). Thus, the page allocator, suffering from its usual wastage issues, ends up allocating far more memory than you actually require, or indeed ever use. What a waste!

The moral: *check and recheck your code that allocates memory with the slab APIs*. Run trials on it using `ksize()` to figure out how much memory is actually being allocated, not how much you think is being allocated.

There are no shortcuts. Well, there is one: if you require less than a page of memory (a very typical use case), just use the slab APIs. If you require more, the preceding discussion comes into play. Another thing: using the `alloc_pages_exact()` / `free_pages_exact()` APIs (covered in the *One Solution – the exact page allocator APIs* section) should help reduce wastage as well.

Graphing it

As an interesting aside, we use the well-known `gnuplot(1)` utility to plot a graph from the previously gathered data. Actually, we have to minimally modify the kernel module to only output what we'd like to graph: the required (or requested) amount of memory to allocate (*x* axis), and the percentage of waste that actually occurred at runtime (*y* axis). You can find the code of our slightly modified kernel module in the book's GitHub repository here: `ch8/slab4_actualsz_wstg_plot` (https://github.com/PacktPublishing/Linux-Kernel-Programming/tree/master/ch8/slab4_actualsize).

So, we build and insert this kernel module, "massage" the kernel log, saving the data in an appropriate column-wise format as required by `gnuplot` (in a file called `2plotdata.txt`). While we do not intend to delve into the intricacies of using `gnuplot(1)` here (refer to the *Further reading* section for a tutorial link), in the following code snippet, we show the essential commands to generate our graph:

```
gnuplot> set title "Slab/Page Allocator: Requested vs Actually
allocated size Wastage in Percent"
gnuplot> set xlabel "Required size"
gnuplot> set ylabel "%age Waste"
gnuplot> plot "2plotdata.txt" using 1:100 title "Required Size" with
points, "2plotdata.txt" title "Wastage %age" with linespoints
gnuplot>
```

Lo and behold, the plot:

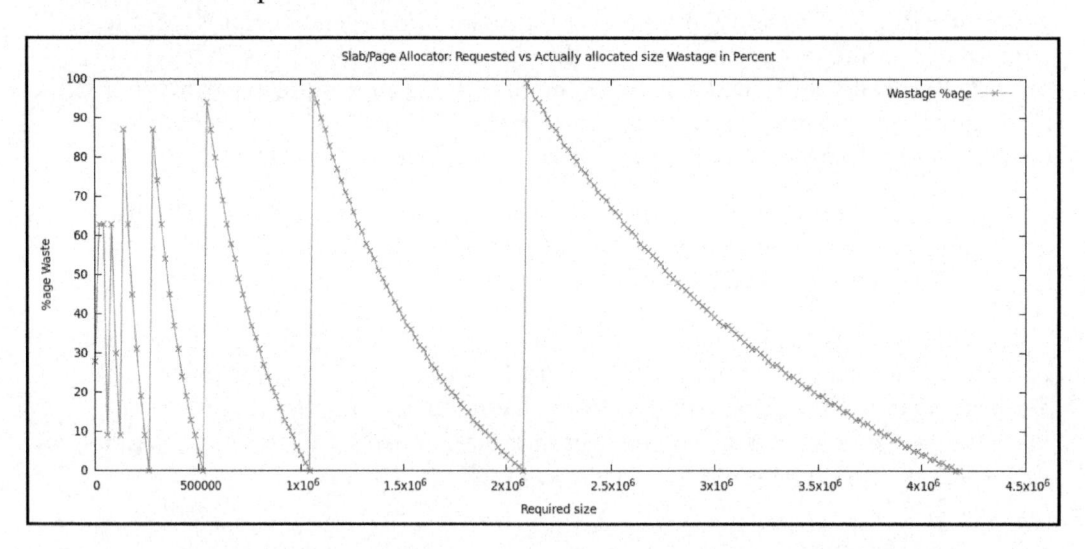

Figure 8.12 – A graph showing the size requested by kmalloc() (x axis) versus the wastage incurred (as a percentage: y axis)

This "saw-tooth"-shaped graph helps visualize what you just learned. The closer a `kmalloc()` (or `kzalloc()`, or indeed *any* page allocator API) allocation request size is to any of the kernel's predefined freelist sizes, the less wastage there is. But the moment this threshold is crossed, the wastage zooms up (spikes) to close to 100% (as seen by the literally vertical lines in the preceding graph).

So, with this, we've covered a significant amount of stuff. As usual, though, we're not done: the next section very briefly highlights the actual slab layer implementations (yes, there are several) within the kernel. Let's check it out!

Slab layer implementations within the kernel

In closing, we mention the fact that there are at least three different mutually exclusive kernel-level implementations of the slab allocator; only one of them can be in use at runtime. The one to be used at runtime is selected at the time of *configuring* the kernel (you learned this procedure in detail in `Chapter 2`, *Building the 5.x Linux Kernel from Source – Part 1*). The relevant kernel configuration options are as follows:

- `CONFIG_SLAB`
- `CONFIG_SLUB`
- `CONFIG_SLOB`

The first (SLAB) is the early, well-supported (but quite under-optimized) one; the second one (SLUB, *the unqueued allocator*) is a major improvement on the first, in terms of memory efficiency, performance, and better diagnostics, and is the one selected by default. The SLOB allocator is a drastic simplification and, as per the kernel config help, "does not perform well on large systems."

Summary

In this chapter, you learned – to a good level of detail – how both the page (or buddy system) as well as the slab allocators work. Recall that the actual "engine" of allocating (and freeing) RAM within the kernel is ultimately the *page (or buddy system) allocator*, the slab allocator being layered on top of it to provide optimization for typical less-than-a-page-in-size allocation requests and to efficiently allocate several well-known kernel data structures ('objects').

You learned how to efficiently use the APIs exposed by both the page and slab allocators, with several demo kernel modules to help show this in a hands-on manner. A good deal of focus was (quite rightly) given to the real issue of the developer issuing a memory request for a certain N number of bytes, but you learned that it can be very sub-optimal, with the kernel actually allocating much more (the wastage can climb to very close to 100%)! You now know how to check for and mitigate these cases. Well done!

The following chapter covers more on optimal allocation strategies, as well as some more advanced topics on kernel memory allocation, including the creation of custom slab caches, using the vmalloc interfaces, what the *OOM killer* is all about, and more. So, first ensure you've understood the content of this chapter and worked on the kernel modules and assignments (as follows). Then, let's get you on to the next one!

Questions

As we conclude, here is a list of questions for you to test your knowledge regarding this chapter's material: https://github.com/PacktPublishing/Linux-Kernel-Programming/tree/master/questions. You will find some of the questions answered in the book's GitHub repo: https://github.com/PacktPublishing/Linux-Kernel-Programming/tree/master/solutions_to_assgn.

Further reading

To help you delve deeper into the subject with useful materials, we provide a rather detailed list of online references and links (and at times, even books) in a Further reading document in this book's GitHub repository. The *Further reading* document is available here: `https://github.com/PacktPublishing/Linux-Kernel-Programming/blob/master/Further_Reading.md`.

9
Kernel Memory Allocation for Module Authors - Part 2

The previous chapter covered the basics (and a lot more!) on using the available APIs for memory allocation via both the page (BSA) and the slab allocators within the kernel. In this chapter, we will delve further into this large and interesting topic. We cover the creation of custom slab caches, the vmalloc interfaces, and very importantly, given the wealth of choice, which APIs to use in which situation. Internal kernel details regarding the dreaded **Out Of Memory** (**OOM**) killer and demand paging help round off these important topics.

These areas tend to be one of the key aspects to understand when working with kernel modules, especially device drivers. A Linux system project's sudden crash with merely a Killed message on the console requires some explanation, yes!? The OOM killer's the sweet chap behind this...

Briefly, within this chapter, these are the main areas covered:

- Creating a custom slab cache
- Debugging at the slab layer
- Understanding and using the kernel vmalloc() API
- Memory allocation in the kernel – which APIs to use when
- Stayin' alive - the OOM killer

Technical requirements

I assume that you have gone through Chapter 1, *Kernel Workspace Setup*, and have appropriately prepared a guest VM running Ubuntu 18.04 LTS (or a later stable release) and installed all the required packages. If not, I highly recommend you do this first.

Also, the last section of this chapter has you deliberately run a *very* memory-intensive app; so intensive that the kernel will take some drastic action! Obviously, I highly recommend you try out stuff like this on a safe, isolated system, preferably a Linux test VM (with no important data on it).

To get the most out of this book, I strongly recommend you first set up the workspace environment, including cloning this book's GitHub repository for the code, and work on it in a hands-on fashion. The GitHub repository can be found at https://github.com/PacktPublishing/Linux-Kernel-Programming.

Creating a custom slab cache

As explained in detail in the previous chapter, a key design concept behind slab caches is the powerful idea of object caching. By caching frequently used objects – data structures, really – performance receives a boost. So, think about this: what if we're writing a driver, and in that driver, a certain data structure (an object) is very frequently allocated and freed? Normally, we would use the usual `kzalloc()` (or `kmalloc()`) followed by the `kfree()` APIs to allocate and free this object. The good news, though: the Linux kernel sufficiently exposes the slab layer API to us as module authors, allowing us to create *our own custom slab caches*. In this section, you'll learn how you can leverage this powerful feature.

Creating and using a custom slab cache within a kernel module

In this section, we're about to create, use, and subsequently destroy a custom slab cache. At a broad level, we'll be performing the following steps:

1. Creating a custom slab cache of a given size with the `kmem_cache_create()` API. This is often done as part of the init code path of the kernel module (or within the probe method when in a driver).
2. Using the slab cache. Here we will do the following:
    1. Issue the `kmem_cache_alloc()` API to allocate a single instance of the custom object(s) within your slab cache.
    2. Use the object.
    3. Free it back to the cache with the `kmem_cache_free()` API.

3. Destroying the custom slab cache when done
   with `kmem_cache_destroy()`. This is often done as part of the cleanup code path of the kernel module (or within the remove/detach/disconnect method when in a driver).

Let's explore each of these APIs in a bit of detail. We start with the creation of a custom (slab) cache.

Creating a custom slab cache

First, of course, let's learn how to create the custom slab cache. The signature of the `kmem_cache_create()` kernel API is as follows:

```
#include <linux/slab.h>
struct kmem_cache *kmem_cache_create(const char *name, unsigned int size,
            unsigned int align, slab_flags_t flags, void (*ctor)(void *));
```

The first parameter is the name of the cache - as will be revealed by `proc` (and hence by other wrapper utilities over `proc`, such as `vmstat(8)`, `slabtop(1)`, and so on). It usually matches the name of the data structure or object being cached (but does not have to).

The second parameter, `size`, is really the key one – it's the size in bytes for each object within the new cache. Based on this object size (using a best-fit algorithm), the kernel's slab layer constructs a cache of objects. The actual size of each object within the cache will be (slightly) larger than what's requested, due to three reasons:

- One, we can always provide more, but never less, than the memory requested.
- Two, some space for metadata (housekeeping information) is required.
- Three, the kernel is limited in being able to provide a cache of the exact size required. It uses the memory of the closest possible matching size (recall from `Chapter 8`, *Kernel Memory Allocation for Module Authors – Part 1*, in the *Caveats when using the slab allocator* section, where we clearly saw that more (sometimes a lot!) memory could actually be used).

Kernel Memory Allocation for Module Authors - Part 2

Recall from Chapter 8, *Kernel Memory Allocation for Module Authors – Part 1*, that the `ksize()` API can be used to query the actual size of the allocated object. There is another API with which we can query the size of the individual objects within the new slab cache:
`unsigned int kmem_cache_size(struct kmem_cache *s);`.
You shall see this being used shortly.

The third parameter, `align`, is the *alignment* required for the objects within the cache. If unimportant, just pass it as 0. Quite often though, there are very particular alignment requirements, for example, ensuring that the object is aligned to the size of a word on the machine (32 or 64 bits). To do so, pass the value as `sizeof(long)` (the unit for this parameter is bytes, not bits).

The fourth parameter, `flags`, can either be 0 (implying no special behavior), or the bitwise-OR operator of the following flag values. For clarity, we directly reproduce the information on the following flags from the comments within the source file, `mm/slab_common.c`:

```
// mm/slab_common.c
[...]
 * The flags are
 *
 * %SLAB_POISON - Poison the slab with a known test pattern (a5a5a5a5)
 * to catch references to uninitialized memory.
 *
 * %SLAB_RED_ZONE - Insert `Red` zones around the allocated memory to check
 * for buffer overruns.
 *
 * %SLAB_HWCACHE_ALIGN - Align the objects in this cache to a hardware
 * cacheline. This can be beneficial if you're counting cycles as closely
 * as davem.
[...]
```

Let's quickly check the flags out:

- The first of the flags, `SLAB_POISON`, provides slab poisoning, that is, initializing the cache memory to a previously known value (`0xa5a5a5a5`). Doing this can help during debug situations.
- The second flag, `SLAB_RED_ZONE`, is interesting, inserting red zones (analogous to guard pages) around the allocated buffer. This is a common way of checking for buffer overflow errors. It's almost always used in a debug context (typically during development).

- The third possible flag, SLAB_HWCACHE_ALIGN, is very commonly used and is in fact recommended for performance. It guarantees that all the cache objects are aligned to the hardware (CPU) cacheline size. This is precisely how the memory allocated via the popular k[m|z]alloc() APIs are aligned to the hardware (CPU) cacheline.

Finally, the fifth parameter to kmem_cache_create() is very interesting too: a function pointer, void (*ctor)(void *);. It is modeled as a constructor function (as in object orientation and OOP languages). It conveniently allows you to initialize the slab object from the custom slab cache the moment it's allocated! As one example of this feature in action within the kernel, see the code of the **Linux Security Module (LSM)** called integrity here:

```
security/integrity/iint.c:integrity_iintcache_init()
```

It invokes the following:

```
iint_cache = kmem_cache_create("iint_cache", sizeof(struct integrity_iint_cache),
    0, SLAB_PANIC, init_once);
```

The init_once() function initializes the cached object instance (that was just allocated). Remember, the constructor function is called whenever new pages are allocated by this cache.

> Though it may seem counter-intuitive, the fact is that the modern Linux kernel is quite object-oriented in design terms. The code, of course, is mostly plain old C, a traditional procedural language. Nevertheless, a vast number of architecture implementations within the kernel (the driver model being a big one) are quite object-oriented in design: method dispatch via virtual function pointer tables - the strategy design pattern, and so on. See a two-part article on LWN depicting this in some detail here: *Object-oriented design patterns in the kernel, part 1, June 2011* (https://lwn.net/Articles/444910/).

The return value from the kmem_cache_create() API is a pointer to the newly created custom slab cache on success, and NULL on failure. This pointer is usually kept global, as you will require access to it in order to actually allocate objects from it (our next step).

Kernel Memory Allocation for Module Authors - Part 2

It's important to understand that the `kmem_cache_create()` API can only be called from process context. A fair bit of kernel code (including many drivers) create and use their own custom slab caches. For example, in the 5.4.0 Linux kernel, there are over 350 instances of this API being invoked.

All right, now that you have a custom (slab) cache available, how exactly do you use it to allocate memory objects? Read on; the next section covers precisely this.

Using the new slab cache's memory

So, okay, we created a custom slab cache. To make use of it, you must issue the `kmem_cache_alloc()` API. Its job: given the pointer to a slab cache (which you just created), it allocates a single instance of an object on that slab cache (in fact, this is really how the `k[m|z]alloc()` APIs work under the hood). Its signature is as follows (of course, remember to always include the `<linux/slab.h>` header for all slab-based APIs):

```
void *kmem_cache_alloc(struct kmem_cache *s, gfp_t gfpflags);
```

Let's look at its parameters:

- The first parameter to `kmem_cache_alloc()` is the pointer to the (custom) cache that we created in the previous step (the pointer being the return value from the `kmem_cache_create()` API).
- The second parameter is the usual GFP flags to pass along (remember the essential rule: use `GFP_KERNEL` for normal process-context allocations, else `GFP_ATOMIC` if in any kind of atomic or interrupt context).

As with the now-familiar `k[m|z]alloc()` APIs, the return value is a pointer to the newly allocated memory chunk – a kernel logical address (it's a KVA of course).

Use the newly allocated memory object, and when done, do not forget to free it with the following:

```
void kmem_cache_free(struct kmem_cache *, void *);
```

Here, take note of the following with respect to the `kmem_cache_free()` API:

- The first parameter to `kmem_cache_free()` is, again, the pointer to the (custom) slab cache that you created in the previous step (the return value from `kmem_cache_create()`).

[452]

- The second parameter is the pointer to the memory object you wish to free – the object instance that you were just allocated with `kmem_cache_alloc()` – and thus have it return to the cache specified by the first parameter!

Similar to the `k[z]free()` APIs, there is no return value.

Destroying the custom cache

When completely done (often in the cleanup or exit code path of the kernel module, or your driver's `remove` method), you must destroy the custom slab cache that you created earlier using the following line:

```
void kmem_cache_destroy(struct kmem_cache *);
```

The parameter, of course, is the pointer to the (custom) cache that you created in the previous step (the return value from the `kmem_cache_create()` API).

Now that you have understood the procedure and its related APIs, let's get hands on with a kernel module that creates its own custom slab cache, uses it, and then destroys it.

Custom slab – a demo kernel module

Time to get our hands dirty with some code! Let's look at a simple demonstration of using the preceding APIs to create our very own custom slab cache. As usual, we show only relevant code here. I urge you to clone the book's GitHub repository and try it out yourself! You can find the code for this file at `ch9/slab_custom/slab_custom.c`.

In our init code path, we first call the following function to create our custom slab cache:

```
// ch9/slab_custom/slab_custom.c
#define OURCACHENAME    "our_ctx"
/* Our 'demo' structure, that (we imagine) is often allocated and freed;
 * hence, we create a custom slab cache to hold pre-allocated 'instances'
 * of it... Its size: 328 bytes.
 */
struct myctx {
```

```
    u32 iarr[10];
    u64 uarr[10];
    char uname[128], passwd[16], config[64];
};
static struct kmem_cache *gctx_cachep;
```

In the preceding code, we declare a (global) pointer (`gctx_cachep`) to the to-be-created custom slab cache – which will hold objects; namely, our fictional often allocated data structure, `myctx`.

In the following, see the code that creates the custom slab cache:

```
static int create_our_cache(void)
{
    int ret = 0;
    void *ctor_fn = NULL;

    if (use_ctor == 1)
        ctor_fn = our_ctor;
    pr_info("sizeof our ctx structure is %zu bytes\n"
            " using custom constructor routine? %s\n",
            sizeof(struct myctx), use_ctor==1?"yes":"no");

  /* Create a new slab cache:
   * kmem_cache_create(const char *name, unsigned int size, unsigned int
       align, slab_flags_t flags, void (*ctor)(void *));  */
    gctx_cachep = kmem_cache_create(OURCACHENAME, // name of our cache
            sizeof(struct myctx),  // (min) size of each object
            sizeof(long),          // alignment
            SLAB_POISON |          /* use slab poison values (explained soon) */
            SLAB_RED_ZONE |        /* good for catching buffer under|over-flow bugs */
            SLAB_HWCACHE_ALIGN,    /* good for performance */
            ctor_fn);              // ctor: here, on by default

    if (!gctx_cachep) {
        [...]
        if (IS_ERR(gctx_cachep))
            ret = PTR_ERR(gctx_cachep);
    }
    return ret;
}
```

Hey, that's interesting: notice that our cache creation API supplies a constructor function to help initialize any newly allocated object; here it is:

```
/* The parameter is the pointer to the just allocated memory 'object'
from
 * our custom slab cache; here, this is our 'constructor' routine; so, we
 * initialize our just allocated memory object.
 */
static void our_ctor(void *new)
{
    struct myctx *ctx = new;
    struct task_struct *p = current;

    /* TIP: to see how exactly we got here, insert this call:
     *  dump_stack();
     * (read it bottom-up ignoring call frames that begin with '?') */
    pr_info("in ctor: just alloced mem object is @ 0x%llx\n", ctx);

    memset(ctx, 0, sizeof(struct myctx));
    /* As a demo, we init the 'config' field of our structure to some
     * (arbitrary) 'accounting' values from our task_struct
     */
    snprintf(ctx->config, 6*sizeof(u64)+5, "%d.%d,%ld.%ld,%ld,%ld",
            p->tgid, p->pid,
            p->nvcsw, p->nivcsw, p->min_flt, p->maj_flt);
}
```

The comments in the preceding code are self-explanatory; do take a look. The constructor routine, if set up (depending on the value of our `use_ctor` module parameter; it's 1 by default), will be auto-invoked by the kernel whenever a new memory object is allocated to our cache.

Within the init code path, we call a `use_our_cache()` function. It allocates an instance of our `myctx` object via the `kmem_cache_alloc()` API, and if our custom constructor routine is enabled, it runs, initializing the object. We then dump its memory to show that it was indeed initialized as coded, freeing it when done (for brevity, we'll leave out showing the error code paths):

```
obj = kmem_cache_alloc(gctx_cachep, GFP_KERNEL);
pr_info("Our cache object size is %u bytes; ksize=%lu\n",
        kmem_cache_size(gctx_cachep), ksize(obj));
print_hex_dump_bytes("obj: ", DUMP_PREFIX_OFFSET, obj,
    sizeof(struct myctx));
kmem_cache_free(gctx_cachep, obj);
```

[455]

Kernel Memory Allocation for Module Authors - Part 2

Finally, in the exit code path, we destroy our custom slab cache:

```
kmem_cache_destroy(gctx_cachep);
```

The following output from a sample run helps us understand how it works. The following is just a partial screenshot showing the output on our x86_64 Ubuntu 18.04 LTS guest running the Linux 5.4 kernel:

```
[25016.805844] slab_custom: inserted
[25016.809108] slab_custom: sizeof our ctx structure is 328 bytes
               using custom constructor routine? yes
[25016.816516] [ker ver > 2.6.38 cache name deprecated...]
[25016.820293] slab_custom:our_ctor(): in ctor: just alloced mem object is @ 0xffff8880537f6440
[25016.823825] slab_custom:our_ctor(): in ctor: just alloced mem object is @ 0xffff8880537f5e40
[25016.827274] slab_custom:our_ctor(): in ctor: just alloced mem object is @ 0xffff8880537f4640
[25016.830510] slab_custom:our_ctor(): in ctor: just alloced mem object is @ 0xffff8880537f6d40
[25016.833210] slab_custom:our_ctor(): in ctor: just alloced mem object is @ 0xffff8880537f6a40
[25016.835664] slab_custom:our_ctor(): in ctor: just alloced mem object is @ 0xffff8880537f4940
[25016.837871] slab_custom:our_ctor(): in ctor: just alloced mem object is @ 0xffff8880537f7340
[25016.840003] slab_custom:our_ctor(): in ctor: just alloced mem object is @ 0xffff8880537f4c40
[25016.841913] slab_custom:our_ctor(): in ctor: just alloced mem object is @ 0xffff8880537f6740
[25016.843975] slab_custom:our_ctor(): in ctor: just alloced mem object is @ 0xffff8880537f5b40
[25016.845800] slab_custom:our_ctor(): in ctor: just alloced mem object is @ 0xffff8880537f5240
[25016.847559] slab_custom:our_ctor(): in ctor: just alloced mem object is @ 0xffff8880537f4340
[25016.849319] slab_custom:our_ctor(): in ctor: just alloced mem object is @ 0xffff8880537f7640
[25016.851086] slab_custom:our_ctor(): in ctor: just alloced mem object is @ 0xffff8880537f4f40
[25016.852843] slab_custom:our_ctor(): in ctor: just alloced mem object is @ 0xffff8880537f5840
[25016.854530] slab_custom:our_ctor(): in ctor: just alloced mem object is @ 0xffff8880537f7040
[25016.856354] slab_custom:our_ctor(): in ctor: just alloced mem object is @ 0xffff8880537f7940
[25016.858110] slab_custom:our_ctor(): in ctor: just alloced mem object is @ 0xffff8880537f6140
[25016.859915] slab_custom:our_ctor(): in ctor: just alloced mem object is @ 0xffff8880537f4040
[25016.861667] slab_custom:our_ctor(): in ctor: just alloced mem object is @ 0xffff8880537f7c40
[25016.863440] slab_custom:our_ctor(): in ctor: just alloced mem object is @ 0xffff8880537f5540
[25016.865210] Our cache object (@ ffff8880537f6440, actual=ffff8880537f6440) size is 328 bytes; ksize=328
[25016.867948] obj: 00000000: 00 00 00 00 00 00 00 00 00 00 00 00 00 00 00 00  ................
[25016.870022] obj: 00000010: 00 00 00 00 00 00 00 00 00 00 00 00 00 00 00 00  ................
[25016.872034] obj: 00000020: 00 00 00 00 00 00 00 00 00 00 00 00 00 00 00 00  ................
[25016.873976] obj: 00000030: 00 00 00 00 00 00 00 00 00 00 00 00 00 00 00 00  ................
[25016.875954] obj: 00000040: 00 00 00 00 00 00 00 00 00 00 00 00 00 00 00 00  ................
[25016.877816] obj: 00000050: 00 00 00 00 00 00 00 00 00 00 00 00 00 00 00 00  ................
[25016.879668] obj: 00000060: 00 00 00 00 00 00 00 00 00 00 00 00 00 00 00 00  ................
[25016.881549] obj: 00000070: 00 00 00 00 00 00 00 00 00 00 00 00 00 00 00 00  ................
[25016.883415] obj: 00000080: 00 00 00 00 00 00 00 00 00 00 00 00 00 00 00 00  ................
[25016.885245] obj: 00000090: 00 00 00 00 00 00 00 00 00 00 00 00 00 00 00 00  ................
[25016.886987] obj: 000000a0: 00 00 00 00 00 00 00 00 00 00 00 00 00 00 00 00  ................
[25016.888742] obj: 000000b0: 00 00 00 00 00 00 00 00 00 00 00 00 00 00 00 00  ................
[25016.890364] obj: 000000c0: 00 00 00 00 00 00 00 00 00 00 00 00 00 00 00 00  ................
[25016.892120] obj: 000000d0: 00 00 00 00 00 00 00 00 00 00 00 00 00 00 00 00  ................
[25016.894500] obj: 000000e0: 00 00 00 00 00 00 00 00 00 00 00 00 00 00 00 00  ................
[25016.896177] obj: 000000f0: 00 00 00 00 00 00 00 00 00 00 00 00 00 00 00 00  ................
[25016.898166] obj: 00000100: 00 00 00 00 00 00 00 00 38 38 37 35 2e 38 38 37  ........8875.887
[25016.900042] obj: 00000110: 35 2c 30 2e 33 2c 39 36 2c 30 00 00 00 00 00 00  5,0.3,96,0......
[25016.901562] obj: 00000120: 00 00 00 00 00 00 00 00 00 00 00 00 00 00 00 00  ................
[25016.903193] obj: 00000130: 00 00 00 00 00 00 00 00 00 00 00 00 00 00 00 00  ................
[25016.904737] obj: 00000140: 00 00 00 00 00 00 00 00                          ........
```

Figure 9.1 – Output of our slab_custom kernel module on an x86_64 VM

Chapter 9

Great! Hang on though, a couple of key points to take note of here:

- As our constructor routine is enabled by default (the value of our `use_ctor` module parameter is 1), it runs whenever a new object instance is allocated by the kernel slab layer to our new cache. Here, we performed just a single `kmem_cache_alloc()`, yet our constructor routine has run 21 times, implying that the kernel's slab code (pre)allocated 21 objects to our brand new cache! Of course, this number varies.
- Two, something very important to notice! As seen in the preceding screenshot, the *size* of each object is seemingly 328 bytes (as shown by all these three APIs: `sizeof()`, `kmem_cache_size()`, and `ksize()`). However, again, this is not really true! The actual size of the object as allocated by the kernel is larger; we can see this via `vmstat(8)`:

```
$ sudo vmstat -m | head -n1
Cache                     Num  Total  Size  Pages
$ sudo vmstat -m | grep our_ctx
our_ctx                     0     21   768     21
$
```

As highlighted in the preceding code, the actual size of each allocated object is not 328 bytes but 768 bytes (the exact number varies; in one case I saw it as 448 bytes). Just as we saw earlier, this is important for you to realize, and indeed check for. We show another way to quite easily check this in the *Debugging at the slab layer* section that follows.

> **TIP**
> FYI, you can always check out the man page of `vmstat(8)` for the precise meaning of each column seen earlier.

We'll round off the discussion on creating and using custom slab caches with the slab shrinker interface.

Understanding slab shrinkers

Caches are good for performance. Visualize reading the content of a large file from disk as opposed to reading its content from RAM. There's no question that the RAM-based I/O is much faster! As can be imagined, the Linux kernel leverages these ideas and thus maintains several caches – the page cache, dentry cache, inode cache, slab caches, and so on. These caches indeed greatly help performance, but, thinking about it, are not actually a mandatory requirement. When memory pressure reaches high levels (implying that too much memory is in use and too little is free), the Linux kernel has mechanisms to intelligently free up caches (aka memory reclamation - it's a continuous ongoing process; kernel threads (typically named `kswapd*`) reclaim memory as part of their housekeeping chores; more on this in the *Reclaiming memory – a kernel housekeeping task and OOM* section).

In the case of the slab cache(s), the fact is that some kernel subsystems and drivers create their own custom slab caches as we covered earlier in this chapter. For the purpose of integrating well and cooperating with the kernel, best practice demands that your custom slab cache code is expected to register a shrinker interface. When this is done, and when memory pressure gets high enough, the kernel might well invoke several slab shrinker callbacks, which are expected to ease the memory pressure by freeing up (shrinking) slab objects.

The API to register a shrinker function with the kernel is the `register_shrinker()` API. The single parameter to it (as of Linux 5.4) is a pointer to a `shrinker` structure. This structure contains (among other housekeeping members) two callback routines:

- The first routine, `count_objects()`, merely counts and returns the number of objects that would be freed (when it is actually invoked). If it returns `0`, this implies that the number of freeable memory objects cannot be determined now, or that we should not even attempt to free any right now.
- The second routine, `scan_objects()`, is invoked only if the first callback routine returns a non-zero value; it's the one that, when invoked by the slab cache layer, actually frees up, or shrinks, the slab cache in question. It returns the actual number of objects freed up in this reclaim cycle, or `SHRINK_STOP` if the reclaim attempt could not progress (due to possible deadlocks).

We'll now wrap up the discussion on the slab layer with a quick summation of the pros and cons of using this layer for memory (de)allocation—very important for you as a kernel/driver author to be keenly aware of!

The slab allocator – pros and cons – a summation

In this section, we very briefly summarize things you have already learned by now. This is intended as a way for you to quickly look up and recollect these key points!

The pros of using the slab allocator (or slab cache) APIs to allocate and free kernel memory are as follows:

- (Very) fast (as it uses pre-cached memory objects).
- A physically contiguous memory chunk is guaranteed.
- Hardware (CPU) cacheline-aligned memory is guaranteed when the `SLAB_HWCACHE_ALIGN` flag is used when creating the cache. This is the case for `kmalloc()`, `kzalloc()`, and so on.
- You can create your own custom slab cache for particular (frequently alloced/freed) objects.

The cons of using the slab allocator (or slab cache) APIs are the following:

- A limited amount of memory can be allocated at a time; typically, just 8 KB directly via the slab interfaces, or up to 4 MB indirectly via the page allocator on most current platforms (of course, the precise upper limits are arch-dependent).
- Using the `k[m|z]alloc()` APIs incorrectly: asking for too much memory, or asking for a memory size just over a threshold value (discussed in detail in Chapter 8, *Kernel Memory Allocation for Module Authors – Part 1*, under the *Size limitations of the kmalloc API* section), can certainly lead to internal fragmentation (wastage). It's designed to only really optimize for the common case – for allocations of a size less than one page.

Now, let's move on to another really key aspect for the kernel/driver developer – effectively debugging when things go wrong with respect to memory allocations/freeing, particularly within the slab layer.

Debugging at the slab layer

Memory corruption is unfortunately a very common root cause of bugs. Being able to debug them is a key skill. We'll now look at a few ways to go about this. Before diving into the details, remember that the following discussion is with respect to the *SLUB* (the unqueued allocator) implementation of the slab layer. This is the default on most Linux installations (we mentioned in `Chapter 8`, *Kernel Memory Allocation for Module Authors – Part 1*, under the *Slab layer implementations within the kernel* section, that current Linux kernels have three mutually exclusive implementations of the slab layer).

Also, our intention here is not to discuss in-depth kernel debug tools with respect to memory debugging—that is a large topic by itself that unfortunately lies beyond the scope of this book. Nevertheless, I will say that you would do well to gain familiarity with the powerful frameworks/tools that have been mentioned, particularly the following:

- **KASAN** (the **Kernel Address Sanitizer**; available for x86_64 and AArch64, 4.x kernels onward)
- SLUB debug techniques (covered here)
- `kmemleak` (though KASAN is superior)
- `kmemcheck` (note though that `kmemcheck` was removed in Linux 4.15)

Don't forget to look for links to these in the *Further reading* section. Okay, let's get down to a few useful ways to help a developer debug code at the slab layer.

Debugging through slab poisoning

One very useful feature is so-called slab poisoning. The term *poisoning* in this context implies poking memory with certain signature bytes or a pattern that is easily recognizable. The prerequisite to using this, though, is that the `CONFIG_SLUB_DEBUG` kernel configuration option is on. How can you check? Simple:

```
$ grep -w CONFIG_SLUB_DEBUG /boot/config-5.4.0-llkd01
CONFIG_SLUB_DEBUG=y
```

The =y seen in the preceding code indicates that it's indeed on. Now (assuming it's turned on) if you create a slab cache with the SLAB_POISON flag (we covered the creation of a slab cache in the *Creating a custom slab cache* section), then, when the memory is allocated, it's always initialized to the special value or memory pattern 0x5a5a5a5a – it's poisoned (it's quite intentional: the hex value 0x5a is the ASCII character Z for zero)! So, think about it, if you spot this value in a kernel diagnostic message or dump, also called an *Oops*, there's a good chance that this is an (unfortunately pretty typical) uninitialized memory bug or **UMR** (short for **Uninitialized Memory Read**), perhaps.

> Why use the word *perhaps* in the preceding sentence? Well, simply because debugging deeply hidden bugs is a really difficult thing to do! The symptoms that might present themselves are not necessarily *the root cause* of the issue at hand. Thus, hapless developers are fairly often led down the proverbial garden path by various red herrings! The reality is that debugging is both an art and a science; deep knowledge of the ecosystem (here, the Linux kernel) goes a really long way in helping you effectively debug difficult situations.

If the SLAB_POISON flag is unset, uninitialized slab memory is set to the 0x6b6b6b6b memory pattern (hex 0x6b is ASCII character k (see Figure 9.2)). Similarly, when the slab cache memory is freed up and CONFIG_SLUB_DEBUG is on, the kernel writes the same memory pattern (0x6b6b6b6b ; 'k') into it. This can be very useful too, allowing us to spot (what the kernel thinks is) uninitialized or free memory.

The poison values are defined in include/linux/poison.h as follows:

```
/* ...and for poisoning */
#define POISON_INUSE    0x5a    /* for use uninitialized poisoning */
#define POISON_FREE     0x6b    /* for use-after-free poisoning */
#define POISON_END      0xa5    /* end-byte of poisoning */
```

With respect to the kernel's SLUB implementation of the slab allocator, let's check out a summary view of **how and when** (the specific circumstances are determined by the following if part) the *slab poisoning occurs*, along with its type in the following pseudocode:

```
if CONFIG_SLUB_DEBUG is enabled
   AND the SLAB_POISON flag is set
   AND there's no custom constructor function
   AND it's type-safe-by-RCU
```

Kernel Memory Allocation for Module Authors – Part 2

Then the slab poisoning occurs as follows:

- The slab memory is set to `POISON_INUSE` (`0x5a` = ASCII `'Z'`) upon initialization; the code for this is here: `mm/slub.c:setup_page_debug()`.
- The slab object is set to `POISON_FREE` (`0x6b` = ASCII `'k'`) upon initialization in `mm/slub.c:init_object()`.
- The slab object's last byte is set to `POISON_END` (`0xa5`) upon initialization in `mm/slub.c:init_object()`.

(So, because of the way the slab layer performs these slab memory initializations, we end up with the value `0x6b` (ASCII `k`) as the initial value of just-allocated slab memory). Notice that for this to work, you shouldn't install a custom constructor function. Also, you can ignore the `it's-type-safe-by-RCU` directive for now; it's usually the case (that is, the "is type-safe-by-RCU" is true; FYI, RCU (Read Copy Update) is an advanced synchronization technology that's beyond this book's scope). As can be seen from how slabs are initialized when running in SLUB debug mode, the memory content is effectively initialized to the value `POISON_FREE` (`0x6b` = ASCII `'k'`). Thus, if this value ever changes after the memory is freed, the kernel can detect this and trigger a report (via printk). This, of course, is a case of the well-known **Use After Free** (**UAF**) memory bug! Similarly, writing before or after the redzone regions (these are in effect guard regions and are typically initialized to `0xbb`) will trigger a write buffer under/overflow bug, which the kernel reports. Useful!

Trying it out – triggering a UAF bug

To help you understand this better, we'll show an example via screenshots in this section. Implement the following steps:

1. Firstly, ensure you enable the `CONFIG_SLUB_DEBUG` kernel config (it should be set to `y`; this is typically the case on distro kernels)
2. Next, boot the system while including the kernel command-line `slub_debug=` directive (this turns on full SLUB debug; or you could pass a finer granularity variant such as `slub_debug=FZPU` (see the kernel documentation here for an explanation of each field: https://www.kernel.org/doc/Documentation/vm/slub.txt); as a demo, on my Fedora 31 guest VM, I passed the kernel command line as follows - the important thing here, the `slub_debug=FZPU` is highlighted in bold font:

```
$ cat /proc/cmdline
BOOT_IMAGE=(hd0,msdos1)/vmlinuz-5.4.0-llkd01
root=/dev/mapper/fedora_localhost--live-root ro
```

```
resume=/dev/mapper/fedora_localhost--live-swap
rd.lvm.lv=fedora_localhost-live/root
rd.lvm.lv=fedora_localhost-live/swap rhgb slub_debug=FZPU 3
```

(More detail on the `slub_debug` parameter is in the next section *SLUB debug options at boot and runtime*).

3. Write a kernel module that creates a new custom slab cache (which of course has a memory bug!). Ensure no constructor function is specified (sample code is here: `ch9/poison_test`; I'll leave it as an exercise for you to browse through the code and test it).

4. We try it out here: allocate some slab memory via `kmem_cache_alloc()` (or equivalent). Here's a screenshot (Figure 9.2) showing the allocated memory, and the same region after performing a quick `memset()` setting the first 16 bytes to z (0x7a):

```
Jul 02 16:14:35 fed31 kernel: poison_test: custom cache destroyed; removed
Jul 02 16:16:42 fed31 kernel: poison_test: inserted
Jul 02 16:16:42 fed31 kernel: poison_test: sizeof our ctx structure is 152 bytes
                              using custom constructor routine? no
Jul 02 16:16:42 fed31 kernel: [ker ver > 2.6.38 cache name deprecated...]
Jul 02 16:16:42 fed31 kernel: Our cache object (@ 0x0000000001549e39, actual=0xffff8f7632123d80) size is 152 bytes; ksize=152
Jul 02 16:16:42 fed31 kernel: obj: 00000000: 6b 6b 6b 6b 6b 6b 6b 6b 6b 6b 6b 6b 6b 6b 6b 6b  kkkkkkkkkkkkkkkk
Jul 02 16:16:42 fed31 kernel: obj: 00000010: 6b 6b 6b 6b 6b 6b 6b 6b 6b 6b 6b 6b 6b 6b 6b 6b  kkkkkkkkkkkkkkkk
Jul 02 16:16:42 fed31 kernel: obj: 00000020: 6b 6b 6b 6b 6b 6b 6b 6b 6b 6b 6b 6b 6b 6b 6b 6b  kkkkkkkkkkkkkkkk
Jul 02 16:16:42 fed31 kernel: obj: 00000030: 6b 6b 6b 6b 6b 6b 6b 6b 6b 6b 6b 6b 6b 6b 6b 6b  kkkkkkkkkkkkkkkk
Jul 02 16:16:42 fed31 kernel: obj: 00000040: 6b 6b 6b 6b 6b 6b 6b 6b 6b 6b 6b 6b 6b 6b 6b 6b  kkkkkkkkkkkkkkkk
Jul 02 16:16:42 fed31 kernel: obj: 00000050: 6b 6b 6b 6b 6b 6b 6b 6b 6b 6b 6b 6b 6b 6b 6b 6b  kkkkkkkkkkkkkkkk
Jul 02 16:16:42 fed31 kernel: obj: 00000060: 6b 6b 6b 6b 6b 6b 6b 6b 6b 6b 6b 6b 6b 6b 6b 6b  kkkkkkkkkkkkkkkk
Jul 02 16:16:42 fed31 kernel: obj: 00000070: 6b 6b 6b 6b 6b 6b 6b 6b 6b 6b 6b 6b 6b 6b 6b 6b  kkkkkkkkkkkkkkkk
Jul 02 16:16:42 fed31 kernel: obj: 00000080: 6b 6b 6b 6b 6b 6b 6b 6b 6b 6b 6b 6b 6b 6b 6b 6b  kkkkkkkkkkkkkkkk
Jul 02 16:16:42 fed31 kernel: obj: 00000090: 6b 6b 6b 6b 6b 6b a5                              kkkkkkk.
Jul 02 16:16:42 fed31 kernel: -------------- after memset s, 'z', 16 : ------------
Jul 02 16:16:42 fed31 kernel: obj: 0000000001549e39: 7a 7a 7a 7a 7a 7a 7a 7a 7a 7a 7a 7a 7a 7a 7a 7a  zzzzzzzzzzzzzzzz
Jul 02 16:16:42 fed31 kernel: obj: 00000000722b8a06: 6b 6b 6b 6b 6b 6b 6b 6b 6b 6b 6b 6b 6b 6b 6b 6b  kkkkkkkkkkkkkkkk
Jul 02 16:16:42 fed31 kernel: obj: 00000000f6326296: 6b 6b 6b 6b 6b 6b 6b 6b 6b 6b 6b 6b 6b 6b 6b 6b  kkkkkkkkkkkkkkkk
Jul 02 16:16:42 fed31 kernel: obj: 0000000068cca351: 6b 6b 6b 6b 6b 6b 6b 6b 6b 6b 6b 6b 6b 6b 6b 6b  kkkkkkkkkkkkkkkk
Jul 02 16:16:42 fed31 kernel: obj: 000000006ef6d99d: 6b 6b 6b 6b 6b 6b 6b 6b 6b 6b 6b 6b 6b 6b 6b 6b  kkkkkkkkkkkkkkkk
Jul 02 16:16:42 fed31 kernel: obj: 00000000248f0168: 6b 6b 6b 6b 6b 6b 6b 6b 6b 6b 6b 6b 6b 6b 6b 6b  kkkkkkkkkkkkkkkk
Jul 02 16:16:42 fed31 kernel: obj: 0000000048099057: 6b 6b 6b 6b 6b 6b 6b 6b 6b 6b 6b 6b 6b 6b 6b 6b  kkkkkkkkkkkkkkkk
Jul 02 16:16:42 fed31 kernel: obj: 00000000fe8d82f0: 6b 6b 6b 6b 6b 6b 6b 6b 6b 6b 6b 6b 6b 6b 6b 6b  kkkkkkkkkkkkkkkk
Jul 02 16:16:42 fed31 kernel: obj: 0000000045f90fe3: 6b 6b 6b 6b 6b 6b 6b 6b 6b 6b 6b 6b 6b 6b 6b 6b  kkkkkkkkkkkkkkkk
Jul 02 16:16:42 fed31 kernel: obj: 00000000ea67ec66: 6b 6b 6b 6b 6b 6b a5                              kkkkkkk.
```

Figure 9.2 – Slab memory after allocation and memset() of the first 16 bytes

Kernel Memory Allocation for Module Authors - Part 2

5. Now, for the bug! In the cleanup method, we free the allocated slab and then reuse it by attempting to do another `memset()` upon it, *thus triggering the UAF bug*. Again, we show the kernel log via another screenshot (Figure 9.3):

```
Jul 02 16:17:27 fed31 kernel: obj: 00000000ea67ec66: 6b 6b 6b 6b 6b 6b a5                         kkkkkk.
Jul 02 16:17:28 fed31 kernel: =================================================================
Jul 02 16:17:28 fed31 kernel: BUG poison_test (Tainted: G    B      OE   ): Poison overwritten
Jul 02 16:17:28 fed31 kernel: -----------------------------------------------------------------
Jul 02 16:17:28 fed31 kernel: INFO: 0x0000000001549e39-0x00000000d178c762. First byte 0x21 instead of 0x6b
Jul 02 16:17:28 fed31 kernel: INFO: Allocated in 0xffffffffc04af0c8 age=45508 cpu=0 pid=7757
Jul 02 16:17:28 fed31 kernel:     __slab_alloc+0x1c/0x30
Jul 02 16:17:28 fed31 kernel:     kmem_cache_alloc+0x23e/0x270
Jul 02 16:17:28 fed31 kernel:     0xffffffffc04af0c8
Jul 02 16:17:28 fed31 kernel:     do_one_initcall+0x6e/0x254
Jul 02 16:17:28 fed31 kernel:     do_init_module+0x5c/0x230
Jul 02 16:17:28 fed31 kernel:     load_module+0x2758/0x2a20
Jul 02 16:17:28 fed31 kernel:     __do_sys_finit_module+0xaa/0x110
Jul 02 16:17:28 fed31 kernel:     do_syscall_64+0x5b/0x180
Jul 02 16:17:28 fed31 kernel:     entry_SYSCALL_64_after_hwframe+0x44/0xa9
Jul 02 16:17:28 fed31 kernel: INFO: Freed in slab_custom_exit+0x13/0xf2d [poison_test] age=15 cpu=0 pid=7785
Jul 02 16:17:28 fed31 kernel:     kmem_cache_free+0x2df/0x300
Jul 02 16:17:28 fed31 kernel:     slab_custom_exit+0x13/0xf2d [poison_test]
Jul 02 16:17:28 fed31 kernel:     __x64_sys_delete_module+0x13f/0x280
Jul 02 16:17:28 fed31 kernel:     do_syscall_64+0x5b/0x180
Jul 02 16:17:28 fed31 kernel:     entry_SYSCALL_64_after_hwframe+0x44/0xa9
Jul 02 16:17:28 fed31 kernel: INFO: Slab 0x000000002a6b69d9 objects=14 used=0 fp=0x0000000001549e39 flags=0xfffe000010200
Jul 02 16:17:28 fed31 kernel: INFO: Object 0x0000000001549e39 @offset=7552 fp=0x000000007b344c6b
Jul 02 16:17:28 fed31 kernel: Redzone 000000003e2471ad: bb bb bb bb bb bb bb bb bb bb bb bb bb bb bb bb  ................
Jul 02 16:17:28 fed31 kernel: Redzone 000000000406be0d4: bb bb bb bb bb bb bb bb bb bb bb bb bb bb bb bb  ................
Jul 02 16:17:28 fed31 kernel: Redzone 00000000001badcd95: bb bb bb bb bb bb bb bb bb bb bb bb bb bb bb bb  ................
Jul 02 16:17:28 fed31 kernel: Redzone 00000000475f60c2: bb bb bb bb bb bb bb bb bb bb bb bb bb bb bb bb  ................
Jul 02 16:17:28 fed31 kernel: Object 0000000001549e39: 21 21 21 21 21 21 21 21 21 6b 6b 6b 6b 6b 6b 6b  !!!!!!!!!kkkkkkk
Jul 02 16:17:28 fed31 kernel: Object 00000000722b8a06: 6b 6b 6b 6b 6b 6b 6b 6b 6b 6b 6b 6b 6b 6b 6b 6b  kkkkkkkkkkkkkkkk
Jul 02 16:17:28 fed31 kernel: Object 00000000f6326296: 6b 6b 6b 6b 6b 6b 6b 6b 6b 6b 6b 6b 6b 6b 6b 6b  kkkkkkkkkkkkkkkk
Jul 02 16:17:28 fed31 kernel: Object 0000000068cca351: 6b 6b 6b 6b 6b 6b 6b 6b 6b 6b 6b 6b 6b 6b 6b 6b  kkkkkkkkkkkkkkkk
Jul 02 16:17:28 fed31 kernel: Object 0000000006ef6d99d: 6b 6b 6b 6b 6b 6b 6b 6b 6b 6b 6b 6b 6b 6b 6b 6b  kkkkkkkkkkkkkkkk
Jul 02 16:17:28 fed31 kernel: Object 00000000248f0168: 6b 6b 6b 6b 6b 6b 6b 6b 6b 6b 6b 6b 6b 6b 6b 6b  kkkkkkkkkkkkkkkk
Jul 02 16:17:28 fed31 kernel: Object 0000000048099057: 6b 6b 6b 6b 6b 6b 6b 6b 6b 6b 6b 6b 6b 6b 6b 6b  kkkkkkkkkkkkkkkk
Jul 02 16:17:28 fed31 kernel: Object 00000000fe8d82f0: 6b 6b 6b 6b 6b 6b 6b 6b 6b 6b 6b 6b 6b 6b 6b 6b  kkkkkkkkkkkkkkkk
Jul 02 16:17:28 fed31 kernel: Object 00000000045f90fe3: 6b 6b 6b 6b 6b 6b 6b 6b 6b 6b 6b 6b 6b 6b 6b 6b  kkkkkkkkkkkkkkkk
Jul 02 16:17:28 fed31 kernel: Object 00000000ea67ec66: 6b 6b 6b 6b 6b 6b a5                             kkkkkk.
Jul 02 16:17:28 fed31 kernel: Redzone 000000008937cab7: bb bb bb bb bb bb bb bb                         ........
Jul 02 16:17:28 fed31 kernel: Padding 00000000c1e31d5b: 5a 5a 5a 5a 5a 5a 5a 5a 5a 5a 5a 5a 5a 5a 5a 5a  ZZZZZZZZZZZZZZZZ
Jul 02 16:17:28 fed31 kernel: Padding 000000001db10a0: 5a 5a 5a 5a 5a 5a 5a 5a 5a 5a 5a 5a 5a 5a 5a 5a   ZZZZZZZZZZZZZZZZ
Jul 02 16:17:28 fed31 kernel: Padding 000000001d18bd2: 5a 5a 5a 5a 5a 5a 5a 5a                          ZZZZZZZZ
Jul 02 16:17:28 fed31 kernel: CPU: 0 PID: 7785 Comm: rmmod Tainted: G    B      OE    5.4.0-llkd01 #2
Jul 02 16:17:28 fed31 kernel: Hardware name: innotek GmbH VirtualBox/VirtualBox, BIOS VirtualBox 12/01/2006
Jul 02 16:17:28 fed31 kernel: Call Trace:
Jul 02 16:17:28 fed31 kernel:  dump_stack+0x66/0x90
Jul 02 16:17:28 fed31 kernel:  check_bytes_and_report.cold+0x40/0x58
Jul 02 16:17:28 fed31 kernel:  check_object+0x20d/0x250
Jul 02 16:17:28 fed31 kernel:  __free_slab+0x9e/0x380
```

Figure 9.3 – The kernel reporting the UAF bug!

Notice how the kernel reports this (the first text in red in the preceding figure) as a `Poison overwritten` bug. This is indeed the case: we overwrote the `0x6b` poison value with `0x21` (which, quite intentionally is the ASCII character !). After freeing a buffer that originated from the slab cache, if the kernel detects any value other than the poison value (`POISON_FREE = 0x6b = ASCII 'k'`) within the payload, it triggers the bug. (Also notice, the redzone - guard - areas are initialized to the value `0xbb`).

The next section provides a few more details on the SLUB layer debug options available.

SLUB debug options at boot and runtime

Debugging kernel-level slab issues when using the SLUB implementation (the default) is very powerful as the kernel has full debugging information available. It's just that it's turned off by default. There are various ways (viewports) via which we can turn on and look at slab debug-level information; a wealth of details is available! Some of the ways to do so include the following:

- Passing the `slub_debug=` string on the kernel command line (via the bootloader of course). This turns on full SLUB kernel-level debugging.
- The specific debug information to be seen can be fine-tuned via options passed to the `slub_debug=` string (passing nothing after the = implies that all SLUB debug options are enabled); for example, passing `slub_debug=FZ` turns on the following options:
    - F: Sanity checks on (enables `SLAB_DEBUG_CONSISTENCY_CHECKS`); note that turning this on can slow down the system.
    - Z: Red zoning.
- Even if the SLUB debug feature has not been turned on via the kernel command line, we can still enable/disable it by writing 1 (as root) to suitable pseudo-files under `/sys/kernel/slab/<slab-name>`:
    - Recall our earlier demo kernel module (ch9/slab_custom); once loaded into the kernel, see the theoretical and actual size of each allocated object like this:

        ```
        $ sudo cat /sys/kernel/slab/our_ctx/object_size /sys/kernel/slab/our_ctx/slab_size
        328 768
        ```

    - Several other pseudo-files are present as well; doing `ls(1)` on `/sys/kernel/slab/<name-of-slab>/` will reveal them. For example, look up the constructor function to our ch9/slab_custom slab cache by performing cat on the pseudo-file at `/sys/kernel/slab/our_ctx/ctor`:

        ```
        $ sudo cat /sys/kernel/slab/our_ctx/ctor
        our_ctor+0x0/0xe1 [slab_custom]
        ```

You can find quite some relevant details in this (very useful!) document here: *Short users guide for SLUB* (https://www.kernel.org/doc/Documentation/vm/slub.txt).

Also, a quick look under the kernel source tree's `tools/vm` folder will reveal some interesting programs (`slabinfo.c` being the relevant one here) and a script to generate graphs (via `gnuplot(1)`). The document mentioned in the preceding paragraph provides usage details on plot generation as well.

> **TIP**: As an important aside, the kernel has an enormous (and useful!) number of *kernel parameters* that can be optionally passed to it at boot (via the bootloader). See the complete list here in the documentation: *The kernel's command-line parameters* (https://www.kernel.org/doc/html/latest/admin-guide/kernel-parameters.html).

Well, this (finally) concludes our coverage of the slab allocator (from the previous chapter continuing into this one). You have learned that it's layered above the page allocator and solves two key things: one, it allows the kernel to create and maintain object caches so that the allocation and freeing of some important kernel data structures can be performed very efficiently; two, this includes generic memory caches allowing you to allocate small amounts of RAM - fragments of a page - with very little overhead (unlike the binary buddy system allocator). The fact is simply this: the slab APIs are the really commonly employed ones by drivers; not only that, modern driver authors exploit the resource-managed `devm_k{m,z}alloc()` APIs; we encourage you to do so. Be careful though: we examined in detail how more memory than you think might actually be allocated (use `ksize()` to figure out just how much). You also learned how to create a custom slab cache, and, importantly, how to go about debugging at the slab layer.

Now let's learn what the `vmalloc()` API is, how and when to use it for kernel memory allocation.

Understanding and using the kernel vmalloc() API

As we have learned in the previous chapter, ultimately there is just one engine for memory allocation within the kernel – the page (or buddy system) allocator. Layered on top is the slab allocator (or slab cache) machinery. In addition, there is another completely virtual address space within the kernel's address space from where virtual pages can be allocated at will – this is called the kernel `vmalloc` region.

Of course, ultimately, once a virtual page is actually used (by something in the kernel or in user space via a process or thread) - it's physical page frame that it's mapped to is really allocated via the page allocator (this is ultimately true of all user space memory frames as well, though in an indirect fashion; more on this later in the *Demand paging and OOM* section).

Within the kernel segment or VAS (we covered all this in some detail in Chapter 7, *Memory Management Internals - Essentials*, under the *Examining the kernel segment* section), is the *vmalloc* address space, extending from VMALLOC_START to VMALLOC_END-1. It's a completely virtual region to begin with, that is, its virtual pages initially are not mapped to any physical page frames.

> For a quick refresher, revisit the diagram of the user and kernel segments – in effect, the complete VAS – by re-examining *Figure 7.12*. You will find this in Chapter 7, *Memory Management Internals - Essentials*, under the *Trying it out – viewing kernel segment details* section.

In this book, our purpose is not to delve into the gory internal details regarding the kernel's vmalloc region. Instead, we present enough information for you, the module or driver author, to use this region for the purpose of allocating virtual memory at runtime.

Learning to use the vmalloc family of APIs

You can allocate virtual memory (in kernel space of course) from the kernel's vmalloc region using the vmalloc() API:

```
#include <linux/vmalloc.h>
void *vmalloc(unsigned long size);
```

Some key points to note on the vmalloc:

- The vmalloc() API allocates contiguous virtual memory to the caller. There is no guarantee that the allocated region will be physically contiguous; it may or may not be (in fact, the larger the allocation, the less the chance that it's physically contiguous).
- The content of the virtual pages allocated is, in theory, random; in practice, it appears to be arch-dependent (the x86_64, at least, seems to zero out the memory region); of course, (at the risk of a slight performance hit) you're recommended to ensure memory zeroing out by employing the vzalloc() wrapper API

- The `vmalloc()` (and friends) APIs must only ever be invoked from a process context (as it might cause the caller to sleep).
- The return value of `vmalloc()` is the KVA (within the kernel vmalloc region) on success or NULL on failure.
- The start of the vmalloc memory just allocated is guaranteed to be on a page boundary (in other words, it's always page-aligned).
- The actual allocated memory (from the page allocator) might well be larger than what's requested (as again, it internally allocates sufficient pages to cover the size requested)

It will strike you that this API seems very similar to the familiar user space `malloc(3)`. Indeed it is at first glance, except that, of course, it's a kernel space allocation (and again, remember that there is no direct correlation between the two).

This being the case, how is `vmalloc()` helpful to us module or driver authors? When you require a large virtually contiguous buffer of a size greater than the slab APIs (that is, `k{m|z}alloc()` and friends) can provide – recall that it's typically 4 MB with a single allocation on both ARM and x86[_64]) – then you should use `vmalloc`!

FYI, the kernel uses `vmalloc()` for various reasons, some of them as follows:

- Allocating space for the (static) memory of kernel modules when they are loaded into the kernel (in `kernel/module.c:load_module()`).
- If `CONFIG_VMAP_STACK` is defined, then `vmalloc()` is used for the allocation of the kernel-mode stack of every thread (in `kernel/fork.c:alloc_thread_stack_node()`).
- Internally, while servicing an operation called `ioremap()`.
- Within the Linux socket filter (bpf) code paths, and so on.

For convenience, the kernel provides the `vzalloc()` wrapper API (analogous to `kzalloc()`) to allocate and zero out the memory region – a good coding practice, no doubt, but one that might hurt time-critical code paths slightly:

```
void *vzalloc(unsigned long size);
```

Once you are done with using the allocated virtual buffer, you must of course free it:

```
void vfree(const void *addr);
```

As expected, the parameter to `vfree()` is the return address from `v[m|z]alloc()` (or even the underlying `__vmalloc()` API that these invoke). Passing `NULL` causes it to just harmlessly return.

In the following snippet, we show some sample code from our `ch9/vmalloc_demo` kernel module. As usual, I urge you to clone the book's GitHub repository and try it out yourself (for brevity, we don't show the whole of the source code in the following snippet; we show the primary `vmalloc_try()` function invoked by the module's init code).

Here is the first part of the code. If the `vmalloc()` API fails by any chance, we generate a warning via the kernel's `pr_warn()` helper. Do note that the following `pr_warn()` helper isn't really required; being pedantic here, we keep it... ditto for the remaining cases, as follows:

```
// ch9/vmalloc_demo/vmalloc_demo.c
#define pr_fmt(fmt) "%s:%s(): " fmt, KBUILD_MODNAME, __func__
[...]
#define KVN_MIN_BYTES     16
#define DISP_BYTES        16
static void *vptr_rndm, *vptr_init, *kv, *kvarr, *vrx;

static int vmalloc_try(void)
{
    if (!(vptr_rndm = vmalloc(10000))) {
        pr_warn("vmalloc failed\n");
        goto err_out1;
    }
    pr_info("1. vmalloc(): vptr_rndm = 0x%pK (actual=0x%px)\n",
            vptr_rndm, vptr_rndm);
    print_hex_dump_bytes(" content: ", DUMP_PREFIX_NONE, vptr_rndm,
            DISP_BYTES);
```

The `vmalloc()` API in the preceding code block allocates a contiguous kernel virtual memory region of (at least) 10,000 bytes; in reality, the memory is page-aligned! We employ the kernel's `print_hex_dump_bytes()` helper routine to dump the first 16 bytes of this region.

Moving on, see the following code employ the `vzalloc()` API to again allocate another contiguous kernel virtual memory region of (at least) 10,000 bytes (it's page-aligned memory though); this time, the memory contents are set to zeroes:

```
/* 2. vzalloc(); memory contents are set to zeroes */
if (!(vptr_init = vzalloc(10000))) {
    pr_warn("%s: vzalloc failed\n", OURMODNAME);
```

Kernel Memory Allocation for Module Authors - Part 2

```
            goto err_out2;
    }
    pr_info("2. vzalloc(): vptr_init = 0x%pK (actual=0x%px)\n",
            vptr_init, (TYPECST)vptr_init);
    print_hex_dump_bytes(" content: ", DUMP_PREFIX_NONE, vptr_init,
            DISP_BYTES);
```

A couple of points regarding the following code: one, notice the error handling with `goto` (at the target labels of multiple `goto` instances, where we use `vfree()` to free up previously allocated memory buffers as required), typical of kernel code. Two, for now, please ignore the `kvmalloc()`, `kcalloc()`, and `__vmalloc()` friend routines; we'll cover them in the *Friends of vmalloc()* section:

```
    /* 3. kvmalloc(): allocate 'kvn' bytes with the kvmalloc(); if kvn is
     * large (enough), this will become a vmalloc() under the hood, else
     * it falls back to a kmalloc() */
    if (!(kv = kvmalloc(kvn, GFP_KERNEL))) {
        pr_warn("kvmalloc failed\n");
        goto err_out3;
    }
    [...]

    /* 4. kcalloc(): allocate an array of 1000 64-bit quantities and zero
     * out the memory */
    if (!(kvarr = kcalloc(1000, sizeof(u64), GFP_KERNEL))) {
        pr_warn("kvmalloc_array failed\n");
        goto err_out4;
    }
    [...]
    /* 5. __vmalloc(): <seen later> */
    [...]
    return 0;
err_out5:
  vfree(kvarr);
err_out4:
    vfree(kv);
err_out3:
    vfree(vptr_init);
err_out2:
    vfree(vptr_rndm);
err_out1:
    return -ENOMEM;
}
```

In the cleanup code path of our kernel module, we of course free the allocated memory regions:

```
static void __exit vmalloc_demo_exit(void)
{
    vfree(vrx);
    kvfree(kvarr);
    kvfree(kv);
    vfree(vptr_init);
    vfree(vptr_rndm);
    pr_info("removed\n");
}
```

We'll leave it to you to try out and verify this demo kernel module.

Now, let's delve briefly into another really key aspect – how exactly does a user space `malloc()`, or a kernel space `vmalloc()`, memory allocation become physical memory? Do read on to find out!

A brief note on memory allocations and demand paging

Without delving into deep detail regarding the internal workings of `vmalloc()` (or the user space `malloc()`), we'll nevertheless cover some crucial points that a competent kernel/driver developer like you must understand.

First and foremost, vmalloc-ed virtual memory has to, at some point (when used), become physical memory. This physical memory is allocated via the one and only way that it can be in the kernel – via the page (or buddy system) allocator. How this happens is a bit indirect and is briefly explained as follows.

Kernel Memory Allocation for Module Authors - Part 2

When using `vmalloc()`, a key point should be understood: `vmalloc()` only causes virtual memory pages to be allocated (they are merely marked as reserved by the OS). No physical memory is actually allocated at this time. The actual physical page frames corresponding to the virtual ones only get allocated – that too on a page-by-page basis – when these virtual pages are touched in any manner, such as for reads, writes, or executions. This key principle of not actually allocating physical memory until the program or process actually attempts to use it is referred to by various names – *demand paging, lazy allocation, on-demand allocation*, and so on. In fact, the documentation states this very fact:

> *"vmalloc space is lazily synchronized into the different PML4/PML5 pages of the processes using the page fault handler ..."*

It's quite enlightening to clearly understand how memory allocation really works for `vmalloc()` and friends, and indeed, for the user space glibc `malloc()` family of routines – it's all via demand paging! Meaning, the successful return of these APIs really does not mean anything in terms of *physical* memory allocation. When `vmalloc()`, or indeed a user space `malloc()`, returns success, all that has really happened so far is that a virtual memory region has been reserved; no physical memory has actually been allocated yet! *The actual allocation of a physical page frame only happens on a per-page basis as and when the virtual page is accessed (for anything: reading, writing, or execution).*

But how does this happen internally? The answer, in brief: whenever the kernel or a process accesses a virtual address, the virtual address is interpreted by the **Memory Management Unit** (**MMU**), which is a part of the silicon on the CPU core. The MMU's **Translation Lookaside Buffer** (**TLB**) *(we don't have the luxury of being able to delve into all of this here, sorry!)* will now be checked for a *hit*. If so, the memory translation (virtual-to-physical address) is already available; if not, we have a TLB-miss. If so, the MMU will now *walk* the paging tables of the process, effectively translating the virtual address and thus obtaining the *physical address*. It puts this on the address bus, and the CPU goes on its merry way.

But, think on this, what if the MMU cannot find a matching physical address? This can happen for a number of reasons, one of them being our case here – we don't (yet) *have* a physical page frame, only a virtual page. At this point, the MMU essentially gives up as it cannot handle it. Instead, it *invokes the OS's page fault handler code* – an exception or fault handler that runs in the process's context – in the context of `current`. This page fault handler actually resolves the situation; in our case, with `vmalloc()` (or indeed even the user space `malloc()`!), it requests the page allocator for a single physical page frame (at order 0) and maps it to the virtual page.

It's equally important to realize that this demand paging (or lazy allocation) is *not the case for kernel memory allocations* carried out via the page (buddy system) and the slab allocator. There, when memory is allocated, understand that actual physical page frames are allocated *immediately*. (In reality on Linux, it's all very fast because, recall, the buddy system freelists have already mapped all system physical RAM into the kernel *lowmem* region and can therefore use it at will.)

Recall what we did in an earlier program, `ch8/lowlevel_mem`; there, we used our `show_phy_pages()` library routine to display the virtual address, the physical address, and **Page Frame Number** (**PFN**) for a given memory range, thereby verifying that the low-level page allocator routines really do allocate physically contiguous memory chunks. Now, you might think, why not call this same function in this `vmalloc_demo` kernel module? If the PFNs of the allocated (virtual) pages are not consecutive, we again prove that, indeed, it's only virtually contiguous. It sounds tempting to try, but it doesn't work! Why? Simply because, as stated earlier (in `Chapter 8`, *Kernel Memory Allocation for Module Authors – Part 1*): do not attempt to translate from virtual to physical any addresses other than direct-mapped (identity-mapped / lowmem region) ones – the ones the page or slab allocators supply. It just doesn't work with `vmalloc`.

A few more points on `vmalloc` and some associated information follow; do read on.

Friends of vmalloc()

In many cases, the precise API (or memory layer) used to perform a memory allocation does not really matter to the caller. So, a pattern of usage that emerged in a lot of in-kernel code paths went something like the following pseudocode:

```
kptr = kmalloc(n);
if (!kptr) {
    kptr = vmalloc(n);
    if (unlikely(!kptr))
        <... failed, cleanup ...>
}
<ok, continue with kptr>
```

Kernel Memory Allocation for Module Authors - Part 2

The cleaner alternative to this kind of code is the `kvmalloc()` API. Internally, it attempts to allocate the requested n bytes of memory like this: first, via the more efficient `kmalloc()`; if it succeeds, fine, we have quickly obtained physically contiguous memory and are done; if not, it falls back to allocating the memory via the slower but surer `vmalloc()` (thus obtaining virtually contiguous memory). Its signature is as follows:

```
#include <linux/mm.h>
void *kvmalloc(size_t size, gfp_t flags);
```

(Remember to include the header file.) Note that for the (internal) `vmalloc()` to go through (if it comes to that), only the `GFP_KERNEL` flag must be supplied. As usual, the return value is a pointer (a kernel virtual address) to the allocated memory, or `NULL` on failure. Free the memory obtained with `kvfree`:

```
void kvfree(const void *addr);
```

Here, the parameter of course is the return address from `kvmalloc()`.

Similarly, and analogous to the `{k|v}zalloc()` APIs, we also have the `kvzalloc()` API, which of course zeroes the memory content. I'd suggest you use it in preference to the `kvmalloc()` API (with the usual caveat: it's safer but a bit slower).

Further, you can use the `kvmalloc_array()` API to allocate virtual contiguous memory for an array of items. It allocates n elements of `size` bytes each. Its implementation is shown as follows:

```
// include/linux/mm.h
static inline void *kvmalloc_array(size_t n, size_t size, gfp_t flags)
{
        size_t bytes;
        if (unlikely(check_mul_overflow(n, size, &bytes)))
                return NULL;
        return kvmalloc(bytes, flags);
}
```

A key point here: notice how a validity check for the dangerous **integer overflow (IoF)** bug is made; that's important and interesting; do write robust code by performing similar validity checks in your code where required.

Next, the `kvcalloc()` API is functionally equivalent to the `calloc(3)` user space API, and is just a simple wrapper over the `kvmalloc_array()` API:

```
void *kvcalloc(size_t n, size_t size, gfp_t flags);
```

We also mention that for code requiring *NUMA awareness* (we covered NUMA and associated topics in Chapter 7, *Memory Management Internals – Essentials*, under the *Physical RAM organization* section), the following APIs are available, with which we can specify the particular NUMA node to allocate the memory from as a parameter (this being the point to NUMA systems; do see the information box that follows shortly):

```
void *kvmalloc_node(size_t size, gfp_t flags, int node);
```

Similarly, we have the `kzalloc_node()` API as well, which sets the memory content to zero.

> In fact, generically, most of the kernel-space memory APIs we have seen ultimately boil down to one *that takes a NUMA node as a parameter*. For example, take the call chain for one of the primary page allocator APIs, the `__get_free_page()` API:
> `__get_free_page() -> __get_free_pages()`
> `-> alloc_pages() -> alloc_pages_current()`
>   `-> __alloc_pages_nodemask()` .
> The `__alloc_pages_nodemask()` API is considered to be the *heart* of the zoned buddy allocator; notice its fourth parameter, the (NUMA) nodemask:
> `mm/page_alloc.c:struct page *`
> `__alloc_pages_nodemask(gfp_t gfp_mask, unsigned int order,`
>   `int preferred_nid, nodemask_t *nodemask);`

Of course, you must free the memory you take; for the preceding `kv*()` APIs (and the `kcalloc()` API), free the memory obtained with `kvfree()`.

Kernel Memory Allocation for Module Authors - Part 2

Another internal detail worth knowing about, and a reason the `k[v|z]malloc[_array]()` APIs are useful: with a regular `kmalloc()`, the kernel will indefinitely retry allocating the memory requested if it's small enough (this number currently being defined as `CONFIG_PAGE_ALLOC_COSTLY_ORDER`, which is 3, implying 8 pages or less); this can actually hurt performance! With the `kvmalloc()` API, this indefinite retrying is not done (this behavior is specified via the GFP flags `__GFP_NORETRY|__GFP_NOWARN`), thus speeding things up. An LWN article goes into detail regarding the rather weird indefinite-retry semantics of the slab allocator: *The "too small to fail" memory-allocation rule, Jon Corbet, December 2014* (https://lwn.net/Articles/627419/).

With regard to the `vmalloc_demo` kernel module we saw in this section, take a quick look at the code again (`ch9/vmalloc_demo/vmalloc_demo.c`). We use `kvmalloc()` as well as `kcalloc()` (*steps 3 and 4 in the comments*). Let's run it on an x86_64 Fedora 31 guest system and see the output:

```
[   65.792406] vmalloc_demo: loading out-of-tree module taints kernel.
[   65.792439] vmalloc_demo: module verification failed: signature and/or required key missing
 - tainting kernel
[   65.792943] vmalloc_demo: inserted
[   65.792949] 1. vmalloc():    vptr_rndm = 0x00000000fcc77e4d (actual=0xffffa858c080d000)
[   65.792951]    content: 4f 00 00 00 00 00 00 00 00 00 00 00 00 00 00 00  O...............
[   65.792955] 2. vzalloc():    vptr_init = 0x00000000c35b38e5 (actual=0xffffa858c0821000)
[   65.792956]    content: 00 00 00 00 00 00 00 00 00 00 00 00 00 00 00 00  ................
[   65.793562] 3. kvmalloc() :      kv = 0x00000000fb2af97f (actual=0xffffa858c2c09000)
                  (for 5242880 bytes)
[   65.793564]    content: ca ef 00 00 00 00 00 00 cc 1a 01 00 00 00 00 00  ................
[   65.793573] 4. kcalloc() :    kvarr = 0x00000000d0418057 (actual=0xffff89f97b49a000)
[   65.793574]    content: 00 00 00 00 00 00 00 00 00 00 00 00 00 00 00 00  ................
[   65.793596] 5. __vmalloc():      vrx = 0x00000000d4d28888 (actual=0xffffa858c1971000)
[   65.793597]    content: 75 70 00 2e 61 6e 6e 6f 62 69 6e 5f 67 72 6f 75  up..annobin_grou
```

Figure 9.4 – Output on loading our vmalloc_demo.ko kernel module

We can see the actual return (kernel virtual) address from the APIs in the preceding output - note that they all belong within the kernel's vmalloc region. Notice the return address of `kvmalloc()` (step 3 in Figure 9.4); let's search for it under `proc`:

```
$ sudo grep "^0x00000000fb2af97f" /proc/vmallocinfo
0x00000000fb2af97f-0x00000000ddc1eb2c 5246976 0xffffffffc04a113d
pages=1280 vmalloc vpages N0=1280
```

[476]

There it is! We can clearly see how using the `kvmalloc()` API for a large quantity of memory (5 MB) resulted in the `vmalloc()` API being internally invoked (the `kmalloc()` API would have failed and would not have emitted a warning, nor retried) and thus, as you can see, the hit under `/proc/vmallocinfo`.

To interpret the preceding fields of `/proc/vmallocinfo`, refer to the kernel documentation here: https://www.kernel.org/doc/Documentation/filesystems/proc.txt.

> Something for you to try out here: in our `ch9/vmalloc_demo` kernel module, change the amount of memory to be allocated via `kvmalloc()` by passing `kvnum=<# bytes to alloc>` as a module parameter.

FYI, the kernel provides an internal helper API, the `vmalloc_exec()` - it's (again) a wrapper over the `vmalloc()` API, and is used to allocate a virtually contiguous memory region that has execute permissions set upon it. An interesting user is the kernel module allocation code path (`kernel/module.c:module_alloc()`); the space for the kernel module's (executable section) memory is allocated via this routine. This routine isn't exported though.

The other helper routine we mention is `vmalloc_user()`; it's (yet again) a wrapper over the `vmalloc()` API, and is used to allocate a zeroed-out virtually contiguous memory region suitable for mapping into user VAS. This routine is exported; it's used, for example, by several device drivers as well as the kernel's performance events ring buffer.

Specifying the memory protections

What if you intend to specify certain specific memory protections (a combination of read, write, and execute protections) for the memory pages you allocate? In this case, use the underlying __vmalloc() API (it is exported). Consider the following comment in the kernel source (`mm/vmalloc.c`):

```
* For tight control over page level allocator and protection flags
* use __vmalloc() instead.
```

The signature of the __vmalloc() API shows how we can achieve this:

```
void *__vmalloc(unsigned long size, gfp_t gfp_mask, pgprot_t prot);
```

[477]

Kernel Memory Allocation for Module Authors - Part 2

> FYI, from the 5.8 kernel, the `__vmalloc()` function's third parameter - `pgprot_t prot` - has been removed (as there weren't any users for page permissions besides the usual ones; https://github.com/torvalds/linux/commit/88dca4ca5a93d2c09e5bbc6a62fbfc3af83c4fca). Tells us another thing regarding the kernel community - if a feature isn't being used by anyone, it's simply removed.

The first two parameters are the usual suspects – the size of the memory required in bytes and the GFP flags for the allocation. The third parameter is the one of interest here: `prot` represents the memory protection bitmask that we can specify for the memory pages. For example, to allocate 42 pages that are set to be read-only (r--), we could do the following:

```
vrx = __vmalloc(42 * PAGE_SIZE, GFP_KERNEL, PAGE_KERNEL_RO);
```

And subsequently, of course, call `vfree()` to free the memory back to the system.

Testing it – a quick Proof of Concept

We'll try a quick Proof of Concept in our `vmalloc_demo` kernel module. We allocate a region of memory specifying the page protection to be read-only (or *RO*) via the `__vmalloc()` kernel API. We then test it by reading *and writing* to the read-only memory region. A code snippet from it is seen as follows.

Note that we have kept the (silly) `WR2ROMEM_BUG` macro in the following code undefined by default, so that you, innocent reader, don't have our evil `vmalloc_demo` kernel module simply crash on you. So in order to try this PoC, please un-comment the define statement (as shown here), thus allowing the buggy code to execute:

```
static int vmalloc_try(void)
{
    [...]
    /* 5. __vmalloc(): allocate some 42 pages and set protections to RO */
/* #undef WR2ROMEM_BUG */
#define WR2ROMEM_BUG    /* 'Normal' usage: keep this commented out, else we
                         * will crash! Read  the book, Ch 9, for details :-) */
    if (!(vrx = __vmalloc(42*PAGE_SIZE, GFP_KERNEL, PAGE_KERNEL_RO)))
    {
```

[478]

```
            pr_warn("%s: __vmalloc failed\n", OURMODNAME);
            goto err_out5;
    }
    pr_info("5. __vmalloc(): vrx = 0x%pK (actual=0x%px)\n", vrx, vrx);
    /* Try reading the memory, should be fine */
    print_hex_dump_bytes(" vrx: ", DUMP_PREFIX_NONE, vrx, DISP_BYTES);
#ifdef WR2ROMEM_BUG
    /* Try writing to the RO memory! We find that the kernel crashes
     * (emits an Oops!) */
    *(u64 *)(vrx+4) = 0xba;
#endif
    return 0;
    [...]
```

Upon running, at the point where we attempt to write to the read-only memory, it crashes! See the following partial screenshot (Figure 9.5; from running it on our x86_64 Fedora guest):

```
[ 1199.357144] vmalloc_demo: inserted
[ 1199.357154] 1. vmalloc():   vptr_rndm = 0x00000000203f6102 (actual=0xffffa858c016d000)
[ 1199.357156]  content: dd 03 00 00 00 00 00 b2 00 00 00 00 00 00 00 00
[ 1199.357163] 2. vzalloc():   vptr_init = 0x000000001f29018a (actual=0xffffa858c0197000)
[ 1199.357165]  content: 00 00 00 00 00 00 00 00 00 00 00 00 00 00 00 00 ................
[ 1199.358586] 3. kvmalloc() :         kv = 0x000000007c676ba4 (actual=0xffffa858c2ba9000)
                    (for 5242880 bytes)
[ 1199.358589]  content: 63 cd 00 00 00 00 00 00 e4 1a 01 00 00 00 00 00  c...............
[ 1199.358591] 4. kcalloc() :       kvarr = 0x000000002829c3ec (actual=0xffff89f97bcee000)
[ 1199.358593]  content: 00 00 00 00 00 00 00 00 00 00 00 00 00 00 00 00 ................
[ 1199.358609] 5. __vmalloc():        vrx = 0x000000008dd6a024 (actual=0xffffa858c1a39000)
[ 1199.358610]  content: 55 16 1f b7 e3 b8 e6 04 00 00 00 00 00 00 00 00  U...............
[ 1199.358615] BUG: unable to handle page fault for address: ffffa858c1a39004
[ 1199.358726] #PF: supervisor write access in kernel mode
[ 1199.358727] #PF: error_code(0x0003) - permissions violation
[ 1199.358729] PGD 7d544067 P4D 7d544067 PUD 7d545067 PMD 341d1067 PTE 8000000075bd6061
[ 1199.358735] Oops: 0003 [#1] SMP PTI
[ 1199.358739] CPU: 1 PID: 3012 Comm: insmod Tainted: G           OE     5.4.0-llkd01 #2
[ 1199.358740] Hardware name: innotek GmbH VirtualBox/VirtualBox, BIOS VirtualBox 12/01/2006
[ 1199.358745] RIP: 0010:vmalloc_demo_init+0x2c9/0x1000 [vmalloc_demo]
[ 1199.358747] Code: d2 b9 10 00 00 00 6a 10 41 b8 01 00 00 00 48 c7 c6 83 c0 49 c0 48 c7 c7 8e c0
               49 c0 e8 f0 07 05 c3 58 5a 48 8b 05 77 d2 ff ff <48> c7 40 04 ba 00 00 00 31 c0 c3 48 8b 3d 75 d2
               ff ff e8 20 13 e1
[ 1199.358749] RSP: 0018:ffffa858c09c7c78 EFLAGS: 00010286
[ 1199.358751] RAX: ffffa858c1a39000 RBX: 0000000000000000 RCX: 0000000000000006
[ 1199.358753] RDX: 0000000000000001 RSI: ffffffff8445c358 RDI: ffff89f97bb17c80
[ 1199.358754] RBP: ffffffffc04a1000 R08: 0000000000000000 R09: 0000000000000000
[ 1199.358756] R10: 0000000000000001 R11: 0000000000000000 R12: ffff89f97842a720
[ 1199.358757] R13: ffff89f933107830 R14: ffffffffc049e140 R15: ffffffffc049e190
[ 1199.358759] FS:  00007ff3faf3d740(0000) GS:ffff89f97db00000(0000) knlGS:0000000000000000
[ 1199.358761] CS:  0010 DS: 0000 ES: 0000 CR0: 0000000080050033
[ 1199.358762] CR2: ffffa858c1a39004 CR3: 0000000072a7a005 CR4: 00000000000606e0
[ 1199.358767] Call Trace:
[ 1199.358772]  do_one_initcall+0x6e/0x254
[ 1199.358789]  ? _cond_resched+0x15/0x30
[ 1199.358792]  ? kmem_cache_alloc_trace+0x1da/0x280
[ 1199.358797]  do_init_module+0x5c/0x230
[ 1199.358804]  load_module+0x2758/0x2a20
[ 1199.358810]  ? vfs_read+0x148/0x170
[ 1199.358816]  ? __do_sys_finit_module+0xaa/0x110
[ 1199.358818]  __do_sys_finit_module+0xaa/0x110
[ 1199.358824]  do_syscall_64+0x5b/0x180
[ 1199.358827]  entry_SYSCALL_64_after_hwframe+0x44/0xa9
[ 1199.358832] RIP: 0033:0x7ff3fb06715d
```

Figure 9.5 – The kernel Oops that occurs when we try and write to a read-only memory region!

This proves that, indeed, the `__vmalloc()` API we performed had successfully set the memory region to read-only. Again, the details on the interpretation of the preceding (partially seen) kernel diagnostics or *Oops* message lie beyond this book's scope. Nevertheless, it's quite easy to see the root cause of the issue highlighted in the preceding figure: the following lines literally pinpoint the reason for this bug:

```
BUG: unable to handle page fault for address: ffffa858c1a39004
#PF: supervisor write access in kernel mode
#PF: error_code(0x0003) - permissions violation
```

> In user space applications, performing a similar memory protection setting upon an arbitrary memory region can be done via the `mprotect(2)` system call; do look up its man page for usage details (it even kindly provides example code!).

Why make memory read-only?

Specifying memory protections at allocation time to, say, read-only may appear to be a pretty useless thing to do: how would you then initialize that memory to some meaningful content? Well, think about it – **guard pages** are the perfect use case for this scenario (similar to the redzone pages that the SLUB layer keeps when in debug mode); it is useful indeed.

What if we wanted read-only pages for some purpose other than guard pages? Well, instead of using `__vmalloc()`, we might avail of some alternate means: perhaps memory mapping some kernel memory into user space via an `mmap()` method, and using the `mprotect(2)` system call from a user space app to set up appropriate protections (or even setting up protections through well-known and tested LSM frameworks, such as SELinux, AppArmor, Integrity, and so on).

We conclude this section with a quick comparison between the typical kernel memory allocator APIs: `kmalloc()` and `vmalloc()`.

The kmalloc() and vmalloc() APIs – a quick comparison

A quick comparison between the `kmalloc()` (or `kzalloc()`) and `vmalloc()` (or `vzalloc()`) APIs is presented in the following table:

Characteristic	`kmalloc()` or `kzalloc()`	`vmalloc()` or `vzalloc()`
Memory allocated is	Physically contiguous	Virtually (logically) contiguous
Memory alignment	Aligned to hardware (CPU) cacheline	Page-aligned
Minimum granularity	Arch-dependent; as low as 8 bytes on x86[_64]	1 page
Performance	Much faster (physical RAM allocated) for small memory allocations (the typical case); ideal for allocations < 1 page	Slower, demand-paged (only virtual memory allocated; lazy allocation of RAM involving the page fault handler); can service large (virtual) allocations
Size limitation	Limited (to typically 4 MB)	Very large (the kernel vmalloc region can even be several terabytes on 64-bit systems, though much less on 32-bit)
Suitability	Suitable for almost all use cases where performance matters, the memory required is small, including DMA (still, use the DMA API); can work in atomic/interrupt contexts	Suitable for large software (virtually) contiguous buffers; slower, cannot be allocated in atomic/interrupt contexts

This does not imply that one is superior to the other. Their usage depends upon the circumstances. This leads us into our next – indeed very important – topic: how do you decide which memory allocation API to use when? Making the right decision is actually critical for the best possible system performance and stability – do read on to find out how to make that choice!

Memory allocation in the kernel – which APIs to use when

A really quick summation of what we have learned so far: the kernel's underlying engine for memory allocation (and freeing) is called the page (or buddy system) allocator. Ultimately, every single memory allocation (and subsequent free) goes through this layer. It has its share of problems though, the chief one being internal fragmentation or wastage (due to its minimum granularity being a page). Thus we have the slab allocator (or slab cache) layered above it, providing the power of object caching and caching fragments of a page (helping alleviate the page allocator's wastage issues). Also, don't forget that you can create your own custom slab caches, and, as we have just seen, the kernel has a `vmalloc` region and APIs to allocate *virtual* pages from within it.

Kernel Memory Allocation for Module Authors - Part 2

With this information in mind, let's move along. To understand which API to use when, let's first look at the kernel memory allocation API set.

Visualizing the kernel memory allocation API set

The following conceptual diagram shows us the Linux kernel's memory allocation layers as well as the prominent APIs within them; note the following:

- Here we only show the (typically used) APIs exposed by the kernel to module/driver authors (with the exception being the one that ultimately performs the allocations – the `__alloc_pages_nodemask()` API right at the bottom!).
- For brevity, we haven't shown the corresponding memory-freeing APIs.

The following is a diagram showing several of the (exposed to module / driver authors) kernel memory allocation APIs:

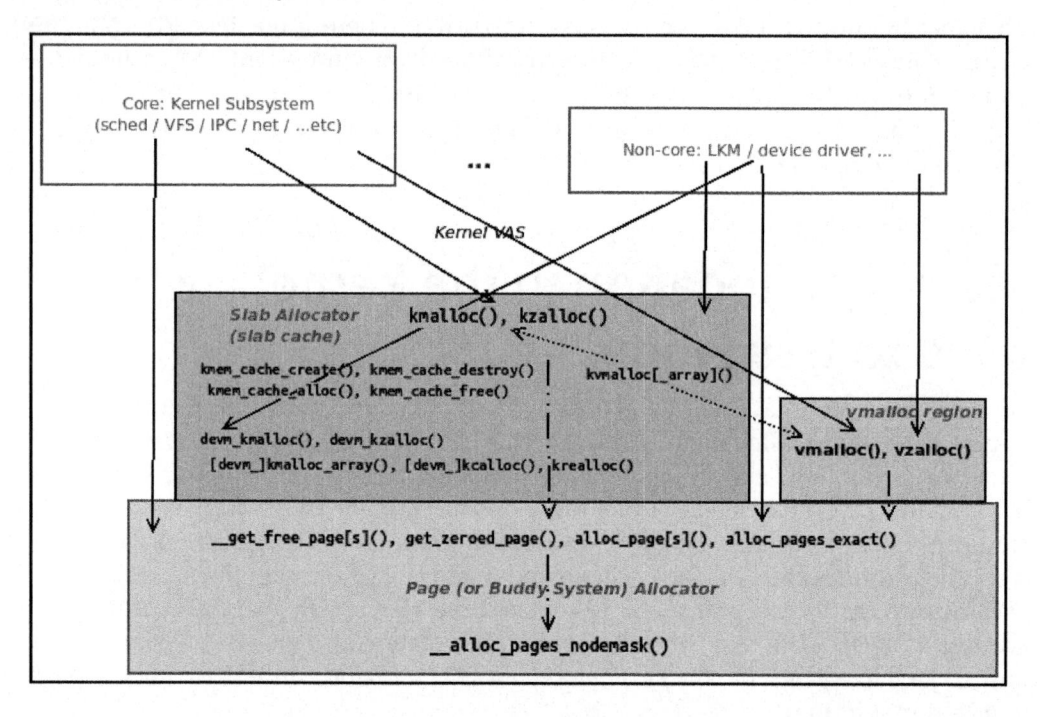

Figure 9.6 – Conceptual diagram showing the kernel's memory allocation API set (for module / driver authors)

Now that you have seen the wealth of (exposed) memory allocation APIs available, the following sections delve into helping you make the right decision as to which to use under what circumstances.

Selecting an appropriate API for kernel memory allocation

With all this choice of APIs, how do we choose? Though we have already talked about this very case in this chapter as well as the previous one, we'll again summarize it as it's very important. Broadly speaking, there are two ways to look at it – the API to use depends upon the following:

- The amount of memory required
- The type of memory required

We will illustrate both cases in this section.

Kernel Memory Allocation for Module Authors - Part 2

First, to decide which API to use by the type, amount, and contiguity of the memory to be allocated, scan through the following flowchart (starting at the upper right from the label **Start here**):

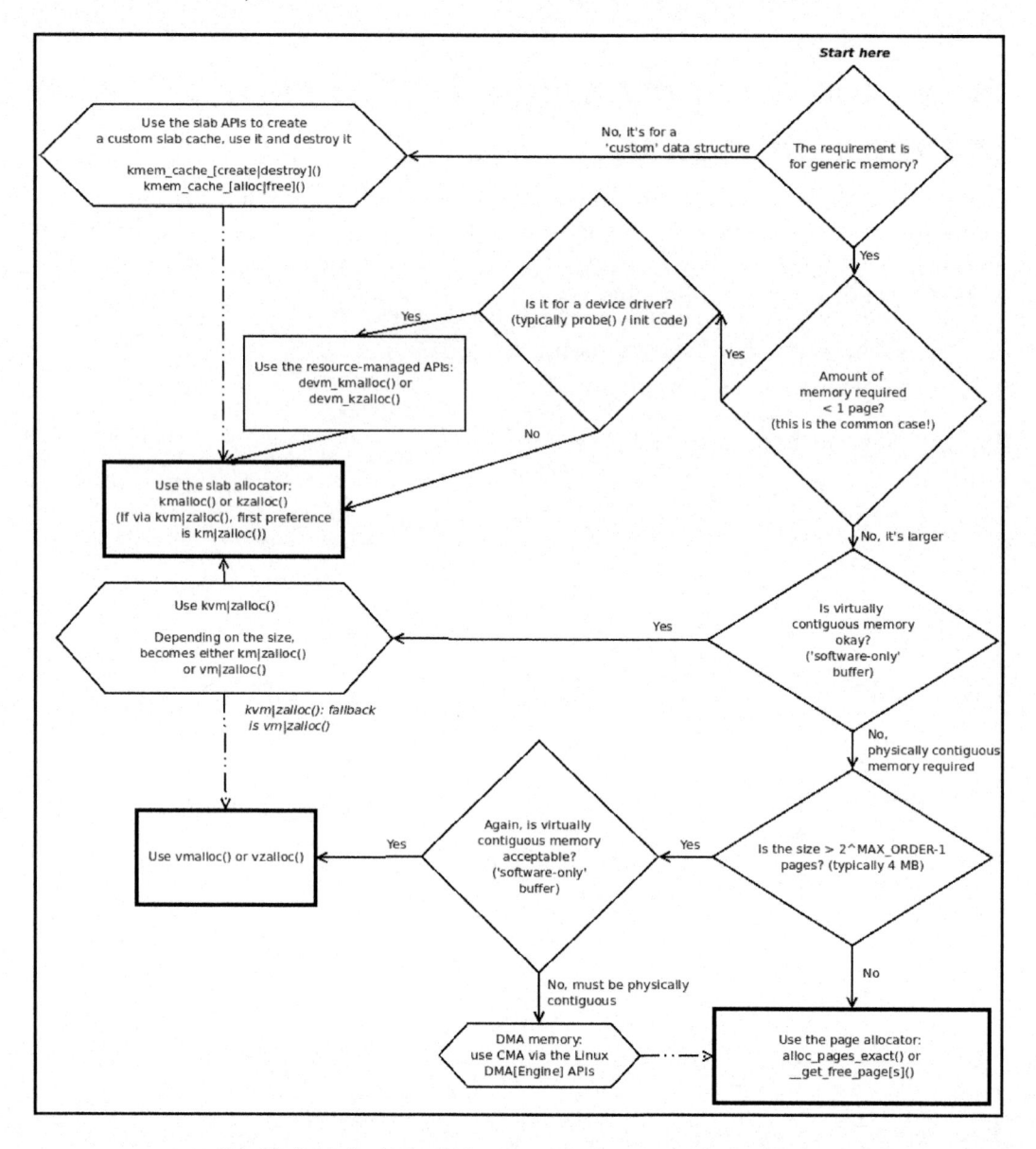

Figure 9.7 – Decision flowchart for which kernel memory allocation API(s) to use for a module/driver

Of course, it's not trivial; not only that, I'd like to remind you to recall the detailed discussions we covered earlier in this chapter, including the GFP flags to use (and the *do not sleep in atomic context* rule); in effect, the following:

- When in any atomic context, including interrupt contexts, ensure you only use the `GFP_ATOMIC` flag.
- Else (process context), you decide whether to use the `GFP_ATOMIC` or `GFP_KERNEL` flag; use `GFP_KERNEL` when it's safe to sleep
- Then, as covered under the *Caveats when using the slab allocator* section: when using the `k[m|z]alloc()` API and friends, make sure to check the actual allocated memory with `ksize()`.

Next, to decide which API to use by the type of memory to be allocated, scan through the following table:

Type of memory required	Allocation method	APIs
Kernel modules, typical case: regular usage for small amounts (less than one page), physically contiguous	Slab allocator	`k[m|z]alloc()`, `kcalloc()`, and `krealloc()`
Device drivers: regular usage for small amounts (< 1 page), physically contiguous; suitable for driver `probe()` or init methods; recommended for drivers	Resource-managed APIs	`devm_kzalloc()` and `devm_kmalloc()`
Physically contiguous, general-purpose usage	Page allocator	`__get_free_page[s]()`, `get_zeroed_page()`, and `alloc_page[s][_exact]()`
Physically contiguous, for **Direct Memory Access (DMA)**	Purpose-built DMA API layer, with CMA (or slab/page allocator)	(not covered here: `dma_alloc_coherent()`, `dma_map_[single|sg]()`, Linux DMA Engine APIs, and so on)
Virtually contiguous (for large software-only buffers)	Indirect via page allocator	`v[m|z]alloc()`
Virtually or physically contiguous, when unsure of runtime size	Either slab or vmalloc region	`kvmalloc[_array]()`

Kernel Memory Allocation for Module Authors - Part 2

| Custom data structures (objects) | Creates and uses a custom slab cache | `kmem_cache_[create|destroy]()` and `kmem_cache_[alloc|free]()` |

(Of course, there is some overlap with this table and the flowchart in *Figure 9.7*). As a generic rule of thumb, your first choice should be the slab allocator APIs, that is via `kzalloc()` or `kmalloc()`; these are the most efficient for typical allocations of less than a page in size. Also, recall that when unsure of the runtime size required, you could use the `kvmalloc()` API. Again, if the size required happens to be a perfectly rounded power-of-2 number of pages ($2^0, 2^1, ..., 2^{MAX\_ORDER-1}$ *pages*), then using the page allocator APIs will be optimal.

A word on DMA and CMA

On the topic of DMA, though its study and usage is beyond the scope of this book, I would nevertheless like to mention that Linux has a purpose-built set of APIs for DMA christened the *DMA Engine*. Driver authors performing DMA operations are very much expected to use these APIs and *not* directly use the slab or page allocator APIs (subtle hardware issues do turn up).

Further, several years back, Samsung engineers successfully merged a patch into the mainline kernel called the **Contiguous Memory Allocator (CMA)**. Essentially, it allows the allocation of *large physically contiguous memory* chunks (of a size over the typical 4 MB limit!). This is required for DMA on some memory-hungry devices (you want to stream that ultra-HD quality movie on a big-screen tablet or TV?). The cool thing is that the CMA code is transparently built into the DMA Engine and DMA APIs. Thus, as usual, driver authors performing DMA operations should just stick to using the Linux DMA Engine layer.

> If you are interested in learning more about DMA and CMA, see the links provided in the Further reading section for this chapter.

Also, realize that our discussion has mostly been with regard to the typical kernel module or device driver author. Within the OS itself, the demand for single pages tends to be quite high (due to the OS servicing demand paging via the page fault handler – what are called *minor* faults). Thus, under the hood, the memory management subsystem tends to issue the `__get_free_page[s]()` APIs quite frequently. Also, to service the memory demand for the *page cache* (and other internal caches), the page allocator plays an important role.

All right, well done, with this you have (almost!) completed our two chapters of coverage on the various kernel memory allocation layers and APIs (for module/driver authors)! Let's finish off this large topic with a remaining important area – the Linux kernel's (fairly controversial) OOM killer; do read on!

Stayin' alive – the OOM killer

Let's first cover a few background details regarding kernel memory management, particularly the reclaiming of free memory. This will put you in a position to understand what the kernel *OOM killer* component is, how to work with it, and even how to deliberately invoke it.

Reclaiming memory – a kernel housekeeping task and OOM

As you will be aware, the kernel tries, for optimal performance, to keep the working set of memory pages as high up as possible in the memory pyramid (or hierarchy).

> The so-called memory pyramid (or memory hierarchy) on a system consists of (in order, from smallest size but fastest speed to largest size but slowest): CPU registers, CPU caches (L1, L2, L3, ...), RAM, and swap (raw disk/flash/SSD partition). In our following discussion, we ignore CPU registers as their size is minuscule.

So, the processor uses its hardware caches (L1, L2, and so on) to hold the working set of pages. But of course, CPU cache memory is very limited, thus it will soon run out, causing the memory to spill over into the next hierarchical level – RAM. On modern systems, even many embedded ones, there's quite a bit of RAM; still, if and when the OS does run low on RAM, it spills over the memory pages that can no longer fit in RAM into a raw disk partition – *swap*. Thus the system continues to work well, albeit at a significant performance cost once swap is (often) used.

The Linux kernel, in an effort to ensure that a given minimum amount of free memory pages are available at all times within RAM, continually performs background page reclamation work – indeed, you can think of this as routine housekeeping. Who actually performs this work? The `kswapd` kernel thread(s) are continually monitoring memory usage on the system and invoke a page reclaim mechanism when they sense that memory is running low.

Kernel Memory Allocation for Module Authors - Part 2

This page reclamation work is done on a per *node:zone* basis. The kernel uses so-called *watermark levels* – min, low, and high – per *node:zone* to determine when to reclaim memory pages in an intelligent fashion. You can always look up `/proc/zoneinfo` to see the current watermark levels. (Note that the unit of watermark levels is pages.) Also, as we mentioned earlier, caches are typically the first victims and are shrunk down as memory pressure increases.

But let's play devil's advocate: what if all of this memory reclamation work doesn't help, and memory pressure keeps increasing to the point where the complete memory pyramid is exhausted, where a kernel allocation of even a few pages fails (or infinitely retries, which, frankly, is just as useless, perhaps worse)? What if all CPU caches, RAM, and swap are (almost completely) full!? Well, most systems just die at this point (actually, they don't die, they just become so slow that it appears as though they're permanently hung). The Linux kernel, though, being Linux, tends to be aggressive in these situations; it invokes a component aptly named the OOM killer. The OOM killer's job – you guessed it! – is to identify and summarily kill the memory-hogger process (by sending it the fatal `SIGKILL` signal; it could even end up killing a whole bunch of processes).

As you might imagine, it has had its fair share of controversy. Early versions of the OOM killer have been (quite rightly) criticized. Recent versions use superior heuristics that work quite well.

> You can find more information on the improved OOM killer work (the kick-in strategy and the OOM reaper thread) in this LWN article (December 2015): *Toward more predictable and reliable out-of-memory handling:* `https://lwn.net/Articles/668126/`.

Deliberately invoking the OOM killer

To test the kernel OOM killer, we shall have to put enormous memory pressure on the system. Thus, the kernel will unleash its weapon – the OOM killer, which, once invoked, will identify and kill some process (or processes). Hence, obviously, I highly recommend you try out stuff like this on a safe isolated system, preferably a test Linux VM (with no important data on it).

Invoking the OOM killer via Magic SysRq

The kernel provides an interesting feature dubbed *Magic SysRq*: essentially, certain keyboard key combinations (or accelerators) result in a callback to some kernel code. For example, assuming it's enabled, pressing the `Alt-SysRq-b` key combination on an x86[_64] system results in a cold reboot! Take care, don't just type anything, do read the relevant documentation here: https://www.kernel.org/doc/Documentation/admin-guide/sysrq.rst.

Let's try some interesting things; we run the following on our Fedora Linux VM:

```
$ cat /proc/sys/kernel/sysrq
16
```

This shows that the Magic SysRq feature is partially enabled (the kernel documentation mentioned at the start of this section gives the details). To fully enable it, we run the following:

```
$ sudo sh -c "echo 1 > /proc/sys/kernel/sysrq"
```

Okay, so to get to the point here: you can use Magic SysRq to invoke the OOM killer!

> Careful! Invoking the OOM killer, via Magic SysRq or otherwise, *will* cause some process – typically the *heavy* one(s) – to unconditionally die!

How? As root, just type the following:

```
# echo f > /proc/sysrq-trigger
```

Look up the kernel log to see whether anything interesting occurred!

Invoking the OOM killer with a crazy allocator program

We'll also demonstrate in the following section a more hands-on and interesting way by which you can (most probably) invite the OOM killer in. Write a simple user space C program that behaves as a crazy allocator, performing (typically) tens of thousands of memory allocations, writing something to each page, and, of course, never freeing up the memory, thus putting tremendous pressure on memory resources.

Kernel Memory Allocation for Module Authors - Part 2

As usual, we show only the most relevant parts of the source code in the following snippet; please refer to and clone the book's GitHub repo for the full code; remember, this is a user-mode app not a kernel module:

```c
// ch9/oom_killer_try/oom_killer_try.c
#define BLK        (getpagesize()*2)
static int force_page_fault = 0;
int main(int argc, char **argv)
{
    char *p;
    int i = 0, j = 1, stepval = 5000, verbose = 0;
    [...]
    do {
        p = (char *)malloc(BLK);
        if (!p) {
            fprintf(stderr, "%s: loop #%d: malloc failure.\n",
                argv[0], i);
            break;
        }

        if (force_page_fault) {
            p[1103] &= 0x0b; // write something into a byte of the 1st page
            p[5227] |= 0xaa; // write something into a byte of the 2nd page
        }
        if (!(i % stepval)) { // every 'stepval' iterations..
            if (!verbose) {
                if (!(j%5)) printf(". ");
            [...]
        }
        i++;
    } while (p && (i < atoi(argv[1])));
```

In the following code block, we show some output obtained when running our *crazy allocator* program on an x86_64 Fedora 31 VM running our custom 5.4.0 Linux kernel:

```
$ cat /proc/sys/vm/overcommit_memory   /proc/sys/vm/overcommit_ratio
0
50
$                                   << explained below >>

$ ./oom-killer-try
Usage: ./oom-killer-try alloc-loop-count force-page-fault[0|1] [verbose_flag[0|1]]
$ ./oom-killer-try 2000000 0
./oom-killer-try: PID 28896
..... ..... ..... ..... ..... ..... ..... ..... ..... .....
```

```
..... ..... ..... ..... ..... ..... ..... ..... ..... ..... .....
..... ..... ..... ..... ..... ..... ..... ..... ...Killed
$
```

The `Killed` message is the giveaway! The user mode process has been killed by the kernel. The reason becomes obvious once we glance at the kernel log – it's the OOM killer, of course (we show the kernel log in the *Demand paging and OOM* section).

Understanding the rationale behind the OOM killer

Glance at the preceding output of our `oom_killer_try` app: (in this particular run) 33 periods (.) appear before the dreaded `Killed` message. In our code, we emit a . (via `printf`) every 5,000 times we make an allocation (of 2 pages or 8 KB). Thus, here, we have 33 times 5 periods, meaning 33 * 5 = 165 times => 165 * 5000 * 8K ~= 6,445 MB. Thus, we can conclude that, after our process (virtually) allocated approximately 6,445 MB (~ 6.29 GB) of memory, the OOM killer terminated our process! You now need to understand why this occurred at this particular number.

On this particular Fedora Linux VM, the RAM is 2 GB *and the swap space* is 2 GB; thus, the total available memory in the *memory pyramid* = (CPU caches +) RAM + swap.

This is 4 GB (to keep it simple, let's just ignore the fairly insignificant amount of memory within the CPU caches). But then, it begs the question, why didn't the kernel invoke the OOM killer at the 4 GB point (or lower)? Why only at around 6 GB? This is an interesting point: the Linux kernel follows a **VM overcommit** policy, deliberately over-committing memory (to a certain extent). To understand this, see the current `vm.overcommit` setting:

```
$ cat /proc/sys/vm/overcommit_memory
0
```

This is indeed the default (0). The permissible values (settable only by root) are as follows:

- 0: Allow memory overcommitting using a heuristic algorithm (see more in the following section); *the default.*

- 1: Always overcommit; in other words, never refuse any `malloc(3)`; useful for some types of scientific apps that use sparse memory.

- 2: The following notes are direct quotes from the kernel documentation (https://www.kernel.org/doc/html/v4.18/vm/overcommit-accounting.html#overcommit-accounting):

  "Don't overcommit. The total address space commit for the system is not permitted to exceed swap plus a configurable amount (default is 50%) of physical RAM. Depending on the amount you use, in most situations this means a process will not be killed while accessing pages but will receive errors on memory allocation as appropriate. Useful for applications that want to guarantee their memory allocations will be available in the future without having to initialize every page"

The overcommit extent is determined by the overcommit ratio:

```
$ cat /proc/sys/vm/overcommit_ratio
50
```

We'll examine two cases in the following sections.

Case 1 – vm.overcommit set to 2, overcommit turned off

Firstly, remember, this is *not* the default. With the `overcommit_memory` tunable set to 2, the formula used to calculate the total (possibly overcommitted) available memory is as follows:

Total available memory = (RAM + swap) * (overcommit_ratio/100);

This formula only applies when `vm.overcommit == 2`.

On our Fedora 31 VM, with `vm.overcommit == 2` and 2 GB each of RAM and swap, this yields the following (in gigabytes):

Total available memory = (2 + 2) * (50/100) = 4 * 0.5 = 2 GB

> **TIP**: This value – the (over)commit limit – is also seen in `/proc/meminfo` as the `CommitLimit` field.

Case 2 – vm.overcommit set to 0, overcommit on, the default

This *is* the default. `vm.overcommit` is set to 0 (not 2): with this, the kernel effectively calculates the total (over)committed memory size as follows:

*Total available memory = (RAM + swap) * (overcommit_ratio + 100)%;*

This formula only applies when `vm.overcommit == 0`.

On our Fedora 31 VM, with `vm.overcommit == 0` and 2 GB each of RAM and swap, this formula yields the following (in gigabytes):

*Total available memory = (2 + 2) * (50+100)% = 4 * 150% = 6 GB*

So the system effectively pretends that there is a grand total of 6 GB of memory available. So now we understand: when our `oom_killer_try` process allocated huge amounts of memory and this limit (6 GB) was exceeded, the OOM killer jumped in!

> We now understand that the kernel provides several VM overcommit tunables under `/proc/sys/vm`, allowing the system administrator (or root) to fine-tune it (including switching it off by setting `vm.overcommit` to the value 2). At first glance, it may appear tempting to do so, to simply turn it off. Do pause though and think it through; leaving the VM overcommit at the kernel defaults is best on most workloads.
>
> **TIP**
>
> (For example, setting the `vm.overcommit` value to 2 on my Fedora 31 guest VM caused the effective available memory to change to just 2 GB. The typical memory usage, especially with the GUI running, far exceeded this, causing the system to be unable to even log in the user in GUI mode!) The following links help throw more light on the subject: Linux kernel documentation: `https://www.kernel.org/doc/Documentation/vm/overcommit-accounting` and *What are the disadvantages of disabling memory overcommit in Linux?* : `https://www.quora.com/What-are-the-disadvantages-of-disabling-memory-overcommit-in-Linux` . (Do see the *Further reading* section for more.)

Kernel Memory Allocation for Module Authors - Part 2

Demand paging and OOM

Recall the really important fact we learned earlier in the chapter, in the *A brief note on memory allocations and demand paging* section: because of the demand paging (or lazy allocation) policy that the OS uses, when a memory page is allocated by `malloc(3)` (and friends), it only actually causes virtual memory space to be reserved in a region of the process VAS; no physical memory is allocated at this time. Only when you perform some action on any byte(s) of the virtual page – a read, write, or execute – does the MMU raise a page fault (a minor fault) and the OS's page fault handler runs as a result. If it deems that this memory access is legal, it allocates a physical frame (via the page allocator).

In our simple `oom_killer_try` app, we manipulate this very idea via it's third parameter, `force_page_fault`: when set as 1, we emulate precisely this situation by writing something, anything really, into a byte - any byte - of each of the two pages allocated per loop iteration (peek at the code again if you need to).

So, now that you know this, let's re-run our app with the third parameter, `force_page_fault`, set to 1, to indeed force page faults! Here's the output that resulted when I ran this on my Fedora 31 VM (on our custom 5.4.0 kernel):

```
$ cat /proc/sys/vm/overcommit_memory /proc/sys/vm/overcommit_ratio
0
50
$ free -h
              total        used        free      shared  buff/cache   available
Mem:          1.9Gi       1.0Gi        76Mi        12Mi       866Mi       773Mi
Swap:         2.1Gi       3.0Mi       2.1Gi
$ ./oom-killer-try
Usage: ./oom-killer-try alloc-loop-count force-page-fault[0|1] [verbose_flag[0|1]]
$ ./oom-killer-try 900000 1
./oom_killer_try: PID 2032 (verbose mode: off)
.... .... .... .... .... .... .... .... .... ....
.... .... .... .... .Killed
$
$ free -h
              total        used        free      shared  buff/cache   available
Mem:          1.9Gi       238Mi       1.5Gi       2.0Mi       192Mi       1.6Gi
Swap:         2.1Gi       428Mi       1.6Gi
```

[494]

```
$
```

This time, you can literally feel the system struggle as it fights for memory. This time, it runs out of memory much sooner *as actual physical memory was allocated*. (From the preceding output, we see in this particular case 15 x 5 + 1 dots (. or periods); that is, 15 times 5 dots + 1 dot => = 76 times => 76 * 5000 loop iterations * 8K per iteration ~= 2969 MB virtually *and physically* allocated!)

Apparently, at this point, one of two things occurred:

- The system ran out of both RAM and swap, thus failing to allocate a page and thus inviting the OOM killer in.
- The calculated (artificial) kernel VM commit limit was exceeded.

We can easily look up this kernel VM commit value (again on the Fedora 31 VM where I ran this):

```
$ grep CommitLimit /proc/meminfo
CommitLimit:     3182372 kB
```

This works out to about 3,108 MB (well over our calculation of 2,969 MB). So here, it's likely that with all the RAM and swap space being used to run the GUI and existing apps, the first case came into play.

Also notice how, before running our program, the amount of memory used by the larger system caches (the page and buffer caches) is significant. The column entitled `buff/cache` in the output of the `free(1)` utility shows this. Before running our crazy allocator app, 866 MB out of 2 GB was being used for the page cache. Once our program runs, though, it applies so much memory pressure on the OS that tremendous amounts of swapping – the paging out of RAM pages to the raw disk partition called "swap" – is performed and literally all caches are freed up. Inevitably (as we refuse to free any memory), the OOM killer jumps in and kills us, causing large amounts of memory to be reclaimed. The free memory and the cache usage right after the OOM killer cleans up are 1.5 GB and 192 MB respectively. (The cache usage right now is low; it will increase as the system runs.)

Kernel Memory Allocation for Module Authors - Part 2

Looking up the kernel log reveals that indeed, the OOM killer has paid us a visit! Note that the following partial screenshot shows only the stack dump on the x86_64 Fedora 31 VM running the 5.4.0 kernel:

```
[  122.685801] oom_killer_try invoked oom-killer: gfp_mask=0x100cca(GFP_HIGHUSER_MOVABLE), order=0, oom_score_adj=0
[  122.685804] CPU: 0 PID: 2032 Comm: oom_killer_try Not tainted 5.4.0-llkd01 #2
[  122.685805] Hardware name: innotek GmbH VirtualBox/VirtualBox, BIOS VirtualBox 12/01/2006
[  122.685806] Call Trace:
[  122.685836]  dump_stack+0x66/0x90
[  122.685847]  dump_header+0x4a/0x27c
[  122.685853]  oom_kill_process.cold+0xb/0x10
[  122.685856]  out_of_memory+0x24d/0x4e0
[  122.685860]  __alloc_pages_slowpath+0xcf1/0xf60
[  122.685871]  __alloc_pages_nodemask+0x368/0x3b0
[  122.685875]  pagecache_get_page+0xc3/0x3a0
[  122.685878]  filemap_fault+0x70b/0xae0
[  122.685885]  ? ext4_filemap_fault+0x25/0x3f
[  122.685889]  ext4_filemap_fault+0x2d/0x3f
[  122.685896]  __do_fault+0x37/0x1a0
[  122.685899]  __handle_mm_fault+0x10b9/0x1ad0
[  122.685905]  handle_mm_fault+0x116/0x240
[  122.685908]  do_user_addr_fault+0x208/0x480
[  122.685912]  do_page_fault+0x31/0x190
[  122.685916]  page_fault+0x3e/0x50
```

Figure 9.8 – The kernel log after the OOM killer, showing the kernel call stack

Read the kernel-mode stack in *Figure 9.8* in a bottom-up fashion (ignoring the frames that start with ?): clearly, a page fault occurred; you can see the call frames:
`page_fault()` | `do_page_fault()` | [...] | `__hande_mm_fault()` | `__do_fault()` | [...] | `__alloc_pages_nodemask()`.

Think about it, this is completely normal: the fault was raised by the MMU as it was trying to service a virtual page with no physical counterpart. The OS's fault handling code runs (in process context, implying that `current` runs its code!); it ultimately leads to the OS invoking the page allocator routine's `__alloc_pages_nodemask()` function, which as we learned earlier is literally the heart of the zoned buddy system (or page) allocator – the engine of memory allocation!

What isn't normal, is that this time it (the `__alloc_pages_nodemask()` function) failed! This is deemed a critical issue and caused the OS to invoke the OOM killer (you can see the `out_of_memory` call frame in the preceding figure).

Toward the latter part of its diagnostic dump, the kernel tries hard to justify its reason for killing a given process. It shows a table of all threads, their memory usage (and various other statistics). Actually, these statistics being displayed occurs due to sysctl : /proc/sys/vm/oom_dump_tasks being on (1) by default. Here's a sampling (in the following output, we have eliminated the leftmost timestamp column of dmesg to make the data more readable):

```
[...]
Tasks state (memory values in pages):
[ pid ]   uid  tgid total_vm      rss pgtables_bytes swapents oom_score_adj name
[   607]    0   607    11774        8         106496      361         -250 systemd-journal
[   622]    0   622    11097        0          90112     1021        -1000 systemd-udevd
[   732]    0   732     7804        0          69632      153        -1000 auditd

              [...]

[  1950] 1000  1950    56717        1          77824      571            0 bash
[  2032] 1000  2032   755460   434468        6086656   317451            0 oom_killer_try
oom-kill:constraint=CONSTRAINT_NONE,nodemask=(null),cpuset=/,mems_allowed=0,global_oom,task_memcg=/user.slice/user-1000.slice/session-3.scope,task=oom_killer_try,pid=2032,uid=1000
Out of memory: Killed process 2032 (oom_killer_try) total-vm:3021840kB, anon-rss:1737872kB, file-rss:0kB, shmem-rss:0kB, UID:1000 pgtables:6086656kB oom_score_adj:0
oom_reaper: reaped process 2032 (oom_killer_try), now anon-rss:0kB, file-rss:0kB, shmem-rss:0kB
$
```

In the preceding output, we have highlighted in bold the rss (*Resident Set Size*) column as it's a good indication of physical memory usage by the process in question (the unit is KB). Clearly, our oom_killer_try process is using an enormous amount of physical memory. Also, notice how its number of swap entries (swapents) is very high. Modern kernels (4.6 onward) use a specialized oom_reaper kernel thread to perform the work of reaping (killing) the victim process (the last line of the preceding output shows that this kernel thread reaped our wonderful oom_killer_try process!). Interestingly, the Linux kernel's OOM can be thought of as a (last) defense against fork bombs and similar **(Distributed) Denial of Service ((D)DoS)** attacks.

Understanding the OOM score

In order to speed up the discovery of what the memory-hogging process is at crunch time (when the OOM killer is invoked), the kernel assigns and maintains an *OOM score* on a per-process basis (you can always look up the value in the `/proc/<pid>/oom_score` pseudo-file).

The OOM score range is `0` to `1000`:

- An OOM score of `0` implies that the process is not using any memory available to it
- An OOM score of `1000` implies the process is using 100 percent of the memory available to it

Obviously, the process with the highest OOM score wins. Its reward – it is instantly killed by the OOM killer (talk about dry humor). Not so fast though: the kernel has heuristics to protect important tasks. For example, the baked-in heuristics imply that the OOM killer will not select as its victim any root-owned process, a kernel thread, or a task that has a hardware device open.

What if we would like to ensure that a certain process will *never be killed* by the OOM killer? It's quite possible to do so, though it does require root access. The kernel provides a tunable, `/proc/<pid>/oom_score_adj`, an OOM adjustment value (with the default being `0`). The *net* OOM score is the sum of the `oom_score` value and the adjustment value:

```
net_oom_score = oom_score + oom_score_adj;
```

Thus, setting the `oom_score_adj` value of a process to `1000` pretty much guarantees that it will be killed, whereas setting it to `-1000` has exactly the opposite effect – it will never be selected as a victim.

A quick way to query (and even set) a process's OOM score (as well as it's OOM adjustment value) is via the `choom(1)` utility. For example, to query the OOM score and OOM adjustment value of the systemd process, just do `choom -p 1`. We did the obvious thing - wrote a simple script (that internally uses `choom(1)`) to query the OOM score of all processes currently alive on the system (it's here: `ch9/query_process_oom.sh`; do try it out on your box). Quick tip: the (ten) processes with the highest OOM score on the system can quickly be seen with (the third column is the net OOM score):

```
./query_process_oom.sh | sort -k3n | tail
```

Chapter 9

With this, we conclude this section and indeed this chapter.

Summary

In this chapter, we continued where we left off in the previous chapter. We covered, in a good amount of detail, how you can create and use your own custom slab caches (useful when your driver or module very frequently allocates and frees a certain data structure), and how to use some kernel infrastructure to help you debug slab (SLUB) memory issues. We then learned about and used the kernel `vmalloc` APIs (and friends), including how to set up given memory protections on memory pages. With the wealth of memory APIs and strategies available to you, how do you select which one to use in a given situation? We covered this important concern with a useful *decision chart* and table. Finally, we delved into understanding what exactly the kernel's *OOM killer* component is and how to work with it.

As I have mentioned before, sufficiently deep knowledge of the Linux memory management internals and exported API set will go a long way in helping you as a kernel module and/or device driver author. The reality, as we well know, is that a significant amount of time is spent by developers on troubleshooting and debugging code; the intricate knowledge and skills gained here will help you better navigate these mazes.

This completes the explicit coverage of Linux kernel memory management in this book. Though we have covered many areas, we have also left out or only skimmed over some of them.

The fact is that Linux memory management is a huge and complex topic, well worth understanding for the purposes of learning, writing more efficient code, and debugging complex situations.

Learning the (basic) usage of the powerful `crash(1)` utility (used to look deep within the kernel, via either a live session or a kernel dumpfile), and then re-looking at this and the previous chapter's content armed with this knowledge is indeed a powerful way to learn!

Great job on having covered Linux memory management! The next two chapters will have you learning about another core OS topic – how *CPU scheduling* is performed on the Linux OS. Take a breather, work on the following assignments and questions, and browse through the *Further reading* materials that capture your interest. Then, revitalized, jump into the next exciting area with me!

Questions

As we conclude, here is a list of questions for you to test your knowledge regarding this chapter's material: https://github.com/PacktPublishing/Linux-Kernel-Programming/tree/master/questions. You will find some of the questions answered in the book's GitHub repo: https://github.com/PacktPublishing/Linux-Kernel-Programming/tree/master/solutions_to_assgn.

Further reading

To help you delve deeper into the subject with useful materials, we provide a rather detailed list of online references and links (and at times, even books) in a Further reading document in this book's GitHub repository. The *Further reading* document is available here: https://github.com/PacktPublishing/Linux-Kernel-Programming/blob/master/Further_Reading.md.

The CPU Scheduler - Part 1

In this chapter and the next, you will dive into the details regarding a key OS topic – that is, CPU scheduling on the Linux OS. I will try and keep the learning more hands-on, by asking (and answering) typical questions and performing common tasks related to scheduling. Understanding how scheduling works at the level of the OS is not only important from a kernel (and driver) developer viewpoint, but it will also automatically make you a better system architect (even for user space applications).

We shall begin by covering essential background material; this will include the **Kernel Schedulable Entity** (**KSE**) on Linux, as well as the POSIX scheduling policies that Linux implements. We will then move on to using tools – perf and others – to visualize the flow of control as the OS runs tasks on CPUs and switches between them. This is useful to know when profiling apps as well! After that, we will dive deeper into the details of how exactly CPU scheduling works on Linux, covering modular scheduling classes, **Completely Fair Scheduling** (**CFS**), the running of the core schedule function, and so on. Along the way, we will also cover how you can programmatically (and dynamically) query and set the scheduling policy and priority of any thread on the system.

In this chapter, we will cover the following areas:

- Learning about the CPU scheduling internals – part 1 – essential background
- Visualizing the flow
- Learning about the CPU scheduling internals – part 2
- Threads – which scheduling policy and priority
- Learning about the CPU scheduling internals – part 3

Now, let's get started with this interesting topic!

Technical requirements

I assume that you have gone through `Chapter 1`, *Kernel Workspace Setup*, and have appropriately prepared a guest **Virtual Machine** (**VM**) running Ubuntu 18.04 LTS (or a later stable release) and installed all the required packages. If not, I highly recommend you do this first.

To get the most out of this book, I strongly recommend you first set up the workspace environment, including cloning this book's GitHub repository for the code and working on it in a hands-on fashion. The repository can be found here: `https://github.com/PacktPublishing/Linux-Kernel-Programming`.

Learning about the CPU scheduling internals – part 1 – essential background

Let's take a quick look at the essential background information we require to understand CPU scheduling on Linux.

> Note that in this book, we do not intend to cover material that competent system programmers on Linux should already be well aware of; this includes basics such as process (or thread) states, the state machine and transitions on it, and more information on what real time is, the POSIX scheduling policies, and so on. This (and more) has been covered in some detail in my earlier book: *Hands-On System Programming with Linux*, published by Packt in October 2018.

What is the KSE on Linux?

As you learned in `Chapter 6`, *Kernel Internals Essentials – Processes and Threads*, in the *Organizing processes, threads, and their stacks – user and kernel space* section, every process – in fact, every thread alive on the system – is bestowed with a task structure (`struct task_struct`) and both a user-mode as well as a kernel-mode stack.

Here, the key question to ask is: when scheduling is performed, *what object does it act upon*, in other words, what is the **Kernel Schedulable Entity**, the **KSE**? On Linux, **the KSE is a thread**, not a process (of course, every process contains a minimum of one thread). Thus, the thread is the granularity level at which scheduling is performed.

An example will help explain this: if we have a hypothetical situation where we have one CPU core and 10 user space processes, consisting of three threads each, plus five kernel threads, then we have a total of (10 x 3) + 5, which equals 35 threads. Each of them, except for the five kernel threads, has a user and kernel stack and a task structure (the kernel threads only have kernel stacks and task structures; all of this has been thoroughly explained in `Chapter 6`, *Kernel Internals Essentials – Processes and Threads*, in the *Organizing processes, threads, and their stacks – user and kernel space* section). Now, if all these 35 threads are runnable, they then compete for the single processor (though it's unlikely that they're all runnable simultaneously, but let's just consider it for the sake of discussion), then we now have 35 *threads* in competition for the CPU resource, not 10 processes and five kernel threads.

Now that we understand that the KSE is a thread, we will (almost) always refer to the thread in the context of scheduling. Now that this is understood, let's move on to the scheduling policies Linux implements.

The POSIX scheduling policies

It's important to realize that the Linux kernel does not have just one algorithm that implements CPU scheduling; the fact is, the POSIX standard specifies a minimal three scheduling policies (algorithms, in effect) that a POSIX-compliant OS must adhere to. Linux goes above and beyond, implementing these three as well as more, with a powerful design called scheduling classes (more on this in the *Understanding modular scheduling classes* section later in this chapter).

> Again, information on the POSIX scheduling policies on Linux (and more) is covered in more detail in my earlier book, *Hands-On System Programming with Linux*, published by Packt in October 2018.

The CPU Scheduler - Part 1

For now, let's just briefly summarize the POSIX scheduling policies and what effect they have in the following table:

Scheduling policy	Key points	Priority scale
SCHED_OTHER or SCHED_NORMAL	Always the default; threads with this policy are non-real-time; internally implemented as a **Completely Fair Scheduling** (**CFS**) class (seen later in the *A word on CFS and the vruntime value* section). The motivation behind this schedule policy is fairness and overall throughput.	Real-time priority is 0; the non-real-time priority is called the nice value: it ranges from -20 to +19 (a lower number implies superior priority) with a base of 0
SCHED_RR	The motivation behind this schedule policy is a (soft) real-time policy that's moderately aggressive. Has a finite timeslice (typically defaulting to 100 ms). A SCHED_RR thread will yield the processor IFF (if and only if): - It blocks on I/O (goes to sleep). - It stops or dies. - A higher-priority real-time thread becomes runnable (which will preempt this one). - Its timeslice expires.	(Soft) real-time: 1 to 99 (a higher number implies superior priority)
SCHED_FIFO	The motivation behind this schedule policy is a (soft) real-time policy that's (by comparison, very) aggressive. A SCHED_FIFO thread will yield the processor IFF: - It blocks on I/O (goes to sleep). - It stops or dies. - A higher-priority real-time thread becomes runnable (which will preempt this one). It has, in effect, infinite timeslice.	(same as SCHED_RR)
SCHED_BATCH	The motivation behind this schedule policy is a scheduling policy that's suitable for non-interactive batch jobs, less preemption.	Nice value range (-20 to +19)
SCHED_IDLE	Special case: typically the PID 0 kernel thread (traditionally called the swapper; in reality, it's the per CPU idle thread) uses this policy. It's always guaranteed to be the lowest-priority thread on the system and only runs when no other thread wants the CPU.	The lowest priority of all (think of it as being below the nice value +19)

> It's important to note that when we say real-time in the preceding table, we really mean *soft* (or at best, *firm*) real time and *not* hard real time as in an **Real-Time Operating System (RTOS)**. Linux is a **GPOS**, a **general-purpose OS**, not an RTOS. Having said that, you can convert vanilla Linux into a true hard real-time RTOS by applying an external patch series (called the RTL, supported by the Linux Foundation); you'll learn how to do precisely this in the following chapter in the *Converting mainline Linux into an RTOS* section.

Notice that a SCHED_FIFO thread in effect has infinite timeslice and runs until it wishes or one of the preceding mentioned conditions comes true. At this point, it's important to understand that we're only concerned with thread (KSE) scheduling here; on an OS such as Linux, the reality is that hardware (and software) *interrupts* are always superior and will always preempt even (kernel or user space) SCHED_FIFO threads! Do refer back to Figure 6.1 to see this. Also, we will cover hardware interrupts in detail in Chapter 14, *Handling Hardware Interrupts*. For our discussion here, we will ignore interrupts for the time being.

The priority scaling is simple:

- Non-real-time threads (SCHED_OTHER) have a real-time priority of 0; this ensures that they cannot even compete with real-time threads. They use an (old UNIX-style) priority value called the **nice value**, which ranges from -20 to +19 (-20 being the highest priority and +19 the worst).

> The way it's implemented on modern Linux, each nice level corresponds to an approximate 10% change (or delta, plus or minus) in CPU bandwidth, which is a significant amount.

- Real-time threads (SCHED_FIFO / SCHED_RR) have a real-time priority scale from 1 to 99, 1 being the least and 99 being the highest priority. Think of it this way: on a non-preemptible Linux system with one CPU, a SCHED_FIFO priority 99 thread spinning in an unbreakable infinite loop will effectively hang the machine! (Of course, even this will be preempted by interrupts – both hard and soft; see Figure 6.1.

The scheduling policy and priorities (both the static nice value and real-time priority) are members of the task structure, of course. The scheduling class that a thread belongs to is exclusive: a thread can only belong to one scheduling policy at a given point in time (worry not, we'll cover scheduling classes in some detail later in the *CPU scheduling internals – part 2* section).

Also, you should realize that on a modern Linux kernel, there are other scheduling classes (stop-schedule and deadline) that are in fact superior (in priority) to the FIFO/RR ones we mentioned earlier. Now that you have an idea of the basics, let's move on to something pretty interesting: how we can actually *visualize* the flow of control. Read on!

Visualizing the flow

Multicore systems have led to processes and threads executing concurrently on different processors. This is useful for gaining higher throughput and thus performance, but also causes synchronization headaches with shared writable data. So, for example, on a hardware platform with, say, four processor cores, we can expect processes (and threads) to execute in parallel on them. This is nothing new; is there a way, though, to actually see which processes or threads are executing on which CPU core – that is, a way to visualize a processor timeline? It turns out there are indeed a few ways to do so. In the following sections, we will look at one interesting way with `perf`, followed later by others (with LTTng, Trace Compass, and Ftrace).

Using perf to visualize the flow

Linux, with its vast arsenal of developer and **Quality Assurance** (**QA**) tools, has a really powerful one in `perf(1)`. In a nutshell, the `perf` toolset is the modern way to perform CPU profiling on a Linux box. (Besides a few tips, we do not cover `perf` in detail in this book.)

> **TIP**
> Akin to the venerable `top(1)` utility, to get a thousand-foot view of what's eating the CPU (in a lot more detail than `top(1)`), the `perf(1)` set of utilities is excellent. Do note, though, that, quite unusually for an app, `perf` is tightly coupled with the kernel that it runs upon. It's important that you install the `linux-tools-$(uname -r)` package first. Also, the distribution package will not be available for the custom 5.4 kernel we have built; so, when using `perf`, I suggest you boot your guest VM with one of the standard (or distro) kernels, install the `linux-tools-$(uname -r)` package, and then try using `perf`. (Of course, you can always manually build perf from within the kernel source tree, under the `tools/perf/` folder.)

With `perf` installed and running, do try out these `perf` commands:

```
sudo perf top
sudo perf top --sort comm,dso
sudo perf top -r 90 --sort pid,comm,dso,symbol
```

(By the way, `comm` implies the name of the command/process, **dso** is an abbreviation for **dynamic shared object**). Using an `alias` makes it easier; try this one (in one line) for even more verbose details (the call stack can be expanded too!):

```
alias ptopv='sudo perf top -r 80 -f 99 --sort pid,comm,dso,symbol --demangle-kernel -v --call-graph dwarf,fractal'
```

The man page on `perf(1)` provides the details; use the `man perf-<foo>` notation – for example, `man perf-top` – to get help with `perf top`.

One way to use `perf` is to obtain an idea of what task is running on what CPU; this is done via the `timechart` sub-command in `perf`. You can record events using `perf`, both system-wide as well as for a specific process. To record events system-wide, run the following command:

```
sudo perf timechart record
```

Terminate the recording session with a signal (^C). This will generate a binary data file named `perf.data` by default. It can now be examined with the following:

```
sudo perf timechart
```

The CPU Scheduler - Part 1

This command generates a **Scalable Vector Graphics (SVG)** file! It can be viewed with vector drawing utilities (such as Inkscape, or via the `display` command in ImageMagick) or simply within a web browser. It can be quite fascinating to study the time chart; I urge you to try it out. Do note, though, that the vector images can be quite large and therefore take a while to open.

A system-wide sampling run on a native Linux x86_64 laptop running Ubuntu 18.10 is shown as follows:

```
$ sudo perf timechart record
[sudo] password for <user>:
^C[ perf record: Woken up 18 times to write data ]
[ perf record: Captured and wrote 6.899 MB perf.data (196166 samples)
]
$ ls -lh perf.data
-rw------- 1 root root 7.0M Jun 18 12:57 perf.data
$ sudo perf timechart
Written 7.1 seconds of trace to output.svg.
```

> It is possible to configure `perf` to work with non-root access. Here, we don't; we just run `perf` as root via `sudo(8)`.

A screenshot of the SVG file generated by `perf` is seen in the following screenshot. To view the SVG file, you can simply drag and drop it into your web browser:

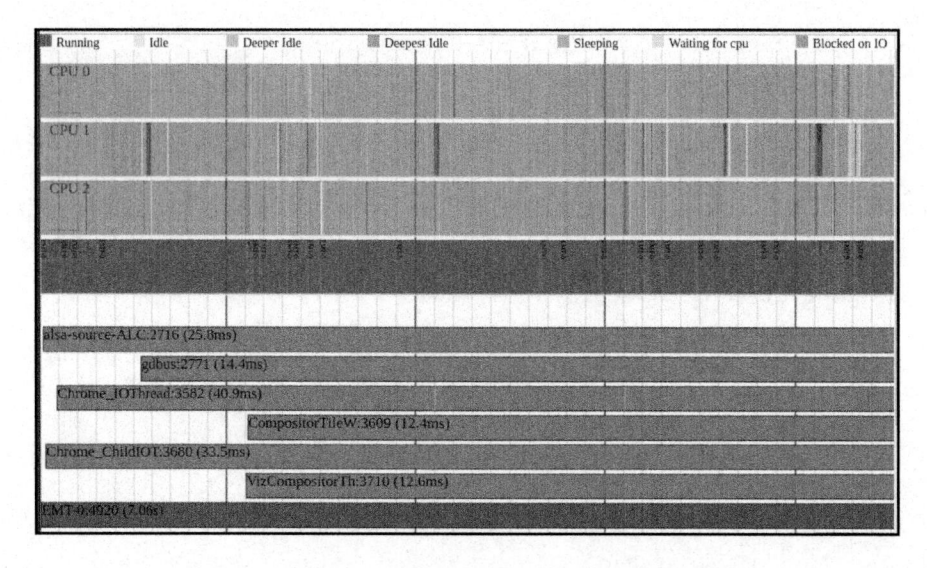

Figure 10.1 – (Partial) screenshot showing the SVG file generated by sudo perf timechart

[508]

Chapter 10

In the preceding screenshot, as one example, you can see that the `EMT-0` thread is busy and takes maximum CPU cycles (the phrase **CPU 3** is unfortunately unclear; look closely in the purple bar below **CPU 2**). This makes sense; it's the thread representing the **Virtual CPU** (**VCPU**) of VirtualBox where we are running Fedora 29 (**EMT** stands for **emulator thread**)!

You can zoom in and out of this SVG file, studying the scheduling and CPU events that are recorded by default by `perf`. The following figure, a partial screenshot when zoomed in 400% to the **CPU 1** region of the preceding screenshot, shows `htop` running on CPU #1 (the purple band literally shows the slice when it executed):

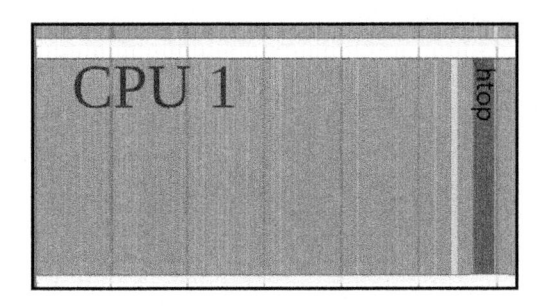

Figure 10.2 – Partial screenshot of perf timechart's SVG file, when zoomed in 400% to the CPU 1 region

What else? By using the `-I` option switch to `perf timechart record`, you can request only system-wide disk I/O (and network, apparently) events be recorded. This could be especially useful as, often, the real performance bottlenecks are caused by I/O activity (and not the CPU; I/O is usually the culprit!). The man page on `perf-timechart(1)` details further useful options; for example, `--callchain` to perform stack backtrace recording. As another example, the `--highlight <name>` option switch will highlight all tasks with the name `<name>`.

The CPU Scheduler - Part 1

You can convert `perf`'s binary `perf.data` record file into the popular **Common Trace Format** (**CTF**) file format, using `perf data convert -- all --to-ctf`, where the last argument is the directory where the CTF file(s) get stored. Why is this useful? CTF is the native data format used by powerful GUI visualizers and analyzer tools such as Trace Compass (seen later in `Chapter 11`, *The CPU Scheduler – Part 2*, under the *Visualization with LTTng and Trace Compass* section).

> **TIP**
>
> However, there is a catch, as mentioned in the Trace Compass Perf Profiling user guide (https://archive.eclipse.org/tracecompass.incubator/doc/org.eclipse.tracecompass.incubator.perf.profiling.doc.user/User-Guide.html): "*Not all Linux distributions have the ctf conversion builtin. One needs to compile perf (thus linux) with environment variables LIBBABELTRACE=1 and LIBBABELTRACE_DIR=/path/to/libbabeltrace to enable that support.*"

Unfortunately, as of the time of writing, this is the case with Ubuntu.

Visualizing the flow via alternate (CLI) approaches

There are, of course, alternate ways to visualize what's running on each processor; we mention a couple here and have saved one other interesting one (LTTng) for `Chapter 11`, *The CPU Scheduler – Part 2*, under the *Visualization with LTTng and Trace Compass* section):

- With `perf(1)`, again, run the `sudo perf sched record` command; this records activity. Stop by terminating it with the `^C` signal, followed by `sudo perf sched map` to see a (CLI) map of execution on the processor(s).
- Some simple Bash scripting can show what's executing on a given core (a simple wrapper over `ps(1)`). In the following snippet, we show sample Bash functions; for example, the following `c0()` function shows what is currently executing on CPU core #0, while `c1()` does the same for core #1:

```
# Show thread(s) running on cpu core 'n' - func c'n'
function c0()
{
```

```
    ps -eLF | awk '{ if($5==0) print $0}'
}
function c1()
{
    ps -eLF | awk '{ if($5==1) print $0}'
}
```

> **TIP**
> While on the broad topic of `perf`, Brendan Gregg has a very useful series of scripts that perform a lot of the hard work required when monitoring production Linux systems using `perf`; do take a look at them here: https://github.com/brendangregg/perf-tools (some distributions include them as a package called `perf-tools[-unstable]`).

Do give these alternatives (including the `perf-tools[-unstable] package`) a try!

Learning about the CPU scheduling internals – part 2

This section delves into kernel CPU scheduling internals in some detail, the emphasis being on the core aspect of the modern design, modular scheduler classes.

Understanding modular scheduling classes

Ingo Molnar, a key kernel developer, (along with others) redesigned the internal structure of the kernel scheduler, introducing a new approach called **scheduling classes** (this was back in October 2007 with the release of the 2.6.23 kernel).

> As a side note, the word *class* here isn't a coincidence; many Linux kernel features are intrinsically, and quite naturally, designed with an **object-oriented** nature. The C language, of course, does not allow us to express this directly in code (hence the preponderance of structures with both data and function pointer members, emulating a class). Nevertheless, the design is very often object-oriented (as you shall again see with the driver model in the *Linux Kernel Programming Part 2* book). Please see the *Further reading* section of this chapter for more details on this.

A layer of abstraction was introduced under the core scheduling code, the `schedule()` function. This layer under `schedule()` is generically called the scheduling classes and is modular in design. Note that the word *modular* here implies that scheduler classes can be added or removed from the inline kernel code; it has nothing to do with the **Loadable Kernel Module (LKM)** framework.

The basic idea is this: when the core scheduler code (encapsulated by the `schedule()` function) is invoked, understanding that there are various available scheduling classes under it, it iterates over each of the classes in a predefined priority order, asking each if it has a thread (or process) that requires scheduling onto a processor (how exactly, we shall soon see).

As of the 5.4 Linux kernel, these are the scheduler classes within the kernel, listed in priority order, with the highest priority first:

```
// kernel/sched/sched.h
[ ... ]
extern const struct sched_class stop_sched_class;
extern const struct sched_class dl_sched_class;
extern const struct sched_class rt_sched_class;
extern const struct sched_class fair_sched_class;
extern const struct sched_class idle_sched_class;
```

There we have it, the five scheduler classes – stop-schedule, deadline, (soft) real time, fair, and idle – in priority order, highest to lowest. The data structures that abstracts these scheduling classes, `struct sched_class`, are strung together on a singly linked list, which the core scheduling code iterates over. (You will come to what the `sched_class` structure is later; ignore it for now).

Every thread is associated with it's own unique task structure (`task_struct`); within the task structure, the `policy` member specifies the scheduling policy that the thread adheres to (typically one of `SCHED_FIFO`, `SCHED_RR`, or `SCHED_OTHER`). It's exclusive - a thread can only adhere to one scheduling policy at any given point in time (it can be changed though). Similarly, another member of the task structure, `struct sched_class`, holds the modular scheduling class that the thread belongs to (which is also exclusive). Both the scheduling policy and priority are dynamic and can be queried and set programmatically (or via utilities; you will soon see this).

So knowing this, you will now realize that all threads that adhere to either the `SCHED_FIFO` or `SCHED_RR` scheduling policy, map to the `rt_sched_class` (for their `sched_class` within the task structure), all threads that are `SCHED_OTHER` (or `SCHED_NORMAL`) map to the `fair_sched_class`, and the idle thread (`swapper/n`, where `n` is the CPU number starting from 0) always maps to `idle_sched_class` scheduling class.

When the kernel needs to schedule, this is the essential call sequence:

```
schedule() --> __schedule() --> pick_next_task()
```

The actual iteration over the preceding scheduling classes occurs here; see the (partial) code of `pick_next_task()`, as follows:

```c
// kernel/sched/core.c
/*
 * Pick up the highest-prio task:
 */
static inline struct task_struct *
pick_next_task(struct rq *rq, struct task_struct *prev, struct rq_flags *rf)
{
    const struct sched_class *class;
    struct task_struct *p;
    /* Optimization: [...] */
    [...]
    for_each_class(class) {
        p = class->pick_next_task(rq, NULL, NULL);
        if (p)
            return p;
    }

    /* The idle class should always have a runnable task: */
    BUG();
}
```

The preceding `for_each_class()` macro sets up a `for` loop to iterate over all scheduling classes. Its implementation is as follows:

```c
// kernel/sched/sched.h
[...]
#ifdef CONFIG_SMP
#define sched_class_highest (&stop_sched_class)
#else
#define sched_class_highest (&dl_sched_class)
#endif
```

The CPU Scheduler - Part 1

```
#define for_class_range(class, _from, _to) \
    for (class = (_from); class != (_to); class = class->next)

#define for_each_class(class) \
    for_class_range(class, sched_class_highest, NULL)
```

You can see from the preceding implementation that the code results in each class, from `sched_class_highest` to `NULL` (implying the end of the linked list they're on), being asked, via the `pick_next_task()` "method", who to schedule next. Now, the scheduling class code determines whether it has any candidates that want to execute. How? That's simple actually; it merely looks up its **runqueue** data structure.

Now, this is a key point: *the kernel maintains one runqueue for every processor core and for every scheduling class*! So, if we have a system with, say, eight CPU cores, then we will have *8 cores * 5 sched classes = 40 runqueues*! Runqueues are in fact implemented as per-CPU variables, an interesting lock-free technique (exception: on **Uniprocessor** (UP) systems, the `stop-sched` class does not exist):

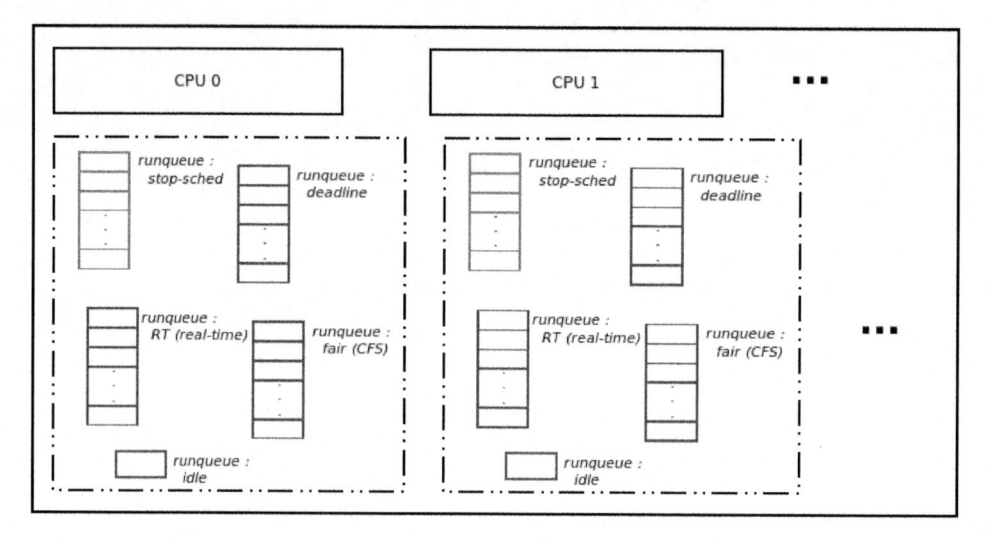

Figure 10.3 – There is a runqueue per CPU core per scheduling class

Please note that in the preceding diagram, the way I show the runqueues makes them perhaps appear as arrays. That isn't the intention at all, it's merely a conceptual diagram. The actual runqueue data structure used depends on the scheduling class (the class code implements the runqueue after all). It could be an array of linked lists (as with the real-time class), a tree - a **red-black (rb) tree** - as with the fair class), and so on.

To help better understand the scheduler class model, we will devise an example: let's say, on an **Symmetric Multi Processor** (**SMP**) or multicore) system, we have 100 threads alive (in both user and kernel space). Among them, we have a few competing for the CPUs; that is, they are in the ready-to-run (run) state, implying they are runnable and thus enqueued on runqueue data structures:

- Thread S1: Scheduler class, `stop-sched` (**SS**)
- Threads D1 and D2: Scheduler class, **Deadline** (**DL**)
- Threads RT1 and RT2: Scheduler class, **Real Time** (**RT**)
- Threads F1, F2, and F3: Scheduler class, CFS (or fair)
- Thread I1: Scheduler class, idle.

Imagine that, to begin with, thread F2 is on a processor core, happily executing code. At some point, the kernel wishes to context switch to some other task on that CPU (what triggers this? You shall soon see). On the scheduling code path, the kernel code ultimately ends up in the `kernel/sched/core.c:void schedule(void)` kernel routine (again, code-level details follow later). What's important to understand for now is that the `pick_next_task()` routine, invoked by `schedule()`, iterates over the linked list of scheduler classes, asking each whether it has a candidate to run. It's code path (conceptually, of course) looks something like this:

1. Core scheduler code (`schedule()`): "*Hey, SS, do you have any threads that want to run?*"
2. SS class code: Iterates over its runqueue and does find a runnable thread; it thus replies: "*Yes, I do, it's thread S1.*"
3. Core scheduler code (`schedule()`): "*Okay, let's context switch to S1.*"

And the job is done. But what if there is no runnable thread S1 on the SS runqueue for that processor (or it has gone to sleep, or is stopped, or it's on another CPU's runqueue). Then, SS will say "*no*" and the next most important scheduling class, DL, will be asked. If it has potential candidate threads that want to run (D1 and D2, in our example), its class code will identify which of D1 or D2 should run, and the kernel scheduler will faithfully context switch to it. This process continues for the RT and fair (CFS) scheduling classes. (A picture's worth a thousand words, right: see Figure 10.4).

The CPU Scheduler - Part 1

In all likelihood (on your typical moderately loaded Linux system), there will be no SS, DL, or RT candidate threads that want to run on the CPU in question, and there often will be at least one fair (CFS) thread that will want to run; hence, it will be picked and context-switched to. If there's none that wants to run (no SS/DL/RT/CFS class thread wants to run), it implies that the system is presently idle (lazy chap). Now, the idle class is asked whether it wants to run: it always says yes! This makes sense: after all, it is the CPU idle thread's job to run on the processor when no one else needs to. Hence, in such a case, the kernel switches context to the idle thread (typically labelled `swapper/n`, where `n` is the CPU number that it's executing upon (starting from `0`)).

Also, note that the `swapper/n` (CPU idle) kernel thread does not show up in the `ps(1)` listing, though it's always present (recall the code we demonstrated in Chapter 6, *Kernel Internals Essentials – Processes and Threads*, here: `ch6/foreach/thrd_showall/thrd_showall.c`. There, we wrote a `disp_idle_thread()` routine to show some details of the CPU idle thread as even the kernel's `do_each_thread() { ... } while_each_thread()` loop that we employed there does not show the idle thread).

The following diagram neatly sums up the way the core scheduling code invokes the scheduling classes in priority order, context switching to the ultimately selected next thread:

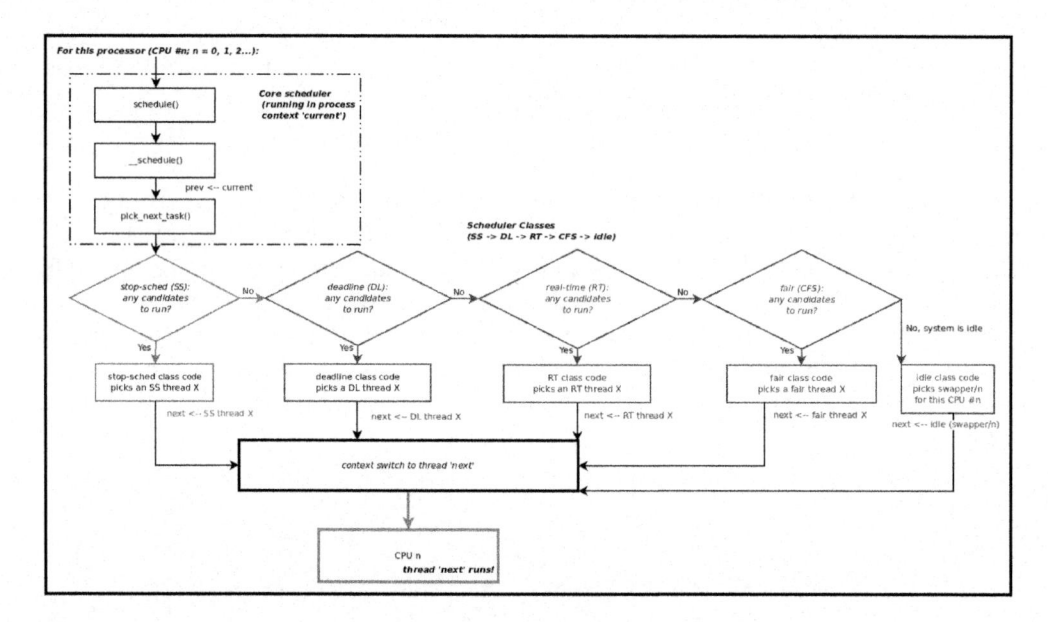

Figure 10.4 – Iterating over every scheduling class to pick the task that will run next

In the following chapter, you shall learn, among other things, how to visualize kernel flow via some powerful tools. There, precisely this work of iterating over modular scheduler classes is actually seen.

Asking the scheduling class

How exactly does the core scheduler code (`pick_next_task()`) ask the scheduling classes whether they have any threads that want to run? We have already seen this, but I feel it's worthwhile repeating the following code fragment for clarity (called mostly from `__schedule()` and also from the thread migration code path):

```
// kernel/sched/core.c
[ ... ]
static inline struct task_struct *
pick_next_task(struct rq *rq, struct task_struct *prev, struct rq_flags *rf)
{
    const struct sched_class *class;
    struct task_struct *p;
    [ ... ]
    for_each_class(class) {
        p = class->pick_next_task(rq, NULL, NULL);
        if (p)
            return p;
    }
    [ ... ]
```

Notice the object orientation in action: the `class->pick_next_task()` code, for all practical purposes, is invoking a method, `pick_next_task()`, of the scheduling class, `class`! The return value, conveniently, is the pointer to the task structure of the picked task, which the code now context switches to.

The preceding paragraph implies, of course, that there is a `class` structure, embodying what we really mean by the scheduling class. Indeed, this is the case: it contains all possible operations, as well as useful hooks, that you might require in a scheduling class. It's (surprisingly) called the `sched_class` structure:

```
// location: kernel/sched/sched.h
[ ... ]
struct sched_class {
    const struct sched_class *next;
    [...]
    void (*enqueue_task) (struct rq *rq, struct task_struct *p, int flags);
    void (*dequeue_task) (struct rq *rq, struct task_struct *p, int
```

The CPU Scheduler - Part 1

```
        flags);
        [ ... ]
        struct task_struct * (*pick_next_task)(struct rq *rq,
                              struct task_struct *prev,
                              struct rq_flags *rf);
        [ ... ]
        void (*task_tick)(struct rq *rq, struct task_struct *p, int queued);
        void (*task_fork)(struct task_struct *p);
        [ ... ]
};
```

(There are many more members to this structure than we've shown here; do look it up in the code). As should be obvious by now, each scheduling class instantiates this structure, appropriately populating it with methods (function pointers, of course). The core scheduling code, iterating over the linked list of scheduling classes (as well as elsewhere in the kernel), invokes - as long as it's not NULL- the methods and hook functions as required.

As an example, let's consider how the fair scheduling class (CFS) implements its scheduling class:

```
// kernel/sched/fair.c
const struct sched_class fair_sched_class = {
    .next          = &idle_sched_class,
    .enqueue_task  = enqueue_task_fair,
    .dequeue_task  = dequeue_task_fair,
    [ ... ]
    .pick_next_task = pick_next_task_fair,
    [ ... ]
    .task_tick     = task_tick_fair,
    .task_fork     = task_fork_fair,
    .prio_changed  = prio_changed_fair,
    [ ... ]
};
```

So now you see it: the code used by the fair sched class to pick the next task to run (when asked by the core scheduler), is the function `pick_next_task_fair()`. FYI, the `task_tick` and `task_fork` members are good examples of scheduling class hooks; these functions will be invoked by the scheduler core on every timer tick (that is, each timer interrupt, which fires – in theory, at least – CONFIG_HZ times a second) and when a thread belonging to this scheduling class forks, respectively.

[518]

> An interesting in-depth Linux kernel project, perhaps: create your own scheduling class with its particular methods and hooks, implementing its internal scheduling algorithm(s). Link all the bits and pieces as required (into the scheduling classes-linked list, inserted at the desired priority, and so on) and test! Now you can see why they're called modular scheduling classes.

Great – now that you understand the architecture behind how the modern modular CPU scheduler works, let's take a brief look at the algorithm behind CFS, perhaps the most used scheduling class on generic Linux.

A word on CFS and the vruntime value

Since version 2.6.23, CFS has been the de facto kernel CPU scheduling code for regular threads; the majority of threads are `SCHED_OTHER`, which is driven by CFS. The driver *behind CFS is fairness and overall throughput*. In a nutshell, within its implementation, the kernel keeps track of the actual CPU runtime (at nanosecond granularity) of every runnable CFS (`SCHED_OTHER`) thread; the thread with the smallest runtime is the thread that most deserves to run and will be awarded the processor on the next scheduling switch. Conversely, threads that continually hammer on the processor will accumulate a large amount of runtime and will thus be penalized (it's quite karmic, really)!

Without delving into too many details regarding the internals of the CFS implementation, embedded within the task structure is another data structure, `struct sched_entity`, which contains within it an unsigned 64-bit value called `vruntime`. This is, at a simplistic level, the monotonic counter that keeps track of the amount of time, in nanoseconds, that the thread has accumulated (run) on the processor.

In practice, here, a lot of code-level tweaks, checks, and balances are required. For example, often, the kernel will reset the `vruntime` value to 0, triggering another scheduling epoch. Also, there are various tunables under `/proc/sys/kernel/sched_*`, to help better fine-tune the CPU scheduler behavior.

The CPU Scheduler - Part 1

How CFS picks the next task to run is encapsulated in the `kernel/sched/fair.c:pick_next_task_fair()` function. In theory, the way CFS works is simplicity itself: enqueue all runnable tasks (for that CPU) onto the runqueue, which is an rb-tree (a type of self-balancing binary search tree), in such a manner that the task that has spent the least amount of time on the processor is the leftmost leaf node on the tree, with succeeding nodes to the right representing the next task to run, then the one after that.

In effect, scanning the tree from left to right gives a timeline of future task execution. How is this assured? By using the aforementioned `vruntime` value as the key via which tasks are enqueued onto the rb-tree!

When the kernel needs to schedule, and it asks CFS, the CFS class code - we've already mentioned it, the `pick_next_task_fair()` function - *simply picks the leftmost leaf node on the tree*, returning the pointer to the task structure embedded there; it's, by definition, the task with the lowest `vruntime` value, effectively, the one that has run the least! (Traversing a tree is a *O(log n)* time-complexity algorithm, but due to some code optimization and a clever caching of the leftmost leaf node in effect render it into a very desirable *O(1)* algorithm!) Of course, the actual code is a lot more complex than is let on here; it requires several checks and balances. We won't delve into the gory details here.

> We refer those of you that are interested in learning more on CFS to the kernel documentation on the topic, at `https://www.kernel.org/doc/Documentation/scheduler/sched-design-CFS.txt`.
>
> Also, the kernel contains several tunables under `/proc/sys/kernel/sched_*` that have a direct impact on scheduling. Notes on these and how to use them can be found on the *Tuning the Task Scheduler* page (`https://documentation.suse.com/sles/12-SP4/html/SLES-all/cha-tuning-taskscheduler.html`), and an excellent real-world use case can be found in the article at `https://www.scylladb.com/2016/06/10/read-latency-and-scylla-jmx-process/`.

Now let's move onto learning how to query the scheduling policy and priority of any given thread.

Threads – which scheduling policy and priority

In this section, you'll learn how to query the scheduling policy and priority of any given thread on the system. (But what about programmatically querying and setting the same? We defer that discussion to the following chapter, in the *Querying and setting a thread's scheduling policy and priority* section.)

We learned that, on Linux, the thread is the KSE; it's what actually gets scheduled and runs on the processor. Also, Linux has several choices for the scheduling policy (or algorithm) to use. The policy, as well as the priority to allocate to a given task (process or thread), is assigned on a per-thread basis, with the default always being the SCHED_OTHER policy with real-time priority 0.

On a given Linux system, we can always see all processes alive (via a simple `ps -A`), or, with GNU `ps`, even every thread alive (`ps -LA`). This does not tell us, though, what scheduling policy and priority these tasks are running under; how do we query that?

This turns out to be pretty simple: on the shell, the `chrt(1)` utility is admirably suited to query and set a given process' scheduling policy and/or priority. Issuing `chrt` with the `-p` option switch and providing the PID as a parameter has it display both the scheduling policy as well as the real-time priority of the task in question; for example, let's query this for the `init` process (or systemd) PID 1:

```
$ chrt -p 1
pid 1's current scheduling policy: SCHED_OTHER
pid 1's current scheduling priority: 0
$
```

As usual, the `man` page on `chrt(1)` provides all the option switches and their usage; do take a peek at it.

The CPU Scheduler - Part 1

In the following (partial) screenshot, we show a run of a simple Bash script (`ch10/query_task_sched.sh`, a wrapper over `chrt`, essentially) that queries and displays the scheduling policy and real-time priority of all the alive threads (at the point they're run):

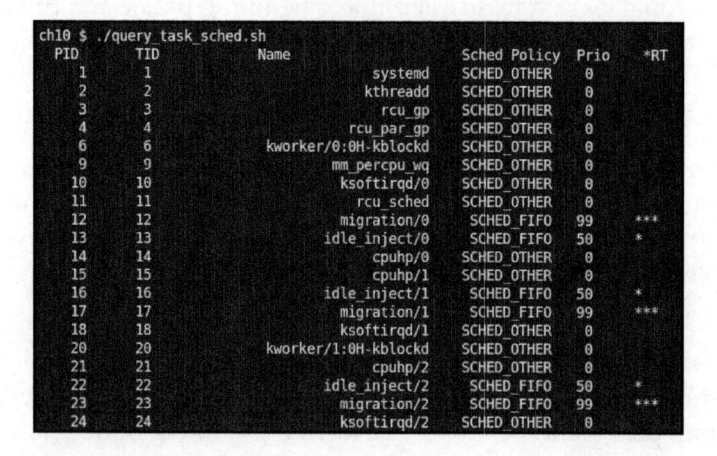

```
ch10 $ ./query_task_sched.sh
 PID      TID          Name              Sched Policy  Prio   *RT
   1       1                  systemd    SCHED_OTHER    0
   2       2                  kthreadd   SCHED_OTHER    0
   3       3                    rcu_gp   SCHED_OTHER    0
   4       4                rcu_par_gp   SCHED_OTHER    0
   6       6        kworker/0:0H-kblockd SCHED_OTHER    0
   9       9                mm_percpu_wq SCHED_OTHER    0
  10      10                ksoftirqd/0  SCHED_OTHER    0
  11      11                  rcu_sched  SCHED_OTHER    0
  12      12                migration/0  SCHED_FIFO    99   ***
  13      13               idle_inject/0 SCHED_FIFO    50    *
  14      14                    cpuhp/0  SCHED_OTHER    0
  15      15                    cpuhp/1  SCHED_OTHER    0
  16      16               idle_inject/1 SCHED_FIFO    50    *
  17      17                migration/1  SCHED_FIFO    99   ***
  18      18                ksoftirqd/1  SCHED_OTHER    0
  20      20        kworker/1:0H-kblockd SCHED_OTHER    0
  21      21                    cpuhp/2  SCHED_OTHER    0
  22      22               idle_inject/2 SCHED_FIFO    50    *
  23      23                migration/2  SCHED_FIFO    99   ***
  24      24                ksoftirqd/2  SCHED_OTHER    0
```

Figure 10.5 – (Partial) screenshot of our ch10/query_task_sched.sh Bash script in action

A few things to notice:

- In our script, by using GNU `ps(1)`, with `ps -LA`, we're able to capture all the threads that are alive on the system; their PID and TID are displayed. As you learned in Chapter 6, *Kernel Internals Essentials – Processes and Threads*, the PID is the user space equivalent of the kernel TGID and the TID is the user space equivalent of the kernel PID. We can thus conclude the following:
    - If the PID and TID match, it - the thread seen in that row (the third column has its name) - is the main thread of the process.
    - If the PID and TID match and the PID shows up only once, it's a single-threaded process.
    - If we have the same PID multiple times (leftmost column) with varying TIDs (second column), those are the child (or worker) threads of the process. Our script shows this by indenting the TID number a bit to the right.

- Notice how the vast majority of threads on a typical Linux box (even embedded) will tend to be non real-time (the SCHED_OTHER policy). On a typical desktop, server, or even embedded Linux, the majority of threads will be SCHED_OTHER (the default policy), with a few real-time threads (FIFO/RR). **Deadline (DL)** and **Stop-Sched (SS)** threads are very rare indeed.
- Do notice the following observations regarding the real-time threads that showed up in the preceding output:
    - Our script highlights any real-time threads (one with policy: SCHED_FIFO or SCHED_RR) by displaying an asterisk on the extreme right.
    - Moreover, any real-time threads with a real-time priority of 99 (the maximum possible value) will have three asterisks on the extreme right (these tend to be specialized kernel threads).
- The SCHED_RESET_ON_FORK flag, when Boolean ORed with the scheduling policy, has the effect of disallowing any children (via fork(2)) to inherit a privileged scheduling policy (a security measure).
- Changing the scheduling policy and/or priority of a thread can be performed with chrt(1); however, you should realize that this is a sensitive operation requiring root privileges (or, nowadays, the preferred mechanism should be the capabilities model, the CAP_SYS_NICE capability being the capability bit in question).

We will leave it to you to examine the code of the script (ch10/query_task_sched.sh). Also, be aware (beware!) that performance and shell scripting do not really go together (so don't expect much in terms of performance here). Think about it, every external command issued within a shell script (and we have several here, such as awk, grep, and cut) involves a fork-exec-wait semantic and context switching. Also, these are all executing within a loop.

> **TIP**: The tuna(8) program can be used to both query and set various attributes; this includes process-/thread-level scheduling policy/priority and a CPU affinity mask, as well as IRQ affinity.

The CPU Scheduler - Part 1

You might ask, will the (few) threads with the SCHED_FIFO policy and a real-time priority of 99 always hog the system's processors? No, not really; the reality is that these threads are asleep most of the time. When the kernel does require them to perform some work, it wakes them up. Now, precisely due to their real-time policy and priority, it's pretty much guaranteed that they will get a CPU and execute for as long as is required (going back to sleep once the work is done). The key point: when they require the processor, they will get it (somewhat akin to an RTOS, but without the iron-clad guarantees and determinism that an RTOS delivers).

How exactly does the chrt(1) utility query (and set) the real-time scheduling policy/priority? Ah, that should be obvious: as they reside within the task structure in kernel **Virtual Address Space (VAS)**, the chrt process must issue a system call. There are several system call variations that perform these tasks: the one used by chrt(1) is the sched_getattr(2) to query, and the sched_setattr(2) system call is to set the scheduling policy and priority. (Be sure to look up the man page on sched(7) for details on these and more scheduler-related system calls.) A quick strace(1) on chrt will indeed verify this!

```
$ strace chrt -p 1
[ ... ]
sched_getattr(1, {size=48, sched_policy=SCHED_OTHER, sched_flags=0,
sched_nice=0, sched_priority=0, sched_runtime=0, sched_deadline=0,
sched_period=0}, 48, 0) = 0
fstat(1, {st_mode=S_IFCHR|0620, st_rdev=makedev(136, 6), ...}) = 0
write(1, "pid 1's current scheduling polic"..., 47) = 47
write(1, "pid 1's current scheduling prior"..., 39) = 39
[ ... ] $
```

Now that you have the practical knowledge to query (and even set) a thread's scheduling policy/priority, it's time to dig a bit deeper. In the following section, we delve further into the internal workings of Linux's CPU scheduler. We figure out who runs the code of the scheduler and when it runs. Curious? Read on!

Learning about the CPU scheduling internals – part 3

In the preceding sections, you learned that the core kernel scheduling code is anchored within the `void schedule(void)` function, and that the modular scheduler classes are iterated over, ending up with a thread picked to be context-switched to. All of this is fine; a key question now is: who and when, exactly, is the `schedule()` code path run?

Who runs the scheduler code?

A subtle yet key misconception regarding how scheduling works is unfortunately held by many: we imagine that some kind of kernel thread (or some such entity) called the "scheduler" is present, that periodically runs and schedules tasks. This is just plain wrong; in a monolithic OS such as Linux, scheduling is carried out by the process contexts themselves, the regular threads that run on the CPU!

In fact, the scheduling code is always run by the process context that is currently executing the code of the kernel, in other words, by `current`.

This may also be an appropriate time to remind you of what we shall call one of the *golden rules* of the Linux kernel: *scheduling code must never ever run in any kind of atomic or interrupt context*. In other words, interrupt context code must be guaranteed to be non-blocking; this is why you cannot call `kmalloc()` with the `GFP_KERNEL` flag in an interrupt context – it might block! But with the `GFP_ATOMIC` flag, it's all right as that instructs the kernel memory management code to never block. Also, kernel preemption is disabled while the schedule code runs; this makes sense.

When does the scheduler run?

The job of the OS scheduler is to arbitrate access to the processor (CPU) resource, sharing it between competing entities (threads) that want to use it. But what if the system is busy, with many threads continually competing for and acquiring the processor? More correctly, what we're really getting at is: in order to ensure fair sharing of the CPU resource between tasks, you must ensure that the policeman in the picture, the scheduler itself, runs periodically on the processor. Sounds good, but how exactly can you ensure that?

The CPU Scheduler - Part 1

Here's a (seemingly) logical way to go about it: invoke the scheduler when the timer interrupt fires; that is, it gets a chance to run `CONFIG_HZ` times a second (which is often set to the value 250)! Hang on, though, we learned a golden rule in Chapter 8, *Kernel Memory Allocation for Module Authors – Part 1*, in the *Never sleep in interrupt or atomic contexts* section: you cannot invoke the scheduler in any kind of atomic or interrupt context; thus invoking it within the timer interrupt code path is certainly disqualified. So, what does the OS do?

The way it's actually done is that both the timer interrupt context, and the process context code paths, are used to make scheduling work. We will briefly describe the details in the following section.

The timer interrupt part

Within the timer interrupt (in the code of `kernel/sched/core.c:scheduler_tick()`, wherein interrupts are disabled), the kernel performs the meta work necessary to keep scheduling running smoothly; this involves the constant updating of the per CPU runqueues as appropriate, load balancing work, and so on. Please be aware that the actual `schedule()` function is *never called here*. At best, the scheduling class hook function (for the process context `current` that was interrupted), `sched_class:task_tick()`, if non-null, is invoked. For example, for any thread belonging to the fair (CFS) class, the update of the `vruntime` member (the virtual runtime, the (priority-biased) time spent on the processor by the task) is done here in `task_tick_fair()`.

> More technically, all this work described in the preceding paragraph occurs within the timer interrupt soft IRQ, `TIMER_SOFTIRQ`.

Now, a key point, it's the scheduling code that decides: do we need to preempt `current`? Within this timer interrupt code path, if the kernel detects that the current task has exceeded its time quantum or must, for any reason, be preempted (perhaps there is another runnable thread now on the runqueue with higher priority than it), the code sets a "global" flag called `need_resched`. (The reason we put the word global within quotes is that it's not really a kernel-wide global; it's actually simply a bit within `current` instance's `thread_info->flags` bitmask named `TIF_NEED_RESCHED`. Why? It's actually faster to access the bit that way!) It's worth emphasizing that, in the typical (likely) case, there will be no need to preempt `current`, thus the `thread_info.flags:TIF_NEED_RESCHED` bit will remain clear. If set, scheduler activation will occur soon; but when exactly? Do read on...

The process context part

Once the just-described timer interrupt portion of the scheduling housekeeping work is done (and, of course, these things are done very quickly indeed), control is handed back to the process context (the thread, current) that was rudely interrupted. It will now be running what we think of as the exit path from the interrupt. Here, it checks whether the TIF_NEED_RESCHED bit is set – the need_resched() helper routine performs this task. If it returns True, this indicates the immediate need for a reschedule to occur: the kernel calls schedule()! Here, it's fine to do so, as we are now running in process context. (Always keep in mind: all this code we're talking about here is being run by current, the process context in question.)

Of course, now the key question becomes where exactly is the code that will recognize whether the TIF_NEED_RESCHED bit has been set (by the previously described timer interrupt part)? Ah, this becomes the crux of it: the kernel arranges for several **scheduling opportunity points** to be present within the kernel code base. Two scheduling opportunity points are as follows:

- Return from the system call code path.
- Return from the interrupt code path.

So, think about it: every time any thread running in user space issues a system call, that thread is (context) switched to kernel mode and now runs code within the kernel, with kernel privilege. Of course, system calls are finite in length; when done, there is a well-known return path that they will follow in order to switch back to user mode and continue execution there. On this return path, a scheduling opportunity point is introduced: a check is made to see whether the TIF_NEED_RESCHED bit within its thread_info structure is set. If yes, the scheduler is activated.

FYI, the code to do this is arch-dependent; on x86 it's here: arch/x86/entry/common.c:exit_to_usermode_loop(). Within it, the section relevant to us here is:

```
static void exit_to_usermode_loop(struct pt_regs *regs, u32 cached_flags)
{
[...]
    if (cached_flags & _TIF_NEED_RESCHED)
        schedule();
```

Similarly, after handling an (any) hardware interrupt (and any associated soft IRQ handlers that needed to be run), after the switch back to process context within the kernel (an artifact within the kernel – `irq_exit()`), but before restoring context to the task that was interrupted, the kernel checks the `TIF_NEED_RESCHED` bit: if it is set, `schedule()` is invoked.

Let's summarize the preceding discussion on the setting and recognition of the `TIF_NEED_RESCHED` bit:

- The timer interrupt (soft IRQ) sets the `thread_info:flags TIF_NEED_RESCHED` bit in the following cases:
    - If preemption is required by the logic within the scheduling class's `scheduler_tick()` hook function; for example, on CFS, if the current task's `vruntime` value exceeds that of another runnable thread by a given threshold (typically 2.25 ms; the relevant tunable is `/proc/sys/kernel/sched_min_granularity_ns`).
    - If a higher-priority thread becomes runnable (on the same CPU and thus runqueue; via `try_to_wake_up()`).
- In process context, this is what occurs: on both the interrupt return and system call return path, check the value of `TIF_NEED_RESCHED`:
    - If it's set (1), call `schedule()`; otherwise, continue processing.

> As an aside, these scheduling opportunity points – the return from a hardware interrupt or a system call – also serve as signal recognition points. If a signal is pending on `current`, it is serviced before restoring context or returning to user space.

Preemptible kernel

Let's take a hypothetical situation: you're running on a system with one CPU. An analog clock app is running on the GUI along with a C program, `a.out`, whose one line of code is (groan) `while(1);`. So, what do you think: will the CPU hogger *while 1* process indefinitely hog the CPU, thus causing the GUI clock app to stop ticking (will its second hand stop moving altogether)?

A little thought (and experimentation) will reveal that, indeed, the GUI clock app keeps ticking in spite of the naughty CPU hogger app! Actually, this is really the whole point of having an OS-level scheduler: it can, and does, preempt the CPU-hogging user space process. (We briefly discussed the CFS algorithm previously; CFS will cause the aggressive CPU hogger process to accumulate a huge `vruntime` value and thus move more to the right on its rb-tree runqueue, thus penalizing itself!) All modern OSes support this type of preemption – it's called **user-mode preemption**.

But now, consider this: what if you write a kernel module that performs the same `while(1)` infinite loop on a single processor system? This could be a problem: the system will now simply hang. How will the OS preempt itself (as we understand that kernel modules run in kernel mode at kernel privilege)? Well, guess what: for many years now, Linux has provided a build-time configuration option to make the kernel preemptible, `CONFIG_PREEMPT`. (Actually, this is merely evolution toward the long-term goal of cutting down latencies and improving the kernel and scheduler response. A large body of this work came from earlier, and some ongoing, efforts: the **Low Latency (LowLat)** patches, (the old) RTLinux work, and so on. We will cover more on real-time (RTOS) Linux - RTL - in the following chapter.) Once this `CONFIG_PREEMPT` kernel config option is turned on and the kernel is built and booted into, we're now running on a preemptible kernel – where the OS has the ability to preempt itself.

> **TIP**: To check out this option, within `make menuconfig`, navigate to **General Setup | Preemption Model**.

There are essentially three available kernel config options as far as preemption goes:

Preemption type	Characteristics	Appropriate for
`CONFIG_PREEMPT_NONE`	Traditional model, geared toward high overall throughput.	Server/enterprise-class and compute-intensive systems
`CONFIG_PREEMPT_VOLUNTARY`	Preemptible kernel (desktop); more explicit preemption opportunity points within the OS; leads to lower latencies, better app response. Typically the default for distros.	Workstations/desktops, laptops running Linux for the desktop

The CPU Scheduler - Part 1

`CONFIG_PREEMPT`	LowLat kernel; (almost) the entire kernel is preemptible; implies involuntary preemption of even kernel code paths is now possible; yields even lower latencies (tens of us to low hundreds us range on average) at the cost of slightly lower throughput and slight runtime overhead.	Fast multimedia systems (desktops, laptops, even modern embedded products: smartphones, tablets, and so on)

The `kernel/Kconfig.preempt` kbuild configuration file contains the relevant menu entries for the preemptible kernel options. (As you will see in the following chapter, when building Linux as an RTOS, a fourth choice for kernel preemption appears.)

CPU scheduler entry points

The detailed comments present in (just before) the core kernel scheduling function `kernel/sched/core.c:__schedule()` are well worth reading through; they specify all the possible entry points to the kernel CPU scheduler. We have simply reproduced them here directly from the 5.4 kernel code base, so do take a look. Keep in mind: the following code is being run in process context by the process (thread, really) that's going to kick itself off the CPU by ultimately context-switching to some other thread! And this thread is who? Why, it's `current`, of course!

The `__schedule()` function has (among others) two local variables, pointer to struct `task_struct` named `prev` and `next`. The pointer named `prev` is set to `rq->curr`, which is nothing but `current`! The pointer named `next` will be set to the task that's going to be context-switched to, that's going to run next! So, you see: `current` runs the scheduler code, performing the work and then kicking itself off the processor by context-switching to `next`! Here's the large comment we mentioned:

```
// kernel/sched/core.c
/*
 * __schedule() is the main scheduler function.
 * The main means of driving the scheduler and thus entering this
function are:
 * 1. Explicit blocking: mutex, semaphore, waitqueue, etc.
 *
 * 2. TIF_NEED_RESCHED flag is checked on interrupt and user space
return
 *    paths. For example, see arch/x86/entry_64.S.
 *
 *    To drive preemption between tasks, the scheduler sets the flag
```

```
  in timer
*     interrupt handler scheduler_tick().
*
* 3. Wakeups don't really cause entry into schedule(). They add a
*    task to the run-queue and that's it.
*
*    Now, if the new task added to the run-queue preempts the current
*    task, then the wakeup sets TIF_NEED_RESCHED and schedule() gets
*    called on the nearest possible occasion:
*    - If the kernel is preemptible (CONFIG_PREEMPTION=y):
*
*    - in syscall or exception context, at the next outmost
*      preempt_enable(). (this might be as soon as the wake_up()'s
*      spin_unlock()!)
*
*    - in IRQ context, return from interrupt-handler to
*      preemptible context
*
*    - If the kernel is not preemptible (CONFIG_PREEMPTION is not
set)
*      then at the next:
*       - cond_resched() call
*       - explicit schedule() call
*       - return from syscall or exception to user-space
*       - return from interrupt-handler to user-space
* WARNING: must be called with preemption disabled!
*/
```

The preceding code is a large comment detailing how exactly the kernel CPU core scheduling code – __schedule() – can be invoked. Small relevant snippets of __schedule() itself can be seen in the following code, reiterating the points we have been discussing:

```
static void __sched notrace __schedule(bool preempt)
{
    struct task_struct *prev, *next;
    [...] struct rq *rq;
    int cpu;

    cpu = smp_processor_id();
    rq = cpu_rq(cpu);
    prev = rq->curr;                     << this is 'current' ! >>

    [ ... ]

    next = pick_next_task(rq, prev, &rf);  << here we 'pick' the task
to run next in an 'object-
                                       oriented' manner, as
```

The CPU Scheduler - Part 1

```
    discussed earlier in detail ... >>
       clear_tsk_need_resched(prev);
       clear_preempt_need_resched();

       if (likely(prev != next)) {
           [ ... ]
           /* Also unlocks the rq: */
           rq = context_switch(rq, prev, next, &rf);
           [ ... ]
    }
```

A quick word on the actual context switch follows.

The context switch

To finish this discussion, a quick word on the (scheduler) context switch. The job of the context switch (in the context of the CPU scheduler) is quite obvious: before simply switching to the next task, the OS must save the state of the previous, that is, the currently executing, task; in other words, the state of `current`. You will recall from Chapter 6, *Kernel Internals Essentials – Processes and Threads*, that the task structure holds an inline structure to store/retrieve the thread's hardware context; it's the member `struct thread_struct thread` (on the x86, it's always the very last member of the task struct). In Linux, an inline function, `kernel/sched/core.c:context_switch()`, performs the job, switching from the `prev` task (that is, from `current`) to the `next` task, the winner of this scheduling round or preemption. This switch is essentially performed in two (arch-specific) stages:

- **The memory (MM) switch**: Switch an arch-specific CPU register to point to the memory descriptor structure (`struct mm_struct`) of `next`. On the x86[_64], this register is called CR3 (**Control Register 3**); on ARM, it's called the TTBR0 (**Translation Table Base Register** 0) register.
- **The actual CPU switch**: Switch from `prev` to `next` by saving the stack and CPU register state of `prev` and restoring the stack and CPU register state of `next` onto the processor; this is done within the `switch_to()` macro.

A detailed implementation of the context switch is not something we shall cover here; do check out the *Further reading* section for more resources.

Summary

In this chapter, you learned about several areas and facets of the versatile Linux kernel's CPU scheduler. Firstly, you saw how the actual KSE is a thread and not a process, followed by gaining an appreciation of the available scheduling policies that the OS implements. Next, you understood that to support multiple CPUs in a superbly scalable fashion, the kernel powerfully mirrors this with a design that employs one runqueue per CPU core per scheduling class. How to query any given thread's scheduling policy and priority, and deeper details on the internal implementation of the CPU scheduler, were then covered. We focused on how the modern scheduler leverages the modular scheduling classes design, who exactly runs the actual scheduler code and when, and ended with a brief note on the context switch.

The next chapter has you continue on this journey, gaining more insight and details on the workings of the kernel-level CPU scheduler. I suggest you first fully digest this chapter's content, work on the questions given, and then move on to the next chapter. Great going!

Questions

As we conclude, here is a list of questions for you to test your knowledge regarding this chapter's material: https://github.com/PacktPublishing/Linux-Kernel-Programming/tree/master/questions. You will find some of the questions answered in the book's GitHub repo: https://github.com/PacktPublishing/Linux-Kernel-Programming/tree/master/solutions_to_assgn.

Further reading

To help you delve deeper into the subject with useful materials, we provide a rather detailed list of online references and links (and at times, even books) in a Further reading document in this book's GitHub repository. The *Further reading* document is available here: https://github.com/PacktPublishing/Linux-Kernel-Programming/blob/master/Further_Reading.md.

11
The CPU Scheduler - Part 2

In this, our second chapter on the Linux kernel CPU scheduler, we continue our coverage from the previous chapter. In the preceding chapter, we covered several key areas regarding the workings (and visualization) of the CPU scheduler on the Linux OS. This included topics on what exactly the KSE on Linux is, the POSIX scheduling policies that Linux implements, using `perf` to see the scheduler flow, and how the design of the modern scheduler is based upon modular scheduling classes. We also covered how to query any thread's scheduling policy and priority (using a couple of command line utilities), and delved deeper into the internal workings of the OS scheduler.

With this background in place, we're now ready to explore more on the CPU scheduler on Linux; in this chapter, we shall cover the following areas:

- Visualizing the flow with LTTng and `trace-cmd`
- Understanding, querying, and setting the CPU affinity mask
- Querying and setting a thread's scheduling policy and priority
- CPU bandwidth control with cgroups
- Converting mainline Linux into an RTOS
- Latency and its measurement

We do expect that you've read (or have the equivalent knowledge of) the previous chapter before tackling this one.

Technical requirements

I assume you have gone through `Chapter 1`, *Kernel Workspace Setup*, and have appropriately prepared a guest **Virtual Machine** (**VM**) running Ubuntu 18.04 LTS (or a later stable release) and installed all the required packages. If not, I highly recommend you do this first.

The CPU Scheduler - Part 2

To get the most out of this book, I strongly recommend you first set up the workspace environment, including cloning this book's GitHub repository for the code, and work on it in a hands-on fashion. The repository can be found here: `https://github.com/PacktPublishing/Linux-Kernel-Programming`.

Visualizing the flow with LTTng and trace-cmd

In the previous chapter, we saw how we can visualize the flow of threads across the processor(s) with `perf` (and a few alternatives). Now, we proceed to do so with more powerful, more visual profiling tools: with LTTng (and the Trace Compass GUI) and with `trace-cmd` (an Ftrace frontend and the KernelShark GUI).

Do note that the intent here is to introduce you to these powerful tracing technologies only; we do not have the scope nor space required to do full justice to these topics.

Visualization with LTTng and Trace Compass

The **Linux Trace Toolkit Next Generation** (**LTTng**) is a set of open source tools enabling you to simultaneously trace both user and kernel space. A bit ironically, tracing the kernel is easy, whereas tracing user space (apps, libraries, and even scripts) requires the developer to manually insert instrumentation (so-called tracepoints) into the application (the tracepoint instrumentation for the kernel is supplied by LTTng as kernel modules). The high-quality LTTng documentation is available online here: `https://lttng.org/docs/v2.12/` (covering version 2.12 as of the time of writing).

We do not cover the installation of LTTng here; the details are available at `https://lttng.org/docs/v2.12/#doc-installing-lttng`. Once installed (it's kind of heavy – on my native x86_64 Ubuntu system, there are over 40 kernel modules loaded up pertaining to LTTng!), using LTTng - for a system-wide kernel session as we do here - is easy and is performed in two distinct stages: recording, followed by data analysis; these steps follow. (As this book is focused on kernel development, we don't cover using LTTng to trace user space apps.)

Recording a kernel tracing session with LTTng

You can record a system-wide kernel tracing session as follows (here, we deliberately keep the discussion as simple as possible):

1. Create a new session and set the output directory to <dir> for saving tracing metadata:

    ```
    sudo lttng create <session-name> --output=<dir>
    ```

2. Simply enable all kernel events (can lead to a large amount of tracing metadata being generated though):

    ```
    sudo lttng enable-event --kernel --all
    ```

3. Start recording a "kernel session":

    ```
    sudo lttng start
    ```

    Allow some time to elapse (the longer you trace for, the more the disk space that's used by the tracing metadata). During this period, all kernel activity is being recorded by LTTng.

4. Stop recording:

    ```
    sudo lttng stop
    ```

5. Destroy the session; don't worry, this does not delete the tracing metadata:

    ```
    sudo lttng destroy
    ```

All the preceding commands should be run with admin privileges (or equivalent).

> **TIP**
> I have a few wrapper scripts to perform tracing with (LTTng, Ftrace, trace-cmd) at https://github.com/kaiwan/L5_debug_trg/tree/master/kernel_debug/tracing; do check them out.

The tracing metadata files (in the **Common Trace Format** (**CTF**) file format) gets saved to the preceding specified output directory.

[537]

The CPU Scheduler - Part 2

Reporting with a GUI – Trace Compass

The data analysis can be performed in two broad ways – using a CLI-based system typically packaged along with LTTng called `babeltrace`, or via a sophisticated GUI called **Trace Compass**. The GUI is far more appealing; we only show its basic usage here.

Trace Compass is a powerful cross-platform GUI application and integrates well with Eclipse. In fact, we quote directly from the Eclipse Trace Compass site (`https://projects.eclipse.org/projects/tools.tracecompass`):

"Eclipse Trace Compass is an open source application to solve performance and reliability issues by reading and analyzing logs or traces of a system. Its goal is to provide views, graphs, metrics, and more to help extract useful information from traces, in a way that is more user-friendly and informative than huge text dumps."

It can be downloaded (and installed) from here: `https://www.eclipse.org/tracecompass/`.

> **TIP**
> Trace Compass minimally requires a **Java Runtime Environment (JRE)** to be installed as well. I installed one on my Ubuntu 20.04 LTS system with `sudo apt install openjdk-14-jre`.

Once installed, fire up Trace Compass, click on the **File | Open Trace** menu, and navigate to the output directory where you saved the trace metadata for your tracing session in the preceding steps. Trace Compass will read the metadata and display it visually, along with various perspectives and tool views made available. A partial screenshot from our brief system-wide kernel tracing session is shown here (*Figure 11.1*); you can literally see the context switch (shown as the `sched_switch` event – see the **Event type** column) from the `gnome-shell` process to the `swapper/1` kernel thread (the idle thread running on CPU #1):

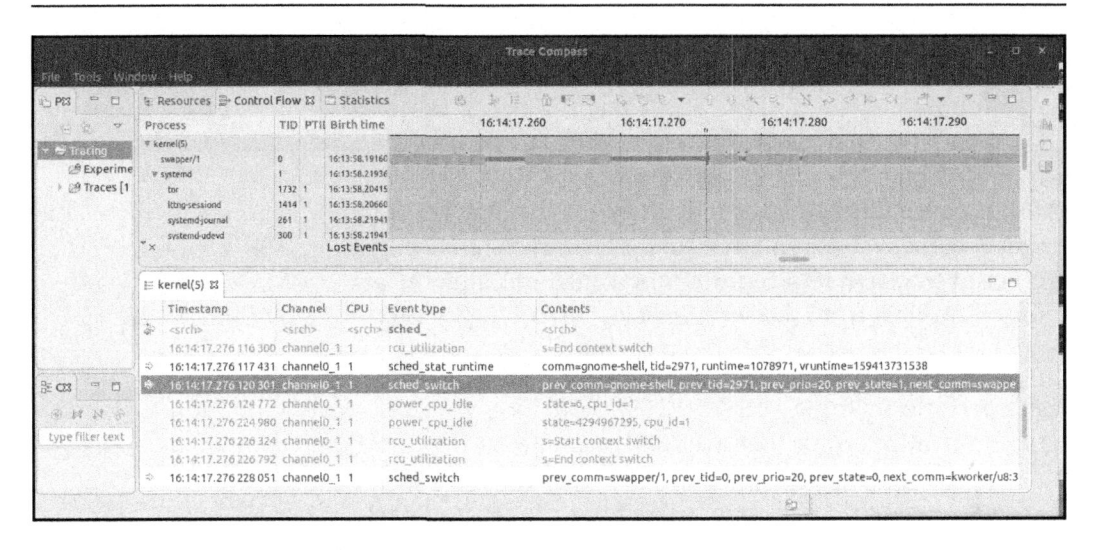

Figure 11.1 – Trace Compass GUI showing a sample kernel tracing session obtained via LTTng

Look carefully at the preceding screenshot (Figure 11.1); in the lower horizontal pane, not only do you get to see which kernel function executed, you *also* get (under the column labeled **Contents**) the parameter list along with the value each parameter had at the time! This can be very useful indeed.

Visualizing with trace-cmd

Modern Linux kernels (from 2.6.27) embed a very powerful tracing engine called **Ftrace**. Ftrace is the rough kernel equivalent of the user space `strace(1)` utility, but that would be short-selling it! Ftrace allows the sysad (or developer, tester, or anyone with root privileges really) to literally look under the hood, seeing every single function being executed in kernel space, who (which thread) executed it, how long it ran for, what APIs it invoked, with interrupts (hard and soft) included as they occur, various types of latency measurements, and more. You can use Ftrace to learn about how system utilities, applications, and the kernel actually work, as well as to perform deep tracing at the level of the OS.

Here, in this book, we refrain from delving into the depths of raw Ftrace usage (as it deviates from the subject at hand); instead, it is just quicker and easier to use a user space wrapper over Ftrace, a more convenient interface to it, called `trace-cmd(1)` (again, we only scratch the surface, showing an example of how `trace-cmd` can be used).

The CPU Scheduler - Part 2

> **TIP**
> For Ftrace details and usage, the interested reader will find this kernel document useful: `https://www.kernel.org/doc/Documentation/trace/ftrace.rst`.

Most modern Linux distros will allow the installation of `trace-cmd` via their package management system; on Ubuntu, for example, `sudo apt install trace-cmd` is sufficient to install it (if required for a custom Linux on, say, ARM, you can always cross-compile it from the source on its GitHub repository: `https://git.kernel.org/pub/scm/linux/kernel/git/rostedt/trace-cmd.git/tree/`).

Let's perform a simple `trace-cmd` session; first, we shall record data samples while the `ps(1)` utility runs; then we shall examine the captured data both via the `trace-cmd report` **Command-Line Interface (CLI)** as well as a GUI frontend called KernelShark (it's in fact part of the `trace-cmd` package).

Recording a sample session with trace-cmd record

In this section, we record a session with `trace-cmd(1)`; we use a few (of the many possible) option switches to `trace-cmd record`; as usual, the man pages on `trace-cmd-foo(1)` (substitute `foo` with `check-events`, `hist`, `record`, `report`, `reset`, and so on) are very useful for finding various option switches and usage details. A few of the useful option switches particularly for `trace-cmd record` are as follows:

- `-o`: Specifies the output filename (if not specified, it defaults to `trace.dat`).
- `-p`: The plugin to use, one of `function`, `function_graph`, `preemptirqsoff`, `irqsoff`, `preemptoff`, and `wakeup`; here, in our small demo, we use the `function-graph` plugin (several other plugins can be configured in the kernel as well).
- `-F`: The command (or app) to trace; this is very useful, allowing you to specify exactly which process (or thread) to exclusively trace (otherwise, tracing all threads can result in a lot of noise when attempting to decipher the output); similarly, you can use the `-P` option switch to specify the PID to trace.
- `-r priority`: Runs the `trace-cmd` threads at the real-time priority specified (the typical range being 1 to 99; we shall cover querying and setting a thread's scheduling policy and priority shortly); this gives a better bet on `trace-cmd` being able to capture samples as required.

Chapter 11

Here, we run a quick demo: we run `ps -LA`; while it runs, all kernel traffic it generates is (exclusively) captured by `trace-cmd` via it's `record` functionality (we employ the `function-graph` plugin):

```
$ sudo trace-cmd record -o trace_ps.dat -r 99 -p function_graph -F ps
-LA
plugin 'function_graph'
PID     LWP TTY          TIME CMD
  1       1 ?        00:01:42 systemd
  2       2 ?        00:00:00 kthreadd
[ ... ]
32701   734 tty2     00:00:00 ThreadPoolForeg
CPU 2: 48176 events lost
CPU0 data recorded at offset=0x761000
[ ... ]
CPU3 data recorded at offset=0xf180000
114688 bytes in size
$ ls -lh trace_ps.dat
-rw-r--r-- 1 root root 242M Jun 25 11:23 trace_ps.dat
$
```

A rather large data file results (as we captured all events and did a `ps -LA` displaying all threads alive, it took a while, and thus the data samples captured are large-ish. Also realize that by default, kernel tracing is performed across all CPUs on the system; you can change this via the `-M cpumask` option.)

> **TIP**
> In the preceding example, we captured all events. The `-e` option switch to `trace-cmd(1)` allows you to specify a class of events to trace; for example, to trace the `ping(1)` utility and capture only events related to networking and kernel memory, run the following command:
> `sudo trace-cmd record -e kmem -e net -p function_graph -F ping -c1 packtpub.com`.

[541]

The CPU Scheduler - Part 2

Reporting and interpretation with trace-cmd report (CLI)

Continuing from the preceding section, on the command line, we can get a (very!) detailed report of what occurred within the kernel when the `ps` process ran; use the `trace-cmd report` command to see this. We also pass along the `-l` option switch: it displays the report in what is referred to as Ftrace's **latency format**, revealing many useful details; the `-i` switch of course specifies the input file to use:

```
trace-cmd report -i ./trace_ps.dat -l > report_tc_ps.txt
```

Now it gets very interesting! We show a few partial screenshots of the (huge) output file that we opened with `vim(1)`; first we have the following:

```
785299    ps-22922    2dN.. 149072.307624: funcgraph_entry:                |    smp_reschedule_interrupt() {
785300    ps-22922    2dN.. 149072.307624: funcgraph_entry:      0.038 us  |      scheduler_ipi();
785301    ps-22922    2dN.. 149072.307625: funcgraph_exit:       0.531 us  |    }
785302    ps-22922    2dN.. 149072.307625: funcgraph_entry:                |    exit_to_usermode_loop() {
785303    ps-22922    2.N.. 149072.307625: funcgraph_entry:                |      schedule() {
785304    ps-22922    2dN.. 149072.307625: funcgraph_entry:                |        rcu_note_context_switch() {
785305    ps-22922    2dN.. 149072.307626: funcgraph_entry:                |          __event_probe__rcu_utilization() {
785306    ps-22922    2dN.. 149072.307626: funcgraph_entry:                |            lttng_event_reserve() {
785307    ps-22922    2dN.. 149072.307626: funcgraph_entry:      0.077 us  |              ktime_get_mono_fast_ns();
```

Figure 11.2 – A partial screenshot showing the output of the trace-cmd report

Look at Figure 11.2; the call to the kernel API, `schedule()`, is deliberately highlighted and in bold font (*Figure 11.2*, on line `785303`!). In order to interpret everything on this line, we must understand each (white-space delimited) column; there are eight of them:

- Column 1: Here, it's just the line number in the file that vim shows (let's ignore it).
- Column 2: This is the process context that invoked this function (the function itself is in column #8); clearly, here, the process is `ps-PID` (its PID is appended after a – character).

[542]

- Column 3: useful! A series of five characters, which shows up in **latency format** (we used the `-l` option switch to `trace-cmd record`, remember!); this (in our preceding case, it's `2.N..`) is very useful and can be interpreted as follows:
    - The very first character is the CPU core it was running upon (so here it was core #2) (note that, as a general rule, besides the first one, if the character is a period `.`, it means it's zero or not applicable).
    - The second character represents the hardware interrupt status:
        - `.` implies the default hardware interrupts are enabled.
        - `d` implies hardware interrupts are currently disabled.
    - The third character represents the `need_resched` bit (we explained this in the previous chapter, in the *When does the scheduler run?* section):
        - `.` implies it's cleared.
        - `N` implies it's set (which implies that the kernel requires rescheduling to be performed ASAP!).
    - The fourth character has meaning only when an interrupt is in progress, otherwise, it is merely a `.`, implying we are in a process context; if an interrupt is in progress – implying we're in an interrupt context – its value is one of the following:
        - `h` implies we are executing in a hardirq (or top half) interrupt context.
        - `H` implies we are executing in a hardirq that occurred within a softirq.
        - `s` implies we are executing in a softirq (or bottom half) interrupt context.

The CPU Scheduler - Part 2

- The fifth character represents the preemption count or depth; if it's a ., it's zero, implying the kernel is running in a preemptible state; if nonzero, an integer number shows up, implying that many kernel-level lock(s) have been taken, forcing the kernel into a non-preemptible state.
- By the way, the output is very similar to Ftrace's raw output except that in the case of raw Ftrace, we would see only four characters – the first one (the CPU core number) does *not* show up here; it shows up as the leftmost column instead; here's a partial screenshot of the raw Ftrace (not `trace-cmd`) latency format:

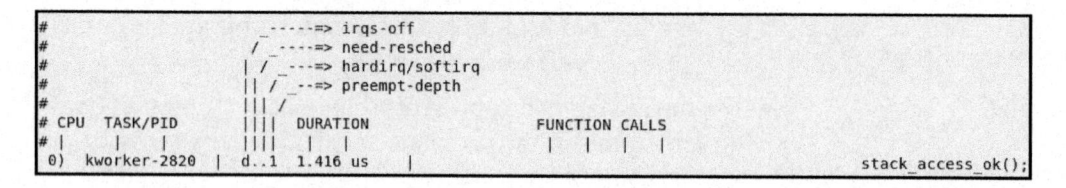

```
#                   _-----=> irqs-off
#                  / _----=> need-resched
#                 | / _---=> hardirq/softirq
#                 || / _--=> preempt-depth
#                 ||| /
# CPU  TASK/PID   ||||  DURATION          FUNCTION CALLS
#  |     |        ||||    |                |   |   |   |
  0)  kworker-2820 | d..1  1.416 us    |              stack_access_ok();
```

Figure 11.3 – A partial screenshot focused on raw Ftrace's four-character latency format (fourth field)

The preceding screenshot was culled directly from the raw Ftrace output.

- So, interpreting our example for the call to `schedule()`, we can see that the characters are `2.N..` implying that the process `ps` with PID `22922` was executing on CPU core #2 in a process context (no interrupts) and the `need-resched` (technically, `thread_info.flags:TIF_NEED_RESCHED`) bit was set (indicating the need for a reschedule ASAP!).

- (Back to the remaining columns in Figure 11.2 now)
  Column 4: Timestamp in *seconds:microseconds* format.
- Column 5: The name of the event that occurred (here, as we've used the `function_graph` plugin, it will be either `funcgraph_entry` or `fungraph_exit`, implying function entry or exit respectively).
- Column 6 [optional]: The duration of the preceding function call with the time taken shown along with its unit (us = microseconds); a prefix character is used to denote whether the function execution took a long time (we simply treat it as part of this column); from the kernel Ftrace documentation (here: https://www.kernel.org/doc/Documentation/trace/ftrace.rst), we have this:
    - `+`, which implies that a function surpassed 10 microseconds
    - `!`, which implies that a function surpassed 100 microseconds
    - `#`, which implies that a function surpassed 1,000 microseconds
    - `*`, which implies that a function surpassed 10 milliseconds
    - `@`, which implies that a function surpassed 100 milliseconds
    - `$`, which implies that a function surpassed 1 second
- Column 7: Just the separator character `|`.
- Column 8: The extreme-right column is the name of the kernel function being executed; an open brace on the right, `{`, implies the function is invoked just now; the column with only a close brace, `}`, implies the preceding function's end (matching the open brace).

This level of detail can be extremely valuable in both troubleshooting kernel (and even user space) issues, and understanding the flow of the kernel in great detail.

> **TIP**: When `trace-cmd record` is used without the `-p function-graph` option switch, we do lose the nicely indented function call graph-like output, but we do gain something as well: you will now see all function parameters along with their runtime values to the right of every single function call! A truly valuable aid at times.

The CPU Scheduler - Part 2

I can't resist showing another snippet from the same report – another interesting example with regard to the very things we learned about how scheduling classes work on modern Linux (covered in the previous chapter); this actually shows up here in the `trace-cmd` output:

```
786463   ps-22922   2dN..  149072.308038: funcgraph_entry:     0.054 us  |    update_rq_clock();
786464   ps-22922   2dN..  149072.308038: funcgraph_entry:     0.221 us  |    pick_next_task_stop();
786465   ps-22922   2dN..  149072.308039: funcgraph_entry:     0.053 us  |    pick_next_task_dl();
786466   ps-22922   2dN..  149072.308040: funcgraph_entry:                |    pick_next_task_rt() {
786467   ps-22922   2dN..  149072.308040: funcgraph_entry:                |      put_prev_task_fair() {
786468   ps-22922   2dN..  149072.308040: funcgraph_entry:                |        put_prev_entity() {
786469   ps-22922   2dN..  149072.308040: funcgraph_entry:                |          update_curr() {
786470   ps-22922   2dN..  149072.308041: funcgraph_entry:     0.125 us  |            update_min_vruntime();
```

Figure 11.4 – A partial screenshot of trace-cmd report output

Interpret the preceding screenshot (*Figure 11.4*) closely: the second line (with the right-most function name column in bold font, as are the two functions immediately following it) shows that the `pick_next_task_stop()` function was invoked; this implies that a schedule occurred and the core scheduling code within the kernel went through its routine – it walks the linked list of scheduling classes in priority order, asking each whether it has a thread to schedule; if they do, the core scheduler context switches to it (as was explained in some detail in the previous chapter, in the *Modular scheduling classes* section).

In Figure 11.4, you literally see this happen: the core scheduling code asks the **stop-sched (SS)**, **deadline (DL)**, and **real-time (RT)** classes whether they have any thread that wants to run, by invoking, in turn,
the `pick_next_task_stop()`, `pick_next_task_dl()`, and `pick_next_task_rt()` functions. Apparently, for all of them, the answer is no, as the next function to run is that of the fair (CFS) class (why doesn't the `pick_next_task_fair()` function show up in the preceding screenshot then? Ah, again, that's code optimization for you: the kernel developers understand that this being the likely case, they check for it and directly invoke the fair class code most of the time).

What we've covered here on the powerful Ftrace framework and the `trace-cmd` utility is just the basics; I urge you to look up the man pages on `trace-cmd-<foo>`(where <foo> is replaced with `record`, `report`, and so on) there are typically good examples shown there. Also, there are several very well-written articles on Ftrace (and `trace-cmd`) – please refer to the *Further reading* section for them.

Reporting and interpretation with a GUI frontend

More good news: the `trace-cmd` toolset includes a GUI frontend, for more human-friendly interpretation and analysis, called KernelShark (though, in my opinion, it isn't as full-featured as Trace Compass is). Installing it on Ubuntu/Debian is as simple as doing `sudo apt install kernelshark`.

Below, we run `kernelshark`, passing the trace data file output from our preceding `trace-cmd record` session as the parameter to it (adjust the parameter to KernelShark to refer to the location where you've saved the tracing metadata):

```
$ kernelshark ./trace_ps.dat
```

A screenshot of KernelShark running with the preceding trace data is shown here:

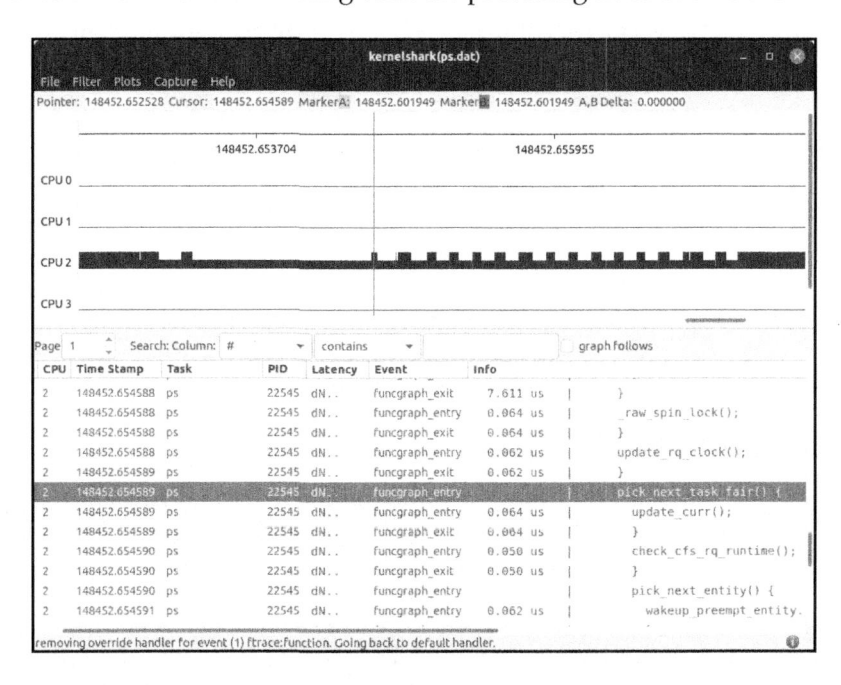

Figure 11.5 – A screenshot of the kernelshark GUI displaying the earlier-captured data via trace-cmd

Interesting; the `ps` process ran on CPU #2 (as we saw with the CLI version previously). Here, we also see the functions executed in the lower tiled horizontal window pane; as an example, we have highlighted the entry for `pick_next_task_fair()`. The columns are quite obvious, with the `Latency` column format (four characters, not five) interpreted as we explained previously for (raw) Ftrace.

[547]

The CPU Scheduler - Part 2

> **Quick quiz**: What does the **Latency** format field `dN..`, seen in Figure 11.5, imply?
>
> Answer: It implies that, currently, right now, we have the following:
>
> - First column `d`: Hardware interrupts are disabled.
> - Second column `N`: The `need_resched` bit is set (implying the need to invoke the scheduler at the next available scheduling opportunity point).
> - Third column `.`: The kernel `pick_next_task_fair()` function's code is running in a process context (the task being `ps` with a PID of `22545`; remember, Linux is a monolithic kernel!).
> - Fourth column `.`: The preemption depth (count) is zero, implying the kernel is in a preemptible state.

Now that we have covered using these powerful tools to help generate and visualize data related to kernel execution and scheduling, let's move on to another area: in the next section, we focus on another important aspect – what exactly a thread's CPU affinity mask is, and how you can programmatically (and otherwise) get/set it.

Understanding, querying, and setting the CPU affinity mask

The task structure, the root data structure containing several dozen thread attributes, has a few attributes directly pertaining to scheduling: the priority (the *nice* as well as the RT priority values), the scheduling class structure pointer, the runqueue the thread is on (if any), and so on.

Among these is an important member, the **CPU affinity bitmask** (the actual structure member is `cpumask_t cpus_allowed`). This also tells you that the CPU affinity bitmask is a per-thread quantity; this makes sense - the KSE on Linux is a thread, after all. It's essentially an array of bits, each bit representing a CPU core (with sufficient bits available within the variable); if the bit corresponding to a core is set (`1`), the thread is allowed to be scheduled on and execute on that core; if cleared (`0`), it's not.

By default, all the CPU affinity mask bits are set; thus, the thread can run on any core. For example, on a box with (the OS seeing) four CPU cores, the default CPU affinity bitmask for each thread would be binary 1111 (0xf). (Glance at Figure 11.6 to see how the CPU affinity bitmask looks, conceptually speaking.)

At runtime, the scheduler decides which core the thread will actually run upon. In fact, think about it, it's really implicit: by default, each CPU core has a runqueue associated with it; every runnable thread will be on a single CPU runqueue; it's thus eligible to run and by default runs on the CPU that it's runqueue represents. Of course, the scheduler has a load balancer component that can migrate threads to other CPU cores (runqueues, really) as the need arises (kernel threads called migration/n, where n is the core number assist in this task).

The kernel does expose APIs to user space (system calls, of course, sched_{s,g}etaffinity(2) and their pthread wrapper library APIs), which allows an application to affine, or associate, a thread (or multiple threads) to particular CPU cores as it sees fit (and by the same logic, we can do this within the kernel as well for any given kernel thread). For example, setting the CPU affinity mask to 1010 binary, which equals 0xa in hexadecimal, implies that the thread can execute *only* upon CPU cores one and three (counting starts from zero).

A key point: though you can manipulate the CPU affinity mask, the recommendation is to avoid doing so; the kernel scheduler understands the CPU topography in detail and can best load-balance the system.

Having said that, explicitly setting the CPU affinity mask of a thread can be beneficial due to the following reasons:

- Cache invalidation (and thus unpleasant cache "bouncing") can be greatly reduced by ensuring a thread always runs on the same CPU core.
- Thread migration costs between cores are effectively eliminated.
- CPU reservation—a strategy to bestow the core(s) exclusively to one thread by guaranteeing all other threads are explicitly not allowed to execute upon that core.

The first two are useful in some corner cases; the third one, CPU reservation, tends to be a technique used in some time-critical real-time systems where the cost of doing so is justified. Performing CPU reservation in practice is quite difficult to do though, requiring OS-level intervention at (every!) thread creation; the cost might be prohibitive. For this reason, this is actually implemented by specifying that a certain CPU (or more) be *isolated* from all tasks; the Linux kernel provides a kernel parameter, isolcpus, for this very job.

The CPU Scheduler - Part 2

In this regard, we quote directly from the man page on the `sched_{s,g}etaffinity(2)` system calls:

> The isolcpus boot option can be used to isolate one or more CPUs at boot time, so that no processes are scheduled onto those CPUs. Following the use of this boot option, the only way to schedule processes onto the isolated CPUs is via sched_setaffinity() or the cpuset(7) mechanism. For further information, see the kernel source file Documentation/admin-guide/kernel-parameters.txt. As noted in that file, isolcpus is the preferred mechanism of isolating CPUs (versus the alternative of manually setting the CPU affinity of all processes on the system).

> **TIP**
>
> Note, though, the previously mentioned `isolcpus` kernel parameter is now considered deprecated; it's preferable to use the cgroups `cpusets` controller instead (`cpusets` is a cgroup feature or controller; we do have some coverage on cgroups later in this chapter, in the *CPU bandwidth control with cgroups* section).
>
> We refer you to more details in the kernel parameter documentation (here: https://www.kernel.org/doc/Documentation/admin-guide/kernel-parameters.txt), specifically under the parameter labeled `isolcpus=`.

Now that you understand the theory behind it, let's actually write a user space C program to query and/or set the CPU affinity mask of any given thread.

Querying and setting a thread's CPU affinity mask

As a demonstration, we provide a small user space C program to query and set a user space process (or thread's) CPU affinity mask. Querying the CPU affinity mask is achieved with the `sched_getaffinity(2)` system call and by setting it with its counterpart:

```
#define _GNU_SOURCE
#include <sched.h>

int sched_getaffinity(pid_t pid, size_t cpusetsize,
                      cpu_set_t *mask);
int sched_setaffinity(pid_t pid, size_t cpusetsize,
                      const cpu_set_t *mask);
```

A specialized data type called `cpu_set_t` is what is used to represent the CPU affinity bitmask; it's quite sophisticated: its size is dynamically allocated based on the number of CPU cores seen on the system. This CPU mask (of type `cpu_set_t`) must first be initialized to zero; the `CPU_ZERO()` macro achieves this (several similar helper macros exist; do refer to the man page on `CPU_SET(3)`). The second parameter in both the preceding system calls is the size of the CPU set (we simply use the `sizeof` operator to obtain it).

To understand this better, it's instructive to see a sample run of our code (`ch11/cpu_affinity/userspc_cpuaffinity.c`); we run it on a native Linux system with 12 CPU cores:

```
$ ./userspc_cpuaffinity
Detected 12 CPU cores [for this process ./userspc_cpuaffinity:335917]
CPU affinity mask for PID 335917:
 335917 pts/11    00:00:00 userspc_cpuaffi
      +--+--+--+--+--+--+--+--+--+--+--+--+
core# |11|10| 9| 8| 7| 6| 5| 4| 3| 2| 1| 0|
      +--+--+--+--+--+--+--+--+--+--+--+--+
cpumask| 1| 1| 1| 1| 1| 1| 1| 1| 1| 1| 1| 1|
      +--+--+--+--+--+--+--+--+--+--+--+--+
$
```

Figure 11.6 – Our demo user space app showing the CPU affinity mask

Here, we have run the app with no parameters. In this mode, it queries the CPU affinity mask of itself (meaning, of the `userspc_cpuaffinity` calling process). We print out the bits of the bitmask: as you can clearly see in the preceding screenshot, it's binary `1111 1111 1111` (which is equivalent to `0xfff`), implying that by default the process is eligible to run on any of the 12 CPU cores available on the system.

The app detects the number of CPU cores available by running the `nproc(1)` utility via the useful `popen(3)` library API. Do note though, that the value returned by `nproc` is the number of CPU cores available to the calling process; it may be less than the actual number of CPU cores (it's usually the same); the number of available cores can be changed in a few ways, the proper way being via the cgroup `cpuset` resource controller (we cover some information on cgroups later in this chapter).

The querying code is as follows:

```
// ch11/cpu_affinity/userspc_cpuaffinity.c

static int query_cpu_affinity(pid_t pid)
{
    cpu_set_t cpumask;

    CPU_ZERO(&cpumask);
```

The CPU Scheduler - Part 2

```
    if (sched_getaffinity(pid, sizeof(cpu_set_t), &cpumask) < 0) {
        perror("sched_getaffinity() failed");
        return -1;
    }
    disp_cpumask(pid, &cpumask, numcores);
    return 0;
}
```

Our `disp_cpumask()` function draws the bitmask (we leave it to you to check it out).

If additional parameters are passed – the PID of the process (or thread), as the first parameter, and a CPU bitmask, as the second parameter – we then attempt to *set* the CPU affinity mask of that process (or thread) to the value passed. Of course, changing the CPU affinity bitmask requires you to own the process or have root privileges (more correctly, to have the `CAP_SYS_NICE` capability).

A quick demo: in Figure 11.7, `nproc(1)` shows us the number of CPU cores; then, we run our app to query and set our shell process's CPU affinity mask. On a laptop, let's say that the affinity mask of `bash` is `0xfff` (binary 1111 1111 1111) to begin with, as expected; we change it to `0xdae` (binary 1101 1010 1110) and query it again to verify the change:

```
$ nproc
12
$ ps
    PID TTY          TIME CMD
 275621 pts/11    00:00:00 bash
 275896 pts/11    00:00:00 ps
$ ./userspc_cpuaffinity 275621 0xdae
Detected 12 CPU cores [for this process ./userspc_cpuaffinity:276018]
CPU affinity mask for PID 275621:
 275621 pts/11    00:00:00 bash
       +--+--+--+--+--+--+--+--+--+--+--+--+
core#  |11|10| 9| 8| 7| 6| 5| 4| 3| 2| 1| 0|
       +--+--+--+--+--+--+--+--+--+--+--+--+
cpumask| 1| 1| 1| 1| 1| 1| 1| 1| 1| 1| 1| 1|
       +--+--+--+--+--+--+--+--+--+--+--+--+

Setting CPU affinity mask for PID 275621 now...
CPU affinity mask for PID 275621:
 275621 pts/11    00:00:00 bash
       +--+--+--+--+--+--+--+--+--+--+--+--+
core#  |11|10| 9| 8| 7| 6| 5| 4| 3| 2| 1| 0|
       +--+--+--+--+--+--+--+--+--+--+--+--+
cpumask| 1| 1| 0| 1| 1| 0| 1| 0| 1| 1| 1| 0|
       +--+--+--+--+--+--+--+--+--+--+--+--+
$
```

Figure 11.7 – Our demo app queries then sets the CPU affinity mask of bash to 0xdae

Okay, this is interesting: to begin with, the app correctly detects the number of CPU cores available to it as 12; it then queries the (default) CPU affinity mask of the bash process (as we pass its PID as the first parameter); it shows up, as 0xfff, as expected. Then, as we've also passed a second parameter – the bitmask to now set (0xdae) – it does so, setting the CPU affinity mask of bash to 0xdae. Now, as the terminal window we're on is this very same bash process, running nproc again shows the value as 8, not 12! That's indeed correct: the bash process now has only eight CPU cores available to it. (This is as we don't revert the CPU affinity mask to its original value on exit.)

Here's the relevant code to set the CPU affinity mask:

```
// ch11/cpu_affinity/userspc_cpuaffinity.c
static int set_cpu_affinity(pid_t pid, unsigned long bitmask)
{
    cpu_set_t cpumask;
    int i;

    printf("\nSetting CPU affinity mask for PID %d now...\n", pid);
    CPU_ZERO(&cpumask);

    /* Iterate over the given bitmask, setting CPU bits as required */
    for (i=0; i<sizeof(unsigned long)*8; i++) {
        /* printf("bit %d: %d\n", i, (bitmask >> i) & 1); */
        if ((bitmask >> i) & 1)
            CPU_SET(i, &cpumask);
    }

    if (sched_setaffinity(pid, sizeof(cpu_set_t), &cpumask) < 0) {
        perror("sched_setaffinity() failed");
        return -1;
    }
    disp_cpumask(pid, &cpumask, numcores);
    return 0;
}
```

In the preceding code snippet, you can see we first set up the cpu_set_t bitmask appropriately (by looping over each bit) and then employ the sched_setaffinity(2) system call to set the new CPU affinity mask on the given pid.

Using taskset(1) to perform CPU affinity

Akin to how (in the preceding chapter) we used the convenient user space utility program, `chrt(1)` to get (or set) a process' (or thread's) scheduling policy and/or priority, you can use the user space `taskset(1)` utility to get and/or set a given process' (or thread's) CPU affinity mask. A couple of quick examples follow; note that these examples were run on an x86_64 Linux system with 4 CPU cores:

- Use `taskset` to query the CPU affinity mask of systemd (PID 1):

    ```
    $ taskset -p 1
    pid 1's current affinity mask: f
    $
    ```

- Use `taskset` to ensure that the compiler – and its descendants (the assembler and linker) – run only on the first two CPU cores; the first parameter to taskset is the CPU affinity bitmask (`03` is binary `0011`):

    ```
    $ taskset 03 gcc userspc_cpuaffinity.c -o userspc_cpuaffinity -Wall
    ```

Do look up the man page on `taskset(1)` for complete usage details.

Setting the CPU affinity mask on a kernel thread

As an example, if we want to demonstrate a synchronization technique called per-CPU variables, we are required to create two kernel threads and guarantee that each of them runs on a separate CPU core. To do so, we must set the CPU affinity mask of each kernel thread (the first one to 0, the second to 1, in order to have them execute on only CPUs 0 and 1 respectively). The thing is, it's not a clean job – quite a *hack*, to be honest, and definitely *not* recommended. The following comment from that code shows why:

```
/* ch17/6_percpuvar/6_percpuvar.c */
/* WARNING! This is considered a hack.
 * As sched_setaffinity() isn't exported, we don't have access to it
 * within this kernel module. So, here we resort to a hack: we use
 * kallsyms_lookup_name() (which works when CONFIG_KALLSYMS is defined)
 * to retrieve the function pointer, subsequently calling the function
 * via it's pointer (with 'C' what you do is only limited by your
 * imagination :).
 */
```

```
    ptr_sched_setaffinity = (void
*)kallsyms_lookup_name("sched_setaffinity");
```

Later, we invoke the function pointer, in effect invoking the `sched_setaffinity` code, like so:

```
    cpumask_clear(&mask);
    cpumask_set_cpu(cpu, &mask); // 1st param is the CPU number, not bitmask
    /* !HACK! sched_setaffinity() is NOT exported, we can't call it
     *   sched_setaffinity(0, &mask); // 0 => on self
     * so we invoke it via it's function pointer */
    ret = (*ptr_sched_setaffinity)(0, &mask);    // 0 => on self
```

Unconventional and controversial; it does work, but please avoid hacks like this in production.

Now that you know how to get/set a thread's CPU affinity mask, let's move on to the next logical step: how to get/set a thread's scheduling policy and priority! The next section delves into the details.

Querying and setting a thread's scheduling policy and priority

In Chapter 10, *The CPU Scheduler – Part 1*, in the *Threads – which scheduling policy and priority* section, you learned how to query the scheduling policy and priority of any given thread via `chrt(1)` (we also demonstrated a simple bash script to do so). There, we mentioned the fact that `chrt(1)` internally invokes the `sched_getattr(2)` system call in order to query these attributes.

Very similarly, setting the scheduling policy and priority can be performed either by using the `chrt(1)` utility (making it simple to do so within a script, for example), or programmatically within a (user space) C application with the `sched_setattr(2)` system call. In addition, the kernel exposes other APIs: `sched_{g,s}etscheduler(2)` and its `pthread` library wrapper APIs, `pthread_{g,s}etschedparam(3)` (as these are all user space APIs, we leave it to you to browse through their man pages to get the details and try them out for yourself).

Within the kernel – on a kernel thread

As you know by now, the kernel is most certainly not a process nor a thread. Having said that, the kernel does contain kernel threads; like their user space counterparts, kernel threads can be created as required (from within the core kernel, a device driver, a kernel module). They *are* schedulable entities (KSEs!) and, of course, each of them has a task structure; thus, their scheduling policy and priority can be queried or set as required..

So, to the point at hand: to set the scheduling policy and/or priority of a kernel thread, the kernel typically makes use of
the `kernel/sched/core.c:sched_setscheduler_nocheck()` (GFP exported) kernel API; here, we show its signature and an example of its typical usage; the comments that follow make it quite self-explanatory:

```
// kernel/sched/core.c
/**
 * sched_setscheduler_nocheck - change the scheduling policy and/or RT
priority of a thread from kernelspace.
 * @p: the task in question.
 * @policy: new policy.
 * @param: structure containing the new RT priority.
 *
 * Just like sched_setscheduler, only don't bother checking if the
 * current context has permission. For example, this is needed in
 * stop_machine(): we create temporary high priority worker threads,
 * but our caller might not have that capability.
 *
 * Return: 0 on success. An error code otherwise.
 */
int sched_setscheduler_nocheck(struct task_struct *p, int policy,
                   const struct sched_param *param)
{
    return _sched_setscheduler(p, policy, param, false);
}
EXPORT_SYMBOL_GPL(sched_setscheduler_nocheck);
```

One good example of the kernel's usage of kernel threads is when the kernel (quite commonly) uses threaded interrupts. Here, the kernel must create a dedicated kernel thread with the SCHED_FIFO (soft) real-time scheduling policy and a real-time priority value of 50 (halfway between), for interrupt handling purposes. The (relevant) code to do this is shown here as an example of setting scheduling policy and priority on a kernel thread:

```
// kernel/irq/manage.c
static int
setup_irq_thread(struct irqaction *new, unsigned int irq, bool secondary)
{
    struct task_struct *t;
    struct sched_param param = {
        .sched_priority = MAX_USER_RT_PRIO/2,
    };
    [ ... ]
    sched_setscheduler_nocheck(t, SCHED_FIFO, &param);
    [ ... ]
```

(Here, we don't show the code that creates the kernel thread via the kthread_create() API. Also, FYI, MAX_USER_RT_PRIO is the value 100.)

Now that you understand to a good extent how CPU scheduling works at the level of the OS, we'll move on to yet another quite compelling discussion – that of cgroups; read on!

CPU bandwidth control with cgroups

In the hazy past, the kernel community struggled mightily with a rather vexing issue: though scheduling algorithms and their implementations – the early 2.6.0 O(1) scheduler, and a little later (with 2.6.23), the **Completely Fair Scheduler (CFS)** – promised, well, completely fair scheduling, it really wasn't. Think about this for a moment: let's say you are logged into a Linux server along with nine other people. Everything else being equal, it is likely that processor time is (more or less) fairly shared between all ten people; of course, you will understand that it's not really people that run, it's processes and threads that run on their behalf.

The CPU Scheduler - Part 2

For now at least, let's assume it's mostly fairly shared. But, what if you write a user space program that, in a loop, indiscriminately spawns off several new threads, each of which perform a lot of CPU-intensive work (and perhaps as an added bonus, allocates large swathes of memory as well; a file (un)compressor app perhaps) in each loop iteration!? The CPU bandwidth allocation is no longer fair in any real sense of the term, your account will effectively hog the CPUs (and perhaps other system resources, such as memory, as well)!

A solution that precisely and effectively allocated and managed CPU (and other resource) bandwidth was required; ultimately, Google engineers obliged with patches that put the modern-day cgroups solution into the Linux kernel (in version 2.6.24). In a nutshell, cgroups is a kernel feature that allows the system administrator (or anyone with root access) to perform bandwidth allocation and fine-grained resource management on the various resources (or *controllers*, as they are called in the cgroup lexicon) on a system. Do note: using cgroups, it's not just the processors (CPU bandwidth), but also memory, network, block I/O (and more) bandwidth that can be carefully allocated and monitored as required by your project or product.

So, hey, you're interested now! How do you enable this cgroups feature? Simple – it's a kernel feature you enable (or disable) at quite a fine granularity in the usual way: by configuring the kernel! The relevant menu (via the convenient `make menuconfig` interface) is `General setup / Control Group support`. Try this: `grep` your kernel config file for `CGROUP`; if required, tweak your kernel config, rebuild, reboot with the new kernel, and test. (We covered kernel configuration in detail back in `Chapter 2`, *Building the 5.x Linux Kernel from Source – Part 1*, and the kernel build and install in `Chapter 3`, *Building the 5.x Linux Kernel from Source – Part 2*.)

> Good news: cgroups is enabled by default on any (recent enough) Linux system that runs the systemd init framework. As mentioned just now, you can query the cgroup controllers enabled by `grep`-ping your kernel config file, and modify the config as desired.

From it's initiation in 2.6.24, cgroups, like all other kernel features, continually evolves. Fairly recently, a point was reached where sufficiently improved cgroup features became incompatible with the old, resulting in a new cgroup release, one christened cgroups v2 (or simply cgroups2); this was declared production-ready in the 4.5 kernel series (with the older one now referred to as cgroups v1 or as the legacy cgroups implementation). Note that, as of the time of this writing, both can and do exist together (with some limitations; many applications and frameworks still use the older cgroups v1 and are yet to migrate to v2).

Chapter 11

> A detailed rationale of why to use cgroups v2 as opposed to cgroups v1 can be found within the kernel documentation here: https://www.kernel.org/doc/html/latest/admin-guide/cgroup-v2.html#issues-with-v1-and-rationales-for-v2

The man page on `cgroups(7)` describes in some detail the interfaces and various available (resource) controllers (or *subsystems* as they are sometimes referred to); for cgroups v1, they are `cpu`, `cpuacct`, `cpuset`, `memory`, `devices`, `freezer`, `net_cls`, `blkio`, `perf_event`, `net_prio`, `hugetlb`, `pids`, and `rdma`. We refer interested readers to said man page for details; as an example, the PIDS controller is very useful in preventing fork bombs (often, a silly but nevertheless deadly DoS attack where the `fork(2)` system call is issued within an infinite loop!), allowing you to limit the number of processes that can be forked off from that cgroup (or its descendants). On a Linux box with cgroups v1 running, peek at the content of `/proc/cgroups`: it reveals the v1 controllers available and their current usage.

Control groups are exposed via a purpose-built synthetic (pseudo) filesystem, typically mounted under `/sys/fs/cgroup`. In cgroups v2, all controllers are mounted in a single hierarchy (or tree). This is unlike cgroups v1, where multiple controllers could be mounted under multiple hierarchies or groups. The modern init framework, *systemd*, is a user of both the v1 and v2 cgroups. The `cgroups(7)` man page indeed mentions the fact that `systemd(1)` auto-mounts a cgroups v2 filesystem during startup (at `/sys/fs/cgroup/unified`).

In cgroups v2, these are the supported controllers (or resource limiters or subsystems, if you will): `cpu`, `cpuset`, `io`, `memory`, `pids`, `perf_event`, and `rdma` (the first five being commonly deployed).

In this chapter, the focus is on CPU scheduling; thus, we do not delve further into other controllers, but limit our discussions to an example of using the cgroups v2 `cpu` controller to limit CPU bandwidth allocation. For more on employing the other controllers, we refer you to the resources mentioned previously (along with several more found in the *Further reading* section of this chapter).

Looking up cgroups v2 on a Linux system

First, let's look up the available v2 controllers; to do so, locate the cgroups v2 mount point; it's usually here:

```
$ mount | grep cgroup2
cgroup2 on /sys/fs/cgroup/unified type cgroup2
```

```
      (rw,nosuid,nodev,noexec,relatime,nsdelegate)
$ sudo cat /sys/fs/cgroup/unified/cgroup.controllers
$
```

Hey, there aren't any controllers present in `cgroup2`!? Actually, it will be this way in the presence of *mixed* cgroups, v1 and v2, which is the default (as of the time of writing). To exclusively make use of the later version – and thus have all configured controllers visible – you must first disable cgroups v1 by passing this kernel command-line parameter at boot: `cgroup_no_v1=all` (recall, all available kernel parameters can be conveniently seen here: https://www.kernel.org/doc/Documentation/admin-guide/kernel-parameters.txt).

After rebooting the system with the preceding option, you can check that the kernel parameters you specified (via GRUB on an x86, or perhaps via U-Boot on an embedded system) have indeed been parsed by the kernel:

```
$ cat /proc/cmdline
 BOOT_IMAGE=/boot/vmlinuz-4.15.0-118-generic root=UUID=<...> ro
console=ttyS0,115200n8 console=tty0 ignore_loglevel quiet splash
cgroup_no_v1=all 3
$
```

Okay; now let's retry looking up the `cgroup2` controllers; you should find that it's typically mounted under `/sys/fs/cgroup/` - the `unified` folder is no longer present (now that we've booted with the `cgroup_no_v1=all` parameter):

```
$ cat /sys/fs/cgroup/cgroup.controllers
cpu io memory pids
```

Ah, now we see them (the exact controllers you see depend on how the kernel's configured).

The rules governing the working of cgroups2 is beyond this book's scope; if you'd like to, I suggest you read through it here: https://www.kernel.org/doc/html/latest/admin-guide/cgroup-v2.html#control-group-v2. Also, all the `cgroup.<foo>` pseudo files under a cgroup are described in detail in the *Core Interface Files* section (https://www.kernel.org/doc/html/latest/admin-guide/cgroup-v2.html#core-interface-files). Similar information is presented, in a simpler way, within the excellent man page on `cgroups(7)` (look it up with `man 7 cgroups` on Ubuntu).

Trying it out – a cgroups v2 CPU controller

Let's try something interesting: we shall create a new sub-group under the cgroups v2 hierarchy on the system. We'll then set up a CPU controller for it, run a couple of test processes (that hammer away on the system's CPU cores), and set a user-specified upper limit on how much CPU bandwidth these processes can actually make use of!

Here, we outline the steps you will typically take to do this (all of these steps require you to be running with root access):

1. Ensure your kernel supports cgroups v2:
    - You should be running on a 4.5 or later kernel.
    - In the presence of mixed cgroups (both legacy v1 and newer v2, which, as of the time of writing, is the default), check that your kernel command line includes the cgroup_no_v1=all string. Here, we shall assume that the cgroup v2 hierarchy is supported and mounted at /sys/fs/cgroup.

2. Add a cpu controller to the cgroups v2 hierarchy; this is achieved by doing this, as root:

   ```
   echo "+cpu" > /sys/fs/cgroup/cgroup.subtree_control
   ```

   > **TIP**: The kernel documentation on cgroups v2 (https://www.kernel.org/doc/html/latest/admin-guide/cgroup-v2.html#cpu) does mention this point: *WARNING: cgroup2 doesn't yet support control of realtime processes and the cpu controller can only be enabled when all RT processes are in the root cgroup. Be aware that system management software may already have placed RT processes into nonroot cgroups during the system boot process, and these processes may need to be moved to the root cgroup before the cpu controller can be enabled.*

3. Create a sub-group: this is done by simply creating a directory with the required sub-group name under the cgroup v2 hierarchy; for example, to create a sub-group called test_group, use the following:

   ```
   mkdir /sys/fs/cgroup/test_group
   ```

4. The interesting bit's here: set up the max allowable CPU bandwidth for the processes that will belong to this sub-group; this is effected by writing into the `<cgroups-v2-mount-point>/<sub-group>/cpu.max` (pseudo) file. For clarity, the explanation of this file, as per the kernel documentation (https://www.kernel.org/doc/html/latest/admin-guide/cgroup-v2.html#cpu-interface-files), is reproduced here:

   ```
   cpu.max
   A read-write two value file which exists on non-root cgroups.
   The default is "max 100000". The maximum bandwidth limit. It's
   in the following format:
   $MAX $PERIOD
   which indicates that the group may consume upto $MAX in each
   $PERIOD duration. "max" for $MAX indicates no limit. If only
   one number is written, $MAX is updated.
   ```

   In effect, all processes in the sub-control group will be collectively allowed to run for `$MAX` out of a period of `$PERIOD` microseconds; so, for example, with `MAX = 300,000` and `PERIOD = 1,000,000`, we're effectively allowing all processes within the sub-control group to run for 0.3 seconds out of a period of 1 second!

5. Insert some processes into the new sub-control group; this is achieved by writing their PIDs into the `<cgroups-v2-mount-point>/<sub-group>/cgroup.procs` pseudo-file:
   - You can further verify that they actually belong to this sub-group by looking up the content of each process's `/proc/<PID>/cgroup` pseudo-file; if it contains a line of the form `0::/<sub-group>`, then it indeed belongs to the sub-group!

6. That's it; *the processes under the new sub-group will now perform their work under the CPU bandwidth constraint imposed*; when done, they will die as usual... you can remove (or delete) the sub-group with a simple `rmdir <cgroups-v2-mount-point>/<sub-group>`.

Chapter 11

A bash script that actually carries out the preceding steps is available here: `ch11/cgroups_v2_cpu_eg/cgv2_cpu_ctrl.sh`. Do check it out! To make it interesting, it allows you to pass the maximum allowed CPU bandwidth – the `$MAX` value discussed in *step 4*! Not only that; we deliberately write a test script (`simp.sh`) that hammers on the CPU(s) – they generate integer values that we redirect to files. Thus, the number of integers they generated during their lifetime is an indication of how much CPU bandwidth was available to them... this way, we can test the script and actually see cgroups (v2) in action!

A couple of test runs here will help you understand this:

```
$ sudo ./cgv2_cpu_ctrl.sh
[sudo] password for <username>:
Usage: cgv2_cpu_ctrl.sh max-to-utilize(us)
 This value (microseconds) is the max amount of time the processes in the sub-control
 group we create will be allowed to utilize the CPU; it's relative to the period,
 which is the value 1000000;
 So, f.e., passing the value 300,000 (out of 1,000,000) implies a max CPU utilization
 of 0.3 seconds out of 1 second (i.e., 30% utilization).
 The valid range for the $MAX value is [1000-1000000].
$
```

You're expected to run it as root and to pass, as a parameter, the `$MAX` value (the usage screen seen previously quite clearly explains it, including displaying the valid range (the microseconds value)).

The CPU Scheduler - Part 2

In the following screenshot, we run the bash script with the parameter `800000`, implying a CPU bandwidth of 800,000 out of a period of 1,000,000; in effect, a quite high CPU utilization of 0.8 seconds out of every 1 second on the CPU (80%):

```
$ sudo ./cgv2_cpu_ctrl.sh 800000
[+] Checking for cgroup v2 kernel support
[+] Adding a 'cpu' controller to the cgroups v2 hierarchy
[+] Create a sub-group under it (here: /sys/fs/cgroup/test_group)

***
Now allowing 800000 out of a period of 1000000 by all processes (j1,j2) in this
sub-control group, i.e., 80.000% !
***

[+] Launch processes j1 and j2 (slinks to /home/llkd/Learn-Linux-Kernel-Development/ch11/cgroups_v2_cpu_eg/simp.sh
) now ...
[+] Insert processes j1 and j2 into our new CPU ctrl sub-group
Verifying their presence...
0::/test_group
Job j1 is in our new cgroup v2 test_group
0::/test_group
Job j2 is in our new cgroup v2 test_group

............... sleep for 5 s ...............

[+] killing processes j1, j2 ...
./cgv2_cpu_ctrl.sh: line 185:  8805 Killed                  ./j1 1 > ${OUT1}
./cgv2_cpu_ctrl.sh: line 185:  8826 Killed                  ./j2 900 > ${OUT2}
cat 1stjob.txt
1 2 3 4 5 6 7 8 9 10 11 12 13 14 15 16 17 18 19 20 21 22 23 24 25 26 27 28 29 30 31 32 33 34 35 36 37 38 39 40 41
42 43 44 45 46 47 48 49 50 51 52 53 54 55 56 57 58 59 60 61 62 63 64 65 66 67 68
cat 2ndjob.txt
900 901 902 903 904 905 906 907 908 909 910 911 912 913 914 915 916 917 918 919 920 921 922 923 924 925 926 927 92
8 929 930 931 932 933 934 935 936 937 938 939 940 941 942 943 944 945 946 947 948 949 950 951 952 953 954 955 956
957 958 959 960 961 962 963 964 965
[+] Removing our cpu sub-group controller
$
```

Figure 11.8 – Screenshot of running our cgroups v2 CPU controller demo bash script with an effective max CPU bandwidth of 80%

Study our script's output in *Figure 11.8*; you can see that it does its job: after verifying cgroup v2 support, it adds a `cpu` controller and creates a sub-group (called `test_group`). It then proceeds to launch two test processes called `j1` and `j2` (in reality, they're just symbolic links to our `simp.sh` script). Once launched, they run of course. The script then queries and adds their PIDs to the sub-control group (as shown in *step 5*). We give the two processes 5 seconds to run; the script then displays the content of the files into which they wrote. It's designed such that job `j1` writes integers starting from 1, and job `j2` writes integers starting from 900. In the preceding screenshot, you can clearly see that, in their lifetime, and under the effectively 80% CPU bandwidth available to it, job `j1` emits numbers from 1 to 68; similarly (under the same constraints), job `j2` emits numbers from 900 to 965 (a similar quantity of work, in effect). The script then cleans up, killing off the jobs and deleting the sub-group.

However, to really appreciate the effect, we run our script again (study the following output), but this time with a maximum CPU bandwidth of just 1,000 (the $MAX value) – in effect, a max CPU utilization of just 0.1%!:

```
$ sudo ./cgv2_cpu_ctrl.sh 1000
[+] Checking for cgroup v2 kernel support
[+] Adding a 'cpu' controller to the cgroups v2 hierarchy
[+] Create a sub-group under it (here: /sys/fs/cgroup/test_group)

***
Now allowing 1000 out of a period of 1000000 by all processes (j1,j2)
in this
sub-control group, i.e., .100% !
***

[+] Launch processes j1 and j2 (slinks to /home/llkd/Learn-Linux-
Kernel-Development/ch11/cgroups_v2_cpu_eg/simp.sh) now ...
[+] Insert processes j1 and j2 into our new CPU ctrl sub-group
Verifying their presence...
0::/test_group
Job j1 is in our new cgroup v2 test_group
0::/test_group
Job j2 is in our new cgroup v2 test_group

.............. sleep for 5 s ...............

[+] killing processes j1, j2 ...
./cgv2_cpu_ctrl.sh: line 185: 10322 Killed    ./j1 1 > ${OUT1}
cat 1stjob.txt
1 2 3
cat 2ndjob.txt
```

```
900 901
[+] Removing our cpu sub-group controller
rmdir: failed to remove '/sys/fs/cgroup/test_group': Device or
resource busy
./cgv2_cpu_ctrl.sh: line 27: 10343 Killed ./j2 900 > ${OUT2}
$
```

What a difference! This time our jobs `j1` and `j2` could literally emit between just two and three integers (the values `1 2 3` for job j1 and `900 901` for job j2, as seen in the preceding output), clearly proving the efficacy of the cgroups v2 CPU controller.

> Containers, essentially lightweight VMs (to some extent), are currently a hot commodity. The majority of container technologies in use today (Docker, LXC, Kubernetes, and others) are, at heart, a marriage of two built-in Linux kernel technologies, namespaces, and cgroups.

With that, we complete our brief coverage of a really powerful and useful kernel feature: cgroups. Let's move on to the final section of this chapter: learning how you can turn regular Linux into a real-time operating system!

Converting mainline Linux into an RTOS

Mainline or vanilla Linux (the kernel you download from `https://kernel.org`) is decidedly *not* a **Real-Time Operating System (RTOS)**; it's a **General Purpose Operating System (GPOS**; as is Windows, macOS, Unix). In an RTOS, where hard real-time characteristics come into play, not only must the software obtain the correct result, there are deadlines associated with doing so; it must guarantee it meets these deadlines, every single time. The mainline Linux OS, though not an RTOS, does a tremendous job: it easily qualifies as being a soft real-time OS (one where deadlines are met most of the time). Nevertheless, true hard real-time domains (for example, military operations, many types of transport, robotics, telecom, factory floor automation, stock exchanges, medical electronics, and so on) require an RTOS.

Another key point in this context is that of **determinism**: an oft missed point regarding real-time is that the software response time need not always be really fast (responding, say, within a few microseconds); it may be a lot slower (in the range of, say, tens of milliseconds); by itself, that isn't what really matters in an RTOS. What does matter is that the system is reliable, working in the same consistent manner and always guaranteeing the deadline is met.

For example, the time taken to respond to a scheduling request, should be consistent and not bounce all over the place. The variance from the required time (or baseline) is often referred to as the **jitter**; an RTOS works to keep the jitter tiny, even negligible. In a GPOS, this is often impossible and the jitter can vary tremendously - at one point being low and the next very high. Overall, the ability to maintain a stable even response with minimal jitter - even in the face of extreme workload pressures - is termed determinism, and is the hallmark of an RTOS. To provide such a deterministic response, algorithms must, as far as possible, be designed to correspond to *O(1)* time complexity.

Thomas Gleixner, along with community support, has worked toward that goal for a long while now; for many years, in fact, ever since the 2.6.18 kernel, there have been offline patches that convert the Linux kernel into an RTOS. These patches can be found, for many versions of the kernel, here: `https://mirrors.edge.kernel.org/pub/linux/kernel/projects/rt/`. The older name for this project was `PREEMPT_RT`; later (October 2015 onward), the **Linux Foundation** (**LF**) took over stewardship of this project – a very positive step! – and renamed it the **Real-Time Linux** (**RTL**) Collaborative Project (`https://wiki.linuxfoundation.org/realtime/rtl/start#the_rtl_collaborative_project`), or RTL (don't confuse this project with co-kernel approaches such as Xenomai or RTAI, or the older and now-defunct attempt called RTLinux).

An FAQ, of course, is "why aren't these patches in mainline itself?" Well, it turns out that:

- Much of the RTL work has indeed been merged into the mainline kernel; this includes important areas such as the scheduling subsystem, mutexes, lockdep, threaded interrupts, PI, tracing, and so on. In fact, an ongoing primary goal of RTL is to get it merged as much as is feasible (we show a table summarizing this in the *Mainline and RTL – technical differences summarized* section).
- Linus Torvalds deems that Linux, being primarily designed and architected as a GPOS, should not have highly invasive features that only an RTOS really requires; so, though patches do get merged in, it's a slow deliberated process.

We have included several interesting articles and references to RTL (and hard real time) in the *Further reading* section of this chapter; do take a look.

The CPU Scheduler - Part 2

What you're going to do next is interesting indeed: you will learn how to patch the mainline 5.4 LTS kernel with the RTL patches, configure it, build, and boot it; you will thus end up running an RTOS – *Real-Time Linux or RTL*! We shall do this on our x86_64 Linux VM (or native system).

We won't stop there; you will then learn more – the technical differences between regular Linux and RTL, what system latency is, and how, practically, to measure it. To do so, we shall first apply the RTL patch on the kernel source of the Raspberry Pi device, configure and build it, and use it as a test-bed for system latency measurement using the *cyclictest* app (you'll also learn to use modern BPF tools for measuring scheduler latencies). Let's get a move on, first building an RTL kernel for our 5.4 kernel on an x86_64!

Building RTL for the mainline 5.x kernel (on x86_64)

In this section, you will learn, in a step-by-step, hands-on fashion, how exactly to patch, configure, and build Linux as an RTOS. As mentioned in the preceding section, these real-time patches have been around a long while; it's time to make use of them.

Obtaining the RTL patches

Navigate to `https://mirrors.edge.kernel.org/pub/linux/kernel/projects/rt/5.4/` (or, if you're on an alternate kernel, go to one directory level above this and select the required kernel version):

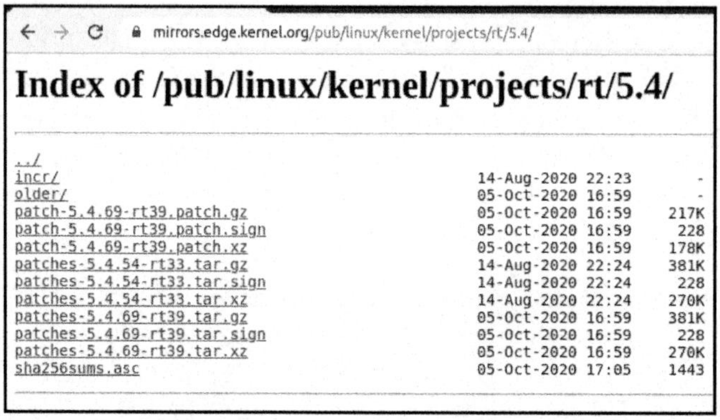

Figure 11.9 – Screenshot of the RTL patches for the 5.4 LTS Linux kernels

You will quickly notice that the RTL patches are available for only some versions of the kernel in question (here, 5.4.y); more on this follows. In the preceding screenshot, you can spot two broad types of patch files – interpret it as follows:

- `patch-<kver>rt[nn].patch.[gz|xz]`: The prefix is `patch-`; this is the complete collection of patches required to patch the mainline kernel (version `<kver>`) **in one unified** (and compressed) file.
- `patches-<kver>-rt[nn].patch.[gz|xz]`: The prefix is `patches-`; this compressed file contains every individual patch (as a separate file) that went into making up the patch series for this version of RTL.

(Also, as you should be aware, `<fname>.patch.gz` and `<fname>.patch.xz` are the same archive; it's just that the compressor differs – the `.sign` files are the PGP signature files.)

We shall use the first type; download the `patch-<kver>rt[nn].patch.xz` file to your target system by clicking on the link (or via `wget(1)`).

Notice that for the 5.4.x kernels (as of the time of writing), the RTL patches seem to be present only for version 5.4.54 and 5.4.69 (and not for 5.4.0, the kernel that we have been working with all along).

> In fact, the particular kernel version that the RTL patches apply against can certainly vary from what I've mentioned here at the time of this writing. That's expected - just follow the steps substituting the release number you're using with what's mentioned here.

Don't be worried – we shall show you a workaround in a moment. This is indeed going to be the case; the community cannot feasibly build patches against every single kernel release – there are just too many. This does have an important implication: either we patch our 5.4.0 kernel to, say, 5.4.69, or, we simply download the 5.4.69 kernel to begin with and apply the RTL patches against it.

The CPU Scheduler - Part 2

The first approach is doable but is more work (especially in the absence of a patching tools such as git/ketchup/quilt or similar; here, we choose not to use git to apply patches, just working on the stable kernel tree instead). As the Linux kernel patches are incremental, we will have to download every single patch from 5.4.0 until 5.4.69 (a total of 69 patches!), and apply them successively and in order: first 5.4.1, then 5.4.2, then 5.4.3, and so on until the final one! Here, to help keep things simple, since we know that the kernel to patch against is 5.4.69, it's just easier to download and extract it instead. So, head on over to `https://www.kernel.org/` and do so. Thus, here, we end up downloading two files:

- The compressed kernel source for mainline 5.4.69: `https://mirrors.edge.kernel.org/pub/linux/kernel/v5.x/linux-5.4.69.tar.xz`
- The RTL patch for 5.4.69: `https://mirrors.edge.kernel.org/pub/linux/kernel/projects/rt/5.4/patches-5.4.69-rt39.tar.xz`

(As explained in detail in Chapter 3, *Building the 5.x Linux Kernel from Source – Part 2*, if you intend to cross-compile the kernel for another target, the usual procedure is to build it on a suitably powerful workstation, so download it there.)

Next, extract both the RTL patch file as well as the kernel code base `tar.xz` file to obtain the kernel source tree (here, it's version 5.4.69; of course, these details have been well covered back in Chapter 2, *Building the 5.x Linux Kernel from Source – Part 1*). By now, your working directory content should look similar to this:

```
$ ls -lh
total 106M
drwxrwxr-x 24 kaiwan kaiwan 4.0K Oct  1 16:49 linux-5.4.69/
-rw-rw-r--  1 kaiwan kaiwan 105M Oct 13 16:35 linux-5.4.69.tar.xz
-rw-rw-r--  1 kaiwan kaiwan 836K Oct 13 16:33 patch-5.4.69-rt39.patch
$
```

(FYI, the `unxz(1)` utility can be used to extract the `.xz`-compressed patch file.) For the curious reader: take a peek at the patch (the file `patch-5.4.69-rt39.patch`), to see all the code-level changes wrought to bring about a hard real-time kernel; it's non-trivial of course! An overview of the technical changes will be seen in the upcoming *Mainline and RTL – technical differences summarized* section. Now that we have things in place, let's begin by applying the patch to the stable 5.4.69 kernel tree; the following section covers just this.

Applying the RTL patch

Ensure you keep the extracted patch file, `patch-5.4.69-rt39.patch`, in the directory immediately above the 5.4.69 kernel source tree (as seen previously). Now, let's apply the patch. Careful – (obviously) don't attempt to apply the compressed file as the patch; extract and use the uncompressed patch file. To ensure that the patch applies correctly, we first employ the `--dry-run` (dummy run) option to `patch(1)`:

```
$ cd linux-5.4.69
$ patch -p1 --dry-run < ../patch-5.4.69-rt39.patch
checking file Documentation/RCU/Design/Expedited-Grace-
Periods/Expedited-Grace-Periods.html
checking file Documentation/RCU/Design/Requirements/Requirements.html
[ ... ]
checking file virt/kvm/arm/arm.c
$ echo $?
0
```

All's well, let's now actually apply it:

```
$ patch -p1 < ../patch-5.4.69-rt39.patch
patching file Documentation/RCU/Design/Expedited-Grace-
Periods/Expedited-Grace-Periods.html
patching file Documentation/RCU/Design/Requirements/Requirements.html
[ ... ]
```

Great – we have the patched kernel for RTL ready now!

Of course, there are multiple ways and various shortcuts that can be employed; for example, you can also achieve the preceding via the `xzcat ../patch-5.4.69-rt39.patch.xz | patch -p1` command (or similar).

Configuring and building the RTL kernel

We have covered the kernel configuration and build steps in detail in `Chapter 2`, *Building the 5.x Linux Kernel from Source – Part 1*, and `Chapter 3`, *Building the 5.x Linux Kernel from Source – Part 2*, hence we shan't repeat it here. Pretty much everything remains the same; the only significant difference being that we must configure this kernel to take advantage of RTL (this is explained on the new RTL wiki site, here: `https://wiki.linuxfoundation.org/realtime/documentation/howto/applications/preemptrt_setup`).

The CPU Scheduler - Part 2

To cut down the kernel features to be built to approximately match the present system configuration, we first, within the kernel source tree directory (`linux-5.4.69`), do the following (we also covered this back in Chapter 2, *Building the 5.x Linux Kernel from Source - Part 1*, under the *Tuned kernel config via the localmodconfig approach* section):

```
$ lsmod > /tmp/mylsmod
$ make LSMOD=/tmp/mylsmod localmodconfig
```

Next, fire up the kernel configuration with `make menuconfig`:

1. Navigate to the `General setup` sub-menu:

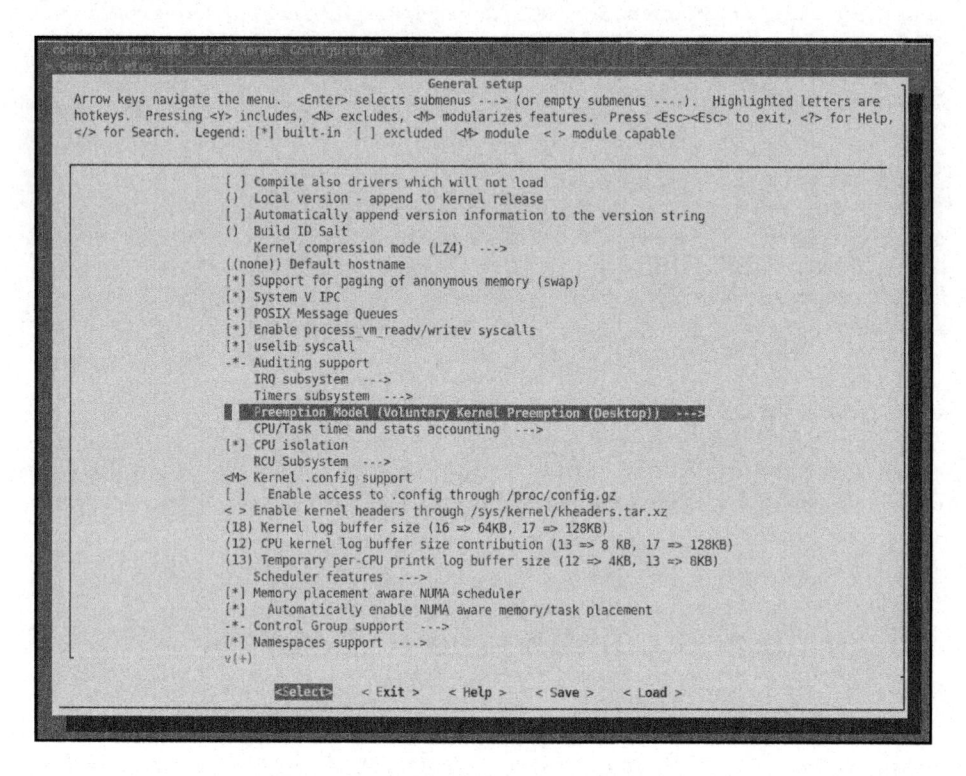

Figure 11.10 – make menuconfig / General setup: configuring the RTL-patched kernel

2. Once there, scroll down to the `Preemption Model` sub-menu; we see it highlighted in the preceding screenshot, along with the fact that the currently (by default) selected preemption model is `Voluntary Kernel Preemption (Desktop)`.

3. Pressing *Enter* here leads us into the `Preemption Model` sub-menu:

[572]

```
           Preemption Model
Use the arrow keys to navigate this window or press the
hotkey of the item you wish to select followed by the <SPACE
BAR>. Press <?> for additional information about this

        ( ) No Forced Preemption (Server)
        (X) Voluntary Kernel Preemption (Desktop)
        ( ) Preemptible Kernel (Low-Latency Desktop)
        ( ) Fully Preemptible Kernel (Real-Time)


              <Select>    < Help >
```

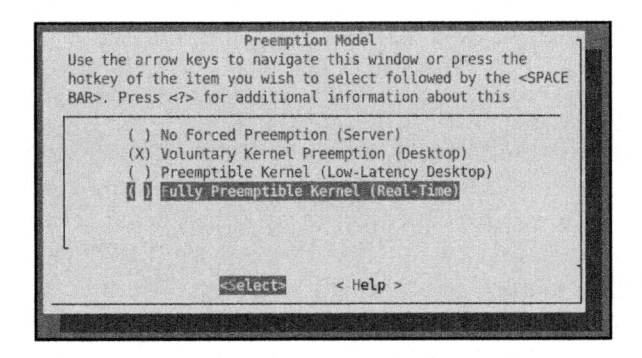

Figure 11.11 – make menuconfig / General setup / Preemption Model: configuring the RTL-patched kernel

There it is! Recall from the previous chapter, in the *Preemptible kernel* section, we described the fact that this very kernel configuration menu had three items (the first three seen in Figure 11.11). Now it has four. The fourth item – the `Fully Preemptible Kernel (Real-Time)` option – has been added on thanks to the RTL patch we just applied!

4. So, to configure the kernel for RTL, scroll down and select the `Fully Preemptible Kernel (Real-Time)` menu option (refer Figure 11.1). This corresponds to the kernel `CONFIG_PREEMPT_RT` config macro, whose `< Help >` is quite descriptive (do take a gander); it does, in fact, conclude with the statement: *select this if you are building a kernel for systems which require real-time guarantees.*

> In earlier versions of the kernel (including 5.0.x), the `Preemption Model` sub-menu displayed five choices; two were for RT: one was termed Basic RT and the other was what we see here as the fourth choice – now (5.4.x) they've simply been folded into one true real-time option.

5. Once you have selected the fourth option and saved and exited the `menuconfig` UI, (re)check that the full preemptible kernel – in effect, RTL – is selected:

```
$ grep PREEMPT_RT .config
CONFIG_PREEMPT_RT=y
```

All right, looks good! (Of course, before building, you can tweak other kernel config options as required for your product.)

6. Let's now build the RTL kernel:

```
make -j4 && sudo make modules_install install
```

7. Once it successfully builds and installs, reboot the system; at boot, press a key to display the GRUB bootloader menu (holding down one of the *Shift* keys can help ensure the GRUB menu is displayed at boot); within the GRUB menu, select the newly built `5.4.69-rtl` RTL kernel (in fact, the kernel just installed is usually the default one selected at boot). It should boot now; once logged in and on a shell, let's verify the kernel version:

```
$ uname -r
5.4.69-rt39-rtl-llkd1
```

Notice `CONFIG_LOCALVERSION` set to the value `-rtl-llkd1`. (Also, with `uname -a`, the `PREEMPT RT` string will be seen.) We're now - as promised - running Linux, RTL, as a hard real-time operating system, an RTOS!

It's very important to understand, though, that for true hard real time, simply having a hard real-time kernel is *not* enough; you must also very carefully design and write your user space (apps, libraries, and tooling) as well as your kernel modules / drivers, to conform to real time as well. For example, frequent page faulting can throw determinism out of the proverbial window and result in high latencies (and high jitter). (Recall what you learned in `Chapter 9`, *Kernel Memory Allocation for Module Authors – Part 2*, in the *A brief note on memory allocations and demand paging* section. Page faulting is a fact of life and can and does often occur; minor page faults will usually cause little to worry about. But in a hard RT scenario? And in any case, "major faults" will hamper performance.) Techniques such as using `mlockall(2)` to lock down all the pages of a real-time application process might well be required. This and several other techniques and tips for writing real-time code are provided here: `https://rt.wiki.kernel.org/index.php/HOWTO:_Build_an_ RT-application`. (Similarly, topics regarding CPU affinity and shielding, `cpuset` management, IRQ prioritization, and so on can be found on the older RT wiki site mentioned previously; `https://rt.wiki.kernel.org/index.php/Main_Page`.)

So, great – you now know how to configure and build Linux as an RTOS! I encourage you to try this out for yourself. Moving along, we'll next summarize the key differences between the standard and RTL kernels.

Mainline and RTL – technical differences summarized

To give you a deeper understanding of this interesting topic area, in this section, we delve further into it: we summarize the key differences between the standard (or mainline) and RTL kernels.

In the following table, we summarize some of the key differences between the standard (or mainline) and RTL kernels. A primary goal of the RTL project is to ultimately become fully integrated into the regular mainline kernel tree. As this process is evolutionary, the merging of patches from RTL into mainline is slow but steady; interestingly, as you can see from the rightmost column in the following table, most of (around 80% at the time of writing) the RTL work has actually been already merged into the mainline kernel, and it continues to be:

Component / Feature	Standard or mainline (vanilla) Linux	RTL (fully preemptible / hard real-time Linux)	RT work merged into mainline?
Spinlocks	The spinlock critical section is non-preemptible kernel code	As preemptible as is humanly possible; called "sleeping spinlocks"! In effect, spinlocks have been converted into mutexes.	No
Interrupt handling	Traditionally done via the top and bottom half (hardirq/tasklet/softirq) mechanism	Threaded interrupts: the majority of interrupt processing is done within a kernel thread (2.6.30, June 2009).	Yes
HRTs (High-Resolution Timers)	Available here due to merge from RTL	Timers with nanosecond resolution (2.6.16, March 2006).	Yes
RW locks	Unbounded; writers may starve	Fair RW locks with bounded writer latency.	No
lockdep	Available here due to merge from RTL	Very powerful (kernel space) tool to detect and prove locking correctness or the lack thereof.	Yes
Tracing	Some tracing technologies available here due to merge from RTL	Ftrace's origins (and to some extent perf's) were with the RT developers attempting to find latency issues.	Yes
Scheduler	Many scheduler features available here due to merge from RTL	Work on real-time scheduling as well as the deadline scheduling class (SCHED_DEADLINE) was first done here (3.14, March 2014); also, full tickless operation (3.10, June 2013).	Yes

(Don't worry – we shall definitely cover many of the preceding details in subsequent chapters of the book.)

Of course, a well-known (at least it should be) rule of thumb is simply this: *there is no silver bullet*. This implies, of course, that no one solution will fit every need.

> **TIP**: Please, if you haven't yet done so, do yourself a huge favor and read the still-so-relevant book *The Mythical Man-Month: Essays on Software Engineering* by Frederick P Brooks.

As mentioned in `Chapter 10`, *The CPU Scheduler – Part 1*, in the *Preemptible kernel* section, the Linux kernel can be configured with the `CONFIG_PREEMPT` option; this is often referred to as the **low-latency** (or **LowLat**) kernel and provides near real-time performance. In many domains (virtualization, telecoms, and so on) using a LowLat kernel might turn out to be better than using a hard real-time RTL kernel, mainly due to RTL's overheads. You often find that, with hard real-time, user space apps can suffer from throughput, reduced CPU availability, and thus higher latencies. (Refer to the *Further reading* section for a whitepaper from Ubuntu that conducts a comparison between a vanilla distro kernel, a low-latency preemptible, and a fully preemptible – effectively an RTL – kernel.)

With latencies in mind, the following section will help you understand what exactly is meant by system latencies; then, you'll learn some ways to measure it on a live system. On, on!

Latency and its measurement

We often come across the term latency; what exactly does it mean in the context of the kernel? A synonym for latency is delay and that's a good hint. *The latency (or delay) is the time taken to react* – in our context here, the time between the kernel scheduler waking up a user space thread (or process), thus making it runnable, and the time when it does actually run on the processor is the **scheduling latency**. (Do be aware, though, the term scheduling latency is also used in another context, to mean the time interval within which every runnable task is guaranteed to run at least once; the tunable is here: `/proc/sys/kernel/sched_latency_ns`, and, at least on recent x86_64 Linux, defaults to 24 ms). Similarly, the time elapsed from when a hardware interrupt occurs (say a network interrupt) to when it's actually serviced by it's handler routine, is the interrupt latency.

The **cyclictest** user space program was written by Thomas Gleixner; its purpose: to measure kernel latencies. Its output values are in microseconds units. The average and maximum latency values are usually the ones of interest – if they fall within the acceptable range for the system, then all's good; if not, it points to perhaps product-specific redesign and/or kernel configuration tweaking, checking other time-critical code paths (including user space), and so on.

Let's use the cyclictest process itself as an example to clearly understand scheduling latency. The cyclictest process is run; internally, it issues `nanosleep(2)` (or, if the `-n` option switch is passed, the `clock_nanosleep(2)` system call), putting itself into a sleep state for the time interval specified. As these `*sleep()` system calls are obviously blocking, the kernel internally enqueues the cyclictest (for simplicity, we refer to it as ct in the following diagram) process into a wait queue, simply a kernel data structure that holds sleeping tasks.

A wait queue is associated with an event; when that event occurs, the kernel awakens all tasks sleeping on that event. Here, the event in question is the expiry of a timer; this is communicated by the timer hardware by emitting a hardware interrupt (or IRQ); this starts the chain of events that must happen to make the cyclictest process wake up and run on the processor. The key point here, of course, is that it's easier said than done: many potential delays might occur on the path to the process actually running on a processor core! This is what the following diagram seeks to convey – the potential sources of latency:

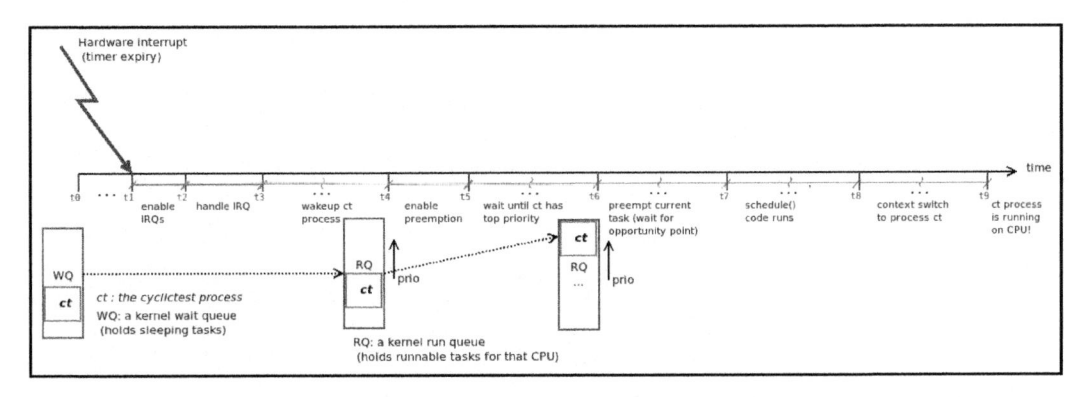

Figure 11.12 – The path to waking, context-switching, and running the cyclictest (ct) process; several latencies can occur

The CPU Scheduler - Part 2

(Some of the preceding inputs stem from the excellent presentation *Using and Understanding the Real-Time Cyclictest Benchmark, Rowand, Oct 2013*.) Study Figure 11.12 carefully; it shows the timeline from the hardware interrupt's assertion due to timer expiry (at time `t0`, as the sleep issued via the `nanosleep()` API by the cyclictest process is done at time `t1`), through IRQ handling (`t1` to `t3`), and the wakeup of the ct process – as a result of which it gets enqueued into the runqueue (between `t3` and `t4`) of the core it will eventually run upon.

From there, it will eventually become the highest priority, or best or most deserving, task for the scheduling class it belongs to (at time `t6`; we covered these details in the preceding chapter), thus, it will preempt the currently running thread (`t6`). The `schedule()` code will then execute (time `t7` to `t8`), the context switch will occur at the tail-end of `schedule()`, and finally(!), and the cyclictest process will actually execute on a processor core (time `t9`). Though it might at first appear complex, the reality is that this is a simplified diagram as several other potential latency sources have been omitted (for example, latencies due to IPI, SMI, cache migration, multiple occurrences of the preceding events, additional interrupts firing at an inopportune moment causing more delays, and so on).

A rule of thumb for determining the maximum latency value of a user space task running with real-time priority is the following:

```
max_latency = CLK_WAVELENGTH x 105 s
```

As an example, the Raspberry Pi Model 3 CPU clock runs at a frequency of 1 GHz; its wavelength (the time between one clock cycle to the next) is the inverse of the frequency, that is, 10^{-9} or 1 nanosecond. So, from the preceding equation, the theoretical maximum latency should be (within) 10^{-7} seconds which is about 10 ns (nanoseconds). As you shall soon discover, this is merely theoretical.

Measuring scheduling latency with cyclictest

To make this more interesting (as well as to run the latency test on a constrained system), we shall perform latency measurements using the well-known cyclictest app – while the system is under some amount of load (via the `stress(1)` utility) – on the equally well-known Raspberry Pi device. This section is divided into four logical parts:

1. First, set up the working environment on the Raspberry Pi device.
2. Second, download and apply the RT patches on the kernel source, configure, and build it.

3. Third, install the cyclictest app, as well as a few other required packages (including `stress`), on the device.
4. Fourth, run the test cases and analyze the results (even plotting graphs to help do so).

The first step and most parts of the second have already been covered in detail in `Chapter 3`, *Building the 5.x Linux Kernel from Source – Part 2*, in the *Kernel build for the Raspberry Pi* section. This includes downloading the Raspberry Pi-specific kernel source tree, configuring the kernel, and installing an appropriate toolchain; we won't repeat this information here. The only significant difference here is that we shall first have to apply the RT patches to the kernel source tree and configure for hard real-time; we cover this in the next section.

Let's get going!

Getting and applying the RTL patchset

Check the mainline or distribution kernel version that is running on your Raspberry Pi device (substitute the Raspberry Pi with any other device you may be running Linux on); for example, on the Raspberry Pi 3B+ I'm using, it's running the stock Raspbian (or Raspberry Pi OS) GNU/Linux 10 (buster) with the 5.4.51-v7+ kernel.

We'd like to build an RTL kernel for the Raspberry Pi with the closest possible matching kernel to the standard one it's currently running; for our case here, with it running 5.4.51[-v7+], the closest available RTL patches are for kernel versions 5.4.y-rt[nn] (`https://mirrors.edge.kernel.org/pub/linux/kernel/projects/rt/5.4/`); we shall come back to this shortly...

Let's go step by step:

1. The steps to download the Raspberry Pi specific kernel source tree onto your host system disk have already been covered in `Chapter 3`, *Building the 5.x Linux Kernel from Source – Part 2*, in the *Kernel build for the Raspberry Pi* section; do refer to it and obtain the source tree.

The CPU Scheduler - Part 2

2. Once this step completes, you should see a directory named `linux`; it holds the Raspberry Pi kernel source for (as of the time of writing) kernel version 5.4.y. What's the value of y? That's easy; just do the following:

   ```
   $ head -n4 linux/Makefile
   # SPDX-License-Identifier: GPL-2.0
   VERSION = 5
   PATCHLEVEL = 4
   SUBLEVEL = 70
   ```

   The `SUBLEVEL` variable here is the value of y; clearly, it's 70, making the kernel version 5.4.70.

3. Next, let's download the appropriate real-time (RTL) patch: the best one would be an exact match, that is, the patch should be named something like `patch-5.4.70-rt[nn].tar.xz`. Lucky for us, it does indeed exist on the server; let's get it (notice that we download the `patch-<kver>-rt[nn]` file; it's simpler to work with as it's the unified patch):
   `wget https://mirrors.edge.kernel.org/pub/linux/kernel/projects/rt/5.4/patch-5.4.70-rt40.patch.xz`

   > **TIP**: This does raise the question: what if the versions of the available RTL patches do *not* precisely match that of the device's kernel version? Well, unfortunately, that does happen. In cases like this, to have the best chance of applying it against the device kernel, select the closest match and attempt to apply it; it often succeeds with perhaps minor warnings... If not, you will have to either manually tweak the code base to suit the patchset, or just switch to using a kernel version for which the RTL patch exists (recommended).

   Don't forget to uncompress the patch file!

4. Now apply the patch (as shown previously, in the *Applying the RTL patch* section):

   ```
   cd linux
   patch -p1 < ../patch-5.4.70-rt40.patch
   ```

5. Configure the patched kernel, turning on the `CONFIG_PREEMPT_RT` kernel config option (as explained previously):
   1. First, though, as we learned in Chapter 3, *Building the 5.x Linux Kernel from Source – Part 2*, it's *critical* that you set up the initial kernel config appropriately for the target; here, as the target device is the Raspberry Pi 3[B+], do this:

      ```
      make ARCH=arm bcm2709_defconfig
      ```

   2. Customize your kernel configuration with the `make ARCH=arm menuconfig` command. Here, of course, you should go to `General setup / Preemption Model`, and select the fourth option, `CONFIG_PREEMPT_RT`, to turn on the hard real-time preemption features.

6. I shall also assume that you have an appropriate toolchain for x86_64-to-ARM32 for the Raspberry Pi installed:

   ```
   make -j4 ARCH=arm CROSS_COMPILE=arm-linux-gnueabihf- zImage modules dtbs
   ```

   > **Hint**: Installing an appropriate toolchain (for x86_64-to-ARM32) can be as simple as `sudo apt install crossbuild-essential-armhf`. Now build the kernel (again, identical to the process we described previously, in the *Configuring and building the RTL kernel* section), with the difference being that we cross-compile it (using the x86_64-to-ARM32 cross-compiler we installed previously).

7. Install the just-built kernel modules; ensure you specify the location as the SD card's root filesystem with the `INSTALL_MOD_PATH` environment variable (else it might overwrite your host's modules, which would be disastrous!). Let's say that the microSD card's second partition (which contains the root filesystem) is mounted under `/media/${USER}/rootfs`, then do the following (in one single line):

   ```
   sudo env PATH=$PATH make ARCH=arm CROSS_COMPILE=arm-linux-gnueabihf- INSTALL_MOD_PATH=/media/${USER}/rootfs modules_install
   ```

The CPU Scheduler - Part 2

8. Copy across the image files (the bootloader files, the kernel `zImage` file, the **Device Tree Blobs** (**DTBs**), the kernel modules) onto the Raspberry Pi SD card (these details are covered in the official Raspberry Pi documentation here: https://www.raspberrypi.org/documentation/linux/kernel/building.md; we have also (lightly) covered this in Chapter 3, *Building the 5.x Linux Kernel from Source – Part 2*).

9. Test: boot the Raspberry Pi with the new kernel image in the SD card. You should be able to log in to a shell (typically over `ssh`). Verify the kernel version and config:

```
rpi ~ $ uname -a
Linux raspberrypi 5.4.70-rt40-v7-llkd-rt1+ #1 SMP PREEMPT_RT
Thu Oct 15 07:58:13 IST 2020 armv7l GNU/Linux
rpi ~ $ zcat /proc/config.gz |grep PREEMPT_RT
CONFIG_PREEMPT_RT=y
```

We are indeed running a hard real-time kernel on the device! So, good – that takes care of the "prep" portion; you are now in a position to proceed with the next step.

Installing cyclictest (and other required packages) on the device

We intend to run test cases via the cyclictest app against both the standard and the newly minted RTL kernel. This implies, of course, that we must first obtain the cyclictest sources and build it on the device (note that the work here is being carried out on the Raspberry Pi).

> **TIP**
> Here's an article that does this very thing: *Latency of Raspberry Pi 3 on Standard and Real-Time Linux 4.9 Kernel*: https://metebalci.com/blog/latency-of-raspberry-pi-3-on-standard-and-real-time-linux-4.9-kernel/.
>
> It mentions an issue faced running the RTL kernel on the Raspberry Pi 3 as well as a workaround (important!): (in addition to the usual ones) pass along these two kernel parameters: `dwc_otg.fiq_enable=0` and `dwc_otg.fiq_fsm_enable=0`. You can put these in the `/boot/cmdline.txt` file on the device.

First, do ensure that all required packages are installed onto your Raspberry Pi:

```
sudo apt install coreutils build-essential stress gnuplot libnuma-dev
```

The `libnuma-dev` package is optional and may not be available on the Raspberry Pi OS (you can proceed even without it).

Let's now get the source code of cyclictest:

```
git clone git://git.kernel.org/pub/scm/utils/rt-tests/rt-tests.git
```

A bit peculiarly, initially, there will exist precisely one file, the README. Read it (surprise, surprise). It informs you how to obtain and build the stable version; it's simple, just do the following:

```
git checkout -b stable/v1.0 origin/stable/v1.0
make
```

Happily for us, the **Open Source Automation Development Lab (OSADL)** has a very useful bash script wrapper over cyclictest; it runs cyclictest and even plots a latency graph. Grab the script from here: https://www.osadl.org/uploads/media/mklatencyplot.bash (explanatory note on it: https://www.osadl.org/Create-a-latency-plot-from-cyclictest-hi.bash-script-for-latency-plot.0.html?no_cache=1sword_list[0]=cyclictest). I have lightly modified it for our purposes; it's here in the GitHub repository for this book: ch11/latency_test/latency_test.sh.

Running the test cases

To get a good idea regarding the system (scheduling) latencies, we shall run three test cases; in all three, the cyclictest app will sample system latency while the stress(1) utility is putting the system under load:

1. Raspberry Pi 3 model B+ (4 CPU cores) running the 5.4 32-bit RTL-patched kernel
2. Raspberry Pi 3 model B+ (4 CPU cores) running the standard 5.4 32-bit Raspberry Pi OS kernel
3. x86_64 (4 CPU cores) Ubuntu 20.04 LTS running the standard 5.4 (mainline) 64-bit kernel

We use a small wrapper script called runtest over the latency_test.sh script for convenience. It runs the latency_test.sh script to measure system latency while running the stress(1) utility; it invokes stress with the following parameters, to impose CPU, I/O, and memory loads on the system:

```
stress --cpu 6 --io 2 --hdd 4 --hdd-bytes 1MB --vm 2 --vm-bytes 128M --timeout 1h
```

The CPU Scheduler - Part 2

(FYI, a later version of `stress` called `stress-ng` is available as well.) While the `stress` app executes, loading the system, the `cyclictest(8)` app samples system latencies, writing its `stdout` to a file:

```
sudo cyclictest --duration=1h -m -Sp90 -i200 -h400 -q >output
```

(Do refer to the man pages on both `stress(1)` and `cyclictest(8)` to understand the parameters.) It will run for an hour (for more accurate results, I suggest you run the test for a longer duration – perhaps 12 hours). Our `runtest` script (and the underlying ones) internally runs `cyclictest` with appropriate parameters; it captures and displays the minimum, average, and maximum latency wall clock time taken (via `time(1)`), and generates a histogram plot. Note that here, we run `cyclictest` for a (maximum) duration of an hour.

> **TIP**
> By default, our `runtest` wrapper script has a variable LAT with the pathname to the `latency_tests` directory set as follows: `LAT=~/booksrc/ch11/latency_tests`. Ensure that you first update it to reflect the location of the `latency_tests` directory on your system.

A screenshot of running the scripts for our test case #1 – on the Raspberry Pi 3B+ running the RTL kernel – is seen here:

```
rpi latency_tests $ ./runtest
======================================================
Thu 15 Oct 11:58:19 IST 2020
stress --cpu 6 --io 2 --hdd 4 --hdd-bytes 1MB --vm 2 --vm-bytes 128M --timeout 1h
stress: info: [1059] dispatching hogs: 6 cpu, 2 io, 2 vm, 4 hdd
-------------------------
Test Title :: "running 'stress'"
-------------------------
Version info:
No LSB modules are available.
Distributor ID: Raspbian
Description:    Raspbian GNU/Linux 10 (buster)
Release:        10
Codename:       buster
Linux raspberrypi 5.4.70-rt40-v7-llkd-rtl+ #1 SMP PREEMPT_RT Thu Oct 15 07:58:13 IST 2020 armv7l GNU/Linux
Linux version 5.4.70-rt40-v7-llkd-rtl+ (kaiwan@kaiwan-7550) (gcc version 9.3.0 (Ubuntu 9.3.0-17ubuntu1~20.04)) #1 SMP PREEMPT_RT Thu Oct 15 07:
58:13 IST 2020

sudo /home/pi/rtl_llkd/rt-tests/cyclictest --duration=1h -m -Sp90 -i200 -h400 -q >output
stress: info: [1059] successful run completed in 3600s
Thu 15 Oct 12:58:19 IST 2020
Thu 15 Oct 12:58:19 IST 2020
rpi latency_tests $ min/avg/max latency: 7 us / 26 us / 256 us
```

Figure 11.13 – Running our first test case for cyclictest on a Raspberry Pi 3B+ on the RTL kernel while under stress

Study the preceding screenshot; you can clearly see the system details, the kernel version (notice it's the RTL-patched `PREEMPT_RT` kernel!), and cyclictest's latency measurement results for the minimum, average, and maximum (scheduling) latency.

Viewing the results

We carry out a similar procedure for the remaining two test cases and summarize the results of all three in Figure 11.14:

DUT (Device Under Test)	System Latency (us)		
	Min	Avg	Max
Raspberry Pi 3B+ ; 5.4.70-rt40 RTL kernel	7 us	26 us	256 us
Raspberry Pi 3B+ ; 5.4.51-v7+ standard kernel	3 us	16.3 us	14,595 us
x86_64 ; Ubuntu 20.04 5.4.0-48-generic standard kernel	1 us	3.8 us	21,027 us

Figure 11.14 – Results of the (simplistic) test cases we ran showing the min/avg/max latencies for different kernels and systems while under some stress

Interesting; though the maximum latency of the RTL kernel is much below the other standard kernels, both the minimum and, more importantly, average latencies are superior for the standard kernels. This ultimately results in superior overall throughput for the standard kernels (this very same point was stressed upon earlier).

The `latency_test.sh` bash script invokes the `gnuplot(1)` utility to generate graphs, in such a manner that the title line shows the minimum/average/maximum latency values (in microseconds) and the kernel the test was run upon. Recollect that test case #1 and #2 ran on the Raspberry Pi 3B+ device, whereas test case #3 ran on a generic (and more powerful) x86_64 system). See here the `gnuplot`-ed graphs (for all three test cases):

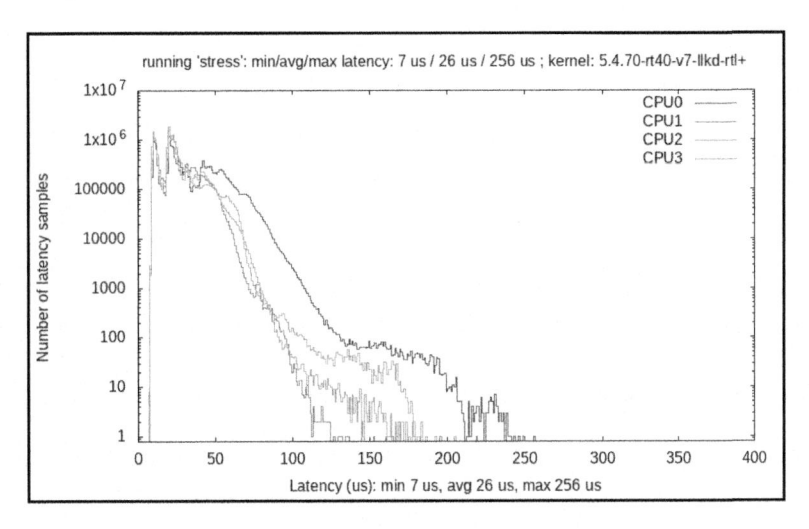

Figure 11.15 – Test case #1 plot: cyclictest latency measurement on Raspberry Pi 3B+ running the 5.4 RTL kernel

The CPU Scheduler - Part 2

Figure 11.15 shows the graph plotted by `gnuplot(1)` (called from within our `ch11/latency_test/latency_test.sh` script) for test case #1. The **Device Under Test (DUT)**, the Raspberry Pi 3B+, has four CPU cores (as seen by the OS). Notice how the graph shows us the story – the vast majority of samples are on the upper left, implying that, most of the time, the latency was very small (between 100,000 to 1 million latency samples (y-axis) fall between a few microseconds to 50 microseconds (x-axis)!). That's really good! Of course, there will be outliers at the other extreme – samples on all CPU cores have much higher latencies (between 100 and 256 microseconds) though the number of samples is much smaller. The cyclictest app gives us the minimum, average, and maximum system latency values. With the RTL-patched kernel, while the max latency is actually excellent (quite low), the average latency can be fairly high:

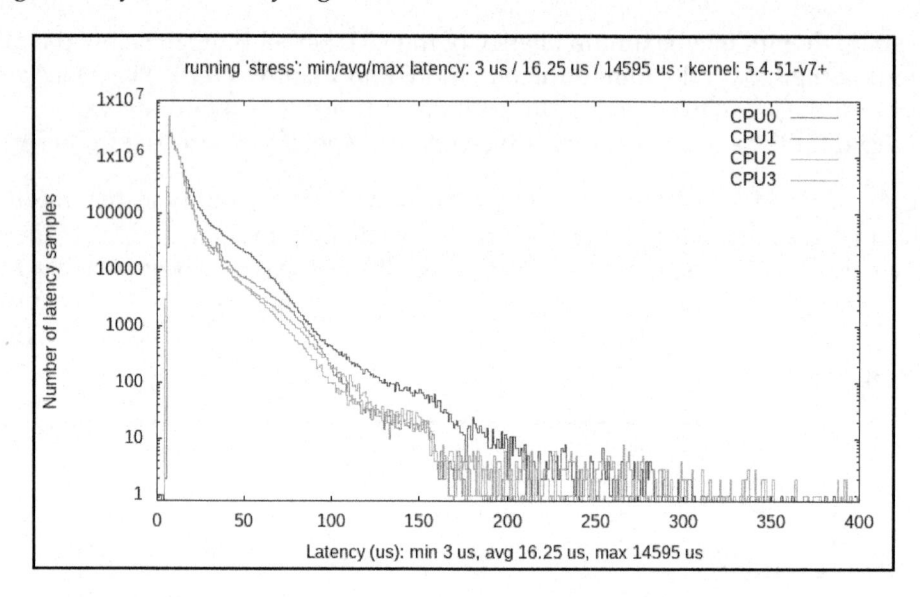

Figure 11.16 – Test case #2 plot: cyclictest latency measurement on Raspberry Pi 3B+ running the standard (mainline) 5.4 kernel

Figure 11.16 shows the plot for test case #2. Again, as with the previous test case – in fact, even more pronounced here – the vast majority of system latency samples exhibit very low latency! The standard kernel thus does a tremendous job; even the average latency is a "decent" value. However, the worst-case (max) latency value can be very large indeed – *showing us exactly why it's not an RTOS*. For most workloads, the latency tends to be excellent "usually", but a few corner cases will tend to show up. In other words, it's *not deterministic* – the key characteristic of an RTOS:

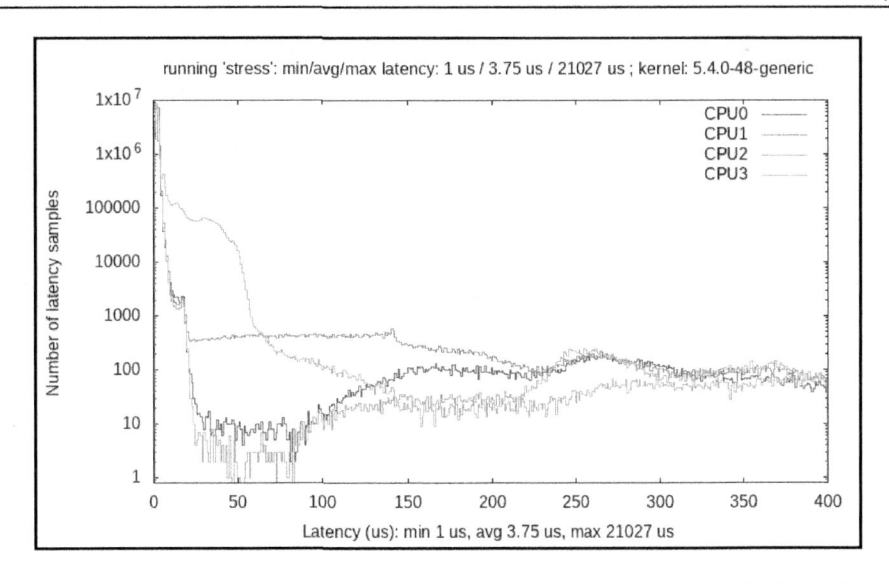

Figure 11.17 – Test case #3 plot: cyclictest latency measurement on an x86_64 Ubuntu 20.04 LTS running the standard (mainline) 5.4 kernel

Figure 11.17 shows the plot for test case #3. The variance – or **jitter** – here is even more pronounced (again, non-deterministic!), though the minimum and average system latency values are really very good. Of course, it's run on a far more powerful system – a desktop-class x86_64 – than the previous two test cases. The max latency value – the few corner cases, although there are more of them here – tends to be quite high. Again, it's not an RTOS – it's not deterministic.

Did you notice how the graphs clearly exhibit *jitter*: with test case #1 having the least amount (the graph tends to drop down to the x-axis quite quickly - meaning a very tiny number of latency samples, if not zero, exhibit high(er) latencies) and test case #3 having the most jitter (with much of the graph remaining well above the x axis!).

Again, we emphasize this point: the results quite clearly show that it's deterministic (a very small amount of jitter) with an RTOS and highly non-deterministic with a GPOS! (As a rule of thumb, standard Linux will result in approximately +/- 10 microseconds of jitter for interrupt processing, whereas on a microcontroller running an RTOS, the jitter will be far less, around +/- 10 nanoseconds!)

Doing this experiment, you will realize that benchmarking is a tricky thing; you shouldn't read too much into a few test runs (running the tests for a long while, having a large sample set, is important). Testing with realistic work loads you expect to experience on the system would be a far better way to see which kernel configuration yields superior performance; it does indeed vary with the workload!

The CPU Scheduler - Part 2

(An interesting case study by Canonical shows statistics for regular, low-latency, and real-time kernels for certain workloads; look it up in the *Further reading* section of this chapter.) As mentioned before, quite often, the superior *max* latency characteristics of an RTL kernel can lead to inferior overall throughput (user space might suffer from reduced CPU due to RTL's rather ruthless prioritization).

Measuring scheduler latency via modern BPF tools

Without going into too many details, we'd be amiss to leave out the recent and powerful [e]BPF Linux kernel feature and it's associated frontends; there are a few to specifically measure scheduler and runqueue-related system latencies. (We covered the installation of the [e]BPF tools back in `Chapter 1`, *Kernel Workspace Setup* under the *Modern tracing and performance analysis with [e]BPF* section).

The following table summarizes some of these tools (BPF frontends); all these tools need to be run as root (as with any BPF tool); they show their output as a histogram (with the time in microseconds by default):

BPF tool	What it measures
`runqlat-bpfcc`	Time a task spends waiting on a runqueue for it's turn to run on the processor
`runqslower-bpfcc`	(read as runqueue slower); time a task spends waiting on a runqueue for it's turn to run on the processor, showing only those threads that exceed a given threshold, which is 10 ms by default (can be tuned by passing the time threshold as a parameter, in microseconds); in effect, you can see which tasks face (relatively) long scheduling delays
`runqlen-bpfcc`	Shows scheduler runqueue length + occupancy (number of threads currently enqueued, waiting to run)

The tools can also provide these metrics on a per-task basis, for every process on the system or even by PID namespace (for container analysis; of course, these options depend on the tool in question). Do look up more details (and even example usage!) from the man pages (section 8) on these tools.

> **TIP**
> There are even more [e]BPF frontends related to scheduling: `cpudist- cpudist-bpfcc`, `cpuunclaimed-bpfcc`, `offcputime-bpfcc`, `wakeuptime-bpfcc`, and so on. See the *Further reading* section for resources.

[588]

So, there you are: by now, you're able to not only understand but even measure system latencies (via both the `cyclictest` app and a few modern BPF tools).

We close this chapter with a few miscellaneous, yet useful small (kernel space) routines to check out:

- `rt_prio()`: Given the priority as a parameter, returns a Boolean to indicate whether it's a real-time task or not.
- `rt_task()`: Based on the priority value of the task, given the task structure pointer as a parameter, returns a Boolean to indicate whether it's a real-time task or not (a wrapper over `rt_prio()`).
- `task_is_realtime()`: Similar, but based on the scheduling policy of the task. Given the task structure pointer as a parameter, returns a Boolean to indicate whether it's a real-time task or not.

Summary

In this, our second chapter on CPU scheduling on the Linux OS, you have learned several key things. Among them, you learned how to visualize kernel flow with powerful tools such as LTTng and the Trace Compass GUI, as well as with the `trace-cmd(1)` utility, a convenient frontend to the kernel's powerful Ftrace framework. You then saw how to programatically query and set any thread's CPU affinity mask. This naturally led to a discussion on how you can programmatically query and set any thread's scheduling policy and priority. The whole notion of being "completely fair" (via the CFS implementation) was brought into question, and some light was shed on the elegant solution called cgroups. You even learned how to leverage the cgroups v2 CPU controller to allocate CPU bandwidth as desired to processes in a sub-group. We then understood that though Linux is a GPOS, an RTL patchset very much exists, which, once applied and the kernel is configured and built, has you running Linux as a true hard real-time system, an RTOS.

Finally, you learned how to measure latencies on the system, via both the cyclictest app as well as a few modern BPF tools. We even tested with cyclictest on a Raspberry Pi 3 device, measuring and contrasting them on an RTL and a standard kernel.

That's quite a bit! Do take the time to properly understand the material, and work on it in a hands-on fashion.

Questions

As we conclude, here is a list of questions for you to test your knowledge regarding this chapter's material: https://github.com/PacktPublishing/Linux-Kernel-Programming/tree/master/questions. You will find some of the questions answered in the book's GitHub repo: https://github.com/PacktPublishing/Linux-Kernel-Programming/tree/master/solutions_to_assgn.

Further reading

To help you delve deeper into the subject with useful materials, we provide a rather detailed list of online references and links (and at times, even books) in a Further reading document in this book's GitHub repository. The *Further reading* document is available here: https://github.com/PacktPublishing/Linux-Kernel-Programming/blob/master/Further_Reading.md.

Section 3: Delving Deeper

Here you will learn about an advanced and critical topic: the concepts behind, the need for, and the usage of kernel synchronization technologies and APIs.

This section comprises the following chapters:

- `Chapter 12`, *Kernel Synchronization - Part 1*
- `Chapter 13`, *Kernel Synchronization - Part 2*

12
Kernel Synchronization - Part 1

As any developer familiar with programming in a multithreaded environment (or even a single-threaded one where multiple processes work on shared memory, or where interrupts are a possibility) is well aware, there is a need for **synchronization** whenever two or more threads (code paths in general) may race; that is, their outcome cannot be predicted. Pure code itself is never an issue as its permissions are read/executed (r-x); reading and executing code simultaneously on multiple CPU cores is not only perfectly fine and safe, but it's encouraged (it results in better throughput and is why multithreading is a good idea). However, the moment you're working on shared writeable data is the moment you need to start being very careful!

The discussions around concurrency and its control – synchronization – are varied, especially in the context of a complex piece of software such as a Linux kernel (its subsystems and related regions, such as device drivers), which is what we're dealing with in this book. Thus, for convenience, we will split this large topic into two chapters, this one and the next.

In this chapter, we will cover the following topics:

- Critical sections, exclusive execution, and atomicity
- Concurrency concerns within the Linux kernel
- Mutex or spinlock? Which to use when
- Using the mutex lock
- Using the spinlock
- Locking and interrupts

Let's get started!

Critical sections, exclusive execution, and atomicity

Imagine you're writing software for a multicore system (well, nowadays, it's typical that you will work on multicore systems, even on most embedded projects). As we mentioned in the introduction, running multiple code paths in parallel is not only safe, it's desirable (why spend those dollars otherwise, right?). On the other hand, concurrent (parallel and simultaneous) code paths within which **shared writeable data** (also known as **shared state**) **is accessed** in any manner is where you are required to guarantee that, at any given point in time, only one thread can work on that data at a time! This is really key; why? Think about it: if you allow multiple concurrent code paths to work in parallel on shared writeable data, you're literally asking for trouble: **data corruption** (a "race") can occur as a result.

What is a critical section?

A code path that can execute in parallel and that works on (reads and/or writes) shared writeable data (shared state) is called a critical section. They require protection from parallelism. Identifying and protecting critical sections from simultaneous execution is an implicit requirement for correct software that you – the designer/architect/developer – must handle.

A critical section is a piece of code that must run either exclusively; that is, alone (serialized), or atomically; that is, indivisibly, to completion, without interruption.

By exclusively, we're implying that at any given point in time, one thread is running the code of the critical section; this is obviously required for data safety reasons.

This notion also brings up the important concept of *atomicity*: a single atomic operation is one that is indivisible. On any modern processor, two operations are considered to always be **atomic**; that is, they cannot be interrupted and will run to completion:

- The execution of a single machine language instruction.
- Reads or writes to an aligned primitive data type that is within the processor's word size (typically 32 or 64 bits); for example, reading or writing a 64-bit integer on a 64-bit system is guaranteed to be atomic. Threads reading that variable will never see an in-between, torn, or dirty result; they will either see the old or the new value.

Chapter 12

So, if you have some lines of code that work upon shared (global or static) writeable data, it cannot – in the absence of any explicit synchronization mechanism – be guaranteed to run exclusively. Note that at times, running the critical section's code *atomically,* as well as exclusively, is required, but not all the time.

When the code of the critical section is running in a safe-to-sleep process context (such as typical file operations on a driver via a user app (open, read, write, ioctl, mmap, and so on), or the execution path of a kernel thread or workqueue), it might well be acceptable to not have the critical section being truly atomic. However, when its code is running in a non-blocking atomic context (such as a hardirq, tasklet, or softirq), *it must run atomically as well as exclusively* (we shall cover these points in more detail in the *Mutex or spinlock? Which to use when* section).

A conceptual example will help clarify things. Let's say that three threads (from user space app(s)) attempt to open and read from your driver more or less simultaneously on a multicore system. Without any intervention, they may well end up running the critical section's code in parallel, thus working on the shared writable data in parallel, thus very likely corrupting it! For now, let's look at a conceptual diagram to see how non-exclusive execution within a critical section's code path is wrong (we won't even talk about atomicity here):

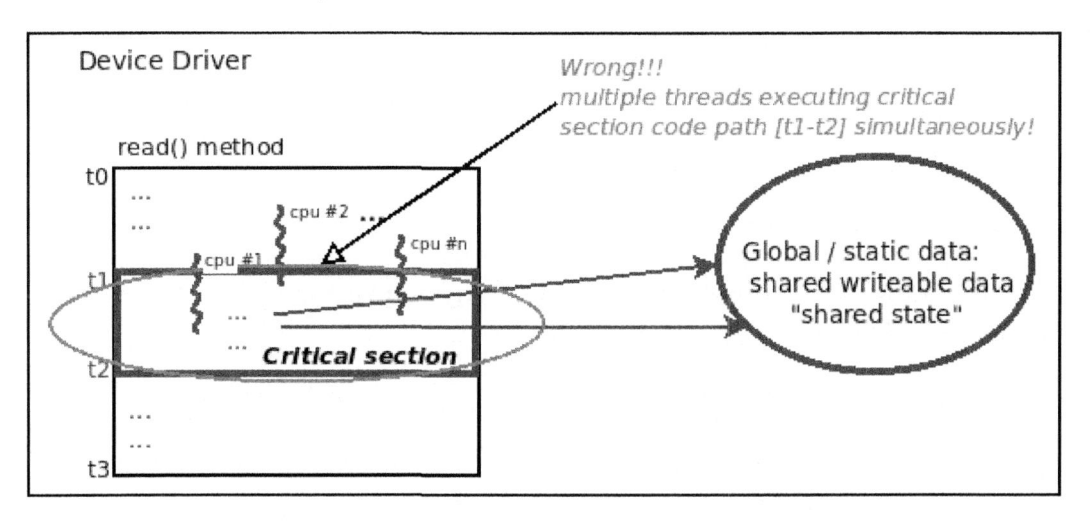

Figure 12.1 – A conceptual diagram showing how a critical section code path is violated by having >1 thread running within it simultaneously

As shown in the preceding diagram, in your device driver, within its (say) read method, you're having it run some code in order to perform its job (reading some data from the hardware). Let's take a more in-depth look at this diagram *in terms of data accesses being made* at different points in time:

- From time `t0` to `t1`: None or only local variable data is accessed. This is concurrent-safe, with no protection required, and can run in parallel (since each thread has its own private stack).
- From time `t1` to `t2`: Global/static shared writeable data is accessed. This is *not* concurrent-safe; it's **a critical section** and thus must be **protected** from concurrent access. It should only contain code that runs exclusively (alone, exactly one thread at a time, serialized) and, perhaps, atomically.
- From time `t2` to `t3`: None or only local variable data is accessed. This is concurrent-safe, with no protection required, and can run in parallel (since each thread has its own private stack).

> In this book, we assume that you are already aware of the need to synchronize critical sections; we will not discuss this particular topic any further. Those of you who are interested may refer to my earlier book, *Hands-On System Programming with Linux (Packt, October 2018)*, which covers these points in detail (especially *Chapter 15, Multithreading with Pthreads Part II – Synchronization*).

So, knowing this, we can now restate the notion of a critical section while also mentioning when the situation arises (shown in square brackets and italics in the bullet points). A critical section is code that must run as follows:

- **(Always) Exclusively**: Alone (serialized)
- **(When in an atomic context) Atomically**: Indivisibly, to completion, without interruption

In the next section, we'll look at a classic scenario – the increment of a global integer.

A classic case – the global i ++

Think of this classic example: a global `i` integer is being incremented within a concurrent code path, one within which multiple threads of execution can simultaneously execute. A naive understanding of computer hardware and software will lead you to believe that this operation is obviously atomic. However, the reality is that modern hardware and software (the compiler and OS) are much more sophisticated than you may imagine, thus causing all kinds of invisible (to the app developer) performance-driven optimizations.

> We won't attempt to delve into too much detail here, but the reality is that modern processors are extremely complex: among the many technologies they employ toward better performance, a few are superscalar and super-pipelined execution in order to execute multiple independent instructions and several parts of various instructions in parallel (respectively), performing on-the-fly instruction and/or memory reordering, caching memory in complex hierarchical on-CPU caches, false sharing, and so on! We will delve into some of these details in Chapter 13, *Kernel Synchronization – Part 2*, in the *Cache effects – false sharing* and *Memory barriers* sections.
>
> The paper *What every systems programmer should know about concurrency* by Matt Kline, April 2020, (https://assets.bitbashing.io/papers/concurrency-primer.pdf) is superb and a must-read on this subject; do read it!

All of this makes for a situation that's more complex than it appears to be at first glance. Let's continue with the classic `i ++`:

```
static int i = 5;
[ ... ]
foo()
{
    [ ... ]
    i ++;      // is this safe? yes, if truly atomic... but is it truly atomic??
}
```

Kernel Synchronization - Part 1

Is this increment safe by itself? The short answer is no, you must protect it. Why? It's a critical section – we're accessing shared writeable data for a read and/or write operation. The longer answer is that it really depends on whether the increment operation is truly atomic (indivisible); if it is, then `i ++` poses no danger in the presence of parallelism – if not, it does! So, how do we know whether `i ++` is truly atomic or not? Two things determine this:

- The processor's **Instruction Set Architecture (ISA)**, which determines (among several things related to the processor at a low level) the machine instructions that execute at runtime.
- The compiler.

If the ISA has the facility to employ a single machine instruction to perform an integer increment, *and* the compiler has the intelligence to use it, *then* it's truly atomic – it's safe and doesn't require locking. Otherwise, it's not safe and requires locking!

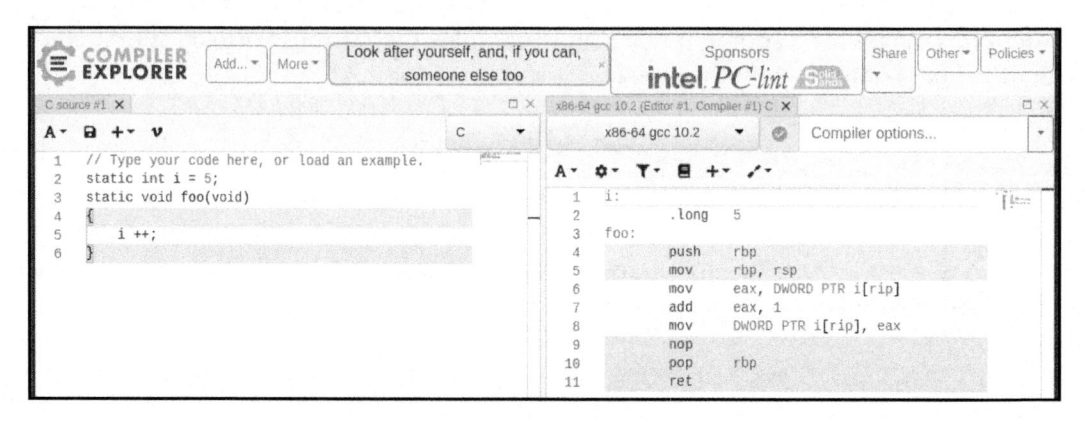

Try this out: Navigate your browser to this wonderful compiler explorer website: `https://godbolt.org/`. Select C as the programming language and then, in the left pane, declare the global `i` integer and increment within a function. Compile in the right pane with an appropriate compiler and compiler options. You'll see the actual machine code generated for the C high-level `i ++;` statement. If it's indeed a single machine instruction, then it will be safe; if not, you will require locking. By and large, you will find that you can't really tell: in effect, you *cannot* afford to assume things – you will have to assume it's unsafe by default and protect it! This can be seen in the following screenshot:

Figure 12.2 – Even with the latest stable gcc version but no optimization, the x86_64 gcc produces multiple instructions for the i ++

The preceding screenshot clearly shows this: the yellow background regions in the left- and right-hand panes is the C source and the corresponding assembly generated by the compiler, respectively (based on the x86_64 ISA and the compiler's optimization level). By default, with no optimization, `i ++` becomes three machine instructions. This is exactly what we expect: it corresponds to the *fetch* (memory to register), the *increment*, and the *store* (register to memory)! Now, this is *not* atomic; it's entirely possible that, after one of the machine instructions executes, the control unit interferes and switches the instruction stream to a different point. This could even result in another process or thread being context switched in!

The good news is that with a quick `-O2` in the `Compiler options...` window, `i ++` becomes just one machine instruction – truly atomic! However, we can't predict these things in advance; one day, your code may execute on a fairly low-end ARM (RISC) system, increasing the chance that multiple machine instructions are required for `i ++`. (Worry not – we shall cover an optimized locking technology specifically for integers in the *Using the atomic integer operators* section).

> Modern languages provide native atomic operators; for C/C++, it's fairly recent (from 2011); the ISO C++11 and the ISO C11 standards provide ready-made and built-in atomic variables for this. A little googling will quickly reveal them to you. Modern glibc also makes use of them. As an example, if you've worked with signaling in user space, you will know to use the `volatile sig_atomic_t` data type to safely access and/or update an atomic integer within signal handlers. What about the kernel? In the next chapter, you'll learn about the Linux kernel's solution to this key issue. We'll cover this in the *Using the atomic integer operators* and *Using the atomic bit operators* sections.

The Linux kernel is, of course, a concurrent environment: multiple threads of execution run in parallel on multiple CPU cores. Not only that, but even on uni-processor (UP/single CPU) systems, the presence of hardware interrupts, traps, faults, exceptions, and software signals can cause data integrity issues. Needless to say, protecting against concurrency at required points in the code path is easier said than done; identifying and protecting critical sections using technologies such as locking – as well as other synchronization primitives and technologies – is absolutely essential, which is why this is the core subject matter of this chapter and the next.

Kernel Synchronization - Part 1

Concepts – the lock

We require synchronization because of the fact that, without any intervention, threads can concurrently execute critical sections where shared writeable data (shared state) is being worked upon. To defeat concurrency, we need to get rid of parallelism, and we need to *serialize* code that's within the critical section – the place where the shared data is being worked upon (for reading and/or writing).

To force a code path to become serialized, a common technique is to use a **lock**. Essentially, a lock works by guaranteeing that precisely one thread of execution can "take" or own the lock at any given point in time. Thus, using a lock to protect a critical section in your code will give you what we're after – running the critical section's code exclusively (and perhaps atomically; more on this to come):

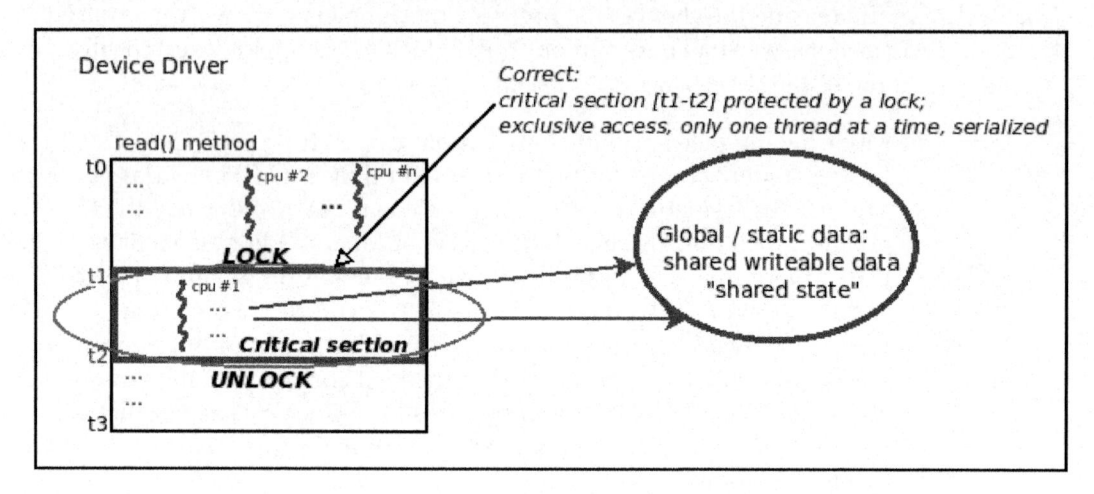

Figure 12.3 – A conceptual diagram showing how a critical section code path is honored, given exclusivity, by using a lock

The preceding diagram shows one way to fix the situation mentioned previously: using a lock to protect the critical section! How does the lock (and unlock) work, conceptually?

Chapter 12

The basic premise of a lock is that whenever there is contention for it – that is, when multiple competing threads (say, n threads) attempt to acquire the lock (the LOCK operation) – exactly one thread will succeed. This is called the "winner" or the "owner" of the lock. It sees the *lock* API as a non-blocking call and thus continues to run happily – and exclusively – while executing the code of the critical section (the critical section is effectively the code between the *lock* and the *unlock* operations!). What happens to the n-1 "loser" threads? They (perhaps) see the lock API as a blocking call; they, to all practical effect, wait. Wait upon what? The *unlock* operation, of course, which is performed by the owner of the lock (the "winner" thread)! Once unlocked, the remaining n-1 threads now compete for the next "winner" slot; of course, exactly one of them will "win" and proceed forward; in the interim, the n-2 losers will now wait upon the (new) winner's *unlock*; this repeats until all n threads (finally and sequentially) acquire the lock.

Now, locking works of course, but – and this should be quite intuitive – it results in (pretty steep!) **overhead, as it defeats parallelism and serializes** the execution flow! To help you visualize this situation, think of a funnel, with the narrow stem being the critical section where only one thread can fit at a time. All other threads get choked; locking creates bottlenecks:

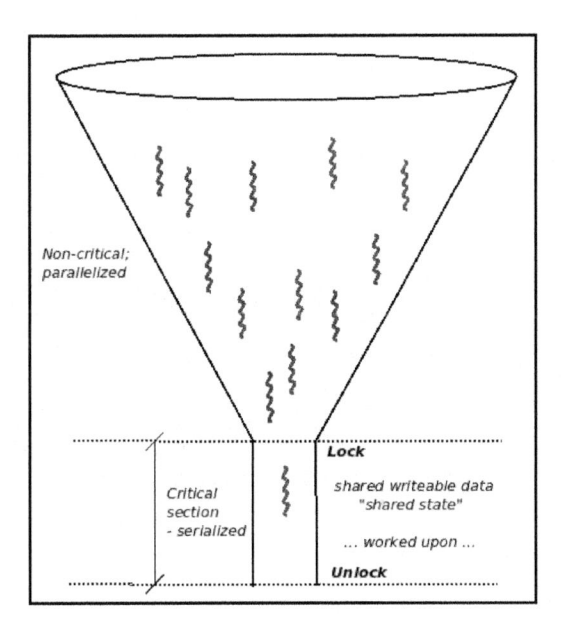

Figure 12.4 – A lock creates a bottleneck, analogous to a physical funnel

Kernel Synchronization - Part 1

Another oft-mentioned physical analog is a highway with several lanes merging into one very busy – and choked with traffic – lane (a poorly designed toll booth, perhaps). Again, parallelism – cars (threads) driving in parallel with other cars in different lanes (CPUs) – is lost, and serialized behavior is required – cars are forced to queue one behind the other.

Thus, it is imperative that we, as software architects, try and design our products/projects so that locking is minimally required. While completely eliminating global variables is not practically possible in most real-world projects, optimizing and minimizing their usage is required. We shall cover more regarding this, including some very interesting lockless programming techniques, later.

Another really key point is that a newbie programmer might naively assume that performing reads on a shared writeable data object is perfectly safe and thus requires no explicit protection (with the exception of an aligned primitive data type that is within the size of the processor's bus); this is untrue. This situation can lead to what's called **dirty or torn reads**, a situation where possibly stale data can be read as another writer thread is simultaneously writing while you are – incorrectly, without locking – reading the very same data item.

Since we're on the topic of atomicity, as we just learned, on a typical modern microprocessor, the only things guaranteed to be atomic are a single machine language instruction or a read/write to an aligned primitive data type within the processor bus's width. So, how can we mark a few lines of "C" code so that they're truly atomic? In user space, this isn't even possible (we can come close, but cannot guarantee atomicity).

> **TIP**: How do you "come close" to atomicity in user space apps? You can always construct a user thread to employ a SCHED_FIFO policy and a real-time priority of 99. This way, when it wants to run, pretty much nothing besides hardware interrupts/exceptions can preempt it. (The old audio subsystem implementation heavily relied on this.)

In kernel space, we can write code that's truly atomic. How, exactly? The short answer is that we can use spinlocks! We'll learn about spinlocks in more detail shortly.

A summary of key points

Let's summarize some key points regarding critical sections. It's really important to go over these carefully, keep these handy, and ensure you use them in practice:

- A **critical section** is a code path that can execute in parallel and that works upon (reads and/or writes) shared writeable data (also known as "shared state").
- Because it works on shared writable data, the critical section requires protection from the following:
    - Parallelism (that is, it must run alone/serialized/in a mutually exclusive fashion)
    - When running in an atomic (interrupt) non-blocking context – atomically: indivisibly, to completion, without interruption. Once protected, you can safely access your shared state until you "unlock".
- Every critical section in the code base must be identified and protected:
    - Identifying critical sections is critical! Carefully review your code and make sure you don't miss them.
    - Protecting them can be achieved via various technologies; one very common technique is *locking* (there's also lock-free programming, which we'll look at in the next chapter).
    - A common mistake is only protecting critical sections that *write* to global writeable data; you must also protect critical sections that *read* global writeable data; otherwise, you risk a **torn or dirty read!** To help make this key point clear, visualize an unsigned 64-bit data item being read and written on a 32-bit system; in such a case, the operation can't be atomic (two load/store operations are required). Thus, what if, while you're reading the value of the data item in one thread, it's being simultaneously written to by another thread!? The writer thread takes a "lock" of some sort but because you thought reading is safe, the lock isn't taken by the reader thread; due to an unfortunate timing coincidence, you can end up performing a partial/torn/dirty read! We will learn how to overcome these issues by using various techniques in the coming sections and the next chapter.
    - Another deadly mistake is not using the same lock to protect a given data item.

- Failing to protect critical sections leads to a **data race**, a situation where the outcome – the actual value of the data being read/written – is "racy", which means it varies, depending on runtime circumstances and timing. This is known as a bug. (A bug that, once in "the field", is extremely difficult to see, reproduce, determine its root cause, and fix. We will cover some very powerful stuff to help you with this in the next chapter, in the *Lock debugging within the kernel* section; be sure to read it!)
- **Exceptions**: You are safe (implicitly, without explicit protection) in the following situations:
    - When you are working on local variables. They're allocated on the private stack of the thread (or, in the interrupt context, on the local IRQ stack) and are thus, by definition, safe.
    - When you are working on shared writeable data in code that cannot possibly run in another context; that is, it's serialized by nature. In our context, the *init* and *cleanup* methods of an LKM qualify (they run exactly once, serially, on `insmod` and `rmmod` only).
    - When you are working on shared data that is truly constant and read-only (don't let C's `const` keyword fool you, though!).
- Locking is inherently complex; you must carefully think, design, and implement this to avoid *deadlocks*. We'll cover this in more detail in the *Locking guidelines and deadlocks* section.

Concurrency concerns within the Linux kernel

Recognizing critical sections within a piece of kernel code is of critical importance; how can you protect it if you can't even see it? The following are a few guidelines to help you, as a budding kernel/driver developer, recognize where concurrency concerns – and thus critical sections – may arise:

- The presence of **Symmetric Multi-Processor (SMP)** systems (`CONFIG_SMP`)
- The presence of a preemptible kernel
- Blocking I/O

- Hardware interrupts (on either SMP or UP systems)

These are critical points to understand, and we will discuss each in this section.

Multicore SMP systems and data races

The first point is pretty obvious; take a look at the pseudocode shown in the following screenshot:

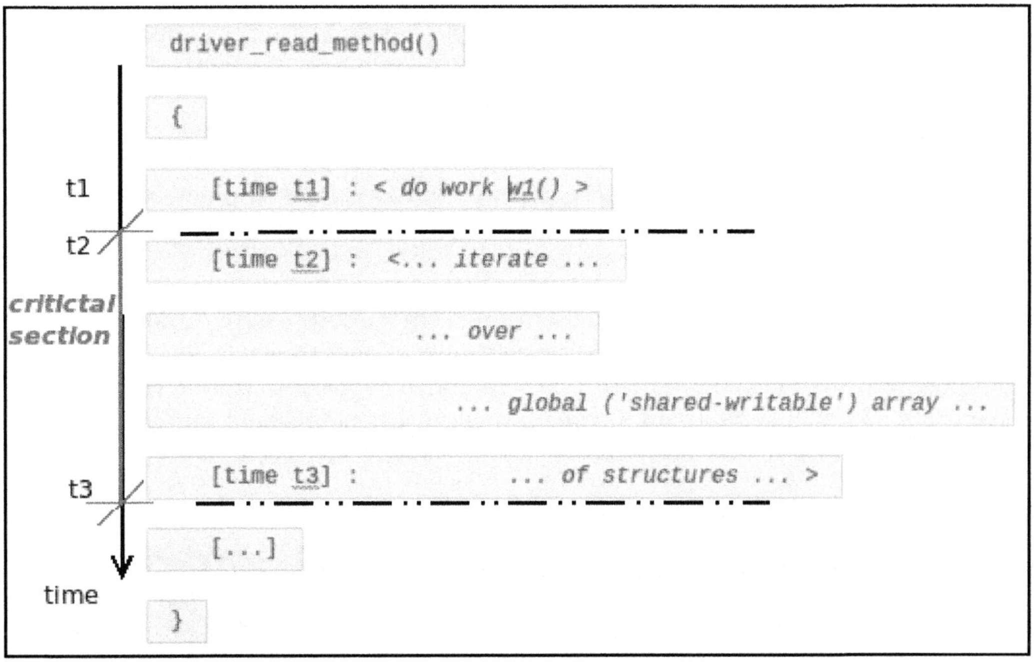

```
driver_read_method()
{
    [time t1] : < do work w1() >
    [time t2] : <... iterate ...
                        ... over ...
                        ... global ('shared-writable') array ...
    [time t3] :         ... of structures ... >
    [...]
}
```

t1
t2
critictal section
t3
time

Figure 12.5 – Pseudocode – a critical section within a (fictional) driver's read method; it's wrong as there's no locking

It's a similar situation to what we showed in *Figures 12.1* and *12.3*; it's just that here, we're showing the concurrency in terms of pseudocode. Clearly, from time `t2` to time `t3`, the driver is working on some global shared writeable data, thus making this a critical section.

[605]

Now, visualize a system with, say, four CPU cores (an SMP system); two user space processes, P1 (running on, say, CPU 0) and P2 (running on, say, CPU 2), can concurrently open the device file and simultaneously issue a `read(2)` system call. Now, both processes will be concurrently executing the driver read "method", thus simultaneously working on shared writeable data! This (the code between `t2` and `t3`) is a critical section, and since we are in violation of the fundamental exclusivity rule – critical sections must be executed by only a single thread at any point in time – we can very well end up corrupting the data, the application, or worse.

In other words, this is now a **data race**; depending on delicate timing coincidences, we may or may not generate an error (a bug). This very uncertainty – the delicate timing coincidence – is what makes finding and fixing errors like this extremely difficult (it can escape your testing effort).

> This aphorism is all too unfortunately true: *Testing can detect the presence of errors, not their absence.* Adding to this, you're worse off if your testing fails to catch races (and bugs), allowing them free rein in the field.

You might feel that since your product is a small embedded system running on one CPU core (UP), this discussion regarding controlling concurrency (often, via locking) does not apply to you. We beg to differ: pretty much all modern products, if they haven't already, will move to multicore (in their next-generation phases, perhaps). More importantly, even UP systems have concurrency concerns, as we shall explore.

Preemptible kernels, blocking I/O, and data races

Imagine you're running your kernel module or driver on a Linux kernel that's been configured to be preemptible (that is, `CONFIG_PREEMPT` is on; we covered this topic in Chapter 10, *The CPU Scheduler – Part 1*). Consider that a process, P1, is running the driver's read method code in the process context, working on the global array. Now, while it's within the critical section (between time `t2` and `t3`), what if the kernel *preempts* process P1 and context switches to another process, P2, which is just waiting to execute this very code path? It's dangerous, and again, a data race. This could well happen on even a UP system!

Another scenario that's somewhat similar (and again, could occur on either a single core (UP) or multicore system): process P1 is running through the critical section of the driver method (between time t2 and t3; again, see *Figure 12.5*). This time, what if, within the critical section, it hits a blocking call?

A **blocking call** is a function that causes the calling process context to be put to sleep, waiting upon an event; when that event occurs, the kernel will "wake up" the task, and it will resume execution from where it left off. This is also known as blocking on I/O and is very common; many APIs (including several user space library and system calls, as well as several kernel APIs, are blocking by nature). In such a case, process P1 is effectively context switches off the CPU and goes to sleep, which means that the code of schedule() runs and enqueues it onto a wait queue. In the interim, before P1 gets switched back, what if another process, P2, is scheduled to run? What if that process is also running this particular code path? Think about it – by the time P1 is back, the shared data could have changed "underneath it", causing all kinds of errors; again, a data race, a bug!

Hardware interrupts and data races

Finally, envision this scenario: process P1 is, again, innocently running the driver's read method code; it enters the critical section (between time t2 and t3; again, see *Figure 12.5*). It makes some progress but then, alas, a hardware interrupt triggers (on the same CPU)! (You will learn about it detail in *Linux Kernel Programming (Part 2)*.) On the Linux OS, hardware (peripheral) interrupts have the highest priority; they preempt any code (including kernel code) by default. Thus, process (or thread) P1 will be at least temporarily shelved, thus losing the processor; the interrupt handling code will preempt it and run.

Well, you might be wondering, so what? Indeed, this is a completely commonplace occurrence! Hardware interrupts fire very frequently on modern systems, effectively (and literally) interrupting all kinds of task contexts (do a quick vmstat 3 on your shell; the column under system labeled in shows the number of hardware interrupts that fired on your system in the last 1 second!). The key question to ask is this: is the interrupt handling code (either the hardirq top half or the so-called tasklet or softirq bottom half, whichever occurred), *sharing and working upon the same shared writable data of the process context that it just interrupted?*

If this is true, then, *Houston, we have a problem* – a data race! If not, then your interrupted code is not a critical section with respect to the interrupt code path, and that's fine. The fact is that the majority of device drivers do handle interrupt(s); thus, it is the driver author's (your!) responsibility to ensure that no global or static data – in effect, no critical sections – are shared between the process context and interrupt code paths. If they are (which does happen), you must somehow protect that data from data races and possible corruption.

These scenarios might leave you feeling that protecting against these concurrency concerns is a really tall order; how exactly can you accomplish data safety in the face of critical sections existing, along with various possible concurrency concerns? Interestingly, the actual APIs are not hard to learn to use; again, we emphasize that **recognizing critical sections** is the key thing to do.

> Again, the basics regarding how a lock (conceptually) works, locking guidelines (very important; we'll recap on them shortly), and the types of and how to prevent deadlocks, are all dealt with in my earlier book, *Hands-On System Programming with Linux (Packt, Oct 2018)*. This books covers these points in detail in *Chapter 15, Multithreading with Pthreads Part II – Synchronization*.

Without further ado, let's dive into the primary synchronization technology that will serve to protect our critical sections – locking.

Locking guidelines and deadlocks

Locking, by its very nature, is a complex beast; it tends to give rise to complex interlocking scenarios. Not understanding it well enough can lead to both performance headaches and bugs – deadlocks, circular dependencies, interrupt-unsafe locking, and more. The following locking guidelines are key to ensuring correctly written code when using locking:

- **Locking granularity**: The 'distance' between the lock and the unlock (in effect, the length of the critical section) should not be coarse (too long a critical section) it should be 'fine enough'; what does this mean? The points below explain this:
    - You need to be careful here. When you're working on large projects, keeping too few locks is a problem, as is keeping too many! Too few locks can lead to performance issues (as the same locks are repeatedly used and thus tend to be highly contended).

- Having a lot of locks is actually good for performance, but not good for complexity control. This also leads to another key point to understand: with many locks in the code base, you should be very clear on which lock protects which shared data object. It's completely meaningless if you use, say, lockA to protect mystructX, but in a code path far away (perhaps an interrupt handler) you forget this and try and use some other lock, lockB, for protection when working on the same structure! Right now, these things might sound obvious, but (as experienced developers know), under sufficient pressure, even the obvious isn't always obvious!
- Try and balance things out. In large projects, using one lock to protect one global (shared) data structure is typical. (*Naming* the lock variable well can become a big problem in itself! This is why we place the lock that protects a data structure within it as a member.)
- **Lock ordering** is critical; **locks must be taken in the same order throughout**, and their order should be documented and followed by all the developers working on the project (annotating locks is useful too; more on this in the section on *lockdep* in the next chapter). Incorrect lock ordering often leads to deadlocks.
- Avoid recursive locking as much as possible.
- Take care to prevent starvation; verify that a lock, once taken, is indeed released "quickly enough".
- **Simplicity is key**: Try to avoid complexity or over-design, especially with regard to complex scenarios involving locks.

On the topic of locking, the (dangerous) issue of deadlocks arises. A **deadlock** is the inability to make any progress; in other words, the app and/or kernel component(s) appear to hang indefinitely. While we don't intend to delve into the gory details of deadlocks here, I will quickly mention some of the more common types of deadlock scenarios that can occur:

- Simple case, single lock, process context:
    - We attempt to acquire the same lock twice; this results in a **self-deadlock**.

- Simple case, multiple (two or more) locks, process context – an example:
    - On CPU 0, thread A acquires lock A and then wants lock B.
    - Concurrently, on CPU 1, thread B acquires lock B and then wants lock A.
    - The result is a deadlock, often called the **AB-BA deadlock**.
    - It can be extended; for example, the AB-BC-CA **circular dependency** (A-B-C lock chain) results in a deadlock.
- Complex case, single lock, and process and interrupt contexts:
    - Lock A takes in an interrupt context.
    - What if an interrupt occurs (on another core) and the handler attempts to take lock A? Deadlock is the result! Thus, locks acquired in the interrupt context must always be used with interrupts disabled. (How? We will look at this in more detail when we cover spinlocks.)
- More complex cases, multiple locks, and process and interrupt (hardirq and softirq) contexts

In simpler cases, always following the *lock ordering guideline* is sufficient: always obtain and release locks in a well-documented order (we will provide an example of this in kernel code in the *Using the mutex lock* section). However, this can get very complex; complex deadlock scenarios can trip up even experienced developers. Luckily for us, **lockdep** – the Linux kernel's runtime lock dependency validator – can catch every single deadlock case! (Don't worry – we shall get there: we'll cover lockdep in detail in the next chapter). When we cover spinlocks (the *Using the spinlock* section), we'll come across process and/or interrupt context scenarios similar to the ones mentioned previously; the type of spinlock to use is made clear there.

With regard to deadlocks, a pretty detailed presentation on lockdep was given by Steve Rostedt at a Linux Plumber's Conference (back in 2011); the relevant slides are informative and explore both simple and complex deadlock scenarios, as well as how lockdep can detect them (`https://blog.linuxplumbersconf.org/2011/ocw/sessions/153`).

> Also, the reality is that not just deadlock, but even **livelock** situations, can be just as deadly! Livelock is essentially a situation similar to deadlock; it's just that the state of the participating task is running and not waiting. An example, an interrupt "storm" can cause a livelock; modern network drivers mitigate this effect by switching off interrupts (under interrupt load) and resorting to a polling technique called **New API; Switching Interrupts** (NAPI) (switching interrupts back on when appropriate; well, it's more complex than that, but we leave it at that here).

For those of you who've been living under a rock, you will know that the Linux kernel has two primary types of locks: the mutex lock and the spinlock. Actually, there are several more types, including other synchronization (and "lockless" programming) technology, all of which will be covered in the course of this chapter and the next.

Mutex or spinlock? Which to use when

The exact semantics of learning to use the mutex lock and the spinlock are quite simple (with appropriate abstraction within the kernel API set, making it even easier for the typical driver developer or module author). The critical question in this situation is a conceptual one: what really is the difference between the two locks? More to the point, under which circumstances should you use which lock? You will learn the answers to these questions in this section.

Kernel Synchronization - Part 1

Taking our previous driver read method's pseudocode (*Figure 12.5*) as a base example, let's say that three threads – **tA**, **tB**, and **tC** – are running in parallel (on an SMP system) through this code. We shall solve this concurrency issue, while avoiding any data races, by taking or acquiring a lock prior to the start of the critical section (time **t2**), and release the lock (unlock) just after the end of the critical section code path (time **t3**). Let's take a look at the pseudocode once more, this time with locking to ensure it's correct:

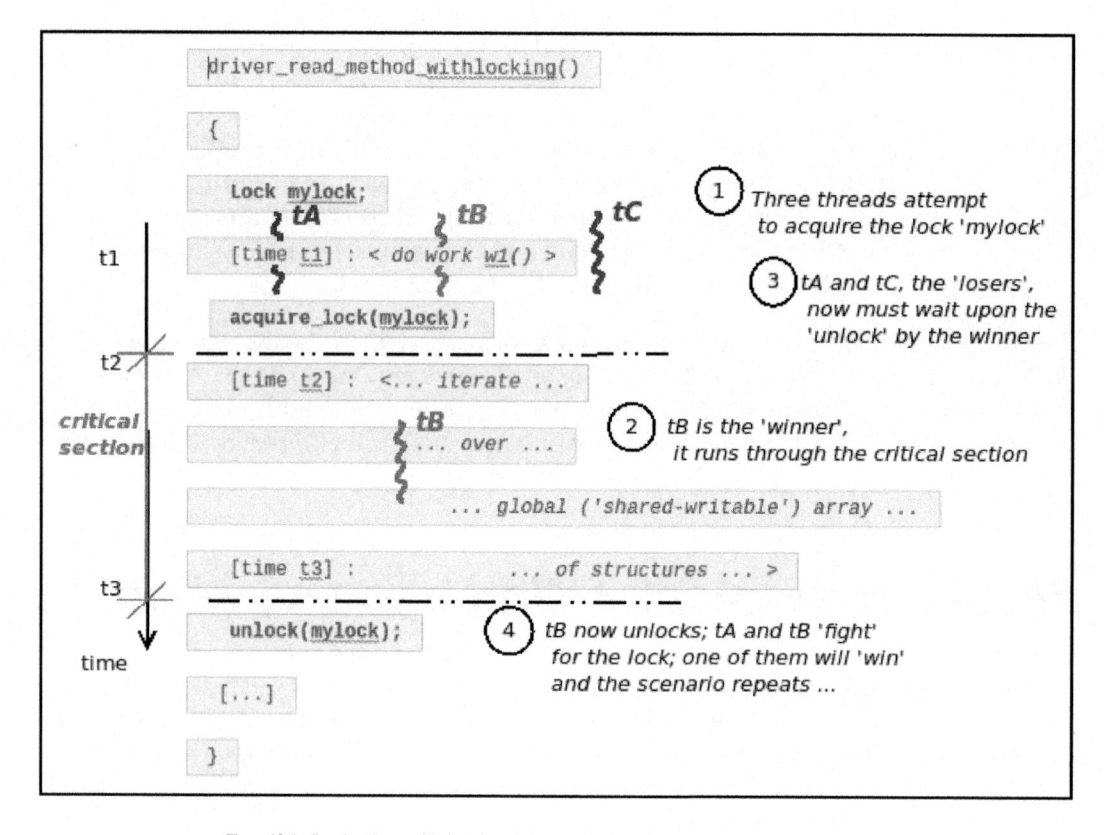

Figure 12.6 – Pseudocode – a critical section within a (fictional) driver's read method; correct, with locking

When the three threads attempt to simultaneously acquire the lock, the system guarantees that only exactly one of them will get it. Let's say that **tB** (thread B) gets the lock: it's now the "winner" or "owner" thread. This means that threads **tA** and **tC** are the "losers"; what do they do? They wait upon the unlock! The moment the "winner" (**tB**) completes the critical section and unlocks the lock, the battle resumes between the previous losers; one of them will be the next winner and the process repeats.

The key difference between the two lock types – the mutex and the spinlock – is based on how the losers wait upon the unlock. With the mutex lock, the loser threads are put to sleep; that is, they wait by sleeping. The moment the winner performs the unlock, the kernel awakens the losers (all of them) and they run, again competing for the lock. (In fact, mutexes and semaphores are sometimes referred to as sleeplocks.)

With the **spinlock**, however, there is no question of sleeping; the losers wait by spinning upon the lock until it is unlocked. Conceptually, this looks as follows:

```
while (locked) ;
```

Note that this is *only conceptual*. Think about it a moment – this is actually polling. However, as a good programmer, you will understand, that polling is usually considered a bad idea. Why, then, does the spinlock work this way? Well, it doesn't; it has only been presented in this manner for conceptual purposes. As you will soon understand, spinlocks only really have meaning on multicore (SMP) systems. On such systems, while the winner thread is away and running the critical section code, the losers wait by spinning on other CPU cores! In reality, at the implementation level, the code that's used to implement the modern spinlock is highly optimized (and arch-specific) and does not work by trivially "spinning" (for example, many spinlock implementations for ARM use the **wait for event** (WFE) machine language instruction, which has the CPU optimally wait in a low power state; see the *Further reading* section for several resources on the internal implementation of spinlocks).

Determining which lock to use – in theory

How the spinlock is implemented is really not our concern here; the fact that the spinlock has a lower overhead than the mutex lock is of interest to us. How so? It's simple, really: for the mutex lock to work, the loser thread has to go to sleep. To do so, internally, the `schedule()` function gets called, which means the loser sees the mutex lock API as a blocking call! A call to the scheduler will ultimately result in the processer being context-switched off. Conversely, when the owner thread unlocks the lock, the loser thread(s) must be woken up; again, it will be context-switched back onto the processor. Thus, the minimal "cost" of the mutex lock/unlock operation is the time it takes to perform two context switches on the given machine. (See the *Information Box* in the next section.) By relooking at the preceding screenshot once more, we can determine a few things, including the time spent in the critical section (the "locked" code path); that is, `t_locked = t3 - t2`.

Kernel Synchronization - Part 1

Let's say that `t_ctxsw` represents the time to context switch. As we've learned, the minimal cost of the mutex lock/unlock operation is `2 * t_ctxsw`. Now, let's say that the following expression is true:

```
t_locked < 2 * t_ctxsw
```

In other words, what if the time spent within the critical section is less than the time taken for two context switches? In this case, using the mutex lock is just wrong as this is far too much overhead; more time is being spent performing metawork than actual work – a phenomenon known as **thrashing**. It's this precise use case – the presence of very short critical sections – that's often the case on modern OSes such as Linux. So, in conclusion, for short non-blocking critical sections, using a spinlock is (far) superior to using a mutex lock.

Determining which lock to use – in practice

So, operating under the `t_locked < 2 * t_ctxsw` "rule" might be great in theory, but hang on: are you really expected to precisely measure the context switch time and the time spent in the critical section of each and every case where one (critical section) exists? No, of course not – that's pretty unrealistic and pedantic.

Practically speaking, think about it this way: the mutex lock works by having the loser threads sleep upon the unlock; the spinlock does not (the losers "spin"). Let's recall one of our golden rules of the Linux kernel: a kernel cannot sleep (call `schedule()`) in any kind of atomic context. Thus, we can never use the mutex lock in an interrupt context, or indeed in any context where it isn't safe to sleep; using the spinlock, however, would be fine. (Remember, a blocking API is one that puts the calling context to sleep by calling `schedule()`.) Let's summarize this:

- **Is the critical section running in an atomic (interrupt) context, or, in a process context, where it cannot sleep?** Use the spinlock.
- **Is the critical section running in a process context and sleep in the critical section is necessary?** Use the mutex lock.

Of course, using the spinlock is considered lower overhead than using the mutex; thus, you can even use the spinlock in the process context (such as our fictional driver's read method), as long as the critical section does not block (sleep).

> [1] The time taken for a context switch is varied; it largely depends on the hardware and the OS quality. Recent (September 2018) measurements show that context switching time is in the region of 1.2 to 1.5 **us (microseconds)** on a pinned-down CPU, and around 2.2 us without pinning (https://eli.thegreenplace.net/2018/measuring-context-switching-and-memory-overheads-for-linux-threads/).
>
> Both hardware and the Linux OS have improved tremendously, and because of that, so has the average context switching time. An old (December 1998) Linux Journal article determined that on an x86 class system, the average context switch time was 19 us (microseconds), and that the worst-case time was 30 us.

This brings up the question, how do we know if the code is currently running in a process or interrupt context? Easy: our PRINT_CTX() macro (within our convenient.h header) shows us this:

```
if (in_task())
    /* we're in process context (usually safe to sleep / block) */
else
    /* we're in an atomic or interrupt context (cannot sleep / block)
*/
```

(The details of our PRINT_CTX() macro's implementation are covered in *Linux Kernel Programming (Part 2)*).

Now that you understand which one – mutex or spinlock – to use and when, let's get into the actual usage. We'll begin with how to use the mutex lock!

Using the mutex lock

Mutexes are also called sleepable or blocking mutual exclusion locks. As you have learned, they are used in the process context if the critical section can sleep (block). They must not be used within any kind of atomic or interrupt context (top halves, bottom halves such as tasklets or softirqs, and so on), kernel timers, or even the process context where blocking is not allowed.

Initializing the mutex lock

A mutex lock "object" is represented in the kernel as a `struct mutex` data structure. Consider the following code:

```
#include <linux/mutex.h>
struct mutex mymtx;
```

To use a mutex lock, it *must* be explicitly initialized to the unlocked state. Initialization can be performed statically (declare and initialize the object) with the `DEFINE_MUTEX()` macro, or dynamically via the `mutex_init()` function (this is actually a macro wrapper over the `__mutex_init()` function).

For example, to declare and initialize a mutex object called `mymtx`, we can use `DEFINE_MUTEX(mymtx);`.

We can also do this dynamically. Why dynamically? Often, the mutex lock is a member of the (global) data structure that it protects (clever!). For example, let's say we have the following global context structure in our driver code (note that this code is fictional):

```
struct mydrv_priv {
    <member 1>;
    <member 2>;
    [...]
    struct mutex mymtx; /* protects access to mydrv_priv */
    [...]
};
```

Then, in your driver's (or LKM's) `init` method, do the following:

```
static int init_mydrv(struct mydrv_priv *drvctx)
{
    [...]
    mutex_init(drvctx->mymtx);
    [...]
}
```

Keeping the lock variable as a member of the (parent) data structure it protects is a common (and clever) pattern that's used within Linux; this approach has the added benefit of avoiding namespace pollution and is unambiguous about which mutex protects which shared data item (a bigger problem than it might appear to be at first, especially in enormous projects such as the Linux kernel!).

> Keep the lock protecting a global or shared data structure as a member within that data structure.

Correctly using the mutex lock

Typically, you can find very insightful comments within the kernel source tree. Here's a great one that neatly summarizes the rules you must follow to correctly use a mutex lock; please read this carefully:

```
// include/linux/mutex.h
/*
 * Simple, straightforward mutexes with strict semantics:
 *
 * - only one task can hold the mutex at a time
 * - only the owner can unlock the mutex
 * - multiple unlocks are not permitted
 * - recursive locking is not permitted
 * - a mutex object must be initialized via the API
 * - a mutex object must not be initialized via memset or copying
 * - task may not exit with mutex held
 * - memory areas where held locks reside must not be freed
 * - held mutexes must not be reinitialized
 * - mutexes may not be used in hardware or software interrupt
 * contexts such as tasklets and timers
 *
 * These semantics are fully enforced when DEBUG_MUTEXES is
 * enabled. Furthermore, besides enforcing the above rules, the mutex
 * [ ... ]
```

As a kernel developer, you must understand the following:

- A critical section causes the code path *to be serialized, defeating parallelism*. Due to this, it's imperative that you keep the critical section as short as possible. A corollary to this is **lock data, not code**.
- Attempting to reacquire an already acquired (locked) mutex lock – which is effectively recursive locking – is *not* supported and will lead to a self-deadlock.

- **Lock ordering**: This is a very important rule of thumb for preventing dangerous deadlock situations. In the presence of multiple threads and multiple locks, it is critical that *the order in which locks are taken is documented and strictly followed by all the developers working on the project*. The actual lock ordering itself isn't sacrosanct, but the fact that once it's been decided on it must be followed, is. While browsing through the kernel source tree, you will come across many places where the kernel developers ensure this is done, and they (usually) write a comment regarding this for other developers to see and follow. Here's a sample comment from the slab allocator code (mm/slub.c):

```
/*
 * Lock order:
 *   1. slab_mutex (Global Mutex)
 *   2. node->list_lock
 *   3. slab_lock(page) (Only on some arches and for debugging)
```

Now that we understand how mutexes work from a conceptual standpoint (and we understand their initialization), let's learn how to make use of the lock/unlock APIs.

Mutex lock and unlock APIs and their usage

The actual locking and unlocking APIs for the mutex lock are as follows. The following code shows how to lock and unlock a mutex, respectively:

```
void __sched mutex_lock(struct mutex *lock);
void __sched mutex_unlock(struct mutex *lock);
```

(Ignore __sched here; it's just a compiler attribute that has this function disappear in the WCHAN output, which shows up in procfs and with certain option switches to ps(1) (such as -l)).

Again, the comments within the source code in kernel/locking/mutex.c are very detailed and descriptive; I encourage you to take a look at this file in more detail. We've only shown some of its code here, which has been taken directly from the 5.4 Linux kernel source tree:

```
// kernel/locking/mutex.c
[ ... ]
/**
 * mutex_lock - acquire the mutex
 * @lock: the mutex to be acquired
 *
 * Lock the mutex exclusively for this task. If the mutex is not
```

```
 * available right now, it will sleep until it can get it.
 *
 * The mutex must later on be released by the same task that
 * acquired it. Recursive locking is not allowed. The task
 * may not exit without first unlocking the mutex. Also, kernel
 * memory where the mutex resides must not be freed with
 * the mutex still locked. The mutex must first be initialized
 * (or statically defined) before it can be locked. memset()-ing
 * the mutex to 0 is not allowed.
 *
 * (The CONFIG_DEBUG_MUTEXES .config option turns on debugging
 * checks that will enforce the restrictions and will also do
 * deadlock debugging)
 *
 * This function is similar to (but not equivalent to) down().
 */
void __sched mutex_lock(struct mutex *lock)
{
    might_sleep();

    if (!__mutex_trylock_fast(lock))
        __mutex_lock_slowpath(lock);
}
EXPORT_SYMBOL(mutex_lock);
```

`might_sleep()` is a macro with an interesting debug property; it catches code that's supposed to execute in an atomic context but doesn't! (Explanation for `might_sleep()` can be found in the *Linux Kernel Programming (Part 2)* book). So, think about it: `might_sleep()`, which is the first line of code in `mutex_lock()`, implies that this code path should not be executed by anything that's in an atomic context since it might sleep. This means that you should only use the mutex in the process context when it's safe to sleep!

> **A quick and important reminder**: The Linux kernel can be configured with a large number of debug options; in this context, the `CONFIG_DEBUG_MUTEXES` config option will help you catch possible mutex-related bugs, including deadlocks. Similarly, under the **Kernel Hacking** menu, you will find a large number of debug-related kernel config options. We discussed this in Chapter 5, *Writing Your First Kernel Module – LKMs Part 2*. There are several very useful kernel configs with regard to lock debugging; we shall cover these in the next chapter, in the *Lock debugging within the kernel* section.

Kernel Synchronization - Part 1

Mutex lock – via [un]interruptible sleep?

As usual, there's more to the mutex than what we've seen so far. You already know that a Linux process (or thread) cycles through various states of a state machine. On Linux, sleeping has two discrete states – an interruptible sleep and an uninterruptible sleep. A process (or thread) in an interruptible sleep is sensitive, which means it will respond to user space signals, whereas a task in an uninterruptible sleep is not sensitive to user signals.

In a human-interactive application with an underlying driver, as a general rule of thumb, you should typically put a process into an interruptible sleep (while it's blocking upon the lock), thus leaving it up to the end user as to whether to abort the application by pressing *Ctrl + C* (or some such mechanism involving signals). There is a design rule that's often followed on Unix-like systems: **provide mechanism, not policy**. Having said this, on non-interactive code paths, it's often the case that you must wait on the lock to wait indefinitely, with the semantic that a signal that's been delivered to the task should not abort the blocking wait. On Linux, the uninterruptible case turns out to be the most common one.

So, here's the thing: the `mutex_lock()` API always puts the calling task into an uninterruptible sleep. If this is not what you want, use the `mutex_lock_interruptible()` API to put the calling task into an interruptible sleep. There is one difference syntax-wise; the latter returns an integer value of `0` on success and `-EINTR` (remember the 0/-E return convention) on failure (due to signal interruption).

In general, using `mutex_lock()` is faster than using `mutex_lock_interruptible()`; use it when the critical section is short (thus pretty much guaranteeing that the lock is held for a short while, which is a very desirable characteristic).

> The 5.4.0 kernel contains over 18,500 and just over 800 instances of calling the `mutex_lock()` and `mutex_lock_interruptible()` APIs, respectively; you can check this out via the powerful `cscope(1)` utility on the kernel source tree.

[620]

In theory, the kernel provides a `mutex_destroy()` API as well. This is the opposite of `mutex_init()`; its job is to mark the mutex as being unusable. It must only be invoked once the mutex is in the unlocked state, and once invoked, the mutex cannot be used. This is a bit theoretical because, on regular systems, it just reduces to an empty function; only on a kernel with `CONFIG_DEBUG_MUTEXES` enabled does it become actual (simple) code. Thus, we should use this pattern when working with the mutex, as shown in the following pseudocode:

```
DEFINE_MUTEX(...);          // init: initialize the mutex object
/* or */ mutex_init();
[ ... ]
    /* critical section: perform the (mutex) locking, unlocking */
    mutex_lock[_interruptible]();
    << ... critical section ... >>
    mutex_unlock();
    mutex_destroy();        // cleanup: destroy the mutex object
```

Now that you have learned how to use the mutex lock APIs, let's put this knowledge to use. In the next section, we will build on top of one of our earlier (poorly written – no protection!) "misc" drivers by employing the mutex object to lock critical sections as required.

Mutex locking – an example driver

We have created a simple device driver code example in the Linux Kernel Programming (Part 2) book in the *Writing a Simple misc Character Device Driver* chapter; that is, `miscdrv_rdwr`. There, we wrote a simple `misc` class character device driver and used a user space utility program (`miscdrv_rdwr/rdwr_drv_secret.c`) to read and write a (so-called) secret from and to the device driver's memory.

However, what we glaringly (egregiously is the right word here!) failed to do in that code is protect shared (global) writeable data! This will cost us dearly in the real world. I urge you to take some time to think about this: it isn't viable that two (or three or more) user mode processes open the device file of this driver, and then concurrently issue various I/O reads and writes. Here, the global shared writable data (in this particular case, two global integers and the driver context data structure) could easily get corrupted.

Kernel Synchronization - Part 1

So, let's learn from and correct our mistakes by making a copy of this driver (we will now call it `ch12/1_miscdrv_rdwr_mutexlock/1_miscdrv_rdwr_mutexlock.c`) and rewriting some portions of it. The key point is that we must use mutex locks to protect all critical sections. Instead of displaying the code here (it's in this book's GitHub repository at `https://github.com/PacktPublishing/Linux-Kernel-Programming`, after all, please do `git clone` it!), let's do something interesting: let's look at a "diff" (the differences – the delta generated by `diff(1)`) between the older unprotected version and the newer protected code version. The output here has been truncated:

```
$ pwd
<...>/ch12/1_miscdrv_rdwr_mutexlock
$ diff -u ../../ch12/miscdrv_rdwr/miscdrv_rdwr.c
miscdrv_rdwr_mutexlock.c > miscdrv_rdwr.patch
$ cat miscdrv_rdwr.patch
[ ... ]
+#include <linux/mutex.h> // mutex lock, unlock, etc
 #include "../../convenient.h"
[ ... ]
-#define OURMODNAME "miscdrv_rdwr"
+#define OURMODNAME "miscdrv_rdwr_mutexlock"

+DEFINE_MUTEX(lock1); // this mutex lock is meant to protect the
integers ga and gb
[ ... ]
+    struct mutex lock; // this mutex protects this data structure
 };
[ ... ]
```

Here, we can see that in the newer safe version of the driver, we have declared and initialized a mutex variable called `lock1`; we shall use it to protect the (just for demonstration purposes) two global integers, `ga` and `gb`, within our driver. Next, importantly, we declared a mutex lock named `lock` within the "driver context" data structure; that is, `drv_ctx`. This will be used to protect any and all access to members of that data structure. It is initialized within the `init` code:

```
+       mutex_init(&ctx->lock);
+
+       /* Initialize the "secret" value :-) */
        strscpy(ctx->oursecret, "initmsg", 8);
-       dev_dbg(ctx->dev, "A sample print via the dev_dbg(): driver
initialized\n");
+       /* Why don't we protect the above strscpy() with the mutex lock?
+        * It's working on shared writable data, yes?
+        * Yes, BUT this is the init code; it's guaranteed to run in
exactly
```

```
+            * one context (typically the insmod(8) process), thus there is
+            * no concurrency possible here. The same goes for the cleanup
+            * code path.
+            */
```

This detailed comment clearly explains why we don't need to lock/unlock around `strscpy()`. Again, this should be obvious, but local variables are implicitly private to each process context (as they reside in that process or thread's kernel mode stack) and therefore require no protection (each thread/process has a separate *instance* of the variable, so no one steps on anyone's toes!). Before we forget, the *cleanup* code path (which is invoked via the `rmmod(8)` process context), must destroy the mutexes:

```
-static void __exit miscdrv_rdwr_exit(void)
+static void __exit miscdrv_exit_mutexlock(void)
 {
+       mutex_destroy(&lock1);
+       mutex_destroy(&ctx->lock);
        misc_deregister(&llkd_miscdev);
 }
```

Now, let's look at the diff of the driver's open method:

```
+
+        mutex_lock(&lock1);
+        ga++; gb--;
+        mutex_unlock(&lock1);
+
+        dev_info(dev, " filename: \"%s\"\n"
         [ ... ]
```

This is where we manipulated the global integers, *making this a critical section*; unlike the previous version of this program (in *Linux Kernel Programming (Part 2)*), here, we *do protect this critical section* with the `lock1` mutex. So, there it is: the critical section here is the code `ga++; gb--;`: the code between the (mutex) lock and unlock operations.

But (there's always a but, isn't there?), all is not well! Take a look at the `printk` function (`dev_info()`) following the `mutex_unlock()` line of code:

```
+    dev_info(dev, " filename: \"%s\"\n"
+         " wrt open file: f_flags = 0x%x\n"
+         " ga = %d, gb = %d\n",
+         filp->f_path.dentry->d_iname, filp->f_flags, ga, gb);
```

Does this look okay to you? No, look carefully: we are *reading* the value of the global integers, `ga` and `gb`. Recall the fundamentals: in the presence of concurrency (which is certainly a possibility here in this driver's *open* method), *even reading shared writeable data without the lock is potentially unsafe*. If this doesn't make sense to you, please think: what if, while one thread is reading the integers, another is simultaneously updating (writing) them; what then? This kind of situation is called a **dirty read** (or a **torn read**); we might end up reading stale data and must be protected against. (The fact is that this isn't really a great example of a dirty read as, on most processors, reading and writing single integer items does tend to be an atomic operation. However, we must not assume such things – we must simply do our job and protect it.)

In fact, there's another similar bug-in-waiting: we have read data from the open file structure (the `filp` pointer) without bothering to protect it (indeed, the open file structure has a lock; we're supposed to use it! We shall do so later).

> The precise semantics of how and when things such as *dirty reads* occur does tend to be very arch (machine)-dependent; nevertheless, our job as module or driver authors is clear: we must ensure that we protect all critical sections. This includes reads upon shared writable data.

For now, we shall just flag these as potential errors (bugs). We will take care of this in the *Using the atomic integer operators* section, in a more performance-friendly manner. Looking at the diff of the driver's read method reveals something interesting (ignore the line numbers shown here; they might change):

```
 static ssize_t read_miscdrv_rdwr(struct file *filp, char __user *ubuf,
-                                 size_t count, loff_t *off)
+                                 size_t count, loff_t *off)
 {
-    int ret = count, secret_len = strnlen(ctx->oursecret, MAXBYTES);
+    int ret = count, secret_len;
     struct device *dev = ctx->dev;
+
+    mutex_lock(&ctx->lock);
+    secret_len = strlen(ctx->oursecret);
+    mutex_unlock(&ctx->lock);
+
     PRINT_CTX();
     dev_info(dev, "%s wants to read (upto) %zd bytes\n", current->comm, count);
@@ -134,17 +140,20 @@
      * member to userspace.
      */
     ret = -EFAULT;
+    mutex_lock(&ctx->lock);
     if (copy_to_user(ubuf, ctx->oursecret, secret_len)) {
         dev_warn(dev, "copy_to_user() failed\n");
-        goto out_notok;
+        goto out_ctu;
     }
     ret = secret_len;

     // Update stats
-    ctx->tx += secret_len; // our 'transmit' is wrt this driver
+    ctx->tx += secret_len; // our 'transmit' is wrt this driver
     dev_info(dev, " %d bytes read, returning... (stats: tx=%d, rx=%d)\n",
-        secret_len, ctx->tx, ctx->rx);
- out_notok:
+            secret_len, ctx->tx, ctx->rx);
+out_ctu:
+    mutex_unlock(&ctx->lock);
+out_notok:
     return ret;
```

Figure 12.7 – The diff of the driver's read() method; see the usage of the mutex lock in the newer version

We have now used the driver context structure's mutex lock to protect the critical sections. The same goes for both the *write* and *close* (release) methods of the device driver (generate the patch for yourself and take a look).

Note that the user mode app remains unchanged, which means for us to test the new safer version, we must continue using the user mode app at `ch12/miscdrv_rdwr/rdwr_drv_secret.c`. Running and testing code such as this driver code on a debug kernel, which contains various locking errors and deadlock detection capabilities, is crucial (we'll return to these "debug" capabilities in the next chapter, in the *Lock debugging within the kernel* section).

In the preceding code, we took the mutex lock just before the `copy_to_user()` routine; that's fine. However, we only release it after `dev_info()`. Why not release it before this `printk`, thus shortening the critical section?

A closer look at `dev_info()` reveals why it's *within* the critical section. We are printing the values of three variables here: the number of bytes read by `secret_len` and the number of bytes that are "transmitted" and "received" by `ctx->tx` and `ctx->rx`, respectively. `secret_len` is a local variable and does not require protection, but the other two variables are within the global driver context structure and thus do require protection, even from (possibly dirty) reads.

The mutex lock – a few remaining points

In this section, we will cover a few additional points regarding mutexes.

Mutex lock API variants

First, let's take a look at a few variants of the mutex lock API; besides the interruptible variant (described in the *Mutex lock – via [un]interruptible sleep?* section), we have the *trylock*, *killable*, and *io* variants.

The mutex trylock variant

What if you would like to implement a **busy-wait** semantic; that is, test for the availability of the (mutex) lock and, if available (meaning it's currently unlocked), acquire/lock it and continue with the critical section code path? If this is not available (it's currently in the locked state), do not wait for the lock; instead, perform some other work and retry. In effect, this is a non-blocking mutex lock variant and is called the trylock; the following flowchart shows how it works:

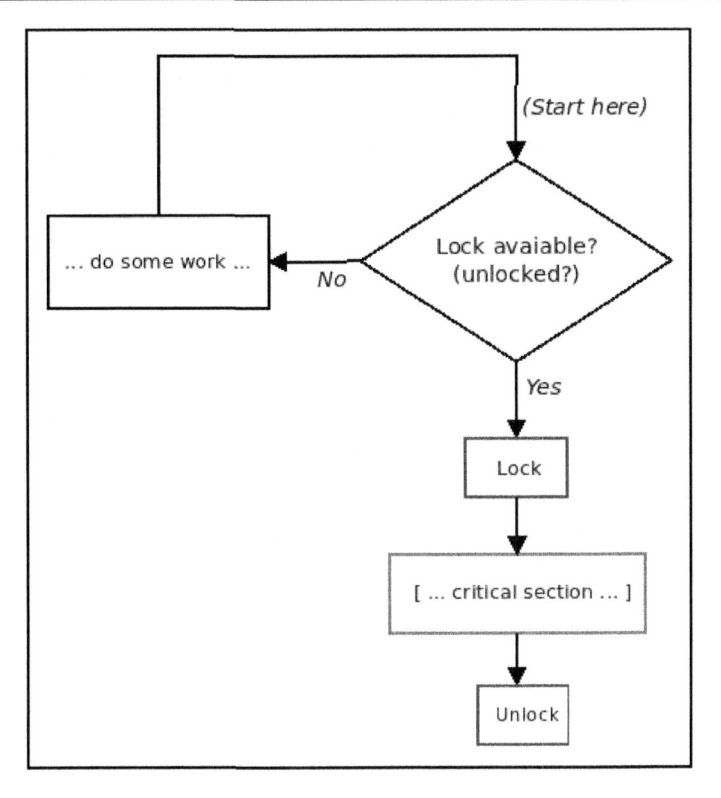

Figure 12.8 – The "busy wait" semantic, a non-blocking trylock operation

The API for this trylock variant of the mutex lock is as follows:

```
int mutex_trylock(struct mutex *lock);
```

This API's return value signifies what transpired at runtime:

- A return value of 1 indicates that the lock has been successfully acquired.
- A return value of 0 indicates that the lock is currently contended (locked).

> **TIP**
> Though it might sound tempting to, do *not* attempt to use the `mutex_trylock()` API to figure out if a mutex lock is in a locked or unlocked state; this is inherently "racy". Next, note that using this trylock variant in a highly contended lock path may well reduce your chances of acquiring the lock. The trylock variant has been traditionally used in deadlock prevention code that might need to back out of a certain lock order sequence and be retried via another sequence (ordering).

Also, with respect to the trylock variant, even though the literature uses the term *try and acquire the mutex atomically*, it does not work in an atomic or interrupt context – it *only* works in the process context (as with any type of mutex lock). As usual, the lock must be released by `mutex_unlock()` being invoked by the owner context.

I suggest that you try working on the trylock mutex variant as an exercise. See the *Questions* section at the end of this chapter for an assignment!

The mutex interruptible and killable variants

As you have already learned, the `mutex_lock_interruptible()` API is used when the driver (or module) is willing to acknowledge any (user space) signal interrupting it (and returns `-ERESTARTSYS` to tell the kernel VFS layer to perform signal handling; the user space system call will fail with `errno` set to `EINTR`). An example can be found in the module handling code in the kernel, within the `delete_module(2)` system call (which `rmmod(8)` invokes):

```
// kernel/module.c
[ ... ]
SYSCALL_DEFINE2(delete_module, const char __user *, name_user,
        unsigned int, flags)
{
    struct module *mod;
    [ ... ]
    if (!capable(CAP_SYS_MODULE) || modules_disabled)
        return -EPERM;
    [ ... ]
    if (mutex_lock_interruptible(&module_mutex) != 0)
        return -EINTR;
    mod = find_module(name);
    [ ... ]
out:
    mutex_unlock(&module_mutex);
    return ret;
}
```

Notice how the API returns `-EINTR` on failure. (The `SYSCALL_DEFINEn()` macro becomes a system call signature; n signifies the number of parameters this particular system call accepts. Also, notice the capability check – unless you are running as root or have the `CAP_SYS_MODULE` capability (or module loading is completely disabled), the system call just returns a failure (`-EPERM`).)

If, however, your driver is only willing to be interrupted by fatal signals (those that *will kill* the user space context), then use the `mutex_lock_killable()` API (the signature is identical to that of the interruptible variant).

The mutex io variant

The `mutex_lock_io()` API is identical in syntax to the `mutex_lock()` API; the only difference is that the kernel thinks that the wait time of the loser thread(s) is the same as waiting for I/O (the code comment in `kernel/locking/mutex.c:mutex_lock_io()` clearly documents this; take a look). This can matter accounting-wise.

> You can find fairly exotic APIs such as `mutex_lock[_interruptible]_nested()` within the kernel, with the emphasis here being on the `nested` suffix. However, note that the Linux kernel does not prefer developers to use nested (or recursive) locking (as we mentioned in the *Correctly using the mutex lock* section). Also, these APIs only get compiled in the presence of the `CONFIG_DEBUG_LOCK_ALLOC` config option; in effect, the nested APIs were added to support the kernel lock validator mechanism. They should only be used in special circumstances (where a nesting level must be incorporated between instances of the same lock type).

In the next section, we will answer a typical FAQ: what's the difference between the mutex and semaphore objects? Does Linux even have a semaphore object? Read on to find out!

The semaphore and the mutex

The Linux kernel does provide a semaphore object, along with the usual operations you can perform on a (binary) semaphore:

- A semaphore lock acquire via the `down[_interruptible]()` (and variations) APIs
- A semaphore unlock via the `up()` API.

> In general, the semaphore is an older implementation, so it's advised that you use the mutex lock in place of it.

An FAQ worth looking at, though, is this: *what is the difference between a mutex and a semaphore?* They appear to be conceptually similar, but are actually quite different:

- A semaphore is a more generalized form of a mutex; a mutex lock can be acquired (and subsequently released or unlocked) exactly once, while a semaphore can be acquired (and subsequently released) multiple times.
- A mutex is used to protect a critical section from simultaneous access, while a semaphore should be used as a mechanism to signal another waiting task that a certain milestone has been reached (typically, a producer task posts a signal via the semaphore object, which a consumer task is waiting to receive, in order to continue with further work).
- A mutex has the notion of ownership of the lock and only the owner context can perform the unlock; there is no ownership for a binary semaphore.

Priority inversion and the RT-mutex

A word of caution when using any kind of locking is that you should carefully design and code to prevent the dreaded *deadlock* scenarios that could arise (more on this in the next chapter in the *The lock validator lockdep – catch locking issues early* section).

Aside from deadlocks, there is another risky scenario that arises when using the mutex: that of priority inversion (again, we will not delve into the details in this book). Suffice it to say that the unbounded **priority inversion** case can be a deadly one; the end result is that the product's high(est) priority thread is kept off the CPU for too long.

> As I covered in some detail in my earlier book, *Hands-on System Programming with Linux*, it's precisely this priority inversion issue that struck NASA's Mars Pathfinder robot, on the Martian surface no less, back in July 1997! See the *Further reading* section of this chapter for interesting resources about this, something that every software developer should be aware of!

Chapter 12

The userspace Pthreads mutex implementation certainly has **priority inheritance** (**PI**) semantics available. But what about within the Linux kernel? For this, Ingo Molnar provided the PI-futex-based RT-mutex (a real-time mutex; in effect, a mutex extended to have PI capabilities. `futex(2)` is a sophisticated system call that provides a fast userspace mutex). These become available when the `CONFIG_RT_MUTEXES` config option is enabled. Quite similar to the "regular" mutex semantics, RT-mutex APIs are provided to initialize, (un)lock, and destroy the RT-mutex object. (This code has been merged into the mainline kernel from Ingo Molnar's `-rt` tree). As far as actual usage is concerned, the RT-mutex is used for internally implementing the PI futex (the `futex(2)` system call itself internally implements the userspace Pthreads mutex). Besides this, the kernel locking self-test code and the I2C subsystem uses the RT-mutex directly.

Thus, for a typical module (or driver) author, these APIs are not going to be used very frequently. The kernel does provide some documentation on the internal design of the RT-mutex at `https://www.kernel.org/doc/Documentation/locking/rt-mutex-design.rst` (covering priority inversion, priority inheritance, and more).

Internal design

A word on the reality of the internal implementation of the mutex lock deep within the kernel fabric: Linux tries to implement a *fast path* approach when possible.

> A **fast path** is the most optimized high-performance type of code path; for example, one with no locks and no blocking. The intent is to have code follow this fast path as far as possible. Only when it really isn't possible does the kernel fall back to a (possible) "mid path", and then a "slow path", approach; it still works but is slow(er).

This fast path is taken in the absence of contention for the lock (that is, the lock is in an unlocked state to begin with). So, the lock is locked with no fuss, pretty much immediately. If, however, the mutex is already locked, then the kernel typically uses a mid path optimistic spinning implementation, making it more of a hybrid (mutex/spinlock) lock type. If even this isn't possible, the "slow path" is followed – the process context attempting to get the lock may well enter the sleep state. If you're interested in its internal implementation, more details can be found within the official kernel documentation: `https://www.kernel.org/doc/Documentation/locking/mutex-design.rst`.

LDV (Linux Driver Verification) project: back in `Chapter 1`, *Kernel Workspace Setup*, in the section *The LDV – Linux Driver Verification – project*, we mentioned that this project has useful "rules" with respect to various programming aspects of Linux modules (drivers, mostly) as well as the core kernel.

> With regard to our current topic, here's one of the rules: *Locking a mutex twice or unlocking without prior locking* (`http://linuxtesting.org/ldv/online?action=show_rulerule_id=0032`). It mentions the kind of things you cannot do with the mutex lock (we have already covered this in the *Correctly using the mutex lock* section). The interesting thing here: you can see an actual example of a bug – a mutex lock double-acquire attempt, leading to (self) deadlock – in a kernel driver (as well as the subsequent fix).

Now that you've understood how to use the mutex lock, let's move on and look at the other very common lock within the kernel – the spinlock.

Using the spinlock

In the *Mutex or spinlock? Which to use when* section, you learned when to use the spinlock instead of the mutex lock and vice versa. For convenience, we have reproduced the key statements we provided previously here:

- **Is the critical section running in an atomic (interrupt) context or in a process context where it cannot sleep?** Use the spinlock.
- **Is the critical section running in a process context and sleep in the critical section is necessary?** Use the mutex lock.

In this section, we shall consider that you've now decided to use the spinlock.

Spinlock – simple usage

For all the spinlock APIs, you must include the relevant header file; that is, `include <linux/spinlock.h>`.

Similar to the mutex lock, you *must* declare and initialize the spinlock to the unlocked state before use. The spinlock is an "object" that's declared via the `typedef` data type named `spinlock_t` (internally, it's a structure defined in `include/linux/spinlock_types.h`). It can be initialized dynamically via the `spin_lock_init()` macro:

```
spinlock_t lock;
spin_lock_init(&lock);
```

Alternatively, this can be performed statically (declared and initialized) with `DEFINE_SPINLOCK(lock);`.

As with the mutex, declaring a spinlock within the (global/static) data structure is meant to protect against concurrent access, and is typically a very good idea. As we mentioned earlier, this very idea is made use of within the kernel often; as an example, the data structure representing an open file on the Linux kernel is called `struct file`:

```
// include/linux/fs.h
struct file {
    [...]
    struct path f_path;
    struct inode *f_inode; /* cached value */
    const struct file_operations *f_op;
    /*
     * Protects f_ep_links, f_flags.
     * Must not be taken from IRQ context.
     */
    spinlock_t f_lock;
    [...]
    struct mutex f_pos_lock;
    loff_t f_pos;
    [...]
```

Check it out: for the `file` structure, the spinlock variable named `f_lock` is the spinlock that protects the `f_ep_links` and `f_flags` members of the `file` data structure (it also has a mutex lock to protect another member; that is, the file's current seek position – `f_pos`).

Kernel Synchronization - Part 1

How do you actually lock and unlock the spinlock? There are quite a few variations on the API that are exposed by the kernel to us module/driver authors; the simplest form of the spin(un)lock APIs are as folows:

```
void spin_lock(spinlock_t *lock);
<< ... critical section ... >>
void spin_unlock(spinlock_t *lock);
```

Note that there is no spinlock equivalent of the `mutex_destroy()` API.

Now, let's see the spinlock APIs in action!

Spinlock – an example driver

Similar to what we did with our mutex locking sample driver (the *Mutex locking – an example driver* section), to illustrate the simple usage of a spinlock, we shall make a copy of our earlier `ch12/1_miscdrv_rdwr_mutexlock` driver as a starting template and then place it in a new kernel driver; that is, `ch12/2_miscdrv_rdwr_spinlock`. Again, here, we'll only show small parts of the diff (the differences, the delta generated by `diff(1)`) between that program and this one (we won't show every line of the diff, only the relevant portions):

```
// location: ch12/2_miscdrv_rdwr_spinlock/
+#include <linux/spinlock.h>
[ ... ]
-#define OURMODNAME "miscdrv_rdwr_mutexlock"
+#define OURMODNAME "miscdrv_rdwr_spinlock"
[ ... ]
static int ga, gb = 1;
-DEFINE_MUTEX(lock1); // this mutex lock is meant to protect the
integers ga and gb
+DEFINE_SPINLOCK(lock1); // this spinlock protects the global integers
ga and gb
[ ... ]
+/* The driver 'context' data structure;
+ * all relevant 'state info' reg the driver is here.
  */
 struct drv_ctx {
     struct device *dev;
@@ -63,10 +66,22 @@
     u64 config3;
 #define MAXBYTES 128
     char oursecret[MAXBYTES];
- struct mutex lock; // this mutex protects this data structure
+ struct mutex mutex; // this mutex protects this data structure
```

```
+       spinlock_t spinlock; // ...so does this spinlock
   };
   static struct drv_ctx *ctx;
```

This time, to protect the members of our `drv_ctx` global data structure, we have both the original mutex lock and a new spinlock. This is quite common; the mutex lock protects member usage in a critical section where blocking can occur, while the spinlock is used to protect members in critical sections where blocking (sleeping – recall that it might sleep) cannot occur.

Of course, we must ensure that we initialize all the locks so that they're in the unlocked state. We can do this in the driver's `init` code (continuing with the patch output):

```
-       mutex_init(&ctx->lock);
+       mutex_init(&ctx->mutex);
+       spin_lock_init(&ctx->spinlock);
```

In the driver's `open` method, we replace the mutex lock with the spinlock to protect the increments and decrements of the global integers:

```
 * open_miscdrv_rdwr()
@@ -82,14 +97,15 @@

       PRINT_CTX(); // displays process (or intr) context info

-       mutex_lock(&lock1);
+       spin_lock(&lock1);
       ga++; gb--;
-       mutex_unlock(&lock1);
+       spin_unlock(&lock1);
```

Now, within the driver's `read` method, we use the spinlock instead of the mutex to protect some critical sections:

```
   static ssize_t read_miscdrv_rdwr(struct file *filp, char __user
   *ubuf, size_t count, loff_t *off)
   {
-       int ret = count, secret_len;
+       int ret = count, secret_len, err_path = 0;
       struct device *dev = ctx->dev;

-       mutex_lock(&ctx->lock);
+       spin_lock(&ctx->spinlock);
       secret_len = strlen(ctx->oursecret);
-       mutex_unlock(&ctx->lock);
+       spin_unlock(&ctx->spinlock);
```

[635]

However, that's not all! Continuing with the driver's `read` method, carefully take a look at the following code and comment:

```
[ ... ]
@@ -139,20 +157,28 @@
     * member to userspace.
     */
    ret = -EFAULT;
-   mutex_lock(&ctx->lock);
+   mutex_lock(&ctx->mutex);
+   /* Why don't we just use the spinlock??
+    * Because - VERY IMP! - remember that the spinlock can only be used when
+    * the critical section will not sleep or block in any manner; here,
+    * the critical section invokes the copy_to_user(); it very much can
+    * cause a 'sleep' (a schedule()) to occur.
+    */
    if (copy_to_user(ubuf, ctx->oursecret, secret_len)) {
[ ... ]
```

When protecting data where the critical section has possibly blocking APIs – such as in `copy_to_user()` – we *must* only use a mutex lock! (Due to lack of space, we haven't displayed more of the code diff here; we expect you to read through the spinlock sample driver code and try it out for yourself.)

Test – sleep in an atomic context

You have already learned that the one thing we should *not do is sleep (block) in any kind of atomic or interrupt context*. Let's put this to the test. As always, the empirical approach – where you test things for yourself rather than relying on other's experiences – is key!

How exactly can we test this? Easy: we shall use a simple integer module parameter, `buggy`, that, when set to 1 (the default value being 0), executes a code path within our spinlock's critical section that violates this rule. We shall invoke the `schedule_timeout()` API (which, as you learned in Chapter 15, *Timers, Kernel Threads, and More*, in the *Understanding how to use the *sleep() blocking APIs* section) internally invokes `schedule()`; it's how we go to sleep in the kernel space). Here's the relevant code:

```
// ch12/2_miscdrv_rdwr_spinlock/2_miscdrv_rdwr_spinlock.c
[ ... ]
```

[636]

```
static int buggy;
module_param(buggy, int, 0600);
MODULE_PARM_DESC(buggy,
"If 1, cause an error by issuing a blocking call within a spinlock
critical section");
[ ... ]
static ssize_t write_miscdrv_rdwr(struct file *filp, const char __user
*ubuf,
                size_t count, loff_t *off)
{
    int ret, err_path = 0;
    [ ... ]
    spin_lock(&ctx->spinlock);
    strscpy(ctx->oursecret, kbuf, (count > MAXBYTES ? MAXBYTES :
count));
    [ ... ]
    if (1 == buggy) {
        /* We're still holding the spinlock! */
        set_current_state(TASK_INTERRUPTIBLE);
        schedule_timeout(1*HZ); /* ... and this is a blocking call!
                 * Congratulations! you've just engineered a bug */
    }
    spin_unlock(&ctx->spinlock);
    [ ... ]
}
```

Now, for the interesting part: let's test this (buggy) code path in two kernels: first, in our custom 5.4 "debug" kernel (the kernel where we have enabled several kernel debug configuration options (mostly from the Kernel Hacking menu in make menuconfig), as explained back in Chapter 5, *Writing Your First Kernel Module – LKMs Part 2*), and second, on a generic distro (we usually run on Ubuntu) 5.4 kernel without any relevant kernel debug options enabled.

Testing on a 5.4 debug kernel

First of all, ensure you've built the custom 5.4 kernel and that all the required kernel debug config options enabled (again, look back to Chapter 5, *Writing Your First Kernel Module – LKMs Part 2*, the *Configuring a debug kernel* section if you need to). Then, boot off your debug kernel (here, it's named 5.4.0-llkd-dbg). Now, build the driver (in ch12/2_miscdrv_rdwr_spinlock/) against this debug kernel (the usual make within the driver's directory should do this; you might find that, on the debug kernel, the build is noticeably slower!):

```
$ lsb_release -a 2>/dev/null | grep "^Description" ; uname -r
Description:    Ubuntu 20.04.1 LTS
```

Kernel Synchronization - Part 1

```
5.4.0-llkd-dbg
$ make
[ ... ]
$ modinfo ./miscdrv_rdwr_spinlock.ko
filename:
/home/llkd/llkd_src/ch12/2_miscdrv_rdwr_spinlock/./miscdrv_rdwr_spinlock.ko
[ ... ]
description: LLKD book:ch12/2_miscdrv_rdwr_spinlock: simple misc char
driver rewritten with spinlocks
[ ... ]
parm: buggy:If 1, cause an error by issuing a blocking call within a
spinlock critical section (int)
$ sudo virt-what
virtualbox
kvm
$
```

As you can see, we're running our custom 5.4.0 "debug" kernel on our x86_64 Ubuntu 20.04 guest VM.

> **TIP**: How do you know whether you're running on a **virtual machine (VM)** or on the "bare metal" (native) system? `virt-what(1)` is a useful little script that shows this (you can install it on Ubuntu with `sudo apt install virt-what`).

To run our test case, insert the driver into the kernel and set the `buggy` module parameter to 1. Invoking the driver's `read` method (via our user space app; that is, `ch12/miscdrv_rdwr/rdwr_test_secret`) isn't an issue, as shown here:

```
$ sudo dmesg -C
$ sudo insmod ./miscdrv_rdwr_spinlock.ko buggy=1
$ ../../ch12/miscdrv_rdwr/rdwr_test_secret
Usage: ../../ch12/miscdrv_rdwr/rdwr_test_secret opt=read/write
device_file ["secret-msg"]
 opt = 'r' => we shall issue the read(2), retrieving the 'secret' form
the driver
 opt = 'w' => we shall issue the write(2), writing the secret message
<secret-msg>
   (max 128 bytes)
$
$ ../../ch12/miscdrv_rdwr/rdwr_test_secret r
/dev/llkd_miscdrv_rdwr_spinlock
Device file /dev/llkd_miscdrv_rdwr_spinlock opened (in read-only
mode): fd=3
../../ch12/miscdrv_rdwr/rdwr_test_secret: read 7 bytes from
/dev/llkd_miscdrv_rdwr_spinlock
```

```
The 'secret' is:
 "initmsg"
$
```

Next, we issue a `write(2)` to the driver via the user mode app; this time, our buggy code path gets executed. As you saw, we issued a `schedule_timeout()` within a spinlock critical section (that is, between the lock and unlock). The debug kernel detects this as a bug and spawns (impressively large) debug diagnostics into the kernel log (note that bugs like this can quite possibly hang your system, so test this on a VM first):

```
[28853.172825] miscdrv_rdwr_spinlock:write_miscdrv_rdwr(): 004)  rdwr_test_secre :23578   |  ...0    /* write_mi
scdrv_rdwr() */
[28853.178231] misc llkd_miscdrv_rdwr_spinlock: rdwr_test_secre wants to write 24 bytes
[28853.181539] misc llkd_miscdrv_rdwr_spinlock: 24 bytes written, returning... (stats: tx=7, rx=24)
[28853.184243] BUG: scheduling while atomic: rdwr_test_secre/23578/0x00000002
[28853.187489] 1 lock held by rdwr_test_secre/23578:
[28853.189904]  #0: ffff8880285c2d60 (&(&ctx->spinlock)->rlock){+.+.}, at: write_miscdrv_rdwr.cold+0xde/0x247 [
miscdrv_rdwr_spinlock]
[28853.195078] Modules linked in: miscdrv_rdwr_spinlock(OE) vboxsf(OE) vboxvideo(OE) crct10dif_pclmul crc32_pcl
mul ghash_clmulni_intel vmwgfx snd_intel8x0 snd_ac97_codec ac97_bus snd_pcm aesni_intel glue_helper crypto_simd
 cryptd joydev snd_seq snd_timer drm_kms_helper snd_seq_device input_leds serio_raw snd syscopyarea sysfillrect
 sysimgblt fb_sys_fops ttm video mac_hid vboxguest(OE) soundcore drm sch_fq_codel parport_pc ppdev lp parport i
p_tables x_tables autofs4 hid_generic usbhid hid psmouse e1000 ahci libahci i2c_piix4 pata_acpi [last unloaded:
 miscdrv_rdwr_spinlock]
[28853.211613] CPU: 4 PID: 23578 Comm: rdwr_test_secre Tainted: G           OE     5.4.0-llkd-dbg #2
[28853.214596] Hardware name: innotek GmbH VirtualBox/VirtualBox, BIOS VirtualBox 12/01/2006
[28853.217244] Call Trace:
[28853.219461]  dump_stack+0xc2/0x11a
[28853.221692]  __schedule_bug.cold+0x2b/0x3c
[28853.223893]  __schedule+0xd4d/0x1090
[28853.226207]  ? firmware_map_remove+0xe9/0xe9
[28853.228428]  ? _raw_spin_unlock_irqrestore+0x51/0x60
[28853.230741]  ? schedule_timeout+0x2b4/0x8c0
[28853.232891]  ? lockdep_hardirqs_on+0x1a2/0x280
[28853.235050]  schedule+0x75/0x140
[28853.237118]  schedule_timeout+0x2b9/0x8c0
[28853.239207]  ? __dev_printk+0xd6/0xf3
[28853.241276]  ? usleep_range+0x100/0x100
[28853.243310]  ? _dev_info+0xcd/0xfb
[28853.245421]  ? __next_timer_interrupt+0xe0/0xe0
[28853.247475]  write_miscdrv_rdwr.cold+0x1ea/0x247 [miscdrv_rdwr_spinlock]
[28853.249726]  ? display_stats+0x80/0x80 [miscdrv_rdwr_spinlock]
[28853.251802]  ? apparmor_file_permission+0x1a/0x20
[28853.253814]  ? security_file_permission+0x65/0x190
[28853.255871]  __vfs_write+0x4f/0x90
[28853.257885]  vfs_write+0x14b/0x2d0
[28853.259744]  ksys_write+0xd9/0x180
[28853.261612]  ? __ia32_sys_read+0x50/0x50
[28853.263388]  ? mark_held_locks+0x29/0xb0
[28853.265119]  ? do_syscall_64+0x19/0x2c0
[28853.266842]  ? entry_SYSCALL_64_after_hwframe+0x49/0xbe
```

Figure 12.9 – Kernel diagnostics being triggered by the "scheduling in atomic context" bug we've deliberately hit here

Kernel Synchronization - Part 1

The preceding screenshot shows part of what transpired (follow along while viewing the driver code in `ch12/2_miscdrv_rdwr_spinlock/2_miscdrv_rdwr_spinlock.c`):

1. First, we have our user mode app's process context (`rdwr_test_secre`; notice how the name is truncated to the first 16 characters, including the `NULL` byte), which enters the driver's write method; that is, `write_miscdrv_rdwr()`. This can be seen in the output of our useful `PRINT_CTX()` macro (we've reproduced this line here):

   ```
   miscdrv_rdwr_spinlock:write_miscdrv_rdwr(): 004)
   rdwr_test_secre :23578 |  ...0 /*  write_miscdrv_rdwr() */
   ```

2. It copies in the new 'secret' from the user space writer process and writes it, for 24 bytes.
3. It then "takes" the spinlock, enters the critical section, and copies this data to the `oursecret` member of our driver's context structure.
4. After this, `if (1 == buggy) {` evaluates to true.
5. Then, it calls `schedule_timeout()`, which is a blocking API (as it internally calls `schedule()`), triggering the bug, which is helpfully highlighted in red:

   ```
   BUG: scheduling while atomic: rdwr_test_secre/23578/0x00000002
   ```

6. The kernel now dumps a good deal of the diagnostic output. Among the first things to be dumped is the **call stack**.

The call stack or stack backtrace (or "call trace") of the kernel mode stack of the process – here, it's our user space app, `rdwr_drv_secret`, which is running our (buggy) driver's code in the process context – can be clearly seen in *Figure 12.9*. Each line after the `Call Trace:` header is essentially a call frame on the kernel stack.

As a tip, ignore the stack frames that begin with the `?` symbol; they are literally questionable call frames, in all likelihood "leftovers" from previous stack usage in the same memory region. It's worth taking a small memory-related diversion here: this is how stack allocation really works; stack memory isn't allocated and freed on a per-call frame basis as that would be frightfully expensive. Only when a stack memory page is exhausted is a new one automatically *faulted in*! (Recall our discussions in `Chapter 9`, *Kernel Memory Allocation for Module Authors – Part 2*, in the *A brief note on memory allocations and demand paging* section.) So, the reality is that, as code calls and returns from functions, the same stack memory page(s) tend to keep getting reused.

[640]

Not only that, but for performance reasons, the memory isn't wiped each time, leading to leftovers from previous frames often appearing. (They can literally "spoil" the picture. However, fortunately, the modern stack call frame tracing algorithms are usually able to do a superb job in figuring out the correct stack trace.)

Following the stack trace bottom-up (*always read it bottom-up*), we can see that, as expected, our user space `write(2)` system call (it often shows up as (something like) `SyS_write` or, on the x86, as `__x64_sys_write`, though not visible in *Figure 12.9*) invokes the kernel's VFS layer code (you can see `vfs_write()` here, which calls `__vfs_write()`), which further invokes our driver's write method; that is, `write_miscdrv_rdwr()`! This code, as we well know, invokes the buggy code path where we call `schedule_timeout()`, which, in turn, invokes `schedule()` (and `__schedule()`), causing the whole `BUG: scheduling while atomic` bug to trigger.

The format of the `scheduling while atomic` code path is retrieved from the following line of code, which can be found in `kernel/sched/core.c`:

```
printk(KERN_ERR "BUG: scheduling while atomic: %s/%d/0x%08x\n",
    prev->comm, prev->pid, preempt_count());
```

Interesting! Here, you can see that it printed the following string:

```
BUG: scheduling while atomic: rdwr_test_secre/23578/0x00000002
```

After `atomic:`, it prints the process name – the PID – and then invokes the `preempt_count()` inline function, which prints the *preempt depth*; the preempt depth is a counter that's incremented every time a lock is taken and decremented on every unlock. So, if it's positive, this implies that the code is within a critical or atomic section; here, it shows as the value 2.

Note that this bug gets neatly served up during this test run precisely because the `CONFIG_DEBUG_ATOMIC_SLEEP` debug kernel config option is turned on. It's on because we're running a custom "debug kernel" (kernel version 5.4.0)! The config option details (you can interactively find and set this option in `make menuconfig`, under the `Kernel Hacking` menu) are as follows:

```
// lib/Kconfig.debug
[ ... ]
config DEBUG_ATOMIC_SLEEP
    bool "Sleep inside atomic section checking"
    select PREEMPT_COUNT
    depends on DEBUG_KERNEL
    depends on !ARCH_NO_PREEMPT
```

```
          help
            If you say Y here, various routines which may sleep will become
very
           noisy if they are called inside atomic sections: when a spinlock is
           held, inside an rcu read side critical section, inside preempt
disabled
            sections, inside an interrupt, etc...
```

Testing on a 5.4 non-debug distro kernel

As a contrasting test, we will now perform the very same thing on our Ubuntu 20.04 LTS VM, which we'll boot via its default generic 'distro' 5.4 Linux kernel that is typically *not configured as a 'debug' kernel* (here, the `CONFIG_DEBUG_ATOMIC_SLEEP` kernel config option hasn't been set).

First, we insert our (buggy) driver. Then, when we run our `rdwr_drv_secret` process in order to write the new secret to the driver, the buggy code path gets executed. However, this time, the kernel *does not crash, nor does it report any issues at all* (looking at the `dmesg(1)` output validates this):

```
$ uname -r
5.4.0-56-generic
$ sudo insmod ./miscdrv_rdwr_spinlock.ko buggy=1
$ ../../ch12/miscdrv_rdwr/rdwr_test_secret w
/dev/llkd_miscdrv_rdwr_spinlock "passwdcosts500bucksdude"
Device file /dev/llkd_miscdrv_rdwr_spinlock opened (in write-only
mode): fd=3
../../ch12/miscdrv_rdwr/rdwr_test_secret: wrote 24 bytes to
/dev/llkd_miscdrv_rdwr_spinlock
$ dmesg
[ ... ]
[   65.420017] miscdrv_rdwr_spinlock:miscdrv_init_spinlock(): LLKD misc
driver (major # 10) registered, minor# = 56, dev node is
/dev/llkd_miscdrv_rdwr
[   81.665077] miscdrv_rdwr_spinlock:miscdrv_exit_spinlock():
miscdrv_rdwr_spinlock: LLKD misc driver deregistered, bye
[   86.798720] miscdrv_rdwr_spinlock:miscdrv_init_spinlock():
VERMAGIC_STRING = 5.4.0-56-generic SMP mod_unload
[   86.799890] miscdrv_rdwr_spinlock:miscdrv_init_spinlock(): LLKD misc
driver (major # 10) registered, minor# = 56, dev node is
/dev/llkd_miscdrv_rdwr
[  130.214238] misc llkd_miscdrv_rdwr_spinlock: filename:
"llkd_miscdrv_rdwr_spinlock"
                wrt open file: f_flags = 0x8001
                ga = 1, gb = 0
[  130.219233] misc llkd_miscdrv_rdwr_spinlock: stats: tx=0, rx=0
```

```
[  130.219680] misc llkd_miscdrv_rdwr_spinlock: rdwr_test_secre wants
to write 24 bytes
[  130.220329] misc llkd_miscdrv_rdwr_spinlock: 24 bytes written,
returning... (stats: tx=0, rx=24)
[  131.249639] misc llkd_miscdrv_rdwr_spinlock: filename:
"llkd_miscdrv_rdwr_spinlock"
                ga = 0, gb = 1
[  131.253511] misc llkd_miscdrv_rdwr_spinlock: stats: tx=0, rx=24
$
```

We know that our write method has a deadly bug, yet it doesn't seem to fail in any manner! This is really bad; it's this kind of thing that can erroneously lead you to conclude that your code is just fine when there's actually a nasty bug silently lying in wait to pounce one fine day!

To help us investigate what exactly is going on under the hood, let's run our test app (the `rdwr_drv_secret` process) once more, but this time via the powerful `trace-cmd(1)` tool (a very useful wrapper over the Ftrace kernel infrastructure; the following is its truncated output:

> The Linux kernel's **Ftrace** infrastructure is the kernel's primary tracing infrastructure; it provides a detailed trace of pretty much every function that's been executed in the kernel space. Here, we are leveraging Ftrace via a convenient frontend: the `trace-cmd(1)` utility. These are indeed very powerful and useful debug tools; we've mentioned several others in Chapter 1, *Kernel Workspace Setup*, but unfortunately, the details are beyond the scope of this book. Check out the man pages to learn more.

```
$ sudo trace-cmd record -p function_graph -F
../../ch12/miscdrv_rdwr/rdwr_test_secret w
/dev/llkd_miscdrv_rdwr_spinlock "passwdcosts500bucks"
$ sudo trace-cmd report -I -S -l > report.txt
$ sudo less report.txt
[ ... ]
```

Kernel Synchronization - Part 1

The output can be seen in the following screenshot:

```
rdwr_tes-2438    4....   1060.741276: funcgraph_entry:                  |  vfs_write() {
rdwr_tes-2438    4....   1060.741276: funcgraph_entry:                  |    rw_verify_area() {
rdwr_tes-2438    4....   1060.741277: funcgraph_entry:                  |      security_file_permission() {
rdwr_tes-2438    4....   1060.741277: funcgraph_entry:                  |        apparmor_file_permission() {
rdwr_tes-2438    4....   1060.741277: funcgraph_entry:                  |          common_file_perm() {
rdwr_tes-2438    4....   1060.741277: funcgraph_entry:       0.244 us   |            aa_file_perm();
rdwr_tes-2438    4....   1060.741277: funcgraph_exit:        0.492 us   |          }
rdwr_tes-2438    4....   1060.741277: funcgraph_exit:        0.715 us   |        }
rdwr_tes-2438    4....   1060.741278: funcgraph_exit:        1.010 us   |      }
rdwr_tes-2438    4....   1060.741278: funcgraph_exit:        1.273 us   |    }
rdwr_tes-2438    4....   1060.741278: funcgraph_entry:                  |    vfs_write() {
rdwr_tes-2438    4....   1060.741278: funcgraph_entry:                  |      write_miscdrv_rdwr() {
rdwr_tes-2438    4....   1060.741278: funcgraph_entry:                  |        dev_info() {
rdwr_tes-2438    4....   1060.741278: funcgraph_entry:                  |          __dev_printk() {
```

Figure 12.10 – A partial screenshot of the trace-cmd(1) report output

As you can see, the `write(2)` system call from our user mode app becomes, as expected, `vfs_write()`, which itself (after security checks) invokes `__vfs_write()`, which, in turn, invokes our driver's write method – the `write_miscdrv_rdwr()` function!

In the (large) Ftrace output stream, we can see that the `schedule_timeout()` function has indeed been invoked:

```
rdwr_tes-2438    4....   1060.746698: funcgraph_entry:                  |  schedule_timeout() {
rdwr_tes-2438    4....   1060.746698: funcgraph_entry:                  |    lock_timer_base() {
rdwr_tes-2438    4....   1060.746698: funcgraph_entry:       0.110 us   |      _raw_spin_lock_irqsave();
rdwr_tes-2438    4d..    1060.746698: funcgraph_exit:        0.318 us   |    }
rdwr_tes-2438    4d..    1060.746698: funcgraph_entry:       0.104 us   |    detach_if_pending();
rdwr_tes-2438    4d..    1060.746699: funcgraph_entry:       0.105 us   |    get_nohz_timer_target();
rdwr_tes-2438    4d..    1060.746699: funcgraph_entry:                  |    __internal_add_timer() {
rdwr_tes-2438    4d..    1060.746699: funcgraph_entry:       0.110 us   |      calc_wheel_index();
rdwr_tes-2438    4d..    1060.746699: funcgraph_entry:       0.161 us   |      enqueue_timer();
rdwr_tes-2438    4d..    1060.746699: funcgraph_exit:        0.588 us   |    }
rdwr_tes-2438    4d..    1060.746699: funcgraph_entry:       0.106 us   |    trigger_dyntick_cpu.isra.0();
rdwr_tes-2438    4d..    1060.746700: funcgraph_entry:       0.117 us   |    lock_text_start();
rdwr_tes-2438    4....   1060.746700: funcgraph_entry:                  |    schedule() {
rdwr_tes-2438    4d..    1060.746700: funcgraph_entry:                  |      rcu_note_context_switch() {
```

Figure 12.11 – A partial screenshot of the trace-cmd(1) report output, showing the (buggy!) calls to schedule_timeout() and schedule() within an atomic context

A few lines of output after `schedule_timeout()`, we can clearly see `schedule()` being invoked! So, there we have it: our driver has (deliberately, of course) performed something buggy – calling `schedule()` in an atomic context. But again, the key point here is that on this Ubuntu system, we are *not* running a "debug" kernel, which is why we have the following:

```
$ grep DEBUG_ATOMIC_SLEEP /boot/config-5.4.0-56-generic
# CONFIG_DEBUG_ATOMIC_SLEEP is not set
$
```

[644]

This is why the bug isn't being reported! This proves the usefulness of running test cases – and indeed performing kernel development – on a "debug" kernel, a kernel with many debug features enabled. (As an exercise, if you haven't done so already, prepare a "debug" kernel and run this test case on it.)

> *LDV (Linux Driver Verification) project:* back in `Chapter 1`, *Kernel Workspace Setup*, in the section *The LDV – Linux Driver Verification – project*, we mentioned that this project has useful "rules" with respect to various programming aspects of Linux modules (drivers, mostly) as well as the core kernel.
>
> With regard to our current topic, here's one of the rules: *Usage of spin lock and unlock functions* (`http://linuxtesting.org/ldv/online?action=show_rulerule_id=0039`). It mentions key points with regard to the correct usage of spinlocks; interestingly, here, it shows an actual bug instance in a driver where a spinlock was attempted to be released twice – a clear violation of the locking rules, leading to an unstable system.

Locking and interrupts

So far, we have learned how to use the mutex lock and, for the spinlock, the basic `spin_[un]lock()` APIs. A few other API variations on the spinlock exist, and we shall examine the more common ones here.

To understand exactly why you may need other APIs for spinlocks, let's go over a scenario: as a driver author, you find that the device you're working on asserts a hardware interrupt; accordingly, you write the interrupt handler for it (You can learn great detail about it in the *Linux Kernel Programming (Part 2)* book). Now, while implementing a `read` method for your driver, you find that you have a non-blocking critical section within it. This is easy to deal with: as you have learned, you should use a spinlock to protect it. Great! But what if, while in the `read` method's critical section, the device's hardware interrupt fires? As you're aware, *hardware interrupts preempt anything and everything*; thus, control will go to the interrupt handler code preempting the driver's `read` method.

Kernel Synchronization - Part 1

The key question here: is this an issue? That answer depends both on what your interrupt handler and your `read` method were doing and how they were implemented. Let's visualize a few scenarios:

- The interrupt handler (ideally) uses only local variables, so even if the `read` method were in a critical section, it really doesn't matter; the interrupt handling will complete very quickly and control will be handed back to whatever was interrupted (again, there's more to it than this; as you know, any existing bottom-half, such as a tasklet or softirq, may also need to execute). In other words, as such, there is really no race in this case.
- The interrupt handler is working on (global) shared writeable data but *not* on the data items that your read method is using. Thus, again, there is no conflict and no race with the read code. What you should realize, of course, is that the interrupt code *does have a critical section and that it must be protected* (perhaps with another spinlock).
- The interrupt handler is working on the same global shared writeable data that your `read` method is using. In this case, we can see that the potential for a race definitely exists, so we need locking!

Let's focus on the third case. Obviously, we should use a spinlock to protect the critical section within the interrupt handling code (recall that using a mutex is disallowed when we're in any kind of interrupt context). Also, *unless we use the very same spinlock* in both the `read` method and the interrupt handler's code path, they will not be protected at all! (Be careful when working with locks; take the time to think through your design and code in detail.)

Let's try and make this a bit more hands-on (with pseudocode for now): let's say we have a global (shared) data structure named `gCtx`; we're operating on it in both the `read` method as well as the interrupt handler (hardirq handler) within our driver. Since it's shared, it's a critical section and therefore requires protection; since we are running in an atomic (interrupt) context, we *can't use a mutex*, so we must use a spinlock instead (here, the spinlock variable is called `slock`). The following pseudocode shows some timestamps (`t1`, `t2`, ...) for this situation:

```
// Driver read method ; WRONG !
driver_read(...)                        << time t0 >>
{
    [ ... ]
    spin_lock(&slock);
    <<--- time t1 : start of critical section >>
... << operating on global data object gCtx >> ...
    spin_unlock(&slock);
    <<--- time t2 : end of critical section >>
```

[646]

```
    [ ... ]
}                                    << time t3 >>
```

The following pseudocode is for the device driver's interrupt handler:

```
handle_interrupt(...)              << time t4; hardware interrupt fires!
>>
{
    [ ... ]
    spin_lock(&slock);
<<--- time t5: start of critical section >>
    ... << operating on global data object gCtx >> ...
    spin_unlock(&slock);
<<--- time t6 : end of critical section >>
    [ ... ]
}                                    << time t7 >>
```

This can be summed up with the following diagram:

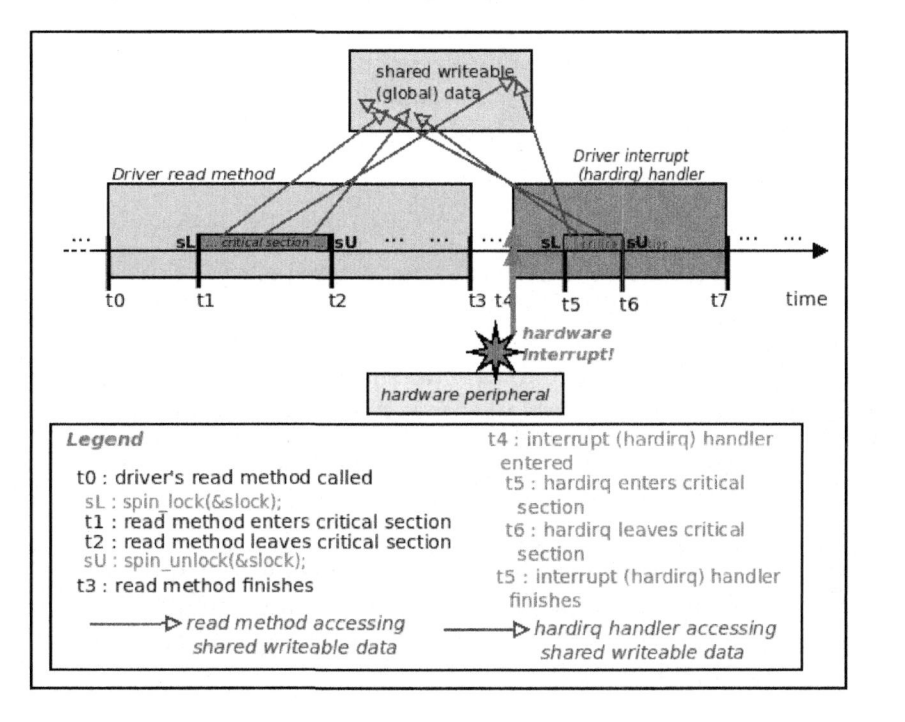

Figure 12.12 – Timeline – the driver's read method and hardirq handler run sequentially when working on global data; there's no issues here

Kernel Synchronization - Part 1

Luckily, everything has gone well – "luckily" because the hardware interrupt fired *after* the `read` function's critical section completed. Surely we can't count on luck as the exclusive safety stamp of our product! The hardware interrupt is asynchronous; what if it fired at a less opportune time (for us) – say, while the `read` method's critical section is running between time t1 and t2? Well, isn't the spinlock going to do its job and protect our data?

At this point, the interrupt handler's code will attempt to acquire the same spinlock (`&slock`). Wait a minute – it cannot "get" it as it's currently locked! In this situation, it "spins", in effect waiting on the unlock. But how can it be unlocked? It cannot, and there we have it: a **(self) deadlock**.

Interestingly, the spinlock is more intuitive and makes sense on an SMP (multicore) system. Let's assume that the `read` method is running on CPU core 1; the interrupt can be delivered on another CPU core, say core 2. The interrupt code path will "spin" on the lock on CPU core 2, while the `read` method, on core 1, completes the critical section and then unlocks the spinlock, thus unblocking the interrupt handler. But what about on **UP (uniprocessor**, with only one CPU core)? How will it work then? Ah, so here's the solution to this conundrum: when "racing" with interrupts, *regardless of uniprocessor or SMP, simply use the* `_irq` *variant of the spinlock API*:

```
#include <linux/spinlock.h>
void spin_lock_irq(spinlock_t *lock);
```

The `spin_lock_irq()` API internally disables interrupts on the processor core that it's running on; that is, the local core. So, by using this API in our `read` method, interrupts will be disabled on the local core, thus making any possible "race" impossible via interrupts. (If the interrupt does fire on another CPU core, the spinlock technology will simply work as advertised, as discussed previously!)

> The `spin_lock_irq()` implementation is pretty nested (as with most of the spinlock functionality), yet fast; down the line, it ends up invoking the `local_irq_disable()` and `preempt_disable()` macros, disabling both interrupts and kernel preemption on the local processor core that it's running on. (Disabling hardware interrupts has the (desirable) side effect of disabling kernel preemption as well.)

`spin_lock_irq()` pairs off with the corresponding `spin_unlock_irq()` API. So, the correct usage of the spinlock for this scenario (as opposed to what we saw previously) is as follows:

```
// Driver read method ; CORRECT !
driver_read(...)                    << time t0 >>
{
    [ ... ]
    spin_lock_irq(&slock);
    <<--- time t1 : start of critical section >>
[now all interrupts + preemption on local CPU core are masked
(disabled)]
... << operating on global data object gCtx >> ...
    spin_unlock_irq(&slock);
    <<--- time t2 : end of critical section >>
    [ ... ]
}                                   << time t3 >>
```

Before patting ourselves solidly on the back and taking the rest of the day off, let's consider another scenario. This time, on a more complex product (or project), it's quite possible that, among the several developers working on the code base, one has deliberately set the interrupt mask to a certain value, thus blocking some interrupts while allowing others. For the sake of our example, let's say that this has occurred earlier, at some point in time t0. Now, as we described previously, another developer (you!) comes along, and in order to protect a critical section within the driver's read method, uses the `spin_lock_irq()` API. Sounds correct, yes? Yes, but this API has the power *to turn off (mask) all hardware interrupts* (and kernel preemption, which we'll ignore for now) on the local CPU core. It does so by manipulating, at a low level, the (very arch-specific) hardware interrupt mask register. Let's say that setting a bit corresponding to an interrupt to 1 enables that interrupt, while clearing the bit (to 0) disables or masks it. Due to this, we may end up with the following scenario:

- time t0: The interrupt mask is set to some value, say, 0x8e (10001110b), enabling some and disabling some interrupts. This is important to the project (here, for simplicity, we're assuming there's an 8-bit mask register) [... *time elapses* ...].
- time t1: Just before entering the driver read method's critical section, call `spin_lock_irq(&slock);`. This API will have the internal effect of clearing all the bits in the interrupt mask registered to 0, thus disabling all interrupts (as we *think* we desire).

- time `t2`: Now, hardware interrupts cannot fire on this CPU core, so we go ahead and complete the critical section. Once we're done, we call `spin_unlock_irq(&slock);`. This API will have the internal effect of setting all the bits in the interrupt mask register to 1, reenabling all interrupts.

However, the interrupt mask register has now been wrongly "restored" to a value of `0xff` (11111111b), *not the value* `0x8e` as the original developer wants, requires, and assumes! This can (and probably will) break something in the project.

The solution is quite straightforward: don't assume anything, **simply save and restore the interrupt mask**. This can be achieved with the following API pair:

```
#include <linux/spinlock.h>
 unsigned long spin_lock_irqsave(spinlock_t *lock, unsigned long flags);
 void spin_unlock_irqrestore(spinlock_t *lock, unsigned long flags);
```

The first parameter to both the lock and unlock functions is the spinlock variable to use. The second parameter, `flags`, *must be a local variable* of the `unsigned long` type. This will be used to save and restore the interrupt mask:

```
spinlock_t slock;
spin_lock_init(&slock);
[ ... ]
driver_read(...)
{
    [ ... ]
    spin_lock_irqsave(&slock, flags);
    << ... critical section ... >>
    spin_unlock_irqrestore(&slock, flags);
    [ ... ]
}
```

> To be pedantic, `spin_lock_irqsave()` is not an API, but a macro; we've shown it as an API for readability. Also, although the return value of this macro is not void, it's an internal detail (the `flags` parameter variable is updated here).

What about if a tasklet or a softirq (a bottom-half interrupt mechanism) has a critical section that "races" with your process-context code paths? In such situations, using the `spin_lock_bh()` routine is likely what's required since it can disable bottom halves on the local processor and then take the spinlock, thus safeguarding the critical section (similar to the way that `spin_lock_irq[save]()` protects the critical section in the process context by disabling hardware interrupts on the local core):

```
void spin_lock_bh(spinlock_t *lock);
```

Of course, *overhead* does matter in highly performance-sensitive code paths (the network stack being a great example). Thus, using the simplest form of spinlocks will help with more complex variants. Having said that, though, there are certainly going to be occasions that demand the use of the stronger forms of the spinlock API. For example, on the 5.4.0 Linux kernel, this is an approximation of the number of usage instances of different forms of the spinlock APIs we have seen: `spin_lock()`: over 9,400 usage instances; `spin_lock_irq()`: over 3,600 usage instances; `spin_lock_irqsave()`: over 15,000 usage instances; and `spin_lock_bh()`: over 3,700 usage instances. (We don't draw any major inference from this; it's just that we wish to point out that using the stronger form of spinlock APIs is quite widespread in the Linux kernel).

Finally, let's provide a very brief note on the internal implementation of the spinlock: in terms of under-the-hood internals, the implementation tends to be very arch-specific code, often comprised of atomic machine language instructions that execute very fast on the microprocessor. On the popular x86[_64] architecture, for example, the spinlock ultimately boils down to an *atomic test-and-set* machine instruction on a member of the spinlock structure (typically implemented via the `cmpxchg` machine language instruction). On ARM machines, as we mentioned earlier, it's often the `wfe` (Wait For Event, as well as the **SetEvent** (**SEV**)) machine instruction at the heart of the implementation. (You will find resources regarding its internal implementation in the *Further reading* section). Regardless, as a kernel or driver author, you should only use the exposed APIs (and macros) when using spinlocks.

Kernel Synchronization - Part 1

Using spinlocks – a quick summary

Let's quickly summarize spinlocks:

- **Simplest, lowest overhead**: Use the non-irq spinlock primitives, `spin_lock()`/`spin_unlock()`, when protecting critical sections in the process context (there's either no interrupts to deal with or there are interrupts, but we do not race with them at all; in effect, use this when interrupts don't come into play or don't matter).
- **Medium overhead**: Use the irq-disabling (as well as kernel preemption disabling) versions, `spin_lock_irq()` / `spin_unlock_irq()`, when interrupts are in play and do matter (the process and interrupt contexts can "race"; that is, they share global data).
- **Strongest (relatively), high overhead**: This is the safest way to use a spinlock. It does the same as the medium overhead, except it performs a save-and-restore on the interrupt mask via the `spin_lock_irqsave()` / `spin_unlock_irqrestore()` pair, so as to guarantee that the previous interrupt mask settings aren't inadvertently overwritten, which could happen with the previous case.

As we saw earlier, the spinlock – in the sense of "spinning" on the processor it's running on when awaiting the lock – is impossible on UP (how can you spin on the one CPU that's available while another thread runs simultaneously on the very same CPU?). Indeed, on UP systems, the only real effect of the spinlock APIs is that it can disable hardware interrupts and kernel preemption on the processor! On SMP (multicore) systems, however, the spinning logic actually comes into play, and thus the locking semantics work as expected. But hang on – this should not stress you, budding kernel/driver developer; in fact, the whole point is that you should simply use the spinlock APIs as described and you will never have to worry about UP versus SMP; the details of what is done and what isn't are all hidden by the internal implementation.

Though this book is based on the 5.4 LTS kernel, a new feature was added to the 5.8 kernel from the **Real-Time Linux** (**RTL**, previously called PREEMPT_RT) project, which deserves a quick mention here: "**local locks**". While the main use case for local locks is for (hard) real-time kernels, they help with non-real-time kernels too, mainly for lock debugging via static analysis, as well as runtime debugging via lockdep (we cover lockdep in the next chapter). Here's the LWN article on the subject: `https://lwn.net/Articles/828477/`.

With this, we complete the section on spinlocks, an extremely common and key lock used in the Linux kernel by virtually all its subsystems, including drivers.

Summary

Congratulations on completing this chapter!

Understanding concurrency and its related concerns is absolutely critical for any software professional. In this chapter, you learned key concepts regarding critical sections, the need for exclusive execution within them, and what atomicity means. You then learned *why* we need to be concerned with concurrency while writing code for the Linux OS. After that, we delved into the actual locking technologies – mutex locks and spinlocks – in detail. You also learned what lock you should use and when. Finally, learning how to handle concurrency concerns when hardware interrupts (and their possible bottom halves) are in play was covered.

But we aren't done yet! There are many more concepts and technologies we need to learn about, which is just what we will do in the next, and final, chapter of this book. I suggest that you digest the content of this chapter well first by browsing through it, as well as the resources in the *Further reading* section and the exercises provided, before diving into the last chapter!

Questions

As we conclude, here is a list of questions for you to test your knowledge regarding this chapter's material: `https://github.com/PacktPublishing/Linux-Kernel-Programming/tree/master/questions`. You will find some of the questions answered in the book's GitHub repo: `https://github.com/PacktPublishing/Linux-Kernel-Programming/tree/master/solutions_to_assgn`.

Further reading

To help you delve deeper into the subject with useful materials, we provide a rather detailed list of online references and links (and at times, even books) in a Further reading document in this book's GitHub repository. The *Further reading* document is available here: `https://github.com/PacktPublishing/Linux-Kernel-Programming/blob/master/Further_Reading.md`.

13
Kernel Synchronization - Part 2

This chapter continues the discussion from the previous chapter, on the topic of kernel synchronization and dealing with concurrency within the kernel in general. I suggest that if you haven't already, first read the previous chapter, and then continue with this one.

Here, we shall continue our learning with respect to the vast topic of kernel synchronization and handling concurrency when in kernel space. As before, the material is targeted at kernel and/or device driver developers. In this chapter, we shall cover the following:

- Using the atomic_t and refcount_t interfaces
- Using the RMW atomic operators
- Using the reader-writer spinlock
- Cache effects and false sharing
- Lock-free programming with per-CPU variables
- Lock debugging within the kernel
- Memory barriers – an introduction

Using the atomic_t and refcount_t interfaces

In our simple demo misc character device driver program's (`miscdrv_rdwr/miscdrv_rdwr.c`) open method (and elsewhere), we defined and manipulated two static global integers, `ga` and `gb`:

```
static int ga, gb = 1;
[...]
ga++; gb--;
```

By now, it should be obvious to you that this – the place where we operate on these integers – is a potential bug if left as is: it's shared writable data (in a shared state) and therefore *a critical section, thus requiring protection against concurrent access.* You get it; so, we progressively improved upon this. In the previous chapter, understanding the issue, in our `ch12/1_miscdrv_rdwr_mutexlock/1_miscdrv_rdwr_mutexlock.c` program, we first used a *mutex lock* to protect the critical section. Later, you learned that using a *spinlock* to protect non-blocking critical sections such as this one would be (far) superior to using a mutex in terms of performance; so, in our next driver, `ch12/2_miscdrv_rdwr_spinlock/2_miscdrv_rdwr_spinlock.c`, we used a spinlock instead:

```
spin_lock(&lock1);
ga++; gb--;
spin_unlock(&lock1);
```

That's good, but we can do better still! Operating upon global integers turns out to be such a common occurrence within the kernel (think of reference or resource counters getting incremented and decremented, and so on) that the kernel provides a class of operators called the **refcount** and **atomic integer operators** or interfaces; these are very specifically designed to atomically (safely and indivisibly) operate on **only integers**.

The newer refcount_t versus older atomic_t interfaces

At the outset of this topic area, it's important to mention this: from the 4.11 kernel, there is a newer and better set of interfaces christened the refcount_t APIs, meant for a kernel space object's reference counters. It greatly improves the security posture of the kernel (via much-improved **Integer OverFlow (IoF)** and **Use After Free (UAF)** protection as well as memory ordering guarantees, which the older atomic_t APIs lack). The refcount_t interfaces, like several other security technologies used on Linux, have their origins in work done by The PaX Team – https://pax.grsecurity.net/ (it was called PAX_REFCOUNT).

Having said that, the reality is that (as of the time of writing) the older atomic_t interfaces are still very much in use within the kernel core and drivers (they are slowly being converted, with the older atomic_t interfaces being moved to the newer refcount_t model and the API set). Thus, in this topic, we cover both, pointing out differences and mentioning which refcount_t API supersedes an atomic_t API wherever applicable. Think of the refcount_t interfaces as a variant of the (older) atomic_t interfaces, which are specialized toward reference counting.

A key difference between the atomic_t operators and the refcount_t ones is that the former works upon signed integers whereas the latter is essentially designed to work upon only an unsigned int quantity; more specifically, and this is important, it works only within a strictly specified range: 1 to UINT_MAX-1 (or [1..INT_MAX] when !CONFIG_REFCOUNT_FULL). The kernel has a config option named CONFIG_REFCOUNT_FULL; if set, it performs a (slower and more thorough) "full" reference count validation. This is beneficial for security but can result in slightly degraded performance (the typical default is to keep this config turned off; it's the case with our x86_64 Ubuntu guest).

Attempting to set a refcount_t variable to 0 or negative, or to [U]INT_MAX or above, is impossible; this is good for preventing integer underflow/overflow issues and thus preventing the use-after-free class bug in many cases! (Well, it's not impossible; it results in a (noisy) warning being fired via the WARN() macro.) Think about it, refcount_t variables are meant to be used *only for kernel object reference counting, nothing else.*

Thus, this is indeed the required behavior; the reference counter must start at a positive value (typically 1 when the object is newly instantiated), is incremented (or added to) whenever the code gets or takes a reference, and is decremented (or subtracted from) whenever the code puts or leaves a reference on the object. You are expected to carefully manipulate the reference counter (matching your gets and puts), always keeping its value within the legal range.

Quite non-intuitively, at least for the generic arch-independent refcount implementation, the `refcount_t` APIs are internally implemented over the `atomic_t` API set. For example, the `refcount_set()` API – which atomically sets a refcount's value to the parameter passed – is implemented like this within the kernel:

```
// include/linux/refcount.h
/**
 * refcount_set - set a refcount's value
 * @r: the refcount
 * @n: value to which the refcount will be set
 */
static inline void refcount_set(refcount_t *r, unsigned int n)
{
    atomic_set(&r->refs, n);
}
```

It's a thin wrapper over `atomic_set()` (which we will cover very shortly). The obvious FAQ here is: why use the refcount API at all? There are a few reasons:

- The counter saturates at the `REFCOUNT_SATURATED` value (which is set to `UINT_MAX` by default) and will not budge once there. This is critical: it avoids wrapping the counter, which could cause weird and spurious UAF bugs; this is even considered as a key security fix (https://kernsec.org/wiki/index.php/Kernel_Protections/refcount_t).
- Several of the newer refcount APIs do provide **memory ordering** guarantees; in particular the `refcount_t` APIs – as compared to their older `atomic_t` cousins – and the memory ordering guarantees they provide are clearly documented at https://www.kernel.org/doc/html/latest/core-api/refcount-vs-atomic.html#refcount-t-api-compared-to-atomic-t (do have a look if you're interested in the low-level details).
- Also, realize that arch-dependent refcount implementations (when they exist; for example, x86 does have it, while ARM doesn't) can differ from the previously-mentioned generic one.

> What exactly is *memory ordering* and how does it affect us? The fact is, it's a complex topic and, unfortunately, the inner details on this are beyond the scope of this book. It's worth knowing the basics: I suggest you read up on the **Linux-Kernel Memory Model (LKMM)**, which includes coverage on processor memory ordering and more. We refer you to good documentation on this here: *Explanation of the Linux-Kernel Memory Model* (https://github.com/torvalds/linux/blob/master/tools/memory-model/Documentation/explanation.txt).

The simpler atomic_t and refcount_t interfaces

Regarding the `atomic_t` interfaces, we should mention that all the following `atomic_t` constructs are for 32-bit integers only; of course, with 64-bit integers now being commonplace, 64-bit atomic integer operators are available as well. Typically, they are semantically identical to their 32-bit counterparts with the difference being in the name (`atomic_foo()` becomes `atomic64_foo()`). So the primary data type for 64-bit atomic integers is called `atomic64_t` (AKA `atomic_long_t`). The `refcount_t` interfaces, on the other hand, cater to both 32 and 64-bit integers.

The following table shows how to declare and initialize an `atomic_t` and `refcount_t` variable, side by side so that you can compare and contrast them:

	(Older) atomic_t (32-bit only)	(Newer) refcount_t (both 32- and 64-bit)
Header file to include	`<linux/atomic.h>`	`<linux/refcount.h>`
Declare and initialize a variable	`static atomic_t gb = ATOMIC_INIT(1);`	`static refcount_t gb = REFCOUNT_INIT(1);`

Table 17.1 – The older atomic_t versus the newer refcount_t interfaces for reference counting: header and init

Kernel Synchronization - Part 2

The complete set of all the `atomic_t` and `refcount_t` APIs available within the kernel is pretty large; to help keep things simple and clear in this section, we only list some of the more commonly used (atomic 32-bit) and `refcount_t` interfaces in the following table (they operate upon a generic `atomic_t` or `refcount_t` variable, v):

Operation	(Older) atomic_t interface	(Newer) refcount_t interface [range: 0 to [U]INT_MAX]
Header file to include	`<linux/atomic.h>`	`<linux/refcount.h>`
Declare and initialize a variable	`static atomic_t v = ATOMIC_INIT(1);`	`static refcount_t v = REFCOUNT_INIT(1);`
Atomically read the current value of v	`int atomic_read(atomic_t *v)`	`unsigned int refcount_read(const refcount_t *v)`
Atomically set v to the value i	`void atomic_set(atomic_t *v, i)`	`void refcount_set(refcount_t *v, int i)`
Atomically increment the v value by 1	`void atomic_inc(atomic_t *v)`	`void refcount_inc(refcount_t *v)`
Atomically decrement the v value by 1	`void atomic_dec(atomic_t *v)`	`void refcount_dec(refcount_t *v)`
Atomically add the value of i to v	`void atomic_add(i, atomic_t *v)`	`void refcount_add(int i, refcount_t *v)`
Atomically subtract the value of i from v	`void atomic_sub(i, atomic_t *v)`	`void refcount_sub(int i, refcount_t *v)`
Atomically add the value of i to v and return the result	`int atomic_add_return(i, atomic_t *v)`	`bool refcount_add_not_zero(int i, refcount_t *v)` (not a precise match; adds i to v unless it's 0.)
Atomically subtract the value of i from v and return the result	`int atomic_sub_return(i, atomic_t *v)`	`bool refcount_sub_and_test(int i, refcount_t *r)` (not a precise match; subtracts i from v and tests; returns `true` if resulting refcount is 0, else `false`.)

Table 17.2 – The older atomic_t versus the newer refcount_t interfaces for reference counting: APIs

You've now seen several `atomic_t` and `refcount_t` macros and APIs; let's quickly check out a few examples of their usage in the kernel.

Examples of using refcount_t within the kernel code base

In one of our demo kernel modules regarding kernel threads
(in `ch15/kthread_simple/kthread_simple.c`), we created a kernel thread and then employed the `get_task_struct()` inline function to mark the kernel thread's task structure as being in use. As you can now guess, the `get_task_struct()` routine increments the task structure's reference counter – a `refcount_t` variable named `usage` – via the `refcount_inc()` API:

```
// include/linux/sched/task.h
static inline struct task_struct *get_task_struct(struct task_struct *t)
{
    refcount_inc(&t->usage);
    return t;
}
```

The converse routine, `put_task_struct()`, performs the subsequent decrement on the reference counter. The actual routine employed by it internally, `refcount_dec_and_test()`, tests whether the new refcount value has dropped to 0; if so, it returns `true`, and if this is the case, it implies that the task structure isn't being referenced by anyone. The call to `__put_task_struct()` frees it up:

```
static inline void put_task_struct(struct task_struct *t)
{
    if (refcount_dec_and_test(&t->usage))
        __put_task_struct(t);
}
```

Another example of the refcounting APIs in use within the kernel is found in `kernel/user.c` (which helps track the number of processes, files, and so on that a user has claimed via a per-user structure):

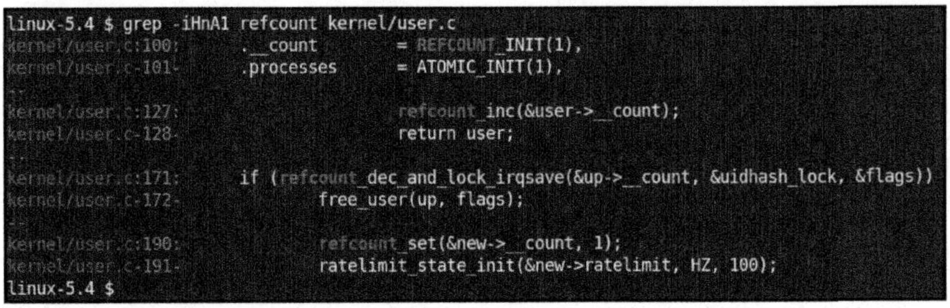

```
linux-5.4 $ grep -iHnA1 refcount kernel/user.c
kernel/user.c:100:        .__count     = REFCOUNT_INIT(1),
kernel/user.c-101-        .processes   = ATOMIC_INIT(1),
--
kernel/user.c:127:            refcount_inc(&user->__count);
kernel/user.c-128-            return user;
--
kernel/user.c:171:    if (refcount_dec_and_lock_irqsave(&up->__count, &uidhash_lock, &flags))
kernel/user.c-172-        free_user(up, flags);
--
kernel/user.c:190:    refcount_set(&new->__count, 1);
kernel/user.c-191-    ratelimit_state_init(&new->ratelimit, HZ, 100);
linux-5.4 $
```

Figure 13.1 – Screenshot showing the usage of the refcount_t interfaces in kernel/user.c

Kernel Synchronization - Part 2

> **TIP**
> Look up the `refcount_t` API interface documentation (https://www.kernel.org/doc/html/latest/driver-api/basics.html#reference-counting); `refcount_dec_and_lock_irqsave()` returns `true` and withholds the spinlock with interrupts disabled if able to decrement the reference counter to 0, and `false` otherwise.

As an exercise for you, convert our earlier `ch16/2_miscdrv_rdwr_spinlock/miscdrv_rdwr_spinlock.c` driver code to use refcount; it has the integers `ga` and `gb`, which, when being read or written, were protected via a spinlock. Now, make them refcount variables and use the appropriate `refcount_t` APIs when working on them.

Careful! Don't allow their values to go out of the allowed range, [0..[U]INT_MAX]! (Recall that the range is [1..UINT_MAX-1] for full refcount validation (CONFIG_REFCOUNT_FULL being on) and [1..INT_MAX] when it's not full validation (the default)). Doing so typically leads to the WARN() macro being invoked (the code for this demo seen in *Figure 13.1* isn't included on our GitHub repository):

```
$ dmesg
[ 7890.344169] miscdrv_rdwr_refcount:miscdrv_init_refcount(): LLKD misc driver (major # 10) registered, minor# = 55, dev node is llkd_miscdrv_rdwr_refcount
[ 7890.345642] misc llkd_miscdrv_rdwr_refcount: A sample print via the dev_dbg(): driver initialized
[ 7904.871029] miscdrv_rdwr_refcount:open_miscdrv_rdwr(): 001) rdwr_test_secre :8519   |  ...0   /* open_miscdrv_rdwr() */
[ 7904.879384] ------------[ cut here ]------------
[ 7904.879735] refcount_t hit zero at open_miscdrv_rdwr+0x194/0x2b0 [miscdrv_rdwr_refcount] in rdwr_test_secre[8519], uid/euid: 1001/1001
[ 7904.880685] WARNING: CPU: 1 PID: 8519 at kernel/panic.c:677 refcount_error_report+0xf1/0x103
[ 7904.881301] Modules linked in: miscdrv_rdwr_refcount(OE) vboxsf(OE) vboxvideo(OE) snd_intel8x0 vmwgfx snd_ac97_codec ac97_bus snd_pcm crct10dif_pclmul crc32_pclmul ghash_clmulni_intel snd_seq aesni_intel glue_helper cryp
to_simd cryptd drm_kms_helper snd_timer snd_seq_device input_leds snd joydev syscopyarea serio_raw sysfillrect sysimgblt fb_sys_fops ttm soundcore vboxguest(OE) video mac_hid sch_fq_codel drm parport_pc ppdev lp parport i
p_tables x_tables autofs4 hid_generic usbhid hid psmouse e1000 ahci libahci i2c_piix4 pata_acpi [last unloaded: miscdrv_rdwr_refcount]
[ 7904.885282] CPU: 1 PID: 8519 Comm: rdwr_test_secre Tainted: G         W  OE     5.4.1-try1 #1
[ 7904.886040] Hardware name: innotek GmbH VirtualBox/VirtualBox, BIOS VirtualBox 12/01/2006
[ 7904.886668] RIP: 0010:refcount_error_report+0xf1/0x103
```

Figure 13.2 – (Partial) screenshot showing the WARN() macro firing when we wrongly attempt to set a refcount_t variable to <= 0

> **TIP**
> The kernel has an interesting and useful test infrastructure called the **Linux Kernel Dump Test Module (LKDTM)**; see `drivers/misc/lkdtm/refcount.c` for many test cases being run on the refcount interfaces, which you can learn from... FYI, you can also use LKDTM via the kernel's fault injection framework to test and evaluate the kernel's reaction to faulty scenarios (see the documentation here: *Provoking crashes with Linux Kernel Dump Test Module (LKDTM)* – `https://www.kernel.org/doc/html/latest/fault-injection/provoke-crashes.html#provoking-crashes-with-linux-kernel-dump-test-module-lkdtm`).

The atomic interfaces covered so far all operate on 32-bit integers; what about on 64-bit? That's what follows.

64-bit atomic integer operators

As mentioned at the start of this topic, the set of `atomic_t` integer operators we have dealt with so far all operate on traditional 32-bit integers (this discussion doesn't apply to the newer `refcount_t` interfaces; they anyway operate upon both 32 and 64-bit quantities). Obviously, with 64-bit systems becoming the norm rather than the exception nowadays, the kernel community provides an identical set of atomic integer operators for 64-bit integers. The difference is as follows:

- Declare the 64-bit atomic integer as a variable of type `atomic64_t` (that is, `atomic_long_t`).
- For all operators, in place of the `atomic_` prefix, use the `atomic64_` prefix.

So, take the following examples:

- In place of `ATOMIC_INIT()`, use `ATOMIC64_INIT()`.
- In place of `atomic_read()`, use `atomic64_read()`.
- In place of `atomic64_dec_if_positive()`, use `atomic64_dec_if_positive()`.

[663]

Kernel Synchronization - Part 2

> Recent C and C++ language standards – C11 and C++11 – provide an atomic operations library that helps developers implement atomicity in an easier fashion due to the implicit language support; we won't delve into this aspect here. A reference can be found here (C11 also has pretty much the same equivalents): `https://en.cppreference.com/w/c/atomic`.

Note that all these routines – both the 32- and 64-bit atomic _operators – are **arch-independent**. A key point worth repeating is that any and all operations performed upon an atomic integer must be done by declaring the variable as `atomic_t` and via the methods provided. This includes initialization and even a (integer) read operation.

In terms of internal implementation, a `foo()` atomic integer operator is typically a macro that becomes an inline function, which in turn invokes the arch-specific `arch_foo()` function. As usual, glancing through the official kernel documentation on atomic operators is always a good idea (within the kernel source tree, it's here: `Documentation/atomic_t.txt`; go to `https://www.kernel.org/doc/Documentation/atomic_t.txt`). It neatly categorizes the numerous atomic integer APIs into distinct sets. FYI, arch-specific *memory ordering issues* do affect the internal implementation. Here, we won't delve into the internals. If interested, refer to this page on the official kernel documentation site at `https://www.kernel.org/doc/html/v4.16/core-api/refcount-vs-atomic.html#refcount-t-api-compared-to-atomic-t` (also, details on memory ordering go beyond the scope of this book; check out the kernel documentation at `https://www.kernel.org/doc/Documentation/memory-barriers.txt` for more on this).

We haven't attempted to show all the atomic and refcount APIs here (it's really not necessary); the official kernel documentation covers it:

- `atomic_t` interfaces:
    - *Semantics and Behavior of Atomic and Bitmask Operations* (`https://www.kernel.org/doc/html/v5.4/core-api/atomic_ops.html#semantics-and-behavior-of-atomic-and-bitmask-operations`)
    - API ref: Atomics (`https://www.kernel.org/doc/html/latest/driver-api/basics.html#atomics`)

- (Newer) `refcount_t` interfaces for kernel object reference counting:
    - `refcount_t` API compared to `atomic_t` (https://www.kernel.org/doc/html/latest/core-api/refcount-vs-atomic.html#refcount-t-api-compared-to-atomic-t)
    - API ref: Reference counting (https://www.kernel.org/doc/html/latest/driver-api/basics.html#reference-counting)

Let's move on to the usage of a typical construct when working on drivers – **Read Modify Write (RMW)**. Read on!

Using the RMW atomic operators

A more advanced set of atomic operators called the RMW APIs is available as well. Among its many uses (we show a list in the coming section) is that of performing atomic RMW operations on bits, in other words, performing bitwise operations atomically (safely, indivisibly). As a device driver author operating upon device or peripheral *registers*, this is indeed something you will find yourself using.

> The material in this section assumes you have at least a base understanding of accessing peripheral device (chip) memory and registers; we have covered this in detail in `Chapter 13`, *Working with Hardware I/O Memory*. Please ensure you understand it before moving further.

Very often, you'll need to perform bit operations (with the bitwise AND & and bitwise OR | being the most commonplace operators) on registers; this is done to modify its value, setting and/or clearing some bits within it. The thing is, merely performing some C manipulation to query or set device registers isn't quite enough. No, sir: don't forget about concurrency issues! Read on for the full story.

RMW atomic operations – operating on device registers

Let's quickly go over some basics first: a byte consists of 8 bits, numbered from bit 0, the **Least Significant Bit (LSB)**, to bit 7, the **Most Significant Bit (MSB)**. (This is actually formally defined as the `BITS_PER_BYTE` macro in `include/linux/bits.h`, along with a few other interesting definitions.)

A **register** is basically a small piece of memory within the peripheral device; typically, its size, the register bit width, is one of 8, 16, or 32 bits. The device registers provide control, status, and other information and are often programmable. This, in fact, is largely what you as a driver author will do – program the device registers appropriately to make the device do something, and query it.

To flesh out this discussion, let's consider a hypothetical device that has two registers: a status register and a control register, each 8 bits wide. (In the real world, every device or chip has a *datasheet* that will provide a detailed specification of the chip and register-level hardware; this becomes an essential document for the driver author). Hardware folks usually design devices in such a way that several registers are sequentially clubbed together in a larger piece of memory; this is called register banking. By having the base address of the first register and the offset to each following one, it becomes easy to address any given register (here, we won't delve into how exactly registers are "mapped" into the virtual address space on an OS such as Linux). For example, the (purely hypothetical) registers may be described like this in a header file:

```
#define REG_BASE       0x5a00
#define STATUS_REG     (REG_BASE+0x0)
#define CTRL_REG       (REG_BASE+0x1)
```

Now, say that in order to turn on our fictional device, the datasheet informs us we can do so by setting bit 7 (the MSB) of the control register to 1. As every driver author quickly learns, there is a hallowed sequence for modifying registers:

1. **Read** the register's current value into a temporary variable.
2. **Modify** the variable to the desired value.
3. **Write** back the variable to the register.

This is often called the **RMW sequence**; so, great, we write the (pseudo)code like this:

```
turn_on_dev()
{
    u8 tmp;

    tmp = ioread8(CTRL_REG);      /* read: current register value into tmp */
    tmp |= 0x80;                  /* modify: set bit 7 (MSB) */
    iowrite8(tmp, CTRL_REG);      /* write: new tmp value into register */
}
```

(FYI, the actual routines used on Linux **MMIO – memory-mapped I/O** – are `ioread[8|16|32]()` and `iowrite[8|16|32]()`.)

A key point here: *this isn't good enough*; the reason is **concurrency, data races!** Think about it: a register (both CPU and device registers) is in fact a *global shared writable memory location*; thus, accessing it *constitutes a critical section*, which you have to take care to protect from concurrent access! The how is easy; we could just use a spinlock (for now at least). It's trivial to modify the preceding pseudocode to insert the `spin_[un]lock()` APIs in the critical section – the RMW sequence.

However, there is an even better way to achieve data safety when dealing with small quantities such as integers; we have already covered it: *atomic operators*! Linux, however, goes further, providing a set of atomic APIs for both of the following:

- **Atomic non-RMW operations** (the ones we saw earlier, in the *Using the atomic_t and refcount_t interfaces* section)
- **Atomic RMW operations**; these include several types of operators that can be categorized into a few distinct classes: arithmetic, bitwise, swap (exchange), reference counting, miscellaneous, and barriers

Let's not reinvent the wheel; the kernel documentation (https://www.kernel.org/doc/Documentation/atomic_t.txt) has all the information required. We'll show just a relevant portion of this document as follows, quoting directly from the `Documentation/atomic_t.txt` kernel code base:

```
// Documentation/atomic_t.txt
[ ... ]
Non-RMW ops:
  atomic_read(), atomic_set()
  atomic_read_acquire(), atomic_set_release()


RMW atomic operations:

Arithmetic:
  atomic_{add,sub,inc,dec}()
  atomic_{add,sub,inc,dec}_return{,_relaxed,_acquire,_release}()
  atomic_fetch_{add,sub,inc,dec}{,_relaxed,_acquire,_release}()


Bitwise:
  atomic_{and,or,xor,andnot}()
  atomic_fetch_{and,or,xor,andnot}{,_relaxed,_acquire,_release}()
```

```
Swap:
  atomic_xchg{,_relaxed,_acquire,_release}()
  atomic_cmpxchg{,_relaxed,_acquire,_release}()
  atomic_try_cmpxchg{,_relaxed,_acquire,_release}()


Reference count (but please see refcount_t):
  atomic_add_unless(), atomic_inc_not_zero()
  atomic_sub_and_test(), atomic_dec_and_test()


Misc:
  atomic_inc_and_test(), atomic_add_negative()
  atomic_dec_unless_positive(), atomic_inc_unless_negative()
[ ... ]
```

Good; now that you're aware of these RMW (and non-RMW) operators, let's get practical – we'll check out how to use the RMW operators for bit operations next.

Using the RMW bitwise operators

Here, we'll focus on employing the RMW bitwise operators; we'll leave it to you to explore the others (refer to the kernel docs mentioned). So, let's think again about how to more efficiently code our pseudocode example. We can set (to 1) any given bit in any register or memory item using the `set_bit()` API:

```
void set_bit(unsigned int nr, volatile unsigned long *p);
```

This atomically – safely and indivisibly – sets the `nr`th bit of `p` to 1. (The reality is that the device registers (and possibly device memory) are mapped into kernel virtual address space and thus appear to be visible as though they are RAM locations – such as the address `p` here. This is called MMIO and is the common way by which driver authors map in and work with device memory. Again, we cover this in *Linux Kernel Programming (Part 2)*)

Thus, with the RMW atomic operators, we can safely achieve what we've (incorrectly) attempted previously – turning on our (fictional) device – with a single line of code:

```
set_bit(7, CTRL_REG);
```

The following table summarizes common RMW bitwise atomic APIs:

RMW bitwise atomic API	Comment
`void set_bit(unsigned int nr, volatile unsigned long *p);`	Atomically set (set to 1) the nrth bit of p.
`void clear_bit(unsigned int nr, volatile unsigned long *p)`	Atomically clear (set to 0) the nrth bit of p.
`void change_bit(unsigned int nr, volatile unsigned long *p)`	Atomically toggle the nrth bit of p.
The following APIs return the previous value of the bit being operated upon (nr)	
`int test_and_set_bit(unsigned int nr, volatile unsigned long *p)`	Atomically set the nrth bit of p returning the previous value (kernel API doc at https://www.kernel.org/doc/htmldocs/kernel-api/API-test-and-set-bit.html).
`int test_and_clear_bit(unsigned int nr, volatile unsigned long *p)`	Atomically clear the nrth bit of p returning the previous value.
`int test_and_change_bit(unsigned int nr, volatile unsigned long *p)`	Atomically toggle the nrth bit of p returning the previous value.

Table 17.3 – Common RMW bitwise atomic APIs

> **Careful**: these atomic APIs are not just atomic with respect to the CPU core they're running upon, but now with respect to all/other cores. In practice, this implies that if you're performing atomic operations in parallel on multiple CPUs, that is, if they (can) race, then it's a critical section and you must protect it with a lock (typically a spinlock)!

Trying out a few of these RMW atomic APIs will help build your confidence in using them; we do so in the section that follows.

Using bitwise atomic operators – an example

Let's check out a quick kernel module that demonstrates the usage of the Linux kernel's RMW atomic bit operators (`ch13/1_rmw_atomic_bitops`). You should realize that these operators can work on *any memory,* both a (CPU or device) register or RAM; here, we operate on a simple static global variable (named `mem`) within the example LKM. It's very simple; let's check it out:

```
// ch13/1_rmw_atomic_bitops/rmw_atomic_bitops.c
[ ... ]
#include <linux/spinlock.h>
#include <linux/atomic.h>
#include <linux/bitops.h>
#include "../../convenient.h"
[ ... ]
static unsigned long mem;
static u64 t1, t2;
static int MSB = BITS_PER_BYTE - 1;
DEFINE_SPINLOCK(slock);
```

We include the required headers and declare and initialize a few global variables (notice how our `MSB` variable uses `BIT_PER_BYTE`). We employ a simple macro, `SHOW()`, to display the formatted output with the printk. The `init` code path is where the actual work is done:

```
[ ... ]
#define SHOW(n, p, msg) do {                                              \
    pr_info("%2d:%27s: mem : %3ld = 0x%02lx\n", n, msg, p, p);            \
} while (0)
[ ... ]
static int __init atomic_rmw_bitops_init(void)
{
    int i = 1, ret;

    pr_info("%s: inserted\n", OURMODNAME);
    SHOW(i++, mem, "at init");

    setmsb_optimal(i++);
    setmsb_suboptimal(i++);

    clear_bit(MSB, &mem);
    SHOW(i++, mem, "clear_bit(7,&mem)");

    change_bit(MSB, &mem);
    SHOW(i++, mem, "change_bit(7,&mem)");

    ret = test_and_set_bit(0, &mem);
```

```
        SHOW(i++, mem, "test_and_set_bit(0,&mem)");
        pr_info("  ret = %d\n", ret);

        ret = test_and_clear_bit(0, &mem);
        SHOW(i++, mem, "test_and_clear_bit(0,&mem)");
        pr_info("  ret (prev value of bit 0) = %d\n", ret);

        ret = test_and_change_bit(1, &mem);
        SHOW(i++, mem, "test_and_change_bit(1,&mem)");
        pr_info("  ret (prev value of bit 1) = %d\n", ret);

        pr_info("%2d: test_bit(%d-0,&mem):\n", i, MSB);
        for (i = MSB; i >= 0; i--)
            pr_info(" bit %d (0x%02lx) : %s\n", i, BIT(i), test_bit(i,
&mem)?"set":"cleared");

        return 0; /* success */
}
```

The RMW atomic operators we use here are highlighted in bold font. A key part of this demo is to show that using the RMW bitwise atomic operators is not only much easier but also much faster than using the traditional approach where we manually perform the RMW operation within the confines of a spinlock. Here are the two functions for both of these approaches:

```
/* Set the MSB; optimally, with the set_bit() RMW atomic API */
static inline void setmsb_optimal(int i)
{
    t1 = ktime_get_real_ns();
    set_bit(MSB, &mem);
    t2 = ktime_get_real_ns();
    SHOW(i, mem, "set_bit(7,&mem)");
    SHOW_DELTA(t2, t1);
}
/* Set the MSB; the traditional way, using a spinlock to protect the RMW
 * critical section   */
static inline void setmsb_suboptimal(int i)
{
    u8 tmp;

    t1 = ktime_get_real_ns();
    spin_lock(&slock);
    /* critical section: RMW : read, modify, write */
    tmp = mem;
    tmp |= 0x80; // 0x80 = 1000 0000 binary
    mem = tmp;
    spin_unlock(&slock);
```

[671]

Kernel Synchronization - Part 2

```
    t2 = ktime_get_real_ns();

    SHOW(i, mem, "set msb suboptimal: 7,&mem");
    SHOW_DELTA(t2, t1);
}
```

We call these functions early in our `init` method; notice that we take timestamps (via the `ktime_get_real_ns()` routine) and display the time taken via our `SHOW_DELTA()` macro (defined in our `convenient.h` header). Right, here's the output:

```
[15186.312399] 2_rmw_atomic_bitops: inserted
[15186.314690]  1:             at init: mem :   0 = 0x00
[15186.315936]  2:       set_bit(7,&mem): mem : 128 = 0x80
[15186.317155] delta: 415 ns (= 0 us = 0 ms)
[15186.318746]  3: set msb suboptimal: 7,&mem: mem : 128 = 0x80
[15186.320096] delta: 110101 ns (= 110 us = 0 ms)
[15186.321285]  4:     clear_bit(7,&mem): mem :   0 = 0x00
[15186.323010]  5:    change_bit(7,&mem): mem : 128 = 0x80
[15186.324379]  6:  test_and_set_bit(0,&mem): mem : 129 = 0x81
[15186.325785]            ret = 0
[15186.327019]  7: test_and_clear_bit(0,&mem): mem : 128 = 0x80
[15186.328396]       ret (prev value of bit 0) = 1
[15186.329868]  8:test_and_change_bit(1,&mem): mem : 130 = 0x82
[15186.331487]       ret (prev value of bit 1) = 0
[15186.333013]  9: test_bit(7-0,&mem):
[15186.334436]      bit 7 (0x80) : set
[15186.335747]      bit 6 (0x40) : cleared
[15186.337013]      bit 5 (0x20) : cleared
[15186.338401]      bit 4 (0x10) : cleared
[15186.339648]      bit 3 (0x08) : cleared
[15186.340825]      bit 2 (0x04) : cleared
[15186.342129]      bit 1 (0x02) : set
[15186.343285]      bit 0 (0x01) : cleared
```

Figure 13.3 – Screenshot of output from our ch13/1_rmw_atomic_bitops LKM, showing off some of the atomic RMW operators at work

(I ran this demo LKM on my x86_64 Ubuntu 20.04 guest VM.) The modern approach – via the `set_bit()` RMW atomic bitwise API – took, in this sample run, just 415 nanoseconds to execute; the traditional approach was about 265 times slower! The code (via `set_bit()`) is so much simpler as well...

On a somewhat related note to the atomic bitwise operators, the following section is a very brief look at the highly efficient APIs available within the kernel for searching a bitmask – a fairly common operation in the kernel, as it turns out.

Efficiently searching a bitmask

Several algorithms depend on performing a really fast search of a bitmask; several scheduling algorithms (such as SCHED_FIFO and SCHED_RR, which you learned about in Chapter 10, *The CPU Scheduler – Part 1*, and Chapter 11, *The CPU Scheduler – Part 2*) often internally require this. Implementing this efficiently becomes important (especially for OS-level performance-sensitive code paths). Hence, the kernel provides a few APIs to scan a given bitmask (these prototypes are found in include/asm-generic/bitops/find.h):

- unsigned long find_first_bit(const unsigned long *addr, unsigned long size): Finds the first set bit in a memory region; returns the bit number of the first set bit, else (no bits are set) returns @size.
- unsigned long find_first_zero_bit(const unsigned long *addr, unsigned long size): Finds the first cleared bit in a memory region; returns the bit number of the first cleared bit, else (no bits are cleared) returns @size.
- Other routines include find_next_bit(), find_next_and_bit(), find_last_bit().

Looking through the <linux/bitops.h> header reveals other quite interesting macros as well, such as for_each_{clear,set}_bit{_from}().

Using the reader-writer spinlock

Visualize a piece of kernel (or driver) code wherein a large, global, doubly linked circular list (with a few thousand nodes) is being searched. Now, since the data structure is global (shared and writable), accessing it constitutes a critical section that requires protection.

Assuming a scenario where searching the list is a non-blocking operation, you'd typically use a spinlock to protect the critical section. A naive approach might propose not using a lock at all since we're *only reading data* within the list, not updating it. But, of course (as you have learned), even a read on shared writable data has to be protected to protect against an inadvertent write occurring simultaneously, thus resulting in a dirty or torn read.

Kernel Synchronization - Part 2

So, we conclude that we require the spinlock; we imagine the pseudocode might look something like this:

```
spin_lock(mylist_lock);
for (p = &listhead; (p = next_node(p)) != &listhead; ) {
    << ... search for something ...
        found? break out ... >>
}
spin_unlock(mylist_lock);
```

So, what's the problem? Performance, of course! Imagine several threads on a multicore system ending up at this code fragment more or less at the same time; each will attempt to take the spinlock, but only one winner thread will get it, iterate over the entire list, and then perform the unlock, allowing the next thread to proceed. In other words, as expected, execution is now *serialized*, dramatically slowing things down. But it can't be helped; or can it?

Enter the **reader-writer spinlock**. With this locking construct, it's required that all threads performing reads on the protected data will ask for a **read lock**, whereas any thread requiring write access to the list will ask for an **exclusive write lock**. A read lock will be granted immediately to any thread that asks as long as no write lock is currently in play. In effect, this construct *allows all readers concurrent access to the data, meaning, in effect, no real locking at all.* This is fine, as long as there are only readers. The moment a writer thread comes along, it requests a write lock. Now, normal locking semantics apply: the writer **will have to wait** for all readers to unlock. Once that happens, the writer gets an exclusive write lock and proceeds. So now, if any readers or writers attempt access, they will be forced to wait to spin upon the writer's unlock.

> Thus, for those situations where the access pattern to data is such that reads are performed very often and writes are rare, and the critical section is a fairly long one, the reader-writer spinlock is a performance-enhancing one.

Reader-writer spinlock interfaces

Having used spinlocks, using the reader-writer variant is straightforward; the lock data type is abstracted as the `rwlock_t` structure (in place of `spinlock_t`) and, in terms of API names, simply substitute `read` or `write` in place of `spin`:

```
#include <linux/rwlock.h>
rwlock_t mylist_lock;
```

The most basic APIs of the reader-writer spinlock are as follows:

```
void read_lock(rwlock_t *lock);
void write_lock(rwlock_t *lock);
```

As an example, the kernel's `tty` layer has code to handle a **Secure Attention Key (SAK)**; the SAK is a security feature, a means to prevent a Trojan horse-type credentials hack by killing all processes associated with the TTY device. This will happen when the user presses the SAK (https://www.kernel.org/doc/html/latest/security/sak.html). When this actually happens (that is, when the user presses the SAK, mapped to the `Alt-SysRq-k` sequence by default), within its code path, it has to iterate over all tasks, killing the entire session and any threads that have the TTY device open. To do so, it must take, in read mode, a reader-writer spinlock called `tasklist_lock`. The (truncated) relevant code is seen as follows, with `read_[un]lock()` on `tasklist_lock` highlighted:

```
// drivers/tty/tty_io.c
void __do_SAK(struct tty_struct *tty)
{
    [...]
    read_lock(&tasklist_lock);
    /* Kill the entire session */
    do_each_pid_task(session, PIDTYPE_SID, p) {
        tty_notice(tty, "SAK: killed process %d (%s): by session\n",
task_pid_nr(p), p->comm);
        group_send_sig_info(SIGKILL, SEND_SIG_PRIV, p, PIDTYPE_SID);
    } while_each_pid_task(session, PIDTYPE_SID, p);
    [...]
    /* Now kill any processes that happen to have the tty open */
    do_each_thread(g, p) {
        [...]
    } while_each_thread(g, p);
    read_unlock(&tasklist_lock);
```

As an aside, you may recall that, back in the *Iterating over the task list* section in Chapter 6, *Kernel Internals Essentials – Processes and Threads*, we did something kind of similar: we wrote a kernel module (`ch6/foreach/thrd_show_all`) that iterated over all threads in the task list, spewing out a few details about each thread. So, now that we understand the deal regarding concurrency, shouldn't we have taken this very lock – `tasklist_lock` – the reader-writer spinlock protecting the task list? Yes, but it didn't work (`insmod(8)` failed with the message `thrd_showall: Unknown symbol tasklist_lock (err -2)`). The reason, of course, is that this `tasklist_lock` variable is *not* exported and thus is unavailable to our kernel module.

Kernel Synchronization - Part 2

As another example of a reader-writer spinlock within the kernel code base, the `ext4` filesystem uses one when working with its extent status tree. We don't intend to delve into the details here; we will simply mention the fact that a reader-writer spinlock (within the inode structure, `inode->i_es_lock`) is quite heavily used here to protect the extent status tree against data races (`fs/ext4/extents_status.c`).

There are many such examples within the kernel source tree; many places in the network stack including the ping code (`net/ipv4/ping.c`) use `rwlock_t`, routing table lookup, neighbor, PPP code, filesystems, and so on.

Just as with regular spinlocks, we have the typical variations on the reader-writer spinlock APIs: `{read,write}_lock_irq{save}()` paired with the corresponding `{read,write}_unlock_irq{restore}()`, as well as the `{read,write}_{un}lock_bh()` interfaces. Note that even the read IRQ lock disables kernel preemption.

A word of caution

Issues do exist with reader-writer spinlocks. One typical issue with it is that, unfortunately, **writers can starve** when blocking on several readers. Think about it: let's say that three reader threads currently have the reader-writer lock. Now, a writer comes along wanting the lock. It has to wait until all three readers perform the unlock. But what if, in the interim, more readers come along (which is entirely possible)? This becomes a disaster for the writer, who has to now wait even longer – in effect, starve. (Carefully instrumenting or profiling the code paths involved might be necessary to figure out whether this is indeed the case.)

Not only that, *cache effects* – known as cache ping-pong – can and do occur quite often when several reader threads on different CPU cores are reading the same shared state in parallel (while holding the reader-writer lock); we in fact discuss this in the *Cache effects and false sharing* section). The kernel documentation on spinlocks (`https://www.kernel.org/doc/Documentation/locking/spinlocks.txt`) says pretty much the same thing. Here's a quote directly from it: "*NOTE! reader-writer locks require more atomic memory operations than simple spinlocks. Unless the reader critical section is long, you are better off just using spinlocks.*" In fact, the kernel community is working toward removing reader-writer spinlocks as far as is possible, moving them to superior lock-free techniques (such as **RCU - Read Copy Update**, an advanced lock-free technology). Thus, gratuitous use of reader-writer spinlocks is ill advised.

Chapter 13

> **TIP**
> The neat and simple kernel documentation on the usage of spinlocks (written by Linus Torvalds himself), which is well worth reading, is available here: https://www.kernel.org/doc/Documentation/locking/spinlocks.txt.

The reader-writer semaphore

We earlier mentioned the semaphore object (chapter 12, *Kernel Synchronization – Part 1*, in the *The semaphore and the mutex* section), contrasting it with the mutex. There, you understood that it's preferable to simply use a mutex. Here, we point out that within the kernel, just as there exist reader-writer spinlocks, so do there exist *reader-writer semaphores*. The use cases and semantics are similar to that of the reader-writer spinlock. The relevant macros/APIs are (within `<linux/rwsem.h>`) `{down,up}_{read,write}_{trylock,killable}()`. A common example within the `struct mm_struct` structure (which is itself within the task structure) is that one of the members is a reader-writer semaphore: `struct rw_semaphore mmap_sem;`.

Rounding off this discussion, we'll merely mention a couple of other related synchronization mechanisms within the kernel. A synchronization mechanism that is heavily used in user space application development (we're thinking particularly of the Pthreads framework in Linux user space) is the **Condition Variable** (**CV**). In a nutshell, it provides the ability for two or more threads to synchronize with each other based on the value of a data item or some specific state. Its equivalent within the Linux kernel is called the *completion mechanism*. Please find details on its usage within the kernel documentation at https://www.kernel.org/doc/html/latest/scheduler/completion.html#completions-wait-for-completion-barrier-apis.

The *sequence lock* is used in mostly write situations (as opposed to the reader-write spinlock/semaphore locks, which are suitable in mostly read scenarios), where the writes far exceed the reads on the protected variable. As you can imagine, this isn't a very common occurrence; a good example of using sequence locks is the update of the `jiffies_64` global.

> For the curious, the `jiffies_64` global's update code begins here: `kernel/time/tick-sched.c:tick_do_update_jiffies64()`. This function figures out whether an update to jiffies is required, and if so, calls `do_timer(++ticks);` to actually update it. All the while, the `write_seq[un]lock(&jiffies_lock);` APIs provide protection over the mostly write-critical section.

[677]

Cache effects and false sharing

Modern processors make use of several levels of parallel cache memory within them, in order to provide a very significant speedup when working on memory (we briefly touched upon this in Chapter 8, *Kernel Memory Allocation for Module Authors – Part 1*, in the *Allocating slab memory* section). We realize that modern CPUs do *not* really read and write RAM directly; no, when the software indicates that a byte of RAM is to be read starting at some address, the CPU actually reads several bytes – a whole **cacheline** of bytes (typically 64 bytes) from the starting address into all the CPU caches (say, L1, L2, and L3: levels 1, 2, and 3). This way, accessing the next few elements of sequential memory results in a tremendous speedup as it's first checked for in the caches (first in L1, then L2, then L3, and a cache hit becomes likely). The reason it's (much) faster is simple: accessing CPU cache memory takes typically one to a few (single-digit) nanoseconds, whereas accessing RAM can take anywhere between 50 and 100 nanoseconds (of course, this depends on the hardware system in question and the amount of money you're willing to shell out!).

Software developers take advantage of such phenomena by doing things such as the following:

- Keeping important members of a data structure together (hopefully, within a single cacheline) and at the top of the structure
- Padding a structure member such that we don't fall off a cacheline (again, these points have been covered in Chapter 8, *Kernel Memory Allocation for Module Authors – Part 1*, in the *Data structures – a few design tips* section)

However, risks are involved and things do go wrong. As an example, consider two variables declared like so: `u16 ax = 1, bx = 2;` (`u16` denotes an unsigned 16-bit integer value).

Now, as they have been declared adjacent to each other, they will, in all likelihood, occupy the same CPU cacheline at runtime. To understand what the issue is, let's take an example: consider a multicore system with two CPU cores, with each core having two CPU caches, L1 and L2, as well as a common or unified L3 cache. Now, a thread, *T1*, is working on variable `ax` and another thread, *T2*, is concurrently (on another CPU core) working on variable `bx`. So, think about it: when thread *T1*, running on CPU 0, accesses `ax` from main memory (RAM), its CPU caches will get populated with the current values of `ax` and `bx` (as they fall within the same cacheline!). Similarly, when thread *T2*, running on, say, CPU 1, accesses `bx` from RAM, its CPU caches will get populated with the current values of both variables as well. *Figure 13.4* conceptually depicts the situation:

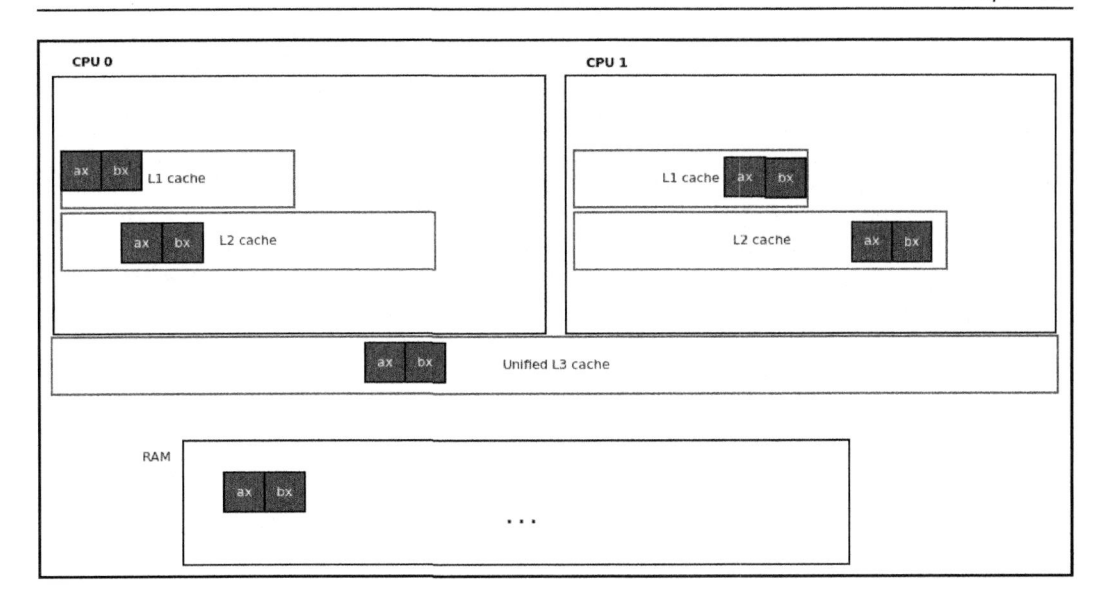

Figure 13.4 – Conceptual depiction of the CPU cache memory when threads T1 and T2 work in parallel on two adjacent variables, each on a distinct one

Fine so far; but what if *T1* performs an operation, say, `ax ++`, while concurrently, *T2* performs `bx ++`? Well, so what? (By the way, you might wonder: why aren't they using a lock? The interesting thing is, it's quite irrelevant to this discussion; there's no data race as each thread is accessing a different variable. The issue is with the fact that they're in the same CPU cacheline.)

Here's the issue: **cache coherency**. The processor and/or the OS in conjunction with the processor (this is all very arch-dependent stuff) will have to keep the caches and RAM synchronized or coherent with each other. Thus, the moment *T1* modifies `ax`, that particular cacheline of CPU 0 will have to be invalidated, that is, a CPU 0-cache-to-RAM flush of the CPU cacheline will occur to update RAM to the new value, and then immediately, a RAM-to-CPU 1-cache update must also occur to keep everything coherent!

But the cacheline contains `bx` as well, and, as we said, `bx` has also been modified on CPU 1 by *T2*. Thus, at about the same time, the CPU 1 cacheline will be flushed to RAM with the new value of `bx` and subsequently updated to CPU 0's caches (all the while, the unified L3 cache too will be read from/updated as well). As you can imagine, any updates on these variables will result in a whole lot of traffic over the caches and RAM; they will bounce. In fact, this is often referred to as **cache ping-pong**! This effect is very detrimental, significantly slowing down processing. This phenomenon is known as **false sharing**.

Kernel Synchronization - Part 2

Recognizing false sharing is the hard part; we must look for variables living on a shared cacheline that are updated by different contexts (threads or whatever else) simultaneously.

> Interestingly, an earlier implementation of a key data structure in the memory management layer, `include/linux/mmzone.h:struct zone`, suffered from this very same false sharing issue: two spinlocks that were declared adjacent to each other! This has long been fixed (we briefly discussed *memory zones* in Chapter 7, *Memory Management Internals – Essentials*, in the *Physical RAM organization/zones* section).

How do you fix this false sharing? Easy: just ensure that the variables are spaced far enough apart to guarantee that they *do not share the same cacheline* (dummy padding bytes are often inserted between variables for this purpose). Do refer to the references to false sharing in the *Further reading* section as well.

Lock-free programming with per-CPU variables

As you have learned, when operating upon shared writable data, the critical section must be protected in some manner. Locking is perhaps the most common technology used to effect this protection. It's not all rosy, though, as performance can suffer. To realize why, consider a few analogies to a lock: one would be a funnel, with the stem of the funnel just wide enough to allow one thread at a time to flow through, no more. Another is a single toll booth on a busy highway or a traffic light at a busy intersection. These analogies help us visualize and understand why locking can cause bottlenecks, slowing performance down to a crawl in some drastic cases. Worse, these adverse effects can be multiplied on high-end multicore systems with a few hundred cores; in effect, locking doesn't scale well.

Another issue is that of *lock contention*; how often is a particular lock being acquired? Increasing the number of locks within a system has the benefit of lowering the contention for a particular lock between two or more processes (or threads). This is called **lock proficiency**. However, again, this is not scalable to an enormous extent: after a while, having thousands of locks on a system (the case with the Linux kernel, in fact) is not good news – the chances of subtle deadlock conditions arising is multiplied significantly.

[680]

So, many challenges exist – performance issues, deadlocks, priority inversion risks, convoying (due to lock ordering, fast code paths might need to wait for the first slower one that's taken a lock that the faster ones also require), and so on. Evolving the kernel in a scalable manner a whole level further has mandated the use of *lock-free algorithms* and their implementation within the kernel. These have led to several innovative techniques, among them being per-CPU (PCP) data, lock-free data structures (by design), and RCU.

In this book, though, we elect to cover only per-CPU as a lock-free programming technique in some detail. The details regarding RCU (and its associated lock-free data structure by design) are beyond this book's scope. Do refer to the *Further reading* section of this chapter for several useful resources on RCU, its meaning, and its usage within the Linux kernel.

Per-CPU variables

As the name suggests, **per-CPU variables** work by keeping *a copy* of the variable, the data item in question, assigned to each (live) CPU on the system. In effect, we get rid of the problem area for concurrency, the critical section, by avoiding the sharing of data between threads. With the per-CPU data technique, since every CPU refers to its very own copy of the data, a thread running on that processor can manipulate it without any worry of racing. (This is roughly analogous to local variables; as locals are on the private stack of each thread, they aren't shared between threads, thus there's no critical section and no need for locking.) Here, too, the need for locking is thus eliminated – making it a *lock-free* technology!

So, think of this: if you are running on a system with four live CPU cores, then a per-CPU variable on that system is essentially an array of four elements: element 0 represents the data value on the first CPU, element 1 the data value on the second CPU core, and so on. Understanding this, you'll realize that per-CPU variables are also roughly analogous to the user space Pthreads **Thread Local Storage** (**TLS**) implementation where each thread automatically obtains a copy of the (TLS) variable marked with the __thread keyword. There, and here with per-CPU variables, it should be obvious: use per-CPU variables for small data items only. This is because the data item is reproduced (copied) with one instance per CPU core (on a high-end system with a few hundred cores, the overheads do climb). We mention some examples of per-CPU usage in the kernel code base (in the *Per-CPU usage within the kernel* section).

Now, when working with per-CPU variables, you must use the helper methods (macros and APIs) provided by the kernel and not attempt to directly access them (much like we saw with the refcount and atomic operators).

Working with per-CPU

Let's approach the helper APIs and macros (methods) for per-CPU data by dividing the discussion into two portions. First, you will learn how to allocate, initialize, and subsequently free a per-CPU data item. Then, you will learn how to work with (read/write) it.

Allocating, initialization, and freeing per-CPU variables

There are broadly two types of per-CPU variables: statically and dynamically allocated ones. Statically allocated per-CPU variables are allocated at compile time itself, typically via one of these macros: `DEFINE_PER_CPU` or `DECLARE_PER_CPU`. Using the `DEFINE` one allows you to allocate and initialize the variable. Here's an example of allocating a single integer as a per-CPU variable:

```
#include <linux/percpu.h>
DEFINE_PER_CPU(int, pcpa);       // signature: DEFINE_PER_CPU(type, name)
```

Now, on a system with, say, four CPU cores, it would conceptually appear like this at initialization:

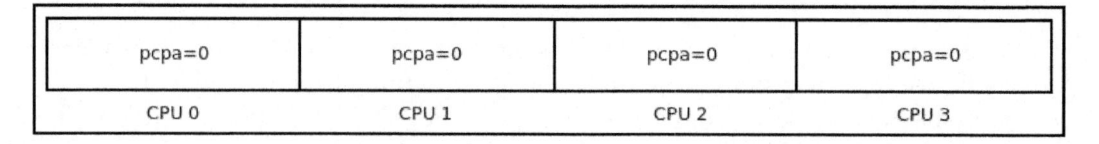

pcpa=0	pcpa=0	pcpa=0	pcpa=0
CPU 0	CPU 1	CPU 2	CPU 3

Figure 13.5 – Conceptual representation of a per-CPU data item on a system with four live CPUs

(The actual implementation is quite a bit more complex than this, of course; please refer to the *Further reading* section of this chapter to see more on the internal implementation.)

[682]

In a nutshell, using per-CPU variables is good for performance enhancement on time-sensitive code paths because of the following:

- We avoid using costly, performance-busting locks.
- The access and manipulation of a per-CPU variable is guaranteed to remain on one particular CPU core; this eliminates expensive cache effects such as cache ping-pong and false sharing (covered in the *Cache effects and false sharing* section).

Dynamically allocating per-CPU data can be achieved via the `alloc_percpu()` or `alloc_percpu_gfp()` wrapper macros, simply passing the data type of the object to allocate as per-CPU, and, for the latter, passing along the `gfp` allocation flag as well:

```
alloc_percpu[_gfp](type [,gfp]);
```

The underlying `__alloc_per_cpu[_gfp]()` routines are exported via `EXPORT_SYMBOL_GPL()` (and thus can be employed only when an LKM is released under a GPL-compatible license).

> **TIP**
> As you've learned, the resource-managed `devm_*()` API variants allow you (typically when writing drivers) to conveniently use these routines to allocate memory; the kernel will take care of freeing it, helping prevent leakage scenarios. The `devm_alloc_percpu(dev, type)` macro allows you to use this as a resource-managed version of `__alloc_percpu()`.

The memory allocated via the preceding routine(s) must subsequently be freed using the `void free_percpu(void __percpu *__pdata)` API.

Performing I/O (reads and writes) on per-CPU variables

A key question, of course, is how exactly can you access (read) and update (write) to per-CPU variables? The kernel provides several helper routines to do so; let's take a simple example to understand how. We define a single integer per-CPU variable, and at a later point in time, we want to access and print its current value. You should realize that, being per-CPU, the value retrieved will be auto-calculated *based on the CPU core the code is currently running on*; in other words, if the following code is running on core 1, then in effect, the `pcpa[1]` value is fetched (it's not done exactly like this; this is just conceptual):

```
DEFINE_PER_CPU(int, pcpa);
int val;
[ ... ]
```

Kernel Synchronization - Part 2

```
val = get_cpu_var(pcpa);
pr_info("cpu0: pcpa = %+d\n", val);
put_cpu_var(pcpa);
```

The pair of `{get,put}_cpu_var()` macros allows us to safely retrieve or modify the per-CPU value of the given per-CPU variable (its parameter). It's important to understand that the code between `get_cpu_var()` and `put_cpu_var()` (or equivalent) is, in effect, a critical section – an atomic context – *where kernel preemption is disabled and any kind of blocking (or sleeping) is disallowed*. If you do anything here that blocks (sleeps) in any manner, it's a kernel bug. For example, see what happens if you try to allocate memory via `vmalloc()` within the `get_cpu_var()`/`put_cpu_var()` pair of macros:

```
void *p;
val = get_cpu_var(pcpa);
p = vmalloc(20000);
pr_info("cpu1: pcpa = %+d\n", val);
put_cpu_var(pcpa);
vfree(p);
[ ... ]

$ sudo insmod <whatever>.ko
$ dmesg
[ ... ]
BUG: sleeping function called from invalid context at mm/slab.h:421
[67641.443225] in_atomic(): 1, irqs_disabled(): 0, pid: 12085, name: thrd_1/1
[ ... ]
$
```

(By the way, calling the `printk()` (or `pr_<foo>()`) wrappers as we do within the critical section is fine as they're non-blocking.) The issue here is that the `vmalloc()` API is possibly a blocking one; it might sleep (we discussed it in detail in Chapter 9, *Kernel Memory Allocation for Module Authors – Part 2*, in the *Understanding and using the kernel vmalloc() API* section), and the code between the `get_cpu_var()`/`put_cpu_var()` pair must be atomic and non-blocking.

Internally, the `get_cpu_var()` macro invokes `preempt_disable()`, disabling kernel preemption, and `put_cpu_var()` undoes this by invoking `preempt_enable()`. As seen earlier (in the chapters on *CPU scheduling*), this can be nested and the kernel maintains a `preempt_count` variable to figure out whether kernel preemption is actually enabled or disabled.

Chapter 13

The upshot of all this is that you must carefully match the `{get,put}_cpu_var()` macros when using them (for example, if we call the `get` macro twice, we must also call the corresponding `put` macro twice).

The `get_cpu_var()` is an *lvalue* and can thus be operated upon; for example, to increment the per-CPU `pcpa` variable, just do the following:

```
get_cpu_var(pcpa) ++;
put_cpu_var(pcpa);
```

You can also (safely) retrieve the current per-CPU value via the macro:

```
per_cpu(var, cpu);
```

So, to retrieve the per-CPU `pcpa` variable for every CPU core on the system, use the following:

```
for_each_online_cpu(i) {
    val = per_cpu(pcpa, i);
    pr_info(" cpu %2d: pcpa = %+d\n", i, val);
}
```

> **TIP**: FYI, you can always use the `smp_processor_id()` macro to figure out which CPU core you're currently running upon; in fact, this is precisely how our `convenient.h:PRINT_CTX()` macro does it.

In a similar manner, the kernel provides routines to work with pointers to variables that require to be per-CPU, the `{get,put}_cpu_ptr()` and `per_cpu_ptr()` macros. These macros are heavily employed when working with a per-CPU data structure (as opposed to just a simple integer); we safely retrieve the pointer to the structure of the CPU we're currently running upon, and use it (`per_cpu_ptr()`).

Per-CPU – an example kernel module

A hands-on session with our sample per-CPU demo kernel module will definitely help in using this powerful feature (code here: `ch13/2_percpu`). Here, we define and use two per-CPU variables:

- A statically allocated and initialized per-CPU integer
- A dynamically allocated per-CPU data structure

[685]

Kernel Synchronization - Part 2

As an interesting way to help demo per-CPU variables, let's do this: we shall arrange for our demo kernel module to spawn off a couple of kernel threads. Let's call them `thrd_0` and `thrd_1`. Furthermore, once created, we shall make use of the CPU mask (and API) to *affine* our `thrd_0` kernel thread on CPU 0 and our `thrd_1` kernel thread on CPU 1 (hence, they will be scheduled to run on only these cores; of course, we must test this code on a VM with at least two CPU cores).

The following code snippets illustrate how we define and use the per-CPU variables (we leave out the code that creates the kernel threads and sets up their CPU affinity masks, as they are not relevant to the coverage of this chapter; nevertheless, it's key to browse through the full code and try it out!):

```
// ch13/2_percpu/percpu_var.c
[ ... ]
/*--- The per-cpu variables, an integer 'pcpa' and a data structure --
- */
/* This per-cpu integer 'pcpa' is statically allocated and initialized
to 0 */
DEFINE_PER_CPU(int, pcpa);

/* This per-cpu structure will be dynamically allocated via
alloc_percpu() */
static struct drv_ctx {
    int tx, rx; /* here, as a demo, we just use these two members,
                ignoring the rest */
    [ ... ]
} *pcp_ctx;
[ ... ]

static int __init init_percpu_var(void)
{
    [ ... ]
    /* Dynamically allocate the per-cpu structures */
    ret = -ENOMEM;
    pcp_ctx = (struct drv_ctx __percpu *) alloc_percpu(struct drv_ctx);
    if (!pcp_ctx) {
        [ ... ]
}
```

Why not use the resource-managed `devm_alloc_percpu()` instead? Yes, you should when appropriate; here, though, as we're not writing a proper driver, we don't have a `struct device *dev` pointer handy, which is the required first parameter to `devm_alloc_percpu()`.

Chapter 13

By the way, I faced an issue when coding this kernel module; to set the CPU mask (to change the CPU affinity for each of our kernel threads), the kernel API is the `sched_setaffinity()` function, which, unfortunately for us, is *not exported*, thus preventing us from using it. So, we perform what is definitely considered a hack: obtain the address of the uncooperative function via `kallsyms_lookup_name()` (which works when `CONFIG_KALLSYMS` is defined) and then invoke it as a function pointer. It works, but is most certainly not the right way to code.

Our design idea is to create two kernel threads and have each of them differently manipulate the per-CPU data variables. If these were ordinary global variables, this would certainly constitute a critical section and we would of course require a lock; but here, precisely because they are *per-CPU* and because we guarantee that our threads run on separate cores, we can concurrently update them with differing data! Our kernel thread worker routine is as follows; the argument to it is the thread number (0 or 1). We accordingly branch off and manipulate the per-CPU data (we have our first kernel thread increment the integer three times, while our second kernel thread decrements it three times):

```
/* Our kernel thread worker routine */
static int thrd_work(void *arg)
{
    int i, val;
    long thrd = (long)arg;
    struct drv_ctx *ctx;
    [ ... ]

    /* Set CPU affinity mask to 'thrd', which is either 0 or 1 */
    if (set_cpuaffinity(thrd) < 0) {
        [ ... ]
    SHOW_CPU_CTX();

    if (thrd == 0) { /* our kthread #0 runs on CPU 0 */
        for (i=0; i<THRD0_ITERS; i++) {
            /* Operate on our perpcu integer */
            val = ++ get_cpu_var(pcpa);
            pr_info(" thrd_0/cpu0: pcpa = %+d\n", val);
            put_cpu_var(pcpa);

            /* Operate on our perpcu structure */
            ctx = get_cpu_ptr(pcp_ctx);
            ctx->tx += 100;
            pr_info(" thrd_0/cpu0: pcp ctx: tx = %5d, rx = %5d\n",
```

[687]

Kernel Synchronization - Part 2

```
                ctx->tx, ctx->rx);
            put_cpu_ptr(pcp_ctx);
        }
    } else if (thrd == 1) { /* our kthread #1 runs on CPU 1 */
        for (i=0; i<THRD1_ITERS; i++) {
            /* Operate on our perpcu integer */
            val = -- get_cpu_var(pcpa);
            pr_info(" thrd_1/cpu1: pcpa = %+d\n", val);
            put_cpu_var(pcpa);
            /* Operate on our perpcu structure */
            ctx = get_cpu_ptr(pcp_ctx);
            ctx->rx += 200;
            pr_info(" thrd_1/cpu1: pcp ctx: tx = %5d, rx = %5d\n",
                ctx->tx, ctx->rx);
            put_cpu_ptr(pcp_ctx);
        }
    }
    disp_vars();
    pr_info("Our kernel thread #%ld exiting now...\n", thrd);
    return 0;
}
```

The effect at runtime is interesting; see the following kernel log:

```
[ 2052.643407] percpu_var:init_percpu_var(): inserted
[ 2052.646162] percpu_var:thrd_work(): *** kthread PID 34971 on cpu 0 now ***
[ 2052.646648] percpu_var:thrd_work():    thrd_0/cpu0: pcpa = +1
[ 2052.647036] percpu_var:thrd_work():    thrd_0/cpu0: pcp ctx: tx =   100, rx =      0
[ 2052.647549] percpu_var:thrd_work():    thrd_0/cpu0: pcpa = +2
[ 2052.647942] percpu_var:thrd_work():    thrd_0/cpu0: pcp ctx: tx =   200, rx =      0
[ 2052.648506] percpu_var:thrd_work():    thrd_0/cpu0: pcpa = +3
[ 2052.648884] percpu_var:thrd_work():    thrd_0/cpu0: pcp ctx: tx =   300, rx =      0
[ 2052.649384] percpu_var:disp_vars(): 000) [thrd_0/0]:34971   |  .N.0  /* disp_vars() */
[ 2052.649979] percpu_var:disp_vars():    cpu  0: pcpa = +3, rx =     0, tx =    300
[ 2052.650486] percpu_var:disp_vars():    cpu  1: pcpa = +0, rx =     0, tx =      0
[ 2052.650999] percpu_var:thrd_work(): Our kernel thread #0 exiting now...
[ 2052.655130] percpu_var:thrd_work(): *** kthread PID 34972 on cpu 1 now ***
[ 2052.655750] percpu_var:thrd_work():    thrd_1/cpu1: pcpa = -1
[ 2052.656255] percpu_var:thrd_work():    thrd_1/cpu1: pcp ctx: tx =     0, rx =    200
[ 2052.656932] percpu_var:thrd_work():    thrd_1/cpu1: pcpa = -2
[ 2052.657440] percpu_var:thrd_work():    thrd_1/cpu1: pcp ctx: tx =     0, rx =    400
[ 2052.658275] percpu_var:thrd_work():    thrd_1/cpu1: pcpa = -3
[ 2052.658746] percpu_var:thrd_work():    thrd_1/cpu1: pcp ctx: tx =     0, rx =    600
[ 2052.659370] percpu_var:disp_vars(): 001) [thrd_1/1]:34972   |  .N.0  /* disp_vars() */
[ 2052.660051] percpu_var:disp_vars():    cpu  0: pcpa = +3, rx =     0, tx =    300
[ 2052.660684] percpu_var:disp_vars():    cpu  1: pcpa = -3, rx =   600, tx =      0
[ 2052.661280] percpu_var:thrd_work(): Our kernel thread #1 exiting now...
```

Figure 13.6 – Screenshot showing the kernel log when our ch13/2_percpu/percpu_var LKM runs

In the last three lines of output in *Figure 13.6*, you can see a summary of the values of our per-CPU data variables on CPU 0 and CPU 1 (we show it via our `disp_vars()` function). Clearly, for the per-CPU `pcpa` integer (as well as the `pcp_ctx` data structure), the values are *different* as expected, *without explicit locking*.

[688]

> The kernel module just demonstrated uses the `for_each_online_cpu(i)` macro to display the value of our per-CPU variables on each online CPU. Next, what if you have, say, six CPUs on your VM but want only two of them to be "live" at runtime? There are several ways to arrange this; one is to pass the `maxcpus=n` parameter to the VM's kernel at boot – you can see if it's there by looking up `/proc/cmdline`:
> ```
> $ cat /proc/cmdline
> BOOT_IMAGE=/boot/vmlinuz-5.4.0-llkd-dbg
> root=UUID=1c4<...> ro console=ttyS0,115200n8
> console=tty0  quiet splash 3 maxcpus=2
> ```
> Also notice that we're running on our custom `5.4.0-llkd-dbg` debug kernel.

Per-CPU usage within the kernel

Per-CPU variables are quite heavily used within the Linux kernel; one interesting case is in the implementation of the `current` macro on the x86 architecture (we covered using the `current` macro in Chapter 6, *Kernel Internals Essentials – Processes and Threads*, in the *Accessing the task structure with current* section). The fact is that `current` is looked up (and set) every so often; keeping it as a per-CPU ensures that we keep its access lock-free! Here's the code that implements it:

```
// arch/x86/include/asm/current.h
[ ... ]
DECLARE_PER_CPU(struct task_struct *, current_task);
static __always_inline struct task_struct *get_current(void)
{
    return this_cpu_read_stable(current_task);
}
#define current get_current()
```

The `DECLARE_PER_CPU()` macro declares the variable named `current_task` as a per-CPU variable of type `struct task_struct *`. The `get_current()` inline function invokes the `this_cpu_read_stable()` helper on this per-CPU variable, thus reading the value of `current` on the CPU core that it's currently running on (read the comment at https://elixir.bootlin.com/linux/v5.4/source/arch/x86/include/asm/percpu.h#L383 to see what this routine's about). Okay, that's fine, but an FAQ: where does this `current_task` per-CPU variable get updated? Think about it: the kernel must change (update) `current` *whenever its context switches* to another task.

[689]

Kernel Synchronization - Part 2

That's exactly the case; it is indeed updated within the context-switching code (`arch/x86/kernel/process_64.c:__switch_to()`; at https://elixir.bootlin.com/linux/v5.4/source/arch/x86/kernel/process_64.c#L504):

```
__visible __notrace_funcgraph struct task_struct *
__switch_to(struct task_struct *prev_p, struct task_struct *next_p)
{
    [ ... ]
    this_cpu_write(current_task, next_p);
    [ ... ]
}
```

Next, a quick experiment to show per-CPU usage within the kernel code base via `__alloc_percpu()`: run `cscope -d` in the root of the kernel source tree (this assumes you've already built the `cscope` index via `make cscope`). In the `cscope` menu, under the `Find functions calling this function:` prompt, type `__alloc_percpu`. The result is as follows:

Figure 13.7 – (Partial) screenshot of the output of cscope -d showing kernel code that calls the __alloc_percpu() API

This, of course, is just a partial list of per-CPU usage within the kernel code base, tracking only use via the `__alloc_percpu()` underlying API. Searching for functions calling `alloc_percpu[_gfp]()` (wrappers over `__alloc_percpu[_gfp]()`) reveals many more hits.

With this, having completed our discussions on kernel synchronization techniques and APIs, let's finish this chapter by learning about a key area: tools and tips when debugging locking issues within kernel code!

[690]

Lock debugging within the kernel

The kernel has several means to help debug difficult situations with regard to kernel-level locking issues, *deadlock* being a primary one.

> Just in case you haven't already, do ensure you've first read the basics on synchronization, locking, and deadlock guidelines from the previous chapter (Chapter 12, *Kernel Synchronization – Part 1*, especially the *Exclusive execution and atomicity* and *Concurrency concerns within the Linux kernel* sections).

With any debug scenario, there are different points at which debugging occurs, and thus perhaps differing tools and techniques that should/could be used. Very broadly speaking, a bug might be noticed at, and thus debugged at, a few different points in time (within the **Software Development Life Cycle (SDLC)**, really):

- During development
- After development but before release (testing, **Quality Assurance (QA)**, and so on)
- After internal release
- After release, in the field

A well-known and unfortunately true homily: the "further" a bug is exposed from development, the costlier it is to fix! So you really do want to try and find and fix them as early as possible!

As this book is focused squarely on kernel development, we shall focus here on a few tools and techniques for debugging locking issues at development time.

> **Important**: We expect that by now, you're running on a debug kernel, that is, a kernel deliberately configured for development/debug purposes. Performance will take a hit, but that's okay – we're out bug hunting now! We covered the configuration of a typical debug kernel in Chapter 5, *Writing Your First Kernel Module – LKMs Part 2*, in the *Configuring a debug kernel* section, and have even provided a sample kernel configuration file for debugging here: ch5/kconfigs/sample_kconfig_llkd_dbg.config. Specifics on configuring the debug kernel for lock debugging are in fact covered next.

Kernel Synchronization - Part 2

Configuring a debug kernel for lock debugging

Due to its relevance and importance to lock debugging, we will take a quick look at a key point from the *Linux Kernel patch submission checklist* document (`https://www.kernel.org/doc/html/v5.4/process/submit-checklist.html`) that's most relevant to our discussions here, on enabling a debug kernel (especially for lock debugging):

```
// https://www.kernel.org/doc/html/v5.4/process/submit-checklist.html
[...]
12. Has been tested with CONFIG_PREEMPT, CONFIG_DEBUG_PREEMPT,
CONFIG_DEBUG_SLAB, CONFIG_DEBUG_PAGEALLOC, CONFIG_DEBUG_MUTEXES,
CONFIG_DEBUG_SPINLOCK, CONFIG_DEBUG_ATOMIC_SLEEP, CONFIG_PROVE_RCU and
CONFIG_DEBUG_OBJECTS_RCU_HEAD all simultaneously enabled.

13. Has been build- and runtime tested with and without CONFIG_SMP and
CONFIG_PREEMPT.

16. All codepaths have been exercised with all lockdep features
enabled.
 [ ... ]
```

> **TIP**
> Though not covered in this book, I cannot fail to mention a very powerful dynamic memory error detector called **Kernel Address SANitizer** (**KASAN**). In a nutshell, it uses compile-time instrumentation-based dynamic analysis to catch common memory-related bugs (it works with both GCC and Clang). **ASan (Address Sanitizer)**, contributed by Google engineers, is used to monitor and detect memory issues in user space apps (covered in some detail and compared with valgrind in the *Hands-On System Programming for Linux* book). The kernel equivalent, KASAN, has been available since the 4.0 kernel for both x86_64 and AArch64 (ARM64, from 4.4 Linux). Details (on enabling and using it) can be found within the kernel documentation (`https://www.kernel.org/doc/html/v5.4/dev-tools/kasan.html#the-kernel-address-sanitizer-kasan`); I highly recommend you enable it in your debug kernel.

As we saw back in `Chapter 2`, *Building the 5.x Linux Kernel from Source – Part 1*, we can configure our Linux kernel specifically for our requirements. Here (within the root of the 5.4.0 kernel source tree), we perform `make menuconfig` and navigate to the `Kernel hacking / Lock Debugging (spinlocks, mutexes, etc...)` menu (see *Figure 13.8*, taken on our x86_64 Ubuntu 20.04 LTS guest VM):

Chapter 13

```
.config - Linux/x86 5.4.0 Kernel Configuration
> Kernel hacking > Lock Debugging (spinlocks, mutexes, etc...)
┌─────────────────── Lock Debugging (spinlocks, mutexes, etc...) ───────────────────┐
│ Arrow keys navigate the menu.  <Enter> selects submenus --->  (or empty submenus ----).  Highlighted │
│ letters are hotkeys.  Pressing <Y> includes, <N> excludes, <M> modularizes features.  Press <Esc><Esc> │
│ to exit, <?> for Help, </> for Search.  Legend: [*] built-in  [ ] excluded  <M> module  < > module │
│ capable                                                                                         │
│   ┌─────────────────────────────────────────────────────────────────────────────────────────┐   │
│   │ [*] Lock debugging: prove locking correctness                                           │   │
│   │ [*] Lock usage statistics                                                               │   │
│   │ -*- RT Mutex debugging, deadlock detection                                              │   │
│   │ -*- Spinlock and rw-lock debugging: basic checks                                        │   │
│   │ -*- Mutex debugging: basic checks                                                       │   │
│   │ -*- Wait/wound mutex debugging: Slowpath testing                                        │   │
│   │ -*- RW Semaphore debugging: basic checks                                                │   │
│   │ -*- Lock debugging: detect incorrect freeing of live locks                              │   │
│   │ [ ] Lock dependency engine debugging                                                    │   │
│   │ [*] Sleep inside atomic section checking                                                │   │
│   │ [ ] Locking API boot-time self-tests                                                    │   │
│   │ < > torture tests for locking                                                           │   │
│   │ < > Wait/wound mutex selftests                                                          │   │
│   └─────────────────────────────────────────────────────────────────────────────────────────┘   │
└─────────────────────────────────────────────────────────────────────────────────────────────────┘
```

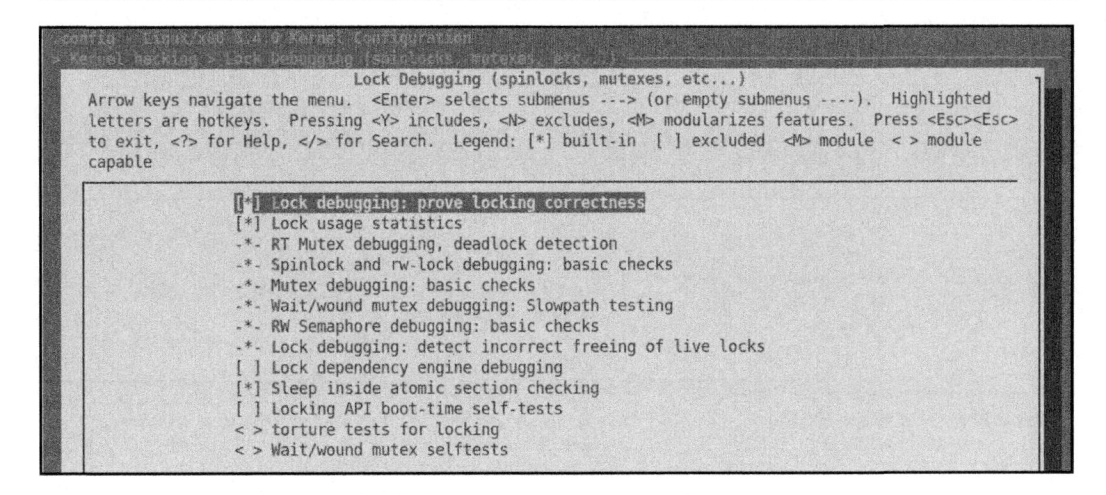

Figure 13.8 – (Truncated) screenshot of the kernel hacking / Lock Debugging (spinlocks, mutexes, etc...) menu with required items enabled for our debug kernel

Figure 13.8 is a (truncated) screenshot of the `< Kernel hacking > Lock Debugging (spinlocks, mutexes, etc...)` menu with required items enabled for our debug kernel.

> **TIP**
> Instead of interactively having to go through each menu item and selecting the `<Help>` button to see what it's about, a much simpler way to gain the same help information is to peek inside the relevant Kconfig file (that describes the menu). Here, it's `lib/Kconfig.debug`, as all debug-related menus are there. For our particular case, search for the menu `"Lock Debugging (spinlocks, mutexes, etc...)"` string, where the `Lock Debugging` section begins (see the following table).

The following table summarizes what each kernel lock debugging configuration option helps debug (we haven't shown all of them and, for some of them, have directly quoted from the `lib/Kconfig.debug` file):

Lock debugging menu title	What it does
Lock debugging: prove locking correctness (CONFIG_PROVE_LOCKING)	This is the `lockdep` kernel option – turn it on to get rolling proof of lock correctness at all times. Any possibility of locking-related deadlock *is reported even before it actually occurs*; very useful! (Explained shortly in more detail.)
Lock usage statistics (CONFIG_LOCK_STAT)	Tracks lock contention points (explained shortly in more detail).
RT mutex debugging, deadlock detection (CONFIG_DEBUG_RT_MUTEXES)	*"This allows rt mutex semantics violations and rt mutex related deadlocks (lockups) to be detected and reported automatically."*

[693]

Spinlock and `rw-lock` debugging: basic checks (`CONFIG_DEBUG_SPINLOCK`)	Turning this on (along with `CONFIG_SMP`) helps catch missing spinlock initialization and other common spinlock errors.
Mutex debugging: basic checks (`CONFIG_DEBUG_MUTEXES`)	"This feature allows mutex semantics violations to be detected and reported."
RW semaphore debugging: basic checks (`CONFIG_DEBUG_RWSEMS`)	Allows mismatched RW semaphore locks and unlocks to be detected and reported.
Lock debugging: detect incorrect freeing of live locks (`CONFIG_DEBUG_LOCK_ALLOC`)	"This feature will check whether any held lock (spinlock, rwlock, mutex or rwsem) is incorrectly freed by the kernel, via any of the memory-freeing routines (`kfree()`, `kmem_cache_free()`, `free_pages()`, `vfree()`, etc.), whether a live lock is incorrectly reinitialized via `spin_lock_init()`/`mutex_init()`/etc., or whether there is any lock held during task exit."
Sleep inside atomic section checking (`CONFIG_DEBUG_ATOMIC_SLEEP`)	"If you say Y here, various routines which may sleep will become very noisy if they are called inside atomic sections: when a spinlock is held, inside an rcu read side critical section, inside preempt disabled sections, inside an interrupt, etc..."
Locking API boot-time self-tests (`CONFIG_DEBUG_LOCKING_API_SELFTESTS`)	"Say Y here if you want the kernel to run a short self-test during bootup. The self-test checks whether common types of locking bugs are detected by debugging mechanisms or not. (if you disable lock debugging then those bugs wont be detected of course.) The following locking APIs are covered: spinlocks, rwlocks, mutexes and rwsems."
Torture tests for locking (`CONFIG_LOCK_TORTURE_TEST`)	"This option provides a kernel module that runs torture tests on kernel locking primitives. The kernel module may be built after the fact on the running kernel to be tested, if desired." (Can be built either inline with 'Y' or externally as a module with 'M')."

Table 17.4 – Typical kernel lock debugging configuration options and their meaning

As suggested previously, turning on all or most of these lock debug options within a debug kernel used during development and testing is a good idea. Of course, as expected, doing so might considerably slow down execution (and use more memory); as in life, this is a trade-off you have to decide on: you gain detection of common locking issues, errors, and deadlocks, at the cost of speed. It's a trade-off you should be more than willing to make, especially when developing (or refactoring) the code.

The lock validator lockdep – catching locking issues early

The Linux kernel has a tremendously useful feature begging to be taken advantage of by kernel developers: a runtime locking correctness or locking dependency validator; in short, **lockdep**. The basic idea is this: the `lockdep` runtime comes into play whenever any locking activity occurs within the kernel – the taking or the release of *any* kernel-level lock, or any locking sequence involving multiple locks.

This is tracked or mapped (see the following paragraph for more on the performance impact and how it's mitigated). By applying well-known rules for correct locking (you got a hint of this in the previous chapter in the *Locking guidelines and deadlock* section), `lockdep` then makes a conclusion regarding the validity of the correctness of what was done.

The beauty of it is that `lockdep` achieves 100% mathematical proof (or closure) that a lock sequence is correct or not. The following is a direct quote from the kernel documentation on the topic (`https://www.kernel.org/doc/html/v5.4/locking/lockdep-design.html`):

> *"The validator achieves perfect, mathematical 'closure' (proof of locking correctness) in the sense that for every simple, standalone single-task locking sequence that occurred at least once during the lifetime of the kernel, the validator proves it with a 100% certainty that no combination and timing of these locking sequences can cause any class of lock related deadlock."*

Furthermore, `lockdep` warns you (by issuing the `WARN*()` macros) of any violation of the following classes of locking bugs: deadlocks/lock inversion scenarios, circular lock dependencies, and hard IRQ/soft IRQ safe/unsafe locking bugs. This information is precious; validating your code with `lockdep` can save hundreds of wasted hours of productivity by catching locking issues early. (FYI, `lockdep` tracks all locks and their locking sequence or "lock chains"; these can be viewed through `/proc/lockdep_chains`).

A word on *performance mitigation*: you might well imagine that, with literally thousands or more lock instances floating around, it would be absurdly slow to validate every single lock sequence (yes, in fact, it turns out to be a task of order $O(N^2)$ algorithmic time complexity!). This would just not work; so, `lockdep` works by verifying any locking scenario (say, on a certain code path, lock A is taken, then lock B is taken – this is referred to as a *lock sequence* or *lock chain*) **only once**, the very first time it occurs. (It knows this by maintaining a 64-bit hash for every lock chain it encounters.)

Kernel Synchronization - Part 2

> **TIP**: Primitive user space approaches: A very primitive – and certainly not guaranteed – way to try and detect deadlocks is via user space by simply using GNU `ps(1)`; doing `ps -LA -o state,pid,cmd | grep "^D"` prints any threads in the D – *uninterruptible sleep* (`TASK_UNINTERRUPTIBLE`) – state. This could – but may not – be due to a deadlock; if it persists for a long while, chances are higher that it is a deadlock. Give it a try! Of course, `lockdep` is a far superior solution. (Note that this only works with GNU `ps`, not the lightweight ones such as `busybox ps`.)
>
> Other useful user space tools are `strace(1)` and `ltrace(1)` – they provide a detailed trace of every system and library call, respectively, issued by a process (or thread); you might be able to catch a hung process/thread and see where it got stuck (using `strace -p <PID>` might be especially useful on a hung process).

The other point that you need to be clear about is this: `lockdep` *will* issue warnings regarding (mathematically) incorrect locking *even if no deadlock actually occurs at runtime*! `lockdep` offers proof that there is indeed an issue that could conceivably cause a bug (deadlock, unsafe locking, and so on) at some point in the future if no corrective action is taken; it's usually dead right; take it seriously and fix the issue. (Then again, typically, nothing in the software universe is 100% correct 100% of the time: what if a bug creeps into the `lockdep` code itself? There's even a `CONFIG_DEBUG_LOCKDEP` config option. The bottom line is that we, the human developers, must carefully assess the situation, checking for false positives.)

Next, `lockdep` works upon a *lock class*; this is simply a "logical" lock as opposed to "physical" instances of that lock. For example, the kernel's open file data structure, `struct file`, has two locks – a mutex and a spinlock – and each of them is considered a lock class by `lockdep`. Even if a few thousand instances of `struct file` exist in memory at runtime, `lockdep` will track it as a class only. For more detail on `lockdep`'s internal design, we refer you to the official kernel documentation on it (https://www.kernel.org/doc/html/v5.4/locking/lockdep-design.html).

Examples – catching deadlock bugs with lockdep

Here, we shall assume that you've by now built and are running upon a debug kernel with `lockdep` enabled (as described in detail in the *Configuring a debug kernel for lock debugging* section). Verify that it is indeed enabled:

```
$ uname -r
5.4.0-llkd-dbg
$ grep PROVE_LOCKING /boot/config-5.4.0-llkd-dbg
CONFIG_PROVE_LOCKING=y
$
```

Okay, good! Now, let's get hands-on with some deadlocks, seeing how `lockdep` will help you catch them. Read on!

Example 1 – catching a self deadlock bug with lockdep

As a first example, let's travel back to one of our kernel modules from Chapter 6, *Kernel Internals Essentials – Processes and Threads*, in the *Iterating over the task list* section, here: `ch6/foreach/thrd_showall/thrd_showall.c`. Here, we looped over each thread, printing some details from within its task structure; with regard to this, here's a code snippet where we obtain the name of the thread (recall that it's in a member of the task structure called `comm`):

```
// ch6/foreach/thrd_showall/thrd_showall.c
static int showthrds(void)
{
    struct task_struct *g = NULL, *t = NULL; /* 'g' : process ptr; 't': thread ptr */
    [ ... ]
    do_each_thread(g, t) { /* 'g' : process ptr; 't': thread ptr */
        task_lock(t);
        [ ... ]
        if (!g->mm) {    // kernel thread
            snprintf(tmp, TMPMAX-1, " [%16s]", t->comm);
        } else {
            snprintf(tmp, TMPMAX-1, " %16s ", t->comm);
        }
        snprintf(buf, BUFMAX-1, "%s%s", buf, tmp);
        [ ... ]
```

[697]

Kernel Synchronization - Part 2

This works, but there appears to be a better way to do it: instead of directly looking up the thread's name with `t->comm` (as we do here), the kernel provides the `{get,set}_task_comm()` helper routines to both get and set the name of the task. So, we rewrite the code to use the `get_task_comm()` helper macro; the first parameter to it is the buffer to place the name into (it's expected that you've allocated memory to it), and the second parameter is the pointer to the task structure of the thread whose name you are querying (the following code snippet is from here: `ch13/3_lockdep/buggy_thrdshow_eg/thrd_showall_buggy.c`):

```
// ch13/3_lockdep/buggy_lockdep/thrd_showall_buggy.c
static int showthrds_buggy(void)
{
    struct task_struct *g, *t; /* 'g' : process ptr; 't': thread ptr */
    [ ... ]
    char buf[BUFMAX], tmp[TMPMAX], tasknm[TASK_COMM_LEN];
    [ ... ]
    do_each_thread(g, t) { /* 'g' : process ptr; 't': thread ptr */
        task_lock(t);
        [ ... ]
        get_task_comm(tasknm, t);
        if (!g->mm) // kernel thread
            snprintf(tmp, sizeof(tasknm)+3, " [%16s]", tasknm);
        else
            snprintf(tmp, sizeof(tasknm)+3, " %16s ", tasknm);
        [ ... ]
```

When compiled and inserted into the kernel on our test system (a VM, thank goodness), it can get weird, or even just simply hang! (When I did this, I was able to retrieve the kernel log via `dmesg(1)` before the system became completely unresponsive.).

What if your system just hangs upon insertion of this LKM? Well, that's a taste of the difficulty of kernel debugging! One thing you can try (which worked for me when trying this very example on a x86_64 Fedora 29 VM) is to reboot the hung VM and look up the kernel log by leveraging systemd's powerful `journalctl(1)` utility with the `journalctl --since="1 hour ago"` command; you should be able to see the printks from `lockdep` now. Again, unfortunately, it's not guaranteed that the key portion of the kernel log is saved to disk (at the time it hung) for `journalctl` to be able to retrieve. This is why using the kernel's **kdump** feature – and then performing postmortem analysis of the kernel dump image file with `crash(8)` – can be a lifesaver (see resources on using `kdump` and crash in the *Further reading* section for this chapter).

Glancing at the kernel log, it becomes clear: `lockdep` has caught a (self) deadlock (we show relevant parts of the output in the screenshot):

```
[ 1021.429110] thrd_showall_buggy: inserted
[ 1021.431264] --------------------------------------------------------------------
                    TGID   PID       current         stack-start     Thread Name    MT? # thrds
                --------------------------------------------------------------------
[ 1021.440804] ============================================
[ 1021.442866] WARNING: possible recursive locking detected
[ 1021.445129] 5.4.0-llkd-dbg #2 Tainted: G           OE
[ 1021.447157] --------------------------------------------
[ 1021.449384] insmod/2367 is trying to acquire lock:
[ 1021.451361] ffff88805de73f08 (&(&p->alloc_lock)->rlock){+.+.}, at: __get_task_comm+0x28/0x50
[ 1021.453676]
                but task is already holding lock:
[ 1021.457365] ffff88805de73f08 (&(&p->alloc_lock)->rlock){+.+.}, at: showthrds_buggy+0x13e/0x6d1 [thrd_showall_buggy]
[ 1021.461623]
                other info that might help us debug this:
[ 1021.465332]  Possible unsafe locking scenario:

[ 1021.468871]        CPU0
[ 1021.470563]        ----
[ 1021.472349]   lock(&(&p->alloc_lock)->rlock);
[ 1021.474591]   lock(&(&p->alloc_lock)->rlock);
[ 1021.476870]
                *** DEADLOCK ***

[ 1021.482086]  May be due to missing lock nesting notation

[ 1021.485550] 1 lock held by insmod/2367:
[ 1021.487884]  #0: ffff88805de73f08 (&(&p->alloc_lock)->rlock){+.+.}, at: showthrds_buggy+0x13e/0x6d1 [thrd_showall_buggy]
```

Figure 13.9 – (Partial) screenshot showing the kernel log after our buggy module is loaded; lockdep catches the self deadlock!

Kernel Synchronization - Part 2

Though a lot more detail follows (including the stack backtrace of the kernel stack of `insmod(8)` – as it was the process context, in this case, register values, and so on), what we see in the preceding figure is sufficient to deduce what happened. Clearly, `lockdep` tells us `insmod/2367 is trying to acquire lock:`, followed by `but task is already holding lock:`. Next (look carefully at *Figure 13.9*), the lock that `insmod` is holding is `(p->alloc_lock)` (for now, ignore what follows it; we will explain it shortly) and the routine that actually attempts to acquire it (shown after `at:`) is `__get_task_comm+0x28/0x50`. Now, we're getting somewhere: let's figure out what exactly occurred when we called `get_task_comm()`; we find that it's a macro, a wrapper around the actual worker routine, `__get_task_comm()`. Its code is as follows:

```
// fs/exec.c
char *__get_task_comm(char *buf, size_t buf_size, struct task_struct *tsk)
{
    task_lock(tsk);
    strncpy(buf, tsk->comm, buf_size);
    task_unlock(tsk);
    return buf;
}
EXPORT_SYMBOL_GPL(__get_task_comm);
```

Ah, there's the problem: the `__get_task_comm()` function *attempts to reacquire the very same lock that we're already holding, causing (self) deadlock*! Where did we acquire it? Recall that the very first line of code in our (buggy) kernel module after entering the loop is where we call `task_lock(t)`, and then just a few lines later, we invoke `get_task_comm()`, which internally attempts to reacquire the very same lock: the result is *self deadlock*:

```
do_each_thread(g, t) {    /* 'g' : process ptr; 't': thread ptr */
    task_lock(t);
    [ ... ]
    get_task_comm(tasknm, t);
```

Furthermore, finding which particular lock this is easy; look up the code of the `task_lock()` routine:

```
// include/linux/sched/task.h */
static inline void task_lock(struct task_struct *p)
{
    spin_lock(&p->alloc_lock);
}
```

[700]

So, it all makes sense now; it's a spinlock within the task structure named `alloc_lock`, just as `lockdep` informs us.

`lockdep`'s report has some amount of puzzling notations. Take the following lines:

```
[ 1021.449384] insmod/2367 is trying to acquire lock:
[ 1021.451361] ffff88805de73f08 (&(&p->alloc_lock)->rlock){+.+.}, at: __get_task_comm+0x28/0x50
[ 1021.453676]
                           but task is already holding lock:
[ 1021.457365] ffff88805de73f08 (&(&p->alloc_lock)->rlock){+.+.}, at: showthrds_buggy+0x13e/0x6d1 [thrd_showall_buggy]
```

Ignoring the timestamp, the number in the leftmost column of the second line seen in the preceding code block is the 64-bit lightweight hash value used to identify this particular lock sequence. Notice it's precisely the same as the hash in the following line; so, we know it's the very same lock being acted upon! `{+.+.}` is lockdep's notation for what state this lock was acquired in (the meaning: + implies lock acquired with IRQs enabled, . implies lock acquired with IRQs disabled and not in the IRQ context, and so on). These are explained in the kernel documentation (https://www.kernel.org/doc/Documentation/locking/lockdep-design.txt); we'll leave it at that.

> A detailed presentation on interpreting `lockdep` output was given by Steve Rostedt at a Linux Plumber's Conference (back in 2011); the relevant slides are informative, exploring both simple and complex deadlock scenarios and how `lockdep` can detect them:
> *Lockdep: How to read its cryptic output* (https://blog.linuxplumbersconf.org/2011/ocw/sessions/153).

Fixing it

Now that we understand the issue here, how do we fix it? Seeing lockdep's report (*Figure 13.9*) and interpreting it, it's quite simple: (as mentioned) since the task structure spinlock named `alloc_lock` is already taken at the start of the `do-while` loop (via `task_lock(t)`), ensure that before calling the `get_task_comm()` routine (which internally takes and releases this same lock), you unlock it, then perform `get_task_comm()`, then lock it again.

Kernel Synchronization - Part 2

The following screenshot (*Figure 13.10*) shows the difference (via the `diff(1)` utility) between the older buggy version (`ch13/3_lockdep/buggy_thrdshow_eg/thrd_showall_buggy.c`) and the newer fixed version of our code (`ch13/3_lockdep/fixed_lockdep/thrd_showall_fixed.c`):

```
-static int showthrds_buggy(void)
+static int showthrds_fixed(void)
{
    struct task_struct *g, *t;  /* 'g' : process ptr; 't': thread ptr */
    int nr_thrds = 1, total = 0;
@@ -60,7 +58,7 @@
    read_lock(&tasklist_lock);
#endif
    do_each_thread(g, t) {       /* 'g' : process ptr; 't': thread ptr */
-        task_lock(t);
+        task_lock(t);  /*** task lock taken here! ***/

        snprintf(buf, BUFMAX-1, "%6d %6d ", g->tgid, t->pid);

@@ -70,12 +68,21 @@
        snprintf(tmp, TMPMAX-1, "  0x%016lx", (unsigned long)t->stack);
        strncat(buf, tmp, TMPMAX);

+        /* In the 'buggy' ver of this code, LOCKDEP did catch a deadlock here !!
+         * (at the point that get_task_comm() was invoked).
+         * the reason: get_task_comm() attempts to take the very same lock
+         * that we just took above: task_lock(t);  !! This is obvious self-deadlock...
+         * So, we fix it here by first unlocking it, calling get_task_comm(), and
+         * then re-locking it.
+         */
+        task_unlock(t);
        get_task_comm(tasknm, t);
-/*--- LOCKDEP catches a deadlock here !! ---*/
+        task_lock(t);
```

Figure 13.10 – (Partial) screenshot showing the key part of the difference between the buggy and fixed versions of our demo thrdshow LKM

Great; another example follows – that of catching an AB-BA deadlock!

Example 2 – catching an AB-BA deadlock with lockdep

As one more example, let's check out a (demo) kernel module that quite deliberately creates a **circular dependency**, which will ultimately result in a deadlock. The code is here: `ch13/3_lockdep/deadlock_eg_AB-BA`. We've based this module on our earlier one (`ch13/2_percpu`); as you'll recall, we create two kernel threads and ensure (by using a hacked `sched_setaffinity()`) that each kernel thread runs on a unique CPU core (the first kernel thread on CPU core `0` and the second on core `1`).

This way, we have concurrency. Now, within the threads, we have them work with two spinlocks, `lockA` and `lockB`. Understanding that we have a process context with two or more locks, we document and follow a lock ordering rule: *first take lockA, then lockB*. Great; so, one way it should *not* be done is like this:

```
kthread 0 on CPU #0                    kthread 1 on CPU #1
    Take lockA                             Take lockB
        <perform work>                         <perform work>
                                               (Try and) take lockA
                                               < ... spins forever :
                                                        DEADLOCK ... >

    (Try and) take lockB
    < ... spins forever :
            DEADLOCK ... >
```

This, of course, is the classic AB-BA deadlock! Because the program (*kernel thread 1, actually*) ignored the lock ordering rule (when the `lock_ooo` module parameter is set to 1), it deadlocks. Here's the relevant code (we haven't bothered showing the whole program here; please clone this book's GitHub repository at https://github.com/PacktPublishing/Linux-Kernel-Programming and try it out yourself):

```
// ch13/3_lockdep/deadlock_eg_AB-BA/deadlock_eg_AB-BA.c
[ ... ]
/* Our kernel thread worker routine */
static int thrd_work(void *arg)
{
    [ ... ]
    if (thrd == 0) { /* our kthread #0 runs on CPU 0 */
        pr_info(" Thread #%ld: locking: we do:"
            " lockA --> lockB\n", thrd);
        for (i = 0; i < THRD0_ITERS; i ++) {
            /* In this thread, perform the locking per the lock
ordering 'rule';
             * first take lockA, then lockB */
            pr_info(" iteration #%d on cpu #%ld\n", i, thrd);
            spin_lock(&lockA);
            DELAY_LOOP('A', 3);
            spin_lock(&lockB);
            DELAY_LOOP('B', 2);
            spin_unlock(&lockB);
            spin_unlock(&lockA);
        }
```

Kernel Synchronization - Part 2

Our kernel thread 0 does it correctly, following the lock ordering rule; the code relevant to our kernel thread 1 (continued from the previous code) is as follows:

```
        [ ... ]
    } else if (thrd == 1) { /* our kthread #1 runs on CPU 1 */
        for (i = 0; i < THRD1_ITERS; i ++) {
            /* In this thread, if the parameter lock_ooo is 1, *violate* the
             * lock ordering 'rule'; first (attempt to) take lockB,
then lockA */
            pr_info(" iteration #%d on cpu #%ld\n", i, thrd);
            if (lock_ooo == 1) {           // violate the rule, naughty boy!
                pr_info(" Thread #%ld: locking: we do: lockB --> lockA\n",thrd);
                spin_lock(&lockB);
                DELAY_LOOP('B', 2);
                spin_lock(&lockA);
                DELAY_LOOP('A', 3);
                spin_unlock(&lockA);
                spin_unlock(&lockB);
            } else if (lock_ooo == 0) { // follow the rule, good boy!
                pr_info(" Thread #%ld: locking: we do: lockA --> lockB\n",thrd);
                spin_lock(&lockA);
                DELAY_LOOP('B', 2);
                spin_lock(&lockB);
                DELAY_LOOP('A', 3);
                spin_unlock(&lockB);
                spin_unlock(&lockA);
            }
        [ ... ]
```

Build and run it with the `lock_ooo` kernel module parameter set to 0 (the default); we find that, obeying the lock ordering rule, all is well:

```
$ sudo insmod ./deadlock_eg_AB-BA.ko
$ dmesg
[10234.023746] deadlock_eg_AB-BA: inserted (param: lock_ooo=0)
[10234.026753] thrd_work():115: *** thread PID 6666 on cpu 0 now ***
[10234.028299] Thread #0: locking: we do: lockA --> lockB
[10234.029606] iteration #0 on cpu #0
[10234.030765] A
[10234.030766] A
[10234.030847] thrd_work():115: *** thread PID 6667 on cpu 1 now ***
[10234.031861] A
[10234.031916] B
[10234.032850] iteration #0 on cpu #1
```

```
[10234.032853] Thread #1: locking: we do: lockA --> lockB
[10234.038831] B
[10234.038836] Our kernel thread #0 exiting now...
[10234.038869] B
[10234.038870] B
[10234.042347] A
[10234.043363] A
[10234.044490] A
[10234.045551] Our kernel thread #1 exiting now...
$
```

Now, we run it with the `lock_ooo` kernel module parameter set to `1` and find that, as expected, the system locks up! We've disobeyed the lock ordering rule, and we pay the price as the system deadlocks! This time, rebooting the VM and doing `journalctl --since="10 min ago"` got me lockdep's report:

```
======================================================
WARNING: possible circular locking dependency detected
5.4.0-llkd-dbg #2 Tainted: G   OE
------------------------------------------------------
thrd_0/0/6734 is trying to acquire lock:
ffffffffc0fb2518 (lockB){+.+.}, at: thrd_work.cold+0x188/0x24c
[deadlock_eg_AB_BA]

but task is already holding lock:
ffffffffc0fb2598 (lockA){+.+.}, at: thrd_work.cold+0x149/0x24c
[deadlock_eg_AB_BA]

which lock already depends on the new lock.
[ ... ]
other info that might help us debug this:

 Possible unsafe locking scenario:

       CPU0                    CPU1
       ----                    ----
  lock(lockA);
                               lock(lockB);
                               lock(lockA);
  lock(lockB);

 *** DEADLOCK ***

[ ... lots more output follows ... ]
```

[705]

Kernel Synchronization - Part 2

The `lockdep` report is quite amazing. Check out the lines after the sentence `Possible unsafe locking scenario:`; it pretty much precisely shows what actually occurred at runtime – the **out-of-order** (**ooo**) locking sequence on `CPU1` : `lock(lockB); --> lock(lockA);`! Since `lockA` is already taken by the kernel thread on CPU 0, the kernel thread on CPU 1 spins forever – the root cause of this AB-BA deadlock.

Furthermore, quite interestingly, soon after module insertion (with `lock_ooo` set to 1), the kernel also detected a soft lockup bug. The printk is directed to our console at log level `KERN_EMERG`, allowing us to see this even though the system appears to be hung. It even shows the relevant kernel threads where the issue originated (again, this output is on my x86_64 Ubuntu 20.04 LTS VM running the custom 5.4.0 debug kernel):

```
Message from syslogd@seawolf-VirtualBox at Dec 24 11:01:51 ...
kernel:[10939.279524] watchdog: BUG: soft lockup - CPU#0 stuck for 22s! [thrd_0/0:6734]
Message from syslogd@seawolf-VirtualBox at Dec 24 11:01:51 ...
kernel:[10939.287525] watchdog: BUG: soft lockup - CPU#1 stuck for 23s! [thrd_1/1:6735]
```

(FYI, the code that detected this and spewed out the preceding messages is here: `kernel/watchdog.c:watchdog_timer_fn()`).

One additional note: the `/proc/lockdep_chains` output also "proves" the incorrect locking sequence was taken (or exists):

```
$ sudo cat /proc/lockdep_chains
[ ... ]
irq_context: 0
[000000005c6094ba] lockA
[000000009746aa1e] lockB
[ ... ]
irq_context: 0
[000000009746aa1e] lockB
[000000005c6094ba] lockA
```

Also, recall that `lockdep` reports only once – the first time – that a lock rule on any kernel lock is violated.

Chapter 13

lockdep – annotations and issues

Let's wrap up this coverage with a couple more points on the powerful `lockdep` infrastructure.

lockdep annotations

In user space, you will be familiar with using the very useful `assert()` macro. There, you assert a Boolean expression, a condition (for example, `assert(p == 5);`). If the assertion is true at runtime, nothing happens and execution continues; when the assertion is false, the process is aborted and a noisy `printf()` to `stderr` indicates which assertion and where it failed. This allows developers to check for runtime conditions that they expect. Thus, assertions can be very valuable – they help catch bugs!

In a similar manner, `lockdep` allows the kernel developer to assert that a lock is held at a particular point, via the `lockdep_assert_held()` macro. This is called a **lockdep annotation**. The macro definition is displayed here:

```
// include/linux/lockdep.h
#define lockdep_assert_held(l) do { \
    WARN_ON(debug_locks && !lockdep_is_held(l)); \
} while (0)
```

The assertion failing results in a warning (via `WARN_ON()`). This is very valuable as it implies that though that lock `l` is supposed to be held now, it really isn't. Also notice that these assertions only come into play when lock debugging is enabled (this is the default when lock debugging is enabled within the kernel; it only gets turned off when an error occurs within `lockdep` or the other kernel locking infrastructure). The kernel code base, in fact, uses `lockdep` annotations all over the place, both in the core as well as the driver code. (There are a few variations on the `lockdep` assertion of the form `lockdep_assert_held*()` as well as the rarely used `lockdep_*pin_lock()` macros.)

[707]

lockdep issues

A couple of issues can arise when working with `lockdep`:

- Repeated module loading and unloading can cause `lockdep`'s internal lock class limit to be exceeded (the reason, as explained within the kernel documentation, is that loading a `x.ko` kernel module creates a new set of lock classes for all its locks, while unloading `x.ko` does not remove them; it's actually reused). In effect, either don't repeatedly load/unload modules or reset the system.
- Especially in those cases where a data structure has an enormous number of locks (such as an array of structures), failing to properly initialize every single lock can result in `lockdep` lock-class overflow.

The `debug_locks` integer is set to 0 whenever lock debugging is disabled (even on a debug kernel); this can result in this message showing up: `*WARNING* lock debugging disabled!! - possibly due to a lockdep warning`. This could even happen due to `lockdep` issuing warnings earlier. Reboot your system and retry.

> Though this book is based on the 5.4 LTS kernel, a powerful feature was (very recently as of the time of writing) merged into the 5.8 kernel: the **Kernel Concurrency Sanitizer (KCSAN)**. It's a data race detector for the Linux kernel that works via compile-time instrumentation. You can find more details in these LWN articles: *Finding race conditions with KCSAN*, LWN, October 2019 (https://lwn.net/Articles/802128/) and *Concurrency bugs should fear the big bad data-race detector (part 1)*, LWN, April 2020 (https://lwn.net/Articles/816850/).
>
> Also, FYI, several tools do exist for catching locking bugs and deadlocks in *user space apps*. Among them are the well-known `helgrind` (from the Valgrind suite), **TSan (Thread Sanitizer)**, which provides compile-time instrumentation to check for data races in multithreaded applications, and lockdep itself; lockdep can be made to work in user space as well (as a library)! Moreover, the modern [e]BPF framework provides the `deadlock-bpfcc(8)` frontend. It's designed specifically to find potential deadlocks (lock order inversions) in a given running process (or thread).

Lock statistics

A lock can be *contended*, which is when, a context wants to acquire the lock but it has already been taken, so it must wait for the unlock to occur. Heavy contention can create severe performance bottlenecks; the kernel provides lock statistics with a view *to easily identifying heavily contended locks*. Enable lock statistics by turning on the CONFIG_LOCK_STAT kernel configuration option (without this, the /proc/lock_stat entry will not be present, the typical case on most distribution kernels).

The lock stats code takes advantage of the fact that lockdep inserts hooks into the locking code path (the __contended, __acquired, and __released hooks) to gather statistics at these crucial points. The neatly written kernel documentation on lock statistics (https://www.kernel.org/doc/html/latest/locking/lockstat.html#lock-statistics) conveys this information (and a lot more) with a useful state diagram; do look it up.

Viewing lock stats

A few quick tips and essential commands to view lock statistics are as follows (this assumes, of course, that CONFIG_LOCK_STAT is on):

Do what?	Command
Clear lock stats	sudo sh -c "echo 0 > /proc/lock_stat"
Enable lock stats	sudo sh -c "echo 1 > /proc/sys/kernel/lock_stat"
Disable lock stats	sudo sh -c "echo 0 > /proc/sys/kernel/lock_stat"

Next, a simple demo to see locking statistics: we write a very simple Bash script, ch13/3_lockdep/lock_stats_demo.sh (check out its code in this book's GitHub repo). It clears and enables locking statistics, then simply runs the cat /proc/self/cmdline command. This will actually trigger a chain of code to run deep within the kernel (within fs/proc mostly); several global – shared writable – data structures will need to be looked up. This will constitute a critical section and thus locks will be acquired. Our script will disable lock stats, and then grep the locking statistics to see a few locks, filtering out the rest:

    egrep "alloc_lock|task|mm" /proc/lock_stat

Kernel Synchronization - Part 2

On running it, the output we obtained is as follows (again, on our x86_64 Ubuntu 20.04 LTS VM running our custom 5.4.0 debug kernel):

```
$ sudo ./lock_stats_demo.sh
[+] Checking that locking statistics config is enabled    [OK]
[+] clearing lock stats ...
[+] enabling lock stats ...
cat/proc/self/cmdline[+] disabling lock stats ...
                       class name     con-bounces       contentions     waittime-min    waittime-max waittime-total    waittime-avg        acq-bo
unces    acquisitions   holdtime-min   holdtime-max holdtime-total    holdtime-avg
                 dup_mmap_sem.rw_sem-R:        0                 0                0.00            0.00           0.00            0.00
   0              1           627.78         627.78           627.78           627.78
                      &mm->mmap_sem/1:         0                 0                0.00            0.00           0.00            0.00
   0              1           624.38         624.38           624.38           624.38
                &(&mm->page_table_lock)->rlock:    0              0                0.00            0.00           0.00            0.00
   0             21             0.34           0.77             9.73            0.46
                      tasklist_lock-W:          0                 0                0.00            0.00           0.00            0.00
   2              3             2.14          20.39            29.36            9.79
                      tasklist_lock-R:          0                 0                0.00            0.00           0.00            0.00
   1              3             0.38           2.51             3.45            1.15
                &(&p->alloc_lock)->rlock:      0                 0                0.00            0.00           0.00            0.00
   2             15             0.32           1.63             8.67            0.58
                      &mapping->i_mmap_rwsem:   0                 0                0.00            0.00           0.00            0.00
   9            104             0.33           2.87            63.88            0.61
                      &mm->mmap_sem#2-W:        0                 0                0.00            0.00           0.00            0.00
   0             32             0.35         626.64           986.59           30.83
                      &mm->mmap_sem#2-R:        0                 0                0.00            0.00           0.00            0.00
   1            328             0.21          51.52          1803.33            5.50
          mmu_notifier_invalidate_range_start:  0                 0                0.00            0.00           0.00            0.00
   0             58             0.22           0.79            14.16            0.24
                      &mm->context.lock:        0                 0                0.00            0.00           0.00            0.00
   0              1             0.53           0.53             0.53            0.53
                 &(&mm->arg_lock)->rlock:       0                 0                0.00            0.00           0.00            0.00
   0              2             0.40           0.61             1.01            0.51
                      &ei->i_mmap_sem-R:        0                 0                0.00            0.00           0.00            0.00
   3              5             1.35           2.13             8.43            1.69
$
```

Figure 13.11 – Screenshot showing our lock_stats_demo.sh script running, displaying some of the lock statistics

(The output in *Figure 13.11* is pretty long horizontally and thus wraps.) The time displayed is in microseconds. The `class name` field is the lock class; we can see several locks associated with the task and memory structures (`task_struct` and `mm_struct`)! Instead of duplicating the material, we refer you to the kernel documentation on lock statistics, which explains each of the preceding fields (`con-bounces`, `waittime*`, and so on; hint: `con` is short for contended) and how to interpret the output. As expected, see, in *Figure 13.11*, in this simple case, the following:

- The first field, `class_name`, is the lock class; the (symbolic) name of the lock is seen here.
- There's really no contention for locks (fields 2 and 3).
- The wait times (`waittime*`, fields 3 to 6) are 0.
- The `acquisitions` field (#9) is the total number of times the lock was acquired (taken); it's positive (and even goes to over 300 for mm_struct semaphore `&mm->mmap_sem*`).

- The last four fields, 10 to 13, are the cumulative lock hold time statistics (`holdtime-{min|max|total|avg}`). Again, here, you can see that mm_struct `mmap_sem*` locks have the longest average hold time.
- (Notice the task structure's spinlock named `alloc_lock` is taken as well; we came across it in the *Example 1 – catching a self deadlock bug with lockdep* section).

> **TIP**
> The most contended locks on the system can be looked up via `sudo grep ":" /proc/lock_stat | head`. Of course, you should realize that this is from when the locking statistics were last reset (cleared).

Note that lock statistics can get disabled due to lock debugging being disabled; for example, you might come across this:

```
$ sudo cat /proc/lock_stat
lock_stat version 0.4
*WARNING* lock debugging disabled!! - possibly due to a lockdep
warning
```

This warning might necessitate you rebooting the system.

All right, you're almost there! Let's finish this chapter with some brief coverage of memory barriers.

Memory barriers – an introduction

Last but not least, let's briefly address another concern – that of the **memory barrier**. What does it mean? Sometimes, a program flow becomes unknown to the human programmer as the microprocessor, the memory controllers, and the compiler *can reorder* memory reads and writes. In the majority of cases, these "tricks" remain benign and optimized. But there are cases – typically across hardware boundaries, such as CPU cores on multicore systems, CPU to peripheral device, and vice versa on **UniProcessor** (**UP**) – where this reordering *should not occur*; the original and intended memory load and store sequences must be honored. The *memory barrier* (typically machine-level instructions embedded within the `*mb*()` macros) is a means to suppress such reordering; it's a way to force both the CPU/memory controllers and the compiler to order instruction/data in a desired sequence.

Memory barriers can be placed into the code path by using the following macros: `#include <asm/barrier.h>`:

- `rmb()`: Inserts a read (or load) memory barrier into the instruction stream
- `wmb()`: Inserts a write (or store) memory barrier into the instruction stream
- `mb()`: A general memory barrier; quoting directly from the kernel documentation on memory barriers (https://www.kernel.org/doc/Documentation/memory-barriers.txt), *"A general memory barrier gives a guarantee that all the LOAD and STORE operations specified before the barrier will appear to happen before all the LOAD and STORE operations specified after the barrier with respect to the other components of the system."*

The memory barrier ensures that unless the preceding instruction or data access executes, the following ones will not, thus maintaining the ordering. On some (rare) occasions, DMA being the likely one, driver authors use memory barriers. When using DMA, it's important to read the kernel documentation (https://www.kernel.org/doc/Documentation/DMA-API-HOWTO.txt). It mentions where memory barriers are to be used and the perils of not using them; see the example that follows for more on this.

As the placement of memory barriers is typically a fairly perplexing thing to get right for many of us, we urge you to refer to the relevant technical reference manual for the processor or peripheral you're writing a driver for, for more details. For example, on the Raspberry Pi, the SoC is the Broadcom BCM2835 series; referring to its peripherals manual – the *BCM2835 ARM Peripherals* manual (https://www.raspberrypi.org/app/uploads/2012/02/BCM2835-ARM-Peripherals.pdf), section 1.3, *Peripheral access precautions for correct memory ordering* – is helpful to sort out when and when not to use memory barriers.

An example of using memory barriers in a device driver

As one example, take the Realtek 8139 "fast Ethernet" network driver. In order to transmit a network packet via DMA, it must first set up a DMA (transmit) descriptor object. For this particular hardware (NIC chip), the DMA descriptor object is defined as follows:

```
// drivers/net/ethernet/realtek/8139cp.c
struct cp_desc {
    __le32 opts1;
```

```
    __le32 opts2;
    __le64 addr;
};
```

The DMA descriptor object, christened `struct cp_desc`, has three "words." Each of them has to be initialized. Now, to ensure that the descriptor is correctly interpreted by the DMA controller, it's often critical that the writes to the DMA descriptor are seen in the same order as the driver author intends. To guarantee this, memory barriers are used. In fact, the relevant kernel documentation – the *Dynamic DMA mapping Guide* (https://www.kernel.org/doc/Documentation/DMA-API-HOWTO.txt) – tells us to ensure that this is indeed the case. So, for example, when setting up the DMA descriptor, you must code it as follows to get correct behavior on all platforms:

```
desc->word0 = address;
wmb();
desc->word1 = DESC_VALID;
```

Thus, check out how the DMA transmit descriptor is set up in practice (by the Realtek 8139 driver code, as follows):

```
// drivers/net/ethernet/realtek/8139cp.c
[ ... ]
static netdev_tx_t cp_start_xmit([...])
{
    [ ... ]
    len = skb->len;
    mapping = dma_map_single(&cp->pdev->dev, skb->data, len,
PCI_DMA_TODEVICE);
    [ ... ]
    struct cp_desc *txd;
    [ ... ]
    txd->opts2 = opts2;
    txd->addr = cpu_to_le64(mapping);
    wmb();
    opts1 |= eor | len | FirstFrag | LastFrag;
    txd->opts1 = cpu_to_le32(opts1);
    wmb();
    [...]
```

The driver, acting upon what the chip's datasheet requires, requires that the words `txd->opts2` and `txd->addr` are stored to memory, followed by the storage of the `txd->opts1` word. As *the order in which these writes go through is important*, the driver makes use of the `wmb()` write memory barrier. (Also, FYI, RCU is certainly a user of appropriate memory barriers to enforce memory ordering.)

Furthermore, using the `READ_ONCE()` and `WRITE_ONCE()` macros on individual variables *absolutely guarantees that the compiler and the CPU will do what you mean*. It will preclude compiler optimizations as required, use memory barriers as required, and guarantee cache coherency when multiple threads on different cores simultaneously access the variable in question.

For details, do refer to the kernel documentation on memory barriers (https://www.kernel.org/doc/Documentation/DMA-API-HOWTO.txt). It has a detailed section entitled *WHERE ARE MEMORY BARRIERS NEEDED?*. The good news is that it's mostly taken care of under the hood; for a driver author, it's only when performing operations such as setting up DMA descriptors or initiating and ending CPU-to-peripheral (and vice versa) communication that you might require a barrier.

One last thing – an (unfortunate) FAQ: will using the `volatile` keyword magically make concurrency concerns disappear? Of course not. The `volatile` keyword merely instructs the compiler to disable common optimizations around that variable (things outside this code path could also modify the variable marked as `volatile`), that's all. This is often required and useful when working with MMIO. With regard to memory barriers, interestingly, the compiler won't reorder reads or writes on a variable marked as `volatile` with respect to other volatile variables. Still, atomicity is a separate construct, *not* guaranteed by using the `volatile` keyword.

Summary

Well, what do you know!? Congratulations, you have done it, you have completed this book!

In this chapter, we continued from the previous chapter in our quest to learn more about kernel synchronization. Here, you learned how to more efficiently and safely perform locking on integers, via both `atomic_t` and the newer `refcount_t` interface. Within this, you learned how the typical RMW sequence can be atomically and safely employed in a common activity for driver authors – updating a device's registers. The reader-writer spinlock, interesting and useful, though with several caveats, was then covered. You saw how easy it is to mistakenly create adverse performance issues caused by unfortunate caching side effects, including looking at the false sharing problem and how to avoid it.

A boon to developers – lock-free algorithms and programming techniques – was then covered in some detail, with a focus on per-CPU variables within the Linux kernel. It's important to learn how to use these carefully (especially the more advanced forms such as RCU). Finally, you learned what memory barriers are and where they are typically used.

Your long journey in working within the Linux kernel (and related areas, such as device drivers) has begun in earnest now. Do realize, though, that without constant hands-on practice and actually working on these materials, the fruits quickly fade away... I urge you to stay in touch with these topics and others. As you grow in knowledge and experience, contributing to the Linux kernel (or any open source project for that matter) is a noble endeavor, one you would do well to undertake.

Questions

As we conclude, here is a list of questions for you to test your knowledge regarding this chapter's material: https://github.com/PacktPublishing/Linux-Kernel-Programming/tree/master/questions. You will find some of the questions answered in the book's GitHub repo: https://github.com/PacktPublishing/Linux-Kernel-Programming/tree/master/solutions_to_assgn.

Further reading

To help you delve deeper into the subject with useful materials, we provide a rather detailed list of online references and links (and at times, even books) in a Further reading document in this book's GitHub repository. The *Further reading* document is available here: https://github.com/PacktPublishing/Linux-Kernel-Programming/blob/master/Further_Reading.md.

Packt>

Packt.com

Subscribe to our online digital library for full access to over 7,000 books and videos, as well as industry leading tools to help you plan your personal development and advance your career. For more information, please visit our website.

Why subscribe?

- Spend less time learning and more time coding with practical eBooks and Videos from over 4,000 industry professionals

- Improve your learning with Skill Plans built especially for you

- Get a free eBook or video every month

- Fully searchable for easy access to vital information

- Copy and paste, print, and bookmark content

Did you know that Packt offers eBook versions of every book published, with PDF and ePub files available? You can upgrade to the eBook version at www.packt.com and as a print book customer, you are entitled to a discount on the eBook copy. Get in touch with us at customercare@packtpub.com for more details.

At www.packt.com, you can also read a collection of free technical articles, sign up for a range of free newsletters, and receive exclusive discounts and offers on Packt books and eBooks.

Other Books You May Enjoy

If you enjoyed this book, you may be interested in these other books by Packt:

Mastering Linux Device Driver Development
John Madieu

ISBN: 978-1-78934-204-8

- Explore and adopt Linux kernel helpers for locking, work deferral, and interrupt management
- Understand the Regmap subsystem to manage memory accesses and work with the IRQ subsystem
- Get to grips with the PCI subsystem and write reliable drivers for PCI devices
- Write full multimedia device drivers using ALSA SoC and the V4L2 framework
- Build power-aware device drivers using the kernel power management framework
- Find out how to get the most out of miscellaneous kernel subsystems such as NVMEM and Watchdog

Hands-On System Programming with Linux
Kaiwan N Billimoria

ISBN: 978-1-78899-847-5

- Explore the theoretical underpinnings of Linux system architecture
- Understand why modern OSes use virtual memory and dynamic memory APIs
- Get to grips with dynamic memory issues and effectively debug them
- Learn key concepts and powerful system APIs related to process management
- Effectively perform file IO and use signaling and timers
- Deeply understand multithreading concepts, pthreads APIs, synchronization and scheduling

Leave a review - let other readers know what you think

Please share your thoughts on this book with others by leaving a review on the site that you bought it from. If you purchased the book from Amazon, please leave us an honest review on this book's Amazon page. This is vital so that other potential readers can see and use your unbiased opinion to make purchasing decisions, we can understand what our customers think about our products, and our authors can see your feedback on the title that they have worked with Packt to create. It will only take a few minutes of your time, but is valuable to other potential customers, our authors, and Packt. Thank you!

Index

/
/proc/buddyinfo pseudo-file
  memory allocation, checking via 433, 434

1
10,000-foot view
  of process VAS 292, 294

6
64-bit atomic integer operators 663, 664
64-bit Linux guest
  installing 15

A
AB-BA deadlock, with lockdep
  catching, example 702, 703, 704, 706
Address Sanitizer (ASan) 692
Address Space Layout Randomization (ASLR) 320
Advanced Linux Sound Architecture (ALSA) 60
Android Open Source Project (AOSP) 303
anonymous mappings 334
Application Binary Interface (ABI) 215
Application Programming Interfaces (APIs) 148
arch-independent 664
atomic context sleep
  testing 636
  testing, on 5.4 debug kernel 637, 638, 640, 641
  testing, on 5.4 non-debug kernel 642, 643, 644, 645
atomic integer operators 656
atomic non-RMW operations 667
atomic RMW operations 667
atomic_t interfaces
  about 659, 660
  using 656
atomicity 594

B
basic input/output system (BIOS) 16, 115
BeagleBone Black (BBB)
  about 23
  reference link 25
Berkeley Packet Filter (BPF) 39
bitmask
  searching, efficiently 673
bitwise atomic operators
  using, example 670, 671, 672
blocking call 413, 607
blocking I/O 606, 607
Board Support Package (BSP) 68, 73
boot process
  basics, on x86 115, 116
bootloader setup 108
Bottom Half (BH) 300
Buffer Overflow (BoF) attack 258
busy-wait semantic 626

C
cache effects 678, 679, 680
cache ping-pong 679
CentOS 8 Linux
  download link 25
cgroups v2 CPU controller
  using 561, 562, 565, 566
cgroups v2
  on Linux system 559, 560
clang 36
Coccinelle
  about 202
  reference link 35
command-line interface (CLI) 540

Common Trace Format (CTF) 510, 537
Completely Fair Scheduler (CFS) 230, 504, 519, 520, 557
Condition Variable (CV) 677
console
  wiring to 183, 185
Contiguous Memory Allocator (CMA) 486
control groups 437
CoverityScan
  reference link 36
Cppcheck
  reference link 35
CPU affinity mask
  about 548, 549, 550
  querying 548, 549, 550
  setting 548, 549, 550
  setting, on kernel thread 554, 555
CPU affinity
  performing, with taskset(1) 554
CPU bandwidth control
  with cgroups 557, 559
CPU scheduler
  context switch 532
  entry points 530, 531, 532
CPU scheduling internals, scheduler code
  preemptible kernels 528, 529, 530
  process context part 527, 528
  running 525
  timer interrupt part 526
CPU scheduling internals
  about 511, 525
  CFS 519, 520
  essential background 502
  flow, visualizing 506
  flow, visualizing via alternate (CLI) approaches 510
  flow, visualizing with perf 506, 507, 508, 509
  KSE, on Linux 502
  modular scheduling classes 511, 512, 513, 514, 515, 516, 517
  need for, running scheduler code 525
  POSIX scheduling policies 503, 505, 506
  vruntime value 519, 520
CPU scheduling policy
  threads 521, 522, 524

CPU scheduling priority
  threads 521, 522, 524
critical section
  about 594, 596
  global i ++ 597, 598, 599
  key points 603, 604
  lock concept 600, 601, 602
  section 595
cross compiler
  installing 29
cross-toolchain
  about 28
  installing 28, 131
  package, installing via apt 132
  package, installing via source repo 132
custom slab cache
  creating 448, 449, 450, 451
  creating, within kernel module 448
  demo kernel module 453, 455, 456, 457
  destroying 453
  memory, using 452
  slab allocator, pros and cons 459
  slab shrinker interface 458
cyclictest
  system latency, measuring with 578

D

data analysis
  performing, with Trace Compass 538, 539
data corruption 594
data races 605, 606, 607
Deadline (DL) 515
deadline (DL) class 546
deadlock 609
deadlock bugs, catching with lockdep
  examples 697, 698, 699, 700, 701
  fixing it 701, 702
debug kernel
  configuring 204, 206
  configuring, for lock debugging 692, 693, 694
demand paging 471, 473, 494, 495, 497
demo kernel module 453, 455, 456, 457
Device Tree Blobs (DTBs) 52, 98, 582
Device Under Test (DUT) 586

Direct Memory Access (DMA) 485, 486
dirty or torn reads 624
dirty reads 602
Discretionary Access Control (DAC) 61
dynamic analysis 204
Dynamic Kernel Module Support (DKMS) 216, 258
dynamic shared object (dso) 507

E

Eclipse Trace Compass
  installation link 538
embedded Linux systems
  kernel configuration for 67, 68
emulator thread (EMT) 509
End Of Life (EOL) 49
entry points 160
Eudyptula Challenge
  URL 266
exact page allocator APIs 411, 412
exclusive execution 594
exclusive write lock 674
Executable and Linkable Format (ELF) 320
exit points 160
extended Berkeley Packet Filter (eBPF) 39, 288

F

false sharing 678, 679, 680
fast path 631
Fedora Workstation
  download link 25
Fedora, as VirtualBox guest
  reference link 21
Flawfinder
  reference link 35
floating-point usage 250, 251
flow
  visualizing 506
  visualizing, via alternate (CLI) approaches 510, 511
  visualizing, with perf 506, 507, 508, 509
Free and Open Source Software (FOSS) 22
Ftrace 539
Ftrace kernel infrastructure 643

G

General Public License (GPL) 224
General Purpose Operating System (GPOS) 505, 566
Get Free Page (GFP) flags
  about 396, 413
  dealing with 397, 398
Git tree
  cloning 55, 56
GNU General Public License (GNU GPL) 62
GNU GRUB bootloader
  used, for booting VM 123, 125
GRand Unified Bootloader (GRUB) bootloader
  about 119
  basics, customizing 120, 121
  customizing 119
  default kernel, selecting to boot 121, 122
  VM, booting via GNU GRUB bootloader 123, 125
GRUB prompt
  experimenting 125, 126
guard pages 480
guest VM
  Linux, running as 15
GUI frontend
  interpretation with 547, 548
  reporting with 547, 548

H

hardware interrupts and data race 607
Hello, world C program
  about 319, 321
  printf() API 321, 323
Hello, world LKM C code 157
high-memory region 347
holes 319

I

I/O (reads and writes)
  performing, on per-CPU variables 683, 685
initial ram filesystem (initramfs) framework
  about 108, 112, 114
  boot process, basics on x86 115, 116
  need for 112

overview 116, 118, 119
initramfs image
  about 107
  generating 108, 110, 111
  generating, on Fedora 30 109, 110
Instruction Set Architecture (ISA) 598
integer overflow (IoF) 474, 657
Inter-Process Communication (IPC) 60
internal fragmentation (wastage) 392
interrupt contexts 272, 273, 274
interrupt handler
  about 645, 647, 648, 649, 650, 651
  scenarios 646
interrupt service routine (ISR) 273

J

Java Runtime Environment (JRE) 36, 538
journalctl 179

K

kaiwanTECH
  reference link 22
Kconfig files
  about 89, 90
  menu item, creating in 90, 91, 92, 93
Kconfig language 93, 94, 95
Kernel Address Sanitizer (KASAN) 351, 400, 460, 692
Kernel Address Sanitizer port 205
Kernel ASLR (KASLR)
  about 368
  status, querying with script 368, 371
  used, for randomizing memory layout 366
kernel build (kbuild)
  about 85, 86
  configuration, differences 86, 88
  dealing with, compiler switch issues 140
  dealing with, missing OpenSSL development headers 140, 141
  executing 138
  for site 137, 138
  minimum version requisites 137
  miscellaneous tips 136
  preliminaries for 44
  shell syntax, for building procedure 139

system 64, 65
using, for Raspberry Pi 129, 130
kernel code base
  refcount_t interfaces, using example 661, 662, 663
Kernel Concurrency Sanitizer (KCSAN) 708
kernel configuration
  creating, with localmodconfig approach 71, 73
  distribution config, using as starting point 68
  for typical embedded Linux systems 67, 68
  starting point, obtaining 66
  tuning, via localmodconfig approach 69, 71
  tuning, via make menuconfig UI 74, 75, 76
kernel developers
  coding style guidelines 264
kernel documentation
  generating, from source 35
  reference link 667
  viewing, on memory layout 365
kernel headers 159
kernel image
  building 98, 99, 100, 102, 103
kernel logging 175, 176
kernel memory allocation API
  selecting 483, 485, 486
  using 481
  visualizing 482, 483
kernel memory allocators 384, 385, 386
kernel memory ring buffer
  using 176, 177
kernel memory
  module, unloading from 172
kernel menu
  customizing 88
kernel messages
  generating, from user space 193, 194
kernel model cross-compilation
  about 213, 215, 216, 217, 218, 219
  environment variables 210
  Makefile, pointing 211, 212
  special environment variables, setting 208
  system, setting up 207
kernel modules
  and security 258

auto-loading 256, 258
auto-loading, on system boot 252, 255
building 98, 99, 100, 102, 103, 166
cross-compiling 206
cryptographic signing 261, 263
custom slab cache, creating 448
custom slab cache, using 448
data types and validation 247
disabling 263
features 105
function 227, 230
getting/setting, after insertion 244, 246
hardware-related kernel parameters 249
installing 104, 106, 107
library emulation, performing via multiple source files 226, 227
library-like features, emulating 226
licensing 224, 225
locating, within kernel source 104
Makefile templates 202, 204
operations 165
parameters name, overriding 248
parameters, declaring 242, 244
parameters, passing 241
parameters, using 242, 244
parameters, validating 247
proc filesystem tunables, that affect system log 259, 261
running 167, 168
stacking 231, 233, 234, 239
URL 261
used, for printing process context info 304
variable scope 227, 230
within kernel source tree 154, 155, 156
writing 157
writing, to use basic slab APIs 426, 427, 429
kernel page allocator
  using 386
kernel printk() 168, 169, 170
Kernel release
  nomenclature 45, 46
  URL 46
Kernel Schedulable Entity (KSE)
  on Linux 502
kernel segment layout

fix map region 350
highmem region 352
KASAN 351
kernel modules 350
lowmem region 351
user VAS 352
vector layout 350
vmalloc region 351
kernel segment
  details, viewing 353, 356, 357
  examining 344
  high memory, on 32-bit systems 347
  information, displaying with kernel module 348
  kernel modules space 346
  kernel VAS, via procmap 357, 361, 362
  kernel vmalloc region 346
  lowmem region 345
  macros and variables, for describing layout 350, 353
  null trap page 364
  user segment 362, 364
  viewing, on Raspberry Pi via dmesg 348
Kernel Self Protection Project (KSPP) 88
kernel slab allocator
  using 415
kernel source trees
  about 58, 59, 60, 62, 63
  cloning 130
  extracting 57, 58
  types 49, 51
kernel space components
  block IO 150
  core kernel 149
  Inter-Process Communication (IPC) support 150
  Memory Management (MM) 149
  network protocol stack 150
  sound support 150
  Virtual Filesystem Switch (VFS) 150
  virtualization support 150
kernel space stack
  about 277
  traditional approach, to viewing 286
  viewing 285

[727]

viewing, of given thread or process 286, 287
viewing, with eBPF 288, 290, 291
kernel space
  about 147
  current situation, summarizing 284, 285
  organizing 277, 278, 279, 282, 283
kernel task structure
  about 294, 295, 296, 297, 298
  accessing 294, 295
  accessing, with current 298, 299
  built-in kernel helper methods 302, 303
  context, determining 299, 300
  optimizations 302, 303
  working with, via current 301, 302
kernel threads (kthreads)
  about 556, 557
  CPU affinity mask, setting on 554, 555
kernel tracing session
  recording, with LTTng 537
Kernel Virtual Address (KVA) 325
Kernel Virtual Machine (KVM) 60, 150
kernel vmalloc() API
  about 473, 474, 476, 477
  demand paging 472, 473
  learning 467
  memory allocation 472, 473
  memory protections, specifying 477
  usage, learning 467, 469, 470, 471
  using 466
kernel's configuration
  verifying 127, 128
kernel's task lists
  code 312, 313, 314, 315
  iterating over 307
  processes, displaying 307, 308
  threads, displaying 308, 310
kernel
  architecture 147, 148
  building 133, 134, 135
  building, from source steps 52, 53
  configuring 133, 134, 135
  development workflow 46, 47, 48, 49
  lock debugging within 691
  per-CPU variables, using within 689, 690
  slab layer implementations 444

killable variant 628
Klocwork
  reference link 36
kmalloc() API
  size limitations 429
  versus vmalloc() API 480
kprobe 191
ksize()
  slab allocation, testing 439, 440

L

Last In, First Out (LIFO) 276
latency
  about 576, 577, 578
  measurement 576, 577, 578
Least Significant Bit (LSB) 324, 665
library 148
Library APIs
  reference link 149
Linux Device Drivers (LDD) 250
Linux distributions 25
Linux Driver Verification (LDV) 40
Linux Foundation (LF)
  about 567
  URL 44
Linux kernel documentation
  locating 33
  reference link 493
Linux Kernel Dump Test Module (LKDTM)
  about 663
  reference link 663
Linux kernel source tree
  downloading 54, 55
  Git tree, cloning 55, 56
  obtaining 53
Linux Kernel Space Verification
  reference link 41
Linux kernel, concurrency concerns
  about 604
  blocking I/O 606, 607
  data races 606, 607
  hardware interrupts and data race 607
  locking guidelines and deadlocks 608, 610
  multicore SMP systems and data race 605, 606

preemptible kernels 606, 607
Linux kernel
  address translation 377, 380
  configuring 63
  default configuration, arriving 65, 66
  direct-mapped RAM 377, 380
  kbuild build system 64, 65
  physical memory 372
  physical RAM organization 372
  static analysis tools 35
Linux man pages
  using 31
Linux OS
  monolithic nature, verifying 305
Linux Security Modules (LSMs) 61, 261, 290, 451
Linux system
  cgroups v2 559, 560
Linux Tracing Toolkit next generation (LTTng)
  about 36, 232, 536
  reference link 36
  used, for recording kernel tracing session 537
  used, for threads flow visualization 536
Linux Verification Center
  URL 41
Linux-Kernel Memory Model (LKMM) 659
Linux
  Kernel Schedulable Entity (KSE) on 502
  running, as guest VM 15
live kernel modules
  listing 171
lkm convenience script 173, 174
LKM framework 152, 153, 154
Loadable Kernel Modules (LKMs)
  about 62, 346
  exploring 152
loader 320
localmodconfig approach
  kernel configuration, creating with 71, 73
  kernel configuration, tuning via 69, 71
lock concept 600
lock debugging
  debug kernel, configuring 692, 693, 694
  within kernel 691

lock proficiency 680
lock statistics
  about 709
  viewing 709, 710, 711
lock validator lockdep 694, 695, 696
lock-free programming
  with per-CPU variables 680, 681
lockdep annotation 707
lockdep
  about 610, 694
  issues 708
locking 645, 647, 648, 649, 650, 651
locking deadlocks 608, 610
locking guidelines 608, 610
Long-Term Stable (LTS) 47
Low Latency (LowLat) kernel 529, 576
lowlevel_mem_lkm kernel module
  deploying 407, 409, 410
LTTng documentation
  reference link 536
LTTng installation
  reference link 536

M

mainline 5.x kernel
  RTL, building for 568
mainline kernel
  contributing to 265, 266
  versus RTL kernel 575, 576
mainline Linux
  converting, into RTOS 566, 568
make menuconfig UI
  kernel configuration, tuning via 74, 75, 76
  using 77, 78, 79, 80, 81, 82, 83, 84
Makefile
  basics 197, 198, 199
Mandatory Access Control (MAC) 61
mappings 319
memory 437
memory allocation
  about 471, 473
  with single call 430, 431, 432, 433
memory barrier
  about 711, 712
  using, in device driver example 712, 714

memory management (mm) 60
Memory Management Unit (MMU) 325, 472
memory ordering 658
memory overcommit in Linux, disadvantages
    reference link 493
memory protection
    PoC, testing 478, 480
    read-only 480
merge window 48
minimal system information
    gathering 219, 221
    security 222, 223
MMIO – memory-mapped I/O 667
modern BPF tools
    scheduler latency, measuring via 588, 589
modular scheduling classes
    about 511, 512, 513, 514, 515, 516, 517
    asking 517, 518, 519
module macros 160
module
    unloading, from kernel memory 172
Most Significant Bit (MSB) 665
multicore SMP systems 605, 606
mutex interruptible 628
mutex io variant 629
mutex lock API variants
    about 626
    mutex interruptible and killable variant 628
    mutex io variant 629
    mutex trylock variant 626, 628
mutex lock, key points
    about 626
    internal design 631
    mutex lock API variants 626
    priority inversion 630
    RT-mutex 630
    semaphore 629
mutex lock
    APIs, unlocking 618, 619
    APIs, usage 618, 619
    device driver, example 621, 623, 624, 626
    initializing 616
    need for 611, 613
    usage, determining in theory 613
    using 615, 617, 618

versus spinlock 613
    via interruptible sleep 620, 621
    mutex trylock variant 626, 628

N

nodes 372, 375
non-canonical addresses 327
Non-Uniform Memory Access (NUMA) systems 372

O

object caching 415, 416, 417, 418
older atomic_t interfaces
    versus newer refcount_t interfaces 657, 658
Open Source Automation Development Lab (OSADL) 583
Open Source Software (OSS) 15
Oracle VirtualBox 6.x 15
Oracle VirtualBox Guest Additions
    installing 18, 19, 20, 27
Oracle VirtualBox kernel modules 232
Oracle VirtualBox
    URL 15
Out Of Bounds (OOB) 351
out-of-memory (OOM) killer
    about 487, 488, 494, 495, 497
    default 493
    invoking 488
    invoking, via Magic SysRq 489
    invoking, with allocator program 489, 490
    memory, reclaiming 487
    output 491
    overcommit on 493
    overcommit turned off 492
    vm.overcommit set to 0 493
    vm.overcommit set to 2 492
out-of-memory (OOM) score 498

P

page allocator APIs
    kernel module, writing to demo 401, 403, 405, 407
    using 395, 396
page allocator
    and internal fragmentation 411

freelist organization 387, 388, 389, 390
internals 393, 394
used, for freeing pages 399, 400
workings 387, 390, 391
Page Frame Numbers (PFNs) 376, 473
Page Global Directory (PGD) 325
per-CPU variables
  about 681, 682
  allocating 682, 683
  freeing 682, 683
  I/O (reads and writes), performing on 683, 685
  initialization 682, 683
  kernel module, example 685, 686, 687
  lock-free programming 680, 681
  using, within kernel 689, 690
  working with 682
perf
  used, for visualizing flow 506, 507, 508, 509
Physical Address (PA) 379
PID
  versus Thread Group IDentifier 310, 311, 312
portability 196
Position Independent Executable (PIE) 140, 370, 371
POSIX scheduling policies 503, 505, 506
pr_debug() kernel messages
  enabling 188, 190
pr_foo convenience macros 182
preemptible kernels 528, 529, 530, 606, 607
printk format specifiers 196
printk instances
  rate limiting 190, 191, 192
printk log levels
  using 180, 181
printk output
  standardizing, via the pr_fmt macro 194, 195
printk
  about 175, 176
  used, for coding security 305, 306
priority inheritance (PI) 631
priority inversion 630
privilege escalation (privesc) attacks 259
proc filesystem (procfs) 78, 366

process context part 527, 528
process contexts 272, 273, 274
process memory map
  /proc/PID/maps output, interpreting 333, 335
  frontends 336
  VAS visualization utility 337, 339, 342
  viewing, with procfs 333
  vsyscall page 336
process VAS
  10,000-foot view of 292, 294
  basics 274, 275, 276
procmap utility 37
Proof of Concept (PoC) 478
Proportional Set Size (PSS) 337

Q
QEMU
  about 22
  installing 28
  URL 28
Quality Assurance (QA) 506, 691
Quick Emulator 22

R
Raspberry Pi console
  output, writing to 185, 186, 187
Raspberry Pi
  kernel build, using 129, 130
  reference link 22, 25, 68
  URL 68
  working with 21, 22
Read Copy Update (RCU) 676
Read Modify Write (RMW) 665
reader-writer semaphore 677
reader-writer spinlock
  about 674
  interfaces 674, 675, 676
  using 673, 674
  word of caution 676
Real Time (RT) 515
real-time (RT) class 546
Real-Time Linux (RTL) 567, 652
Real-Time Operating System (RTOS)
  about 505
  mainline Linux, converting into 566, 568

red-black (rb) tree 514
Reduced Instruction Set Computer (RISC) 299
refcount 656
refcount_t interfaces
  about 659, 660
  using 656
  using, within kernel code base example 661, 662, 663
  versus atomic_t interfaces 657, 658
release candidate (rc) 47
release kernels, types
  -next tress kernels 50
  -rc kernels 50
  distribution kernels 50
  LTS kernels 50
  mainline kernels 50
  prepatches kernels 50
  stable kernels 50
  super LTS (SLTS) kernels 50
Request For Comments (RFCs) 60
Resident Set Size (RSS) 337
resource-managed memory allocation APIs
  using 435, 436
return values
  0/-E return convention 161, 162, 163
  __exit keyword 165
  __init keyword 164
  about 161
  ERR_PTR macro 163
  PTR_ERR macro 163, 164
Return-Oriented Programming (ROP) 371
RMW atomic operators
  device registers, operating 665, 666, 667
  using 665
RMW bitwise operators
  using 668, 669
RT-mutex 630
RT-mutex implementation design
  reference link 631
RTL kernel
  building 571, 572, 574
  configuring 571, 572, 574
  versus mainline kernel 575, 576
RTL patches
  applying 571
  obtaining 568, 569, 570
RTL
  building, for mainline 5.x kernel 568
RTLinux 567

S

Scalable Vector Graphics (SVG) 508
scenarios, page allocator
  complex case 392
  downfall case 392
  simplest case 392
scheduler latency
  measuring, via modern BPF tools 588, 589
scheduling classes 511
Secure Attention Key (SAK)
  about 675
  reference link 675
segments 319
semaphore 629
shared state 594
shared writeable data 594
Simple Embedded ARM Linux System (SEALS) 39
Simultaneous Multi-Threading (SMT) 99
Single-Board Computer (SBC) 21, 129, 206
slab allocation, testing with ksize()
  about 440, 441
  output, graphing 443, 444
  output, interpreting 442, 443
slab allocation
  testing, with ksize() 439, 440
slab allocator APIs
  data structures 423
  using 419
slab allocator
  about 384, 435
  background details 438
  caveats 438
  conclusions 438
  cons 459
  pros 459
slab caches
  about 384
  using, for kmalloc 424, 425
slab helper APIs 436, 437

slab layer implementations
  within kernel 444
slab layer
  debugging 460
  debugging, through slab poisoning 460, 462
  SLUB debug options, at boot and runtime 465, 466
  UAF bug, triggering 462, 464
slab memory
  allocating 419, 421
  freeing 421, 422
slab poisoning 460
slab shrinker interface 458
SLUB debug options
  at boot and runtime 465, 466
Smatch
  reference link 35
Software Development Life Cycle (SDLC) 691
software packages
  installing 26, 27
SonarQube
  reference link 36
Source Code Management (SCM) tool 47
source lines of code (SLOC) 99
sparse regions 319
Sparse
  reference link 35
SPDX license identifier
  URL 225
Sphinx 35
spinlock
  about 610
  atomic context sleep, testing 636
  device driver, example 634, 635, 636
  key statements 632
  medium overhead 652
  need for 611, 613
  simplest, lowest overhead 652
  strongest, high overhead 652
  usage 632, 634
  usage, determining in practice 614
  usage, determining in theory 613
  using 632, 652
  versus mutex 613
Stack Pointer (SP) 283

static analysis 204
stop-sched (SS) class 515, 546
swapper 504
Symmetric Multi Processor (SMP) 515, 604
system call 149
system call APIs
  reference link 149
system latency measuring, with cyclictest
  about 578
  cyclictest, installing 582, 583
  results, viewing 585, 586, 587
  RTL patchset, applying 579, 581, 582
  RTL patchset, obtaining 579, 581, 582
  test cases, running 583, 584
System on Chip (SoC) 21, 323
systemd 116, 178

T

taskset(1)
  using, to perform CPU affinity 554
thrashing 614
Thread Group IDentifier
  about 310
  versus PID 310, 311, 312
Thread Local Storage (TLS) 681
Thread Sanitizer (TSan) 708
thread's CPU affinity mask
  querying 550, 551, 552, 553
  setting 550, 551, 552, 553
threads flow visualization
  with LTTng 536
  with Trace Compass 536
thread's scheduling policy
  querying 555
  setting 555
thread's scheduling priority
  querying 555
  setting 555
timer interrupt part 526
tldr variant 32
torn reads 602
Trace Compass GUI
  reference link 36
Trace Compass
  about 538

    used, for performing data analysis 538, 539
    used, for threads flow visualization 536
trace-cmd record
    sample session, recording with 540, 541
trace-cmd report (CLI)
    interpretation with 542, 543, 545, 546
    reporting with 542, 543, 545, 546
trace-cmd
    used, for threads flow visualization 536, 539
tracepoints 536
Translation Lookaside Buffer (TLB) 326, 472

U

UAF bug
    triggering 462, 464
Ubuntu 18.04 LTS Desktop 24
Uninitialized Memory Reads (UMR) 461
Unique Set Size (USS) 337
UNIX process model 277
Use After Free (UAF) 41, 351, 462, 657
user space stack
    about 277, 284
    traditional approach, to viewing 286
    viewing 285
    viewing, of given thread or process 287, 288
    viewing, with eBPF 288, 290, 291
user space
    about 147
    kernel messages, generating from 193, 194
    organizing 277, 278, 279, 280, 281
user VAS
    examining 332
    process memory map, viewing with procfs 333
User Virtual Address (UVA) 320
user-mode ASLR 367
user-mode preemption 529
Userspace IO Drivers (UIO) 78

V

Virtual Address Spaces (VASes)
    about 37, 149, 524
    layout process 330, 331
    process, examining 331
    user VAS 332
Virtual CPU (VCPU) 509
Virtual Filesystem Switch (VFS) 60, 150, 344
Virtual Machine (VM)
    about 100, 638
    booting, via GNU GRUB bootloader 123, 125
Virtual Memory Areas (VMAs) 342, 344
VM overcommit policy 491
VM split, on 64-bit Linux systems
    about 324
    address translation 324, 328, 329
    virtual addressing 324, 328, 329
VM split
    about 318, 321
    on 64-bit Linux systems 324
vmalloc() API
    versus kmalloc() API 480
VMware Workstation 15
vruntime value 519, 520

X

x86 system
    virtualization extension support 16, 18

Y

Yocto
    URL 141
Your Mileage May Vary(YMMV) 349

Z

zones 375, 377

Printed in Great Britain
by Amazon